Finding the Walls of Troy

Frank Calvert reflecting. Thymbra Farm, 1892. By Francis Henry Bacon. Courtesy Elizabeth Bacon.

Finding the Walls of Troy

Frank Calvert and Heinrich Schliemann at Hisarlık

Susan Heuck Allen

UNIVERSITY OF CALIFORNIA PRESS
Berkeley   Los Angeles   London

University of California Press
Berkeley and Los Angeles, California

University of California Press, Ltd.
London, England

© 1999 by
The Regents of the University of California

Library of Congress Cataloging-in-Publication Data

Allen, Susan Heuck, 1952–
    Finding the walls of Troy : Frank Calvert and Heinrich Schliemann
at Hisarlık / Susan Heuck Allen.
        p.   cm.
    Includes bibliographical references and index.
    ISBN 0-520-20868-4 (alk. paper)
    1. Calvert, Frank, 1828–1908—Contributions in archaeology.
2. Schliemann, Heinrich, 1822–1890—Professional ethics.
3. Archaeologists—Great Britain—Biography. 4. Consuls—Turkey—
Biography. 5. Archaeologists—Germany—Biography. 6. Excavations
(Archaeology)—Turkey—Troy (Extinct city). 7. Troy (Extinct city).
I. Title
DF212.C35A67   1998
930.1′092—dc21   98-13101
                                                              CIP

Printed in the United States of America
9 8 7 6 5 4 3 2 1

The paper used in this publication meets the minimum requirements of American National
Standard for Information Sciences—Permanence of Paper for Printed Library Materials,
ANSI Z39.48-1984.

I dedicate this book to my family.

TABLE OF CONTENTS

ACKNOWLEDGMENTS

During a long association with Troy through the University of Cincinnati and later a doctoral dissertation on Late Bronze Age pottery from the site, I became acquainted with Frank Calvert, author of brief excavation reports in the 1850s and 1860s of prehistoric sites in the Troad, the northwesternmost area of Anatolia, where Troy is located. Years later, I found a cache of objects that a Frank Calvert had sold to the Worcester Art Museum in Massachusetts in 1905. Intrigued, I began following the loose strands that were later woven together to form this book.

Frank Calvert had executed the sale through a middleman named Francis Henry Bacon. A letter preserved in the museum's files from Bert Hodge Hill, former director of the American School of Classical Studies at Athens, noted that both Bacon and his younger brother, Henry, the architect of the Lincoln Memorial in Washington, D.C., had married Calvert's nieces and had brought them to the United States. Hence, the family's Boston connection resulted in the Worcester acquisition. Informed by Cornelius and Emily Vermeule of the Museum of Fine Arts, Boston, and Harvard University that the Bacons still lived near Boston, I resolved to find them. In casual conversation with Jeremiah M. Allen, I found that I already knew the great-great-grandnephew of Frank Calvert, Kendall Bacon, a childhood friend of my husband's. Immediately I telephoned Bacon and inquired if the name Frank Calvert meant anything to him. After a long pause Bacon replied that the story of Calvert and Troy was "a family myth because no one had ever given him credit for his discoveries." Bacon's statement inspired the writing of this book. Through Bacon and Calvert descendants and with the help of other scholars, Calvert's story has moved from myth to history.

I should like to thank the American Philosophical Society for a generous grant that enabled me to do initial research at museums and archives in Britain, Germany, Turkey, and Greece. I also wish to thank the descendants of Frederick

Calvert and his son-in-law, Francis Henry Bacon, for their generosity in sharing with me diaries, photographs, and letters saved by Bacon. I thank Dyfri Williams, keeper of Greek and Roman Antiquities at the British Museum, for permission to publish correspondence between Calvert and Charles T. Newton. I also thank J. Lesley Fitton for considerable help in facilitating my research there. I thank Haris Kalligas, director of the Gennadius Library of the American School of Classical Studies in Athens, for permission to publish diaries and correspondence belonging to Calvert, Schliemann, and others in the Schliemann Archive, where David Jordan, the acting director, and archivists Christina Vardas and Natalia Vogeikoff were of great help. I thank W. Knobloch, director of the Berlin-Brandenburgische Akademie der Wissenschaften, for permission to publish the Calvert-Virchow correspondence. I thank the Center for American History, University of Texas, the Avery Rare Books Library, Columbia University, and the Mitchell Library, Glasgow, for permission to publish hitherto unpublished or partly published letters. Thanks also to the Public Record Office, Kew, and to Milton Gustafson and David Pfeiffer of the National Archives for assistance and permission to publish relevant diplomatic correspondence.

I thank Nurten Sevinç of the Çanakkale Archaeological Museum for permission to examine museum accessions registers and the unpublished "Katalog der Sammlung Calvert in den Dardanellen und in Thymbra" compiled by Hermann Thiersch in 1902 and the late John M. Cook for entrusting his notes and Nicholas Bayne's on that manuscript to me. I am grateful to Kum Kale T.I.G.E.M. and the Çanakkale Museum's Ömer Bey for trips to the Calvert farm at Akça Köy and to Pınarbaşı. Bülent Cetin and Ibrahim Aksu of Çanakkale have helped facilitate my work in Çanakkale. I have also benefited from communications with Pierre Amandry, William M. Calder III, Donald F. Easton, Elena Frangakis-Syrett, Brian Giraud, Peter Harrington, R. Ross Holloway, John Iatrides, Manfred Korfmann, George S. Korres, the late Olivier Masson, Kenneth Mayer, Paul G. Naiditch, Andras Riedlmayer, Claudia Rockenmeyer, C. Brian Rose, David S. Thomas, David A. Traill, and Penny Wilson. Many students and friends, the American School of Classical Studies, the British School at Athens, Brown University Interlibrary Loan, the Gennadius Library, the Providence Athenaeum, and the Blegen Library, University of Cincinnati, have also contributed to this book. I happily acknowledge my debt to the readers of this manuscript and to Marie Mauzy, photographer at the American School of Classical Studies, and Bill Rice, for help with photography. Special thanks go to Peter S. Allen.

This volume grew from the enthusiastic response to a paper delivered at the 1993 annual meeting of the A.I.A. and subsequent articles in *Archaeology, Anatolian Studies,* and the *American Journal of Archaeology* and has come to fruition thanks to Mary Lamprech.

MAPS AND FIGURES

Frontispiece. Frank Calvert reflecting. Thymbra Farm, 1892.

Prologue

Who discovered Troy? Until fairly recently, everybody thought they knew the answer: the archaeologist Heinrich Schliemann discovered the ruined walls of Troy at Hisarlık, in modern Turkey, and found there the fabulous cache known as "Priam's Treasure." Everybody knew this because Schliemann himself made absolutely certain that the story of his discovery became part of modern mythology: the heroic archaeologist connecting the quotidian present with a golden, legendary past. In his archaeological publications, he reinvented his own life to create this myth. A series of ever-evolving autobiographies produced a *"Wunschbild,* a picture that he created for himself and wished posterity to accept," as one critic put it.[1] In an early autobiography, he is captivated by the spell of Homer's *Iliad* as recited in the original Greek by a drunken miller.[2] The next version is further enhanced. After seeing a printed image of Priam's blazing city, he promises his father that one day he will excavate Troy.[3] And he triumphs, realizing in his adulthood his childhood dreams—an autobiographical fiction that was wildly successful. Even Freud envied Heinrich Schliemann.[4] As a matter of fact, Schliemann discovered the walls of Troy several times. Unfortunately, after each triumphant proclamation, troubling discrepancies arose to put the putative discovery into question. But scholars were slow to suspect the myth that Schliemann erected around himself. Most of his biographers used Schliemann's published autobiographies as their chief source material, occasionally augmenting their accounts with his numerous unpublished diaries and letters. For the most part, they did not look much further than Schliemann's own writings.[5] And few mastered the entire corpus of his material, including eighteen diaries written in eleven languages.

Despite the success of the myth of himself that Schliemann promoted, biographies of the archaeologist, of which more than forty exist in book length, have not escaped controversy. Sanctioned by Schliemann's widow, Emil Ludwig (1881–1948), Schliemann's first biographer, had access to almost all of his papers. In

1931, the popular biographer published a best-seller: *Schliemann of Troy: The Story of a Gold Seeker,* which unified its subject's life around the story of a rags-to-riches-to-ruins quest for gold by an enlightened amateur who beat the solid experts. Because of the venality of Ludwig's Schliemann, the book did not please the family.[6] Scholars also recoiled from Ludwig's portrayal.[7] One American Homerist described it as "a life which has knocked off [Schliemann's] halo."[8] What is more, Ludwig was a Jew criticizing a German hero, and his books were burned in Nazi Germany in 1933.

Simultaneously, Ernst Meyer (1888–1968) began publishing Schliemann's letters, which now number around eighty thousand.[9] Around nine hundred of these appeared in three major volumes in 1936, 1953, and 1958. Meyer censored the letters, suppressing some documents damaging to Schliemann and selectively editing others, leaving uncomplimentary portions unpublished. As a teacher in the Gymnasium Carolinum, Schliemann's own school, Meyer understandably presented a flattering picture of this alumnus.[10] Meyer's idealized biography of Schliemann was commissioned by an official of the National Socialist Party in Mecklenburg, who had other reasons for perpetuating the myth of the visionary German who reconnected the modern world with the Homeric past.[11] In redeeming Schliemann, Meyer sought to discredit Ludwig's portrayal, believing that "Ludwig lacked the organ to detect the German in Schliemann."[12] Because most of the biographers who followed Meyer used his publications, they celebrated Meyer's mythic Schliemann and perpetuated the myth that Schliemann himself created.

Ironically, it was the celebration of Schliemann's 150th birthday in 1972 that touched off a critical investigation of Schliemann's life and his discoveries. An American classicist, William M. Calder III, announced that he had found discrepancies in Schliemann's autobiographies and had become suspicious,[13] calling for a reexamination of Schliemann's corpus and urging the necessity of corroborating Schliemann's autobiographies and archaeological writings with independent sources. He also declared that Schliemann's mendacity was "exceeded only by the gullibility of his biographers."[14] What actually had happened a hundred years earlier during Schliemann's excavations in the Troad, the northwestern corner of Asia Minor bounded by the Gulf of Edremit, the Aegean Sea, and the Hellespont, was itself about to be dug up and examined.

Another American classicist, David A. Traill, began to investigate the Schliemann case with the training of a philologist. He attacked the huge corpus of Schliemann's writings, looking for problems, inconsistencies, revisions, and errors in fact and language.[15] The result of his thorough scrutiny of Schliemann's diaries, letters, and publications is a significant contribution to the understanding of Schliemann's complexities.[16] His effort to unravel Schliemann from his "cocoon of myth" has culminated in a masterful biography, *Schliemann of Troy: Treasure and Deceit,* that is no less controversial than its subject.[17]

Investigations by archaeologists into the veracity of Schliemann's writings began in Athens, where the Gennadius Library of the American School of Classical Studies houses the Schliemann Archive of letters, diaries, and other papers. A Greek archaeologist, George S. Korres, who has compiled an exhaustive bibliography of Schliemann's writings as well as those that concern Schliemann studics, has examined details surrounding some of Schliemann's questionable archaeological claims where private and public accounts did not match, establishing grounds for doubting the accuracy of some of Schliemann's archaeological writings.[18] While concentrating on Schliemann's excavation records of the 1870–72 seasons, a British archaeologist, Donald F. Easton, has studied and synthesized the archaeological finds of Schliemann and his successors, contributing to the reappraisal of Schliemann's work by reconstructing provenances and stratigraphy, bringing thousands of finds excavated by Schliemann back into discussion.[19] In so doing, Easton and other archaeologists have responded to Traill's accusations by generally supporting the authenticity of Schliemann's claims.[20]

Unexpectedly, the end of the Cold War opened the way for inquiries into another aspect of the Schliemann case: the whereabouts of Priam's Treasure, the hoard of gold, silver, and bronze jewelry, vessels, implements, and weapons taken from Schliemann's excavations at Hisarlik. In 1991, an art historian-journalist and a former museum curator and inspector from Russia broke the story of its fate.[21] Two years later, Russia formally confirmed that the phenomenal hoard discovered by Schliemann, then smuggled out of Turkey to Athens, given to Berlin, and eventually listed among items lost during the capture of Berlin in May 1945, still existed, hidden deep underground in the basement of the Pushkin State Museum of Fine Arts in Moscow. In April 1996, the notorious treasure was exhibited for the first time in half a century.

Easton and Traill have pored over Schliemann's varied accounts of the controversial treasure, arriving at different reconstructions of this sensational find in a number of articles.[22] Historically, like Easton, most archaeologists have approved the authenticity of the treasure, if not of his dramatic tale of its discovery. With its appearance, governments of all the nations involved in the vexed history of the treasure have staked competing claims to its ownership. But there is another claim to be staked, both to some of Schliemann's treasures and to the honor of actually having found the site of Troy. That claim belongs to the man who owned half the land on which Troy eventually was found, the man who informed and educated Heinrich Schliemann about the site and persuaded him to dig there.

The story of the discovery of Troy is but partly told by those who have penetrated the deceptions with which Schliemann surrounded himself in his accounts of the event. Schliemann's self-aggrandizement cast into the shadows a man whose claim to having discovered Troy is just as strong, if not stronger: Frank Calvert.

In contrast to the voluminous material left behind by Schliemann and written about him after his death, few clues remain to illuminate the life of Frank Calvert (1828–1908). He left no autobiography. Only a small cache of letters, preserved by his niece, survived the vicissitudes of his life at the Dardanelles, modern

Çanakkale,[23] the city near the strait of the same name between Europe and Turkey. Only the occasional letter offers details of his unpublished achievements, the manuscripts for which rarely have been found. Calvert was a self-effacing, private person. His published scientific works reveal little about him as an individual. Largely forgotten at the end of the nineteenth century, Calvert was a victim of his own temperament, his financial situation, and his scanty publications, all of which assisted Schliemann's successful campaign of self-aggrandizement. Even the small cache of letters preserves only a select part of the history.

Until 1973, when Calder and Traill began to question the authenticity of Schliemann's claims, almost no attention whatsoever had been paid to Calvert in half a century. In 1911, three years after Calvert's death, Walter Leaf (1852–1927), a British avocational scholar of Homer, traveled the Troad for five weeks. Not himself an archaeologist, Leaf explored the region and visited some of the sites that Calvert had discovered, excavated, and identified. In his first book, *Troy: A Study in Homeric Geography* (1912), he reconciled Homer's landscape with modern research and praised Schliemann and his successor, Wilhelm Dörpfeld (1853–1940). In the second, *Strabo on the Troad* (1923), Leaf examined the ancient geographer Strabo's account of the Troad and accepted every one of Calvert's identifications, giving him credit for the discoveries he published and referring to him as "a pioneer as usual in the scientific topography of the Troad."[24]

Less than ten years after Leaf's second book, Ludwig called attention to Calvert in his biography of Schliemann. With access to Schliemann's private papers, he was able to point out that Calvert had introduced Schliemann to the theory that Troy lay at Hisarlık and to the writings of its armchair proponents. Quoting Calvert's own criticism of Schliemann's method, Ludwig noted his subject's overly hasty destruction of the upper strata at Hisarlık, inexactitude in recording depths of finds and strata, superficial descriptions of walls, and precipitate announcements that he had found Troy.[25] But few followed his provocative lead.[26].

Things began to change in 1973, when the British archaeologist John M. Cook (1910–1994) published his comprehensive archaeological and topographical study, *The Troad*. Cook addressed a much more circumscribed area than Leaf, one that he had studied in much greater detail over ten years. He was able to specify Calvert's contributions more accurately because in 1960 he had learned of the discovery of the unpublished manuscript catalogue to the Calvert Collection, "Katalog der Sammlung Calvert in den Dardanellen und in Thymbra," which documented Calvert's many identifications and excavations at over twenty-eight sites in the Troad and the Gallipoli Peninsula to the north.[27] A Turkish schoolteacher had saved and later given it to the Istanbul Archaeological Museum, where Cook studied and mined it for information concerning Calvert's many unpublished excavations. He was sympathetic to Calvert and regretted that because Calvert had "regarded his knowledge as of value only in so far as it was relevant to a problem or an argument . . . he left behind only the skeleton of what he must have known." Furthermore, he made the importance of Calvert's research and fieldwork clear by observing unequivocally that Calvert "is our principal authority for the field archaeology of much of the Troad. Permanently resident at the Dardanelles, and a familiar figure in the countryside, Calvert had advantages that no other archaeologist in the Troad has enjoyed. . . . He was much respected by visitors and scholars of all nations who came to the Troad."[28] Later Cook remarked that "Calvert alone knew what classical city sites looked like; by comparison his successors have been groping in the dark."[29] Following Ludwig, Cook, too, drew attention to Schliemann's indebtedness to Calvert for the discovery of Troy and for encouraging him to excavate there.[30]

A. C. Lascarides reviewed several of Frank Calvert's archaeological publications in an exhibition of important books, articles, and maps on Troy, published as *The Search for Troy* in 1977. One was Calvert's critical refutation in 1864 of the popular theory that Pınarbaşı was the site of Troy. Lascarides concluded that "there is no longer any doubt that Frank's intimate knowledge of the antiquities of the Troad played the greatest part in directing Schliemann to Hissarlik and supplying him not only with a wealth of personal experience gained through years of digging here and there, but also in guiding Schliemann's reading to appreciate the works of those who had abandoned Bunarbashi [Pınarbaşı] altogether."[31]

In the 1980s, several of the articles that Traill published on Schliemann shed light on Calvert.[32] Traill discovered some of the damning correspondence between Calvert and Schliemann that had been consciously glossed over by Meyer and left unpublished. Concerned mainly with a correct assessment of Schliemann, Traill published portions of Schliemann's 1868 diary and those episodes in letters that shed light on Schliemann's unsavory character during his early acquaintance with Calvert. Chief among these was Schliemann's repeated attempt to diminish the significance of Calvert's excavations at Troy and deny Calvert's persuasion of him to dig at Hisarlık.

But because Traill's early articles, along with the books by Cook and Lascarides, reached a limited audience composed primarily of classical scholars, they had little impact outside the field of classics. In 1982, the BBC publicized Calder's and Traill's research in a documentary, "The Man behind the Mask."[33] Three years later, Michael Wood brought some of these revisionist views to an even wider audience in the 1985 BBC series *In Search of the Trojan War* and suggested that Schliemann had appropriated Calvert's childhood dream of finding Troy.[34] He and Easton by now had discovered critical correspondence between Calvert and the British Museum.[35] In order to make Traill's scattered research more easily accessible, Calder collected Traill's articles and published them in 1993 as *Excavating Schliemann*. Yet this and Traill's 1995 biography of Schliemann, designed to reach a wider audience, devoted little time to Calvert and left much critical documentation unpublished. Only in the 1990s have new archival sources been found that enable a comprehensive study of Calvert's relationship with Schliemann.[36]

The story of Calvert's life and of his contributions to modern archaeology would have been very different if a series of chance events had not brought him face-to-face with Heinrich Schliemann during the summer of 1868. Schliemann was not then the visionary archaeologist he was to claim he was, but a businessman and tourist developing an enthusiasm for antique treasures and sites. In the midst of a grand tour of the ancient world, he came across an architect in Athens, Ernst Ziller. Ziller steered Schliemann toward Pınarbaşı, a site then assumed to be Troy by most of the scholarly community, where Ziller had participated in excavations a few years earlier. He gave Schliemann excellent information on the Troad and must have encouraged him to meet the expert on Trojan archaeology when he traveled to the Dardanelles.[37] That expert was Frank Calvert.

In fact, Schliemann would meet Calvert only at the end of his journey. In the meantime, Ziller's information had excited him so much that on the day of their meeting, 25 July 1868, Schliemann tried to book a passage from Athens to the Dardanelles.[38] But because he could not be guaranteed a disembarkation there, he chose to wait for a later ship and to visit Mycenae and Argos instead.[39] On 31 July he entered the Treasury of Atreus at Mycenae and noted potsherds and tile fragments on the citadel of Agamemnon.[40] After visiting Mycenae and Argos on 31 July, he followed *Murray's Handbook of Greece* to other sites in the Argolid.

Armed with Nicoläides' *Topographie et plan stratégique de l'Iliade, Murray's Handbook,* and an excavation report prepared by von Hahn, Schliemann eagerly anticipated his pilgrimage to the plain of Troy, but the visit did not start well.[41] Arriving at the Dardanelles at 10:00 P.M. on 7 August, he was not allowed to disembark from this ship, either, but had to go all the way to Constantinople and catch another steamer headed back to the Hellespont. This he did undeterred, arriving at the Dardanelles at 6:30 A.M. on 8 August. Rather than searching out Frank Calvert, whose imposing office-residence would have been hard to miss,[42] he went instead directly to the Russian consul, who gave Schliemann an indifferent guide and horses as far as Erenköy, where he could get a Greek guide and fresh horses.[43] But when he arrived, neither were available.[44] At the end of a long and frustrating day Schliemann finally reached his goal, Pınarbaşı, the supposed site of Troy. He ascended the bluff above the Scamander River and was transfixed by the dramatic view at dusk. "It was for me a strange feeling, when, from the mountain, I saw in front of me the great plain of the Troad with two large monuments near the shore," he told his diary.[45]

Schliemann wasted part of 9 August looking for a guide and better horses. Later, in a nearby village, a combination innkeeper and barber who spoke fair Arabic guided him to ruins that he does not name in the diary: "on a hill which is almost 100 feet high, he showed me, covered with a great deal of soil, but recently partly excavated,[46] a temple or palace of excellently worked cyclopean stones. From there I had a fine view over the plain of the Troad. Nearby lie the remains of fine stelai."[47] If this was Hisarlık, it did not claim Schliemann's attention, suggesting he was at that point unaware of its having a claim to be Troy. Neither Murray nor Nicoläides mentioned the site, and it was sheer chance that the Turkish barber had led him there at all.[48] Schliemann then continued on to Rhoeteum, on the north coast, where, following his guide book, he noted a monumental tomb excavated by "Calvart" and, following Nicoläides, the tumuli of Achilles and Patroclus.[49]

In the meantime, Schliemann set out to do some excavating where he was certain the site of ancient Troy lay. On 11 August, with a crew of one he began to dig at Pınarbaşı in various spots in the ancient city, but results were disappointing. "We did not find even the slightest traces of bricks or pieces of pots," he wrote.[50] Schliemann prospected in one of the three tumuli where Nicoläides noted Calvert had dug,[51] finding some sherds there, and in another that also had been opened.

On 12 August, after a day of exertion with two diggers, Schliemann confessed: "Dug today all day at the site of the ancient city but I did not find even a trace of bricks or anything else which could prove that a city existed there of old."[52] He had begun that day's diary entry differently, using the dates of both the Julian and Gregorian calendars, a practice that he continued until he reached Constantinople five days later. The Gregorian calendar was in use throughout Europe at the time, while the Julian calendar was still employed in Greece, Russia, and the Ottoman Empire.[53] Whereas Traill noted that Schliemann used both dates to remove ambiguity, in fact, the seemingly meticulous and self-conscious recording with multiple dates was a clever screen behind which he reworked the important events of the next few days.[54]

Schliemann had gotten behind on his diary entries, beginning with 12 August, after excavating for two days at Pınarbaşı and traveling through the Troad to the Dardanelles. Then he met Calvert. All those entries that he double-dated reflect a self-conscious attempt to render the altered course of events more official, more historical. By writing entries 31/12 August, 2/14 August, and 4/16 August after his meeting with Calvert, he could incorporate all of Calvert's information and opinions into his own diary as if he himself had come to them independently, days before Calvert persuaded him that Troy most probably lay not at Pınarbaşı, but at Hisarlık.

It is at this point, understandably, that it becomes difficult to trust Schliemann's account, thanks to all his ex post facto revisions of the story of how he alone found Troy. And it is at this point that he broke with his previously unquestioned acceptance of Pınarbaşı as Troy, declaring it was a "conjectured city" and reiterating, "The city was never on this site."[55] His confident rejection is curious. Surely the excavation results were not sufficient to change his mind so abruptly. To bolster his entry, he reported that characteristic features of Homeric sites, such as the cyclopean walls and pot sherds such that he had just seen at Mycenae, were missing there.

After touring the Troad on his own and with considerable difficulty, Schliemann quit and again headed north. He later would record the uneventful day's ride: "2/14 August, at the Dardanelles," noting as an afterthought and without any previous mention of the site, "We passed the plain of the ancient Troad which I looked at with great curiosity, especially the hill of Haserlik where, in my opinion, Homer's Pergamos [the acropolis of Troy] used to be."[56] He does not mention stopping there, which is odd if in fact he then believed it to be Homeric Troy's citadel. If he visited Hisarlık at all in 1868, the only possible place would have to be the unnamed site that the barber had shown him five days earlier.[57] The preponderance of the evidence certainly indicates that until Schliemann met Calvert, he in fact had conceived of no alternative to Pınarbaşı for the true location of ancient Troy.[58]

After stopping at Erenköy Schliemann returned to the Dardanelles on 14 August. Having lingered along the road to remove an inscription, on arriving at his destination he was told that he was one hour late for the afternoon steamer to Constantinople. Obliged to spend the nights of 14 and 15 August waiting for the next steamer, Schliemann found shelter in a filthy establishment where he coated himself with "Persian dust" to keep the bugs at bay.[59] Schliemann now was marooned for a day and a half at the Dardanelles. According to his diary, he was just killing time when he finally met Frank Calvert.

Schliemann called on Calvert, and Calvert invited him to dinner. For generations, the Calvert family graciously had entertained Europeans passing through. Frank Calvert did not record his first meeting with Schliemann, but according to the radically telescoped account preserved in later family tradition, "a dinner was given for Mr. Schlemann, the Archaeologist, and a number of . . . treasures were shown to him. He was then searching for the ruins of ancient Troy in quite another locality. On seeing the fragments which had been found by Mr. Calvert, he called off his force, dug some trial trenches and found the site of Troy."[60] Actually, Schliemann did not commence excavations at Troy until two years later, in 1870.

Frank Calvert strongly believed in the historicity of Homer's account of Troy. Years previously he publicly had dismissed Pınarbaşı as its site, along with other theories of its location. He had become convinced, instead, that Troy lay at Hisarlık. He believed that over the preceding years, while excavating small sections of the land that he owned there, he had made finds that would prove it, although at present he was unable to afford the effort to do so. Calvert, the experienced excavator who understood stratigraphy and the buildup of cultural debris, convinced the defeated Schliemann, who had resources more than adequate for the task of excavation. Calvert always had been generous with his knowledge. Now, on the spur of the moment, he seized on Schliemann's financial strength to carry out the excavations he had hoped to conduct himself. "In the interest of science," as he later put it, he made "a sacrifice of personal considerations, urging Dr. Schliemann to carry out what had been for years my particular ambition."[61] In the space of an evening, he had given away his cherished ambition to an unknown, unproven, unannounced stranger. After his meeting with Calvert, Schliemann's head must have spun. Suddenly, at the end of a journey that had been vexed with difficulties and doomed to fail, he had stumbled upon a knowledgeable ally who could foster his interests at a scarcely dug, yet immensely promising, site.

Now reinvigorated, he caught up on his diary, which he had forgotten in his discouragement. He wrote the double-dated entries for 12 and 14 August, confidently rejecting Pınarbaşı. The myth-making process had begun. Schliemann recorded his meeting with Frank Calvert in his diary entry for 4/16 August, Dardanelles:[62] "Yesterday I made the acquaintance of the famous Archaeologist Frank Calvert who thinks, as I do, that the Homeric Troad was nowhere else but at Hessarlik. He advises me strongly to dig there. He says that the whole mound is man-made. He showed me his large collection of vases and other antiquities which he has found during his excavations amongst which was a bronze lion with Punic letters indicating its use as a weight measuring a talent."[63] The quality of Calvert's collection of artifacts and Calvert's generosity and enthusiastic description of his own excavations at Hisarlık caused Schliemann to drop Pınarbaşı and commit his fortune to the excavation of Homer's Troy at Hisarlık.[64] The rest, as the saying goes, is history, but it is a history of a very different kind than people long have been led to believe. At the center of that history is an unassuming scholar and gentleman, Frank Calvert.

CHAPTER ONE

"Levantine English families"
The Calverts of the Dardanelles

The Dardanelles strait, the narrowest part of the Hellespont channel connecting the Aegean and the Sea of Marmara, stretches for roughly a mile, connecting and separating Europe and Asia [Map 1]. It was naturally dangerous for navigation before the advent of steam-powered vessels. For most of the summer sailing season, a prevailing northeast-southwest wind blows down the channel from the Sea of Marmara, adding to an already strong current of as much as four miles an hour that prevented access to sailing ships wishing to pass northward to the Black Sea.[1] Sometimes boats would be detained for as long as a month, waiting for a south wind to allow them to surmount the formidable current.[2] As many as two to three hundred ships thus could be gathered below the Hellespont.[3] And when the south wind blew in the late fall and winter, it often resulted in gales that churned the dangerous waters flowing in the opposite direction.[4]

This critical passage in ancient times was controlled by Troy, according to Homer. In Ottoman times, it was guarded by castles. Originally known as Kale-i Sultaniye, or Sultan Kalaahsi,[5] the fortress on the Asiatic side was, by the 1800s, "called by the Turks Channákálasy, or *Pot Castle*, from the extensive potteries carried on in the town; the other, on the European side, is called *Kalidbakar* [Kilid Bahr], or Lock of the Sea." Here batteries faced each other and could unite in firing to make the strait unpassable.[6] Pencil sketches of both sides of the Dardanelles by William "Crimean" Simpson (1823–1899), Queen Victoria's war artist on his way to Balaclava in November 1854, document the twin forts and the towns that grew up around them [Figures 1a and 1b].[7]

The Rhodius River bordered the castle "Channákálasy" on the west. To the northeast grew the town of Çanakkale, named for the fortress that defended it, "a sort of advanced post to 'Stamboul." A picture of the town can be pieced together from eighteenth-century views and the memoirs of a fairly steady stream of European visitors.[8] The British called the town "the Dardanelles," a term that other-

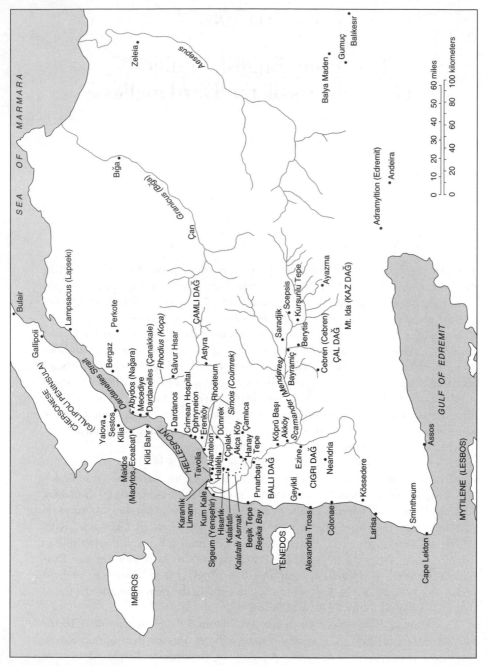

Map 1. The Troad.

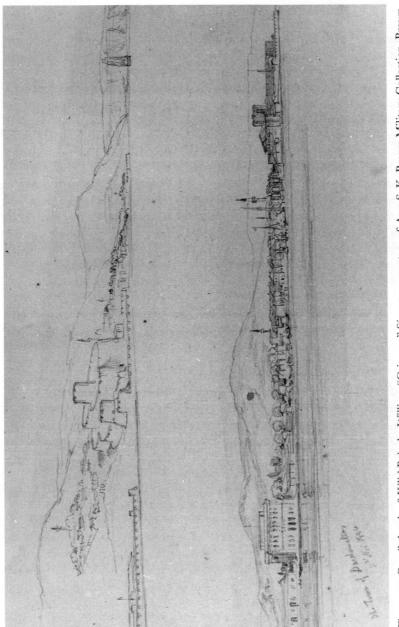

Figure 1a. Pencil sketch of Kilid Bahr by William "Crimean" Simpson, courtesy of Ann S. K. Brown Military Collection, Brown University Library. Figure 1b. Pencil sketch of Çanakkale (the Dardanelles) by William "Crimean" Simpson, courtesy of Ann S. K. Brown Military Collection, Browr University Library.

wise referred to the strait alone, and observed that its strongly fortified position made it "the portal to the sultan's capital."[9]

Second only to its strategic importance was its value as a buffer zone against outside influences. One British traveler noted that "the *cordon sanitaire* has a post here, a hundred miles from Constantinople, to prevent the introduction of plague to the city."[10] For just this purpose, a quarantine station, or lazaretto, was constructed northeast of the city to monitor and hinder the passage of persons coming from afflicted parts of the realm, sequestering those who were ill or without papers. Still, the city was occasionally plagued by cholera morbus, carried by ships and spread from the fort at Abydos (Nağara), which lay dangerously close to the lazaretto and the city itself.[11] Pestilential fevers spread quickly in summer through the low-lying town and its marshy outskirts.

Because of its location, by 1875 this city was in more constant contact with Europe than any other place in Turkey except Constantinople, according to the *John Murray Handbook for Travellers*.[12] Ships of one nationality or another visited almost every day, and each was compelled to stop and show its papers. Because of this traffic, the Dardanelles became the outlet for all goods produced in the Troad and neighboring regions, from Ayvalık on the Gulf of Edremit to Gallipoli on the Chersonese, including several Aegean islands. Not surprisingly, many of the local industries serviced shipping: the production of cotton and manufacture of sail cloth, as well as boat building.[13] Local pottery was exported to Greece, Cyprus, and Romania.[14] Other exports were wool,[15] timber, leeches, hides, and especially grain and valonia, an important product of the Eurasian evergreen oak, used in preparing and dyeing leather in tanneries. Of these, hides, wool, and grain went chiefly to England and France and valonia to Russia and Austria.[16] Although a telegraph office was operative by 1854, most mail continued to be carried by ship.[17] Curiously, however, there were no wharves or docks or even good anchorages. Instead, all of the vessels anchored out in the harbor, where they would land the mail and transact other business, with loading and unloading facilitated by locals in caiques, or small boats, and lighters.[18] Ships would at the same time load choice oysters, cockles, scallops, and various species of fish available in local waters.[19]

The Dardanelles was the seat of a civil and military governor, a "pasha of three tails,"[20] an exceedingly wealthy landowner with vast estates.[21] From the sultan on down, the Turks were eager to be hospitable to the British, Ottoman allies in the Battle of the Nile in 1798, when Lord Nelson had bested the French fleet. The British traveler and antiquary Edward Daniel Clarke (1769–1822) described his audience with the colorful pasha of the Dardanelles. While the Russian consul interpreted on his knees, the elegantly accoutered pasha, hereditary lord over the entire district, reclined on a superb green divan. Clarke noted that his generous host wished to escort him all over the region and was willing to give "all the antiquities of Troas" for some English pistols.[22]

The city was the administrative capital, first of the Archipelago and later of the Biğa *sançak*, or province.[23] For this reason, as well as because of its singular location, the

Dardanelles was home to the vice-consuls or consular agents of most European countries and the United States. Their consular offices constituted a bright line of structures along the sea, painted in various colors, "with the flags of every nation fluttering gaily in the breeze" [Figure 1b].[24] It also was home to the Russian and British consuls.

One visitor in the 1870s noted that this fair front of diplomatic edifices "hid from view the usual medley of shipping agencies, restaurants, and thievish-looking dens which constitute a seaport town of Asia Minor." Nevertheless, it was "a cleanlier town than many others on that coast . . . the numerous shops for jugs of a peculiar green glaze give it an air of industry, if not of art, unusual at least in a Graeco-Turkish town."[25] The city, with its densely packed houses, was prone to fires, which devastated it in 1800, 1838 (twice), 1857, 1860, and 1865.[26] In 1838, a visitor noted that one-half of the town, "the court end, was completely destroyed last year, but is rapidly rising again, formed entirely of wooden houses, which, while new and uniform, have a peculiar and somewhat pleasing effect."[27] Other travelers described the primitive conditions that still prevailed in 1849: the "dreary little town" is "badly built, and the streets very narrow and dirty."[28] In 1854, the *John Murray Handbook* described it as "miserable."[29]

Each long-standing ethnic community had its own quarter, within which clustered one-story houses of wood or mud brick lacking in comfort. The Franks, or Europeans, were on the seaside. The Armenians, there since 1529, were centered around their church. The large community of Sephardic Jews who immigrated to the area in 1660 spoke Hebraicized Spanish and had three hundred houses and a synagogue.[30] The Greek Orthodox population by 1740 had its own distinct area with about eighty houses and by 1793 a church. Of these, the Frank quarter was devastated in the fire of 1860 and the Greek, Jewish, and Armenian communities were consumed by the fire of 1865.[31]

The Ottomans had made benevolent, but inefficient, attempts at city planning.[32] These included widening the streets and segregating wooden and stone houses in 1857, after that year's fire, which had left some forty families homeless.[33] Another measure to help preclude destruction by fire was the removal of the pottery kilns, which were dangerously located in a neighborhood of wooden houses, to an area outside the town. After the fire of 1865, the city finally expanded across the wooden bridge over the ancient Rhodius River and took over the dried marshland to the south.[34]

By contrast with the squalor of the crowded town, rich and beautiful environs surrounded the area. Nearby gardens were lush and well cultivated, with cotton, sesame, vines, olives, citrus, and other fruits.[35] Sycamores shaded the picturesque riverbanks, home to colorful Greek and Turkish festivals.[36] Behind the town lay cemeteries for Turks, Jews, and Christians.[37] To the northeast rose vine-colored hills; to the south, the plain terminated at a low mountain. On these hills behind the Dardanelles, British travelers noted unusually dense habitation in comparison with that of the plain of Troy and elsewhere in Asia Minor or Turkey. In these forested hills roamed wild boar, deer, hares, partridges, and woodcocks.[38]

Although actual population estimates vary wildly, at the end of the eighteenth century there were approximately two thousand houses sheltering a population of around ten thousand, most of whom were agriculturalists. In 1816, an English observer noted that among the *raya*, or non-Muslim Ottoman subjects,[39] there were 80 Jewish houses, 150 Armenian, and 300 Greek.[40] The rest were Turkish. According to one report, in 1844 there were twenty British subjects.[41] General population estimates rose to eleven thousand in 1842 and to twelve thousand in 1856, after the Crimean War.[42] By 1857, the population was in a considerable state of flux, with the Turkish population declining, and the number of Greeks, many of them immigrants from European Turkey, increasing.[43]

Small businesses, such as tanneries, rope, soap, and jam producers, and forges, were run by Greeks, Armenians, and Jews. The Turks were armorers and shipbuilders. All residents could speak Turkish, although among themselves the Greeks, Armenians, and Sephardic Jews spoke their own languages. The Europeans and Levantines of the diplomatic community spoke French.[44] The Jewish community provisioned ships and exported red wines, supplied by vineyards of neighboring towns,[45] to Constantinople, Smyrna, Aleppo, France, and England.[46] From time to time they dealt in antiquities brought from the Troad in the hope of selling them to English travelers.[47] For more than a century, the Jews of the Dardanelles had acted as agents for the British Levant Company.[48] The Tarragano and Gormezano families were among the more prominent in the community, providing dragomen, or interpreters, for European travelers and consular agents for the various European nations.[49] The Tarraganos alone filled the posts of British viceconsul and Russian consul for generations.[50] It was not uncommon for one individual or family to represent several nations at once. This model also was followed by the Calvert family.

It was in and around the consular offices of the Dardanelles that the Calvert family lived and made a living. Charles Alexander Lander (1786–1846), their maternal uncle, had become the British consul by 1829.[51] In the decades that followed, several of his nephews found employment as consuls and vice-consuls, including Frank Calvert.

Simpson's sketch of the Asiatic shore reveals the newly built Calvert house [Figure 1b]. With its tremendous length facing the strait and lapped by the waves, the conspicuous building dominated the cityscape from the sea, dwarfing every other structure on the waterfront, including the fort. It was constructed in 1852.[52] The house projected into the harbor on land reclaimed from the strait in front of it.[53] Family members testify that the local pasha was irate as the house was being built because he saw its imposing form as a challenge to his own status.[54] Low warehouses lined the landward side of the street, further accentuating its scale.[55] To the west lay the old town, with its windmills and mosques, the diminutive seaside structures upstaged by the formal European-style consular mansion.

At the center of the Calvert family's presence at the Dardanelles—and in many ways, at the center of Frank Calvert's life and his efforts to discover the true site of

Homeric Troy—stood his older brother, Frederick William Calvert (1819–1876), who had become British consul in 1847.[56] An "extremely intelligent and agreeable man," Frederick Calvert spoke Greek, Turkish, Italian, and French, in addition to his native tongue.[57] He was a great sportsman who used to go shooting with one of the local pashas and was well liked by the Turks.[58] He dispensed loans to the local population, and on Sundays, sick peasants came to him for advice and simple surgical operations.[59]

Pragmatic and ambitious, he consolidated his position by quickly purchasing two farms on the Chersonese, or Gallipoli Peninsula, and in the Troad, as well as prime waterfront real estate in the Dardanelles.[60] There he gradually introduced European livestock and agricultural equipment, experimenting with new crops and techniques.[61] According to British observers, men such as he served as examples to the local community and pioneers in agricultural reform.[62]

On the eve of the Crimean War, George William Frederick Howard (1802–1864), the seventh earl of Carlisle, toured the area in the summer and autumn of 1853, when the British fleet was stationed at Beşika Bay, the final anchorage before the Dardanelles strait.[63] Carlisle was a frequent guest of Stratford Canning (1786–1880), who was made Viscount Stratford de Redcliffe in 1852 and who was the British ambassador to the Sublime Porte (Constantinople) from 1842 to 1858.[64] The earl moved in high circles, flitting from ship to ship, tasting the culinary delights of the area, "turtle from Alexandria, partridge from Imbros, grapes from Lesbos."[65] Thus accustomed to every luxury, the noted British statesman found "the excellent Mr. Calvert" a hospitable host. The earl also described Frederick's wise benevolence, gentle energy, and "inventive utilitarianism," and he suggested that "such a class of men would be more real regenerators of this bright, but still barbarous region, than either fleets or protocols."[66] Inspired by the landscape, Carlisle reread the *Iliad* in the original. After "a delicious ride at dusk" with Frederick Calvert, Carlisle praised him in words Homer had reserved for one of his ancient "ex-neighbours," an ally of Priam's.[67] A subsequent visitor topped this accolade by remarking that Frederick Calvert could be called "a latter day Priam" for his widespread estates.[68]

At least one foreign visitor referred to the Calverts' fine stone house in town as a small "palace by the sea" [Figure 2].[69] Neoclassical in style and grand in proportion, it was designed to impress. The mansion was well located for transacting maritime business, one of the chief roles of the consular agent. British and American flags flew from the terrace on the flat roof. There Frederick Calvert, consul for England, vice-consul for Prussia, and agent for Belgium and Holland, and his brother James (1827–1896), consular agent for the United States, would collect fees from all ships bearing British, U.S., Prussian, Belgian, and Dutch flags that passed through the strategic strait.[70]

The foyer was formal, with symmetrical pillars on either side of the majestic stone staircases that flanked the entrance from the street [Figure 3]. Vases from the family's collection of antiquities stood on columnar pedestals high above the visitor, on the

Figure 2. Calvert mansion at the Dardanelles. By Francis Henry Bacon, courtesy of Elizabeth Bacon.

Figure 3. Interior of Calvert mansion. Frank Calvert stands by the staircase in the foyer. By Francis Henry Bacon, courtesy of Candace Bacon Cordella.

Figure 4. Landward view of the Calvert mansion. By Francis Henry Bacon, courtesy of Elizabeth Bacon.

staircase landings. In the central hall, which must have doubled as a waiting room, the family provided comfortable wicker chairs for clients, visitors, and petitioners. Here Schliemann would await his initial meeting with Frank Calvert in August 1868.

Enchanted visitors fondly remembered tea and conversation in the English salon, where the Calvert ladies performed pleasing musicales and sang for their distinguished guests.[71] Photographs of the family's private quarters show a richly appointed and colorful interior, with lavish use of Oriental carpets, kilims, and inlaid tables from Damascus. The walls of the large drawing room were decorated with paintings and tapestries. Stacks of books lay on the tables, and a guitar rested on a comfortable divan strewn with pillows. A marble statue of a goddess stood on a tapestry-decked chest, marking the central axis of the building. In the dining room, an elaborately carved marble mantle bore numerous antiquities and curiosities. On the other side of the entrance, a silver service with gleaming samovars was exhibited on a generous sideboard. In the center of the room, a table with candelabra and six chairs awaited family and guests.

On the landward facade, a shaded second-floor balcony rose above the arched doorway to the street [Figure 4]. Here the family could look out on their lush English gardens with over six acres of tree-lined avenues, fragrant orchards of peach, apricot, and plum, resplendent pools and cool fountains, exotic plants, and winding paths. Family photographs depict an all-encompassing space of great natural beauty. On the perimeter were a stable, a tennis court, greenhouses, and numerous storerooms and outbuildings. Beyond the gardens lay the family cemetery, begun in 1846, a lovely walled enclosure shaded by cypress trees and the resting place of most of the clan.[72]

Figure 5. View of Erenköy. Choiseul-Gouffier (1822), plate 51. Courtesy of Brown
University Library.

Francis H. Bacon, who later would marry Frederick's eldest daughter, Alice,
reminisced about the lifestyle of Frederick Calvert, whom he never met, his family, and his class in his diary in 1883:

> He had been quite wealthy. . . . When he died, the house was unfinished.[73] Here the
> three girls live with their mother and their father's brother, Mr. Frank Calvert, our
> consul . . . [and] Mr. Calvert's sister . . . also unmarried! The girls all ride horse-back
> splendidly, each having her own horse. Then they play tennis, going winters to
> Smyrna, Egypt, or Constantinople, where they have relatives! These old Levantine
> English families form quite an aristocracy! They are nearly all well to do, and all
> seem to be related to each other.[74]

On vine-covered slopes overlooking the Hellespont some 12 miles southwest of
the Dardanelles stood the family's country house at Erenköy, where Lander had
bought a country residence in an old Turkish town recently taken over by
Greeks.[75] An early-nineteenth-century view of the village and a map of its environs portray it as a sleepy hamlet in the midst of olive and oak orchards and fields
of cotton, barley, and wheat [Figures 5 and 6].[76] A large tumulus crowned the hill
to the southeast behind the town. In 1816, the village had about two hundred
neatly built stone houses with flat roofs, and by 1842 an inn, or *han*.[77] It prospered
from the passage through the village of all land traffic from the south. Because of
treacherous wind at the strait, the Russian consul kept a resident secretary stationed there to service ships stranded along the coast below.[78] Here the Landers
and the Calverts sought refuge and relief from the dirty city.[79]

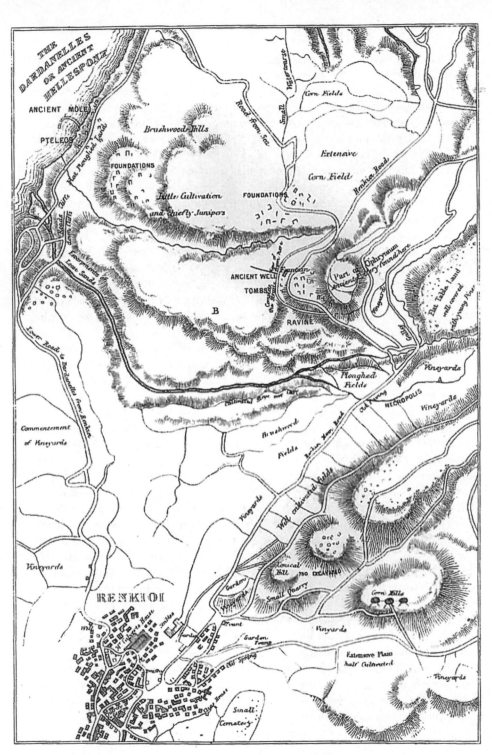

Figure 6. Plan of Erenköy and environs. From Calvert (1860b).

Once the property of a Turkish *aga,* or local official, their house stood at the high point in the center of the village opposite the village square and consisted of two Turkish houses joined together, surrounded by gardens, orchards, and vineyards.[80] One guest wrote: "The view of the Hellespont from Mr. Lander's windows is really beautiful—covered as it is with vessels of all nations ascending and descending its current, which in this part is extremely rapid."[81] Sir Adolfus Slade (1802–1877), British admiral of the Turkish fleet, who was surveying the fortifications of the Dardanelles, reminisced that "at times we had a noble sight from our windows of sixty or seventy vessels, of all nations, making sail together from . . . the various points, where they had lain wind-bound for weeks or months, and running past the little town, which on its part displayed, from the various consulates, all the colours of Europe."[82]

The estate came into Frederick's control after Lander's death in 1846.[83] It was held in the name of Frederick's wife, since foreign males were not allowed to hold property in the Ottoman realm. During the 1840s and early 1850s, it was the family seat and official residence of the British consul, where he received visitors.[84] It was here that Frederick entertained the earl of Carlisle, who was charmed by evening walks down the lanes and through the vineyards. Impressed, Carlisle wrote in his journal that the house was "airy and spacious . . . with a very wide view over the Hellespont, the Aegean, and the islands—all the waters in intense blue."[85] The "classical" view encompassed the Chersonese to the north, Imbros, Samothrace, and Mount Athos to the west, and Kum Kale, Sigeum, the tumuli, and Tenedos to the south.[86] On the plain below the house, as part of his contribution to the Crimean War effort, Frederick aided in the construction of a model British military hospital with 3000 beds in 1855.[87] With the buildup of British troops at the Dardanelles bound for or returning from the Crimea, and with a large community of British located at the hospital, the family frequently entertained at the villa.[88] After the war, the family used Erenköy much less often. Because of financial difficulties, Frederick mortgaged the estate in 1858.[89] More than a decade later, Frank Calvert offered it to Schliemann as a residence during the first Hisarlık excavations, but the property by then was dilapidated.[90]

While Erenköy and its visual beauty provided an escape, the Dardanelles structure was home and office to Frank Calvert for more than fifty years. Here he was firmly grounded in a community where there existed access to Europe and frequent travelers and scholars. But it was in the Troad that Frank Calvert found his true life's work, his greatest fulfillment, and his greatest frustration [Map 1]. More than any other archaeologist before or since, he was blessed with the opportunity to wander through this historic landscape, allowing it to reveal its mysteries to him slowly. In the words of a contemporary, he "drank in the privileged silence in keeping with indulgent daydreams of Troy and its heroes."[91]

To the north rushes the Hellespont, a "salt river," the mouth of which stretches for five miles between the cliffs of the Chersonese and the Sigeum ridge of the Troad. To the west lies the Aegean Sea, to the south laps the Adramyttion Gulf, and to the south and southeast soars the mighty mass of Ida (Kaz Dağ), which rises ridge on ridge, its forested slopes home to deer, wolves, jackals, hyenas, bears, foxes, and wildcats.[92] Lagoons mark the northern shore and give way to promontories and gentle hills to the east, many crowned with ancient sites. Hills girdle the plain of Troy, which extends nine miles from north to south and three from east to west. The plain, too, abounded in wildlife: hares, boar, jackals, partridge, woodcock, quails, and tortoises.[93] One observer remarked laconically of a bleak winter in the Troad, "Nothing breaks the monotony of the horizon but the vast tumuli which appear at intervals against the sky, marking the grave of some Homeric hero . . . the roads in the Plain of Troy have long strings of camels on their way to some far country, and an occasional horseman armed to the teeth."[94] Another noted the springtime beauty of fields clothed in poppies and star-of-Bethlehem, with hovering clouds of almond blossoms.[95]

Three principal streams or winter torrents flow through the plain: the Dümrek, or Simois, the Kemer, or Thymbrios, and the Menderes, or Scamander, River.[96] Fresh-water turtles basked along the riverbanks while large herds of water buffalo and mares grazed in marshy areas teeming with snipe and water fowl.[97] In the western part of the plain, where the Scamander changed its course over millennia, lay a pestilential marsh, treacherous for fever.

Unlike most English abroad, the Calverts were not content simply to reside in town with the Europeans. Frederick, in particular, had the zeal of a colonist.[98] His dispatches show that between 1830 and 1860 the resident British were paving the way for an influx of their countrymen, and that they planned to develop the countryside. Thus, the family spread into the hinterland, purchasing acreage and pioneering European agricultural techniques. Frederick bought up land on both sides of the strait and was considering the purchase of yet another estate at Dardanos.[99] One large farm lay on the Chersonese, beyond the Ottoman fortress of Kilid Bahr.[100] The other lay on the plain of Troy.

Frederick's Troad farm extended for approximately 2,000 to 3,000 acres through fine valleys and gentle hills.[101] The farm buildings straddled a ridge at the southern limit of the Trojan plateau, 4 miles southeast of Hisarlık, at the confluence of the Kemer (Strabo's ancient Thymbrios)[102] and Menderes Rivers [Figure 7]. Also known as Batak Chiflik, or "marsh estate," it lay dangerously close to a wetland area known for its fevers.[103] A small Turkish town, Akça Köy, had stood on the spot until 1814, when plague killed most of the inhabitants.[104] By 1839, a farm was in operation there, near ground honeycombed with tombs from an ancient cemetery.[105] Frederick Calvert purchased the estate in 1847.[106]

Family photographs show a large, rambling farmhouse built of stone and partly stuccoed [Figure 7]. With five bays of windows across the front, it overlooked the rich farmland and reached out into the countryside with artful trellises and shaded verandahs. Several additions marked the growth of the family and its economic status. The living quarters were surrounded by an elegant fence, whose gateposts were surmounted by urns. In a landscaped court, the family kept large antiquities, which they had gathered in their excursions or had excavated in the Troad [Figures 8 and 9]. The house itself was appointed with colorful kilims, tapestries, wicker chairs, and comfortable divans.

Figure 7. Distant view of Batak Chiflik, later known as Thymbra Farm, at Akça Köy. By Francis Henry Bacon, courtesy of Candace Bacon Cordella.

Figure 8. Eveline Abbott Calvert in courtyard at Batak, or Thymbra, Farm, with the Calvert Stele on the right and the Aeolic capital from Neandria on the left (1892). By Francis Henry Bacon, courtesy of Elizabeth Bacon.

Figure 9. Frank Calvert stands among inscriptions and sculptures in the courtyard at Batak, or Thymbra, Farm. By Francis Henry Bacon, courtesy of Elizabeth Bacon.

This was a working farm, where the family cultivated valonia oak, the chief agricultural export of the Troad, harvesting the cup of the acorn for use in the tanning and dyeing industries of England.[107] They also grew cotton and wheat. Frederick, an agricultural pioneer for profit, not only introduced English plows, but engineered the draining of the marsh, thereby reclaiming 240 acres of pasture. Family members always had seasonal work at the farms, bringing in the harvest and coping with recurrent problems, such as locust infestations.[108]

A high stone wall protected the family compound and farm buildings from brigands. A string of low, subsidiary buildings formed a continuous line crowning the ridge to the left of the main house. These housed a superintendent, servants, and farm workers, as well as animals and equipment. Valonia oaks dotted the ridge, and horses grazed in the plain, which stretched out below.

Francis Henry Bacon described this residence and the Calverts' life there:

> We reached the Chiflik about ten o'clock, a long court surrounded by sheds and farm buildings, and a gate at the lower end leads to the house where the Calverts live when at the farm! The roof was covered with stork nests and the storks were sailing about in the moonlight in all directions, clapping their bills! The house is on the edge of a hill looking off over a vineyard to the valley of the Scamander! It was just lovely

and we all said, Oh! Ah! and sat down to enjoy it while Athenasius unloaded the luggage! . . . a servant took the best care of us! Everything was spick and span—spindle legged chairs, comfortable divans, old fashioned books in a case, and it seemed almost like a New England farm house; a porch overgrown with vines, gravel walks under the trees, with flower pots set about, etc. That night we each had a snug little bedroom which smelled of herbs![109]

For almost a century, this renowned homestead, later known as Thymbra Farm, attracted scholars who traveled through the Troad in search of Homer's Troy. In 1890, the German archaeologist Carl Schuchhardt (1859–1943) recalled: "this lovely spot is the only oasis in the deserted plain of the Skamander, and every visitor to Troy who gains admission here will in his later reminiscences forget the sandy ride and the melancholy clay huts of the villages in the recollection of the 'Villa Thymbra' and its friendly host," Frank Calvert.[110]

Frank Calvert had been born on Malta in 1828 to James Calvert (1778–1852), a lateral descendant of the barons of Baltimore,[111] and Louisa Ann Lander (1792–1867), daughter of John and Mary Campbell Lander, a lineal descendant of the Glenlyon and Duneaves branch of the Campbell family of Argyll. They married in Smyrna (present-day Izmir) in 1815, and then moved to Malta, the central point of departure for all travelers to the Levant and a very important entrepôt for British goods sent to the south of France and to the eastern Mediterranean [Map 2].[112] Malta then was recovering from an economic slump brought on by a devastating plague in 1813 and the subsequent withdrawal of Europeans and European capital. British citizens were sent to stabilize conditions there. In Valletta, the English capital of the island, Mr. Calvert worked in shipping and conveying mail between England and India and served with the grain department.[113] There, on the wide but steep Strada Zecca, the Calverts began to raise a large family, a daughter and six sons.[114] Frank Calvert was their youngest child.

The Calverts, and on their mother's side, the Landers, occupied a privileged, yet precarious, social position, one central to the operation of Britain's imperial interests in the eastern Mediterranean, yet located at a problematic overlap between two very different social spheres in Victorian society. In 1853, Charles Thomas Newton (1816–1894), then British vice-consul at Mytilene, wrote that the Calvert house at Erenköy contained "a few stray relics of European civilization," which, in addition to "a piano forte, a bagatelle-table, some of the new books published last year in England and various other little luxuries unknown to Mytilene," included a portrait gallery that boasted, among others, "a grim picture of Sir Thomas Maitland, flanked by two family portraits of beauties of George III's time."[115] These portraits taken together help to begin to paint another sort of picture, that of the Calverts' social class.

The paintings included ancestral portraits of the Calvert clan, as well as the portrait of Maitland (1759–1824), commander-in-chief of the Mediterranean and governor of Malta from 1813 to 1824, a personal gift to their father, James Calvert, "to whom Sir Thomas was a true friend." There was no portrait of the father in

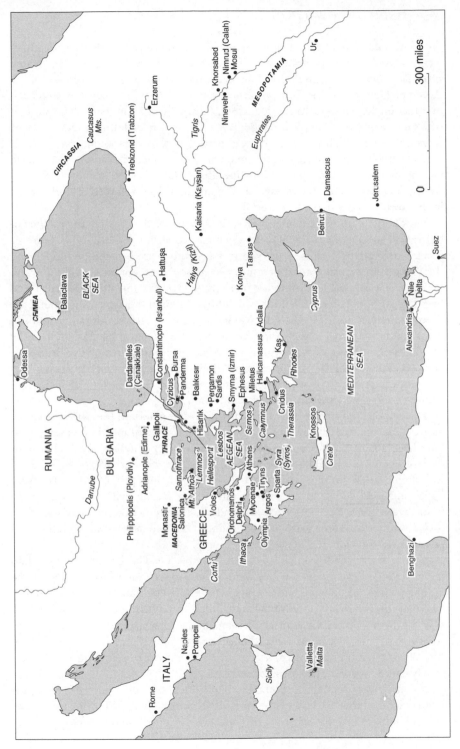

Map 2. The central and eastern Mediterranean.

the house; the family found itself in reduced circumstances after his death.[116] There were, however, portraits of his father, William Calvert (1739–1807), "with a silver-lace collar," his grandfather, John Calvert (1704–1774), great-grandson of the Reverend George Calvert, B.A., vicar of Stanwell, shown in a "figured waistcoat," his great-uncle, James Calvert (1702–1786), shown "with a fur coat collar," and his wife's mother, Mary Campbell Lander (1752–1846), wife of John Lander of Poole, Dorset.[117] These highly respectable and gentrified ancestors, themselves descendants of nobility, had produced by the beginning of Victoria's reign what was to be one of the recurring topoi of its literature: unpropertied younger offspring who, despite possessing the lineage of a "gentleman," were forced to find a living in the world of commerce [Figure 10].

Back home in the British metropolis, the spheres of the gentleman and the entrepreneur seeking the main chance were regarded as inherently at odds, however much—or perhaps because—the gentry frequently were in need of money and the rising commercial classes were in need of social acceptance. In the Levant, however, it was possible for families such as the Calverts and the Landers to lead lives that seemingly reconciled the two. Thus, although they were not among the Victorian elite who traveled to the Mediterranean at leisure, migrating south in the autumn and north in the spring, because of their geographical position at the Dardanelles, they occasionally came into contact with the apex of the British social pyramid: government ministers, peers, heirs to landed fortunes, and members of the royal family, all of whom flocked to the area in the footsteps of their eighteenth-century predecessors on the Grand Tour.

Because of their lineage, the Calverts thus could entertain the earl of Carlisle, and for that matter, Victoria's son, Prince Arthur, something they never would have been able to do at home. And in the Levant, they could enjoy a higher standard of living than would have been possible in England. Servants provided them with ample leisure for the intellectual and cultural pursuits proper to the class from which they had come. In addition to interacting socially with those who, back home, would have been regarded as decidedly their superiors in social standing, they also entertained the European consular set. And their relations with the local peasants were decidedly paternalistic.

Yet they were indeed compelled to earn a living. The Calverts and Landers had traveled to the Levant because they were obliged to seek their fortune. They were among the host of colonial bureaucrats, service officers, traders, and missionaries who had come there for professional and commercial purposes. What made it possible for them to live the lives of gentlemen and ladies while actually working constantly to support a style of living that otherwise would have been denied them was the occupation into which, sooner or later, most of the men in the Calvert family found their way, the consular service.

A consul was uniquely positioned to acquit the office of a gentleman by providing aid and service to his countrymen in a foreign clime, yet at the same time he held in his hands the very reins of commerce. The consular service had arisen

THE CALVERT FAMILY

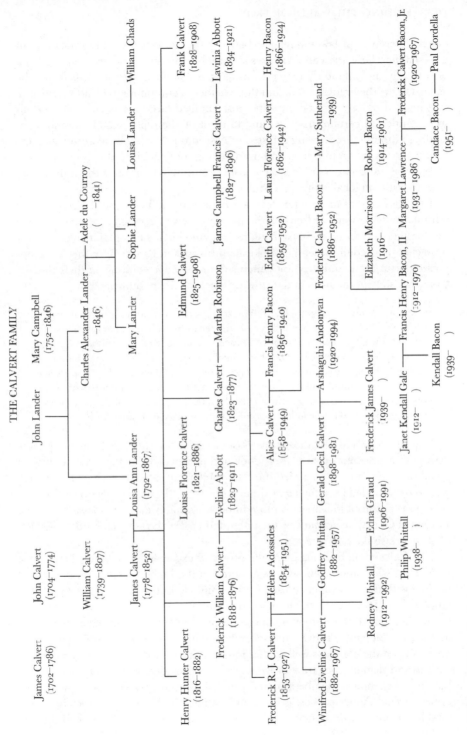

Figure 10. Calvert family tree.

out of differences of law and religion between the Levant and the European countries that had large mercantile interests there. In general, consular duties were not
of a strictly diplomatic character. Consuls were "political agents," officers of the
governments they represented, and thus wielded a combination of administrative
and judicial powers. Yet because the post entailed large responsibilities, consuls
were entitled to certain privileges and to most of the diplomatic immunities, including immunity from being arrested or cast into prison by local authorities, except for some atrocious crime, and from having soldiers billeted upon them, invi-
olability of their papers unless the consul was a merchant, and the right not to
have to testify in local courts as a witness.

Consuls acted as interpreters for their countrymen. They also settled civil and
criminal suits between citizens of the nation they represented, disputes between
the masters and crews of ships flying its flag, and claims for small debts.[118] They
protected their countrymen before local authorities in cases where they were op-
pressed or injured, and they appointed subordinate vice-consuls in their district.
Consuls also kept the birth and death registries for their countries.

> How many things a man must know to make a good consul, for his duties are endless
> in their variety, and of quite a different character from those of other officials of the
> Foreign Office; they demand a mass of practical knowledge for which special educa-
> tion is required. Consuls should be able to fulfill, in the event of necessity, the duties of
> judge, arbitrator, and reconciler. They must be able to do the work of a notary, some-
> times that of a commissioner of the navy. They have to look after sanitary matters, and
> from them is expected, owing to their general relations a clear idea of the state of trade
> and navigation, and of the industry peculiar to their place of residence.[119]

In western Asia Minor, those consuls or vice-consuls who had the arms of a foreign power emblazoned over their door had attained the highest social position
possible locally, one that entitled them to appear on public occasions in uniform
and to be attended by armed guards, or *kavasses*.[120] "In fact," wrote one observer,
"the post of consul in Turkey is more important than that of ambassador at any
European Court; on account of the unlimited power they exercise independently
of the Turkish laws."[121]

The Calverts' upbringing on Malta provided excellent training for the life of a
gentleman who simultaneously was at home in the highest circles, yet capable of
dealing with the varying circumstances of daily life in the Levant, and in need of
employment. James Calvert, Frank's father, had worked there as a civil servant and
minor diplomat in the cosmopolitan community.[122] Valletta provided a good living
at a reasonable cost. Primary and secondary schools were good, and there was a
university on the island, as well as a famous botanical garden.[123] "Amusements are
various and elegant," one traveler wrote: "a club, provided with papers, periodicals;
billiards, &c., unites members of the professions and travellers; an opera three
times a week; dinner parties; riding and boating. . . . The English society is hospitable, inclined to do honour to their country in the due entertainment of for-

eigners, and, barring the foibles inherent in a confined circle . . . very pleasant."[124] There was little intercourse between English and Maltese families, and, although fluent in Italian, very few Maltese spoke acceptable English.[125] "You meet travellers of all sorts—antiquarians, missionaries, yachtsmen, Italian patrols, Barbary exiles, and occasionally a cargo from Naples. . . . Giraffes from Egypt for the Zoological, and lions from Barbary for the Tower. . . . Without moving, you have the élite of the whole world brought to you."[126] But there were drawbacks to a life in the Levant, as well. Despite the clean town and the healthy climate, cholera broke out in 1813, and in 1830 and 1831, malaria and smallpox ravaged the population when the entire Calvert family was still resident on Malta.[127] The well-built and handsome town of stepped streets lay on a neck of land between two harbors—the eastern one for commerce, the western one for quarantine, the sequestration of ill travelers and those without proper health papers. This purgatory was called "the abomination of travelling," "the nightmare of horror to all travellers to the east."[128]

The Calvert sons all left home at sixteen to seek their fortunes. The few careers open to gentlemen of limited means who "did not wish to suffer loss of caste by entering trade" included law, medicine, the church, and the military, in addition to the diplomatic and consular services. The eldest, Henry Hunter Calvert (1817–1882), initially chose the navy, and then moved from the military to the diplomatic corps.[129] From 1838 on, he resided within the Ottoman Empire, serving in the British consulate in Erzerum in 1851 and later as British vice-consul of Alexandria, Egypt, where he remained for twenty-five years.[130] Edmund (1825–1908) went east and began an itinerant diplomatic career at Trebizond on the Black Sea coast of Turkey, Konya, and Kaisaria (Kayseri) in 1842.[131] In 1852, he worked under Stratford de Redcliffe at the British embassy in Constantinople, and he later served as secretary to the British ambassador (from 1858 to 1865), and still later as the acting British vice-consul of Constantinople.[132] After serving as acting British consul at various posts in the Ottoman Empire, he finally became the British vice-consul at Rhodes.[133]

The other sons could not avoid the taint of commerce so easily. They were sent to the Dardanelles to go to work for their maternal uncle, Charles Alexander Lander, who also was their father's business partner.[134] Lander had moved to the Dardanelles in 1829, presumably attracted by the favorable economic conditions that followed the end of the Greek War of Independence.[135] Though he and his sister, Mrs. Calvert, were descended from a noble line, Lander himself had had to make his way as a trader.[136] At the Dardanelles, Lander was well positioned to take advantage of the immense opportunities for free trade caused by the abolishing of the Levant Company, which hitherto had monopolized commerce between England and the Ottoman Empire.[137] Aided by the plummeting value of the Ottoman piaster relative to the British pound sterling, by 1842, Lander and Frank Calvert's brother Frederick had established a successful valonia-processing business.[138] Initially living at Erenköy, Lander had completed a house in town for business purposes by 1833.[139]

But Lander, too, was a gentleman. It was Charles Lander who showed the younger Calverts how the consular service could help resolve the conflict between the status of a gentleman and the need to make money in business. He had become British consul at the Dardanelles in 1829.[140] By all accounts he was gracious and hospitable, meeting British ships anchoring offshore with fine fruit and inviting admirals,[141] scholars, and travelers to dine and stay with him and his wife, the former Adèle de Courroy, "an accomplished Frenchwoman," according to the admiring Admiral Slade.[142] The admiral believed that a representative of the crown was obliged to maintain appearances and should be supported adequately to do so: "The principal officers of Great Britain's possessions should be able to live on a par with the principal natives," and "high salaries" are "an allurement to proper men. . . . Opinion depends as much on appearances as on character . . . so no Englishman . . . should be employed in a foreign possession without an adequate salary."[143]

But not all consuls enjoyed such salaries. There were two distinct consular classes in Turkey—those who received a fixed salary and were prohibited from engaging in trade, and those who got only a small stipend but were allowed "to follow some commercial pursuit to enable them to support the dignity of their station." The Calvert clan that followed in Lander's footsteps may have lived as gentlemen, but they supported that lifestyle by earning their livelihood as merchants.

Whereas the system of trader-consuls seemed to work well in Europe, where courts could protect the rights of British subjects and where, consequently, the consul did not exercise judicial power, many felt it was dangerous in the Levant, where Turkish tribunals had no jurisdiction over a foreign resident. There, a consul took on a higher rank, invested with judicial authority, the "guardian of his country's honour and the protector of the rights of her citizens, from whose fiat there is no appeal." It was of this grade that it was thought critical that they "receive adequate salary to enable them to uphold the dignity of their station, without having recourse to commercial employments."[144] The latter grade was less preferable. It carried the onus associated with all "commercial employments"— and it was more open to corruption.[145]

Frank Calvert's brother Frederick succeeded Lander after assisting him in both business and consular matters for over a decade, first as acting consul in 1845 and 1846 and then as British consul.[146] Charles Calvert (1823–1877) [Figure 11] had joined Frederick at the Dardanelles by 1840. By 1843, he had revived the consular office of the United States there, and he served as U.S. consular agent until 1849, when he left the family enclave for a successful diplomatic career abroad.[147] He became acting British consul at Damascus in 1850 and later at Beirut, moving to Salonica as British consul in 1856. By 1860, he was posted to Monastir (in present Macedonia), and later he was sent to Naples.[148] Unlike Henry and Edmund, who also served far from home, Charles did not keep in close contact with the family.

James Campbell Francis Calvert (1827–1896) and the youngest brother, Frank, both moved to the Dardanelles with their spinster sister Louisa Florence (1821–

Figure 11. Family portrait, 1866. Courtesy Elizabeth Bacon. From left: Frank Calvert, seated; Lavinia Abbott Calvert and James Calvert, standing; Louisa Lander Calvert (Mrs. James Calvert, Sr.), seated in wheelchair; Charles Calvert, standing; Martha Robinson Calvert (Mrs. Charles Calvert), with Alice Calvert on lap; Eveline Abbott Calvert (Mrs. Frederick W. Calvert) seated, with Laura on her lap; Edith Calvert, Frederick R. J. Calvert, and Louisa Florence Calvert, seated on right.

1886) around 1845, after Frank had completed school [Figure 11].[149] James was trained by Frederick and often stood in as acting British consul when Frederick was away. A talented linguist, James inherited Charles's post as U.S. consular agent.[150] After the Crimean War ended in 1856, James married Lavinia Abbott of Smyrna, the third daughter of a family much like the Calverts and Landers. He remained at his post until 1874, when he finally left the closed community of the Dardanelles and moved permanently to Constantinople.[151]

By the time that Frank Calvert arrived at the Dardanelles, his brothers were occupied with their diplomatic activities, and Frederick was active in Lander's commercial affairs, probably already having taken over unofficially the British consulship from his uncle.[152] Lander was well read and knowledgeable about the landscape and its ruins. Among his prized possessions was a valuable library, which burned in the fire of 1838 that devastated the town. He deplored the great quantity of ancient marbles, sarcophagi, and columns that had been removed during his time by the Ottomans[153] to carry on their building of the forts at the Dardanelles and for fashioning enormous cannonballs that were shot at the strait.[154] He had accompanied travelers to Mount Ida and Samothrace while his assistant, Frederick Calvert, had guided others to archaeological sites along the Asiatic coast of the Dardanelles.[155] Thus, Calvert was welcomed into the region by a man who appreciated the historical importance of his adopted land.

Initially, Frank Calvert seems not to have involved himself in the family business or consular offices. But by 1852 and 1853 he was helping his brothers Frederick and James in their consular duties, writing 50 percent of the letters in French and English generated for his brothers, which they would sign as officers.[156] He did the same in 1855, while Frederick was completely engrossed in affairs related to the Crimean War.[157] In 1856 and 1857, he would write only occasional letters, implying increased free time. On occasion in 1856 and 1858, he stood in for Frederick as acting British consul.[158] After standing in for James, eventually Frank succeeded him as United States consular agent in 1874, an unpaid position that he held for the rest of his life.[159] Occasionally, he served on local mixed European and Turkish tribunals, assuming from time to time the title of acting British consul. Quite involved in the shipping industry, he became local agent for the Moss Steamship Company, whose steamers sailed between Liverpool and the Mediterranean, and member of an important commission investigating shipping at the strategic port.[160] He and James were partners in two mining ventures.[161] In later life, when his elder brothers had left the Dardanelles, Frank managed the family business and the farm. Like his sister and brothers Edmund and Henry, he never married.[162]

Instead, he fell in love with his adopted land. The Calverts hunted on the Trojan plain and fished in the Simois River, which ran right by the site of Hisarlık, which already was connected with Ilium Novum in their day. They picnicked on ancient sites in abandoned Roman quarries and explored ancient clay storage jars large enough to hold six men. They had tea at Pınarbaşı on the bluff overlooking the Scamander River at the site most scholars thought was Homer's Troy. Frank Calvert achieved an intimate knowledge of topography that never has been matched. In a landscape synonymous with mythic deeds, this displaced young man found himself at home.

CHAPTER TWO

"Indulgent daydreams of Troy and its heroes"
Early Explorations of the Troad

The Troad and the landscape surrounding what became known as Thymbra Farm was an archaeological site on a grand scale—the site not just of ancient ruins, but of a privileged time and place in the imagination of the West, a "landscape of the mind." Where Europe and Asia meet, history and poetry, war and epic had left behind successive layers of fact and myth about the genealogy of Western civilization and its self-representations. It was rich in legends of noble purpose and tragic death. The very name Hellespont derives from an old tale connected with the saga of Jason and the Argonauts. As the story goes, a Greek king, left with a son and a daughter named Helle, remarried. When his new queen tried to rid herself of the stepchildren, a magical ram with golden fleece transported the children through the air from Europe into Asia. As they were flying eastward, Helle fell off and was drowned in the waterway that subsequently bore her name.

Romantics were attracted to the strait because of the tale of the lovers Hero and Leander.[1] Hero was the priestess of Aphrodite at Sestos on the European shore and Leander a young man from Abydos on the Asiatic coast. By night, he secretly would swim the strait to be with Hero. One night, a storm blew out Hero's light and Leander became lost and drowned. Hero hurled herself from the heights of Sestos to join him in death.[2] Gazing out over this landscape of magnified possibilities and mystical revelations, on 3 May 1810, Byron imitated Leander and swam the Hellespont from Sestos to Abydos.[3] Others followed. For anyone arriving as a teenager in such a landscape, as Frank Calvert had done, it was difficult not to be stimulated imaginatively and galvanized into curiosity.

The privileged story of the Troad, the narrative of treachery and retribution, of heroism and victory and defeat and conflagration that lay at the center of it all, was of course Homer's.[4] Like every upper- or middle-class British schoolboy in the early 1800s, Frank Calvert had read the classics of Greek and Latin literature and knew them well. He knew that the *Iliad*, composed in the eighth century B.C., did not tell the whole story. It focused on events taking place in the tenth year of the Trojan War, omitting major episodes before and after the action of the poem, which were told in later epics. Later poems—the *Odyssey*, the *Little Iliad*, the *Cypria*, and the *Sack of Troy*, or the *Iliupersis*—gave many of the other familiar aspects of the story, such as the Trojan Horse, the Judgment of Paris, and the Sack of Troy.

Living in the setting of the story itself had to have made the tale doubly gripping. On the level of the imagination, at least, Troy was present all around Calvert. The gods Apollo and Poseidon had built the first walls of Troy. But, cheated of their due by the Trojan king, Laomedon, they afterward sent Herakles to destroy the citadel. With a small band of Greeks, he sacked the palace and slaughtered the Trojans, leaving only a very young prince, later called Priam, who one day would rebuild the citadel's walls (*Iliad* 5.640). And so the events began to unfold.

The cast of characters, their actions, and their fates were part of the *genius loci* of the Troad: Priam, now survived into old age; his queen, Hecuba, and fifty sons and twelve daughters; Hector, the eldest son, the warrior, who with his wife Andromache had reared Priam's grandson Astyanax; Paris, the scourge of Troy, who had abducted Helen, the queen of Sparta, while enjoying the hospitality of her husband Menelaus; Helen, the sister of Clytemnestra and wife of Menelaus, brother of Agamemnon, king of Mycenae; Agamemnon's assault on the "strong-walled citadel of Troy" to regain Helen; the combat between Patroclus, Achilles' friend, and Hector, magnificent warriors of both sides of the struggle; the death of Achilles; the Trojan Horse and the sack of the city; its final destruction. And always, the gods looking down from snowy Ida and Samothrace, championing their favorites.

Patroclus and Hector were cremated on huge pyres, according to Homer, their bones and ashes placed in urns or caskets. In their honor, mourning comrades raised earthen mounds over their graves, with "stones laid close together," making barrows, or tumuli, on the plain of Troy. Achilles, too, was cremated and buried with Patroclus in a prominent position overlooking the Hellespont. These mounds haunted the Troad like sentinels, at the entrance to the Hellespont, along the western coast, and inland, especially at Pınarbaşı on the Ballı Dağ.

That was the story, and in his daily life, Frank Calvert was living in the middle of it. But was Homer's Troy a real place or a myth, and if it was real, exactly where was it located? The vexing question *Ubi Troja fuit?* marshaled scholars, travelers, and armchair antiquarians into opposing camps for centuries. If a historical Troy could be found, he was in the right place to join in the search.

The family's prominent position and wide-ranging interests brought Frank Calvert into contact with the theories of most if not all of the major European scholars who had addressed the issue of Trojan topography. Several of these scholars were houseguests. While Frederick Calvert was serving European dignitaries in his capacity of British consul, Frank Calvert guided foreign scholars, lords, and princes through the Troad and occasionally much farther afield to various archaeological sites. In addition, he encouraged scholars to peruse the family's growing collection of antiquities. It was an apprenticeship in a vocation that, like his family's consular positions, would allow him to employ his time usefully and respectably, as well as gainfully, as a gentleman. It became an apprenticeship in archaeology.

Some visitors, such as the Russian envoy Peter de Tchihatcheff (1808–1890)[5] and Charles Maclaren (1782–1866),[6] founder and from 1817 to 1847 editor of the *Scotsman*, the leading political journal in Scotland, were interested in the geology and geography and passed along an appreciation for natural science as well as archaeology to the young Calvert. Several engaged Frank Calvert in discussions while traveling through the plain.

Maclaren, who visited the Calvert family in 1847, the same year as the purchase of Batak Farm and shortly after Frank Calvert's arrival, treated the Trojan War as a real event. Maclaren was a polymath, keenly interested in a wide variety of subjects from American Indians to Homer. In his words: "Ilium was, for a considerable period to the Heathen world, what Jerusalem is now to the Christian, a 'sacred' city which attracted pilgrims by the fame of its wars and its woes, and by the shadow of ancient sanctity reposing upon it . . . a voice speaking from this hill, three thousand years ago sent its utterance over the whole ancient world, as its echoes still reverberate over the modern."[7] The articulate and persuasive journalist must have made a deep impression on his host's teenage brother. Frank Calvert soon would devote his leisure time to proving that Troy had existed and to locating it and the towns of its allies. The landscape was littered with remains of the past. But which, if any, of these belonged to Homer's Troy was not easy to say. One way to tell was to dig for evidence of earlier civilizations—but how much earlier?

Calvert knew that the Greeks thought of the Trojan War as their own ancient history. Through lists of kings and aristocratic genealogies, the Greeks extended their awareness of history back from the eighth century B.C. to the beginning of the first millennium B.C. Beyond that lay an abyss difficult to bridge, "where the heroes could dwell at ease."[8] Opinions ranged from 1334 to the tenth century B.C.[9] Herodotus, "the father of history," had suggested around 1300 B.C.,[10] but in Hellenistic times the officially accepted date was 1184 to 1183 B.C., the date given by Eratosthenes, the learned third-century astronomer and geographer of Alexandria, and accepted by Calvert himself.[11]

Through his study of Herodotus, Xenophon, and Thucydides, Calvert also knew that the ancient authors never had lost sight of Troy, recounting numerous later chapters in its history. But those later chapters were written over the Homeric narrative like a palimpsest, inscribing the actions of other heroes pursuing their own fates and ends. In the first millennium B.C., Greeks had established a small colony at a spot in the Troad and called it "Ilion."[12] Centuries later, as Xerxes was preparing to conquer the Greeks in 480 B.C., he constructed a pontoon bridge from Abydos to Sestos.[13] Before crossing the Hellespont from Asia to Europe, the Persian king arrived at the Scamander and ascended the "Pergamos" to pay homage to Priam. There, "he sacrificed 1000 oxen to Iliean Athena and the Magi poured out libations in honor of the heroes," according to Herodotus.[14] And this was not just a simple gesture of respect. He claimed that his reason for invading Greece was to right the wrongs inflicted on the Trojans.[15] While surveying the strait that Xerxes bridged at Abydos, the young Calvert would claim to visitors that he had found the throne of the Persian potentate.[16] A generation earlier, a misty-eyed British traveler spied the blackened timbers of ships wrecked at Abydos and seriously thought these might actually be remnants of Xerxes' fleet.[17]

One hundred and fifty years after the Persian invasion, Alexander the Great, who claimed for himself descent from Achilles and slept with an annotated *Iliad* beside his dagger, made the reverse crossing from Europe into Asia in 334 B.C., a millennium after the fall of Troy, according to one calculation.[18] Reverently, he slaughtered a bull for Poseidon and poured libations to the nymphs in midstream. The first of his army to touch Trojan soil, he planted his spear and claimed the land for the gods. Alexander then marched his troops to Ilion, where, having "sacrificed to Trojan Athena, and dedicated his full armor in the temple, he took down in its place some of the dedicated arms yet remaining from the Trojan war, which, it is said, the hypaspists [targeteers] used to carry before him into battle. Then he sacrificed also to Priam at the altar of Zeus, praying Priam not to vent his anger on the race of Neoptolemos, of which he himself was a scion." At Troy, his pilot crowned him with a golden wreath. Before he left the Troad, Alexander emphasized his genealogical claim by anointing himself with oil, running naked to Achilles' grave, and laying a garland on it.[19] His friend Hephaistion did likewise for Patroclus. "Later, he reenacted the dragging of Hector's corpse [*Iliad* 22.395–404] by dragging one of his own enemies around the city by thongs which pierced his ankles."[20]

According to Alexander's wishes, his successors patronized the town. Alexander had raised Ilion to the status of a polis and made its cult of Athena fashionable. In 306 B.C. it became the capital of a league of Troad cities focused on this cult.[21] A local benefactor built a theater, and Alexander's general, Lysimachus (361–281 B.C.), began a marble Doric temple to Athena, and according to Strabo, he also built a fortification wall.[22] Ilion at this time saw itself as the heir to Athens, even instituting Panathenaic games. After a brief occupation by the Gauls, the site was overshadowed by the newly founded coastal city of Alexandria Troas.[23] In 86 B.C., after the Roman rebel Fimbria besieged and gained admission to Ilion, he immediately massacred the Ilians and sacked the town.[24] But Julius Caesar, who traced *his* own lineage back through Iulus to the lesser Trojan prince Aeneas, revived Ilion and patronized the site as Ilium after visiting it in 48 B.C. After crossing over from the Sigeum promontory and the Simois, Caesar was moved by the sight of the plain "where so many heroes died, where no stone is nameless," and he wandered about, looking for the remains of the great citadel and Apollo's walls.[25] He found this site overgrown with trees, and "even the ruins had been destroyed." Vowing to rebuild the home of his ancestors as the Roman capital, he struck a silver coin commemorating his bloodline.[26] Caesar was succeeded by Octavian, later Augustus, who visited Ilium in 20 B.C. Under his eye the most enduring Roman monument to Troy was created, Virgil's *Aeneid,* the epic poem linking the Trojan Aeneas and the found-ing of Rome. As Roman engineers leveled the Pergamos, or acropolis, Augustus restored the temple and theater and built a concert hall, or *odeion,* and a council chamber, or *bouleuterion,* to celebrate the legendary connection between the two cities.[27] Imperial visits were commemorated by gifts of imperial portraits.[28] In A.D. 215, the Roman emperor Caracalla, who traced his Macedonian-Epirote roots to Achilles,[29] surveyed Ilium and its antiquities and paid his respects at Achilles' tomb by allegedly cremating his friend Festus so that he could reenact Achilles' mourning for Patroclus. Since the Panathenaic games continued until the third century A.D., a continuous stream of travelers visited the temple and honored the tumuli until the Goths plundered the city in A.D. 267.[30] After touring the area in the late fourth century, Constantine considered shifting his capital to Ilium or Sigeum on the coast.[31] He tried to found his new capital at the mouth of the Hellespont on the western coast of the Sigeum ridge.[32] But because it had no port, he later trans-ferred it from the impractical spot to Byzantium, or Constantinopolis.[33]

For eight hundred years, then, the ancients had both honored Ilion, or Ilium, as the site of Troy and associated themselves with the events and heroes of Homer's narrative to further their own ends. In spite of the early Christian at-tempts to stamp out paganism, in A.D. 355 altars were still burning in Hector's shrine and his statue was still being anointed. Even Achilles' tomb was intact. In the West, with the incipient rise of nationalism, nations again strove to construct genealogies that connected them with the illustrious heroes of Troy, inventing he-roes such as Brutus, descended from Aeneas, who had fled Rome for Britain, lead-ing the last of the Trojans to that western island and calling it "Britain" from his own name.[34] Another even went so far as to claim that this Brutus, descended from Ilius, founder of Troy, had founded London as "Troynovant," or New Troy.[35] Throughout England and Wales, early mazes and labyrinths called "the walls of Troy" further celebrate this kinship. So the British had established a national affili-ation with the Trojans long before the Tudors embraced the Trojans as their an-cestors and Shakespeare wrote them into his plays.[36]

Troy also was dear to the Ottoman sultans for the same reasons. There was a contemporary identification of the Osmanlis (Turks) with the Trojans.[37] After conquering Constantinople in 1453 and Athens in 1456, Sultan Mehmet II visited what he thought was the site of Troy in 1462, inspecting its ruins, viewing its fa-vorable advantages, and paying his respects at the tombs of the heroes Achilles, Hector, and Ajax. "It is to me," he said, "that Allah has given to avenge this city and its people."[38] Thus, over the years, Homer's heroes had invested the land-scape of the Troad with power. Their deeds and their motivations had been hon-ored, denied, constantly reinvented, adapted, and adopted. If Homer's Troy was real and not a myth, its historical reality lay not only under the accumulated phys-ical strata of the centuries somewhere in the Troad, but also under the accumu-lated histories that both pointed to it and obscured it. And when it came to the question of the actual site of Homeric Troy, the ancient historians disagreed.

Almost all the ancient authors believed that Troy lay under the Greek and Roman city of Ilion, or Ilium. Herodotus, Xenophon, Arrian, and Plutarch were among them. Strabo (63 B.C.–A.D. 19), the geographer who wrote around the time of Augustus, stood alone among major authors in his insistence that it lay elsewhere.[39] In this he followed Demetrius of Scepsis, a local geographer from the town of Scepsis in the Troad who had lived around 180 B.C. and who wrote a work in thirty books on the sixty-two-line passage in the *Iliad* concerning Priam's allies.[40] Apparently Scepsis had pretensions of being the home of Aeneas and therefore coveted lucrative Roman patronage.[41] Perhaps jealous of the attention that Ilion had received, Demetrius argued that Homer's Troy, in his day called Ilion Kome, or the "village of the Ilians," lay "some thirty stades higher up to the east," on a low ridge between the Scamander and the Thymbrios.[42] His inventive account and Strabo's transmission of it would prove to be the bane of generations of modern travelers looking for the true ancient site.

Later residents preserved the memory of the name of Troy, but its location varied within the western Troad.[43] Two coastal sites, Alexandria Troas and Sigeum, both significantly later than Homer's epic, vied for the honor. Until the nineteenth century, European visitors making a pilgrimage to the plain of Troy while reading Homer would be taken to one or the other and would keep diaries of their trips. If travelers disembarked on the west coast, they would be taken to the site of Alexandria Troas,[44] unfortunately a city founded only at the end of the fourth century B.C.[45] If travelers put in on the north coast near the mouth of the Hellespont at Kum Kale, they would be taken to Sigeum, or Yenişehir, where stood the ruins of Constantine's even later aborted capital. If the travelers stopped at both, they could decide for themselves which rival had the better claim.[46] In 1599, one visitor, Thomas Dallam, who was conveying an organ from Elizabeth I of England to Sultan Mehmet III,[47] saw both sites, which are separated by about sixty miles, and thought that *both* were Troy and that at the second site he simply had seen the ruins of Troy in more detail.[48] Both of these sites thus suffered by being accessible, and Sigeum virtually disappeared in the seventeenth century, plundered for its stones.[49]

The British traveler Aaron Hill, who visited the Sigeum area around 1700, mused over its antiquity and quoted the chorus of an old English ballad: "Wast lie those Walls, which were so good / And Grass now grows, where Troy town stood." He dug with swords into a "heap of stones" and discovered one, carved with a knife in 1631, that read:

> *I do suppose that here stood Troy.*
> My name it is William, a *jolly Boy.*
> My other name it is Hudson, and so,
> God Bless the Sailors, wherever they do go.[50]

The British poet Lady Mary Wortley Montagu visited the Troad in 1718 and pronounced that "all that is now left of Troy is the ground on which it stood."[51]

In 1580, Elizabeth I and Murat III established diplomatic relations and opened up Turkey to merchants and individual travelers.[52] With the advent of the Levant Company, which promoted trade between England and the Ottoman Empire, European travelers, inspired by Homeric associations, began to tour this land.[53] George Sandys, a translator of Ovid who ventured to the Troad in 1610, identified the Sigeum ruins with Constantine's capital, recognized the Scamander River in the Menderes, and correctly placed Troy in the vicinity of its lower plain.[54] But travelers rarely penetrated beyond the coastal sites because of brigands, who haunted the desolate plain of Troy until as late as the end of the nineteenth century.

It was not until the Enlightenment, with its intellectual self-confidence, its spirit of inquiry, and its enthusiasm for all things classical, that the issue of the possible location of the true, historical Homeric Troy gradually began to take on the shape in which Frank Calvert found it. Eighteenth-century travelers were indefatigable inquirers. The Irish traveler Robert Wood (ca. 1717–1771), for example, later a member of the British Society of the Dilettanti, visited the Troad in 1742 and for a fortnight in 1750.[55] He discovered the springs at Pınarbaşı, scaled the heights of Çığrı Dağ, and journeyed up the Scamander River.[56] His conclusion that the bay of Troy had been silted up by the Scamander had important repercussions on the candidacy of hitherto unknown inland sites.

It was the appointment of Marie Gabriel Florent Auguste, Comte de Choiseul-Gouffier (1752–1817), to the post of French ambassador to the Sublime Porte in 1784, however, that marked the most significant advance in the study of the Troad.[57] He funded a major cartographic expedition to map the northeastern Aegean, including the western coastline of the Troad, that of the Dardanelles, and the interior of the Troad for his volumes entitled *Voyage pittoresque de la Grèce*. For this purpose, he recruited an expert staff of scholars, engineers, artillery officers, artists, and marines, including Jean-Baptiste Chevalier (1752–1836), who became his personal secretary.[58] Beginning with the investigations undertaken by in quirers that Choiseul-Gouffier sponsored, the question of the site of Troy began to take on a new focus. His team illuminated two sites not hitherto considered, Pınarbaşı and Hisarlık.

In 1785, on his first, brief visit, Chevalier sought the warm and cold springs that Homer placed at the gate of Troy (*Iliad* 22.147–56). Local guides took him to the Kırk Göz, or Forty Eyes, a series of springs near the modern village of Pınarbaşı. Convinced that these springs also were the source of the Scamander River, Chevalier placed Homer's Troy near the village, on the heights of the dramatic bluff named Ballı Dağ overlooking the Menderes, 9 miles from the Hellespont. This novel thesis quickly gained acceptance with those who wished Troy to be real, and the ambassador sent him out again in 1786 to map the area. But in order to claim that Troy lay near Pınarbaşı, Chevalier had to rearrange the rivers rather arbitrarily, with the Menderes becoming the Simois and a lesser stream, the Pınarbaşı Çay, which began at the famous springs, transformed into the Scamander. In 1786, he compiled these findings in a map and stated categorically that he was the first to reconcile perfectly the present topography of the Troad with Homer's text. Because of the positive reaction to his theories, Choiseul-Gouffier accompanied Chevalier to the Troad in 1787.[59]

After acquainting his patron with his research, Chevalier left on a diplomatic mission and took his map with him. When the French Revolution intervened, he traveled to Scotland, where in March 1791, he presented an account of his theories to the Royal Society of Edinburgh, published under the title *Description of the Plain of Troy*.[60] Meanwhile, his patron, Choiseul-Gouffier, left Constantinople in 1793 for Russia, where he sought refuge. There he served as imperial librarian for Catherine the Great and her son, Czar Paul I.[61] In 1802, Choiseul-Gouffier returned to France to work on the second part of *Voyage pittoresque*, which dealt with the Troad. This final volume was not completed until 1822, five years after his death.[62]

The first to discover the mound at Hisarlık was Franz Kauffer, an engineer employed by Choiseul-Gouffier to survey the interior of the Troad and the plain of Troy in 1787. Perhaps prompted by Chevalier's publication, he had located ancient remains at Hisarlık by 1793. His 1793 map was the first to include the site (as Hissardgik or Hissarlik), some 650 yards to the west of Çıplak (Tchiblak) at Old Kalafatlı, between the Dümrek (Simois) and the Kalafatlı Asmak, with the Menderes or Scamander some 1.5 miles to the south [Map 3].[63] The same map showed tumuli and *dedeliks*, or Turkish cemeteries, old roads, and the village at Akça Köy. It detailed the swampy nature of the plain of Troy and the fields worked in the area. The telling archaeological details, such as the line of fortification walls, the location of the citadel, and the higher position of the northern spur and steep slope to the north, as well as the general remains in the area were added to Kauffer's map by Léon Jean Joseph Dubois in the emended version of 1819.[64] This remained the principal map of the Troad for almost fifty years. Meanwhile, the artist Jean Baptiste Hilaire (1753–1820) drew the first published views of Hisarlık and made a detailed survey of the site [Figure 12].[65]

In 1787, Choiseul-Gouffier ordered the earliest documented excavation in the Troad at the "tumulus of Achilles" on the Sigeum promontory overlooking the coast. Chevalier no longer was present. Salomon Gormezano, the son of the French consul, or dragoman, Moisé Gormezano, dug at night there for two weeks, presumably without permission, in order to avoid being seen by the *aga*. He sank a shaft into the mound and proclaimed that he was seeking a spring. Gormezano dug from the top through strata of clay, sand, and stone to a "granite block," which apparently shielded a small pit below ground level.[66] In it were a great quantity of ash and a cremation burial in a small rectangular cavity enclosed by walls of rough construction.[67] Finds consisted of charcoal and ash, calcined bones, fragments of two *lekythoi*, Attic funerary oil vessels, part of an elaborate bronze mirror, iron and bronze fragments, and a piece of an alabaster oil flask.[68]

Because there were no witnesses, Kauffer was dispatched to check Gormezano's claims and examine the finds. Later scholars, after viewing the site, claimed

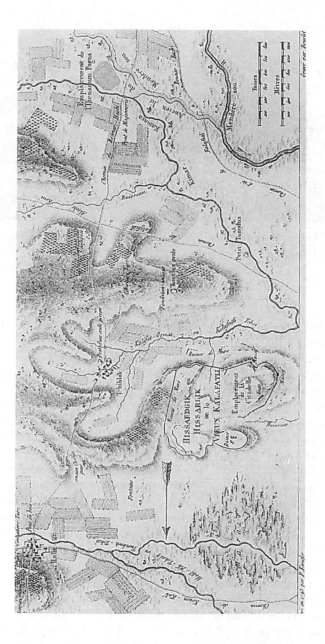

Map 3. Kauffer's map of the plain of Troy. Choiseul-Gouffier (1822), plate 35. Courtesy of the Brown University Library.

Figure 12. View of Hisarlık. By J. B. Hilaire. Choiseul-Gouffier (1822), plate 36. Courtesy of Brown University Library.

that Gormezano had not dug down far enough, indeed only slightly more than one-third of the depth of the tumulus.[69] When the fifth-century finds could not be brought into harmony with those of Achilles' time, the Jewish agent, Gormezano, was maligned by scholars wishing to believe this was the final resting place of Achilles. Some suggested that they had been acquired in Alexandria.[70]

Sir William Gell (1777–1836), one of the next round of travelers, spent five days sketching the topography of the Trojan plain in December 1801. He followed Chevalier's theories and favored Pınarbaşı in his *Topography of Troy and Its Vicinity*, published quickly in 1804.[71] However, his enthusiasm was far from universal. George Hamilton Gordon, the fourth earl of Aberdeen (1784–1860), who visited the plain in 1803, savaged the Pınarbaşı theory in his review of Gell's work and referred to it as "speculation . . . no more than a gay dream of a Classical enthusiast." He likened his determination of Pınarbaşı as Ilion to "determining the true longitude and latitude of the Garden of Eden."[72] In 1810, George Gordon, Lord Byron (1788–1824)[73] made his pilgrimage with John Cam Hobhouse, Lord Broughton (1786–1869).[74] For a month they lived at Abydos and visited sites in the Troad, which Byron noted "was a fine field for conjecture and snipe-shooting."[75]

At that time, the average philologist regarded Homer's poems as constituting "a moment in European intellectual development, not a literal account of ancient geography, warfare, or private life."[76] But not Byron. He paid his respects to the legendary Leander and years later defended the historicity of Troy.

> We do care about the authenticity of the tale of Troy! I have stood upon that plain *daily*, for more than a month, in 1810. . . . I venerated the grand original as the truth

of *history* (in the material facts) and of *place*. Otherwise, it would have given me no delight. Who will persuade me, when I reclined upon a mighty tomb, that it did not contain a hero?—its very magnitude proved this. Men do not labour over the ignoble and petty dead—and why should not the dead be Homer's dead?[77]

Edward Daniel Clarke, the traveler and antiquary who had called on the pasha of the Dardanelles in 1801 while collecting manuscripts, marbles, and antiquities throughout the Ottoman Empire between 1799 and 1802, cast further doubt on Chevalier's thesis that Troy lay at Pınarbaşı.[78] Clarke, later a professor of mineralogy at Cambridge, pronounced the ruins at Pınarbaşı to be "very inconsiderable . . . with no character of remote antiquity."[79] He also recognized the Menderes as the Scamander. When Clarke measured the temperature of the supposedly warm and cold springs at the head of Pınarbaşı Çay that Chevalier contended were evidence that Pınarbaşı was Troy, he found them to be consistently around sixty-two degrees, thus appearing cold in summer and warm in winter. Proceeding to the vicinity of Çıplak, he stopped at a Greek village called Kalafat, where the Kalafatlı Asmak joins the Menderes. Walking through the streets and courtyards in which Corinthian columns were strewn about, he was shown bronze coins of Ilium and told that they had come from Palaio Kalafatlı.[80] This was Hisarlık, the mound previously mapped by Kauffer [Map 3]. In his *Travels in Various Countries of Europe, Asia, and Africa*, Clarke described the ruins as he saw them in March 1801:

> We came to an elevated spot of ground, surrounded on all sides by a level *plain*, watered by the *Callifat Osmack*, and which there is every reason to believe was the *Simoïsian Plain*. Here we found, not only the traces, but also the remains of an antient citadel. *Turks* were then employed raising enormous blocks of marble, from the foundations which surrounded this eminence; and the foundations may have been the identical works constructed by *Lysimachus*, when he fenced *New Ilium* with a wall. The appearance of the structure exhibited that colossal and massive style of architecture which bespeaks the masonry of the early ages of *Grecian* history. All the territory within these foundations was covered by broken pottery, whose fragments were parts of those antient terra-cotta vases which are now held in such high estimation. Here the peasants said they had found the *medals* which they had offered to us; and that after heavy rains. Many had been discovered in consequence of the recent excavations made there by the *Turks*, who were removing the materials of the old foundations, for the purpose of constructing works at the *Dardanelles*.[81]

After justifying the position of Palaio Kalafatlı with Strabo's description of Greco-Roman Ilium Novum, he concluded on the basis of coins and inscriptions that Hisarlık was the Greco-Roman site.[82] He declared rightly that "a light breaks in upon the dark labyrinth of TROAS; we stand with *Strabo* upon the very spot whence he deduced his observations. . . . From the natural or the artificial elevation of the territory . . . we beheld almost every land-mark to which that author has alluded."[83] Yet this was just part of the puzzle. It concerned only Ilion, the first-millennium town, not Homer's Troy.

Dr. Philip Hunt (1772–1838), chaplain and factotum to Lord Elgin (1766–1841), British ambassador to the Sublime Porte from 1799 to 1802, visited the Troad a few days behind Clarke in 1801.[84] At Pınarbaşı, which then was considered the site of Homer's Troy, he mentioned a hill called Hector's Tomb, "a heap of rough stones, thrown confusedly together," as if from a quarry.[85] He noted critically that on digging around the nearby foundations of walls, he found both tiles and mortar, although he saw "no fragments of vases or pottery, so generally abundant on the sites of ancient cities in Asia Minor and Greece." Nor were there "remains of art of a cyclopean kind similar to those seen at Tiryns, Argos, Mycenae, and other parts of Greece."[86] Peter Oluf Bröndsted (1780–1842), a professor at the University of Copenhagen who visited the Troad between 1810 and 1813, declared, "Our actual guide was an honest Turc from the Dardanelles, our spiritual guides were no more than three, first and foremost Homer, next Strabo, and finally, Le Chevalier's famous book." Clearly inspired, Bröndsted mused, "By watching these monuments it is easy to fall upon the idea to excavate one of these tumuli in order to find the bronze urn."[87] But although Bröndsted was the first Dane to excavate on Greek soil, he did not follow his inclination at Pınarbaşı.[88] Instead, he paid homage to Chevalier but, like Hunt, concluded that at Pınarbaşı there was "nothing, absolutely nothing, to indicate that there ever was a very old town in this area, not e.g. any walls stylistically similar to the Cyclopian style so well known from the ruins of Mycenae, Tiryns, and Ithaca."[89] Rather than two springs, there were many, and all were warm. Finally, he suggested that the settlement above Pınarbaşı on the Ballı Dağ was a "Greco-Roman hamlet," and he declined to speculate further about it, not identifying any other location as being Homer's Troy.

Major James Rennell (1742–1830), a geographer and the surveyor general of Bengal, India, was skeptical about Pınarbaşı's identity as the site of Troy as well. Although Rennell never visited the Troad, he published an account of Trojan topography in 1814 comparing the claims made by Chevalier, Clarke, and others. Railing against the liberties that Chevalier had taken with the landscape, Rennell reasserted the original identification of the Scamander with the Menderes[90] and dismissed the claim that Pınarbaşı was Homer's Troy for three chief reasons: because of its distance from the sea, because it was "entirely hilly" on the Ballı Dağ, whereas Homer described Troy in the midst of a plain, and because Homer had described only two springs and at Pınarbaşı there were many, all of the same temperature.

Chevalier's system, he asserted, was based on a "*most erroneous* topography; in which not only the *principal part* of the extensive plain, lying on the east of the Mender, is converted into a *hilly tract;* but a *river* and its *valley* are entirely omitted; and *others* of a *different name* are substituted for them."[91] From a close analysis of Strabo and modern writers, he concluded, "one cannot help believing, that the ancient city of TROY, or ILIUM, stood somewhere in the quarter between Atchekui and Kalafatli which site must also have included that of the Iliean village [Strabo's Troy of Homer]. But no traces of either are recognized in these times.

. . . Nor is it at all wonderful: since there was so vast a demand for materials for the building of cities in its neighbourhood."[92]

By this point, then, the claim for Pınarbaşı as the site of Homer's Troy had been both asserted and questioned, although it remained the conventional wisdom on the subject for want of a better alternative. Even after Clarke located Ilion/Ilium Novum at Hisarlık, no one thought to place Homer's Troy there because of Strabo's assertion that they were in two different locations. Still, Homer's Troy and the Troad continued to cast their spell on visitors, who could roam the landscape and give their imaginations free play without being constrained by any certain knowledge of what they were seeing, generally more disposed to credit the experts than to investigate the matter themselves. As it had for centuries, the area encouraged "indulgent daydreams of Troy and its heroes."[93]

During the course of his employment at the British embassy in Constantinople, for example, William Turner (1792–1867) visited the Troad in 1812 and 1816 with a copy of Clarke's work. Like Romantics before him, he tried to swim the Hellespont (unsuccessfully) and then had a lock of hair cut and placed on Achilles' tomb, as Achilles had done for Patroclus.[94] Of Pınarbaşı, Turner noted in his *Journal of a Tour in the Levant* (1820) only that eighteen years earlier, someone had dug up a barrow known as Hector's Tomb, but by 1812 it had been filled up.[95] He also left a clear description of the diminished remains at Hisarlık, Clarke's Palaio Kalafatlı.

> The hill, containing the ruins supposed by us to be those of New Ilium, is called by the Turks Issarlik. The ruins . . . consist of small stones, among which are some morsels of marble and brick scattered over the hill, of which not one stone remains upon another. . . . If these ruins were New Ilium, that city stood *on* the limestone range, which Clarke states to have been behind it, and on the extremity of a range of hills which reach to Dombrik and Tchiblak. Issarlik has a gradual ascent on every side but the north, where it is very steep, and about seventy feet of perpendicular height.[96]

In general, Turner confirmed Clarke's observations about the position of the site in connection with the rivers, but he also said nothing in his account about Homeric Troy. That would await the next generation of gentleman scholars. Among them was Frank Calvert.

CHAPTER THREE

From Antiquary to Archaeologist
Frank Calvert's "Contributions
to the Ancient Geography of the Troad"

By the time Frank Calvert set foot in the Troad around 1845, his brothers Frederick and Charles were well established. Although he probably helped at the farms,
it was seven years before Calvert entered into family consular duties in 1852.[1] Prior
to his archaeological investigations, Calvert knew that previous identifications
often had been founded on conjecture, not proof. Sure that traces must still exist,
he tested the earlier theories about the locations of those ancient towns with the
spade.[2] Through his own efforts and with help from educated travelers, he developed a sound methodology, quickly surpassing any other family members in the
field. From a local antiquarian, by 1862 he rose to the status of an archaeological
authority respected in European circles of London, Paris, and Rome.

Calvert came of age as an excavator amid fast-paced developments in the field
of archaeology. A century earlier, the quest for the past had been driven by a variety of motives and developments. One was a simple desire to corroborate literary
works such as the Bible and Homer's epics. Another was the rise of neoclassicism.
After visiting the remarkable excavations that began at Herculaneum in 1731 and
Pompeii in 1748, British travelers from the Society of the Dilettanti, for example,
inspired interest in classical antiquity back home with their illustrated journeys.[3]
In addition, Lord Elgin's removal to London of the marble sculpture of the
Parthenon in Athens and the Greek War of Independence (1821–1828) inspired
further interest in Greek antiquities. The fabulous wealth of the Scythian grave tu-
muli in the Crimea gave Europeans a taste for Greek jewelry.[4]

Meanwhile, although isolated individuals had been studying the ancient remains
of Egypt for two centuries, Napoleon's attempted conquest in 1798 had touched off
a passion for Egyptian antiquities and Egyptian styles in architecture, furniture, and
jewelry in Europe. A sustained interest grew after the Rosetta Stone arrived in London. Scholars and young aristocrats journeyed to Egypt as part of the Grand Tour.
Egypt became a popular vacation spot, while French and British consuls vied for the

most precious antiquities. The deciphering of hieroglyphs in 1822 opened up Egyptian literature to scholars and revealed a mystifyingly complex civilization.

It was the desire to substantiate biblical accounts that had fired interest in the ancient Near East. Again, French and English consuls scrambled for the best sites. The support and enthusiasm previously devoted to the discovery of classical and Egyptian antiquities now shifted to the Tigris and Euphrates. Soon, ancient Mesopotamian wedge-shaped cuneiform writing was deciphered. In 1843, the French consul in Mosul, Paul Botta (1802–1870), hit pay dirt at Khorsabad in a tell, or artificial mound, with the discovery of sculpted wall reliefs and huge, human-headed winged bulls in the palace of Sargon II, an ancient Assyrian king.[5]

The first articles in English on Botta's Mesopotamian finds appeared in the *Malta Times* of 1845, written by a young Englishman, Austen Henry Layard (1817–1894). Soon, Layard began his own excavations at the tell of Nimrud, with funds advanced by Ambassador Stratford Canning and later with support from the British Museum.[6] Layard's object, given the tremendous area involved and the amount of funding he received, was "to unearth the largest number of well-preserved objects of art at the least possible outlay of time and money."[7] Beginning with six men in two different parts of the site, he found two palaces of Assyrian kings in twelve hours.[8] In 1849, he published *Nineveh and Its Remains*, an immediate best-seller that Calvert read. Layard followed Henry Creswicke Rawlinson's identification of the site as Nineveh. After Layard published his excavations, Rawlinson changed his mind and identified Nimrud as biblical Calah (Genesis 10:11–12). The exotic sculpted reliefs and colossal sculpted bulls that Layard discovered captivated the English people.[9] By 1849, Layard, excavating at the actual site of Nineveh (Kuyunjik), found sculpted reliefs detailing the biblical sieges of Lachish and Jerusalem and an archive that was more than a foot deep in cuneiform clay tablets.[10] In the northern half of the mound, his successor found another palace and archive. Between them, they had discovered more than twenty thousand clay tablets, many of which went to the British Museum. Layard established a chronology for Mesopotamia, providing scholars with the opportunity to study changes in architectural and sculptural style, and gave written records to establish an historical framework for the material remains.[11] By 1851, having set an impressive precedent, Layard was internationally famous and left archaeology for politics and diplomacy. European museums soon sated themselves on Mesopotamian finds, and the Crimean War put a stop to all excavations in the Fertile Crescent. But Egypt and Mesopotamia had added three thousand years to human history.[12]

Canning continued to promote archaeological conquests in the Ottoman realm. In 1846, he secured twelve reliefs from the frieze of the mausoleum of Halicarnassus, one of the seven wonders of the ancient world, as a personal gift from the sultan. Canning had the sculptured reliefs extracted from the fortress of Bodrum and sent to the British Museum.[13]

But these were classical finds, which were familiar and understood. At this point and for decades to come, classical archaeology, Egyptology, and Assyriology were strongly oriented toward epigraphy—the study of inscriptions—and art history. One could study them within a comfortable historical or Biblical framework. Prehistoric archaeology, however, was another matter, at first a matter of sheer speculation, and then later strongly influenced by the sciences.

One Danish scholar, R. Nyerup, wrote of prehistory in 1806 that "everything which has come down to us from heathendom is wrapped in a thick fog; a space of time we cannot measure."[14] European antiquarians knew that all pre-Roman finds were not contemporary, but how could they subdivide them? In the mid-seventeenth century, a British antiquarian had suggested that humans had used stone tools before learning to work metals. European colonization brought opportunities to observe tribes using similar technologies. By 1655, a French scholar had contested the account of creation in Genesis, saying that stone tools were used by a "pre-Adamite" race. By the mid-nineteenth century, it was conceded in England that they were at least pre-Roman.[15]

Danish scholars made great strides in establishing an analytical framework for the study of prehistoric artifacts. In 1816, Christian Thomsen (1788–1865), a founder of the new Danish royal commission on antiquities, classified hundreds of prehistoric stone, bronze, and iron artifacts in the University of Copenhagen collection, later in the National Museum, using what would become the widely used scheme of three technological stages of tool production through which humankind had evolved. He called them the Stone, Bronze, and Iron Ages in a guide to the collections translated into English in 1848.[16] His student, the historian and archaeologist Jens Worsaae (1821–1885), used Thomsen's chronology to group and date the prehistoric burial mounds of Denmark in the 1840s.[17] Worsaae suggested further that the materials characterized different races, since the artifacts in varying media had been used in contrasting burial practices. Worsaae recommended that barrows "should be dug by a large hole from the top or by a trench eight feet broad from southeast to northwest."[18] In addition, he urged the accurate description and classification of antiquities and advocated that all artifacts be collected—even "trifling objects," declaring that "antiquities have a value with reference to the spot in which they are found."[19] An English antiquarian translated his book in 1849, and the Society of Antiquaries invited him to speak in London in 1852, thus spreading the influential ideas to an interested group in England.[20]

Archaeology was evolving from a nobleman's hobby into a science, although the evolution took different forms in different places. Serious excavation was emerging as a way to understand the past, not just to fill up museums with exotica and the cabinets of antiquarians with curiosities. This commitment would inform Frank Calvert's approach. British geologists such as Charles Lyell (1797–1875) had proved the worth of stratigraphy, or the vertical succession of levels, where the oldest is the lowest, in dating natural features.[21] By the 1860s, the Three Age System had been proven stratigraphically and gradually was adopted across Europe. Thus, historical understanding slowly extended itself backward in time through the use of the archaeological and geological methods.

At the same time, unthinkable new finds pushed back the antiquity of humankind to considerably earlier than the accepted date for creation of 4004 B.C. established in 1650 by Archbishop Ussher and accepted by all of Christendom. In 1853 and 1855, a young Englishman named John Lubbock (1834–1913) found the remains of a mammoth and a musk ox in the gravel pits of southern England.[22] Similar remains of long-extinct animals were discovered in pits in France and England in association with stone tools of human manufacture.[23] In 1857, the discovery of an early human skull in the Neander Valley of Germany began to overturn Ussher's creationist dogma.[24] Scholars took notice when in 1858–59 further primeval finds of rhinoceros and mammoth appeared with flint tools sealed under a stalagmite sheet from three to eight inches in depth at Windmill Hill Cave in England.[25] Proof of the great antiquity of humanity existed, and the acceptance of the Three Age System offered a reasonable framework for studying the remote past. These advances culminated in 1859, when Charles Darwin (1809–1882) published *On the Origin of Species.*

Darwin provided an explanatory model that enabled the development of many of the modern "human sciences," including archaeology. In place of creationism's appeals to religious revelation, it offered a purely material explanation of the origin of biological forms. It also substituted for the stasis of divine fiat the notion that such forms change and develop over time. Transposed into the social realm and used to study the development of civilization, the Darwinian model resulted in a "shift from traditional ethnological, comparative philological, or historical orientations toward a more systematically 'developmental' point of view" among archaeologists, as one historian of the field has put it.[26] In 1859, which has been called the annus mirabilis of archaeology, with the advent of the developmental model for scientific explanation, prehistoric archaeology came into being. It also was the year when Frank Calvert made his debut in the scientific world with the publication of his first archaeological report.

Then, as now, it was critical for those pursuing an understanding of the past to belong to a community of scholars. In England during the middle years of the nineteenth century, learned societies allowed those with such interests to show and discuss their new discoveries or acquisitions and receive responses to them, as well as to learn of exciting new finds in a fast-developing field. They pursued diverse investigations into local topographies, botanical studies, local history, natural history, or paleontology with remarkable industry and zeal, believing that "the science of the real antiquary is not of a narrow and limited character. To him, every relic which he picks up or secures, is pregnant with instruction, bearing upon the history of the social life or habits of some past age. . . . [He is] a man of large and liberal mind."[27] Practitioners tried to combine literary and material remains as they collected, preserved, and transmitted the past.

Antiquarian studies in England attracted a highly motivated, self-taught group of scholars who pooled their knowledge, working cooperatively and subscribing to a belief in the collective importance of the research to which each added. Middle-class members followed their interests on a part-time basis, while those from the elite classes could afford more extended research. But all behaved as gentlemen engaged on a common, important task. The attentiveness paid to any individual's work was reciprocated, and competition was rare. Each depended on others for filling in gaps in their own research. Because not all members were leisured, and because of pressures of work and time, it remained largely "an amateur sport."[28]

The informal networks established by these gentleman antiquarians and archaeologists have been called "an invisible college." Higher education was not an opportunity open to many of them,[29] but not even the university-educated could have studied their chosen pursuit in England. The Disney Professorship of Archaeology at Cambridge, the first of its kind in that country, was not established until 1851.[30] Instead, in addition to the formal meetings of their societies, they relied on the informal communications that they maintained with each other to spur them on intellectually as they requested information, passed on discoveries, and corrected facts. In turn, letters exchanged in this way often were read at the meetings of the learned societies on behalf of those who could not be present.

As was the case in so many fields in the nineteenth century, classical archaeology flourished in the philhellenic humanism of the Enlightenment. It first became established within the institutional framework of the German academy, where departments were created at the major universities. Academic credentials, less important in the gentlemen's societies in England, consequently became critical to success. In the rigid, professionalized *cursus honorum* that developed, "antiquarianism" was an epithet applied to "the mistakes of humanistic science."[31] The German approach to archaeology entailed a text-oriented, rather than a fieldwork-oriented method, a "philology of monuments." Working in this tradition, Johann Joachim Winckelmann (1717–1768) established a periodization of ancient sculpture in his *History of Ancient Art* (1764). Only four years later it was translated into English. In 1830, the German philologist and historian Karl Otfried Müller (1797–1840) wrote his epoch-making, comprehensive work on the evolution of art in antiquity, from architecture through painting and sculpture to vase painting.[32] He was the first great German classicist to visit England, and his book was translated into English in 1847 as *Ancient Art and Its Remains; or, A Manual of the Archaeology of Art.*[33]

Because material remains, in the German approach to archaeology, were considered inferior to texts, German scholars, so far ahead in terms of the critical analysis of classical art and archaeology, were slow to enter into actual excavations in the East. Not much concerned with archaeological field work, they tended to practice archaeology as "a matter of acquiring antiquities in a more or less orderly and expensive way," as one commentator has put it, and of interpreting the remains in terms of *Kulturgeschichte*, the history of culture.[34]

Those British excavators who worked in the East, though not known as antiquarians, began their work very much in the manner of their antiquarian compatriots back home, although they later outgrew the tradition. However, their social and intellectual situation differed considerably from that of their colleagues, both in England and on the Continent, for they could not enjoy the same pleasures and peer support, attending meetings of like-minded individuals and regularly hearing of the latest breakthroughs, nor did they have the institutional backing of a university or museum behind their work. As Frank Calvert did, they had to rely more on chance meetings with scholars passing through, on correspondence with those scholars they were privileged to encounter, and on published accounts in the journals of the learned societies. Furthermore, like Calvert, most individuals living permanently in the exotic East began to excavate while otherwise employed. Thus, they could not often conduct research on a full-time basis. Finally, because there was no community of scholars in the East, individuals had to rely on private patronage, public funding, or their own limited resources to carry out projects that, had they been in England, perhaps would have drawn on the communal resources of the antiquarian community.

The effects of this difference in intellectual, social, and economic support between archaeologists working within a tight network of colleagues in the metropolis and their compatriots working at the margins of the British Empire can be seen in the difference between Frank Calvert's opportunities and those enjoyed by his near-contemporary, John Lubbock, the discoverer of prehistoric animal remains in southern England.

Like Calvert, Lubbock also left school at sixteen, in his case to work at his father's bank. But Lubbock was "singularly fortunate in his friends," who included Charles Darwin himself. Darwin became his neighbor when the boy was eleven and greatly encouraged him in the area of scientific inquiry.[35] Lubbock wrote his first four articles in 1853 and 1854 on species in Darwin's own collection and trained his eye by illustrating Darwin's books. Through Darwin, he was introduced to Charles Lyell, who proposed the twenty-year-old for membership in the Royal Geological Society.[36] Through his discovery of the first fossil musk ox, he came into contact with the leading prehistorians of the day, Joseph Prestwich and Sir John Evans (1823–1908).[37] Even before the publication of *On the Origin of Species,* Lubbock was part of the "Darwinian inner circle." By 1860, when he toured the gravel pits of France, he had become a leading member of the "prehistoric movement."[38] This clique, which represented the cutting edge of scientific scholarship in mid-nineteenth-century England, encouraged and supported Lubbock. His articles went to press immediately. At age twenty-three he was elected a Fellow of the Royal Society.[39] This is the sort of career that could happen in London. But recognition and support were harder to come by on the intellectual periphery at the Dardanelles.

Less than twenty years after he, too, left school, through careful research and diligent sleuthing, Frank Calvert had made several important discoveries and was elected to membership in learned archaeological societies in London and Rome. But Calvert constantly had to contend with the limitations imposed on him by his isolation. He did not have a resident mentor who could help steer him in useful directions, directing his focus to profitable research, as Lubbock did. Nor did he enjoy firm institutional support, like Charles Newton, or private patronage, like Austen Henry Layard. He had to prove his maturity as an excavator and scholar on his own, on his own schedule, with his own or his family's modest resources.

For the sons of diplomats and entrepreneurs in the British Empire's farther reaches who were born in the first quarter of the nineteenth century, it was by no means standard to have a university education, let alone an education at Oxford or Cambridge, and neither Frank Calvert nor his siblings did.[40] However, before he finished school, like other upper-class and middle-class English youths in Malta and the Ionian islands, Frank Calvert would have learned mathematics, navigation, cartography, Italian, and English, in addition to history, geography, Latin, and Greek. This five-year course was designed to prepare students for the moderately priced university in Malta, which conferred degrees in divinity, law, and medicine, all avenues by which the sons of local gentlemen could hope to make a respectable living.[41] An extensive public library in Valletta possessed more than sixty thousand volumes by 1790 and in 1840 contained, according to one researcher, almost every work that had been published on the topic of Troy, which was, he mused, intimately connected with British "schoolboy and college associations."[42] Frank Calvert's knowledge of languages, along with his own family's excellent library, afforded him access to the literary sources necessary for his later work. Standard reference works in English were not published until midcentury.[43] It was only later that an Oxbridge education became the rule. Calvert thus was on the cusp of both the transition of archaeology from a gentleman's avocation to a scientific discipline and its absorption into the institutions and practices of the academy. But he began as an antiquarian.

Because of their extensive land holdings on both sides of the Hellespont, all of the Calverts were understandably intrigued with local topography. Lander knew some archaeological sites of the Hellespont coast, and locals reported new finds to him.[44] His excellent resources enabled the Calverts to augment their formal education with shared interests and avid reading. Likewise, the Calvert estates provided thousands of acres as a private archaeological proving ground, giving the family easy access to the tumuli and other visible archaeological riches of the Troad. When their residences provided hospitality for eminent guests, they also served as showcases for the Calverts' nascent hobby of collecting ancient artifacts.

Each Calvert brother maintained intellectual pursuits associated with antiquity. The eldest, Henry Calvert, visited Mycenae and sketched the Lion Gate in 1835 [Figure 13]. Later, he met Charles Newton and donated a Coptic inscription to the British Museum.[45] He was a fine draftsman with an eye for detail.[46] While working in eastern Turkey at Erzerum (Armenia), he built up a well-known collection of plants and shells and corresponded with Layard, advising him on how to collect and dry plants successfully,[47] a talent that Henry passed on to his youngest brother.[48] Edmund Calvert, three years Frank's senior, "was a great Oriental and classical scholar, and well-versed in Egyptological lore." His notebooks preserve his studies of Egyptian inscriptions on scarabs and sarcophagi.[49] Charles Calvert

Figure 13. The Lion Gate at Mycenae. By Henry Calvert (1835). Courtesy of Ziya Ulucr.

informed the British Museum about an ancient statue just uncovered in his consular district,[50] and James Calvert corresponded with Newton and the Anglo-
French epigrapher and numismatist William-Henry Waddington (1826–1894)
about the family's important new finds.[51] While he was U.S. consular agent at the
Dardanelles, James conducted an informed correspondence with Heinrich Schliemann concerning his excavations.

Only Frank Calvert and his elder brother Frederick ever excavated, however. In
1853, the earl of Carlisle described Frederick as a knowledgeable antiquarian, but
his involvement seems to have been only casual, at the most sponsoring some of
Frank's small excavations in the area after being stimulated by his brother's modest successes. In cases where visitors noted Frederick Calvert's excavations, it
seems that as its patron he often took credit for his brother's work. Frederick thus
successfully created the impression of a cultivated antiquarian. Knowing Stratford
Canning's own patronage of archaeological pursuits and the spectacular success
of his protégé Layard in archaeology and politics, Frederick no doubt also was inspired by social and professional ambition.

Frederick did dig into a tumulus located behind the villa at Erenköy in 1857.[52]
He found little: earth mixed with stones and accidental fragments of pottery and
some boars' tusks.[53] Next he plumbed one of the most famous tumuli, that of Patroclus, which stood on the northwest tip of the Troad next to the "Tomb of

Achilles" that Gormezano had "excavated" in 1787.[54] This was another disappointment. Both were essentially barren.[55] Because Frederick left no record of his excavations, it is impossible to know if they proceeded deep enough to be conclusive. In any case, the outcome was negligible, and it appears that he did not excavate again.[56] For Frederick, digging did not repay the effort and expense needed. Just as Frank Calvert's excavations antedate Frederick's earliest work, they exceeded them in care, execution, and reporting.

The Calvert women also followed archaeology, although they seem never to have excavated.[57] The Calverts' sister, Louisa Calvert, and James's wife, Lavinia, visited Schliemann's excavations and corresponded with him.[58] Much later, Frederick's daughter, Edith (1859–1952), was very close to her "Uncle Frank" and enjoyed his archaeological pursuits. Through his influence, she became quite involved and well read on Trojan subjects.

Of the visitors who passed through the Calverts' residence in the Dardanelles, three were particularly important in Frank Calvert's education as an archaeologist: the self-educated journalist Charles Maclaren, whom we already have met, Peter de Tchihatcheff, and William-Henry Waddington. Maclaren spent ten days laid up by a cold with the Calverts in early May 1847.[59] Frank was eighteen. Maclaren must in many ways have been a role model for the youngest Calvert. Apparently, like Calvert, Maclaren had "a modest disposition, never prominent or forward."[60] He received only a parish-school education before he went to work as a clerk and a bookkeeper. But during these years he taught himself French, Greek, and later German. He was an avid mineralogist and took geological excursions all over Scotland, hammer in hand. Although his career was in journalism, Maclaren made time for serious scientific research and published regularly. In short, he was "a gentleman scholar" in much the same way Frank Calvert was. In 1839 he wrote an article entitled "The Geology of Fife and the Lothians" and established a reputation as a sound, practical geologist. As a member of the Royal Geological Society of Edinburgh (1837) and the Geological Societies of London and of France (1846), he kept up with and participated in recent developments in the field, particularly controversies regarding the significance of geology for understanding the remote antiquity of man (1861).[61]

Maclaren made the Grand Tour to France and Italy in 1839 and again in 1846–47, after which he continued on to Greece and the Troad. On both trips, he visited and wrote on the antiquities of Rome, Campania, and Pompeii, reporting that on his second trip he had witnessed Vesuvius erupting. From there, he sojourned in Greece, targeting the Homeric sites of Argos, Tiryns, and Mycenae, among others, and remarking on the devastation caused by the War of Independence that "the only things unruined were the ruins."[62]

In April 1849, the Russian diplomat, traveler, and naturalist Peter de Tchihatcheff (1808–1890) was touring Anatolia and gathering information for his work on the geography, climate, geology, and archaeology of Asia Minor.[63] Tchihatcheff met Frank Calvert, then aged twenty, and together they climbed Erciyas Dağ, near

Kayseri. Tchihatcheff wrote that he had enjoyed Calvert's company immensely. In turn, he left a lasting impression on his "young friend Calwert," instilling in him a love for natural science that permeated all of Calvert's later publications.[64]

In 1850–51, William-Henry Waddington toured Asia Minor with his new bride. As a Cambridge man, he was well acquainted with the collections of the Fitzwilliam and British Museums and well read in Greek literature. His archaeological tour quickly changed into a hunt for coins for his growing collection.[65] Wanting to avoid high prices by going to the source, he visited village goldsmiths, who would buy old pieces of gold or silver by weight for the forge. Whenever he beat the coins to the crucible, he made a coup.[66] After nine months, he returned to France with hundreds of coins, all acquired on the spot.[67] In each case, he tried to discover the provenance or source of the coins because he believed that numismatics, the study of coins, was a science auxiliary to history, and that coins could be used to solve historical and geographical problems.[68]

Waddington transcribed and took impressions of inscriptions along his route. Later letters show that in 1855, the Calverts helped Waddington export inscriptions that, presumably, he had located during his 1850–51 trip.[69] Subsequently, Calvert wrote letters of inquiry to Waddington, who replied concerning the value of certain coins or statues on the Parisian art market and later on proposed excavations of Hisarlık.[70] As a scholar and collector, Waddington clearly was a very valuable contact. In 1872, Waddington published numerous of the Calverts' inscriptions in his magnum opus on Greek and Latin inscriptions from Asia Minor, *Explication des inscriptions grecques et latines recuillies en Grèce et en Asie Mineure* (1872). He referred to stones from Ilium Vetus, Ilium Novum, Ilium, and Abydos that were found at Pınarbaşı, Haliléli, Çıplak, Yeni Köy, Ilium, Akça Köy, Hanay Tepe, Saradjik, and Gangherli.[71] Regarding one of the inscriptions, Waddington noted that an employee of the British consulate (possibly Frank Calvert) had made a copy of the inscription in 1846.[72] As a result of this association, Calvert developed an appreciation for coins and inscriptions for identifying and dating sites, a technique that he put to use as early as 1853.

By spring 1853, Frank Calvert had a standard itinerary of sites with which he was quite familiar, perhaps through sherding or casual prospecting, if not because of actual excavation. Presumably Calvert had begun by excavating the sites that were on family land. Villagers tipped him off to other sites, such as Dardanos and Abydos, after they discovered graves there.[73] In the course of his guiding, he eventually would have sherded and tested historic sites farther from home, such as Pınarbaşı, Alexandria Troas, and Çığrı Dağ.[74] Proud of his discoveries and eager for corroborating information, he shared his finds with the Europeans passing through. The earl of Carlisle described his archaeological experiences with Calvert,[75] and Carlisle, Charles Newton, and the Reverend Henry Fanshawe Tozer (1829–1916), referred to Calvert's earliest dated excavation at Hanay Tepe, a tumulus at Batak Farm on the plain of Troy.[76]

Of these, Charles Newton had the most significant influence on the young archaeologist. After completing his studies at Oxford, Newton [Figure 14] worked as

Figure 14. Sir Charles Thomas Newton, bust by Sir John Boehm. Courtesy of the British Museum.

an assistant in the department of antiquities at the British Museum from 1840 to 1852, publishing the vase collections and the frieze sculptures from Halicarnassus acquired through the generosity of Stratford Canning and witnessing the flood of riches into the museum from Layard's Mesopotamian excavations.[77] The most brilliant acquisitions from the Ottoman Empire had passed through his hands.

Newton had read Worsaae and Lyell and had lectured on archaeology in 1850. Although he recognized the importance of the archaeology of art for reading and interpreting remains, Newton, through his exposure to the ideas of Worsaae and Lyell, had a much more broadly based approach to his field than many who had preceded him. The purpose and function of archaeology, he insisted, is "to collect, classify, and interpret all of the evidence of man's history not already incorporated in Printed Literature." Artifacts are "vouchers for Printed History," he believed, and "to collect the implements, weapons, pottery, costume, and furniture of races is to contribute materials not only to the history of mining, metallurgy, spinning, weaving, dyeing, carpentry, and the like, arts which minister to civilisation, but also to illustrate the physical history of the countries." Newton advised that to "master the manifold subject-matter of Archaeology and appreciate its whole range and compass, [one] must possess a mind in which the reflective and perceptive faculties are duly balanced; he must combine with the aesthetic culture of the Artist, and the trained judgment of the Historian, not a little of the learning of the Philologer." He continued that "plodding drudgery" must not blunt the critical acuity necessary for the classification and interpretation of remains, and that healthy suspicion should not breed skepticism. "The Archaeologist cannot, like the Scholar, carry on his researches in his own library, almost independent of outward circumstances. . . . He must travel, excavate, collect, arrange, delineate, decipher, transcribe" before he can understand his subject. Newton urged that he must not do this single-handedly, but with the help of museum collections and societies, which could gather resources and which could preserve, register, and publish finds systematically.[78] Shortly thereafter, Newton followed his own advice and left for the Mediterranean.

Newton was an academically privileged individual, backed by both the British Museum and the Foreign Office. He became vice-consul at Mytilene (Lesbos) in 1852, charged with acquiring antiquities for the museum.[79] In February 1853, Newton toured the Troad. He visited various sites with Calvert, including Pınarbaşı,[80] Hisarlık,[81] Ophryneion,[82] Çığrı,[83] and Hanay Tepe.[84] He acutely observed that the ceramics of Pınarbaşı did not "resemble the very early pottery so abundant on the Homeric sites of Mycenae and Tiryns," probably sparking Calvert's interest in testing Newton's observations through excavation.[85] Newton commented on "the suggestive irregularities of the ground" at Ilium Novum, again a statement that would have encouraged Calvert, but noted that "the remains visible above the ground are very trifling."[86]

Newton recorded one of Frank Calvert's first excavations—at the mound of Hanay Tepe, conveniently situated only 500 meters from the verandah of the family farm house at Akça Köy [Figure 15]. In Newton's presence and as if following Worsaae's methodology, in the center of the mound, which was 3 to 4 meters deep, Calvert sank a shaft and then drove a horizontal gallery through the mound from the south to the shaft.[87] Although Newton had not yet begun to excavate himself, he commented on Calvert's work. "Nothing was found in the interior ex-

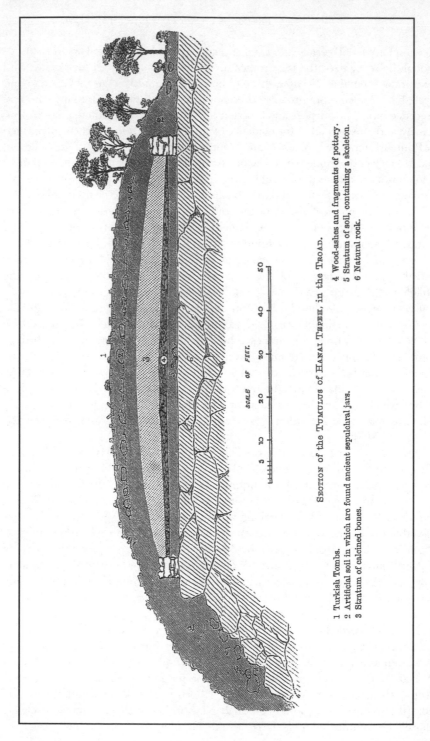

SECTION of the TUMULUS of HANAI TEPEH, in the TROAD.

1 Turkish Tombs.
2 Artificial soil in which are found ancient sepulchral jars.
3 Stratum of calcined bones.
4 Wood-ashes and fragments of pottery.
5 Stratum of soil, containing a skeleton.
6 Natural rock.

SCALE OF FEET.

5   10   20   30   40   50

Figure 15. Hanay Tepe section. Calvert (1859).

cept a layer of ashes near the bottom, but the excavation was not carried low enough to obtain a conclusive result." Then he added, somewhat academically, "It is well known that the most important remains have been found in Greek tumuli below their apparent base."[88] Later, in his own publication, Newton referred to Calvert's site report.[89]

Following the Hanay Tepe foray, Newton witnessed Calvert excavating *pithos*, or jar burials [Figure 16], in the "Hellenic cemetery" nearby,[90] the rich necropolis from the Archaic and Classical periods that stretched along the banks of the Thymbrios, a few hundred meters to the east of the mound.[91] Here Calvert dug deep enough. Newton noted conclusively: "Below these was native rock, proof that no earlier interments had taken place in this cemetery." Through Newton, who was knowledgeable but equally inexperienced, Calvert had learned to dig down to virgin soil or bedrock.

Calvert clearly knew other sites as well. According to the German scholar August Baumeister (1830–1922), who toured in 1854,[92] four tumuli around the Troad recently had been excavated prior to his visit: that of Antilochus at Sigeum,[93] another further south on the Aegean coast, the middle tumulus at Pınarbaşı, and Hanay Tepe.[94] According to Baumeister, the mounds produced no ancient finds, bones, pottery, or coins, although Calvert had opened them in the center and had carried on below the level of artificial stratification. Just south of the Batak farmhouse, Baumeister added, Calvert had uncovered an area 60 feet square where he found rows of vases, mostly broken, with cremated remains. Baumeister also mentioned Calvert excavations of graves at Dardanos and Ophryneion near Erenköy.[95] Although Baumeister began his account by acknowledging his debt to "Mr. Calvert, the English Consul at the Dardanelles," which would have been Frederick, all of the excavations that he mentioned that can be corroborated by independent sources are Frank's.

By 1853, Frank Calvert had located Ophryneion,[96] a town that Herodotus had mentioned in connection with Xerxes' departure from Ilion.[97] He had found the acropolis, city, harbor, and necropolis north-northeast of Erenköy, on the border of a hill bounded by deep ravines. He clinched the identification with a number of bronze coins inscribed with ОФРΥ, the city's name,[98] and identified the site to the British Admiralty, which included it on subsequent maps of the Dardanelles.[99] But by then the Crimean War had intervened, and Calvert was writing up his research for publication. Baumeister noted that "because of the care with which Calvert set to work, it would be of great use to science." Nevertheless, it would be years before it appeared.

It is certain that with the tremendous amount of consular work at the Dardanelles before and during the Crimean War, Frank Calvert had very little leisure time for archaeological excavations between autumn 1853 and spring 1856. However, during the war, he may have been able to excavate the graves at Ophryneion. They were, after all, only walking distance from the family's country house, in the vineyards at Erenköy. But from July 1855 on, bands of mutinous troops and brig-

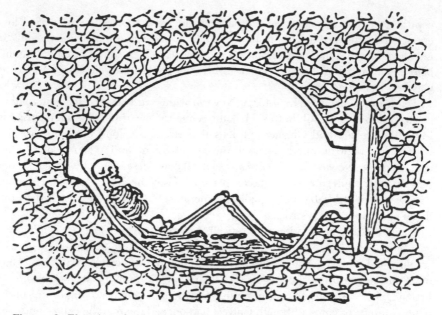

Figure 16. Elevation of *pithos* burial. *Illustrated London News,* 26 April 1856, and Calvert (1859).

ands ravaged the countryside, making travel dangerous.[100] He certainly would have had trouble venturing much further afield.

Calvert's wartime duties probably account for the hiatus between his excavations at Hanay Tepe and Pınarbaşı and the writing of the excavation reports. Calvert had tested Chevalier's theory that Pınarbaşı was Troy by excavating the middle tumulus, the largest on the plateau below the acropolis. He found it virtually empty except for a stone chamber in the center. Both the pottery (just accidental fragments) and the masonry were late. With nothing before the sixth century B.C., it couldn't possibly be Homeric.[101] Nor was there evidence of a burial. The setting was indeed dramatic, but also improbable—so far away from the Hellespont. Calvert sat on his important findings, not yet ready to challenge Chevalier on the subject, for he had not yet probed the settlement remains.

When Calvert resumed work at Hanay Tepe in 1856, after the war, he clearly had learned from Newton. He took up the challenge laid down by the Kiel classics professor Peter Wilhelm Forschammer (1801–1894), who had written that Hanay Tepe must be a natural hill because of its size. Forschammer had suggested that excavation alone could settle the point,[102] so Calvert resolved to dig to disprove him.

Calvert's stratigraphic excavations of the site were exemplary by the standards of the day and an undoubted improvement over his earlier foray, as well as Hills's, Gormezano's, and Hunt's attempts. Calvert clearly understood the geological features of the site, probably the legacy of his association with Maclaren and Tchihatcheff. His horizontal trench illuminated the mound's construction as he then understood it, while his section drawing showed the superimposed strata [Figure 15].[103] He determined that the lowest three were prehistoric levels of calcined bone, ash, and earth. This time he excavated down to bedrock and was rewarded with numerous finds.

Calvert noted the clustering of burials and the different treatment of adults and children in his test shaft.[104] He described the distinctive *pithos* burials of the Troad and depicted one in an elevation drawing [Figure 16].[105] After considering the alignment, disposition, and condition of skeletons, he dated the burials from the Archaic and Classical periods by their associated grave goods, illustrated in scale drawings [Figure 17].

Calvert assumed that the *Iliad* preserved the main design of certain historical facts and that these could be corroborated by the remains left by those ancient peoples it recorded. Homer's truth, though established by poetry, was for Calvert clearly illustrated and confirmed by the topography around him. At the same time, he knew this assumption was an act of faith, necessary for useful research in periods beyond the reach of history. He needed proof—facts, or rather, artifacts—to substantiate his ideas and found evidence in the layer of calcined bones with "three or four vases of coarse pottery and rude form."[106] These were the first prehistoric vessels from the Troad ever published and illustrated. Presciently, Calvert associated the layer of coarse pottery beneath that of the Archaic period burials with Homer's heroes. Inasmuch as any of the events of Homer can be connected with archaeological remains in the Troad, Calvert dated the prehistoric ash layer correctly. But in 1856, the Calverts professed the belief that Homer's Troy lay at Pınarbaşı, a belief expressed to the Oxford don and political economist Nassau William Senior (1790–1864) in 1857.[107] Reasoning that Hanay Tepe must be contemporary with Troy, Frank Calvert argued that it represented the communal burial of Trojan heroes after the first truce in the *Iliad*, as for example with the Achaeans (*Iliad* 7.331), and he quoted *Iliad* 23.225 for the method of creation of the pyre.[108]

By September 1856, Calvert had explored *pithos* graves at various spots in the Chersonese and the Troad.[109] Then, in 1856–57, he turned his focus to the north coast, near the family's villa at Erenköy, excavating a tomb that had been discovered by villagers at Dardanos and the site of Ophryneion.

The critical year in the development of archaeology, 1859, also was a year in which Calvert made great strides as an archaeologist. By 1859, Calvert had perfected his method: start with the ancient sources, analyze modern scholarship, and then tramp through the countryside, taking note of critical features such as proximity to the coast and to a water source, the size and shape of a hill, actual remains, and local knowledge. He had great success. That summer he chose the southwestern area of the Troad, the coast from Cape Lecton to Alexandria Troas.[110]

Using Strabo, Xenophon, and Thucydides as guides,[111] he identified the sites of Larisa and Colonae,[112] two coastal towns whose inhabitants later were trans-

Figure 17. Grave goods from Hanay Tepe. Calvert (1859).

ferred to Alexandria Troas.[113] He began with Colonae, which according to Strabo once belonged to Tenedos and lay next to Alexandria Troas. Calvert dismissed the claims of Richard Chandler (1738–1810), who had put Colonae inland, and followed Lord Broughton, who placed it somewhere on the coast opposite Tenedos.[114] Within walking distance on the coast south of Alexandria Troas,[115] Calvert found an oval hill (Beşik Tepe) with abrupt slopes and evidence of an ancient site in heaps of stones, black-glaze pottery sherds, and a necropolis. To the south lay the acropolis, with foundations for a square stone tower, inside which he found a bronze coin of Colonae with ΚΟΛΟΝΑΩΝ inscribed around the figure of the sun, proof of the identity of a city. Because most of the fortification wall of

Colonae, the Temple of Apollo Cillaeus, and other buildings had been pillaged, first for the construction of Alexandria Troas and later for buildings in several nearby Turkish villages, Calvert conducted excavations in the necropolis, where he found built stone tombs, cist graves, and *pithos* burials.

During the same summer, he also excavated graves on the summit of Çığrı Dağ, at the site he had known for a decade. His career as an archaeologist was gaining momentum. His article "The Tumulus of Hanai Tepeh in the Troad," written three years previously, finally was published in the *Archaeological Journal*, the publication of the Royal Archaeological Institute.[116] There were not many venues for archaeological publication at that time.[117] Newton, or possibly Frederick during a two-and-a-half-year stay in London in 1858 and 1859, may possibly have suggested this one. The Archaeological Institute had been founded in 1843 for the promotion of field archaeology, so publication in its journal was a happy choice. Dr. John Anthony communicated Calvert's article, and the gathering clearly appreciated it, commending "the first fruits of the interesting researches which Mr. Frank Calvert . . . has prosecuted with unusual advantages." The editor expressed the hope that he soon would contribute "further results of his valuable investigations."[118] In April 1860, Newton wrote to Calvert, presumably congratulating him on the Hanay Tepe article.[119] His discovery was recognized at the time as "very remarkable," and indeed it was. Not only had Calvert proven that at least one of the tumuli in the Troad was constructed for funerary purposes, he also had dated it to the Homeric era.[120]

By 1860, Frank Calvert had hit his stride as an archaeologist. First he published a brief report on a bronze lion weight that had been found by a peasant farming the ancient site of Abydos [Figure 18].[121] In December, he published his excavations at both Colonae and Ophryneion under the general title "Contributions to the Ancient Geography of the Troad," which signaled his lifelong interest in the topography of the region. Calvert's publication of Colonae treated his process of identification and described his 1859 excavation of a large built tomb in the necropolis, the contents of which greatly added to his growing collection.[122] Calvert was equally confident with Ophryneion. After an analysis of ancient sources, Calvert refuted the ideas of Philip Barker Webb (1793–1854), who had placed Hector's tomb there incorrectly, and Forschammer, who had located the town too far west.[123] He proceeded to use important topographical data to place the site on the ridge north-northeast of the village. He also demonstrated his knowledge of geology and paleontology in a subsequent discussion of the ancient geological deposits comprising the hill, which contained the remains of mastodons and other ancient pachyderms.[124]

Calvert described Ophryneion's architectural features on land and underwater harbor installations, near which he found bronze fish hooks and netting needles. He accompanied his descriptions with a plan [Figure 6][125] showing plentiful remains: 2-meter-thick fortification walls enclosing a Greek settlement, and on the upper acropolis, Roman buildings and mosaics.[126] In the rock of the ravine, he excavated eight to ten wells containing Attic black-glaze pottery. The necropolis con-

Figure 18. Lion weight from Abydos. Calvert (1860a).

tained *pithos* burials and a few stone coffins.[127] With Herodotus in hand and using bronze coins of Ophryneion as evidence, Calvert successfully identified the site and then dated it using pottery.[128] Both articles confidently had analyzed the literary testimonia and modern arguments, combining them with keen observation of pertinent topographical, geological, and vestigial architectural features.

The London barrister and antiquarian Charles Sprengel Greaves wrote to congratulate him on "the favorable manner in which his memoir was received at [the] May meeting."[129] Calvert gained confidence from the warm reception of his articles. By the time of the publication of Colonae and Ophryneion in December 1860, Calvert was made an honorary corresponding member of the Royal Archaeological Institute of Great Britain in London.[130]

In 1861, Calvert published an article in the *Archaeological Journal* identifying Larisa, another town mentioned by Strabo, again under the title "Contributions to the Ancient Geography of the Troad." His deduction of the location of Larisa involved the refutation of all modern scholars (including Gell and Lord Broughton) to arrive at a completely original identification,[131] based both on a complete knowledge of ancient sources and a keen eye for topography. He chose Liman Tepe, a low, flat-topped, partly artificial hill just off the beach and near Colonae, the right distance from Ilium Novum, according to Strabo.[132] Apparently chosen in antiquity for its harbor, the bay adjacent to the site still was used for shipping in the nineteenth century. Larisa had been completely pillaged, leaving only fragments of black-glazed pottery and some building foundations. Although Calvert did not personally explore the necropolis, he recounted the testimony of local inhabitants as to its location and character.

Calvert now was becoming known in London. His paper, once again read by Greaves, was reviewed in the *Athenaeum*.[133] This literary journal, begun in 1828 "to lay a foundation of solid and useful knowledge" by recording the work of the most distinguished philosophers, historians, and orators of the day, had become the fashionable paper, attracting a readership among privileged society. It gave complete coverage of every cultural interest and thus serves as an index of current thought and taste from 1830 to 1900. It also was authoritative in its reporting of scientific advances and controversies.[134] From now on, Frank Calvert's achievements would be chronicled in its "Proceedings of Learned Societies," which discussed discoveries in the principal branches of scientific inquiry.

Between 1860 and 1862, Calvert engaged in a flurry of activity. His publications were appreciated and, indeed, anticipated. But at the same time, he was becoming aware of his relative isolation. He was looking for community, for sources of information on current ideas of leading archaeologists, as well as for information on the latest archaeological discoveries. During this time he wrote twice to Newton, who was serving from 1859 to 1861 as British consul in Rome or local secretary for the Papal States, responding to Newton's letter in 1860 and including archaeological queries for his learned colleague.[135]

In passing, he mentioned that after he had inquired of Newton how to subscribe to and get the publications of the Archaeological Institute in Rome, an apparent mix-up had occurred, and his brother had received the diploma of membership that probably was intended for him.[136] Clearly, Calvert previously had inquired about subscribing to the Archaeological Institute in Rome. The institute, known as the Instituto di Corrispondenza Archeologica and the Institut für archäologische Korrispondenz, was founded in 1829, the first international association of classical archaeologists. Its purpose was "to gather and make known all archaeologically significant facts and finds—that is, from architecture, sculpture, and painting, topography, and epigraphy—that are brought to light in the realm of classical antiquity, in order that these might be saved from being lost, and by means of concentration in one place may be made accessible for scientific study."[137] Its articles appeared in Italian, French, and occasionally Latin and generally addressed Roman, Etruscan, and Greek art, rarely anything Egyptian or Near Eastern.[138]

Only after reading in the newspaper of Newton's return to the British Museum as first keeper of the newly created department of Greek and Roman antiquities did Calvert write again, on 12 February 1862, with exciting news of his discoveries.[139] Because he had written twice before without response, it is not known exactly when the discoveries were made in the two-year period. But they were important, and Newton had part of the letter published in the *Transactions of the Royal Society for Literature*.[140] The *Athenaeum* also reported the discoveries on 19 April 1862.[141]

In the interior, Calvert wrote, he had found the city of Cebrene (Cebren) and other sites about which he was then occupied in writing.[142] Then he told of his dis-

covery of the Cave of Andeira, described in Strabo, 13.1.56. In his letter to Newton, Calvert shared the excitement of his descent into the cave but probably consciously omitted the precise location and the fact that Strabo had associated it with
silver deposits.[143] He also described a rich necropolis, with amber beads and
Egyptian scarabs of faience inscribed with cartouches, and another of gilt blue
material.[144] He mentioned trying to date the deposit with these, using utterly
sound archaeological technique. Appealing to Newton's interest in acquisitions,
Calvert reported that travelers were spoiling the market for cheap coins. Calvert
also apprised the new keeper that he recently had written to Waddington concerning a bronze coin of Rhoeteum, which he had used to identify yet another
site.[145] With confidence and pride, Calvert asked if Newton might come out to the
area again. He wanted to take Newton over the new sites he had brought to light
and about which he was already occupied in writing. One can only imagine which
sites those might have been. Although Hisarlık and Pınarbaşı may have been
among these, Calvert did not specify them in his letter.

Calvert clearly looked forward to an equally intense pace of exploration, confiding in Newton his intention that spring to go up the Aesepus River valley, which
formed the eastern boundary of Strabo's Troad. He would investigate the interior
from the southern shore of the Sea of Marmara between Abydos and Cyzicus to
the east to discover Strabo's sites, including Zeleia, where the Persians had awaited
Alexander.[146] Then he would cross the country southwest to Assos and work his
way back up the coast, in effect covering the entirety of the area mentioned in
Strabo's book 13. This was a very ambitious plan that required considerable prepa-
ration and time. It is not clear whether he ever got the chance to implement it.

One result of all this activity was the beginning of the Calvert Collection of antiquities. It is hard to determine whether Frederick or Frank Calvert first started
collecting antiquities because the sources frequently confuse them by omitting
their given names or ignoring the younger brother in favor of the older. Most
likely both actively collected as Frank discovered sites while exploring and Frederick developed his estates. Frederick also may have been spurred on by the sort of
career advancement and patronage that Stratford Canning was offering.

Farmers brought the Calverts important pieces, just as they had Lander.[147] The
collection grew steadily. Artifacts became part of a cabinet of curiosities, where
ancient vases stood alongside items from the natural world. In 1849, Tchihatcheff
noted that the Calverts already possessed a notable botanical collection.[148] They
housed their eclectic collection of antiquities at their three residences.[149] Occasionally, travelers noted the location of specific pieces. Baumeister recorded material at Erenköy[150] and Schliemann noted finds at Batak Farm[151] and the Dardanelles consular house.[152] By 1862, the brothers had amassed the preeminent
collection of antiquities from the Troad.[153]

When the family began to collect is not known. Newton does not mention seeing a collection in February 1853, although he does mention Calvert family heirlooms and amenities from England, and during his travels, Newton noted several

other collections of antiquities in Asia Minor, including the Constantinople coin collection of "M. Michanowitz"[154] and that of Ismail Pasha, kept "in great sacks,"[155] of which part was later purchased by James Whittall, the Calverts' colleague at Smyrna.[156]

Knowing his interests and considerable expertise in antiquity, the Calverts certainly would have shown Newton what treasures they had found to that point. Yet he mentions only a bronze mouse.[157] Considering Newton's strong impact on Calvert the archaeologist, one also should attribute to Newton the Calverts' interest in forming an antiquities collection.[158]

Within six months, the earl of Carlisle remarked in his journal that, along with various innovative agricultural practices and engineering feats such as the draining of the malarial marsh on the plain of Troy, the Calverts were starting to collect antiquities. "Mr. Calvert is beginning to form a museum, which will have much interest from the fragments he is gradually picking up; and as he proposes to drain extensively, the utilitarian and antiquarian operations may materially assist each other." There already were several small vases from the Akça Köy necropolis that Calvert had assigned to the time of Philip of Macedon. Frederick gave one of these, from a tomb excavated in Carlisle's presence, to the earl as a memento.[159] Presumably, most of these came from Frank's sizable excavations at Akça Köy.[160] Carlisle's memoir suggests that Frederick's approach was casual, yet pragmatic.

The collection appears to have grown rapidly at this point, fueled on the one hand by Frank's growing intellectual and Frederick's financial interest in antiquities and by the attention paid to it by prominent visitors. By November 1854 it contained material from sites throughout the Troad. At Erenköy, Baumeister saw the Calverts' substantial collection of vases from the necropolis of Ophryneion, Dardanos, Alexandria Troas, and other points of the Troad,[161] confirming Calvert's early excavations there. In 1859, Calvert's excavations at Colonae greatly enriched the collection.[162] In one tomb alone, Frank wrote, more than "sixty vases of different shapes were found, of which one half were broken." The tomb contained vases of yellow and blue glass, terra-cotta figurines, coins, and an iron spearhead.[163] These and other vases from Akça Köy were kept in a china cabinet in the dining room at Batak Farm [Figure 19].

In September 1871, a group of important Prussian and Swiss scholars journeyed to Asia Minor on reconnaissance. The unification of Germany that year had inspired a keen desire to establish the new nation's standing as a patron of major works of classical art. The Calvert Collection had grown in extent and reputation and was a major stop on their itinerary.[164] The scholars mentioned it prominently in their accounts, took copious notes, and made rubbings of its inscriptions.[165] Among those present were the famous classical philologist and archaeologist Ernst Curtius (1814–1896),[166] the Swiss philologist and historian Heinrich Gelzer (1847–1906),[167] one of Curtius's students, the archaeologist Gustav Hirschfeld (1847–1895), the architect Friedrich Adler (1827–1908),[168] and the classical archaeologist Karl Bern-

Figure 19. Cabinet display of vases excavated by Frank Calvert at Batak or
Thymbra Farm (1892). By Francis Henry Bacon, courtesy of Elizabeth Bacon.

hard Stark (1824–1895).[169] They already had visited the Imperial Ottoman Museum
in the Church of St. Irene[170] and two private collections in Constantinople.[171] In the
Troad, they stopped first at the Calvert house, where they hoped to discuss the
topography and archaeology of the region with the expert, Frank Calvert.

Curtius wrote his wife that the Calverts' collection was "very remarkable."[172]
Gelzer later lauded the collection and Calvert himself to his Swiss colleagues.
Calvert's "name has become famous in the learned world through his antiquarian
researches of the Trojan Plain. He has, at his own cost, conducted excavations at
several locations, and possesses the richest collection of antiquities from the Trojan territory. The personal reports imparted by such a thoroughly informed man
were for us of the greatest worth." Gelzer understood the importance of Calvert's
collection, the product of one man's excavations and research, whose artifacts and
works of art had a provenance and, in some cases, contextual data that enriched
their significance.[173]

The scholars reserved the last two days of their trip for an examination of the
collection. Stark published the fullest treatment of the collection itself, speaking

warmly of the generosity and hospitality of their host, Frank Calvert, who patiently showed them his finds, displayed on the wide landing of the columned stairwell, [Figure 3] in the vestibule, and in narrow attics of the consular house at the Dardanelles,[174] where it was poorly installed and "very unfavorably crowded for the visitor."[175]

The rich collection included Greek and Roman inscriptions, especially a long one from Sestos; Greek grave and votive reliefs from Cyzicus and Akça Köy; marble architectural fragments from Alexandria Troas and the Temple of Athena at Ilion;[176] terra-cottas from Neandria and Akça Köy; hundreds of Attic vases; abundant glass vessels;[177] the bronze lion weight from Abydos [Figure 18];[178] the bronze mouse that Newton had seen; a spectacular gold diadem depicting Dionysos and Ariadne and jewelry from a grave at Abydos;[179] and gold and silver coins.[180] Of these pieces, the Sestos inscription and the lion weight were most noteworthy. Aside from the Greek and Roman antiquities, the collection included many prehistoric items: stone tools of jasper and flint,[181] fossils,[182] geological specimens, querns, spindle whorls, and sherds from Calvert's assays into prehistory at Hanay Tepe and Ophryneion. These artifacts and natural specimens reflected Frank's personal interests in the natural sciences.

Summing up the collection as a whole, Stark declared, "Its importance lies first of all in its absolute coherence, in which the objects come without exception from the region of the Hellespont."[183] Upon his return, Curtius spoke of Calvert and his preeminent collection to a gathering of scholars at the Archaeological Society in Berlin, noting that the Calvert house at the Dardanelles was "the headquarters of all Trojan research," where there existed a rich museum of antiquities of the region, the greatest detailed knowledge of all building remains, finds, and find spots.[184] Apparently Frederick (and presumably Frank) originally intended to display these antiquities, but there is no evidence that a formal space was ever created for such a purpose. The Dardanelles mansion would have functioned well, but the dream never was realized. Instead, the antiquities remained in the residences until long after both brothers had died.

CHAPTER FOUR

"Progress in discovering . . .
the real site of old Troy"
Pınarbaşı, Akça Köy, or Hisarlık?

As Calvert became active in archaeology, he evolved from an antiquarian to an archaeologist, systematically confirming or disproving past identifications of ancient cities and filling in the blanks in the archaeological record of the Troad. By 1860, he had gained enough stature in the field to begin to tackle the big question—where was Troy? With respect to the two principal sites connected with Troy, Pınarbaşı and Hisarlık, the majority still believed Strabo and expected the prehistoric Troy to lie somewhere other than historic Ilion/Ilium Novum, that is, somewhere other than Hisarlık. The majority view, which scholars clung to as late as 1874, was that Chevalier was generally correct, no matter how flawed his testimony: Pınarbaşı, or the site on the nearby summit of the Ballı Dağ, marked the site of Priam's city. Chief among the qualifications that favored Pınarbaşı was its simply spectacular commanding situation, dominating the lower plain of Troy, from which its inhabitants could view the entire area. Second was the presence of springs near the base of the Ballı Dağ and Chevalier's claim that they, in fact, did run warm and cold as Homer had described. Third was the compelling presence below the acropolis of four heroic tumuli, two known by different authors as the "Tomb of Hector," the middle one as the "Tomb of Priam," plus a fourth on the lower plateau, as well as the presence of a considerable number of antiquities.

Forschammer, who had traveled for a month in July 1839 with Captain (later Admiral) Thomas Abel Brimage Spratt (1811–1888) of the British navy,[1] was among those who argued for Pınarbaşı. Forschammer noted that the remains on the acropolis on the heights at Pınarbaşı were second only to those at Ilium Novum. "The traces of the acropolis walls are continuous," he wrote, and were preserved to three courses in situ [Map 4, detail].[2] He could make out terrace walls on the south side rising one above the other and a wall once "of considerable height and thickness" that crossed the promontory. On both sides of it were what he assumed to be large cisterns. Farther west, another wall of large dimensions extended across the promontory. Between the two were indications of buildings. On a lower plateau stood the tumuli. Unfortunately, Forschammer followed Chevalier's skewed system in calling the Menderes River the Simois and the diminutive Pınarbaşı Çay the Scamander.[3]

Although Chevalier's thesis that Homer's Troy lay at Pınarbaşı quickly had been questioned by Clarke and Rennell, those who protested Chevalier's neat arrangement were in a decided minority. Many were happy simply to be able to stand on the promontory and dream of the epic past. For those who dissented, however, a new topography had to be suggested, and few were willing to wager where that would put Troy. The general consensus, with which Calvert agreed, was that Clarke had discovered the Greco-Roman city of Ilium Novum at Hisarlık (Palaio Kalafatlı).[4] Since Strabo was adamant that Homer's Troy did not lie beneath it, the British botanist and traveler Philip Barker Webb, who had visited the plain in 1819, put Homer's Troy near Hisarlık at Çıplak.[5] Charles Maclaren was bolder still.

Without having ever set foot in the Troad, Charles Maclaren had deduced that Strabo was wrong and that Homer's Troy must have lain at Hisarlık. Maclaren wrote more than once about Troy. His first work was an essay published in *Edinburgh Magazine* in 1820. Next he wrote *A Dissertation on the Topography of the Plain of Troy* in 1822. But his hypothesis went largely unnoticed for forty years.[6] One of the problems impeding the search was the lack of a good map. When Maclaren finally visited Hisarlık in 1847, he was greatly aided by the cartographic work of Spratt, who had surveyed from Erenköy to Alexandria Troas with Forschammer in 1839 and who had compiled the most accurate map of the Troad, which was published in 1840.[7] The Calvert family hosted Maclaren and guided him around the sites.[8] Maclaren probably confided his theories to them and may have presented them with a copy of his 1822 work at that time,[9] but his ideas did not persuade them to abandon Pınarbaşı. After his brief visit to the Troad, Maclaren returned to Scotland. Frank Calvert continued to profess that Troy lay at Pınarbaşı.

When Nassau W. Senior visited Pınarbaşı in 1857, a decade later, he noted that the whole surface of the site on the Ballı Dağ was "covered with stones and in many parts the foundations of walls" were distinct [Map 4]. He traced the walls and found two gates. The southern one he called the "Scaean."[10] Elsewhere, he noted the place where "Mr. Calvert" supposed the wild-fig wood lay, the most accessible part of the town, according to Andromache. Senior drank from the springs and noted little difference in temperature, quoting current opinion that they were the source of the Scamander. He mentioned "Mr. Calvert's" earlier excavation of the tomb of Priam, but no discussion ensued as to the barrow's relevance in discussions of Pınarbaşı's likelihood as Homer's Troy.[11]

For Senior as for Calvert, the remains suggested the past presence of a "considerable city and an acropolis." Convinced that Troy lay here, Senior was only bothered that it would have been impossible for Achilles to have chased Hector three times around these walls, but he attributed the impossibility to the story, not

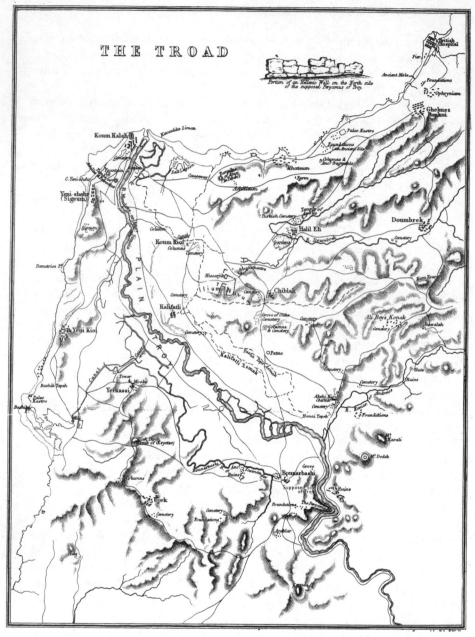

Map 4. The Troad (Senior, 1859).

the site. The distance from the sea was not an insurmountable objection because it was known that the land had encroached on the sea.[12] According to Senior, who was for the most part repeating what was told him by Calvert, Ilium Novum could not possibly be the site of Troy because of its proximity to the Hellespont. For some reason, Senior never even visited it.[13] Alexandria Troas was too near the Aegean and was not near the source of a river.

There also was now a third alternative. Assuming that Strabo was correct in differentiating the locations of prehistoric Troy and Ilion/Ilium Novum, Rennell suggested, following Homer, that Troy (the "Ilian village" of Strabo) lay in the plain somewhere between Akça Köy and Kalafatlı, but he was not in the Troad himself and could find no reference to remains equal to the epic city.[14] One location that fit Rennell's qualifications, although it was not mentioned by Senior, was Akça Köy itself, the site of Frederick Calvert's farm. In 1824, Palaio Akça Köy had been suggested by the British antiquarian and classical topographer William Martin Leake (1777–1860) as the site of Ilion Kome, Strabo's "village of the Ilians."[15] This idea, mentioned in passing by Leake, was further developed by Heinrich Nikolaus Ulrichs, the first professor of Latin at Athens University, who visited the area in 1843. Fortunately for the Calverts, who did not speak or read German, his 1845 article was translated from German into English in 1847. Like Leake, Ulrichs quoted Strabo's passage on Ilion Kome and concluded that Troy must lie on the Akça Köy ridge.[16]

Frederick Calvert took notice. Perhaps the theory even influenced him to buy the Akça Köy farm known as Chiflik, or Batak, in the same year. But few architectural remains had survived the villagers' quarrying in the early nineteenth century, and Frank Calvert found only Hanay Tepe and a rich necropolis of historical times on a nearby ridge.[17] Frank Calvert did not quickly abandon the theory that the walls of Homer's Troy could be found at Pınarbaşı. Eventually the careful archaeologist would excavate all three, Pınarbaşı, Akça Köy, and Hisarlık, before he concluded which site had the rightful claim.

By the time of Senior's visit in 1857, Frank Calvert and a "Mr. Freeman" from Erenköy had purchased 2000 acres of ground, including part of the site of Ilium Novum, for £300.[18] They had purchased the acreage between 1853 and 1856.[19] The exact year of the purchase is not known, although by 1856 Frederick had encountered financial trouble that only worsened in 1857,[20] so it appears most probable that they bought it during the war. From Senior's account, it seems that the Calvert brothers formed a partnership, with Frederick investing the capital and expecting a good return.

In the beginning, the Calverts' decision to purchase Hisarlık must have seemed simply to be a profitable land speculation. Both Frederick and Frank Calvert must have recognized Hisarlık's potential as an investment. The site was surrounded by good farmland and was only a mile and a half from Frederick's other estate at Akça Köy. The two properties were divided along the plateau of which Ilium Novum formed the spur. The farm lay in the valley of the Dümrek, or Simois,

River and along the ridges to the north and south, as well as across the stream of the Kemer, or Thymbrios [Map 4].[21]

The partners had succeeded in overcoming a number of obstacles, among which were Moslem neighbors who objected to Christians living and working in their midst.[22] Near the Turkish village of Çıplak, in what was perhaps the western and southern limit of Calvert's property, Senior saw "rough buildings which Calvert and his partner had put up as the beginning of their farm." Calvert told Senior that they expected to lay out another £1700 for outbuildings, one hundred cattle, and twenty oxen, but that expenses would be paid out of the produce. He projected that soon they would make £1000 annually. The purchase itself seems consistent with Frederick's tendency to overextend himself with land acquisitions. There is no further evidence of Calvert's ambitious plans for farming the Ilium Novum land, and given subsequent financial problems, he may never have had the chance.[23] Presumably the Calverts would have wished to buy more land at Hisarlık as its potential became clear.[24]

Viewed as an archaeological site, rather than as an investment, Hisarlık showed considerably less promise, at least on the surface. By Calvert's time, the archaeological remains there had deteriorated steadily for fifty years. Leake noted in 1800 that villagers resorted to it as a stone quarry for neighboring villages, farms, and cemeteries.[25] Already in Clarke's day, the Turks were dismantling the walls of the recently noted remains.[26] Yet in 1839, Forschammer noticed extensive ruins: an acropolis, a theater, an aqueduct, a city wall, and the foundations of a bath.[27] As late as 1840–41, Gustav von Eckenbrecher, a German physician from Smyrna, described remains of destroyed buildings above ground: columns, architraves, triglyphs, and other fragments of a temple.[28] But just a few years later, Maclaren noted far fewer. "It was strewed with innumerable small morsels of pottery and tile, and some bits of marble, and bore, in patches, in the first week of May 1847, a miserably thin crop of wheat or barley." The pillaging had not stopped in 1847, and by 1853, Newton could remark that the remains above ground were "very trifling."[29] Still, from Newton's assessment as well as their own, they knew that the site would provide antiquities, at least of historical Ilion/Ilium Novum. Prehistoric antiquities from the Troad were unknown prior to Calvert's 1856 excavation at Hanay Tepe.

Maclaren gave the fullest treatment of Hisarlık's physical appearance prior to excavation. To the north lay the acropolis; "the eminence seemed nearly square and its breadth little more than a furlong, say 700 feet . . . with a few scattered trees." He noted that the summit of the hill stood some 110 feet above the plain [Figures 20a, 20b, and 20c]. Along the north face, the eastern end was sheer as it dropped to the plateau below; the west fell straight to the plain.[30] Maclaren further noted that the northern edge of the acropolis inclined between 24 and 10 feet down to a plateau that sloped off to the south. The plateau, in turn, stood some 84 feet above the plain.

Thanks to the Crimean War, virtually all the sites Frank Calvert would excavate in search of Troy recently had been disturbed. As the war dragged on, and more and more support services were needed for the wounded, the British government ordered

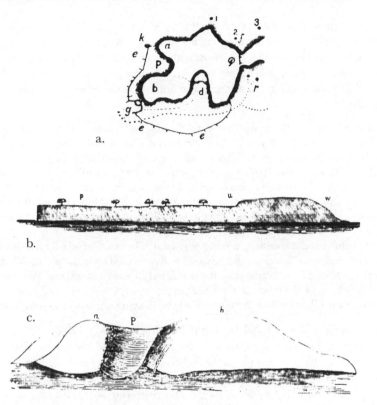

Figures 20 a–c. Hisarlık. Maclaren (1863), 70, 72, and 76. a. Plan of Hisarlık; b. western part of Çıplak ridge (u–w: Hisarlık); c. outline of Hisarlık from the west.

the London railway engineer John Brunton (1812–1899) to build a hospital to provide sanitary facilities for British troops. After surveying the south coast of the Black Sea and the Sea of Marmara for suitable sites, in 1855, Brunton chose to build on the narrow coastal strip below and 2 miles northeast of Erenköy.[31] While working with Frederick Calvert, he developed close relations with the Calverts.[32] By winter, the exemplary hospital was functioning and all but finished.[33] Then the War Office notified Brunton of the impending peace with Russia and ordered him to stop all work. Rather than turning loose some 150 idle soldiers from the Army Works Corps under his command,[34] on the spur of the moment, Brunton "camped them out on the plains of Troy, determining to commence some excavations at the Necropolis." Since Brunton probably knew Frank Calvert's theory that Hanay Tepe was the burial mound of the Trojans, Brunton's "Necropolis" of Troy would have been the mound at Hanay Tepe or the nearby classical necropolis.[35]

Brunton was not an archaeologist by any means. This was not excavation to test the historical record, but, apparently, more of a lark or a treasure hunt. To motivate his men, Brunton bribed them with an extra pint of stout and wrote of his army corps: "When we came on ancient tombs, sarcophagi, amphorae &c they got much interested and worked away with great zest. We found a great many things,—vases, armlets, anklets, earrings &c." At this point in the narrative he becomes a bit more specific, mentioning the actual sites where he had ordered his men to dig.

> I detached a section of my men to Illium Novum, and put them to excavate there.
>
> I found the ruins of a temple, the Corinthian capital of one of the columns, evidently shaken down by an earthquake, was the most beautiful piece of carving in white marble I ever saw. It weighed over 3 tons—we had some difficulty in getting it out of the hole in which we discovered it. There were no roads to the place along which a cart could be brought to convey it away—so I was forced to roll it up the mound under which I had found it, set it up on end, and to my great regret leave it there.
>
> We came upon the walls of a house very near this spot. The plaster was still on the walls, and we could see the colour which had been used upon the plaster. We dug down a little deeper and came upon the tessellated pavement of a room. We cleared the whole area of the room. In the centre of the room was a large oval tessellated picture,—the subject a Boar hunt, beautifully worked in variously tinted marbles.

Called back to the hospital by dispatches from the War Office, Brunton was prevented from cutting out the mosaic. He interrupted his assault on the mound and ordered the Roman mosaic backfilled and all the earth and material that had been dug up to be thrown in. He never excavated there again. When he returned a fortnight later to retrieve the mosaic, it had been removed, and he had to content himself with a bit of border that had been left behind.[36] Soon thereafter, peace was declared, and the hospital was dismantled and sold,[37] leaving the coastal plain almost deserted when Brunton sailed for England.[38] Upon his return, Brunton wrote, "I presented the Trojan relics to the British Museum, the Authorities there sent Panici,[39] the Curator of Antiquities to inspect the collection."[40]

From the point of view of sound archaeology, there are a number of problems with Brunton's "excavations." To busy his men, Brunton had them digging simultaneously at as many as seven sites on the plain and the coast, thus making supervision impossible. Since he mentioned no one else in a supervisory capacity, one imagines a complete free-for-all. During a very brief period of time, perhaps only a day, Brunton's men worked all over the Troad. His artifacts, now in the British Museum, are labeled "Dardanos," "Old Dardanos," "the cemetery near Troy," "Troy," "Ilium Novum," "a tomb at Troy," and "Ophryneion (?)."[41] Because of the changing identifications between sites and ancient cities, it is quite difficult to pin down just where these identified find spots were. Brunton's Troy, for instance, could refer to Pınarbaşı, according to Chevalier's theory, which was still current in 1855–56,[42] or to Akça Köy, according to Ulrichs.

Brunton probably excavated at most of these sites because they were owned by the Calverts or their clients and hence accessible. Frederick clearly owned the land at Akça Köy, and his vineyards at Erenköy may have encompassed some of the site at Ophryneion. Frank Calvert probably already was the proprietor of the farm at Ilium Novum,[43] and Frederick might have controlled some property at Dardanos.[44] Either way, Frederick may casually have given Brunton carte blanche, welcoming the free labor force, and steered Brunton to the most profitable locations, where Frank Calvert had made the only scientific excavations.

It is odd that Frank Calvert never once mentioned Brunton's work at Hisarlık or elsewhere—all the more so because he did note that of Gormezano at the tomb of Achilles.[45] Although the Brunton excavations were cursory, they are significant in being the first documented work at Ilium Novum, albeit with no notion of finding Homer's Troy—indeed, just to keep his men out of trouble.[46]

One can only conjecture why Frank Calvert failed to note Brunton's work.[47] Whether or not Frederick had given Brunton permission without asking his brother, Frank may have been justifiably outraged that an interloper had first probed his most important site. Furthermore, the digging was so far removed from being a scientific excavation that Calvert may have felt it did not merit comment. One must surmise that Frank jealously suppressed Brunton's excursion.

A few months after Brunton's sortie, the French archaeologist Georges Perrot (1832–1914) toured Hisarlık in dismay, noting the scatter of column shafts, capitals, and trimmed blocks in disarray, probably left by generations of quarrying Turks.[48] In the midst of this chaos he noted some "superficial excavations" from which a group of Greeks from Kalafatlı had removed an unremarkable mosaic for the floor of their church.[49] He mentioned the remains of a temple, apparently with features of both Ionic and Doric orders.[50] Noting that ruins were visible everywhere that pits had been dug, he observed that well-conducted excavations over a large area at the site could be interesting.

The Reverend Henry Fanshawe Tozer documented the site in 1861 as it appeared after Brunton's assault and presumably prior to Calvert's excavations. Of his visit to Ilium Novum, he noted that at "Hisarlik or the Place of the Castle . . . remains of the ancient city are few, being principally composed of lines of walls and pieces of mosaic pavement, which had been excavated. At the extreme angle was the acropolis and close to this is the form of a theatre excavated in the hillside." He dismissed its ancient claim to be Homer's Troy.[51]

Brunton's finds suggest that he worked on the southern and southeastern slope of the mound and perhaps the lower city on that part of the site owned by Calvert prior to 1857.[52] At the very least, Brunton had proven the archaeological wealth of the site, and even if his sojourn had been little more than a looting expedition, he had probed the mound first.

For reasons of security as well as pressures of work at the consulate,[53] Calvert could not have begun to excavate Ilium Novum during the Crimean War. As it was, Frederick Calvert's farm at Akça Köy was attacked and ransacked in the summer of 1855. But seven years intervened from 1856 until he began to excavate in earnest in 1863. If it is true, as Calvert later claimed, that he had purchased the land because he believed that he would find the walls of Troy there, then it is hard to understand why he did not begin to excavate his prize sooner. He knew at the very least it represented the Greco-Roman city honored by Alexander and Augustus. Both Calvert brothers probably knew Maclaren's theory that Homer's Troy lay beneath classical Ilium, but Frank Calvert's conversion from Pınarbaşı to Hisarlık cannot be documented in the 1850s. It seems clear that he did not switch allegiance from Pınarbaşı before 1860.

What also seems clear is that significant excavation at Hisarlık would mean a considerable outlay of money. Given the effort he expended in small excavations and inquiries throughout the Troad between 1856 and 1862 at the classical cities of Ophryneion, Colonae, Larisa, Cebrene, Pınarbaşı, and at Akça Köy and the Aesepus Valley, it may simply have been that the magnitude of the task, the size and the complexity of the mound, prevented him from undertaking it. Although he lacked money, he did have time. After all, until he changed his mind, it was just another classical city mentioned by Strabo, and it already had been identified by Clarke.

While in London in 1860, Frederick Calvert, who undoubtedly enjoyed the recognition his brother was receiving for his research, had numerous discussions on Troy with Greaves and reported his "brother's strong doubts" respecting the site near Pınarbaşı as an acceptable Troy. At the same time, he and Greaves agreed that if Homer's warm and cold springs could be found, the site would be fixed conclusively. When Frederick returned in 1860, he would have assessed his estates and perhaps proceeded with the draining of the pestilential marsh to the west of Akça Köy. This activity would have demanded Frank's assistance and energies and pulled his attention away from antiquarian pursuits elsewhere in the Troad, focusing them on the plain.

A year later, in 1861, Frederick Calvert wrote Greaves, confiding the brothers' shift in allegiance away from Pınarbaşı and mentioning their "progress in discovering . . . the real site of old Troy," although he noted that they had not yet "actually discovered" it. Frederick continued, "Since my return we have gone thoroughly into the question (as to the precise location of Troy), and have become convinced that the theory of Professor Ulrich . . . which places the site of Troy at Aktchiheni (my farm buildings) is nearly correct." So at this point, Frank Calvert seems to have been focusing on the Akça Köy hypothesis.

Frederick told Greaves that he had noted two springs in the center of a deep marsh in the immediate neighborhood that he had visited with the Reverend Hugh A. J. Munro (1815–1885), an English classicist, as witness and found between them a difference of twenty-two and one-half degrees Fahrenheit.[54] An ancient hill immediately above and close to the springs answered well to Homer's description as being on a spur of Ida advancing into the plain (*Iliad* 20.216). The location of the site can be reconstructed by examining Schliemann's later map, which puts it to the north of the marshy area to the west of Akça Köy, about 3 miles to the southeast of Ilium Novum.[55] Greaves concluded that the site "agreed in every respect with Homer's site of Troy" based on Frederick's information and presumably on the added authority of his brother, and he immediately communicated the finding to the Archaeological Institute on 5 July 1861.[56]

It is curious that Frederick, rather than Frank, Calvert made the disclosure of this claim to Greaves, a claim that Frank Calvert had not yet publicized, but then Frederick had enjoyed the companionship of his brother's correspondent during his extended stay in London. Perhaps Frederick had lost patience with his younger brother's cautiousness. Knowing from his recent visit to London that the subject was hotly contested in antiquarian circles, Frederick Calvert may have acted impulsively, not wanting the family to be left out of the debate. Here was their opportunity to contribute something original to the continuing dialogue on Troy's true location. The locale fit with Rennell's prophetic statement of 1814—it did lie in the plain, on a promontory of a ridge that descended from Ida, and it was in the specified area between Akça Köy and Kalafatlı. This could be Strabo's Troy, "Ilion Kome."

Greaves's approbation certainly would have stimulated Frank Calvert to look more deeply into the Trojan question, having already had himself put on record as taking a position on it. But he would need hard proof before he himself published such controversial conclusions refuting the theory of the day. Whether or not Frank Calvert ever excavated the site north of the Batak marsh, he never publicly corroborated Frederick's claim. The lack of prehistoric remains probably disqualified it for him on closer inspection. Frank Calvert did, however, go so far as to measure the temperature of the Duden spring himself.[57] In the end, neither Frank nor James Calvert agreed with Frederick.[58] In the interim, however, Frank Calvert would first expose Chevalier's claim that Pınarbaşı was Homeric Troy as the fraud he felt it to be.

Early in 1863, Frank Calvert fired a decisive salvo into the Pınarbaşı camp with a concise refutation of Chevalier's theory based on his own excavations and a critique of ancient and modern writers.[59] In it, he laid out his earlier excavation of the "tumulus of Priam" at Pınarbaşı on the Ballı Dağ [Figure 21],[60] To determine the true character of the tumuli on the bluff, Calvert had excavated the central one, opening a shaft at the base of the mound and continuing along the surface of the natural rock through a mixture of earth and stones. He concluded that the rectangular foundations were those of a stone tower or statue base and illustrated them in a section drawn to scale [Figure 22].[61] Through excavation, Calvert disproved once and for all Chevalier's romantic supposition that the tumuli of Pınarbaşı were the burial mounds of Trojan heroes. The "heap of stones" Chevalier had called the "Tomb of Hector" Calvert confidently dismissed as "heaps of refuse stone thrown out during quarrying." The remaining two smaller tumuli remained unexcavated.

Calvert also refuted Chevalier's theory about the settlement at Pınarbaşı.[62] He had examined the fortification wall carefully, and though "the roughness of the stones" in the massive wall foundations was indicative of an "early age," now Calvert specifically (and correctly) cited the stonework of the fortifications as "posterior to that of Homeric Troy." His evidence: "the comparatively small hewn

Figure 21. Frank Calvert and Alice Calvert Bacon at Pınarbaşı on the Ballı Dağ, courtesy of Candace Bacon Cordella.

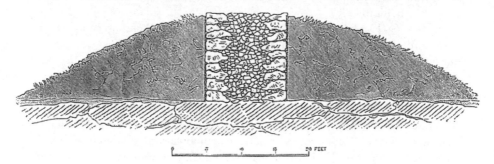

Figure 22. Tumulus of Priam, Pınarbaşı. Calvert (1864).

stones in regular layers being dissimilar to the more massive masonry that characterize the remains of Tiryns, Larisa (at Argos) and Mycenae, true Homeric cities."

By this time, Calvert had located the settlement's necropolis outside the acropolis walls and noted that it contained only *pithos* graves and much later pottery.[63] In fact, there was no pottery whatsoever that resembled the rude ceramics of a prehistoric, Homeric era, such he had excavated at Hanay Tepe. On the basis of pottery styles, Calvert dated the site to around 500 B.C.[64] For this reason, he sought to identify it with a later settlement. Rather than abdicating the responsibility of identifying the site as his predecessors had done, Calvert researched the possibilities and finally settled on Gergis on the basis of ancient testimonia and coins.[65] Xenophon had described Gergis as a place of great strength with lofty towers and an acropolis. This was a town settled by Trojans who had emigrated to Cyprus and had returned "to colonize their ancient fatherland." Thus, Calvert not only had disproved Chevalier's theory by excavating, but also had offered an attractive alternative, based on scholarly research. Gergis was itself linked with Homer's Troy, for Herodotus claimed that its inhabitants were "all the remnant that is left of the ancient Teucri" (5.122).

If Troy was probably not at Akça Köy and definitely not at Pınarbaşı, the last alternative site was at Hisarlık, under Ilion/Ilium Novum. The case for Hisarlık got a renewed hearing when in 1863, at the age of eighty, Charles Maclaren published *The Plain of Troy Described*.[66] Because his first book had not been widely read, he once again refuted Strabo and Demetrius, restating his 1822 thesis reviving the ancient idea that Homer's Troy and classical Ilion were on the same spot.

After having visited the plain of Troy, he now spoke more authoritatively about its topography. "The more the poet's local details are investigated, the more exact and exclusive is the coincidence to be found between the hill of Issarlik, and the position of his Troy." He used his own topographical observations to augment those of Kauffer and Forschammer, whose map and article he followed, emending his own identifications [Figures 20a, 20b, and 20c].[67] Maclaren had no time for Demetrius of Scepsis, a "mere antiquarian speculator" envious of the prosperity of Ilium.[68]

Nor did he put any stock in the thesis advanced by Chevalier, whom he accused of distorting the facts to hide the inconsistency of his own narrative.[69] He spoke of "the seductive error of the plausible Frenchman," whose "very gross errors [were only] . . . slightly corrected in a second edition." Furthermore, he brought attention to the "suspicious fact that all the errors tend to bolster his theory."[70] Instead, Maclaren urged that "number and measure . . . supply the only pure test of truth and consistency."[71]

Calvert had demolished Pınarbaşı and Maclaren had made a strong case for Hisarlık in the same year, 1863. Although it is difficult to prove, it is likely that Calvert read Maclaren's book before he commenced his own excavations at Ilium Novum.[72] Considering Maclaren's thesis, the damage resulting from Brunton's predations at Hisarlık took on a much more serious cast. Not one prone to making snap judgments, Calvert had excavated Pınarbaşı, and presumably he had further investigated the site west of Akça Köy. Now he tested Hisarlık and concurred with Maclaren that Hisarlık had the rightful claim. Calvert acted immediately. Before, Hisarlık had been to him no more than a large classical site with considerable remains. Now he thought of the rich prehistoric remains of Priam's city below.

Even though he was the proprietor, he could not easily excavate it on his own. Eager to proceed, Calvert considered his next move carefully. Cautious as always, he began to consider his financial constraints. Mindful of his need to garner private patronage or institutional support, and perhaps simply for moral support, Calvert wrote to his most influential archaeological contact in Paris. He told Waddington, the accomplished epigrapher and member of the Numismatic Society of London, about his ownership of Hisarlık, that is, of Ilium Novum, what remains had been exposed, and his desire to excavate. Waddington, who was chiefly interested in classical remains, responded that he believed important discoveries could indeed be made in the area of the temple.[73] But Calvert knew he would need meticulous documentation before publishing any claim that, Strabo to the contrary, Ilium Novum was Homer's Troy. He was fully cognizant of the scholars railing against one another on behalf of their pet theories, and if they could be wrong, so could he. Bolstered by Waddington's positive response, Calvert stood on the brink of one of the century's great archaeological achievements.

CHAPTER FIVE

"The imputation of serious frauds"
Disgrace and Disappointment

As everyone knows, the fame for finding the walls of Homer's Troy went not to Frank Calvert, but to Heinrich Schliemann. Yet it was Calvert who was poised to make the discovery. What went wrong? In effect, the two worlds that overlapped in the Calvert family's employment as consuls in the Dardanelles began to pull apart. For Frederick Calvert, the linchpin of the Calvert family and the genial gentleman who also had to be a businessman eager for the main chance, the outcome was disastrous. After the end of the Crimean War, he stood accused of actions no gentleman ever should undertake. His catastrophe affected the fortunes of the rest of the family, especially those of his brother Frank.

When Frederick William Calvert had joined his maternal uncle, Charles Lander, at the Dardanelles in 1834, at the usual age of sixteen, he simultaneously had learned diplomacy and entrepreneurship.[1] On at least one occasion he was mistaken for Lander's son.[2] He showed such promise that when Lander's wife died, in 1841, Lander appointed Frederick Calvert his trustee and coexecutor, and the guardian of his three daughters. After Lander died, late in 1846, Frederick assumed control not only of Lander's property at the Dardanelles and Erenköy and the inheritance held in trust for his cousins,[3] but also his position as British consul.[4] In the same year, he married Eveline Eugenie Abbott (1829–1911), the fair-haired second daughter of Richard B. and Helen Abbott of Smyrna, an accomplished linguist.[5] In 1847, Frederick became Prussian vice-consul, and to his consular titles he soon added the Belgian and Dutch vice-consulships, as well.[6] He also served from time to time as acting French consul.[7]

Frederick's marriage allied him socially and economically with "the prolific house of Abbott" in Constantinople and Smyrna,[8] the "Marseilles of the Levant."[9] The Abbotts were commercial leaders, and through them the Calverts were linked to the "best society" of Smyrna, known for its hospitality and splendid lifestyle.[10] This aristocracy was purely mercantile: although many had princely

fortunes, they clung to the countinghouse.[11] Whereas the houses of the local population were of wood, those of the Europeans were of stone, enclosed in a courtyard with a fountain in the center. The houses were so close that the eaves almost
met.[12] Just as at the Dardanelles, European merchants in Smyrna had houses in
town for transacting business and villas or hillside retreats in the neighboring
towns to which they escaped, surrounded by portraits of their ancestors and by
English gardens.[13] Like the Calverts, these Smyrna merchants collected antiquities. They spoke Greek, French, Italian, and English, and many knew Turkish, but
there was no lingua franca.[14] They gave concerts and elegant balls and soirées at
the European casino, where they could play cards, chess, or billiards and read the
latest European newspapers and literary periodicals.[15] As at the Dardanelles, each
ethnic group had its own quarter of the city.[16] The British attended services at the
Anglican church in the "Frank," or Christian, quarter.[17] In "the grand emporium
of the commerce of Turkey," the Franks, or Europeans, occupied Frank Street,
which extended half the length of the city.[18] Parallel to this lay the "English Scala"
in front of the British consulate and Anglican church and a marina, with a range
of edifices running along the shore.[19]

Frederick Calvert strove to be on a par with these gentlemen merchants. His
consular position demanded a show of respect from those around him. Travelers
and dignitaries, on arriving at the Dardanelles, expected to be entertained, and
Frederick Calvert was quite solicitous with his well-connected visitors. Carlisle
and Senior both dined with his superior, Stratford Canning, in Constantinople
and could be relied upon to convey a good report.[20] In fact, Senior described his
visit as "the most agreeable and most instructive week of the whole tour."[21]

As a young and ambitious man, in 1847 Frederick Calvert requested to be a
consul with trading privileges.[22] As such, he actively pursued the advantages provided by British economic domination in the Levant and his own strategic location, dealing under the aegis of Calvert Bros. and Co., an "extended family company,"[23] in commodities such as grain, valonia, cotton, and timber.[24] At the same
time, he dispensed high-interest loans to the local population[25] and further sup-
plemented his modest income by being the local agent for Lloyd's.[26] Clearly, a
consular salary was not high enough to maintain a family at the Dardanelles at his
elevated standard of living.

James Whittall (1819–1883), a prominent British trader in Smyrna,[27] spoke of
him as a man of talent, energy, and public spirit who could speak Turkish and
"whose opportunities of doing good, or rather preventing evil," were enormous.
He remarked that Calvert was a more important person than the local pasha. He
was glamorous and sharp, and "the whole province looks up to him and all the
Pasha's merits are justly ascribed to his influence."[28] But because of their power
and high profile, consuls like Frederick Calvert, who acted like watchdogs against
local Ottoman abuses, drew a great deal of jealous criticism.[29]

As England prepared for war, Frederick Calvert was drawn into the actions that
were his downfall. The proud man previously had sought to enhance his status by

hobnobbing with the pasha, speculating in real estate, and showing a fashionable interest in antiquarian matters. Now, the war offered him a chance for greatness—a chance to serve his country as a true gentleman should. His younger brother Edmund already was working under Canning, now Viscount Stratford de Redcliffe, in Constantinople. From 1853 to 1856, Frederick put his own business affairs on hold. When the combined British and French fleets arrived at Beşika Bay in July 1853, Erenköy was strategically located for entertaining admirals and other dignitaries between the bay, the strait, and the Dardanelles. By October 1853, troop ships lay anchored off the fort at Abydos (Nağara). Britain expected a brief campaign and was ill prepared for the war.[30]

Because of a lack of foresight, there was a vacuum of experienced leadership in the Commissariat, a civilian department at first under the control of the Treasury Department and then under the War Office, Foreign Office, and Colonial Office. To serve ten thousand troops, a total of forty-four largely untrained men were appointed. Four went to Gallipoli and Constantinople in the spring of 1854, charged with billeting and provisioning British troops, but without any knowledge of Turkish.[31] Although each of these deputy assistant commissaries general was to have a clerk to help serve the assigned brigade, none were sent. Instead, Sir Charles Trevelyan of the Treasury Department admitted that "we relied upon getting subordinates in the countries where the force was to act."[32]

In March, Frederick Calvert stepped into this vacuum and made arrangements for the troops there and at the Abydos lazaretto northeast of the Dardanelles.[33] Reports referred to "our excellent consul at the Dardanelles" who detailed the available supplies so that within days Deputy Assistant Commissary General Bagot Smith could sign contracts with Turkish individuals "for a supply of every requisite for the army."[34] Frederick offered the family's waterfront warehouses for the storage of Britain's war supplies.[35] In 1855, he also served the British Land Transport Corps at a feverish pace, traveling to Constantinople, Salonica, and the scene of battle in the Crimea.[36] To prevent the loss of valuable time due to inclement weather conditions, he had tugs tow British supply ships through the dangerous strait.[37] Using his vast network of contacts in the area, he procured saddles, drivers, horses, and mules by the thousands, hay and straw by the tons.[38]

Frederick Calvert boasted of "a large establishment of sub-agents, clerks, and other employees engaged between Scutari [on the shore of the Bosphorus] and Tarsus in Asia and Constantinople and Volo in Europe who are paid exclusively by me." According to Calvert, Colonel McMurdo (1819–1894), responsible for forming the Land Transport Corps,[39] noted that, "but for the timely and efficacious service" rendered by Calvert, "the Land Transport Corps in the Crimea, and at a very critical period of the campaign, might have broken down."[40] Others commended him for the most substantial contribution of any person in Turkey in the supply of British troops. Noblesse oblige.

To secure his supplies, however, Frederick Calvert frequently went beyond accepted channels and, like others who lacked liquid capital, took out loans "at a high rate of interest to carry out . . . various contracts with the Commissariat." In doing so, he overextended himself.[41] Whittall noted that "Calvert . . . rendered great services to our army; and, if the Commissariat would have allowed him, would have rendered much greater."[42] But the Commissariat system was a logistical shambles. It broke down, and in the process broke independent contractors like Frederick Calvert who served it.

Because the contractors were trading on credit, the Commissariat paid the funds that were due to the contractors to their bankers, instead. The bankers, in turn, were hesitant to make additional advances to the contractors to pay their suppliers. Contractors like Calvert were caught in the middle, having contracted to provide supplies, including hay for forage, but neither being paid for attempting to fulfill their contracts nor being able to pay those with whom they had contracted. In May 1855, Calvert promised several thousand tons of hay.[43] By the fall, he had gathered the hay at Salonica. But the Commissariat could not transport the hay and left it on the quay unused.[44] Moreover, the Commissariat would not allow contractors like Calvert to sell the hay to anyone else after claiming the hay for its own use. Consequently, the British army, unable to use 60 percent of the hay that had been collected, let it rot on the dock.[45]

When the system broke down in the winter of 1854–55, want of forage caused mass starvation among the animals, and the Treasury Department refused to accept responsibility.[46] In late 1855, Lord Panmure, war secretary from 1855 to 1858, directed John McNeill and Colonel Alexander M. Tulloch "to inquire into the whole arrangement and management of the Commissariat Department" in order to investigate "the sources of supply" and alleged delays.[47] They found that the elderly commissary general, James Filder, had been "unwilling to depart from specified processes and find local substitutes for lost rations."[48] He was replaced. During the investigation, the Commissariat blamed the independent contractors for failing in their deliveries.[49] Deputy Assistant Commissary General Smith at Constantinople, criticized for his inability to transport forage, in turn fingered Calvert, vaguely saying that he had shown "less regard for public than private interests."[50]

Whittall told Senior that "they hated him, and tried to ruin him. Some, because he required from them more exertion than men with their torpid routine habits could make, or could ever conceive; others, because he interfered with their jobs."[51] McNeill and Tulloch finally published their final report on 20 January 1856. Because of Smith's allegations, by 26 January, Calvert had to answer to charges of alleged profiteering to Brigadier General Mansfield.[52]

According to Frederick Calvert's version of the story, his trade and properties suffered tremendously during the Crimean War. Both Batak Farm and his Chersonese estate had been assaulted and plundered by marauding Bashi Bazouks, native irregulars in the service of the British cavalry, who also had threatened Erenköy.[53] He had had increased social obligations and constantly had been moving about the country. He had lost his trading partners and had mortgaged all his property.[54] After peace was declared, Frederick complained that his personal affairs and those of his family "imperatively" required his attention and requested leave to put his "affairs in order in Europe to be released from further liability in a commercial undertaking."[55] He left Frank in charge of the consulate. By July, Frederick was trying to "attain with respect to his private affairs a position more compatible with his public duties" than the one he had "unwillingly and unavoidably occupied for the last few years."[56] He had begun to encounter the problems involved in being a consul-trader.

Whittall had articulated the problems of consular service in Asia Minor: "In this country almost everyone turns jobber. The opportunities are incessant, the immunity is almost perfect. Public opinion is in favor of corruption. Englishmen who might have been honest anywhere else, caught the endemic." He continued: "The consuls and vice-consuls should not only be better chosen, but better paid. Their salaries have not been raised, while everything has doubled in price. If Calvert were not agent for Lloyd's, he could not maintain his position." Whittall lamented the moral collapse of inhabitants of the East: "even Englishmen are the worse for twenty or thirty years of residence among us."[57]

After peace was declared, John Brunton, who had worked so closely with Calvert in building the British military hospital below Erenköy, was ordered to sell or dismantle it. Frederick saw a chance to make a financial coup and tried to purchase supplies and equipment being auctioned by the army at a drastically reduced price.[58] But Brunton thwarted him and accused him of being an opportunist, scheming to defraud the War Office for his own gain. Brunton portrayed him as so extremely powerful that local people were afraid to cross him.[59] They had a serious falling out in late summer 1856. Frederick did not get the supplies, but he did purchase the land. Smith's innuendo haunted Calvert's future career.

Calvert was brought before the Supreme Consular Court in Constantinople in March 1857 for debts owed to the War Office.[60] He left in February 1858 for London, where he spent two and a half years. He stayed there trying to clear his name and appeared before a parliamentary committee on consular service.[61] Although he begged to be knighted by the queen for his suffering, in 1859 he was "imprisoned for ten weeks on account of a debt contracted for the sole benefit of Her Majesty's Government." The War Office had withheld payment of several thousand pounds, and in 1859 it disallowed the 3 percent commission to which Frederick was entitled for his wartime service to the Land Transport Corps. Calvert responded that his imprisonment had had "a disastrous effect" on his private affairs, which were otherwise fast recovering their previously prosperous position. Later he lamented, "My official position at the Dardanelles has also been seriously compromised."[62]

Again in 1860, Calvert begged for advancement or some other marked token of approbation from the queen.[63] Foreign Office communiqués asserted that the character of the consular service and that of the Foreign Office had "been affected by the imprisonment of one of HM Consuls for alleged misconduct. . . .

Either the Consul should be proved to have done wrong or he must be exonerated from blame. The War Office have not proved the wrong, but will not admit the right . . . [they] have no positive knowledge of anything to the Consul's prejudice. . . . How can a stain of fraudulent conduct be allowed to rest on his character?"[64] Eventually his name was cleared, after a full investigation in 1860.[65] He received commendation from the British government and both houses of Parliament.[66] Four and a half years after the end of the war, the War Office finally paid him several thousand pounds of back commission and reimbursements, with interest. He returned home to the Dardanelles with considerable capital in October 1860.[67]

In many ways Frederick Calvert's problems reflected the tenuous hold of Europeans in that area. Their constant land acquisitions in western Anatolia,[68] which frequently were held in the name of local *rayas*, were quite risky, and few prospered.[69] Soon after purchasing *çiftliks*, or large tracts of land (often entire villages), foreigners went bankrupt, left the property vacant, as it appears Frank Calvert did with his farm, or leased it out to local peasants in small units.[70] On the Chersonese and in Smyrna, British gentleman-merchants like Frederick Calvert had settled huge estates, brought technology from England at great expense, and then lost everything.[71] Thus, the "Trojan Colonisation Society," which Senior at one point envisioned, and, in general, British imperial hopes for western Anatolia, which Whittall had foreseen as an "English and German colony,"[72] did not become realities. Between 1858 and 1860, debt-related cases accounted for close to half of the civil suits tried at the British consular court in Smyrna, and Foreign Office bankruptcy files were full of proceedings against foreign residents in Turkey.[73] One British traveler remarked that "Levant trade is becoming slippery and unsafe, a trick and a chicane that no English house can compete with the [locals] . . . or continue any time in the Levant trade without being ruined or reduced to the necessity of *Levanting*."[74]

Frederick Calvert continued to suffer from the exigencies of his position as an English gentleman in the East in need of ready profits. Despite his complaint that his "salary was barely sufficient to cover expenses of subsistence even on the most reduced scale,"[75] he had been forced for reasons of health and because of the vulnerability of his commercial interests to reject a lucrative promotion involving a move to Syria in 1860.[76] He clearly was overextended by his land acquisitions and must have found it difficult to keep up his lifestyle, being the main provider for his mother, sister, wife, brother Frank, and small children,[77] as well as being responsible for his business interests and farms and for the weight they lent him in local society. The cost of living at the Dardanelles, thrice inflated during the Crimean War, was still twice that of other cities in Asia Minor because of the frequency of ships provisioning there.[78] His incarceration had injured his status with the local Turkish officials,[79] and Frederick's correspondence with his superiors at the British consulate in Constantinople in 1860 and 1861 betrays his frustration with the system and the corruption of local authorities. Later that year, local officials complained to the Porte that Frederick was appropriating offshore land to construct a quay without permission.[80] Frederick needed to make a killing, and he was becoming willing to take a few risks to do so.

Early in January 1861, Calvert was approached by Hussein Aga, a Turkish friend who managed the olive groves of several of the great pashas of Constantinople. He wished to ship a very profitable cargo of olive oil for sale in England and wanted Calvert to contact a man of integrity in London. The Turk required only moderate advances of capital from him to join the enterprise, and Frederick was enticed by promises of an easy profit. He decided to confide the business to his wife's uncle, William Abbott, with whom he had lived in London. In doing so, Frederick Calvert drew his extended family into another spiraling scandal, this time one that had even more dire consequences.

Known at the time as the "*Possidhon* Affair,"[81] it concerned the insuring of a new brig of that name, whose seaworthiness had been vouchsafed in legalized certificates by Calvert himself. On 23 January 1861, Frederick approached Abbott, a London timber merchant, to insure its cargo in his own name at market value and to obtain an advance on the sale of the oil once he had received a bill of lading.[82] On 6 March, Frederick notified Abbott that he had borrowed £500 and advanced it to Hussein Aga, and he advised Abbott to obtain £2500 in cash as soon as possible, which Calvert also would forward to the Turk. Two weeks later, Abbott sent this money to Hussein Aga via Calvert. Without actually inspecting the ship, Calvert signed the ship's clean bill of health on 4 April, and with the ship's bill of lading, Abbott insured its cargo for £1200. His insurance agent was Lloyd's.

Loaded with 200 tons of top-grade olive oil, the ship left Adramyttion (Edremit), a port on the coast of Turkey opposite Lesbos, on 6 April, but it never reached its London destination. On 8 May, Abbott received an advance of £1500 against the cargo. When the ship failed to arrive in London, Abbott became concerned. Calvert reported that the captain of an Ottoman vessel had spotted a ship "furiously burning" off the island of Lemnos on 8 April.[83] Although it never occurred to him at the time, he later surmised that the burning brig was the *Possidhon*. Calvert did not hear from Hussein Aga for months and thought he was "somewhere between this and Syria." By October, Abbott suspected foul play, and on 21 November, Calvert forwarded the ship's papers to him so that he could make a claim with Lloyd's for the "total loss."

In early January 1862, Lloyd's Salvage Association sent an agent to investigate the claim. Frederick then wrote a series of letters to Abbott noting suspicious circumstances relating to the ship.[84] On 5 February, Frederick wrote Abbott that he would make a "strict investigation" into Hussein Aga. By the 12th, he questioned whether a shipment was made at all. Soon it appeared that the *Possidhon* itself never had existed. Hussein had taken a total of £3000 from Calvert and Abbott and disappeared. By March 1862, the office of the consulate general in Constantinople recorded documents regarding the firm of Abbott Bros. versus Consul Frederick Calvert.[85] Abbott and Calvert ceased writing to each other, and in the same month, Abbott, unable to pay back the advance he had secured, went bankrupt.

The consulate general in Constantinople began to investigate the *Possidhon* matter. On 6 March 1862, Frederick Calvert requested leave to go to London "on urgent private business." He was granted it a week later, but then Sir Henry L. Bulwer (1801–1872), the British ambassador at Constantinople from 1858 to 1865, telegraphed him to remain at his post.[86] His superiors, who supported him, were baffled by his behavior in the affair. "You admit that you have been led into error by false informations . . . yet you took no precautions to ascertain the truth he had certified how and by who were you led into error," the consul general wrote him.[87] But by the time the consul general's letter arrived, Calvert had disappeared.

Others quickly stepped forward with conflicting stories as to his whereabouts. The *Levant Herald,* an English-language newspaper in Constantinople, published an inflammatory article on 1 April by the Lloyd's agent, who was recognized at the time as biased against Calvert, while the consul general wrote the Foreign Office, repeating that Calvert "had simply been led into error."[88] Chaos reigned, and his absence naturally tended to implicate him in the fraud. Even though Calvert had been exonerated completely of the previous charges of questionable dealings during the war, old prejudices now contributed to the current mistrust. As the Foreign Office put it, "Calvert's antecedents and his connexion with Mr. Abbott tend to raise suspicions. . . . Mr. Calvert's absence from his post and the contradictory statements regarding his whereabouts cannot fail to add doubts to his complicity in the fraud."[89]

Suddenly, Frederick reappeared on 30 April and accounted for his actions. He had been set up, he asserted, and because he had "unconsciously been made to play such a prominent role" in the "nefarious transaction," he had wished to find and convict those who had "so completely abused his good faith with their deep laid plot."[90] But those he said had set him up could not be found. This explanation satisfied no one. The Foreign Office observed that there was "great irregularity in the conduct of his consular business" and recommended that it be "narrowly investigated."[91] The consul general replied to Earl Russell that "much is left unexplained" and ordered an examination of his correspondence with Abbott, recommending that inquiries be undertaken on the spot in London and the Dardanelles.[92]

Ambassador Bulwer, who went to the Dardanelles to investigate the "Supposed Case of Barratry," could not get past Calvert's inability to locate those he said had deceived him. In his report, he praised Calvert as "a most excellent and useful public servant," but he noted that "the affair is a strange one; and what speaks against Calvert is that none of the people he speaks of can be produced."[93] During the intervening six weeks, Calvert had been hunting for them unsuccessfully around Smyrna. Bulwer believed Calvert "innocent of complicity," but guilty of indiscretion and negligence.[94] Within days, he vented his frustration: "It is impossible to acquit Mr. Calvert of great carelessness," he wrote, although he still believed that Calvert was the "victim of a conspiracy rather than the agent in one." He noted that the matter was cleverly managed, if by foreigners, including the

Turkish officials who wanted to blame Calvert, and "most stupidly," if by Calvert, who would have known the extent to which a claim for such a large sum would be investigated under British law. For this reason, he still thought Calvert's alleged complicity "highly improbable," but in the absence of proof of the existence of the plot's other characters, Bulwer continued to maintain that he would be forced to regard them as "imaginary persons under whose name Mr. Calvert himself carried on the conspiracy."[95] Meanwhile, Frederick Calvert was gearing up for an imminent visit by the Prince of Wales, apparently thinking the whole thing would blow over.[96]

Instead it blew up. The whole affair quickly took on overtones of the larger religious and political conflicts that characterized the British imperial presence within the Ottoman Empire: Muslim versus Christian, and Turk versus European. One group had lied. The agent for the underwriters, who was biased against Calvert from the beginning, collected testimony from Turkish harbor and health officials hostile to the British consul in which they charged that he had forged their sealed documents. The "*Possidhon* Affair" and the behavior of Frederick Calvert were becoming issues concerned with British political and economic policy in the East. Lloyd's declared it was "determined thoroughly to investigate" the case because "many other cases which had given rise to suspicions of fraud had occurred in the Levant," and it was concerned for "the future security of Underwriters." Its opinion was "unfavourable to Mr. Calvert," their own agent.

More—or less—than simple justice for Frederick Calvert was at stake. The underwriters wanted a prosecution, and they never would have been able to secure one against Hussein Aga in Ottoman courts. Like Calvert, they could not even find him. Instead, they went after Calvert, who already had enemies and doubters and who could be—and had been—prosecuted in Consular Court. Travelers long had been cynical about the likelihood of a fair trial in this court. One noted that especially for the British,

> in criminal matters, [consular] proceeding not infrequently degenerates into arbitrary acts . . . tantamount to a denial or evasion of justice . . . the evil proceeds from the limited authority of the ambassadors, and their rigid adherence to the elements of British law. All these systems require modification, —but none is so frequently vicious and ineffective than that of Great Britain. All responsibility falls on the consul-general and however zealous, laborious, and conversant with business he may be, finds himself utterly unable to administer justice in a manner suitable to the objects in view.[97]

Here, the underwriters could argue that Calvert had masterminded the scheme by first inventing the ship and then mustering individuals to bear false witness on his behalf, even though, as Bulwer noted to Earl Russell, their case was based on the testimony of local port officials who were the guilty persons if Calvert was not.[98]

Shortly after Bulwer departed the Dardanelles, Calvert panicked. With Lloyd's building a case against him and faced with the prospect of undergoing another long consular inquiry, he abandoned the Dardanelles a second time, despite orders to the contrary. By 7 June, he had gone into hiding.[99] For Bulwer, this was as good as a confession, and Bulwer suspended him immediately. He wrote the Foreign Office that "circumstances have transpired which leave little or no doubt" as to Calvert's guilt.[100] The Foreign Office combed London for him in vain.[101] Immediately, he lost both the British consulship and his Prussian position.[102] Philip Francis, legal vice-consul of the Supreme Consular Court in Constantinople, issued a warrant for his arrest but could not serve it because he had absconded.[103] In August, Bulwer asked Calvert's successor to freeze his assets, Lloyd's made their inquiry public, and within a week the London *Times* published their damaging exposé under the headline "Extraordinary Fraud." Calvert soon lost the Belgian and Dutch consulships and was stricken from the membership list of the Archaeological Institute in Rome, as well.[104]

Crushing stress fell on his brothers, particularly James, who also was related to the Abbotts by marriage.[105] Frank, Edmund, and James Calvert had to hold the family together and manage the farms and Calvert business at the Dardanelles in Frederick's absence. Edmund was dropped from the list of embassy attachés in October.[106] Creditors appeared from nowhere, and Turkish authorities harassed the family business.[107] Publicly shamed both in the small community of the Dardanelles and in metropolitan London society, the Calverts tried to continue their lives. Frank, who had just tasted the pleasures of his scholarly accolades, must have been deeply mortified. A warrant had been issued for his brother's arrest and then suspended, and bankruptcy proceedings had begun.

Before the end of the year, Frederick's empire had collapsed, and Frank's hopes had collapsed with it. Frederick's successor, John Fraser, acting as consul, had denied James the right to represent Frederick in bankruptcy proceedings and precipitously had declared him bankrupt.[108] When Fraser unjustly arrested a Calvert servant and slandered Frederick, Frank, then acting Belgian consul, lost his self-control and at the casino accused Fraser of "making bankruptcies to order."[109] Although Calvert quickly apologized, Fraser appealed to Supreme Consular Court in Constantinople. The legal vice-consul, Philip Francis, the acting judge in the 20 October trial, was eager to punish the elusive ex-consul and declared that "a severe sentence was necessary . . . to teach a lesson that was needed at the Dardanelles." Siding with his "brother official" in the case of *The Queen* v. *Frank Calvert*, Francis found that Calvert had "scandalized and vilified" Fraser. If the insult had occurred in a court or on the way to a court, the punishment would have been £50 or one week's incarceration, but as Earl Russell noted, "it was just a billiard room squabble." In England, it was not necessarily even a misdemeanor. Yet at the Supreme Consular Court in Constantinople, Francis fined him £20, made him pay court costs, and sentenced him to two weeks' imprisonment, twice the prescribed term. The judge's arbitrariness and injustice were publicized in the *Levant Herald* on 5 November and subsequently were decried in the London *Daily News*, which recommended "disciplinary action" for Francis. The thoroughly humiliated

Frank Calvert, however, was described as "having the misfortune to be the brother of ex-Consul Calvert . . . under the imputation of serious frauds."[110]

Frank Calvert had begun to pay for Frederick's alleged crimes. And in the end, the price was Troy itself. Frank Calvert believed he knew where it lay and owned a share of the very land under which he thought it slumbered. But now he could not muster the resources to prove it. Those institutions and individuals to whom he might look for help and patronage never had given him the sort of support an archaeologist in the metropolis might enjoy. Now they positively turned their backs on him. Not least among these were Charles Newton and the British Museum.

Although Calvert had kept up with Newton over the years, the correspondence had been one-sided, and the collegiality Calvert had hoped for never grew between them.[111] After Mytilene, Newton had proceeded to Rhodes as acting consul. While there, he investigated several sites in the Dodecanese islands and excavated the mausoleum of Halicarnassus, Cnidus, and later Miletus,[112] each time enriching the British Museum. Newton had not replied to Calvert in 1862. Not willing to give up on this valuable contact, Calvert wrote again about some coins in the spring of 1863.[113] Again, Newton did not reply.

By then, Calvert had completed his Pınarbaşı article and, probably as a result of reading Maclaren's book, had decided to begin probing Hisarlık. The British historian George Grote (1794–1871) had written of Homer's Troy that it was "a past which never was present . . . a legend and nothing more."[114] But Calvert, envisioning "windy Ilion," commenced looking for Priam's "well-founded stronghold" with its wide ways, "fine towers," and strong walls. Would the uneven terrain disclose the "towering ramparts" that had loomed above the Greeks fighting in the plain below, the four gates to the citadel, most famous of which was the Scaean Gate near the "great tower of Ilios"? Would he find Priam's castle of "smoothed stone," in front of which elders and young men gathered in assembly?[115] At the peak of the citadel of "sacred Ilion" Athena's temple had stood, tended by Hecuba and the royal women. Elsewhere in the citadel, according to Homer, there was a temple to Apollo and an altar where Zeus would receive burnt offerings. Could he find them? Homer distinguished the "Pergamos," the acropolis, from the lower city at large, where the Trojans and their allies gathered and kept their famous horses.[116] Hisarlık's topography promised an acropolis, or upper city, and broad plateau beneath. The rough picture seemed to fit, but could he prove it? Nothing earlier than classical remains had yet been found at Ilium. This would be his big chance.

Calvert began his work just in from the north slope, along the perimeter of the tell for easy disposal of refuse, and on the southeastern slope of the mound where Brunton had already cleared away much overlying material. By September 1863, Calvert himself already had excavated in a fan-shaped trench in the theater, later determined to be a *bouleuterion*, or council chamber,[117] on the southeastern slope, probably the site of Brunton's Corinthian capital [Figure 26a].[118] The new acting

British consul, Randall Callander, arrived in midmonth with the news that Newton soon would be leaving London for Rhodes in order to commence excavations for the British Museum.[119] Quickly, Calvert wrote Newton an informal letter asking Newton's "opinion regarding a proposal . . . for a similar purpose." The 24 September 1863 letter proceeded: "You are aware of my proprietorship to a large portion of the site of Ilium (Novum) which contains many remains of antiquity buried below its surface." Calvert's subtle bracketing of "Novum" in reference to Ilium at Hisarlık was as far as he would go toward identifying Hisarlık as Troy.[120]

Calvert wrote of the northern trench where locals had quarried for cut stone since Clarke's time: "I have discovered that the site of the temple of Pallas occupied the prominent mound which rises out of the plain—an excavation I made twelve feet long by eight feet broad and three deep, disclosed a number of fluted columns, a capital, an inscription, and friezes whilst others appear underneath and on all sides."[121]

Evoking Waddington, Calvert continued to validate Hisarlık's significance. "Our mutual friend W. Waddington thinks important discoveries may be made in this temple. The field containing the actual site [the higher western part?], I am in treaty for and hope soon to secure."[122] Calvert mentioned enticingly that "a short time since whilst clearing out brushwood from the theatre, a torso, and two forepaws of a lion were brought to light—just below the surface."[123] Then he came to the point with Newton and introduced his remarkable proposition to the keeper.

> Now if anything could be managed with the British Museum to carry on excavations here (and elsewhere if they desired it) I would be happy to offer my services.
>
> I would allow any part of my lands to be turned over, and all objects found to become the property of the British Museum (with the exception of any duplicates which the Turkish government would probably claim as their right in granting the firman of excavation).

According to Ottoman law, Calvert as proprietor had a right to all antiquities discovered on his land, excepting the duplicates he had mentioned, so this was an exceedingly generous offer. Because Calvert's finances were in a desperate state, it is even more notable that he was willing to hand over all finds to the museum.

He continued, "I would however wish to have the direction of the excavation, so that my name might be attached to any discoveries made. My services would be gratuitous [unless] . . . the British Museum on the results of the excavation being known, might think it fit to make me a compensation—but this is a matter I leave entirely to them." The informal proposal was in effect a gentlemanly solicitation of the kind of financial support that already had been given to Layard and to Newton himself.

But given the family's straitened circumstances, Newton may have found such a casual proposal presumptuous. After all, as some believed, the Calverts seemed to have demonstrated that they were not, in fact, gentlemen. Furthermore, Stratford de Redcliffe had left Constantinople in the 1850s and Frederick had squandered the powerful support of his successor as ambassador. Instead, the suspended warrant for his brother's arrest hung over the family like the sword of Damocles, and the bankruptcy proceedings already had frozen their assets. Distancing himself from Frederick's alleged impropriety, Calvert cautioned that "the funds could be under the control, or not, of HM's Consul as the British Museum might deem preferable." He also tried to reassure the trustees as to his own character and standing within the local community: "My relations with the Authorities here are very good—filling as I do the post of European member in the Turkish tribunal."[124]

He then concluded as humbly and selflessly as he began. "This I think is a liberal proposal, which combined with my knowledge and experience, that could be brought to bear favourably on the enterprise, makes me entertain a hope that the British Museum may be disposed to accept it."

Finally, an amalgam of entrepreneurial spirit and avowed patriotism, he subtly tried to pressure Newton to respond with due haste before he looked for other patrons. "You would greatly oblige me by letting me know as soon as possible whether there is any chance of my proposal being entertained, for in the negative case, my intention is to apply to the Prussian or French government as I confess my means for carrying on excavations are limited. This is an alternative I am loathe to have recourse to, preferring infinitely to serve my own government."[125]

Calvert realized that he needed considerable assistance to excavate the richly stratified mound. His 1863 excavation had produced the finds to entice Newton and the museum to offer that assistance. But could these potentialities persuade them to enter into a partnership with Frederick Calvert's brother? It is curious that he did not mention Maclaren's new book if he had, in fact, read it before writing to Newton, since doing so certainly would have strengthened his proposal. But then he did not mention Brunton, either. He wanted Hisarlık to be *his*. Calvert's willingness to work for free and to forego the lucrative antiquities that belonged to him by law thus underscores the gravity and desperation of his move to involve the British Museum in his undertaking. He wanted to rehabilitate the Calvert name in England and passionately desired his own name to go down in history next to the discovery of Homer's Troy.[126]

Newton quickly forwarded Frank Calvert's letter of offer to the trustees of the British Museum on 6 October 1863 with the following recommendations:

> Mr. Newton sees no reason to doubt that Ilium Novum would prove a good site for excavations. The ground, which he himself visited in 1853, is free from all encumbrances of houses or enclosures and is broken up in irregular mounds which most probably contain the ruins of the ancient city under herbage. Mr. Newton, therefore, thinks that a grant of money placed under the control of Her Majesty's Consul at the Dardanelles, as Mr. Calvert suggests, might be employed with advantage in an experimental excavation on this site. Mr. Newton does not think that this sum should in the first instance exceed £100. Mr. Calvert having been long resident in the Troad,

having much local influence and having been engaged for many years in small excavations on various sites near the Dardanelles would probably be able to explore the
site of Novum Ilium at a very moderate cost. It would be necessary to apply for a
firman from the Porte empowering Mr. Calvert to export any marbles or other antiquities discovered.

Considering the recent family scandals, Newton's letter offered guarded support
tempered by his own experience.[127] Newton endorsed an experimental excavation
and volunteered to meet with Calvert at Smyrna or proceed to the Dardanelles to
the excavation itself.[128] At this time, the excavation permit mentioned at the end
of the letter was essentially a formality, for the British still had carte blanche with
the Ottomans.

After forwarding the letter and his own recommendation to the trustees, Newton responded to Calvert promptly on 8 October, assuring him that the proposition respecting Ilium Novum would be laid before the trustees at their next meeting and that he would inform Calvert of the outcome as soon as possible.
Although Newton mentioned that the meeting was "to-morrow," it actually took
place on 17 October. He informed Calvert that he was leaving London for Smyrna
on 14 October and would arrive around the end of the month, "which will give
you an opportunity of seeing me, if an interview is needed."[129] His formality is
understandable, considering the family's situation.

When the standing committee of the trustees met, they mentioned Calvert's
proposal to excavate Ilium Novum "for the Benefit of the British Museum" and
Newton's recommendation that "the requested sum be granted and placed at the
disposal of the British Consul at the Dardanelles for this purpose."[130] They ordered the principal librarian to "report to the Trustees when he shall have received
further information from Mr. Newton on the subject of the excavations proposed
by Mr. Calvert."[131] What additional information the trustees sought is unclear.
There is no record of the trustees receiving more data concerning the Ilium
Novum project. Apparently none was forthcoming because Newton already had
departed London for Smyrna on leave. In his absence, and apparently not hearing more from Newton, the museum trustees voted the "consideration postponed."[132]

In December, Calvert found out that Newton was traveling from Rhodes to
Constantinople on a French vessel. Anxious over the outcome of his "liberal proposal" and hungry for a response from Newton, Calvert rowed out by night and
tried to board the ship when it was anchored at the strait. But the ship's steward,
thinking Newton was asleep, would not permit Calvert to come aboard.

Throughout this period, Calvert kept his eye on the local antiquities market,
writing to Newton about newly surfaced coins and sculpture.[133] On 6 November,
he notified Newton that he had found a new site, a large town on the Granicus
River that he thought might be Sidene.[134] As late as 21 January 1864, Calvert
wrote enthusiastically to Newton about the great growth of the Calvert Collection
with more than four hundred vases alone.[135] At the same time, he requested to

know the museum's decision as soon as possible so as to be able to make his plans accordingly. But Newton was still absent.

In February 1864, Newton finally wrote to Calvert. After regretting the missed rendezvous at the Dardanelles, when, in fact, he had been standing on deck, he proceeded formally to deal the death blow to Frank Calvert's hopes:

> With regard to your proposal to the Trustees, I am desired by M. Panizzi to inform you that the Trustees decline entertaining the project of digging at Ilium novum at present, but that they are obliged to you for making them the offer.
>
> I hope on some future occasion to have the pleasure of seeing your collection.[136]

This rejection has to be seen in context.[137] Calvert had had reason to hope. Newton's own assistant at the mausoleum excavations subsequently had received support to excavate the classical site of Cyrene in 1860–61.[138] John Turtle Wood (1821–1890), who had come to Turkey as an architect for the Smyrna-Aydin Railway in 1857, had received a small grant from the trustees of the British Museum and had begun excavating at Ephesus by 1863.[139] And Calvert knew Newton. Newton had visited Hisarlık. These things had a way of working out. Prospects looked good indeed.

In fact, local British consuls were excavating throughout the Near East. Excavations by George Dennis (1814–1898) in Sicily in 1862–63 and at Benghazi in 1866–67 and by Alfred Bilotti on Rhodes in 1864 and 1868 were supported by the British Museum, undoubtedly on the recommendation of Newton, who knew each of them personally. Wood's at Ephesus would continue for years. As an advocate for classical archaeology, Newton secured nearly £100,000 in special grants from the British Treasury, and from these excavations, made through his influence or inspiration, the museum obtained many valuable acquisitions. Yet the British Museum had outgrown itself, pressed for space and overextended with material pouring in from Sicily, Cyprus, and Rhodes.[140] The director wrote that there literally was no space in the present building in which they could accommodate, still less exhibit to the public, these important remains. Even Newton's own sculptures from the mausoleum at Halicarnassus would not be installed for twenty years.

Why, then, did the museum trustees reject Calvert's offer? It can't be that Newton thought Frank Calvert was incapable of excavating such a complex site.[141] Although he had witnessed Calvert excavating when Calvert was only a novice and not the seasoned excavator of 1863, Newton himself had not excavated at all at this point. If Newton doubted Calvert's expertise, he would not have referred Calvert's letter on Andeira for publication in 1862 and would not have cited Calvert's articles in his own publication.[142] Nor would he have recommended Calvert to the trustees if he considered him incompetent. Calvert's stature at the time of his proposal was not inconsiderable. He was respected as an authority on the archaeology and topography of the Troad and had identified sites for the British Admiralty for inclusion on their maps. He was a member of the Archaeological Institutes of London and Rome. He was a published author with at least five articles to his credit and more in gestation. His local knowledge, standing in the community, and command of ancient and modern literature on his subject augured well.

The only compelling reason for the postponement and subsequent failure of Calvert's proposal and thus of his archaeological career can be the widely publicized scandal caused by Frederick's alleged fraud and subsequent bankruptcy.[143] Frank's own conviction on criminal slander, which also had made the London papers, even though they treated it as a travesty of justice, helped confirm the museum's decision to have nothing to do with the disgraced family. The very terms of Calvert's proposal—the courtly disavowal of interest in whatever patronage he might nonetheless desire from them, the insistence that all he wanted was his name to be connected with the discoveries and with the museum—would have been unthinkable to them. Calvert's offer could not have been more miserably timed. The museum trustees would have been reading about the Calvert family's misfortunes and Frederick's alleged felony only months before they received Frank Calvert's overgenerous offer.

Still, the finality of Newton's language is curious, since the trustees simply had mentioned postponement. Because no further communication exists among the board of trustees, from them to Panizzi, and from Panizzi to Newton, the rejection seems to have been a private decision of Panizzi's, perhaps influenced by earlier conversations with Brunton. It is no wonder that Panizzi chose not to become associated with the scandal-plagued family. Presumably Panizzi himself just said "hands off."

Following this stunning rejection, Calvert withdrew. Just when he had the pleasure of seeing his refutation of Chevalier in print, he was rebuffed by the British Museum and his friend Newton. He must have known the reason. Everyone else would have. Life for the Calverts at the Dardanelles must have been hell at this time, living so conspicuously in their "palace by the sea." The shame only could have deepened with time. While Frederick was in hiding, investigators seeking details in Frederick's bankruptcy compared the quest for justice to "a search for a fossil in the British Museum."[144] As proceedings dragged on, they reported that the family was "not disposed to aid in frankly assisting the creditors."[145] Frank Calvert did not correspond with Newton for more than two years, and then, in 1866, the purpose was to introduce his brother Henry and, at the same time, to corroborate his own identification of the site on Çığrı Dağ as Neandria.[146] No response is recorded.

This was the state of affairs when in April 1864, Calvert escorted Johann Georg von Hahn from Kum Kale to Pınarbaşı. There, the Austrian consul for eastern Greece at Syra (Syros) excavated the ancient settlement for several weeks, accompanied by Julius Schmidt (1825–1884), director of the observatory in Athens, and Ernst Ziller (1837–1923), the German neoclassical architect working from 1861 onward in Athens who so inflamed Heinrich Schliemann's interest in Troy.[147] Von Hahn reflected Calvert's stature in Trojan studies at the time by naming an area of his excavation the "Calvert Nische"[Figure 23].[148] Aware of Calvert's conclusion that the site was too late for Homeric Troy and could only be Georgis, von Hahn persisted in claiming that some of the walls were "prehistoric or pre-Homeric." Calvert maintained that they were later. In the end, von Hahn concluded that the topography of the Ballı Dağ had inspired Homer's descriptions of Troy but that there was no historical city called Troy there.

In the face of his crushing failure to involve the British Museum, Frank Calvert persevered as time and money permitted. Despite financial limitations occasioned by the loss of Frederick's salary and mounting family difficulties, he attempted to purchase more of the acropolis in 1864 but still did not succeed in purchasing the western half.[149] Calvert decided to continue probing the tell without sponsor or patron on his own schedule and, it appears, without much hope.

For the first time, Frank Calvert considered selling antiquities to fund his dream. By 1865, he had excavated three trenches on the northern and northeastern flanks of the mound, as well as the large area of the *bouleuterion* to the southeast.[150] Everywhere he dug, he hit classical remains. Nowhere did he reach virgin soil.[151] If he hoped he would find prehistoric pottery similar to that at Hanay Tepe, he was disappointed. With so much overlay, he must have despaired of ever reaching the early levels he knew still lay buried.

Presumably Calvert chose these areas because they were highest on the part of the mound that he owned. He still did not own most of the highest part. To his credit, he scrupulously did not extend his excavations onto his neighbors' land to the west. Calvert had revealed in his two northern trenches what survived of the temple of Athena: Doric columns, lion-head water spouts from the *sima*, or marble gutter,[152] and elegantly carved sections of the roof course.[153] "Although the building stones were, in truth, for the most part displaced and scattered, I came . . . upon part of the foundation *in situ*."[154] In the same area were what he considered to be remains of the "Lysimachean Wall," the wall that Strabo believed had been built by Alexander's general.[155] The northern trenches were not inconsiderable in size: 30 by 5 meters and 18 by 12 meters, and he had dug down 3 to 4 meters.[156] He probably designed the northeastern trench to trace the "Lysimachean Wall" farther.[157] Instead, Calvert found a massive wall of the Roman era and was forced to quit. He later said he missed the famous northeast bastion of the Late Bronze Age walls by a meter.[158] Calvert also dug into the plateau to the south, where he explored a long underground passage, a quarry, or "latomie," beneath a large protruding rock 200 yards west of Hisarlık, where the plateau slopes down to the plain. In his trenches, on the citadel, which reached a depth of 3 to 4 meters, Calvert excavated layers of "accumulated rubbish" with no pottery earlier than that of the Archaic period, from the seventh to the sixth centuries B.C. Without having reached virgin soil, Calvert noted that at the very least he had proven that Greek Ilion predated the earliest known references to it by one hundred and fifty to two hundred and fifty years.[159] Because he had not found pottery that he could recognize as prehistoric, he still was hesitant to claim publicly his conviction that Homer's Troy lay at Hisarlık. Instead, he mentioned only the architectural finds from the temple of Minerva. He did not discuss the dating of artifacts and never dared mention that he had found the Troy of Priam.

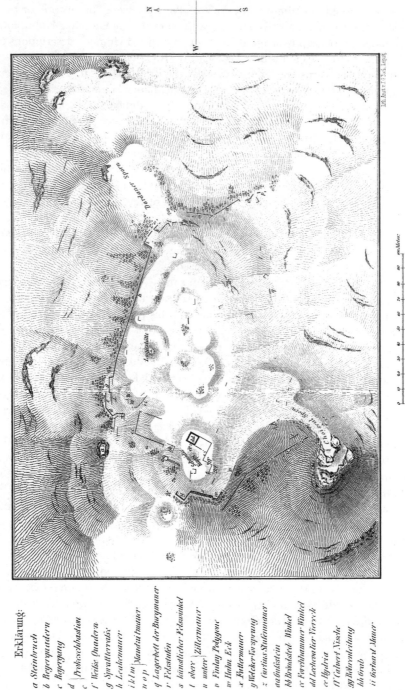

Figure 23. Pınarbaşı. Von Hahn (1865), plate 1.

Having discreetly kept the news of his earlier finds private while awaiting the museum's decision, he finally gave a brief summary of his Hisarlık excavations to Charles Sprengel Greaves. At the 7 July 1865 meeting of the Archaeological Institute in London, Greaves announced the "extensive excavations."[160] Because of the importance of the subject in the continuing debate, the institute published Calvert's summary communication immediately in the *Archaeological Journal* for 1865. Ironically, it appeared after a long account by Newton of his discoveries at the mausoleum of Halicarnassus. Calvert reported "extensive excavations at Ilium Novum, and also the discovery of ruins as supposed, of a temple of Minerva [Athena], consisting of marble columns, architraves, and portions of bas-reliefs, one of them being part of the figure of a gladiator."[161] But Calvert's earlier confidence regarding his archaeological career was gone. The very brief paragraph did not begin to describe the enormity or significance of his findings at the site.

Once again, the *Athenaeum* covered his announcement. But in what can only be described as a perverse turn of fortune, it mistakenly noted that Calvert had found the temple of Minerva at Cebrene. It never even mentioned Ilium Novum. Calvert's announcement of his most important excavation—at Troy—had been botched and damned to obscurity.[162]

Despite his propitious finds, Calvert seems subsequently to have had little time for the site. The continuing lack of financial resources and the ongoing family dilemma compounded his problems. It took a decade for Calvert to refer publicly to the rejection of his offer by the British Museum. Then, in the pages of the *Athenaeum* he noted that "I suggested to the British Museum the advisability of making excavations in this promising field, but my proposal was declined."[163]

At the same time, he labored to bring other projects to fruition. In 1864, Calvert submitted to the Archaeological Institute his 1862 discovery and identification of the remote stronghold of Cebrene (Cebren) at Çal Dağ, where Strabo claimed that Paris was buried.[164] It appeared in 1865 and was reviewed in the *Athenaeum* in May.[165] As he did in his earlier articles, he surveyed and dismissed modern scholarship,[166] analyzed ancient authors,[167] and noted topographical and geological features of the site. Then he assessed the architectural remains of the fortified town, whose walls he found reminiscent of the cyclopean masonry of Tiryns and Mycenae. The topography and character of the site matched ancient descriptions; and he identified it with coins found at the site. The confidence and excitement inherent in the article suggest that he wrote most of it much earlier.[168]

Perhaps because he subsequently had lost heart or no longer could afford his archaeological vocation, at the last minute, in his splintered leisure, he embedded two other important identifications in the previously written Cebrene article, rather than giving them the full attention they deserved. Calvert referred to Kurşunlu-Tepe as the site of ancient Scepsis, the home of the Demetrius who had tried to prove that Homer's Troy could not be at Ilium and who had tried to trace the history of Scepsis back to the sons of Hector and Aeneas.[169] Calvert surveyed or excavated the site prior to February 1862.[170] The fact that Calvert just threw this identification out without any discussion indicates the extent to which he was completely embroiled in other affairs at the time.[171] In another twist of fate, Calvert's identification, published in 1865, was credited to another archaeologist, the English architect Richard Popplewell Pullan (1825–1888), who never even had visited the area before 1866.[172] Once again, the identification gained wide acceptance.[173]

The second identification that Calvert embedded in the Cebrene article was that of Neandria, which Calvert placed "in the neighbourhood of Çığrı Dağ,"[174] the site on the summit of the mountain to which he had brought Newton and Carlisle in 1853. Here Calvert had excavated graves, noted the remains of houses, and studied the architecture of the impressive fortification walls, recording the presence of a series of successive styles. Indeed, he never published his manuscript, although as with Scepsis, in 1866 a skeletal treatment appeared in the *John Murray Handbook*.[175] Again, his identification found acceptance. Calvert continued to explore the site and its environs, perhaps due to mineral riches that he discovered in the area.[176]

Frank Calvert needed an excavation permit to make sure that all of his future excavations would be absolutely legitimate, but he no longer had Frederick's clout to back his application.[177] It is one measure of the extent to which Frank's fortunes had fallen along with his brother's that in January 1865, he had to ask his friend Randall Callander, the acting British consul at the Dardanelles, to apply for an excavation permit for him to excavate throughout the province and request permission to export the finds. No doubt he feared that if he applied in his own name, he probably would be denied. "I am very anxious to have the required authority before applications are made by other Governments for the same purpose," Callander told the Turkish officials, because he had heard "from a trustworthy source" about Turks excavating for building stone at Assos and Nağara, ancient Abydos, in connection with the building of fortifications.[178] Callander wished to have some of these sites excavated before they were obliterated altogether. He noted, "I do not seek any pecuniary assistance from the British Government. . . . I have a fit person to attend to all that is necessary." There is no doubt that Calvert was Callander's source and would do the excavating.[179] Calvert probably cautioned Callander against asking for funds. Shortly after receiving the *firman*, Callander left the area. But Calvert now could excavate with impunity as his agent.

Despite prejudice against the family in the Foreign Office, Frank Calvert was still the unimpeached expert on the archaeology of the Troad. Prince Arthur (1850–1942) therefore asked Frank Calvert to escort him throughout the area in April 1865.[180] During the same year, John Murray II asked Calvert to contribute information, advice, and suggestions concerning the Troad to the popular *John Murray Handbook for Travellers*. These red Murray handbooks, the first series of systematic guidebooks for travelers, were revered to the point of "Murrayolatry."[181] Soon Calvert would be the local correspondent for the *Levant Herald*, the newspaper in which his brother first had been accused by Lloyd's. Frederick Calvert's scandal did not affect those areas of Frank's life in which his knowledge was indispensable, though it had effectively ruined others.

In 1865, Calvert secured a long inscription, later known as the "Sestos Inscription," from the wall of a mosque on the Chersonese. He sent a facsimile of the important Greek inscription from the ancient town of Sestos to Greaves, who later forwarded a copy to William Ewert Gladstone (1809–1898), the future British prime minister, who had a keen interest in the Troad.[182] This coup was covered in the pages of the *Athenaeum*.[183]

From February 1862 to 1865, there are no attestable excavations by Calvert other than those at Hisarlık, which were carried out between 1863 and 1865. Rather, in 1864 and 1865 he published his earlier finds. Calvert continued to putter around as he could, exploring new regions in his diminished spare time. "In the interest of science" and buoyed up by his association with Prince Arthur and John Murray, he applied successfully for a *firman* in his own name to excavate in the neighboring province of Balıkesır.[184] By June 1866, he had extended his explorations there, but to what extent is not known, for he never published these investigations. There is no record of him excavating at Hisarlık after May and June 1865. In fact, his archaeological career had stalled. A family portrait of 1866 (in which Frederick is conspicuously absent) shows the beleaguered clan huddled around the foundation of the consular mansion, which now perhaps seemed more like a fortress [Figure 11].[185]

At the same time, another British consul, George Dennis of Etruscan fame, was casting about for a new site to excavate. He wrote to the trustees of the British Museum about the prospect of carrying out limited excavations on their behalf "on the sites of various ancient Greek cities on the coast . . . and cemeteries of Asia Minor."[186] Ironically, Newton reported to the trustees that he considered Asia Minor a "very promising field for researches such as those proposed by Mr. Dennis, the cemeteries of the Greek cities of the Troad, Ionia, Caria . . . having as yet been very slightly explored by competent persons." Newton was particularly interested in the Lydian tumuli around Sardis. The trustees then decided that it would be "difficult to find a person more competent than Mr. Dennis for carrying out the enterprise." But, the principal librarian added, "The Trustees have no funds at their disposal." It is difficult to read this correspondence and not think of Calvert's plight four years earlier. In the end, Dennis received £500 from the British Treasury.[187] One can only assume that had there been no scandal, funds also would have been found for Frank Calvert.

In June 1867, Frederick Calvert emerged from five years of hiding, one month before his mother's death.[188] After living at the Erenköy villa and Dardanelles mansion for several months, he was arrested in October on a charge of "conspiring to defraud certain underwriters of £12,000."[189] He later accounted for his disappearance by saying that he was being sued for bankruptcy by a gentleman in London and that he had been unable to fight both suits at once. As a result, he had to wait for the gentleman to stay his suit, which he had just done. He also spoke of the very bad treatment he had endured at the hands of the Foreign Office with regard to Crimean War transactions.[190]

Once again, British officials approached Frederick's case from the point of view of its effect on British political and economic interests in the Levant. In theory, he may have been presumed innocent until proven guilty, but in fact, those who administered the consular system were convinced of his guilt and, worried about the perception of corruption in its ranks, eager to make an example of him for "Levanting": Frederick had become "a person who, by absconding and remaining so many years in obscurity, may be considered to have confessed his crime." Should the matter be allowed to drop, they asserted, Frederick, taking it as "an admission of his innocence," might "readily find some Post in the East where he can plant himself and once more prey on the commerce of this and other countries." The British government was zealous to prosecute him, or, as they put it, grant him the opportunity he demanded for "clearing his character."[191]

For the trial, the Foreign Office tried to get Philip Francis to preside, the same legal vice-consul who had issued the warrant for Frederick's arrest and who precipitously had sentenced Frank to jail five years earlier. They even promised him a promotion to consul general, but he stalled and said he was unavailable.[192] In December, the trial was postponed so that the accused could gather witnesses, and Frederick was released on bail set at £2000 in securities and the same amount in Calvert's "own recognizance of his appearance" at the trial.[193] Finally, less than five weeks before the trial, the Foreign Office reluctantly notified James Lane, a junior judge, that he would be the one to try the Calvert case in Supreme Consular Court.[194]

Such a complicated and well-publicized case strained the limits of the consular judicial system. The prisoner was bound to be tried according to British law; however, this was by no means Britain. Those implicated by Calvert as perpetrators of the fraud did not fall under the jurisdiction of the court. The Turkish port and health officials were in no way bound by oaths delivered by infidels. There also was no power to compel them to appear, and if they did appear, to testify. Furthermore, the British Criminal Appeal Act did not extend to Turkey, so that the prisoner was "placed in a singularly disadvantageous position," lacking the rights of ordinary British citizens under these conditions.

The trial, which began on 13 February 1868 and lasted six days, turned on the difficulties of Calvert's position. The judge noted that the prosecution's case was constructed of "necessarily presumptive or circumstantial evidence," with no actual proof of guilt or complicity. A conspiracy had been proved, but had Calvert been a party to it? The evidence adduced, the judge admitted, was based on "wholly presumptive statements" by two local Turks denying their own complicity in the conspiracy. Moreover, "two Christian witnesses, who had testified for the prosecution, had also deposed on oath that bribes had been offered to them to give false evidence against Mr. Calvert." And several natives and foreigners required as witnesses for the defense had failed to attend. Finally, the defense complained that it was hampered by the strict application of the "English law of evidence," which was "ill-adapted to the social conditions" of the Ottoman realm.[195] Much of Calvert's evidence was dismissed by the judge as inadmissible. And the judge in his summing up spoke subtly yet persuasively against Calvert. After a short deliberation, the jury found Frederick Calvert guilty.[196]

When Calvert was asked to say why sentence should not be passed, he declared that he had not been fairly tried, that the "inexperienced" judge, who was prejudiced against him, "did not know the country sufficiently to distinguish between a judicial enquiry, here and in England." He intimated that the three Turkish officials had not been bound by their oaths and that the judge had swayed the jury in his summing up.[197] More than the judge, however, it was the system that was against Calvert. Pressured by economic interests, which by 1868 were becoming shaky in the Levant, the consular officials sought to set an example, "to teach a lesson," as Francis had done with Frank Calvert in 1862. Calvert again was the scapegoat.

In fact, acting judge Lane was more sympathetic than Francis would have been. Resolving to treat Calvert's remarks "with all the consideration that might be felt for a gentleman in his mournfully distressing situation," Lane reassured Calvert of his "most dispassionate judgment" and his "poignant personal regrets that the large promises made by his counsel to produce evidence which would triumphantly refute the charges, had not been fulfilled." The judge reduced the sentence from three to two years' imprisonment.

Lane appealed to British foreign secretary Lord Stanley (1826–1893) that "in so far as legal and moral justice were satisfied by a conviction," he might be disposed "to avoid inflicting needless pain on one in Mr. Calvert's rank in life."[198] The young judge reflected that "there may be in the nature of things and in the infirmity of human judgment, a possibility of his innocence, and that something which was not urged could have been urged as suggesting such a possibility." But he declined to pursue this and assured Lord Stanley that "every opportunity was afforded the defence for preparing and collecting their evidence." Because Frederick Calvert wished to serve his term in Constantinople, presumably to be near his young family, Lane so recommended.[199]

It was a cause célèbre. Those Europeans who supported Calvert were horrified at the "unexpected result" of the trial. When Francis finally arrived back in Constantinople, where he took over as consul general, he was concerned about "scandal, charges of favoritism . . . and interference with discipline" arising from the trial and from the preferential treatment of the imprisoned ex-consul. He thought Calvert was being portrayed "as a martyr instead of a convict."[200] Consequently, Francis requested that Calvert be moved from Constantinople to Corradino Prison on Malta.[201] Apparently because of the outrage that Calvert's conviction had elicited, the Foreign Office consulted with "the Law Officers of the Crown" before agreeing to Francis's request.[202] Against his wishes, Frederick Calvert was transferred to Malta in May.[203]

Still trying to prove his innocence, Calvert wrote from prison to Lord Stanley to indict three Muslim witnesses for perjury. On 31 July, Stanley notified Francis that he "did not intend to reply." Even Francis later noted the possibility of an unjust conviction but repeated that there was "only his word for it and I attach no value whatever to his declaration."[204] The British government had invested money and prestige in this decision. The trial already had cost the unheard-of sum of £1035.[205]

There was an outpouring of support for Frederick Calvert that cut across ethnic boundaries. The Turks alone remained silent, in support of the Muslim witnesses and those who had not appeared. By 3 May, eight petitions had been received in favor of Calvert, including one from the British consular chaplain at Smyrna, Reverend William B. Lewis, who had married the Calverts in 1846. Besides members of the Abbott family, British residents of Constantinople, the Dardanelles, and Smyrna, Armenian residents of the Dardanelles, and Greek residents of Erenköy, Yenişehir (Troad), and Maditos (Maidos, or Eceabat, on the Chersonese) protested the verdict and signed petitions in English, Greek, and Turkish, praying that Queen Victoria (1819–1901) would pardon the consul: "all alike looked to him as a guiding hand, his singular disinterestedness and integrity endeared him to all." He had rendered valuable services during the Crimean War, services "which had elicited the commendation of Your Majesty's Government and both houses of Parliament." With such "irreproachable antecedents we felt confident that unless positive and undeniable proof of guilt were adduced against him, he must be acquitted," one declared.[206] But the petitions never reached the queen. They were returned by the Foreign Office with a curt request that the consulate "make the petitioners aware of the decision of Her Majesty's Government." There would be no absolution for Frederick Calvert.

Frederick Calvert was not a saint, but neither was he clearly guilty of the crime for which he was convicted. In the exigencies of his double position as gentleman-consul and consul-trader, he had made a bid for a quick profit, and it went awry, but even the presiding judge did not rule out the possibility of his innocence. Doubts remained about his having been framed. The justice and relevance of British judicial procedure in the Supreme Consular Court of Constantinople had been questioned. The daring entrepreneur had balanced precariously his elevated, baronial lifestyle, the maintenance of an extended family, his Byzantine finances, and the acquisition of antiquities and acreage in his quest for financial security and status in the Victorian world. In his collapse, he mortgaged his family's future.

His younger brother could not have been more different. Instead of dramatically staking his claim, Frank Calvert hesitated when he made his tentative bid for immortality, his claim to be known as the excavator of Troy. In writing to Newton, he did not state straightforwardly that he believed he was excavating Homer's Troy. Nor did he do so in the brief that he forwarded to the Archaeological Institute in 1865. Instead, he hoarded his treasured convictions. Because he made no substantial claims, his announcement was little noticed.

In the context of these events, it is understandable that Frank Calvert could not focus on the complexities of Hisarlık. Burdened by increased responsibilities to his family and scarred by scandal, Calvert had considerable work to attend to aside from archaeology. His duties had distracted him from his archaeological pursuits and must have forced him to admit his own inability to pursue his dream. He had sought aid from his homeland but was rebuffed by the British Museum. As long as Frank Calvert alone had access to Hisarlık, he could excavate at his own pace and publish his findings as time permitted. He was the only one who could address the historical significance of Hisarlık from an archaeological point of view, being the only archaeologist ever to excavate the mound. His life's tragedy was that he never fully plumbed, described, or analyzed his most important excavation. His quest to find Homer's Troy, first articulated by the more glamorous and outgoing elder brother who often spoke for him, would be realized by another who, like Frederick Calvert, had the knack for self-promotion and the hunger for worldly status that Frank Calvert lacked. Calvert would be swept aside by Heinrich Schliemann's search for recognition and approval, his entrepreneur's talent, and his quest for Victorian respectability, all of which came to hang on his own claim to be the discoverer of Homer's Troy.

CHAPTER SIX

"In the interest of science . . .
a sacrifice of personal considerations"
Calvert and Schliemann

Few people could have been as different, yet equally aspiring to the status conferred by the discovery of Homeric Troy, as Frank Calvert and Johann Ludwig Heinrich Julius Schliemann [Figure 24]. Calvert was a gentleman-scholar who needed money to complete his archaeological researches, but whose family had fallen from a measure of social prominence into disgrace. Schliemann was an unabashed entrepreneur from a lowly family who had made plenty of money and who aspired to the status of gentleman-scholar by means of the respectability that archaeological research could provide. The discovery of Troy could catapult either man to prominence and erase the disgraces brought on the family of each by other family members.

Heinrich Schliemann, born to Ernst and Louise Schliemann on 6 January 1822 in Neubukow, in Mecklenburg-Schwerin, was destined to be a volatile, rootless drifter looking for recognition.[1] In 1823, his father gave up being a schoolmaster for a position as pastor of the Lutheran church in the town of Ankershagen. The family moved, and Heinrich Schliemann spent his childhood there.[2] His mother was the well-educated, musical daughter of a Protestant clergyman. But she died when Heinrich was nine, having just given birth to her ninth child in twenty years. Shortly thereafter, his father lost his position due to an injudicious affair with their maid and a suspected misappropriation of church funds. At this time, Heinrich went to live with his uncle, who had him tutored in Latin. Schliemann entered Gymnasium Carolinum in Neustrelitz, where boys were prepared for university studies, but spent only one term there because of financial hardship brought on by his father's suspension without pay in 1833.[3] Subsequently, he transferred to the Realschule, which catered to the entrepreneurial and commercial classes. There he learned practical subjects to prepare him for business and earned "satisfactory" marks in English and French and "unsatisfactory" in Latin.[4] Had he stayed at the Gymnasium Carolinum, Schliemann would have been bound for a career in the civil service or academia. As it was, according to the harsh realities of the system,

Figure 24. Heinrich Schliemann (1880). Courtesy of G. Kastriotis.

he was excluded from any humanistic intellectual pursuit. The elitist German system did not embrace amateurs, and professionalization and specialization at an
early age only widened the social and intellectual gap between classes.[5]

In 1836, at the age of fourteen, Schliemann went to work as a grocer's apprentice in Fürstenburg. When according to his own story he heard a drunken miller

recite Homer in ancient Greek and was so enthralled that he bought him whiskey just to have the man continue over and over again, Schliemann claimed that "from that moment, I never ceased to pray God that by His grace I might yet have the happiness of learning Greek."[6] After five and a half years of hard work there, he injured himself on the job, necessitating a change in employment.

Schliemann had a taste for work and study, the gift of good luck, and an ability to rebound from ill fortune. In 1841, Schliemann, who had been prevented from sailing to the New World by his recently remarried father, moved to Hamburg, where a friend of his parents gave him a position as cabin boy on a ship headed for Columbia. He had accepted a job there writing business letters in English, French, and German.[7] The vessel sank in a hurricane off the coast of Holland, with only the captain, one crew member, and Schliemann surviving. After this brush with untimely death, Schliemann made his way to Amsterdam, where he began working as a clerk. Ambitious and driven, he set aside half his salary for education to improve his handwriting and his language skills, beginning with English and French and progressing to Dutch, Spanish, Italian, and Portuguese.

At the age of twenty-two, in 1844, Schliemann secured the position of correspondent and bookkeeper with the firm of B. H. Schröder & Company, one of Europe's leading merchant banks, at more than double his clerk's salary.[8] In anticipation of handling some of their indigo trade with Russia, Schliemann began to learn Russian and six weeks later was corresponding in the language. Within two years he was supervising fifteen clerks, and Schröder's promoted him at age twenty-four to be their agent in Saint Petersburg. There he started his own business as a wholesale trader of indigo and quickly rose among the ranks of commodities dealers handling indigo, sugar, tea, coffee, and Rhine wines, eventually working for several companies.[9] In 1846, while on a business trip to London and Paris, he visited the British Museum's Egyptian collection.

On hearing of his brother's death in California, Schliemann traveled to the United States in order to recoup some of the fortune Louis Schliemann had made as a San Francisco innkeeper during the Gold Rush. He arrived in 1851, just three years after gold was discovered, when the state's population was rising from fourteen thousand to two hundred and fifty thousand. Within months of his arrival, Schliemann had set up a bank, where he bought gold dust and sold it to an agent of a London firm. In five and a half months he had sold $1.35 million in gold dust, with a profit according to today's values of roughly £162,000, or about $243,000.[10] When the Rothchild agent in San Francisco threatened to break off relations with Schliemann because of consistently short-weight consignments, Schliemann sold the bank and, feigning fever, left in a hurry.[11] He returned to Saint Petersburg and quickly married Ekaterina Lyshin in 1852. With her he had a son, Sergei, and two daughters, born in 1855, 1858, and 1861.[12]

Schliemann made yet another fortune as a profiteer on the Russian side in the Crimean War.[13] He capitalized on shortages during the British blockade of Russian ports and invested all his cash in a risky venture whereby supplies would be off-loaded in Prussia and transported overland to Saint Petersburg. When it paid off, he repeatedly turned over his money and doubled his investment in a year. Schliemann learned modern Greek during the war to facilitate his commercial dealings with Greeks in the Crimea.[14]

On the business trip in 1854 during which Schliemann again visited the British Museum, he saw a scale model of Ramses II's temple at Abu Simbel at the Crystal Palace in London and became enthralled with Egypt.[15] Foreseeing a diminution in profits, he considered retiring in 1856, at the end of the war. In March, he wrote his father that he would like to visit the land of "his beloved Homer."[16] That summer, in his language exercise book he wrote that he would like to visit Greece and the Pyramids.[17] In October, he began to learn ancient Greek in a process of cultural self-improvement.[18] In December, he started a literary salon, and after curtailing his business to dealing in secured loans, he resumed studying Latin in 1858.[19] Sometime before January of the next year he again wrote in his language exercise book:

> I yearn to travel and visit Greece. Until now, I never was satisfied with my travels, always being caught up in business matters. . . . Now I can travel for other purposes involved with my beloved sciences, and in particular with philology. . . . I plan to go to Greece and Egypt with Homer and Thucydides in hand, and visit Ithaca, the Peloponnese, the plain of Troy, the Skamander . . . and other worthy ruins of antiquity . . . of which there are now only paltry remains.[20]

In November 1858, he began his first Grand Tour, visiting Sweden, Denmark, and Germany and finally traveling to ancient lands—Italy, Egypt, Petra, Jerusalem, Syria, Smyrna, and Greece[21]—returning seven months later to Saint Petersburg because he was being sued by a former business associate.[22] He may have seen the accumulation of cultural capital as a way to advance in Saint Petersburg society, the Grand Tour being an essential part of every gentleman's education, but his language exercise book betrays strong private desires, as well.[23] Thinking it too late to enter a scholarly career,[24] he reluctantly went back into business.[25] After winning his court case and subsequent appeal, he was appointed judge in a commercial court.[26] During the American Civil War, he again made tremendous profits by dealing in indigo and olive oil and by speculating in cotton, since the blockade of Southern ports a scarce and very profitable commodity.[27]

Schliemann effectively retired in 1864.[28] Leaving his family at home a third time, he set out on an ambitious world tour from 1864 to 1866. Beginning at ancient Carthage,[29] he proceeded via Egypt to India and the Himalayas.[30] He concluded his Asian adventure with sojourns in Ceylon, Singapore, Java,[31] China, and Japan, writing a travelogue about the last two countries during his fifty-day Pacific crossing to the Americas.[32] While on his tour, he developed a respect for ancient monuments and ruins and, considering that he had carried off a piece of the Great Wall, what one can only characterize as a hypocritical disrespect for governments that did not concern themselves with their preservation.

In January 1866, Schliemann again abandoned his family, visiting London and the British Museum, where he noted not only the Egyptian Collection, but also Layard's Mesopotamian finds. He then spent a month studying literature, philology, philosophy, and Egyptian archaeology at the Sorbonne. At the same time, he moved his assets from Saint Petersburg to Paris, investing heavily in real estate. He wrote his wife of the cultural activities to be found there and asked her to join him, but she not surprisingly refused. Twice he threatened divorce. During 1866 and 1867 he remained in Paris, absorbed by studies of geography and philosophy. In 1867 he attended the Universal Exhibition and a lecture on George Nicoläides' new book, *La topographie et plan strategique de l'Iliade*, at the Geographical Society, where Waddington had been a member since 1865.[33] The insatiable Schliemann fed on the social camaraderie and intellectual ferment of the learned societies. He wrote his son, "I am surrounded by fanatics for knowledge, who have made me a fanatic also."[34]

In February 1868, Schliemann took courses at the Sorbonne and the Collège de France and attended meetings of the geographical, ethnographical, and archaeological societies.[35] There he began life-long relationships with a number of important scholars and aristocrats. He planned to visit his children in Saint Petersburg at the end of a proposed Mediterranean tour but was prevented by the threat of a subsequent lawsuit. On 4 April, he wrote his son that among the places he proposed to visit, Switzerland, Italy, Ithaca, Corfu, Corinth, Athens, the Dardanelles, the "battleground of Troy," Constantinople, Odessa, Kiev, Moscow, and Saint Petersburg, he was most interested in seeing Rome and Pompeii.[36] He planned to visit as "a normal tourist," self-conscious of the fact that he "lacked the knowledge necessary for scientific investigations."[37]

Schliemann spent almost two months in Rome, where the pope was sponsoring excavations on the Palatine Hill (5 May–6 June) and around the Bay of Naples (7–30 June). He recorded all in his diary for 1868.[38] In Pompeii, he met the pioneering excavator Giuseppe Fiorelli (1823–1896), hard at work recovering the city plan.[39] As Schliemann traveled, his diary began to express a personal interest in antiquity.[40] At Pompeii, with its marvelous preservation, urban city plan, and relation to the coastline, he was awakened to the possibilities of archaeology.[41] On 16 June, he recorded Fiorelli's innovative method of reclaiming the incinerated bodies of Pompeians.[42] Schliemann was impressed by Fiorelli's use of a railway to dispose of unwanted debris and by the sheer history of archaeological exploration there.[43] Yet the impatient Schliemann could not stomach the amount of time, two weeks, that Fiorelli took to clear one house.

On 8 July Schliemann continued east, arriving at "Odysseus' Kingdom" on Ithaca.[44] Schliemann's long separation from his own home and long-suffering wife seems to have compounded his identification with the hero.[45] Yet in spite of his appreciation of the Homeric landscape, he again began his diary by parroting his guidebook. Perhaps his intellectual insecurity encouraged his thorough, dogged approach, following routes suggested by Murray.[46] He began to purchase antiquities.[47]

But on the summit of Mount Aetos, identified as "Odysseus' Castle" in a later autobiographical statement, Schliemann found walls, and to understand "the interior arrangement," he resolved then and there to excavate.[48] Later, when he returned to dig there, he expected to find the palace of Odysseus but instead found only pieces of brick. He noted several cinerary urns and, on the second day, a small building.[49] Within months he would envision Odysseus's palace in the scrappy walls and the hero and Penelope in the ashes. But for the time being, he recorded just what he saw. By the time he reached the Troad, he already had experienced his first taste of dirt archaeology, excavating what he imagined were the remains of Priam's enemy, who had conceived the deadly stratagem of the Trojan Horse.

Exciting developments in archaeology had preceded Schliemann's incipient interest in the field and Calvert's preliminary work at Troy. Most revolutionary were those of the "prehistoric movement" in archaeology that grew out of the developmental approach to scientific inquiry pioneered by Darwin. In 1863, in *The Antiquity of Man*, Sir Charles Lyell had discussed at great length Darwin's evolutionary view of human development, although he did not commit himself to it. In the same year, Thomas Huxley had published *Man's Place in Nature*, where he argued, "We must extend by long epochs the most liberal estimate that has yet been made of the Antiquity of Man." But prehistoric archaeology really came into its own in 1865 with the publication of Sir John Lubbock's *Prehistoric Times*, an instant and long-lived best-seller.[50]

In this manifesto of the prehistoric movement, Lubbock proclaimed, "A new branch of knowledge has arisen . . . which deals in times and events far more ancient than any which have yet fallen within the province of the archaeologist. . . . Archaeology forms," he declared, "the link between geology and history."[51] He had coined the terms "Neolithic" and "Paleolithic" for later and earlier eras in the Stone Age, when indigenous peoples crafted humble stone tools. But for the European Bronze Age he espoused the "Aryanist/diffusionist" idea that civilization had come from the east in the form of an Indo-European race. His book synthesized and projected human prehistory back from the Bronze Age to the primeval gravel beds. To understand the earliest peoples, he recommended studying modern savages.[52] Lubbock was asked to chair the first session on primeval antiquities at the annual meeting of the Archaeological Institute.[53] Following Lubbock's lead, the Crystal Palace showed a reconstruction of a Paleolithic site from the Dordogne in 1866. Building on this, the Universal Exhibition of Paris in 1867 exhibited collections of prehistoric tools and fossils from every region of Europe. Prehistory had become the rage, and Schliemann, who had attended both these events, knew it.

In the autobiographical notice he published in 1874, Schliemann referred to his 1868 tour as the "dream of my whole life." He also stated that he had "not had the ambition of publishing a work on the subject." He had decided upon doing so only when he "found what errors almost all the archaeologists had spread about Ithaka, Mycenae, and Troy."[54] Here, all of a sudden, was a chance to prove the experts wrong, thanks to his almost accidental encounter with Calvert.

The "sacrifice of personal considerations" that Calvert had made "in the interest of science" would haunt him the rest of his life.[55] When Calvert shared with Schliemann the results of his excavations at Hisarlık—the great depth of deposits, the richness of the finds, the fact that in digging through 3 to 4 meters of debris he had not yet touched the prehistoric levels that must lie below—Schliemann was well prepared to recognize the significance of what he was hearing and what it could mean for him. Not only was the site rich, but it would encompass prehistoric material, now the darling of European scholars—and, even better, it was Troy. The archaeologist who knew more about the area than anyone else had said so. Calvert may even have told Schliemann that he had not yet confided his treasured conviction to anyone else. Perhaps it was not too late for Schliemann to pursue a scholarly career after all. He would try to o'erleap the educational handicap of his youth. With a goal like finding Homer's Troy, he could strive against the scholarly disdain that German academic circles reserved for dilettantes, amateurs, and those who had not studied philology.

Before he left Turkey after his meeting with Frank Calvert and his conversion to Hisarlık as the true site of Troy, on 22 August Schliemann wrote his sister of the plans he already had formed: "Next April I intend to lay bare the entire hill of Hissarlik, for I consider it certain that I will find there Pergamos, the citadel of Troy."[56] Back in Paris in September 1868, he sought to impress Calvert with his credentials and quickly sent him a copy of his travelogue on China and Japan, published in 1867. In response, Calvert wrote enthusiastically, "Truth ungarnished appears in all the descriptions you give. The work you have in hand will doubtless prove as interesting."[57] By November, Schliemann may even have discussed a publication project with Calvert.

Realizing that he had stumbled on an opportunity to achieve greatness in scholarly pursuits, Schliemann bombarded Calvert with queries concerning the site, which he himself had scarcely noticed. On 10 October, Schliemann wrote a long letter to Calvert inquiring about basic facts, such as the location of Hisarlık. Was it north of Pınarbaşı or between it and the coast to the west? Was it connected to hills, or isolated?

After some prodding,[58] Calvert responded, answering Schliemann's questions and reassuring him. He quoted recent authors' opinions, gave information on many topographical points concerning the Troad, and responded to Schliemann's specific topographical inquiries on Hisarlık, stating:

> The artificial mound is larger than you suppose. It has taken its elevated form from being kept in on all sides by a wall made of the debris of temples & of the rubbish accumulating therein. . . . It is however only a spur of the flat table land immediately connected with it. The spur on which we find the elevated mound is the most remarkable on this range & its commanding position would at once point it out as the most eligible spot on the plateau. It has been built on over and over again until it was raised to its present elevation—but this does not preclude the possibility of the Acropolis having in the more ancient times extended far beyond this to the east, west, and south.

Genuinely flattered by Schliemann's enthusiasm, he then continued:

> It will give me much pleasure and satisfaction in giving you all the assistance I can in
> carrying on your excavations at Ilium Novum to settle the ground question "*ubi Troja
> fuit.*" All my lands are at your disposal, to examine as you may think best.—and if
> you have no permit from the Turkish Government to excavate (although such can be
> obtained through your ambassador at Cons[tantino]ple), you can carry on your
> works in virtue of the one I possess. All the ancient authors (subsequent to Homer)
> place the site of Troy at Ilium Novum until Strabo's time when he starts the theory
> given him by Demetrios of Scepsis.[59]

In his letter of 11 November 1868 he reiterated his enthusiastic offers of help:
"It will give me great pleasure to assist you in carrying out your researches."[60] To
this Schliemann responded on 26 December 1868: "It gives me pleasure to inform
you that I am now *quite decided* to dig away the whole of the artificial mount of
Hissarlik."[61] In the same letter, Schliemann requested all sorts of practical information, such as the right kind of hat, where to get workers and tools, and whether
to carry a gun.

Calvert wrote back on 13 January 1869. "The decision you have come to regarding the excavation of Hissarlik has given me great pleasure. You may be sure
you will have my hearty cooperation as far as lays in my power to carry out this interesting exploration—& let us hope the results may crown the hopes of our expectations in finding the walls of Troy."[62] Note his reference to shared expectations. In answer to a specific question regarding ownership of the mound, he
responded: "Part of the artificial mound is my property and . . . you have my consent to clear it out. For the remainder of the mound I will use my influence with
the other proprietor to allow the excavation & I have no reason to expect any serious difficulty in persuading him."[63]

This was a gentleman's agreement, based on the assumption of honorable,
generous, and responsible behavior, and Calvert went to great lengths to uphold
his end of the bargain. In response to Schliemann's letters dated 21 and 22 January, Calvert continued on 3 February:

> It has taken me years to become possessor of the part of the mound, with the express
> purpose of excavating it. . . . My ideas were based on finding the walls of Troy, the
> antiquities in the shape of marbles, coins, [e]tc paying for the expenses of excavation
> and value of field which would be rendered useless for agricultural or any other pur-
> pose. When you stated to me your wish to find the *walls of Troy* I at once consented,
> for to tell you the truth I cannot spare the necessary amount for excavating the
> mound at present—and as it is generally understood and your not mentioning any-
> thing to the contrary, the objects found remain to the proprietor of the land. I am
> willing nevertheless to meet you halfway, if you agree to it, which is that half of the
> objects found are to be my property after deduction made of duplicates which may
> or may not be claimed by Turkish Govt. The division to be made as follows the ob-
> jects to be separated into two portions of as equal value as possible and then to draw
> lots—afterwards exchanges can be made between us.[64]

According to preserved documents, this is the first time Calvert committed himself to sharing finds with Schliemann.[65] He may have made a vague promise of doing so earlier, for Schliemann was not one to invest heavily without a good return. But here Calvert spelled out the terms of their gentleman's agreement.

In the same letter he informed Schliemann of some difficulties with the Turk who owned the western half and, more importantly, of a change in permit regulations that had caught him off guard, noting ominously:

> Since last writing to you I am very sorry to say there has been very bad news for us, no less than that a new law has been promulgated by which excavations have been prohibited throughout the Turkish dominions, thus virtually reducing my firman to a nullity. As yet I have had no intimation but am expecting to receive it daily. I have been quite upset by this change of affairs and am now turning it over in my mind as to what course had better be pursued to attain our object under the present adverse circumstances.

Calvert had applied for a new *firman* on 18 January, explaining that he previously had been excavating under Callander's permit, but that Callander had returned to England.[66] Before leaving, he had requested Hakki Pasha of the Dardanelles to consider Calvert "as his representative."[67] But Hakki Pasha had just died. In his letter of application, Calvert stressed that he wanted to verify the ancient topography of the neighborhood. Then he mentioned that an archaeologist was proposing to commit a considerable sum to extensive research, identifying the site of Troy and examining various tumuli and other remains in the province. With the death of the pasha and the new archaeologist's proposals, Calvert simply wanted to make sure that he had an operative permit.[68] His letter was forwarded from the Dardanelles to the British ambassador on 20 January by Vice-Consul William H. Wrench with a strong recommendation that it be approved:[69] "Mr. Calvert's scientific labours have for many years attracted great interest among archaeologists." Wrench stressed, in support of Calvert, "the important nature, from a topographical and archaeological point of view, of operations he now contemplates."

But requests such as these were not granted as easily now as they had been in the past. The *firman* soon would prove to be a serious stumbling block. To the cover letter sent by Wrench to Ambassador Elliot, a reply was appended on 28 January: "I have been informed by H. E. Safvet Pasha Minister for Foreign Affairs ad interim that by a Law recently promulgated the excavation for exportation of antiquities is for the future prohibited throughout Turkish dominions."[70] The Ottomans now wished to protect their archaeological heritage and exhibit it in the new Imperial Ottoman Museum, formally created in Constantinople in 1869.[71] Presumably Calvert's 1866 permit for Balıkesır was unaffected, but the status of his continued right to excavate as Callander's agent was debatable. Since both he and Schliemann might want to export antiquities, the former permit was insufficient.[72] Meanwhile, Calvert would wait through 1869 and 1870, trying to placate

Schliemann in the midst of prolonged problems of acquiring a firman from the Ottoman government and access to the other half of the site from its Turkish owners. At this point, Schliemann still wished to begin in April.

Schliemann had certain misgivings, asking Calvert to clarify why he thought the hill was artificial.[73] On 13 January Calvert shared his observations concerning the complex stratigraphy with Schliemann, who had little if any understanding of the site or much concept of the layering of cultural debris over time. "Wherever I have excavated in this mound the soil is artificial—(not only on the slopes but on its summit)—in some places deeper than others. The average I should say would be 10 to 12 feet. The pavement of the temple of Minerva I found at this depth and I naturally conclude the rest of the flat hill is similarly composed of artificial soil."[74] Calvert had not reached virgin soil in any of his own trenches, so this was a safe (and correct) assumption. On 22 January 1869, Schliemann, still unclear, asked Calvert whether the mound was 20 or 120 meters high and requested that Calvert telegraph him with descriptions of the stratigraphy. He did so.[75] Calvert then took great pains in his letter of 3 February to clear up Schliemann's hazy understanding of the tell, because it was clear that he "had not seized the right idea of the true nature of the Hissarlik mound." In this letter, Calvert gave Schliemann minute descriptions of the site and a very rough section [Figure 25] showing the depth of artificial soil on the tell as it had appeared from Calvert's own excavations.

On 13 January 1869, Calvert eagerly counseled Schliemann on appropriate excavation methods for testing the large mound to determine a suitable location for concentrating his effort: "The plan I would adopt would be to make open trenches across the mound down to the natural soil, and others at right angles and only when anything interesting comes to view to open out the structure or foundation. In this manner much unprofitable ground might be left untouched. I believe it was in this manner that Layard excavated the Nineveh mounds."[76] He continued to advise him on accepted digging procedure and his own experience excavating in the Troad: "The method adopted in this country is for one man to dig and another to shovel the loose soil."[77] In a letter of 3 February he cautioned Schliemann, "You will find 10 to 12 feet of soil very heavy work removing and many things may be found at this depth." This was the depth at which Calvert had stopped.

Trusting completely in Schliemann, Calvert shared his passionate conviction that Hisarlik was the site of Troy and volunteered not only this land and half of the artifacts found therein, but also his expert knowledge. Schliemann's extreme ignorance of Trojan topography and ancient and modern literary sources is readily apparent in letters exchanged between October 1868 and January 1869. Particularly revealing is Calvert's response to the lost letter of 10 October 1868 in which Schliemann had requested all sorts of information, both topographical and literary. Calvert supplied Schliemann with all the ancient sources and works of modern scholars bearing on the question of the location of Troy and later recalled, "Until I mentioned them to him, Dr. Schliemann knew nothing of Maclaren or

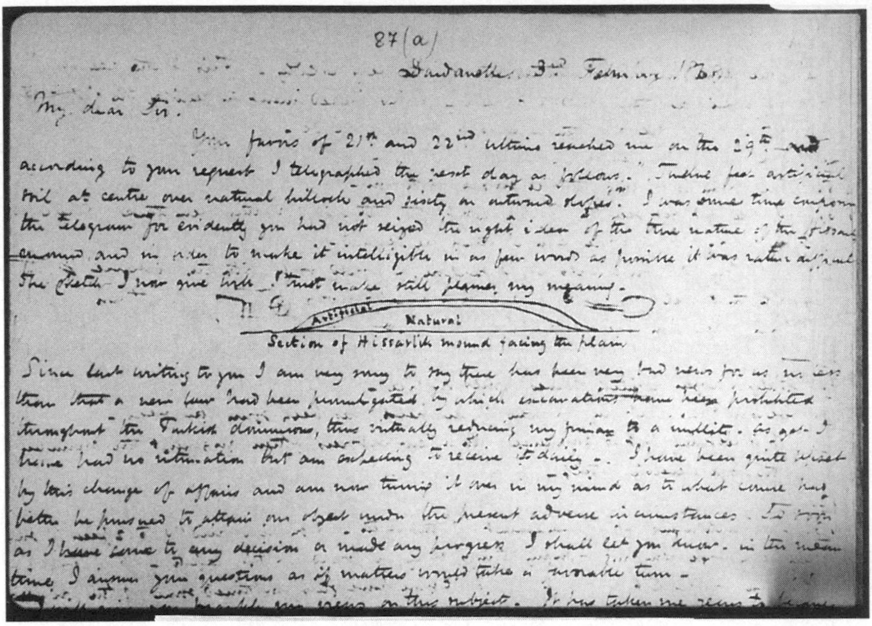

Figure 25. Frank Calvert's section of Hisarlık, from the south looking north. Courtesy of the Gennadius Library of the American School of Classical Studies, Athens.

Eckenbrecker, the only two writers who hit upon the theory that Hissarlik was the site of Homer's Troy. . . . From me he took note of their works."[78] When Schliemann could not secure them through the booksellers of Paris, Calvert copied passages by hand for him, including ones from Maclaren. On 22 January 1869, Schliemann had further requested a reading list for the field, "a mem. of the ancient classics and modern publications which you advise me to take with me for consultation."[79]

Schliemann's efforts to minimize Calvert's role in the discovery of Troy in order to maximize his own began immediately after their first meeting and continued throughout their relationship of over twenty years. This was not just "leeway he allowed himself to elevate his report to a scholarly level," as some of his modern defenders have claimed.[80] From the moment Schliemann left Calvert on 15 August, he deliberately began to rewrite the record. It is clear that he recast events in his diary to make it appear that he believed Hisarlık was the site of Homer's Troy prior to his influential meeting with Calvert. Nothing in his diary suggests that he had any knowledge of the theory that Hisarlık was either Ilium Novum or Homer's Troy before that historic encounter.

Although he had used von Hahn's work earlier, Schliemann did not critique von Hahn until 12 August, when he began double-dating his diary entries. From then on, a new confidence drives the diary. He rejected von Hahn's conclusions not on the basis of two days spent scratching the surface at Pınarbaşı, but rather as a result of his interview with Calvert.[81] Schliemann wrote this diary entry after his meeting with Calvert, and therefore in the white heat of excitement. Only this can explain his out-and-out rejection of von Hahn after he'd been parroting him earlier word for word.

Schliemann back-dated not only the diary entries, but also a letter to his father from Pınarbaşı in which he mentioned the artificial hill where he hoped to find the Pergamos, the citadel of Troy.[82] This and the letter he wrote to his sister and brother-in-law on 22 August conveniently omit any mention of Calvert. Schliemann clearly wrote the letter to his father to corroborate the diary he already was writing for posterity. He had laid the groundwork for the campaign of deception by which he would convince himself and others that he had adopted the Hisarlık theory on his own.

The questions remain whether Schliemann wrote the entries at the Dardanelles or in Constantinople and before or after he heard of the Calvert family scandals. He certainly learned of them immediately. The family had enemies in both cities, and knowledge of the scandals was widespread. A day at the Dardanelles or a week in the capital only months after the notorious trial would have provided plenty of opportunities for Schliemann to hear of them. Less than a year after the conviction, even the U.S. secretary of state knew of Frederick Calvert "having been convicted of forgery" and sentenced to two years' imprisonment, which he was serving on Malta.[83] Schliemann's later references to Frederick as a "convict" whose theft had caused an "immense clamor" and "would remain forever unique in the annals of crime" probably reflected the vicious reports circulating after the trial. In any case, Schliemann remarked that the scandal was "universally known at Constantinople and throughout the world."[84]

Frederick's conviction made a deep impression on Schliemann. His original agreement with Frank Calvert may have been more cooperative, but the two men did indeed have different ideas about how the excavations would proceed. Vicious gossip against the Calverts probably caused Schliemann to take a different line with Frank Calvert than originally had been arranged and may have freed him to dare his own deception, keeping Calvert and his family at arm's length.

While Frank Calvert was taking depositions for James at the U.S. consular agency,[85] Schliemann was making copious notes and, within weeks of his meeting Calvert, pompously writing friends and family members about a book he was composing on his excavations on the battlefield of Troy. With this book, which appeared as *Ithaque, le Péloponnèse et Troie*, he hoped to create a small reputation as an author. Surviving in his letter copybooks are letters he wrote to Mr. Bétolaud de la Drable on 17 September 1868, barely a month after he had met Calvert, concerning "my excavations at Ithaca and at Troy."[86] Next he corresponded with a New York banker named Janssen on 30 September 1868 and reported his imminent transformation into a man of letters: "I am in the process of writing a book on my archaeological researches in Ithaca and the Plain of Troy."[87] He wrote his cousin

Adolph about the project in October, saying he hoped he would not dishonor the family with his "bad publications."[88]

Wanting additional information, Schliemann sought rather duplicitously to reassure Calvert that "my book treats almost exclusively of Ithaca, but I must add something ab[ou]t the Plain of Troy."[89] A November letter to his son, Sergei, notes that he was working "day and night," that he had read thirty pages of the manuscript to the geographical and archaeological societies in Paris, of which he was by then a member, and that he thought he had been well received.[90] That Schliemann was able to rehearse his manuscript and ideas with a learned audience was a benefit of membership in the learned societies, and it certainly provided important intellectual reinforcement for the former grocer's apprentice. By November he had found a publisher and wrote to his son that "I have gloriously refuted the writings of Strabo on Ithaca and Troy and I am finishing once and for all, *the absurd dogma of modern archaeologists to find in the heights of Bounarbaschi the site of ancient city of Troy.*"[91] In December he wrote to his father triumphantly that he was circulating a manuscript among friends and soliciting comments.[92] Within months of Schliemann's visit with Calvert he had published it. Contrary to what he had told Calvert, the focus of *Ithaque, le Péloponnèse et Troie* was on Troy. There he claimed, "I completely share the conviction of this savant [Calvert] that the citadel of Hissarlik is the location of ancient Troy and the aforesaid hill is the site of its Pergamos."[93] He noted, as he had in the diary, that Calvert had excavated a large building—a palace or a temple.

Meticulous analyses of the 1868 diary and the text of the 1869 book have shown how many contradictions exist.[94] Schliemann recast the events concerning his 1868 trip to the Troad in order to show himself in a more scholarly light and to garner the glory of the scientific discovery for himself. In fact, Calvert supplied the literary sources and most of the documentation for Troy. Calvert's ideas became Schliemann's in a process of assimilation. His original motive may have been less malice than self-deception. He was creating a compelling narrative centered on himself as protagonist. He wrote that he had leaped across one hundred generations to a world of heroes. The book appeared more than a year before Schliemann ever put spade to earth at Troy. In a gigantic effort of intellectual imperialism Schliemann assimilated, synthesized, and shaped the vast mass of knowledge that Calvert had shared with him. But until he began to excavate at Hisarlık, he was still operating like all scholars before Calvert, in the realm of conjecture.

In prepublication letters, Schliemann thanked his benefactor for the "highly interesting and valuable communications . . . of which I have largely made use for my work." In the same letter, because he needed more information, Schliemann flattered Calvert and assured him that "the name of the great scholar Frank Calvert to whom the science of archaeology is greatly indebted for so many important discoveries, has been frequently mentioned in the book."[95] In fact, Schliemann did mention Calvert in his book, but nowhere did he clarify the extent to which he was indebted to his predecessor. Nor did he ever admit that it was Calvert who had led him by the hand to the Hisarlik hypothesis, confirming it with the visual evidence of finds from his own excavations and sealing it with his passionate conviction.

Calvert surely was unprepared for the avalanche of self-promotion, the prodigious outpouring of energy, and the broken trust that followed from his first association with Schliemann. But at the Dardanelles, Calvert was far from the antiquarian community, and Schliemann was not yet part of the tradition of gentlemanly understanding in which one's ideas and discoveries were protected from encroachment by others, although he aspired to attach himself to it, nor was he a gentleman, as his behavior had shown. Calvert graciously wrote to thank Schliemann for the volume: "I have read the book through and find it highly interesting—it is evident the author is thoroughly acquainted with Homer and has made it his 'vade mecum'[96]—The Preface has excited my warmest admiration . . . I am highly flattered by the manner in which you have made mention of me in your work—you have given me more praise than is my due for the services rendered to archaeology."[97] The gentle tone of the letter was perhaps due as much to his later request of Schliemann to intercede on his behalf in the acquiring of the Prussian vice-consulship for the Dardanelles as to his unassuming gentlemanly demeanor. Although Calvert did note differences of interpretation between himself and Schliemann, on the whole, he was quite positive. It was his turn to ask a favor.

Perhaps Calvert did not respond more vehemently because of his own unfortunate experience of losing his composure in 1862 with John Fraser, a lesser man than Schliemann. Mindful also of the family scandal, he probably wanted to reduce unpleasantness in his life at any cost. If his "partnership" with Schliemann was not what he had expected, he could make the most of it or sever relations.

Schliemann perceived Calvert's gentlemanly, passive, noncombative nature and exploited it, successfully motivating Calvert to do his bidding long after there existed any sense of partnership. Instead of becoming the enabler of Calvert's dream, Schliemann would appropriate the dream and live the destiny to which Calvert had aspired.

Following Frederick's conviction, Frank Calvert was forced to devote more and more time to official work, now for his brother James. Local merchants and Turkish authorities continued to harass the family.[98] Within the Foreign Office, the brothers were penalized and denied promotion.[99] Since Frederick's conviction, the Calverts had taken a more pragmatic view of their valuable collection,[100] seeing it as one way out of their current difficulties. When Schliemann appeared at the Dardanelles in 1868, Frank Calvert may have assumed that the millionaire enthusiast who clearly appreciated the collection might one day prove to be a buyer. Less than a fortnight after Schliemann's visit, James Calvert wrote to Newton concerning the two statues recently found at Cyzicus, which he simultaneously was offering to Waddington, who was now a member of the Institut de France. He requested help in determining their values, which obviously was difficult to do at the Dardanelles, far from the market. He added a note about having sold a gold coin from Lampsacus that would have brought twice as much if he had waited. Since the letter dates to just after Schliemann's visit, it may be inferred that James was referring to a price that the latter had offered for the coin.[101] If so, then Schliemann may have lured the Calverts into partnership with the implied promise of inflated prices for their antiquities. But there is no preserved record of their oral communication.

Although Schliemann was an archaeological novice, he was, if not a buyer himself, a man with contacts in Saint Petersburg and Berlin, two European capitals in which the Calverts knew no collectors, and given what they knew of Schliemann's background, they reasonably assumed that he could act as a conduit to the beau monde of European patrons and collectors. Frank Calvert explored the possibilities of marketing his finds by asking Schliemann "for any information as to the best place for disposing of marble statues, bas reliefs, and other antiqu[iti]es. Both Paris & London do not give good prices, I mean the Louvre & the British Museum. I have heard Saint Petersburg and Berlin as offering the best market for antiquities—but have no means of ascertaining the correctness or mode of communicating."[102] Although thanks to his own long-standing contacts with Newton and Waddington Calvert could speak confidently of the prospects for sales in London and Paris, he obviously was looking for more profitable, hitherto inaccessible markets.

To his credit, Schliemann did attempt to help. Capitalizing on the entrées provided by his membership in the intellectual societies of the French capital, Schliemann could tap into the highest echelons of French intelligentsia. Trying to assess Calvert's chances, he wrote to J. Lichtenstein of Königsberg and Baron de Witte (coincidentally a close friend of Waddington's) in Paris on 16 December 1868.

> Excellency, my friend, *Mr. Frank Calvert*, at the Dardanelles has a large collection of statues, bas-reliefs, and other antiquities which he desires to sell. It would appear that he has already sold to the museums in London and Paris, because he writes me that these museums give bad prices. He asks me if he could not obtain a more advantageous price for his goods in Saint Petersburg or Berlin. But as I know no one in these two cities who takes charge of antiquities sales, I permit myself to ask you: if you perhaps know someone at Paris whom one might address in complete confidence to attend to the sale of antiquities? But the person who would wish to take charge ought to have the necessary acquaintance with archaeology for a mission such as this.[103]

Schliemann then closed the earnest letter most humbly. "I would not address this question to you for anyone else, but I must for Mr. Frank Calvert, to whom the science of Archaeology is indebted for all important discoveries."

But Calvert's hopes were misplaced. Schliemann responded in a letter dated 24 December 1868 to Calvert's inquiries concerning the disposal of his collection. He

wrote: "I have taken informations both here and in Berlin as to the sale of antiquities and particularly statues. Unfortunately, my friends in Berlin can give me no advice in the matter and though I have been in Saint Petersburg yearly ever since 1845
I do not know of any person there likely to be useful to you for selling antiquities."
In those cities, Schliemann was just a businessman, shut out by his lack of education from elite intellectual circles. Yet, unwilling to betray his inexperience in the art
world, he added, obviously trying to impress Calvert with his social position in
Paris, "I have therefore addressed myself here to the 'Institut de France,' with many
of whose members I am well acquainted. They answered me, that it is a delicate
matter and that they cannot indicate the best plan to be pursued without more
ample information as to your intentions. They ask for instance whether you intend
addressing catalogues of your antiques to the directors of the museums?"

Clearly unaware of Calvert's own connections, Schliemann continued, "They
maintain that *no* museum is richer gifted than the British Museum, whose director,
Mr. Newton, is a friend of several of the members of said Institut de France and
they assure that for *really interesting* objects Mr. Newton pays more generously than
anyone in the world."[104] Wishing to be helpful, he continued: "They say, that, if
you might wish to sell here by public competition, it would be adviseable to give
previously minute information as to the Collection you wish to dispose of, the
charges of freight, storage, etc. being very considerable." Finally, he urged Calvert
to action. "I advise you to come yourself if you want to . . . and I hardly need to
assure you that I shall be delighted to assist you in every possible way."[105] Calvert
thanked Schliemann for his trouble and swallowed his disappointment. For him,
Newton was a closed door.[106]

Next, Calvert tried in vain to use his powerful new friend's connections and
asked Schliemann to intercede on his behalf to try to secure the office of Prussian
vice-consul at the Dardanelles, which Frederick had held for many years until his
removal in 1862. The Calverts wished to recoup the fees generally accruing to the
consuls from ships of that country passing through the Dardanelles. At age forty,
Calvert naturally enough wanted a secure position and thought Schliemann well-
enough connected, at least in the world of international trade, to be able to facilitate this small request, which he, as Frederick Calvert's brother, was reluctant to
make directly so soon after his brother's conviction. Calvert cited his experience as
an elected member of a mixed tribunal and his wide-ranging diplomatic responsibilities in the consular offices of every major European nation at the Dardanelles.
Moreover, he reasoned, "The post would give me greater facilities for carrying on
my archaeological researches and Prussia is known as one of the ardent patrons of
archaeology."[107] Berlin represented a potential market for the sale of antiquities.
Schliemann responded, "It would have afforded me very great joy to assist you at
Berlin to obtain the vice-Consulate, but since I have no powerful friends there I can
alas not act on your behalf."[108] In this case, however, there is no evidence to suggest
that he ever followed up on the request. Knowing the history of Frederick's alleged fraud, Schliemann did not want to risk damaging his commercial reputation

by recommending this brother of a convicted felon and begged off. Neither he nor Calvert ever brought up Frederick's name in these letters.

Meanwhile, with the *firman* stalled, Schliemann did not waste time; he left for the United States in March to secure U.S. citizenship. Saint Petersburg and Berlin represented the past for Schliemann, and he was flinging himself into the future. Part of this involved divorcing his Russian wife, which he did by fraudulent means after traveling to Indianapolis, where he hired lawyers and obtained perjured testimony attesting to his residence in the United States.[109] But before he left, he laid careful plans to establish himself in the ranks of German intellectual life. Knowing that he would require scholarly credentials to survive in his chosen field, he submitted *Ithaque* and asked to be considered as a candidate for the Doctor of Philosophy at the University of Rostock.[110] His doctorate was awarded in absentia on 27 April.[111] He was equally successful in Indiana and obtained his divorce on 30 June and official copies by mid-July.[112] While waiting for his boat to Europe, he addressed the first meeting of the American Philological Association on the day of their founding.[113] Welcoming the future, Schliemann wooed and married Sophia Engastromenos in September.[114] All was going according to plan for him. He just needed to wait for the *firman*.

Back at work in the American consular agency,[115] Frank Calvert did not correspond with Schliemann again until the end of the year, probably responding to a letter from Schliemann about the permit status.[116] When Calvert did write, his enthusiasm had evaporated. He had learned a lot from Schliemann in a year and a half and was more reserved now. With some distance, Calvert formally restated his position, aims, and motivation when he wrote Schliemann on 27 December 1869,[117] "Allow me to inform you that I have not come to any arrangement with any other party for excavating—it is true that I have been and am seeking opportunities for carrying on other excavations independently of the one in view and clear up as much as possible during my lifetime the archaeology of the Troad— still as to Hissarlik I have given you my promise and there is nothing now to prevent our views from being carried out except the firman." He planned to honor his pledge, but the warmth and enthusiasm of his earlier letters had cooled within a year.

Calvert had reason to be depressed. His hard-won claim to the life of a gentleman-scholar had been overwhelmed by the need to survive as a merchant. His intellectual confidence had been undermined by the treatment he received from the British Museum. His position in the scientific community had been shaken and his financial resources had evaporated when Frederick fled. In the midst of the family scandals, the one ray of light had been Hisarlık. Now he himself had given it away. And for what? He had received nothing in return. When he had made his offer to the British Museum, Calvert had stipulated certain conditions. He would direct the excavations, and it was his name that would be linked with the discoveries. With Schliemann, he had stipulated no such conditions, and moreover had volunteered an equal division of finds. By the end of 1869, Calvert had yielded the dream of having his name intertwined with that of Troy for posterity. The purely accessory role that Calvert would play in the actual excavations would not become clear to him until 1870. And then it would be painfully obvious.

Calvert was caught in the fissure between commerce and gentility, but he also was caught up in the changes affecting the emerging science of archaeology in the second half of the nineteenth century. Schliemann, by contrast, was assisted by those changes. By means of his scrappy commercial endeavors, he had built a secure financial foundation that would fund his bid for intellectual respectability. He could devote himself to his field without the distractions of another vocation. And in pursuing it, Schliemann made the right choices. Antiquarian pursuits could be a means of upward mobility for the nouveau riche and could lead all the way to the highest intellectual circles, to the academic credentials that increasingly separated amateur from professional and antiquarian from archaeologist. The entrepreneurial Schliemann was able to position himself at the center of these developments, and to capitalize on social and intellectual contacts in the clubs and learned societies of all the capitals of Europe, unlike Calvert, who always would remain on the periphery. He had the means to transform himself at a time when there was an opportunity for such transformations to succeed.

Schliemann was on his way. He had traveled widely and had begun his archaeological career by excavating two sites, albeit for less than two days each. His book was out, and while not a success, it was sufficient to earn him a doctorate at a German university. The proud author was now Doktor Schliemann, an almost unthinkable achievement in Germany given his humble origins. He had rid himself of his disaffected wife and married a girl less than half his age. Furthermore, he had allied himself with a young country whose industrious citizens he admired. Schliemann had accomplished much in less than two years, and he had done so in the very teeth of German disdain for dilettantism. All while waiting for a permit.

CHAPTER SEVEN

"Troy, Hell, or China!"
Excavation and Recrimination

From the very beginning of the relationship between Schliemann and Frank Calvert, Schliemann's behavior caused problems. The giving was all one-sided. In 1868, Calvert had given Schliemann permission to excavate on his own land, and in 1869 he had volunteered an equal division of finds between the excavator and the landowner. But after all Calvert's generosity and help and as soon as this agreement had been arranged, Schliemann instead began to look covetously at the western half of the mound, which belonged to two Turks from the neighboring village of Kum Kale.[1] By owning this other half, Schliemann reasoned, he would have complete control of the site, and since he would be excavating on his own land, he would not have to relinquish any of the finds to a local proprietor. He became fixated on securing the Turks' land and ignored that belonging to Calvert, which he had agreed to excavate.

Instead, he excavated the Turks' land—without purchasing it, without the owners' permission, and without a government permit. In a long letter announcing the results of his first week of excavations at Hisarlık to the president of the Institut de France on 21 April 1870, Schliemann explained the rash move to excavate without a permit and without permission of the landowners: "Knowing in advance that the Turkish owners would refuse to give me permission I did not ask them."[2] In fact, according to his diary, he was surprised to find that he was on their land.[3] He rationalized his choice because the western half of the mound was higher. Moreover, its imposing position had a much better view of the surrounding plain than the part of the mound on Calvert's side. For these reasons, he had thought that he would find Priam's Palace and Athena's Temple there.[4] He never mentioned that Calvert already had found and identified Athena's Temple elsewhere, seven years earlier.

In response to a previous inquiry from Schliemann regarding the stalled excavation permit and the equally fruitless attempt to acquire the Turks' land,[5] Calvert had admitted that excavations might be undertaken without a permit, but cautioned that they could be halted by the government in such a case, and Calvert clearly advised against it.[6]

Schliemann wished to commence excavations at once, first threatening Calvert that he would switch his efforts to Mycenae if he could not and then ignoring Calvert's advice against proceeding.[7] He had planned a tour of Turkey with Sophia, but when she refused to accompany him, he struck out alone for the Troad. Arriving at the Dardanelles on 8 April, he found Frank Calvert sick in bed with a fever; he then continued on to Erenköy, beginning excavations at Hisarlık the following day.[8] Looking around the surface of the mound, he followed the first wall that came to light, without any particular plan and without regard to whose land he was on. At this point, he became embroiled in a continually changing scenario with the Turkish landowners. First they only wanted baksheesh, then 40 francs, which Schliemann paid. Then the Turks were willing to let him excavate for £12 to £13, but they wanted him to backfill his trenches when he finished.[9] They wanted to have any cut stone that he discovered so they could use it for building. Then, on 16 April, the Turks returned with the barber from Çıplak who originally had shown Schliemann the site and told Schliemann that unless he gave them $3,000 he should quit at once. Because Schliemann already had given them 40 francs, he regarded this demand as an affront and kept on digging.[10]

He had begun excavations on the Turks' land on 9 April 1869. He dug with ten to fifteen workmen on the highest (northwestern) part of the mound, which the men affectionately referred to as "the grandmother of the excavations."[11] There he found cemented stones and a wall of cut stone. The next day, he found a large rectangular building of stone but noted that the work of excavation was so boring he couldn't bear it for more than three hours and took a field trip to Hanay Tepe and Akça Köy. The following day, he found another late building on the heights with mosaic pavement at a depth of 2 meters from the surface. One of the walls he found had cut stones 60 by 43 centimeters and 65 centimeters high. It was covered by a wall with marble blocks.[12]

Schliemann then moved farther west and dug eastward in two perpendicular 30-meter-long trenches on the western side of the tell [Figure 26a, no. 3]. On the second day, after doubling his workmen, in the western area where he had found a network of walls of uncertain date, he discovered coins, clay pots, fragments of a cup, and a leather ring. The cold weather and rain took a toll on Schliemann's spirits, and he declared that he had "lost all hope of finding the cyclopean walls of temples and palaces sung in the *Iliad*." He resolved to cut a deep trench on the summit, where he had seen such a mass of well-worked columns that he expected sumptuous finds. But instead, he wrote, "I find only trash."[13]

On 13 April, he discovered Homer's Troy—or so he thought. Schliemann correctly had assessed that he would find important architecture on the higher, western slope. In one of the western trenches, he found a building with a 2-meter-wide room, the upper part of its walls of large cut stone [Figures 26a and 26b, no. 36].

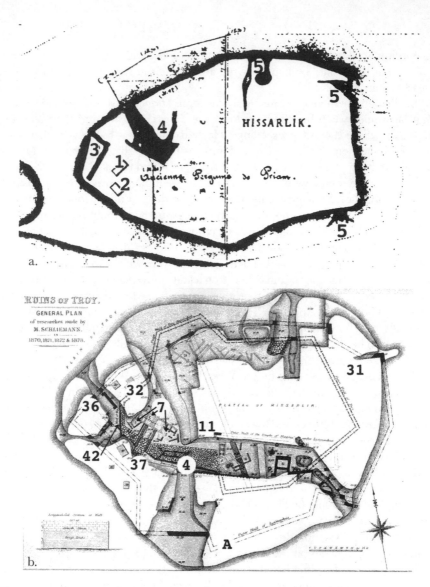

Figures 26a–b. Laurent's plans. 26a: Laurent's plan before the 1872 excavations.
1: Schliemann's house; 2: Storage magazine; 3: Schliemann's excavations in 1870;
4: Schliemann's excavations in 1871; 5: Excavations of Frank Calvert. Schliemann (1874b),
plate 116. 26b: Laurent's plan of Schliemann's excavations, 1873. 4: Great Tower of Ilium;
7: Ruins of the Palace of Priam and later superincumbent constructions; 11: Remains of
the Temple of Minerva (Athena); 31: Excavations of Frank Calvert; 32: Outer Wall of
Troy; 36: Hellenic Tower; 37: Scaean Gate and paved road; 42: Place where Priam's
Treasure was found. A: Outer Wall of Lysimachus. Schliemann (1875a), plate 2.

In his diary he wrote: "One recognizes the walls of Ilium Novum and perhaps a part of that of the Troy of Priam at a small elevation to the east and the north of the hill [where they were digging]." Two walls formed a right angle and he attributed them to a house or a temple that seemed from the immense mass of burned matter to have been repeatedly destroyed by fire. Elsewhere he posited earthquake damage to walls of cut stone, 2 meters high. In the masses of ash were animal bones and teeth. He concluded, "This seems certainly to belong to the Pergamos of Priam . . . most of the stones in the ancient wall are of cut stone, but there are also many which are uncut." He dug under the threshold of the building, looking "for vases dedicated to Apollo, but found none," and stopped at a depth of 1.5 meters. On 19 April, he again noted the very fine stone work of the 2-meter-wide room and again attributed the building to a palace or temple because of the fine masonry. He never specified a date for this structure in his diary or in the newspaper article announcing his putative find.[14]

Schliemann thought the only impressive architecture he had uncovered at Hisarlık was in the western trenches, where the house, or *megaron*, did indeed date to the Late Bronze Age, although he later referred to it as "the Hellenic Tower." In the northwestern trench below the marble wall lay the northern face of the massive Late Bronze Age fortification wall, with its regularly cut stones, although he did not recognize it.[15] He suggested that other walls there represented the ruins of the ancient Temple of Ilian Athena so often mentioned in the *Iliad,* a predecessor of the temple that Calvert had identified on his own land to the east.

Although Schliemann's diary reads as a reasoned account of the digging, when it came to writing up his reports for publication, he abandoned modesty and made sweeping assertions without much proof. A terra-cotta statuette, for example, became "a bust of Helen."[16] He also claimed in his published accounts to have dug deeper than his diary would suggest.

This initial, hasty excavation, equivocal discovery, and precipitous assertion of its significance was the beginning of a pattern that Schliemann was to repeat many times in the years that followed. Schliemann was obsessed with finding "Troy" and understandably dismayed by what he actually uncovered. His zeal caused him to make precipitous announcements long before he had had time to analyze and interpret the significance of his discoveries. Determined to find the city Homer had described, he repeatedly was discovering "the walls of Troy" and associating King Priam and the Trojan War with different levels of the excavation. It is true that there were few who were qualified to comment on his work from their own experience. One who was eminently qualified to do so, however, was Frank Calvert. Eventually, the problems associated with his claims would be exposed; when that happened it was Frank Calvert who did so.[17]

When Schliemann came upon his first solid wall, he rushed to the Calverts, exclaiming, as Calvert recalled, "Three cheers for Troy. I have discovered Priam's Palace and I have already sent off the glorious news to the A.Z.," the *Augsburger Allgemeine Zeitung.*[18] Calvert logically pointed out that, since Schliemann had found them at the top of the accumulated debris of the town, they must be from "a much later period than the Heroic Age."[19] Calvert assessed Schliemann's discoveries in the northwestern trench as best he could and wished him "interesting finds," but by 16 April, when Calvert wrote that he was still afflicted by fever, in fact, he may have been suffering from sheer shock at Schliemann's hasty and arrogant pronouncements.[20]

It would not be the last shock that the gentlemanly consul and careful archaeologist would receive. All Calvert had wanted was to see the excavation of Hisarlık undertaken by someone who could fund it properly and carry it out scientifically. He had been made to suffer, both in the Dardanelles and in England, by his brother's disgrace. Now he was going to have to put up with Schliemann's blatant abrogation of their agreement. For one and a half years Calvert had helped Schliemann, thinking that Schliemann would soon excavate *his* land at Hisarlık. Now he knew that Schliemann had abandoned his professed plan to dig in the temple and avoided his land altogether.[21] Where was the partnership now? Schliemann justified his actions in anticipation of Calvert's concerns: "It would neither do for me to begin excavations on your part of the acropolis," he wrote, "for if I did so the Turks would certainly not sell at any price . . . the land has literally been ruined by my diggings."[22] Schliemann's rash actions soon would jeopardize Calvert's relations with the Turks, as well.

Although he was to claim that the Turks eventually evicted him from this first excavation, according to his diary, he came to terms with them, put his assistant, Nicholas Yannakis, in charge, and left because he wanted to catch the next steamer for Athens. Once there, he picked up Sophia and brought her back to Constantinople for sightseeing.[23] After this, they left for Europe but returned weeks later because of growing hostilities between Prussia and France.

During Schliemann's absence, James Calvert, who was personally quite interested in Schliemann's results, went out to the site and wrote to him of his impressions, noting that Schliemann's walls were "undoubtedly earlier than the time of Lysimachus because of burials from the time of Alexander that had been dug into the debris beside them.[24] Frank Calvert also wrote in May, but Schliemann did not receive either letter.[25] Desperate at not having received any communications from the Calverts and "thunderstruck at the loss" of the letters, Schliemann was furious not to have "a line" from Calvert about the diggings. He begged Frank to inspect the exposed remains and give him his candid opinion about the different walls he had brought to light.[26] But by July, Schliemann was still waiting "with great anxiety" for a word from Calvert.[27] Frank Calvert had not returned to Hisarlık by 20 July.[28] Perhaps he demurred out of concern for the local political fallout or dismay at Schliemann's lack of adherence to their gentleman's agreement, and he continued to avoid Schliemann's excavations.

Immediately after Schliemann returned home, he began to rail defensively about the depredations that his excavations suffered, pillaged at an alarming rate by the local inhabitants for building projects such as bridges. He enlisted the

Calvert family's help to fight this prevailing custom. Frank Calvert, long active in the preservation of ancient sites in the Troad, such as Assos, Abydos, and Alexandria Troas, took on this mission with some success.[29] It seems that by preventing the Turkish landowners from "pillaging" Hisarlık, Schliemann hoped to encourage them to sell. But while Schliemann offered £100 for the land, Calvert wrote that they would not accept less than £500.[30] When Calvert counseled patience and "some tactics" with the Turks, Schliemann insulted his gentlemanly code by offering him a commission for his labors.[31]

For Calvert, Schliemann's behavior had immediate consequences, no less disastrous for the Calvert Collection than for Calvert himself. When Schliemann had raced into print in the *Augsburger Allgemeine Zeitung* on 24 May, declaring that he had found Priam's Palace, he had mentioned his "learned friend" Frank Calvert, as well as James.[32] This would have passed without notice in Germany, but, as was customary, the *Levant Herald* reprinted the article in June.[33]

It thus became a matter of public record by July that the Calverts had counseled Schliemann. From the beginning, Frank Calvert had worked hard through all possible channels to obtain an excavation permit for Schliemann, had recommended village workers and what to pay them, and even had offered his personal library and his family's house as a residence. Now he was associated with Schliemann's illegal efforts in the Troad, and the Ottoman government immediately penalized Calvert for his part in Schliemann's transgressions.

As Calvert told Schliemann, not only was there little hope of Schliemann obtaining a permit, but the Turks also had denied Calvert's own permit application, thanks to the article reproduced in the local papers in which "Mr. Schliemann *boasts* of his arbitrary proceedings and having acted without the authorization either of the Govt. or of the private individual who owned the site of the excavation." As a result, they implicated Calvert as being "as much to blame as Mr. Schliemann." At this point, utterly outraged, Calvert wrote, "I cannot conceal from you how injudicious I think it is for you to have made a boast of what you did—and we must suffer the consequences."[34] Calvert did not take this slight to his own integrity lightly, for Frederick would have just finished his prison term, and the last thing he wanted was more scandal.

Much more serious for Calvert were the repercussions that his finances suffered from the eleven days of illicit excavations. Earlier in 1870, Calvert had entered into negotiations with the year-old Imperial Ottoman Museum in Constantinople, which was eager to acquire ancient art for display. But by 10 August, all negotiations had ceased. Although Calvert had been in treaty with the Ottoman government for the sale of his collection, because of Schliemann's article advertising his excavations at Ilium Novum, they had withdrawn from the negotiations and they would have nothing more to do with him. Calvert had lost the chance to sell his collection to the Ottoman government at a time when he desperately needed cash.

The Turks now explicitly warned Calvert not to excavate until he had a permit. Moreover, "They stated I never had a firman and my collection was made by deceitful means," he told Schliemann. He immediately responded to them that he had had, in fact, not one, but two, although they might have lapsed. With an attitude conditioned by decades of living with Ottoman bureaucracy, he hoped that the present difficulties would be surmountable with time and patience. The Turks had become very averse to granting *firmans*, he told Schliemann, "but as you say with baksheesh all their scruples can be overcome."[35] It was becoming clear to Calvert that Schliemann had few scruples of his own.

By this time, Schliemann had enlisted the help of Frank Calvert's more powerful elder brothers, James at the Dardanelles and Edmund in Constantinople, in getting the *firman*. To bind them to him, Schliemann showered them with gifts to help their own research and with pieces of artwork—baksheesh in another form.[36] This was unnecessary, since they aided Schliemann out of both noblesse oblige and a genuine intellectual interest in his excavations. For Edmund, who was a serious avocational scholar, it also was an invaluable opportunity to obtain through Schliemann information from the various savants, libraries, and museums of Europe for his own research.[37] Neither, however, succeeded in getting the permit, despite considerable effort.

On 17 August, Frank Calvert wrote to the minister of public instruction, Safvet Pasha (1814–1883), with the purpose of disassociating himself from Schliemann and the ill-advised excavations. Edmund Calvert had explained Schliemann's motives to the Ottoman authorities and also had advised Schliemann to write a conciliatory letter "to soften down Safvet Pasha." "Entre nous it has been *privately* stated no notice wd have been taken of your proceedings had you not unfortunately made matters so public + as it were allowed the construction to be interpreted that you bearded the authorities—The new regulations have been shelved for a time." Frank Calvert noted that Edmund thought he would have a better chance of securing a *firman* through the French embassy and cautioned questioning about the permit.[38]

In response, but almost ignoring the impact of his actions on Calvert, Schliemann focused principally on himself, his own *firman*, and his efforts to acquire the Turks' land. Pressing Calvert and his brothers to accomplish his objectives for him, he again threatened Calvert that if he did not receive his permit by March 1871, he would turn his attention to Mycenae. Then he addressed Calvert's concerns, continuing confidently that if, as Calvert had said, he had had a chance to sell his collection of antiquities to the new museum of Constantinople, that chance would be made better than ever as soon as Schliemann came to Constantinople, "for I shall explain *everything* myself."[39] It was a classic "trust me" reply, coupled with a direct threat. However queasy it might have made him feel, Calvert's fortunes and reputation now were at Schliemann's mercy.

A master of obsequiousness, Schliemann was confident that he could persuade the landowners and the minister of culture to see things his way if he could speak their language. With Edmund Calvert's help, he began to study Turkish in order to negotiate for the permit and the property directly with the Ottomans and returned to the Dardanelles in December to consult with the Calverts over strategy.[40] But in the same month, Safvet Pasha deftly sidestepped Schliemann and purchased the western half of Hisarlık from the Turkish landowners on behalf of the government.[41] As the excavator of state property, Schliemann now would have to give his finds to the state and thus channel them to the new museum. Safvet Pasha acted protectively to safeguard the mound from the predations of Schliemann, who clearly had shown that he considered himself above the law. It was unlikely that he would be as generous as Calvert had been, volunteering to share what was found. By March 1871, Schliemann and Calvert had made little progress with either permit or pasha.

Schliemann was not pleased, and he continued to harass Calvert regarding the purchase of land, threatening not to renew excavations unless he got ownership of the western half of the mound. For his part, seeing how desperate Schliemann was to purchase the land and how intransigent the Turks were,[42] and considering his own need for money, Calvert reasoned that Schliemann would want the eastern half as well. It is a measure of Frank Calvert's financial distress that he was willing to sell the land on which he believed a major part of Homeric Troy to lie.

As early as May 1870, immediately following Schliemann's illicit excavations, Calvert had suggested that Schliemann seek institutional backing by forming a society along the lines of the Palestine Exploration Fund to finance the purchase and carry out the work.[43] If he was successful, Calvert then would sell his land, offering between 500 and 600 *dounoms*, or between roughly 125 and 150 acres, for £1200. Calvert mentioned two coin hoards of two thousand and five hundred coins each that had been found on the land in the last fifteen to twenty years, as well as temples, mosaics, a theater, and a bath.[44] Following the tactics of his Turkish neighbors, Calvert inflated his purchase price considerably, thinking the rich man would pay. But as for the classical remains, Schliemann replied that "only the heroic age interests Europe in Troy."[45]

Schliemann hedged in responding to Calvert's offer, saying that he was sure that he easily could get up a society for the excavations at Troy—but only after he had finished excavating where he had begun. "Then it would be easy to purchase your land provided of course you consent to include the portion of the hill in which I have been digging."[46] But Calvert did not own the half where Schliemann had been digging. Schliemann was turning the "tactics" that Calvert had recommended using with the Turks on Calvert himself.[47] Schliemann would continue to string Calvert along in this manner for two years.

Following the government's purchase of the western half of the mound in December 1870, Calvert again offered to sell Hisarlık.[48] He had been busy setting up his mining operations, and clearly he needed capital for their development.[49] Considering his opinion of Schliemann at this point, he hardly would have considered another "partnership." He began by appealing to Schliemann's passion, saying that he would certainly prefer to see the fields fall into good hands that would turn them to the intention he had had on purchasing them, which was "to unbury old

Troy." He also appealed to Schliemann's ego: "There is no one who would take up the affair more warmly or be so fitted to bring the undertaking to a successful issue as yourself." Finally, he spoke to the businessman. From his first, impossibly high offer of £1200, Calvert came down to a fair price of £500 and conveyed to Schliemann that this was indeed a bargain that did not take into account the years it had taken him to purchase the fields piecemeal and the time he had lost. "I name this moderate price solely with the view to tempt you to become the sole owner of Troy," he wrote.[50] Later he also pointed out that as possessor of the property, Schliemann would be free (as he was not in the other half) to make any excavations without impediment from the government. And he would be sole owner of everything found. He then added cynically that this excepted duplicates (never discovered), which could be claimed by the government.[51]

After a year and a half of stalling, Schliemann finally said "no" to this proposal. He wrote very formally that as Calvert was aware, Schliemann, as an American citizen, could not hold land in Turkey, and he had been advised that he would have endless trouble if he possessed property there. Then, in the same breath, Schliemann audaciously asked him to exclude from possible sales to others the hill and the land close to it, to use as a dumping ground.[52] Having by this time exhausted his good will toward Schliemann, Calvert responded two months later, when he returned from the interior, that he was quite occupied. If he found a suitable purchaser, agricultural or archaeological, he would sell to them, since money was his object under present circumstances.[53]

It is difficult to understand why Schliemann did not take Calvert up on this offer. True, he already had access to Calvert's land, but he was not interested in working on it. Yet it is abundantly clear from the wild promises that he was making to Safvet Pasha for the other half that he did want sole control of the site. Although the first offer had been inflated, the offer of 23 February seems to have been reasonable. Moreover, as Schliemann himself had bruited about, money was not an object. But Schliemann's treatment of Calvert in this matter is consistent with his treatment of him throughout: it kept Calvert bound to him, yet at a distance, dependent and motivated to help. If Schliemann had purchased Calvert's land, he no longer would have had any way to keep up this dependence. And Schliemann needed Calvert.

Indeed, owning Hisarlık continued to bind Calvert to Schliemann, especially given Calvert's need for funds. On 4 May 1872, Calvert once again wrote to Schliemann, this time an impassioned plea detailing again and at length his investment in the twenty-three fields or pieces of land that he had assembled and that had cost him £600, not considering the time he had invested acquiring them from various owners and overcoming their prejudice against having a Christian in their midst. He then reminded Schliemann of his own lack of success in purchasing even one and pointed out that without Calvert's connections, Schliemann could not have secured all these fields for less than £1000. "Do buy the property . . . for £450 Stg," he begged. "[It is] a great sacrifice. If you resell it, hereafter, you will make £2–3000 by the transaction. It is a good speculation doing a good stroke of business and at the same time a friendly act towards myself."[54] Schliemann apparently felt no indebtedness to his benefactor, and as a result, by 7 May 1872 Calvert realized that there was no hope.[55]

At the same time, Schliemann doggedly kept trying to acquire the western half of Hisarlık from the government. After noting that Safvet Pasha believed "the ground is pregnant with treasures," Schliemann wrote that he would guarantee Safvet Pasha in writing that he had the ownership not only of all treasures in gold and silver Schliemann might discover, but also of all and every coin he might find, and that he could watch his excavations with two men. The desperate Schliemann even promised to give him double the value of the precious metals he might find, professing that he had "no other object in view than to solve the mighty problem of Troy's real site" and that he was ready to sacrifice for its excavation years of his life and a vast amount of money in this undertaking. But he added that the field must be his property, and as long as this was not the case, he never would recommence excavations. He foresaw that if he dug on government ground, he would be exposed to "everlasting vexations and trouble."[56]

On the same day, he embellished the theme of the sacrifices he was willing to make in a letter to Wayne Mac Veagh (1833–1917), U.S. minister to the Sublime Porte, whom he barraged with appeals.[57] The letter is classic Schliemann: it effaces Calvert's work at Hisarlık and Calvert's influence on Schliemann while condescendingly treating the Turks as being incapable of being motivated by the enthusiasms of civilized men:

> for 2000 years scholars of all countries have disputed about the real site of Homer's Troy none has ever found it, no man has ever gone to the trouble and expense to dig for it although there is no spot on earth in which the world takes a deeper interest than this. And now that I have discovered it and laid bare the walls of Priamus' Pergamus, now that I am willing to sacrifice 5 years of my life and to spend a vast sum of money to bring to light those most interesting pages of history, a mere thought of which fills every civilized man with an immense enthusiasm, now the Minister of Public Instruction stops me, he who ought to think it is a great favor from Heaven that during his administration the great problem of Troy was solved, and he does not stop me because he wants to make those excavations himself; but because he is afraid I might carry away the gold and silver I find.[58]

In a final attempt to obtain the land, Schliemann wrote a conciliatory letter to Safvet Pasha as Calvert had recommended, trying to reassure him: "My entire task will be restricted to archaeological verifications based on the writings of the poet Homer," he declared virtuously.[59] But Safvet Pasha was a keen judge of character. He wouldn't sell.

Calvert, too, had had enough of Schliemann—enough of his broken promises and his unsubstantiated, self-serving claims to have discovered Priam's Palace. In May 1871, one year after Schliemann had begged for them, Calvert finally conveyed to Schliemann his views on Schliemann's 1870 excavations.[60] He declared that "the thick walls on the exterior face of the mound are without a doubt" the same as those that he himself had uncovered "at the northern extremity." The structure, the material, even the "builders' monograms" were the same. Calvert had assumed that these were Lysimachean on good grounds, that is, because of the inscriptions. Indeed they date to among the latest structures on the mound. "As to the structures within the above, viz. those attatched to the same, and the square building . . . some feet below the soil, they are certainly not more ancient than the defensive walls—probably of still more recent date." He threw down the gauntlet, noting that because of their relative elevation on the mound, none of the structures Schliemann had disclosed could be as ancient as Calvert's previously excavated Temple of Athena. He reasoned that the temple, which he thought was built on bedrock, antedated those structures founded on "the accumulated debris of fallen buildings." He included a rough section drawing [Figure 27] in order to elucidate the relative elevations of buildings and to clarify which important features had been excavated by him and to distinguish them from those dug by Schliemann. In it, he noted a late structure found by Schliemann, the earlier Temple of Minerva (Athena) that he himself had found, and artificial soil and debris overlying the virgin soil of the mound.[61] Most importantly, he implied that because Schliemann had found nothing earlier than the material Calvert had found, he was nowhere near the level of Priam's Palace. "To discover the walls of *Troy*," he challenged Schliemann, "I think you must go deeper still," below the Lysimachean walls, "which may possibly have been built on them."

Although Calvert was right in believing that some of the walls Schliemann had found were contemporary with or later than the "Lysimachean Wall" that he had discovered, he was wrong in thinking them all to be later than the Heroic Age. Calvert's reasoning was sound, but Hisarlık is an unusually complex site with very irregular terrain, which complicated the stratigraphy. Schliemann had uncovered a number of buildings on the summit of Hisarlık that certainly were later than the Lysimachean temple to Athena that Calvert had discovered. The cemented stones, builders' marks, and buildings with mosaic floors are ample testimony to this. But he also had discovered fragmentary earlier structures in both the northwestern and western areas.[62] These Calvert did not discuss and may not have recognized; perhaps they were obscured by earth washed down by winter rains. Although distracted by the birth of his first child with Sophia, Schliemann responded that Calvert had not visited his "deep ditch," where he had laid bare a wall 2 meters thick.[63]

Calvert was unmoved and repeated his belief that because of their relative elevation on the mound, the northern walls and the rectangular building were contemporary and late structures, not Priam's Pergamos and Homer's Troy. He said the same thing to Ernst Curtius and the group of scholars who visited him in 1871. The group clearly respected Calvert's authority and wished to see Schliemann's 1870 excavations and to compare these with those of the Austrian consul von Hahn at neighboring Pınarbaşı. Schliemann, who had alerted Calvert of their arrival, was quite anxious that Calvert persuade the eminent archaeologist Curtius

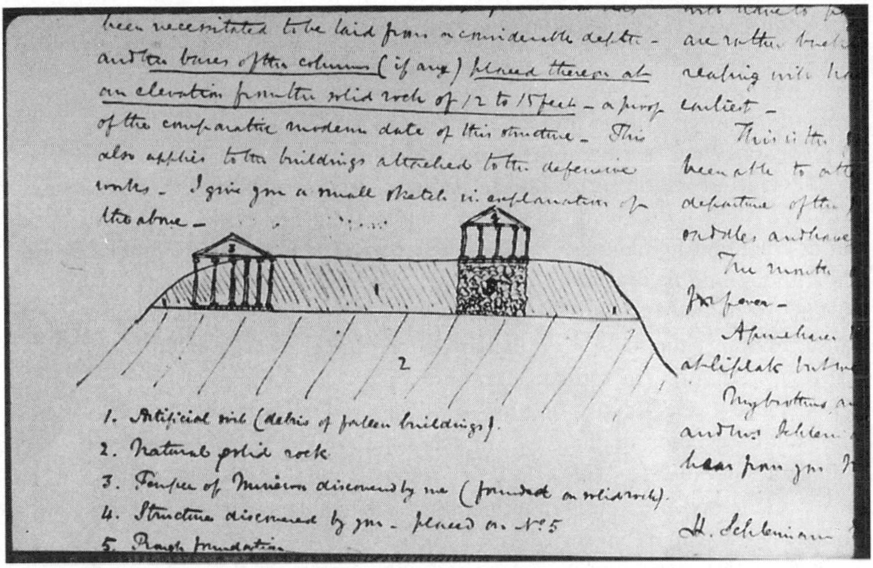

Figure 27. Frank Calvert's section of Hisarlık, showing his and Schliemann's architectural finds. Courtesy of the Gennadius Library of the American School of Classical Studies, Athens.

that he was correct in his placement of Troy. Instead, Calvert repeated to Schliemann what he had told Curtius: "when Hissarlik is excavated . . . the ancient walls of the far famed city might still be found."[64] Calvert also told Schliemann that Gustav Hirschfeld believed that Schliemann's walls, as well as those excavated by Calvert himself, were of comparatively recent date and certainly not of ancient Troy, "in which opinion, as you know, I agree." Schliemann could not have been pleased, already having claimed to the press a year before that he had found the Pergamos of Priam.

To substantiate his claims, Schliemann set out once again to discover the walls of Troy and Priam's Pergamos in 1871. He had big plans. As Schliemann began to hope that the elusive permit at last was on its way, he wrote to Calvert about his future excavations with unbridled enthusiasm. He and Mrs. Schliemann would publish in Greek, French, and German the description of their own diggings.[65] But in June 1871, Safvet Pasha and Mr. Goold, director of the new Imperial Museum from 1869 to 1871, informed him that he would have to file a regular permit application,[66] a process that would take two to three months.[67] Schliemann accused Goold of impeding the process so as to "enrich the non-existing Imperial Museum of which he is the ill-fated director."[68] Schliemann placed all his confidence in John P. Brown, chargé d'affaires of the U.S. legation in Constantinople.[69]

The year's delay profoundly frustrated Schliemann, to the point that he would not heed Calvert's cautionary advice on excavation methodology. He boasted to Calvert that he would recommence excavations on a large scale at His-arlık and "take away the whole hill."[70] In letters to others, he described the great north-south trench that he planned to cut through the mountain, "a tremendous trench thirty metres broad and at least 122 m long."[71] Yet he had absorbed much from Calvert, such as the importance of digging down to virgin soil. Remembering Calvert's advice on stratification, Schliemann reasoned that the lowest range of buildings on virgin soil must be the most ancient.[72] So struck was he by this idea that at one point he planned to begin the excavation from the foot of the mountain and dig until he reached the virgin soil, and then follow that up.

With the help of Wayne Mac Veagh and especially John P. Brown of the American legation, Schliemann eventually obtained his excavation permit, on 12 August 1871.[73] Although he estimated commencing work at the end of September, by 5 October he was still stalled because of problems having to do with the local governor's interpretation of the terms of the *firman*, which did not specify on which half of the mound Schliemann was permitted to dig.[74] Yet Schliemann persisted because he feared the humiliation he might suffer if he returned to Athens without having excavated that year. On 8 October he wrote, "so much has been written in the newspapers of the ensuing excavations that . . . the whole press would describe me as a ridiculous fool."[75]

Correspondence between Frank Calvert and Schliemann was interrupted that autumn while Calvert was away for two months in the interior, engrossed in mining ventures. He was absent, perhaps by choice, during Schliemann's entire six-week season. Thus, Schliemann addressed all letters during the excavation season to Calvert's brothers.

Schliemann commenced excavations at the northern edge of the mound with workmen from Erenköy on 11 October and continued until 24 November.[76] But again he worked on the western half and ignored Calvert's land. Schliemann himself was everywhere at once: supervising seventy to eighty workmen, receiving finds, and writing up reports when it rained.[77] As the number of workmen increased, equipment broke and supplies ran low. In his haste, he ignored the terms of the *firman*, which stipulated that he must leave walls in place, and instead removed great blocks of stone and sent them thundering to the plain below.[78]

Within a month, he was 4 meters down from the summit, in a level characterized by stone tools. There was no indication of cyclopean walls.[79] He wrote to James Calvert on 30 October that to his horror there seemed to be nothing remotely Homeric in his finds. They were older than any he had seen in the British Museum, and he hoped that these stone tools dated to a "temporary invasion of barbarians." "Since I find again civilization below the hundreds of stone implements," he continued, "I feel for these excavations a paramount interest, an interest that words cannot describe."[80] Yet a week later he also candidly confessed, "[it] perplexes me everyday more and more."[81] Knowing, as did Calvert, that Homer had spoken only of bronze and iron, Schliemann felt more and more desperate—he wrote Frederick Calvert that if he did not find a cyclopean wall, a characteristic of Heroic Age citadels in Greece, he would abandon Hisarlık and dig at Frederick's site at Akça Köy, the Ilion Kome, or "village of the Ilians," of Demetrius and Strabo, in a last-ditch effort to locate Troy.[82]

Frank Calvert, the one person who could have given Schliemann wise counsel, was away, and his absence was "much regretted" by Schliemann.[83] The elder Calvert brothers tried to help him interpret the puzzling material.[84] Frederick and Eveline Calvert suggested that "the stone period debris" had been brought in as fill and placed on top of the later remains. But as early as 26 October 1871, Schliemann knew better and reported distinct strata at the mound [Figure 28]. In the top meter of earth lay coins, cemented buildings of hewn stone, and huge blocks of stone. The next meter of deposit contained no more huge blocks, but instead a quadrangular structure of uncemented hewn stone and three Greek inscriptions.[85] The next stratum occurred at a depth of from 2 to 4 meters and had very little stone and the remains of wooden buildings destroyed by fire. The following stratum, which was third from the bottom, lay 4 to 7 meters down. Here he encountered the "stone period," with its myriad spindle whorls, stone hammers, hand mills, axes, knives, terra-cotta vases with owls' faces, one piece of wire, and copper nails.[86] He originally suggested that this stratum must date to an age "thousands of years before the Trojan War."

Schliemann was lost. Nothing was as he had envisioned: no palace on the summit, no bronze tools of which Homer had sung. Most importantly, he could connect no level at Hisarlık with Homer's bronze-hurling warriors. Instead, there were Hellenistic and Classical period strata related to the Iron Age of Alexander and his predecessors and the "stone period," which he thought must represent the Stone Age. And the stratigraphy was not straightforward. "How strange that I come on the summit of the hill in 4 metres depth into the stone period, whilst only 20 m distant I found that Roman wall in a depth of 5 metres and no trace of the stone period even at 8 metres."[87] Where was the Bronze Age stratum? This was where Frank Calvert had stopped, thinking that he had hit bedrock below the temple foundations [Figure 27].[88] To his credit, Schliemann did not. Instead he rationalized his disappointment. Finding himself in the dark, he made a virtue of it, writing in his diary,

> I am not digging to find works of art although I accept them with joy when I find them. I am digging only to enhance knowledge and I am doing it profoundly in the darkness of time—in the strata of debris that must antedate Homer by thousands of years. All the archaeologists that have visited the Plain of Troy have decided the question of the site . . . theoretically. . . . No-one so far has ever taken the trouble to resolve this great question practically, as I am doing.[89]

Schliemann's appeal to "the darkness of time" recalls Nyerup's "thick fog" of prehistory, "a space of time we cannot measure." And it is true that although Calvert's excavations had preceded his, Schliemann was breaking new ground in the archaeological understanding of the prehistorical past. Whereas a great effort

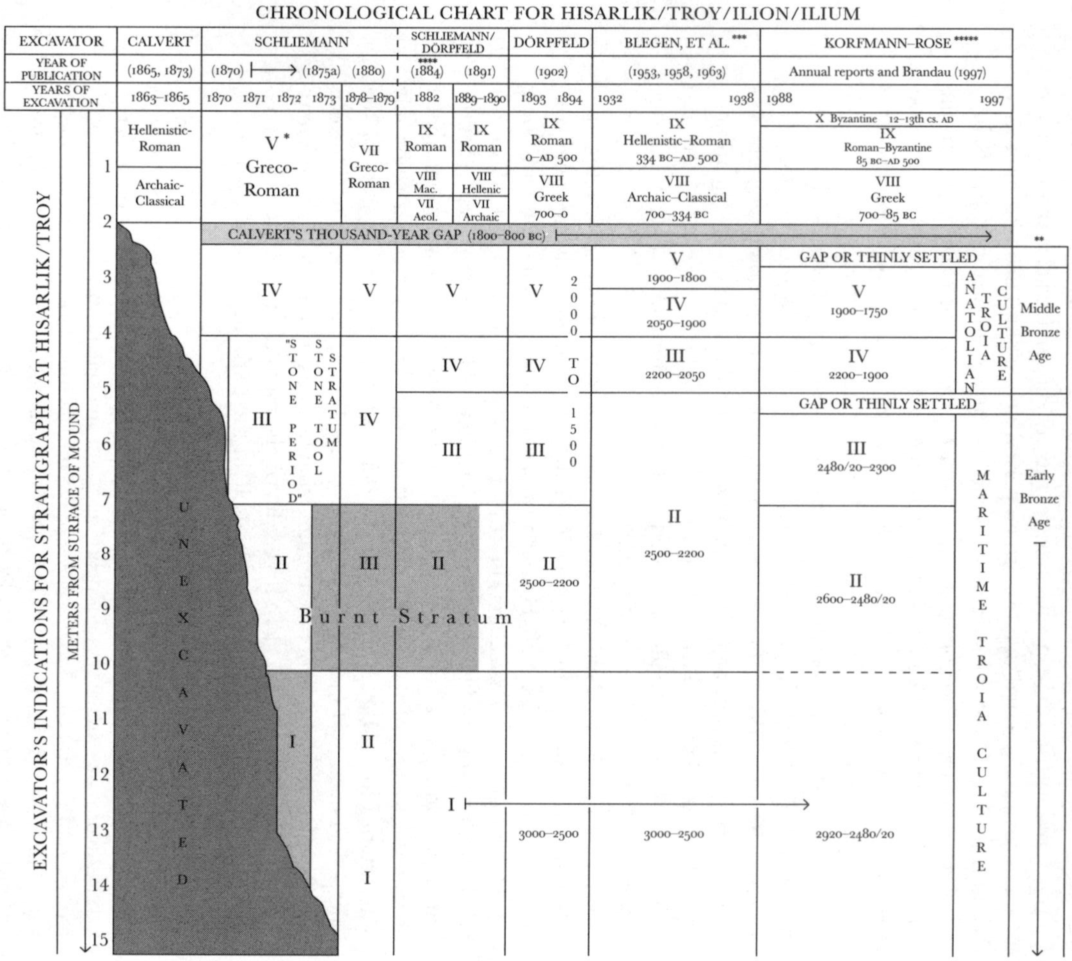

* Roman numerals indicate the relative position of excavated strata or settlements; I is the lowest, earliest, or first stratum.

** See companion chart.

*** As interpreted by Easton (1990), 436 and fig. 13, and Blegen, et al. (1958), 248.

**** Dörpfeld to F. Adler, 18 June 1882. Traill (1995), 309 n. 2. There Dörpfeld notes that Schliemann distinguished nine cities: five prehistoric ones, a sixth—Lydian, a seventh—Aeolian, an eighth—Macedonian, and a ninth—Roman.

***** Considerable fluctuations have occurred in the dating of the Bronze Age levels I–V as the present excavations have progressed. These dates reflect those of Korfmann, Brandau (1997) and (1998).

▒ Indicates the stratum that the excavator believed was Homer's Troy.

Figure 28. Chronology in the search for Homer's Troy.

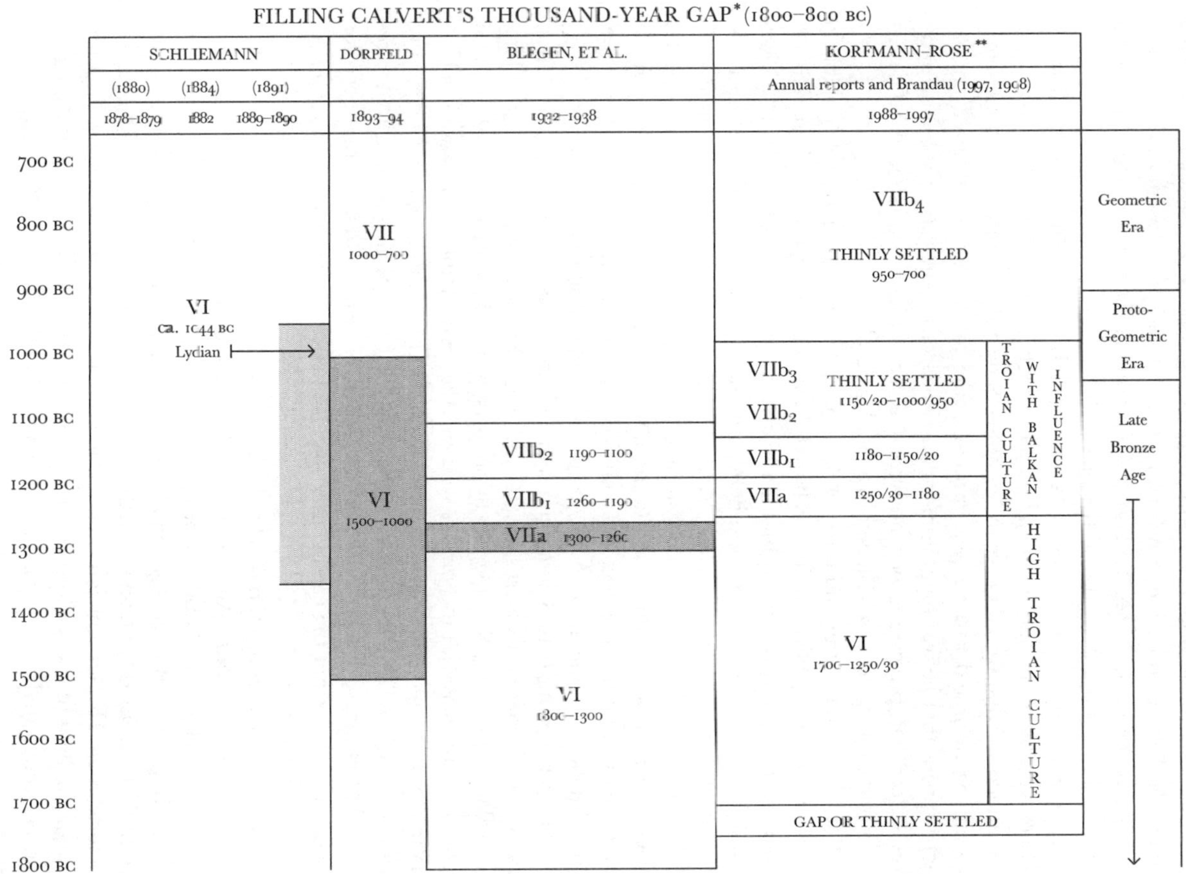

FILLING CALVERT'S THOUSAND-YEAR GAP* (1800–800 BC)

SCHLIEMANN	DÖRPFELD	BLEGEN, ET AL.	KORFMANN–ROSE **	
(1880) (1884) 1882 1889–1890 (1891) 1878–1879	1893–94	1932–1938	Annual reports and Brandau (1997, 1998) 1988–1997	

* These levels were largely discerned on the slopes of the citadel. They had been removed in antiquity from the summit.

** For information on Protogeometric and Geometric material, see Rose (1998), 100. "We now have found enough evidence to demonstrate that the site was probably never abandoned after the end of the Bronze Age."

☐ (shaded) Level excavator believed was Homer's Troy.

☐ Schliemann realized but did not publish the association with Troy VI and Homer.

Geometric Era

Proto-Geometric Era

Late Bronze Age

VIIb₄ — THINLY SETTLED 950–700

VIIb₃ — THINLY SETTLED 1150/20–1000/950
VIIb₂ — 1180–1150/20
VIIb₁ — 1250/30–1180
VIIa

VI — 1700–1250/30

GAP OR THINLY SETTLED

VII 1000–700

VI 1500–1000

VIIb₂ 1190–1100
VIIb₁ 1260–1190
VIIa 1300–1260

VI 1800–1300

VI ca. 1044 BC
Lydian

TROIA WITHIN — BALKAN CULTURE

HIGH TROIAN CULTURE

700 BC
800 BC
900 BC
1000 BC
1100 BC
1200 BC
1300 BC
1400 BC
1500 BC
1600 BC
1700 BC
1800 BC

Figure 29. Filling the thousand-year gap.

had been made in the sixty-five years since Nyerup wrote to shed light on the pre-history of northern Europe, few had attempted to lift the veil of Mediterranean or Aegean prehistory. Schliemann also was correct in initially assuming that the "stone period debris" preceded Homer's Troy significantly. But his belief that the strata actually were of the Stone Age was immediately questioned by the astute James Calvert.[90] Schliemann noted that even if he managed to prove that Troy never had existed, he would be happy to be recognized by the scholarly world for having resolved the question. Since Frank Calvert had been absent during his en-tire digging season and again had not helped him in his hour of need, Schliemann continued to write Calvert out of the picture.

Then Schliemann's persistence was rewarded. Before he halted his excavations, Schliemann began to find the metal he had sought in a level 7 to 10 meters from the surface, in what would prove to be the second stratum from the bottom. On 8 November, he noted two copper brooches, and on the next day, three copper tools—proof that he was digging in metal-rich Bronze Age remains. Schliemann now indeed had progressed beyond what Calvert had accomplished, for Calvert never had claimed to have reached Bronze Age levels.

But what Schliemann had uncovered posed a further problem. He had found proof of a higher civilization in which metalworking was common. He had found weapons, tools, and the stone molds for casting them in bronze.[91] But he had found them at a level beneath and hence antedating the "stone period" remains. How could he account for Bronze Age remains, which he now associated with Homer, beneath the debris of the "stone period"? Resolving this dilemma would prove critical to any ultimate substantiation of Schliemann's claims. To John P. Brown, Schliemann wrote: "All this confusion of ages instead of discouraging me, only stimulates me the more to go ahead and reach virgin soil at any price."[92]

Still, to hedge his bets, Schliemann sent a group of workmen to excavate "Ilion Kome" on Frederick Calvert's land,[93] although Frank and James Calvert long since had abandoned this identification. Regarding Frederick's hypothesis that Troy lay at the site with the springs west of Akça Köy, James had written Schlie-mann that he would "find Demetrius of Skepsis' Troy on my brother's farm—but not Homer's Troy."[94] After about a week's digging there, Schliemann, who had re-mained at Hisarlık, dispatched Frederick Calvert's beloved Ilion Kome thesis for good, concluding that the earthworks once thought to enclose a fortification wall were, in fact, barren.[95]

Despite the conundrum posed by the interposition of the remains of the "stone period" over the Bronze Age stratum he had discovered, Schliemann had every reason to be elated. Although at this point he believed that the stratum in which he had found these Bronze Age remains in the western part of Hisarlık was not yet Homer's, he seemed to be on the right track.[96] Confidently, he repeated his earlier rhetoric about Homer's ancient city, "which no one before me has ever thought of bringing to light by excavations."[97] He vowed to dig deeper, convinced that he had not yet "penetrated to the period of the Trojan War."[98] To James Calvert, he confided: "I am approaching Troy. Yes I have some strange forebodings that at the bottom I shall find something very curious, in fact, that I shall find the real Pergamus."[99] Again.

Now cocky, Schliemann sought to distance himself from those who had helped him come this far and those who wanted to assist him in the future. He wrote to James Calvert on 21 November 1871 that he had rejected help of exactly the sort of society that Frank had suggested forming in 1870, the Ellenikos Philologikos Syllogos of Constantinople, which was ready and enthusiastic to support him and his excavations. Perhaps later, if the project were enlarged, he might give it to them and be merely the director of the project.[100] His arrogance certainly would have galled the Calverts, particularly Frank, who desperately had hoped for this type of sponsorship.

Frank Calvert went out to Schliemann's excavations as soon as possible after returning from the necessary time in quarantine. Immediately, he wrote Schliemann with his impressions of the remains. Calvert correctly advised Schliemann that the "stone period" artifacts that had so perplexed him were later than the Stone Age. Trying to be of help to the flailing Schliemann, Calvert explained the principle of dating respective strata by associated artifacts and suggested that Schliemann could date the levels more precisely by noting the pottery found therein. But he demurred from doing so himself since Schliemann had left only unwanted debris by the trenches and it was not diagnostic.[101] Schliemann responded coolly: "Many scholars have seen my antiquities; all of them exclaim that they *never* saw anything like them; some think that my vases (even those from strata 4 to 7 m deep) are *prehomeric*, others think with me that now only in a depth of 10 metres I have reached the epoch of the Trojan War, but all concur that *all* my trojan antiquities are prehistoric."[102] If Schliemann now could date these strata, it would be a true advance.

From the beginning, Calvert had tried to share such information on archaeological methods with Schliemann, as well as his interpretations of Schliemann's discoveries, but during the 1871 excavation, Schliemann had continued to plow through the mound, rarely modifying his own opinions in the face of Calvert's constructive criticism. In 1872, the squabbles, contentions, and betrayals continued. Schliemann returned with two Greek foremen, Spyros Demetriou and Theodorus Makrys, as well as a railway engineer, Adolphe Laurent, hired to draw up site plans.[103] Again he began at the northern edge and worked into the western half of the mound, eventually swallowing his 1871 excavations [Figure 26b]. Schliemann intended to bisect the mound by driving a great trench, 79 meters broad and 14 meters deep, through the mound from north to south. Laurent reckoned he would move 91,000 cubic meters of earth.[104] To do this he engaged 120 workmen to move 60 cubic meters a day.[105] Much more ambitious than the short campaign of 1871, Schliemann's 1872 excavations would extend over four and a half months, from 1 April to 13 August. Optimistically, he requested an American flag from Brown because he had a presentiment that he would discover Troy the day it flew over his dig house.[106]

As in 1871, the finds from these excavations were unusual, with few parallels, and they piled up fast. To press forward his "gigantic progress," Schliemann planned "to blow up all the earthen walls with gunpowder."[107] By 24 April his engineer noted that he had removed 8500 cubic meters of debris.[108] "The work of one day would often yield objects from almost all the strata, from the present surface of the hill to the virgin soil."[109] More molds for copper tools and ornaments appeared in the same stratum in which he previously had found them, again bringing him in touch with the Bronze Age civilization he had encountered the previous year.[110] Schliemann rewarded his men for every object "belonging to the dark night of pre-Hellenic times, and bearing traces of human skill in art."[111]

As soon as Schliemann began to dig, tempers flared, over everything from minor annoyances to major differences in how to proceed. In one letter, Calvert complained that he had been to the customs house a dozen times on account of Schliemann's wheelbarrows![112] Schliemann retorted on 21 April: "Excuse me that I trouble you so much but I am working for the glory of Troy and you cannot but benefit yourself by my success."[113] To some, Schliemann denied his grandiose claims.[114] Later, he again countered Calvert's negative remarks with a profession of faith, declaring that he must firmly believe in finding Troy, for otherwise he would be "a crazy man" to work with 120 and 125 men, and to spend 300 francs daily. He added, as if to placate Calvert, that as soon as he found Troy, not only Calvert's half of the hill but also his neighboring fields and, in fact, the whole Troad would be very precious.[115] On 30 April, Calvert responded that had Schliemann commenced in his field as they had originally agreed, he would have saved himself a lot of money.[116] On 2 May, Schliemann agreed that he would have solved the riddle of Troy much sooner by running a platform through Calvert's field and that he could have done it at much less expense and without any trouble. But since the other half was higher, he reiterated, it had struck him as the more likely spot for the king's palace.[117] Calvert wrote back on 3 May that Schliemann's excavations must be "very interesting" and that he would visit them sometime when he had come to something decisive, the implication being, of course, that he had not. Three days later, obviously in despair, Schliemann wrote that he was going to abandon the other field for Calvert's side and that he wept that he had not begun there two years ago.[118]

Schliemann understandably was suffering, digging through a very hard stratum of ash on the northwestern side of the mound and expecting at any moment to reach the bedrock that Calvert had hit at 3 to 3.6 meters, directly below the temple foundations on his half of the mound [Figure 27].[119] But Calvert had mistaken the rock-hard ash layer for bedrock.[120] Further troubled by the smallness of the citadel, Schliemann also soon agreed with Calvert that the Pergamos must have extended beyond the confines of the citadel and onto the plateau to the south.[121]

In the western area, he found a large stone structure of the third stratum with 2-meter-thick walls.[122] Below this, at a depth of 9 meters, on 17 May 1872, at the west end of the north platform, he found his first treasure: a dress pin, a ring, and three earrings.[123] He suppressed this find and, although he recorded it in his diary, he never mentioned it to the Turks or to Frank Calvert, with whom he was in almost daily contact.[124] Invigorated by the discovery of the gold in the second stratum, where he had made his other bronze discoveries, he wrote confidently to Calvert a month later that he was now progressing much faster than before and hoped to accomplish in two months a 23-meter-wide cut down to virgin soil through the whole hill. If he then saw any encouragement, he could attack the remainder from three sides at once.[125]

Schliemann wrestled with the critical problem of chronology as his excavations descended, a problem that haunted his claims from the 1870 excavation onward throughout the rest of his life [Figure 28]. If this was indeed the site of Homer's Troy, in which stratum was it to be found? The uppermost meter of debris in the topmost stratum, the fifth from the bottom, 2 meters deep, where he had found the coins, clearly was of the Roman era. Below this in the fifth stratum he found painted Greek pottery associated with beautifully hewn walls that he suggested had been built by Greek colonists who had founded a new city there. There was a big break in continuity between this historic, Greco-Roman stratum and the fourth, below it. He interpreted this fourth stratum from the bottom, 2 to 4 meters from the top, as the last pre-Hellenic level. There then was continuity between the fourth stratum and those below it in the owlish marble idols, bronze and stone tools, and the *depas*, or drinking cup, he found.[126] But that continuity posed problems of its own. The strata below the fourth seemed more advanced—a notion that was abhorrent to anyone who subscribed to the Darwinian idea of progressive development.

In both 1871 and 1872, Schliemann discovered that the four lower strata had been destroyed by fire, making their basic divisions clear, with "signs of a higher civilisation increasing with the greater depth."[127] The fourth stratum had much less pottery than its predecessors below it, and what existed was smaller and coarser still. The remains of the third stratum from the bottom were more impressive than those of the fourth, yet inferior to those below: its stone implements were rougher, its terra-cottas coarser, its owlish vessels inferior. Metal, though known, was much rarer in this stratum than it was below it, and stone was far more common.[128] Yet in the second stratum from the bottom, he found copper tools, gold, silver, and bronze pins and knives, and terra-cotta tankards.[129] He dug down to the first stratum with great expectations. Then, when he reached the first stratum above virgin soil, 10 to 15.5 meters below the surface, he found only black lustrous vessels, copper nails and rings, a silver hairpin, a stone saw, and millstones.[130] He wrote in his diary: "Nothing to be found in lowest levels and I am beginning to be discouraged. . . . I don't know what to make of the splendid pottery in the lowest levels."[131] Which stratum held Troy?

In 1871, Schliemann had written up his finds every week or two and submitted a total of five dispatches in Greek and German to an Athenian newspaper *Ephemeris ton syzeteseon* and the *Augsburger Allgemeine Zeitung*,[132] reports that, preserved in draft in the diaries and in final copies in the copybooks, Schliemann re-worked slightly and published as *Troy and Its Remains* in 1875.[133]

Evidence in favor of the metal-rich second stratum included terra-cotta vases with owlish facial features that Schliemann believed must have represented Homer's *glaukopis* Athena.[134] And the terra-cotta tankards he found there he sur-mised must be examples of Homer's two-handled drinking cup, the *depas am-phikypellon*. Yet throughout much of the 1872 season, he favored the lowest, or first stratum, with its glossy pottery. Once again he had publicized dramatic claims without proof.

In his uncertainty, Schliemann thus continued to need Calvert, and Calvert continued to offer assistance and counseling on archaeological methodology. Schliemann, as a field archaeologist, was not the autodidact he liked to claim he was. Nor was he the first to consider the implications of the stratigraphic remains at Hisarlık. He certainly was not digging at a time when "scientific methods of ex-cavation did not yet exist or were only in their very first stages," as some have claimed.[135] Although he recently has been praised for "his careful observation of pottery," he was in large part educated by Calvert. In response to Schliemann's re-peated pleas for help, Calvert again tried to guide him in the dating of strata by looking at the style of associated pottery, for which the only parallels were those Calvert had excavated at Hanay Tepe almost two decades earlier.[136] Calvert shared his views on the leveling activities in antiquity, which had affected the stratigraphy of the mound, noting the edge of the plateau, where the ashes and re-mains appeared to have been cleared off the rock and thrown down the hill toward the plain.[137]

In June 1872, almost four years after Calvert had given him permission, and midway through his third season at Hisarlık, Schliemann finally began to dig on Calvert's land, with Georgios Photidas in charge.[138] Again he worked from the steep northern slope, but this time into Calvert's field. With seventy men he opened a third platform 33 meters broad and an upper terrace 34 meters broad, quickly obliterating Calvert's earlier trenches, which Laurent already had recorded [Figures 26a, no. 5, and 26b, no. 31].[139] Schliemann described Calvert's land as completely covered with marble blocks and a square depression (34 by 23 meters) left by the ransacking of the "marble-seeking Turks."[140] Immediately, he set to work among the foundations of the early Hellenistic temple that Calvert had identified as belonging to Athena and began looking for its predecessor, the one visited by Xerxes and later by Alexander the Great during his invasion of Asia.[141] On 11 June, Schliemann hit upon a splendid piece of architectural sculpture, a marble metope bearing an image of Helios, or Apollo, in a chariot and flanked by triglyphs [Figure 30].[142] It was an important find, but it added to the stress that had been building in the relationship between Calvert and Schliemann.

As they debated the identity of the figure, Calvert considered the legal impli-cations of such a significant find occurring on his land. Because Schliemann's permit applied only to the field belonging to the government, he advised Schlie-

Figure 30. Helios Metope. Schliemann (1874b), plate 30.

mann to obtain a second permit for excavating on private property with the pro-prietor's consent to "prevent marbles from falling into the hands of the Phillistines." With a second permit he could "snap your fingers at the Govt. and they will get nothing . . . at present we ought to try and prevent anything falling into the hands of the Authorities."[143] His advice reflects the general reaction of Europeans to the more stringent antiquities legislation and the bias that many Europeans held against the Turks. Calvert's previous good relations with the Ottomans soured after 1870.

Immediately, the pragmatic businessman wanted to lighten the metope for transport and suggested that they hire a marble sawyer to cut off the triglyphs on either side of the sculpture, which was 2 meters long and 86 centimeters high. Horrified, Calvert prevailed upon him to turn it over and leave it intact lest he destroy its aesthetic value. At this point the haggling began, for by the terms of their gentleman's agreement and its equal division of finds, with a unique sculpture, one would have to buy the other out or both would have to sell to a third party. Having no means of evaluating the sculpture locally, Schliemann, knowing Calvert's view of Newton, slyly volunteered to have him look at it.[144] Calvert responded that Newton was "one of the greatest screws," someone who always offered a tenth of the real price of a thing and then asked for something to be deducted or some other object to be thrown into the bargain.[145] From his behavior toward Calvert concerning the Helios Metope, it seems that Schliemann decided to emulate Newton. In the same letter, Calvert suggested £500 as a reasonable price, or even "under the mark." Discounting the £20 expenses of transporting it to London, Calvert estimated the worth of his half-interest at £240 but generously volunteered to take £125. Schliemann countered with an appallingly low estimate of 200 francs, or £80, as the total value, offering £40 for Calvert's half and adding magnanimously that he never would have made the offer had he not found it himself.[146] Remarkably, Calvert, though offended,[147] agreed to accept £50 for his share, which Schliemann assured him was more than half the price the metope would bring on the European market. Out of this Schliemann made Calvert assume transportation expenses to the port.[148] After Frederick Calvert facilitated the loading of the marble on 3 August and the Calverts smoothed its way with the port authorities, in the end, Calvert received only £49.[149]

During the problematic negotiations on how to handle the Helios Metope and Schliemann's aggressive behavior, Calvert's enthusiasm permanently slumped. Concerned about the treatment of his part of the site, he resumed his cautionary statements concerning excavation,[150] advising Schliemann to test the eastern portion with a narrow trench as a reconnaissance. Schliemann should not open large trenches, but small ones, in which two men might work abreast and throw out earth on each side. Only if he saw anything promising might he expand the cutting.[151] These remarks went unheeded; in six weeks, Schliemann had destroyed all but one of Calvert's original trenches, rendering all but invisible the history of Calvert's own inquiry at the site.

In spite of the magnificent discovery of the Helios Metope, Schliemann was not satisfied. He had not found the predecessor of Athena's temple. Instead, where Calvert had suggested that the foundations were laid on rock, Schliemann had found only rock-hard ash—debris from animal sacrifices—as his excavations descended deeper and deeper. He still had not found the Troy that he was seeking. Nothing yet had appeared that was comparable to the architecture or pottery of Mycenae or Thera. Schliemann was plagued with self-doubt and fear of being made a laughingstock. Having now twice declared that he had found Troy and having built up unrealistic expectations in the academic world, Schliemann feared the subsequent ridicule and humiliation. "To stop my excavation now . . . would not do, for the whole civilized world, and you [Calvert] more than anybody else would laugh at me."[152] But on 19 July, he struck a 6-meter-high wall built on bedrock. With great excitement, he immediately christened it "The Great Tower of Ilium" [Figure 26b, no. 4] and assigned it to his first stratum, although he subsequently changed his mind.[153] To strengthen the claim that his first stratum contained Homer's Troy, he bundled together the gold jewelry found on 17 May in the second stratum and attributed it, together with a skeleton found in August in the first, to the first stratum, allowing him to romanticize his find as "Ilium." When Schliemann subsequently chastised Calvert for lack of interest in his "godly wall," the latter responded tactfully on 24 July that he was not indifferent to the discovery of the Trojan walls, and it was only because he had not been sure whether Schliemann's labors had been crowned with success that he had not offered him his congratulations. After all, Calvert had endured several such claims. He then ended on a hopeful note, saying that he would be glad to see the mystery of Troy solved and that he truly commended Schliemann for his perseverance and expenditures: "You have succeeded in doing what no other person has attempted on such a large scale." Here was Schliemann's strength—his total commitment of time and resources as well as his persistence.[154]

By the end of the season, Calvert was so disillusioned with Schliemann that he did not even care to be present at the distribution of the finds. Instead, he recommended that Schliemann's major domo, Nicholas Yannakis, choose for him.[155] Schliemann, by contrast, was both exhausted and exhilarated. He now wistfully claimed that he wished that some government or society might undertake the burden of the excavations. "The expenses of excavating Ilium are . . . too great for private means, and I hope that a company will be formed, or that some government will decide to continue my excavations."[156]

With the acquisition of the Helios Metope, the most important sculpture Schliemann ever found at Hisarlık, the scales had begun to tip toward Schliemann. In Berlin, Ernst Curtius wrote to ask Schliemann for a photograph of the metope, asking for a plaster cast of it and suggesting that with the promise of sculpture in return, the German government might be interested in underwriting his excavations.[157] Schliemann declared proudly, "As regards the more than a hundred thousand objects which I have brought to light . . . used by ancient tribes, I venture to say that I have revealed a new world to archaeology." From this point on, he began to take a new responsibility toward his finds.[158]

His pride was not without justification. His excavation of four major pre-Hellenic strata at Hisarlık was pioneering. His persistence in plowing through the rock-hard ash beneath the temple had rewarded him with the riches of Anatolian prehistory. He had surpassed Calvert and had discovered a relative chronology in more than 15 meters of successive strata of human habitation. This was indeed a tremendous achievement. Yet he was determined to push his achievement further in order "to prove that the Iliad was based on facts."[159] He hoped "that, as a reward for my enormous expense and all my privations, annoyances, and sufferings in this wilderness, but above all for my important discoveries, the civilized world will acknowledge my right to re-christen this sacred locality; and in the name of divine Homer. . . . I give it the name of Troy and Ilium, and I call the Acropolis . . . by the name of the Pergamos of Troy."[160]

Excavations stopped on 14 August, and Schliemann returned to Athens, where the metope now ornamented his garden. Back in Athens, he anticipated the next season, when he would work from west to east, hoping to uncover one kilometer of the "divine walls of Troy."[161] Most of all, he wished to find the predecessor of Lysimachus's Temple of Athena and a temple to Apollo that he believed lay in the southeast area. Then he would clear the "Scaean Gate."

In October, the Calverts hosted Sir John Lubbock, the acclaimed author of *Prehistoric Times,* at Batak Farm. After visiting Hisarlık at sunset, Calvert arranged a tour of the Troad for him, during which he excavated the tumulus of Hector at Pınarbaşı.[162] Calvert delighted in the presence of the eminent prehistorian, who most likely shared his broad research interests in entomology and botany with his avid host. Subsequently, Calvert developed interests in these areas, and Lubbock would facilitate his research and publication in these fields.

Having heard from Calvert about Lubbock's visit, Schliemann wrote Lubbock himself, promising to send him in the coming year a weekly report on his progress at Hisarlık. In the course of describing his own work at the site, he referred to the southeastern area of the mound (Calvert's one extant trench) as a "small excavation . . . almost on the surface," with no mention of Calvert as excavator of that or any other area.[163]

In November 1872, Mac Veagh's successor, the recently appointed U.S. minister George Henry Boker (1823–1890), stopped in Athens on the way to his new post and visited Schliemann and his collection. In December, Boker reacted to the unprecedented effort that Schliemann had expended at Hisarlık: "The photographs give me a very distinct idea of the magnitude of your works. You seem to have engaged in an effort to disembowel the earth. The air of the figure leaning on his spade, and gazing at the tower of Ilium, seems to say: 'Troy, Hell, or China!' " [See lithograph, Figure 31.][164]

Schliemann had begun to collect antiquities casually in 1865, picking up curios from the Orient, and more seriously in 1868 in Ithaca. These he kept in a little collection in

Figure 31. Lithograph of the great north-south trench. Schliemann (1874b), plate 110.

Paris. In 1870 he bought inscriptions, vases, and stone implements on Thera and Therassia, as well as coins from the plain of Troy.[165] If Calvert had ever had delusions of selling his collection to Schliemann, these hopes were dashed by the man himself, who blandly explained his modus operandi in August 1871: "I never offered to buy your things for I did not want to cheat you because you have many very valuable objects whilst I only buy if I can do so exceedingly cheap."[166] Schliemann then closed his letter on a somewhat self-righteous note: "I prefer spending my money on excavations."

By the end of his 1872 season, Schliemann claimed to have unearthed more than one hundred thousand objects. He boasted about his Trojan museum, which contained a vast collection of objects from all depths of the mound. He wrote to John Turtle Wood that he had bought a house where he would establish his "pre-historic museum."[167] With the acquisition of the Helios Metope, his competitive efforts to create a collection were beginning to pay off, and they received the attention of various dignitaries. To publicize and celebrate his achievement, Schliemann was having casts of the Helios Metope sent to major museums and offered one to Charles Newton, who once had greeted Schliemann's announcement that he would excavate Hisarlık "with scepticism and a hearty laugh."[168] By November 1872, Newton wished to visit the Schliemanns at Troy.[169] Now those travelers who stopped at the Dardanelles to see the Calvert Collection would stop in Athens to see Schliemann's rival collection as well.[170]

Schliemann had built up his collection, as Calvert had, primarily from his own excavations. Reneging on their agreement of splitting the finds equally, Schliemann coveted and kept the most important finds for himself,[171] shortchanging Calvert of his share of the finds or manipulating him, as, for instance, with regard to the undervalued Helios Metope in 1872. He maintained this approach with important historical inscriptions found in 1873, denying their importance to get a better deal.[172] In fact, Schliemann was treating Calvert much as he was treating the Ottoman government, the proprietor of the other half of the mound.

In addition to their numerous squabbles and antagonisms, a more serious rift had developed between Calvert and Schliemann, caused by important differences in their interpretation of Schliemann's excavations. As a gentleman, Calvert had shared his opinions with Schliemann privately. As early as the Curtius visit in September 1871, Calvert had reminded Schliemann that he disagreed with his dating of later walls to Homer's era. On 24 February 1872, as a response to Schliemann's dating of significantly earlier material to the time of Homer, Calvert again made it clear that he did not support all of Schliemann's ideas. In that letter, he declared that he was sure that the Homeric site would be found, but that he could not reconcile the vases found in any of the "stone implement strata" with the Homeric period. "They are too remote in age." Consequently, he concluded, there must be a "great gap missing in the history of Ilium or Hissarlik."[173] A year later, Calvert would prove there was: in Schliemann's excavations, he pointed out, "a most important link was missing between 1800 and 700 B.C., forming a gap of over a thousand years, including the date of the Trojan War, B.C. 1193–1184" [Figure 28].[174] It was a gap that Schliemann never satisfactorily could explain and that required much labor by his successors to understand [Figure 29].

Only after the accelerating series of betrayals by Schliemann did Calvert speak up publicly to set the record straight at the urging of his friends.[175] In a 4 February 1873 article, "Excavations in the Troad," in the *Levant Herald*, Calvert addressed his own contribution to the Troy debate, as well as the results so far attained by Schliemann.[176]

After summarizing the ancient authors on the subject of the location of Troy and discussing modern writers' opinions, Calvert announced that he would confine himself to recent archaeological work in the Troad and to deductions to be drawn from it.[177] Noting the work at Pınarbaşı, he focused on his own excavations at Hisarlık, where he had found "pottery of different ages; but none anterior to the Greek of the seventh to sixth centuries B.C.," pushing back the history of Ilium by "150 to 250 years prior to the visit of Xerxes." He noted further, with regard to his own excavations, that the foundations of the Athena temple and the wall of Lysimachus were built on "accumulated rubbish," beneath which, although he dug to a total depth of 3 to 4 meters, he never reached virgin soil.

"Mr. H. Schliemann, in 1870–1872, continued the excavations I had commenced, reaching bed rock at sixty-seven feet" he declared. Below rubbish mixed with sherds of pottery of the sixth and seventh centuries B.C., which Calvert had found in a stratum equivalent to the lower meter of Schliemann's fifth, or uppermost, stratum, Schliemann had found "vases of an earlier date" in "a continuous superposition of stratum on stratum of rubbish, with remains of an entirely different character." Here were numerous coarse and fine polished vases, both handmade and thrown on a wheel, along with innumerable flint flakes and saws and polished stone celts or axheads, hammers, hand mills, or querns, spindle whorls, bone tools, and shells. He compared this accumulation to those in the shell mounds of Denmark cited by Lubbock in *Prehistoric Times*. This was clearly prehistoric material such as he recently had found washed by rain out of the lower level of Hanay Tepe. In these strata, metals were "scarce." Beyond the several molds for casting tools and weapons, Calvert noted a few weapons, tools, and other small objects in bronze, as well as "some trifling ornaments in gold and silver wire." As to the houses of the lower strata, Calvert observed that they were "roughly put together," some hardly deserving to be designated as walls, and mud brick structures whose forms had not been preserved.[178] He characterized the workmanship on Schliemann's great Tower of Ilium as "inferior."

To arrive at a date for the earlier strata, Calvert adroitly invoked parallels from the ancient Near East. Since implements of chipped and polished flint such as knives, arrowheads, axes, and hammers "were found together with bronze, gold, lead, and even iron in the tombs at Ur,[179] the capital of ancient Chaldea (B.C. 2,200–1,800), it is to be inferred by analogy, that the stone implement strata discovered by Mr. Schliemann are not referable to a later date." By using the meager sources available in 1873, Calvert indeed hit upon the correct dating of contemporary materials. And as a further proof of the early date of the stratum, Calvert remarked that Homer never mentioned stone tools, but only metal ones.[180] Thus, Calvert saw incontestable proof of the existence of a prehistoric settlement at Hisarlık "at a very early date, several centuries prior to the Trojan War."

Here lay the crux of the problem that plagued all of Schliemann's claims to have discovered the location of Homeric Troy, both those he had made to date and those he was to make in the future, a problem that also had troubled Calvert as early as the 1860s. The Greco-Roman levels of the fifth stratum lay directly over the prehistoric strata of the fourth, and Schliemann could not place any relics of an intervening epoch between that indicated by the presence of prehistoric stone implements and that shown by the Greek pottery of the Archaic period. Characteristically, Calvert dropped this bombshell quietly. His prescient assessment of the Hisarlık excavations was balanced, not malicious. Calvert's observation of the gap was incredibly astute, even more so since it was made prior to the major excavations at Ur.[181] Because of the similar finds in the prehistoric levels at Hisarlık and at Hanay Tepe, he concluded that because of its partial contemporaneity with the prehistoric remains found at Hisarlık, Hanay Tepe could not be a Homeric tomb of the Trojans.

It was possible, he continued circumspectly, that Hisarlık had been a ruin when Homer wrote. Anticipating the results of the excavations in the plateau below the citadel more than a century later, Calvert wrote that the large excavations at Hisarlık "are but a trifle" in comparison with the vast extent of accumulated artificial soil elevated above the plain and extending far beyond the hill.[182]

Calvert closed his article with the generous wish that his "energetic friend Mr. Schliemann, in his further contemplated researches, may be able to complete the missing link, and discover the lost Homeric Troy, for if ever the world-famed city existed, the probability is that Hissarlik marks its site." In this newspaper article of less than two pages, Calvert had demolished Schliemann's basic premise and reduced his excavations to "a trifle." What seems to have been a well-intentioned attempt to set the record straight, however, soon had major repercussions, mainly for its author.

Amazingly, Calvert notified Schliemann of the article and promised to send him a copy. In the same letter, he warned Schliemann of the new orders "to prevent the exportation of antiquities."[183] At first puzzled at the content of Calvert's article, Schliemann responded on 9 February that he had read the article with "*very great interest.*" Then he proceeded to debate all of Calvert's points. But because he was trying to secure historical inscriptions from Calvert, he toned down his initial reaction.[184]

Apparently unaware of the impact of his article on Schliemann,[185] Calvert answered some of Schliemann's objections and digressed rather pedantically to explain the concept of *terminus post quem* dating to his colleague: "It is not the *most ancient article* found in a rubbish heap that proves its date, but the most modern—this is an accepted fact by all archaeologists." Then he frankly challenged Schliemann's claim that his four prehistoric levels represented four different nations at Hisarlık. "I consider the *prehistoric* remains of the different strata to be of *one race*—and the accumulation of ages." Schliemann weakened his own argument, "for if the wall you discovered is of Homeric Troy, what nations could you assign as the subsequent occupants of the site + prior to the Lydian kings?" Finally, he declared, "In these days of materialism everything must be *proved* and the days of enthusiasm are past—and what alone is now accepted, is *fact.* . . . My ideas solely are to establish the truth." He closed with a recommendation that Schliemann read the works published on prehistoric remains.[186] One can only imagine how insulted Schliemann would have been at that.[187]

Calvert's article pointing out the thousand-year gap soon was reprinted back in Germany in the *Augsburger Allgemeine Zeitung*. At the time, Schliemann had been haggling with Calvert over the sale of three inscriptions from Calvert's field. Characteristically, Schliemann waited until he had secured and shipped them before venting his rage for what he considered high treason on Calvert's part.[188] He wrote to Calvert that it would require long articles from Mr. Burnouf and other scholars "to let evaporate the wrong [Calvert] had done to the sake of Troy" and to him in his tremendous labors.[189] Schliemann was affronted: "You thought that a man in my position could write anything else but the sacred truth?" Calvert, however, knew better.

After almost five years of increasing friction between these two very different men, the seemingly inevitable breach finally occurred when Calvert stood up for himself in public and questioned Schliemann's claims. The outraged Schliemann furiously accused Calvert of having trampled his excavation results into the mud by his erroneous reports at a time when the whole civilized world was waiting with feverish anxiety for the result of his three-year struggle. He continued that he was preparing to upset the errors contained in Calvert's article and to counteract "the immense wrong it was calculated to produce to science." To prevent the lifelong rupture of their friendship, Schliemann offered to give Calvert a hundred men with which to dig. But if Calvert refused to accept Schliemann's proposal, Schliemann would consider it "a fearful insult and would rather die."[190] On the same day, Schliemann damned Calvert in his report to the press,[191] ridiculing Calvert's excavations as two small cuttings and denying that he had continued Calvert's excavations. Furthermore, he said that he had dug the site of the Athena temple only because a depression 33.9 by 22.8 meters left by pillagers had betrayed it to him and denigrated Calvert's work by saying that it by no means gave any idea of the existence of such a temple.[192] On 1 April, he wrote a scathing letter to Heinrich Brockhaus, his publisher, claiming that Calvert's article was "crawling with false assertions" and "rubbish."[193]

The violence of Schliemann's reaction masked his own equivocal treatment of the pre-Hellenic strata. Although he had spoken of Andromache watching the plain from his "Great Tower of Ilium," he himself had once claimed that the material of that level predated Homer by millennia. He was well aware of the weaknesses in his claims, but in his search for a quick solution, he had had to choose a level as Priam's. Continually vacillating in his choice of the stratum he would claim to contain Homeric Troy, he had done his best to make sense of the truncated stratigraphy, with its thousand-year gap. He even in some cases had bundled his finds from different levels to augment his argument.

As Calvert had suspected as early as 1872, leveling had occurred above the ash layer, just beneath the temple foundations, shaving off exactly the level that

Calvert and Schliemann had sought. Later builders had removed the previous stratum's palace, temples, and archives to prepare a level space for their own structures.

Just over a week after their break, Calvert would begin to discover the full extent of the duplicity that Schliemann had used to ensnare him. While staying with Ernest Abbott, the wealthy mining entrepreneur, in Constantinople in late March,[194] he met many antiquarian and professional people and learned from them that Schliemann had not only swindled him with regard to negotiations over the Helios Metope, but also boasted of it. He wrote to Schliemann that "they informed me the value you fixed on it was £150,000 but that was too high a figure as frs. 25,000 to 30,000 [£1000–£1200] was its market value." Ever the gentleman, Calvert still tried to allow Schliemann the benefit of the doubt: "This latter estimate however, is 10 to 12 times the amount you *swore* to me was the value, and I cannot believe you could have been aware at the time of its great worth." The latter figure would have been worth £14,000, or $21,000, today.[195]

Calvert apparently had a good case against Schliemann under English and American law if he pressed a claim.[196] But any claim would have been settled in a consular court between British and American consul generals. Calvert understandably was loathe to submit himself to the indignity and danger of appearing before the same Constantinople court officials who had convicted him and his brother.[197] In addition, Calvert may have been aware of Schliemann's considerable experience in the courts of the United States and Russia, where he had briefly acted as judge. Schliemann knew how to use the courts and lawyers and had done so to obtain favorable decisions in the past.

Calvert's only recourse seemed to be to try to recover his losses by attempting to hold Schliemann to the code of a gentleman, a code that, however much Schliemann yearned for respectability, it was not part of his character to honor. He told Schliemann on 14 April that his friends were

> of the opinion that you are in no ways *morally* released to give me half the value of this marble—the assertion on your oath as per letter of 18th July last being sufficient between gentlemen to decide the value of an object, notwithstanding previous ideas on the subject entertained on either side . . . you are not morally released . . . otherwise you leave yourself open to the accusation that you have taken undue advantage of me and I would be sorry to be obliged by my friends to publish your letters and show how you obtained the bas relief in question for £49 Stg.[198]

Calvert's suspicions are confirmed by a letter Schliemann wrote to Emile Burnouf in which he offered the relief to France for 100,000 French francs.[199] As the disagreement escalated, Schliemann began writing his correspondence in French, the formal language of diplomatic correspondence, and thus a signal of chilly remoteness.

> I do not sell antiquity, in effect, you can be sure that one who is in the state of expending each year, during five months, 400 francs daily to realize the grand idea of

his life of discovering Troy, you can be sure that this man does not sell antiquities that he has reclaimed with pains from the depths of Ilium. . . . Nothing will ever be sold of my Trojan antiquities, because I leave all my collection by will to the charming Greek nation, one estimates 200,000 francs for constructing a grand museum for installing part of my collection. . . . A deal made is sacred one does not go back and one cannot, such is the usage of the world.[200]

Calvert volleyed back in English three days later. "You are mistaken, I think, in making the affair of the marble a commercial transaction, for it is not one, the basis of our agreement being founded on mutual confidence as gentlemen . . . when you gave me your word of honour, that it was not worth more than the latter sum—as a gentleman, I accepted your statement." He proposed a gentleman's solution: "I regret exceedingly the misunderstanding that has arisen between us and would suggest some method by which it might be removed. Suppose we each ask a friend to meet the other and discuss the matter—and abide by the decision (that is if they agree) they may come to."[201]

The quarrel became increasingly nasty. After Schliemann rejected Calvert's proposal, on 20 April Calvert wrote Schliemann a more blunt letter. "You are mistaken in considering a bargain cannot by law be rescinded under any circumstances for there are several exceptions to this general rule, and which are applicable in the present instance," he threatened, reiterating that it had been concluded "on your solemn oath and word of honour as a gentleman. . . . I therefore hold you both legally and morally responsible for the difference in value of the marble and of the amount paid to me by you."

He now told Schliemann that future finds on his land would not suffer the same fate as the Helios Metope. He wanted to reconsider "the best mode of disposal of any future marbles that may be discovered for I wish to counsel the matter, as your mode of dealing makes me take all due precaution."[202] At this point, perhaps worried about a lawsuit, Schliemann ceased excavating in Calvert's field.[203]

After two months of bitter recrimination concerning Calvert's article and Schliemann's underhandedness, Schliemann set out to attack the one thing Calvert valued most, his reputation. In late April, Frank Calvert, acting as *gérant*, or manager, for his brother James, opened another scathing letter from Schliemann. In it, the excavator complained about Calvert's odious harassments and threatened to appeal for protection to George Henry Boker, the United States minister in Constantinople, James's superior and Schliemann's ally, if James Calvert would not represent him against his own brother.[204] James responded to Schliemann that he would not interfere but regarded Schliemann's method of appraisal of objects distant from a market as "erroneous."[205] The very next item in Schliemann's copybook was a letter to Boker protesting Calvert's actions, complaining that he was making "a fearful row" and invoking Boker's "power of protection." Schliemann threatened a lawsuit of his own. After noting "the continued vexations" and "the attacks of Mr. Frank Calvert," he let Boker know that James, the U.S. consul, was no longer resident at the Dardanelles, where he was supposed to be, but was rather in Constantinople.[206] Boker responded, "I shall not permit that you shall suffer injustice at the hands of anyone. If Mr. Calvert should press you in the above affair, you can receive protection and redress by an appeal to the Court of the Consulate General."

An original draft of Calvert's own response shows his tortured reaction to Schliemann's treachery and ingratitude.

> With regard to future excavations in my field in the interest of science, I shall not stop them on account of the misunderstanding between us. . . . I feel much hurt by the expressions you make use of in your letter to my brother. If I give you "tracasseries" [pin pricks—an amazingly condescending term, in this context], you must remember that it is in upholding what I consider my right, and that I have done all in my power to assist you in your works since you first arrived—and always sacrificed my time when your interests were concerned—if now, you consider you have no further need of me, it is very ungracious of you to use that word, in recompense for all that I have done for you—and remember *if it was not for me* and the excavations made previously in my field (purchased *expressly* for the purpose) you would never have undertaken the work and reaped the benefit of my experience. . . . At the same time, for the sake of science, I assure you I will not distract you in your work, nor bring an action against you before consulting a lawyer, and if he sees that justice is on my side, not until you have finished your labours and returned to Athens—I would prefer infinitely to leave the affair to Mr. Boker's decision. . . . I place this confidence in you, that, if I am present or not, at the excavations, the result will be the same.[207]

On 4 May 1873, Schliemann haughtily answered this poignant letter from Frank Calvert with a formal response, again in French. In it he feigned interest in reopening excavations along the north slope of Calvert's field and in his theater but demurred, having been dissuaded by his wife: "We cannot handle this gigantic enterprise in view of the process whereof you threaten us at the end of our excavations."[208] Before the month was out, Schliemann had discovered Priam's Treasure. Schliemann's desperation over the problems with his claim to have found the walls of Troy and his clear loathing of the man who pointed them out may have contributed to the vehement zeal with which he promoted that discovery. After that, he had no need of Calvert. Relations between them broke down for more than five years.

CHAPTER EIGHT

"A little broken pottery"
Priam's Treasure and Its Repercussions

Just as Schliemann publicly had staged himself as the discoverer of Homeric Troy, obscuring Frank Calvert's contributions to his efforts and denying the questions Calvert raised about them, he also wished to eclipse the Calvert Collection, the premier collection of antiquities of the Troad for more than two decades. With the discovery of Priam's Treasure, Schliemann attained that goal. With it, as well, he not only consolidated his claim in the public mind to be the discoverer of Troy, but eclipsed Calvert's own professional reputation as the premier archaeologist of the Troad. The golden jewelry captivated the public and the professionals alike.[1]

By spring 1873, British interest in Troy was increasing. Sir John Lubbock read a paper on his visit to the Troad and tumulus excavation to the Society of Antiquaries on 6 March 1873. Although the meeting passed a resolution recommending to have the tumuli excavated, one member protested, "In the case of the Troad there is little or no chance of acquiring any possession for the public which would repay the search. . . . The question is: are excavations undertaken for the purpose of illustrating the "Iliad" a proper object for the expenditure of public money? . . . In my judgment they are not."[2] Hisarlık soon would prove him wrong.

Characteristically, with the benefit of hindsight, Schliemann later said that in 1873 he had had a premonition of great things to come. He had gone out to the Troad on 31 January and sat at his writing desk in February with the ink freezing in his pen and "nothing to keep us warm except our enthusiasm for the great work of discovering Troy."[3] Beginning in February on the south slope of the western half of the mound, he employed 158 workmen; he estimated that he had removed 8,400 cubic meters of debris from the temple alone.[4] He had a tough time keeping up with the tremendous volume of finds but managed to send reports of his excavations and finds to the London *Times* and the *Augsburger Allgemeine Zeitung*.

Schliemann excavated simultaneously in the northeast, southeast, and northwest areas of the citadel. Desperate to find more architectural sculpture from the early Hellenistic temple, he even dug through his own dump in vain.[5] And once again, he discovered Homer's Troy. Beneath the temple he once again found four strata, or "cities." Earlier, he had thought the lowest, or first, level was that of Priam. Now he changed his mind, admitting that in 1871 and 1872 he had destroyed a large portion of the city in digging down to the first level, "for I broke down all the house walls in the higher strata which obstructed my way."[6] Now he assigned the second level from the bottom of the mound to the time of Homer. It was in this burned stratum that he had found the owl-faced vessels he had identified with Ilian Minerva and the *depas amphikypellon* mentioned by Homer, the gold, silver, and lead objects, and copper molds and stone tools. But Calvert had written that none of these prehistoric "stone implement-bearing strata" could date later than 1800 B.C., and since this was the second from the bottom, it necessarily predated 1800 B.C. by a considerable margin. Thus, it also antedated the time of the Trojan War by perhaps as much as a millennium. The thousand-year gap simply would not go away.

In the southwest, he uncovered more of the fortification wall discovered the previous year, which he now associated with the second level and Homer's Troy, a gateway that he quickly dubbed "the Scaean Gate," and a paved street that ascended from the exterior into the citadel [Figure 26b, no. 37].[7] He dug deep trenches right up to the front doors of the houses he had constructed for the excavation. A stone building to the northwest of the gateway and contemporary with it he called "the Palace of Priam" [Figure 26b, no. 7].[8] "Everywhere I find the ashes of destruction," he declared dramatically.[9] In March and April, he excavated on Calvert's land to the southeast and found a gold leaf-shaped pendant, also in the rich second stratum.[10] All the time he was closely watched by his so-called "dirty, Argus-eyed" watchman, the government representative who kept track of discoveries.

During the course of his 1873 excavations, Schliemann made twenty borings into the plateau where Calvert had indicated a lower city must exist. But his southerly *sondages* from west to east uncovered only first-millennium remains postdating the thousand-year gap. Against his will, he was forced to admit that if this was Priam's famous city, as he claimed, it encompassed only that small area within the second-stratum fortification walls on the citadel of Hisarlık. "I had wished to be able to make it a thousand times larger, but I value truth above everything," he now piously declared. "Homer is an epic poet, and not an historian. . . . [He] made no excavations to bring [those remains] to light. He knew of these monuments of immortal fame only from hearsay."[11] By 30 May, Schliemann was exhausted and ready to quit, having moved 250 cubic meters of debris. He had just found a small "treasure" on 23 May at the southeast end of his northwestern trench. Needing positive publicity, he published the silver jar and cup and fragments of a bronze teapot immediately in his next report.[12] He wrote his son Sergei that his finds would make a beautiful museum, with never-before-seen artifacts collected in the depths of Ilium. "Now that we have realized the great idea of our lives, we will close the excavations here in Troy forever on the 15 June." He would create a Museum Schliemann in Athens and give the entire collection to the Greek nation.[13]

Before breakfast on 31 May, while work was proceeding simultaneously in five trenches,[14] Schliemann uncovered a remarkable assemblage as he straightened the side of his trench near the site of the treasure he had found a week earlier, behind the "hellenic tower" and northwest of the "Scaean Gate" [Figure 26b, no. 42].[15] Outside the fortification wall of his second stratum he had found a "little place built around with stones and having flat stones to cover it."[16] First he saw a large copper vessel, with the glint of gold behind: Priam's Treasure.

Working quickly, with the help of Yannakis, Schliemann removed what he had found before it drew the attention of the workmen or the government representative. In a later account he rewrote the circumstances, replacing Yannakis with Sophia. Describing the danger of extracting the treasure in secret, he remarked that it would have been impossible "without the help of my dear wife, who stood by me ready to pack the things which I cut out in her shawl and to carry them away."[17] But Sophia was not there. She had, in fact, been present for only a month, from mid-April, when she had been assaulted by Schliemann's overseer, Photidas, to 7 May, when she fled back to Athens upon receiving news that her father had suddenly died. But Schliemann added Sophia to the story because he was "endeavoring to make an archaeologist of her" and sensed that she would enhance the romantic drama he was creating.[18]

According to his own story, Schliemann exclaimed that it was his birthday and plied the representative with cognac while he attended to the find, carried it to his wooden house, and locked it up. Alerted by one of the workers, the representative immediately demanded in the name of the sultan that Schliemann open all his chests and cupboards, but Schliemann refused and threw him out.[19] As Schliemann watched him leave for the Dardanelles to secure authority and reinforcements, a German scholar, Heinrich Bulthaupt from Bremen, arrived with a letter of introduction from Frederick Calvert.[20] Immensely distracted, Schliemann gave him a tour around the site and then penned a desperate and duplicitous letter to Frederick, who was in the habit of storing material for Schliemann at his farm and who had facilitated the export of his Helios Metope.

> I am closely watched and expect that the turkish watchman who is angry at me, I do not know for what reason, will search my house tomorrow. I therefore take the liberty to deposit with you 6 baskets and a bag begging you will kindly *lock* them up and *not* allow by any means the turks to touch them. . . . The villagers betray me to the turk so that I cannot anymore take their horses. So, when I want to remove the baskets, pray, lend me for three hours in the night three horses . . . please do not refuse for I am quite in despair; having spent here more than 100,000 franks I cannot take away a little broken pottery.[21]

As he returned to his packing, Schliemann was again interrupted, this time by the visit of Gustav von Eckenbrecher, the Smyrna physician who had theorized thirty years earlier that Troy must lay near Ilium Novum. Schliemann gave him lodgings and then excused himself and returned to packing the treasure.[22] After sending off the treasure with Yannakis to asylum at Akça Köy [Figure 7], he relaxed with Eckenbrecher and Bulthaupt.[23] Later that day he reported to his publisher Heinrich Brockhaus that he had found a large copper container filled with silver and gold vases and cups that he had not even had time to count, a "champagne-glass" of solid gold with two handles and a rounded foot, flat pieces of silver, and knives. To this he added a thick silver vase that he had found eight days earlier.[24] Two days later, he described the treasure briefly from memory in his diary: "copper cauldron, a shallow bronze pan, bronze kettle, eight spearheads, 13 bronze daggers, 14 flat axes, 3 chisels and silver and gold."[25]

On 6 June, Yannakis went by night to Frederick Calvert's farm with Demetriou, one of Schliemann's Greek foremen, and transported the material that Frederick had kept for one week to the north-coast inlet whence they were loaded, using the same ship and harbor as before with the Helios Metope.[26] Again Schliemann avoided Ottoman customs officials. He enjoined the shipping agent at Syros, Tzerlent, to guard the cargo and to keep the crates from being opened, explaining, "I am a benefactor of Greece, because everyone is stealing antiquities from Greece, but I have been working for three years in the Troad on behalf of the glory of Greece and I send all the antiquities I excavate to Greece and am bequeathing them to the Greek nation."[27] Demetriou accompanied the treasure to Athens. Once the treasure was safely out of Turkey, Schliemann confided news of his coup to Boker. But because he had been forced to send it off immediately "to save it from the Turkish watchman," he confessed that he had "only a faint idea of what it contains." He mentioned "a huge goblet with two gigantic handles and a round basis . . . of pure gold."[28]

Before returning to Athens himself, Schliemann demolished the wooden dig house where he had been living, which was surrounded by deep excavation trenches, to make sure he was leaving no part of the treasure behind.[29] By 26 June, he was back in Athens, unpacking and cataloguing the immense treasure, which included, besides the bronze items and the golden sauceboat or "champagne-glass": "two gold vessels, one of electrum, and nine of silver, six silver ingots, six gold bracelets, two gold headdresses, one golden diadem, four golden basket-earrings with pendant chains, 56 golden shell-earrings, and 8750 gold beads, sequins, and studs."[30] He set up the finds on shelves and had them photographed [Figure 32].[31] Schliemann then invited Athenians to come to his house and see the treasure of Priam.[32] Later, he had Sophia photographed in the headdress and earrings and distributed the famous photo to family and friends [Figure 33].[33]

The discovery and successful smuggling of Priam's Treasure was a tonic to Schliemann's sense of self-worth. He wrote to Frederick that "this treasure of a mythic city's mythic king of the mythic heroic age . . . is much larger than I was led to believe" and "wherever I may excavate you may rest assured that I shall do nothing on a small scale, because having past all my former life in vast commercial operations, I cannot live without working now to the same extent in the field of science."[34]

One must place Schliemann's smuggling of the treasure in the context of the times and customary practice and also consider European bias against the Turks.

Trésor de Priam découvert à 8½ mètres de profondeur

Figure 32. Priam's Treasure on the shelves of the Schliemann house in Athens.
Schliemann (1874b), plate 204.

Figure 33. Sophia Schliemann wearing a Trojan diadem. Courtesy of the
Gennadius Library of the American School of Classical Studies, Athens.

Since 1869, when Schliemann had acquired American citizenship in order to divorce his first wife, he had looked to the American legation for advice and help.
Since Mac Veagh had been recalled in June 1871 and for nine months the legation
was without a minister, John P. Brown acted as the senior official.

Brown was an "old hand" in Constantinople, having served as dragoman, or
interpreter, to the U.S. legation since at least 1840. The post of dragoman carried

great power because linguistically crippled diplomats who rarely learned Turkish helplessly entrusted the momentous affairs of state, as well as their individual concerns, to members of this local elite who were fluent in speaking and writing Turkish and savvy in the ways of negotiation. "The dragomans may be considered . . . as the nobility of the kings. No aristocracy . . . equals them in self-importance," as one traveler put it. All *rayas* employed by ambassadors regarded them as "the ambassadors' prime minister." The office was virtually hereditary, and the powerful families all intermarried. Thus, they knew all the secrets of embassy affairs and the ambassadors were "impotent without them."[35] Because of their power and high profile, dragomen drew a great deal of jealous criticism, particularly those at Constantinople and Smyrna.[36] Although within the confines of the U.S. legation Brown was distrusted by American colleagues, in the local community he was respected as a man of letters intimately familiar with the Ottoman world.[37]

In the midst of considerable correspondence with Brown, Schliemann looked for a loophole that would allow him to avoid dividing the finds equally with the government, since he had paid for the excavations himself. He inquired of Brown about possible exceptions to the Ottoman antiquities law. His permit said he was entitled to export half his finds, yet Brown had sent him Article 2 of the Law Code, which stipulated that those excavating with government authorization could not "export the antiquities found."[38] Brown's advice reflected sentiments all too common at the time. On 19 March 1872, the career diplomat counseled Schliemann: "When you find any *small* objects, put them in your pocket. If you do happen to fall upon any fancy statues, we will see about it here." Wood, he said, was exporting his finds at Ephesus for the British Museum, and "the Imperial Museum, here, is a dead letter like anything else which does not make money. Money is the first question of the day, so that you must *not* find any large amount of Gold or Silver in your diggings." He went on to say that he believed that the pasha was not interested in any ancient objects. "I carry them off for all they can earn!"[39]

Schliemann would have received Brown's advice on how to proceed with precious small finds only two months before his first known discovery of gold jewelry, which he subsequently neglected to publicize until the time was right and which he never shared with the Turks or with Calvert as the landowner.[40] In 1873, the situation differed. Schliemann did not have the luxury of being able to withhold his best finds, and he published them as soon as they were safely arrived in Athens.[41]

Privately, both Brown and Boker encouraged Schliemann to abuse the Ottoman government. Boker responded to Schliemann's private announcement of the smuggled treasure trove with a letter marked *"Personal and Confidential"* on 28 June. "If you intend to continue your excavations, it would be the height of imprudence to give publicity to your recent discoveries," he told Schliemann. After quoting the Ottoman law on antiquities, he then advised:

> It would be worse than throwing away the articles which you have discovered to permit any part of them to go into the absurd collection of rubbish which the Turks call their "Museum." My advice to you therefore is to give no publicity to your discoveries until you have finished your labors in Turkey, and given up this field of explo-

ration forever. As sure as you do, you will be prevented from continuing the work, as you will be obliged to turn over to ignorant barbarians objects which in your hands may become precious archaeological illustrations.

Of course, if you once get your treasures to America, they will be safe from Turkish pursuit, as I have little doubt they are in Athens. . . . I therefore advise you to keep quiet, and let no man know the facts and discoveries of your recent researches.

You must understand that all which I have written above is unofficial and personal. If I wrote you as Minister of the U.S., I should be obliged to use very different language, and to advise you to conform yourself to Turkish law [e]tc. But in my sympathy with you as a man of science, I cannot be guilty of the hypocrisy of giving you such advice, knowing that it would be better for the world of letters that you should re-bury the objects than to turn them over to the Turks.[42]

After Brown's death in 1872, Schliemann opened similar "unofficial" communications with Boker. Archaeologists customarily lobbied diplomats with the fruits of their labors,[43] and Boker requested that Schliemann send him one of the owl-headed Minerva idols of the golden headdress from Priam's Treasure.[44] To his credit, Schliemann refused, saying that "the head veils of gold" were constructed in such a way that "the chains and idols cannot be separated" and begging his forgiveness.[45]

Of course, Charles Newton was far too discreet to request antiquities from Schliemann. He inquired of a Greek colleague, one of Schliemann's enemies, whether or not the Greek courts were going to abandon Schliemann and the treasure to the Turks. With a superior attitude, Newton deprecated Schliemann's abilities as an excavator and reiterated Boker's anti-Turkish sentiment, veiled in a Horatian allusion, "aurum irrepertum et sic melius situm," that the gold would have been better left undiscovered than gathered for human uses with a hand that plunders everything.[46]

These remarks were hardly out of character with the omnipresent Western bias against the Orient in general and Turks in particular. Whereas the exoticism of the Orient was, to a degree, alluring, the Westerners felt repulsed by what was other, what they could not understand. Thus, as John Pemble puts it, "they judged and denigrated the Turks from a vantage point of political and moral superiority, particularly the British, who were hostile to what they saw as a civilization in decline."[47]

Senior, the Oxford economist who had stayed with the Calverts in 1857, chronicled the general feeling of Europeans in the Levant as "uniform repugnance . . . to the Turks. Hatred, contempt, disgust . . . to be the feelings which they excite among all the Christians who come into contact with them." He reported James Whittall's remark that the Turks did not even belong to the same species and that "their brains were smaller than those of Europeans."[48] Prominent nineteenth-century archaeologists were no better. The British Egyptologist Sir Gardner Wilkinson believed the Turks utterly incapable of feelings of real civilization: "they are the only instance of a nation that has reached the zenith of its power and fallen again, without ever having become civilized."[49]

As soon as Schliemann returned to Athens, news leaked out about the find. The 2 July 1873 *Levant Herald* documented Schliemann's return to Athens "laden with valuable trophies of his zeal, liberality, and perseverance . . . with valuable silver and gold ornaments . . . dug out of what the learned doctor considers the very Palace of Priam." A week later, an "occasional correspondent" from the Dardanelles deplored the "non-observance by Mr. Schliemann of the terms of the concession under which his excavations of Ilium were carried on . . . this measure will render the Government more than ever mistrustful of scientific men, and tend to the imposition of more stringent conditions upon the prosecution of archaeological research."[50] Forwarding Schliemann a *Levant Herald* clipping, Boker wrote that "your enemies at the Dardanelles are at work endeavoring to get you into trouble with the Turks." Having received as yet no official complaint from the Turks, Boker hoped the matter would "go quietly to sleep, as things of the kind generally do in Turkey." Because Schliemann had admitted to the director of the Imperial Ottoman Museum that he had not adhered to the terms of his petition, if he returned, he would be vulnerable to proceedings that could be instituted against him by the Ottomans in a consular court for a breach of contract. Consequently, Boker advised Schliemann to keep safely beyond Ottoman jurisdiction "until the whole affair has blown over."[51] Schliemann asked Boker to send his rebuttal to the newspaper and claimed that Frank Calvert "can['t] and will never pardon me to have discovered Troy and he does not shrink from resorting to the foulest of all foul means to take vengeance."[52]

Schliemann's appropriation of Priam's Treasure indeed got him into trouble. Frederick Calvert wrote to Schliemann that the government had instituted a crackdown. The provincial governor was investigating by order of the Sublime Porte everything connected with his operations at Hisarlik. Frederick, too, recommended that Schliemann avoid returning to Turkey "until the matter will have been arranged or forgotten." He also advised Schliemann that if he wished to excavate, to acquire his future excavation permit in someone else's name and to get an Ottoman subject to guarantee that the government would receive its share.[53]

Schliemann didn't do much to alleviate the problem. Just as he had done with his illicit excavations in 1870 and his export of the Helios Metope and bearding of Frank Calvert in 1872, he bragged to the press. Against Boker's advice, Schliemann published a description of the treasure in the *Augsburger Allgemeine Zeitung* on 5 August 1873.[54] Again Schliemann asked Boker to forward his rebuttal to the *Levant Herald* and begged Boker's assistance in smoothing things over with the Turks.[55]

But Boker was furious and wished to disassociate himself from such an unscrupulous individual. He sent back the stone idol given him by Schliemann, writing: "The effects on future explorations will be, I fear, most damaging, tending to increase the jealousy of the government to such a degree that all permissions to excavate may be refused for foreigners."[56] Three days earlier, Frederick Calvert had rejected Schliemann's gift of his share of the 1873 finds, suggesting that it was "right and expedient that the whole lot go intact to increase the museum" of his brother Frank.[57]

Thanks to Boker, on 10 September Schliemann's response was published, in which he defended himself against the charge of not treating the private landowners fairly. But on the same day, the *Levant Herald* published an editorial sympathetic to "the aggrieved proprietors" of Hisarlık and noted that its information, in which the editor had "entire confidence," differed in every essential feature from Schliemann's description of the discovery. The proprietors, he suggested, could obtain proper redress legally. Schliemann had abrogated his agreement with the government. This abrogation the author criticized on moral grounds. The government's "trust in Mr. Schliemann as a gentleman and a man of science" had been betrayed and "virtually scoffed at." He "boasts of the artifices" by which he smuggled the objects out of Turkey. "It is bad enough that the Ottoman Government should have been defrauded of its due, but it is far worse that that fraud should have been practised in the name of science; for it will render the Turkish Government excusably jealous and suspicious of archaeologists, and thus close to the latter the very field in which they would most naturally desire to pursue their researches, but it casts a slur upon science itself, by making its name a cloak for deception, and degrading its pursuit to the level of predatory traffic."[58]

If the article was not actually written by Calvert, it certainly was reminiscent of Calvert's rhetoric, and Schliemann assumed that Calvert was the author.[59] To Boker, he blasted "the author of all those foul and false calumnies regarding me in the Levant Herald . . . Frank Calvert, who—*a disgrace to our great country* is acting U.S. consul at the Dardanelles. [He thinks] I will pay him a big ransom in order to stop his ignominious calumnies. He makes them *anonymous,* knowing that I would at once attack him in our consular court at Constantinople if he signed his name to them." Then he noted that the local press was not disinterested in the matter, since the editor, whom he alleged was Calvert's brother-in-law, would print anything. In answer to Boker's desire for an explanation, Schliemann alluded to Boker's 28 June letter in a coercive inducement to act on his behalf.[60]

Schliemann later accused Calvert of repeatedly insinuating to a "great luminary" in London and the *Levant Herald* that "Priam's Treasure had been made, by my order, by a goldsmith of Athens."[61] Ironically, however, it was Calvert, the man who had the biggest ax to grind with Schliemann, who stood up in his defense when the genuineness of his find was questioned. Calvert indeed had written to the "luminary" in question, Sir John Lubbock, on 4 November, but what he wrote was supportive:

> a portion of the press ridicule the idea that Dr. S. has brought to light the so-called Priam's Treasure,—and even go so far as to insinuate it to have been made in the *ateliers* of Athens. Although I have not seen the objects themselves—only photographs of them—I believe that Dr. Schliemann did discover a number of gold and silver ornaments at Hissarlik. . . . I do not agree with him in identifying them as the property of the Trojan king.[62]

Other scholars were less generous. The Oxford professor and Orientalist Friedrich Max Müller (1823–1900) thought Schliemann's claim ridiculous and protested:

"To look for the treasure of the Homeric Priamos at Hissarlik would be like [looking] for . . . the bracelet of Helle in the Dardanelles."[63]

Meanwhile, treasure fever set in. Locals, including Schliemann's workmen, were found to be plundering the site.[64] In December 1873, Ottoman authorities at Kalafatlı and Yenişehir seized many pieces of gold jewelry: necklaces, bracelets, rings, earrings, and a diadem, which workmen had found in two places in Schliemann's trenches. In an article in the *Levant Herald,* Calvert pointed out that this pilfering of treasures by the workmen substantiated Schliemann's claim that his find was genuine. "Dr. Schliemann has now the clearest proofs . . . refuting the invidious assertions . . . that the gold ornaments at Troy . . . had been manufactured under his personal direction by a goldsmith in Athens. The scientific world will now be enabled to pronounce upon the true nature and probable age of this most interesting long buried treasure." They had been found the previous March, 8.75 meters down—in the second stratum, "six yards to the south of an ancient wall not yet entirely cleared." This spot, according to Calvert, lay 150 yards apart from that of Priam's Treasure—in the eastern half of the mound—the southeastern area where Schliemann's men had indeed been excavating the previous March [Figure 26b] and near where he had found the gold pendant.[65] Not only were these further testimony to the wealth of the second-stratum settlement, they were also the first gold finds demonstrably from Calvert's land. Boker forwarded the supportive article to Schliemann, but Schliemann could not respond graciously, since it was "from the pen of Mr. Calvert," and Calvert had told and written him "too many lies and falsehoods."[66]

The disagreement concerning Schliemann's claims to have found Homeric Troy thus continued unabated. Whereas Schliemann claimed that Priam's Treasure showed that Hisarlık "was, in spite of all her thousands of stone weapons and implements, immensely rich and being rich . . . powerful," he also admitted privately that his Troy had no acropolis and was forced to assert that "the Pergamos is a pure invention of the poet."[67] Even while supporting the genuineness of Priam's Treasure in the *Levant Herald,* Calvert once again questioned the date of Schliemann's second stratum. Since Homer mentioned only bronze and iron, the second stratum at Hisarlık, with its bronze and stone tools, must be transitional "from the stone age to that of bronze." Thus, if one accepted Homer's description, one could not accept Hisarlık as the "immortal city." He lamented that Schliemann and von Hahn were so locked into their preconceived ideas that their interpretations merely confirmed their earlier notions.[68]

Although the date for the end of the Bronze Age generally was thought to coincide with the Trojan War, there was no fixed point for the beginning. The transition from the Stone Age to the Bronze Age in the Aegean was virtually unknown outside Hisarlık. Newton wrote that they were "vaguely groping in the twilight of an uncertified past."[69] The result was a series of vague terms—"Heroic," "Homeric," "prehistoric," and "pre-Hellenic"—that Schliemann and others used to describe this uncharted era and its material culture.

After visiting Schliemann's collection, Newton summed up the position taken by his colleagues in England, Germany, France, and Greece with respect to the finds by declaring there was "a *prima facie* case for considering the Schliemann antiquities as prehistoric and consequently antecedent to the earliest Greek antiquities as yet discovered." He affirmed that they were genuine, but because there was not a single sherd similar to the painted pottery of Mycenae, he would not yet accept that Hisarlık was Homeric Troy. Meanwhile, the eminent French archaeologist François Lenormant (1837–1883) suggested dates similar to Calvert's for Schliemann's prehistoric levels. Lenormant noted that he and Newton believed that Schliemann's objects belonged to "a really barbarous state," "a stage of culture less advanced" than that of Homeric Troy. He dated them to between 2000 and 1900 B.C.[70] The thousand-year gap still plagued Schliemann.

With their fundamental disagreement over whether Schliemann actually had discovered the walls of Homer's Troy continuing, the feud between Calvert and Schliemann went on. Schliemann never had tolerance for Calvert espousing any ideas in print about Hisarlık and Troy, especially those that did not agree with his own.[71] Now he prepared to silence Calvert for his original *Levant Herald* article and also for subsequent anonymous ones (July and September 1873 and 3 January 1874) that he attributed to the same author. He did this in his publication in early 1874 of *Antiquités troyennes* in French, and a German edition, *Trojanische Alterthümer.* Eventually published in England and America in 1875 as *Troy and Its Remains,* it reached a tremendous audience.[72] The book comprised Schliemann's reports, with few revisions and an introduction.[73] One can trace the deterioration of their relationship from a tone of respect to ridicule in Schliemann's dated reports, which became chapters in the book. Schliemann dismissed Calvert's work completely in the 29 March 1873 report, claiming that he, not Calvert, had discovered the Temple of Athena and denigrating Calvert's four trenches as "two small cuttings which still exist, and he is wrong in saying that I have continued his excavations."[74] In the introduction, written last, Schliemann summarized all work at Hisarlık and archaeological work in the Troad as a whole without mentioning Calvert at all. He had written Calvert out of history.[75]

At the same time, Schliemann was not blind to the vast differences between his finds and those from Homeric sites in Greece and to the significance of the thousand-year gap. To his friend John M. Francis, former U.S. minister to Greece and now editor of the *Daily Times* in Troy, New York, Schliemann confided: "No doubt the site of Troy has been abandoned and uninhabited for centuries before the age of Homer for the objects and particularly the idols found even in the highest prehistoric layers of the ruins show an immense difference in age when compared to those described by Homer."[76] But he never would admit this publicly.

Calvert, now U.S. consular agent at the Dardanelles,[77] reviewed Schliemann's book in the *Athenaeum* and rejected Schliemann's portrayal of him as an adversary of the explorations and of the identity of Hisarlık as Troy: "It was in truth I myself who first convinced him of that identity and persuaded him to make the ex-

cavations which have yielded such interesting results. Having a turn for archaeological pursuits, and as a resident of many years standing, I have made a special
study of the topography and antiquities of this region."[78] After reviewing the history of his own inquiry at Hisarlık, he noted his unsuccessful proposal to the
British Museum for support in excavating the site.

Calvert continued:

> In 1868 Dr. Schliemann first visited the Troad. He asked me my opinion as to the
> true site of Troy, admitting that he had not as yet given any attention to the problem.
> I, on my part, frankly communicated to him the results of my researches and the
> grounds on which I had arrived at the conviction, regarding the location of Homer's
> Troy, that if Troy ever existed, it must have been at Hissarlik.

Calvert noted in passing how he had guided Schliemann to Maclaren and
other authors, not looking for acknowledgment, but out of collegial courtesy between fellow archaeologists. To set the record straight, he enumerated all of the
finds that he had made himself and that Schliemann had claimed were his own,
such as the Temple of Athena and the "Lysimachean Wall." Calvert refuted the
preposterous claim of "two small cuttings" by referring to the plan that Schliemann himself had published in his 1874 atlas of plans and photographs, which accompanied *Trojanische Alterthümer,* clearly marked with four "trenches dug by Frank
Calvert," all but one obliterated by Schliemann's excavations [Figure 26a, no. 5].[79]
In a second installment of the review, Calvert referred to dietary details of the
early peoples of Hisarlık noted in his 4 February 1873 article that Schliemann had
ignored in his book: "It is likely they never came under his notice, as he says, for
prehistoric remains offered no attractions to Dr. Schliemann, his only aim was to
discover Homeric Troy; and his explorations, the earlier part of them especially,
were marked by the indiscriminate destruction of such relics." Schliemann had
admitted as much himself.

Calvert distinguished between Schliemann's "prehistoric stratum" and the
"Heroic or Homeric Age of Troy" and once again referred to the discontinuity
apparent in the lack of an intermediate cultural link between the prehistoric material and "the deposit above it from historical times, represented by archaic Greek
pottery of the seventh to sixth centuries B.C." Either "the semi-barbarous relics of
Dr. Schliemann's collection" represented "the real state of art during the heroic
period" or there existed "a total absence so far, not only at Hissarlik, but throughout the explored sites of Greece, of any relics of the civilization depicted, or invented by Homer."

> Dr. Schliemann has taken occasion to express his surprise that, as proprietor of part
> of Hissarlik, I should, against my material interest, have published my doubts as to
> the age and origin of the antiquities discovered by him. He seems unable to under-
> stand that in a question of this kind no personal considerations whatsoever ought to
> have any weight, and that it is simply childish to hope that they can be made to pre-
> vail against scientific truth. Whilst fully recognizing his enterprise, devotion, and en-

ergy in carrying out these excavations, I cannot but express the regret that Dr. Schliemann should have allowed the "enthusiasm," which, as he himself admits, "borders on fanaticism," to make it so paramount an object with him to discover the Troy described by Homer, as to induce him either to suppress or to pervert every fact brought to light that could not be reconciled with the *Iliad*.[80]

Schliemann railed to Boker that "Frank Calvert has published a monstrous libel against me. . . . It is below my dignity to answer *libels*. . . . It is the fate of all discoverers to be envied, illtreated, pursued and libelled and all this will cease only at my death. I am firmly resolved not to lose any more [of] my time in controversy and least of all to answer libels."[81] But he continued to do so, responding to an 1874 review of *Trojanische Alterthümer* by Karl Bernhard Stark with an article in the 8 January 1875 *Augsburger Allgemeine Zeitung* and in several letters.[82]

Schliemann undermined and ridiculed Calvert publicly in the 31 March 1875 issue of the *Guardian*. He admitted that Calvert had told him in 1868 that "in one of the small ditches at Hissarlik he had found a temple," but that that discovery had been upset by the "criticism" of his pickax. "Not the least funny thing in Mr. Calvert's article is the assertion that it was *he* who *first* indicated to me Hissarlik as the site of Troy, and that I avowed him that I had not previously given any attention to the subject."

He now proclaimed that Homeric topography always had been of paramount interest to him. To establish his prior interest, he asserted that he had thoroughly studied and restudied all that had been written on the subject long before he met Calvert. Moreover, he claimed that when he had first set foot in the Troad, he had long ago decided that the *Iliad* confirmed the ancient sources that identified Greek Ilion with the place *"ubi Troja fuit."* "I first saw Mr. Calvert on my return from the Plain of Troy, was happy to hear that he shared my opinion regarding the identity of the Homeric Ilion with the posterior city of that name."[83] In a quasi-generous postscript in which he noted that Calvert was his friend, but truth was dearer, he described Calvert's excavations as "mere depressions" three feet square and one deep in the midst of excavations made by the Turks before he was born and claimed that he had put them on the map only because he was, at that time, "on very friendly terms with him."

Not willing to drop the affair, Calvert rebutted Schliemann in the same paper in August 1875. Amazed that Schliemann could so pervert their history together as to demand that Calvert disclaim finding the Temple of Athena and his own excavation trenches, illustrated in Schliemann's own publication, Calvert observed since "Schliemann can accommodate scientific facts to personal feelings, it is at least presumable that his facts may be similarly accommodated in a contrary direction, now that he is on terms with me that are not 'very friendly.'" He ended by quoting Schliemann's 22 January 1869 letter to him: "Had anybody else proposed to me to dig away a hill at my own cost, I would not even have listened to him."[84] Schliemann, tired of the public squabble, wrote privately to Newton on 3 September 1875 complaining of Calvert's "foul and ignominious accusations."[85]

Eternally thin-skinned, Schliemann felt besieged by critics. Overwhelmed, he sometimes took them on, responding point by point to their arguments and eventually swaying them to his side, as in the case of Friedrich Max Müller. Max Müller, who never admitted to agreeing with everything Schliemann proposed,[86] nevertheless became his ally and later deflected criticism from him, though he used to say of Schliemann, "He destroyed Troy for the last time."[87]

While Calvert and Schliemann fought their battle in newspapers and journals, the Ottoman government predictably sought redress. After the close of the 1873 excavations, the director of the Imperial Ottoman Museum, Philipp Déthier, had asked Schliemann merely to send some of the owl-faced vessels that he had found in great abundance. Schliemann refused this modest request and countered on 30 July with a proposal to excavate at Hisarlik for three months with 100 to 150 workmen at his own expense, a scheme similar to the one he had offered to Calvert in the spring of 1873. If the museum acknowledged that everything found before the proposed dig belonged to Schliemann, he offered, he would yield up all subsequent finds to the museum.[88]

Expecting trouble from the government, in June 1873, less than a month after the discovery, Schliemann secretly had investigated the possibility of having copies made in Paris of the gold and silver pieces in the treasure, perhaps thinking that the Turks would be interested only in these.[89] And upon the publication of his discovery of Priam's Treasure and his self-declared abrogation of his agreement with the Ottomans, the trouble he had anticipated arrived. The government asked Boker for an explanation of Schliemann's actions. Schliemann justified his rash announcement to the infuriated U.S. minister as a moral imperative because of the uniqueness of the finds, "things of such an immense importance and of such an incalculable value to science . . . which make all hearts overflow with joy." Since the Ottomans had broken their contract by issuing in midseason the 1872 ministerial decree that forbade the export of antiquities, he argued, he was legally exempted from any obligation. But, he confided, he had suggested the joint excavation plan to the museum so as to "make friends," his ulterior motive being additional Ottoman *firmans* to dig on Crete and Samos. He pleaded with Boker to intercede on his behalf.[90]

Boker reiterated that the Ottoman government sought an explanation from Schliemann and had accused him of considerable abuses against the brother of the British consul at the Dardanelles, who had given Schliemann permission to dig on his land. To defend himself, Schliemann replied with a letter to be sent to Reschid Pasha defaming both Frank Calvert and his brother Frederick, whom he maligned as "bankrupt and condemned to the galleys at Malta for 5 years because of a formidable theft which he had committed against Lloyds of London for which he was an agent."[91] This theft had caused "an immense clamor and would remain forever unique in the annals of crime." Then he told the whole story of the fraud, exaggerating the sums involved, just as he had his prison sentence. Moreover, he added, the fact was "universally known at Constantinople and throughout the whole world." Regarding his own behavior, he alleged that the deal struck for the Helios Metope was legitimate. With regard to other finds from the 1872 season, he accused "the freed convict of Malta" of robbing him of his rightful share by trickery during the process of division. Professing to know the way the Calverts operated, in 1873 he did not wish to make a division with them, and so in recompense for "some small service" that Frederick had rendered him, Schliemann gave his own share to him. That "small service" was, in fact, Frederick's hiding of Priam's Treasure at his farm.[92] Boker informed Schliemann that the Turks were not amused by his letter and thought that he "should be brought here in chains for punishment."[93]

By April 1874, the Ottomans had given up on efforts to negotiate with Schliemann and had launched a lawsuit against him in Greece.[94] A battle ensued in the courts of Athens, wherein the Ottomans, through Déthier, whom Safvet Pasha had sent there to try to resolve the dispute, sought to regain their half of the treasure. Initially, the tribunal of the first instance supported Schliemann, declaring itself incompetent to adjudicate a dispute between two foreigners, and once again Schliemann talked of leaving his collection to Greece. Looking ahead, he already had begun to excavate Mycenae, again without a permit.[95] Then the Royal Court reversed the earlier decision and ordered the precautionary seizure of the treasure. Trying to buy the support of the Greek courts, Schliemann issued a proclamation to the Athenians that he had made them heirs of Priam's Treasure and appealed to the Supreme Court, or Areopagus. But it became known through the *Athenaeum* and other foreign newspapers that Schliemann was negotiating a sale of Priam's Treasure, "now to London, now to Paris."[96] Schliemann wished to remove it from the jurisdiction of the court and sought the protection of a foreign embassy.[97] He quickly hid the treasure, once again, for if he lost the case, he would have to return half of it or pay reparations for half its estimated value.[98] When his appeal was denied and the authorities came to confiscate the collection, they found nothing.[99] As a result, the court placed a sequestration order on his house, furniture, and bank shares.[100] Furious with the action of the Greek judicial system, Schliemann then disinherited the Athenians and made the Louvre his legatee, for he had been able to hide Priam's Treasure at the Ecole Française d'Athènes, thanks to its director from 1867 to 1875, Emile Burnouf (1821–1907).[101] Exasperated with Schliemann's arrogant sophisms and his argument that the finds could not be separated, Déthier supported the Greek regulation that no antiquities be exported. Otherwise, he said, one would need "to make a trip around the whole world and visit all the museums just to study Greek antiquities."[102]

Engaging in every manner of secret bargaining with various European countries for the ownership of the collection, Schliemann even considered giving it to the United States in return for protection.[103] In April 1874, Schliemann interrogated Boker on his ability to keep the Trojan Collection "beyond any attack. . . . Would it be possibly safe if I put on it the U.S. seal and I donate it to the U.S. I have to think for the Turks would always find plenty of unscrupulous lawyers in the U.S.

who love money and who would do anything to get all of the Trojan antiquities back to Turkey." In the same letter he considered giving it to France and the Louvre. One month later, he asked Boker "if the Turks bombard Piraeus and take the Trojan Collection by force, would not the American fleet intervene?" In October, Schliemann finally asked Boker to protect him and the treasure and foresaw himself "on the shores of Massachusetts, or perhaps in Boston; of course we take the Trojan Collection along."[104] In December 1874, calling Safvet Pasha "a bitter old devil," Boker promised Schliemann that he would "cover him with the American eagle's powerful protection" and asked if he had "ever heard the American eagle scream." He told Schliemann he was making "a great mistake in not at once carrying your collection to the land of your adoption and giving our country all the credit and the advantages of your disinterested labors."[105] Schliemann responded:

> I cannot think of leaving [Greece] before the arrangement is made with Turkey, for until then I cannot bring out anything of my Trojan collection from its hiding places. It is my firm intention to settle down in the U.S. and I am sure it will please Mrs. Schliemann, for *that* is the earthly paradise of the ladies . . . the result of my excavations has excited in the U.S. an immense enthusiasm . . . we want to live in a society where we are not tortured to death by the libels of our so called friends. I think it will be wise if we leave the Trojan collection here until we have chosen our abode in the U.S., for the objects are too fragile. I think Boston is the place for us. . . . I am sure we shall not be sneered and laughed at and nobody will libel us in the United States.[106]

At the same time, he boasted to others that he could "sell it to the United States for 200,000 dollars."[107]

By 12 April 1875, the Ottoman government had terminated its lawsuit because Schliemann had paid a total of 50,000 francs (£2000) as compensation for Priam's Treasure.[108] In return, he got to keep the Trojan Collection intact. Schliemann now removed the objects from their hiding places and placed most of the collection in his house and Priam's Treasure in Athenian bank vaults.[109] Everyone seemed satisfied, but the court case never addressed the issue of illegal export of antiquities, which had been strictly forbidden since 1872.[110] In what must have been a surprise to Schliemann, the agreement stipulated that he was not to continue excavating at Hisarlık.[111] He had relied on Boker to finesse a future excavating season there, but Boker had left Constantinople for his new post in Saint Petersburg before the suit was over. Emile Burnouf, who had played an active role in the negotiations, said that the Ottomans wished to reserve the excavation for themselves. They had left Schliemann only the right of publication. In a rare case of the shoe being fitted to the other foot, Schliemann had been duped by the Ottomans, who had gotten 20,000 francs for their half of the treasure and the additional 30,000 francs with which Schliemann had intended to finance his next season of excavations at Hisarlık.[112] But this was nothing compared with the value of one million francs that Schliemann placed on the collection.[113]

Priam's Treasure brought Schliemann both public and professional acclaim, and the collection of which it formed the centerpiece caused the Calvert Collection of antiquities to be forgotten. Once Schliemann had settled the court case with the Ottoman government,[114] he was invited to come to London, where he soon found himself being lauded by the once and future prime minister. *Troy and Its Remains,* the English edition of his 1874 work on the Troy excavations, had just appeared, published by the prestigious house of John Murray.[115] A year before, Newton had paved the way for Schliemann by addressing the elite Society of Antiquaries on his excavations on "non-Hellenic and pre-Hellenic" finds at Hisarlık.[116] Newton had brought Schliemann's work to William Ewart Gladstone's attention as early as October 1873 and had forged a bond between the two men so bent on proving the historicity of Homer.[117] Gladstone was a true Homeric scholar who "let no day pass without having Homer in his hand." The politician, who had been writing volumes on Homer since 1847,[118] praised Schliemann's book as a "real objective Troy," declaring that the "excavations and poems greatly fortify one another."[119] Schliemann himself read an address to the Society of Antiquaries, "The Discovery of Homeric Troy," on 24 June 1875, at which he was accompanied by Gladstone. At the same time, he enjoyed the Kentish hospitality of Sir John Lubbock, whose best-seller had done so much to interest the public in prehistoric archaeology ten years earlier. Feted continually through June and July, Schliemann claimed it was as if he had "discovered a new portion of the globe for England."

Schliemann left London in August for a quiet visit with his family in Germany. There he first met Rudolf Virchow (1821–1902), a pathologist from the University of Berlin and excavator of prehistoric remains in Germany, founder of the German Society of Anthropology, Ethnography, and Prehistory and an opposition member of the Prussian parliament, who had been recommended to him by Gladstone.[120] At the same time, he visited Ludwig Lindenschmidt, an archaeologist working on Franconian graves near Selzen in Rheinhessen, Germany.[121]

While he was in London, Schliemann had taken advantage of his fame to try to find a way around the settlement prohibiting him from further excavations at Troy. Before tackling other excavations, he confided to Newton, he was "wishing to find first Troy," implying a gnawing personal doubt as to whether he had, in fact, located the correct level.[122] Following Frederick Calvert's suggestion to apply under someone else's name, he expressed interest in continuing the Hisarlık excavations and lobbied Lord Stanhope to solicit an excavation *firman* for the entire Troad in the name of the British government. He then would excavate for the British Museum, assuming all expenses himself and splitting the finds equally with them.[123] But these terms were less attractive than those that Calvert had offered twelve years earlier when he, as landowner, had volunteered to give the museum all of the finds. Schliemann's scheme would yield at the most only one-quarter of the finds. Half would go to the Ottoman government and the other quarter to Schliemann himself. The museum postponed its decision, as it had with Calvert. But Schliemann did not wait to be rejected.[124] He withdrew the offer and asked Gladstone himself to apply for the permit. Schliemann would pay all expenses.[125]

When this, too, came to naught, Schliemann resorted to another plan—to have diplomats pressure the Sublime Porte on his behalf.[126]

This plan succeeded. In 1876, after Schliemann had worked tirelessly for four months, he secured permission to excavate again at Hisarlık. During this time, Schliemann complained to Gladstone about the tremendous difficulties he had had when "jealous ennemies again upset everything by their anonymous libels." By the time Schliemann received the *firman,* he claimed to have suffered more than Odysseus in the ten years of the Trojan War.[127] The *firman* he had secured was for two years' work, and Schliemann began immediately preparing the site for a new, expanded season. In the same month, Schliemann was elected an Honorary Fellow of the Society of Antiquaries for his work at Hisarlık.[128]

Because Schliemann intended to commence excavations at once, he again needed Calvert. But by this point, their antagonism had quite a history. For more than a month, he requested Calvert's assistance on mundane problems such as the duty charged on wheelbarrows, getting a bodyguard of five soldiers for protection in the Troad, and securing permission to erect buildings on the site: "I am not an animal to bed down for all this time in the open."[129] After protesting the wages that he was forced to pay government representatives, "the governor's spies," Schliemann tried unsuccessfully to heal their relationship by giving Calvert a copy of Gladstone's new book *Homeric Synchronism: An Enquiry into the Time and Place of Homer.*[130]

On the same day Calvert, unmoved, returned the book unopened, with a coldly polite note:

> You will remember that in the controversy which arose between us you did not confine yourself to scientific argument but advanced a most unfounded and uncalled for accusation against my brother and myself—I have already intimated to you through your man Nicola that in any private capacity I could enter into no negotiations with you until you had made reparation for this wrong—committed though it may perhaps have been in the heat of argument—still less can I think of accepting any favour at your hands until the satisfaction I demand has been given—at the same time I shall in my official capacity, assist you as an American citizen in your dealings with the local authorities and uphold your rights to the best of my power.[131]

By "accusation," Calvert must have meant Schliemann's libelous letter to Reschid Pasha via Boker, who was at that time James Calvert's superior at Constantinople. The contents of his letter may have helped to sour James's promising career with the American diplomats.[132] They cannot have helped Frederick or Frank. But now, as always, Schliemann was determined. Once again, Schliemann responded, "After all what has happened between us it is painful to me indeed to be obliged to apply to you and to trouble you. But since you are U.S. consul, I can only look to you for protection."[133]

Calvert's reaction to this missive is not known, but Schliemann wrote Calvert on 28 June to complain about the local governor, Ibrahim Pasha, who was obstructing his work and claiming that he had no order from the grand vizier. As a result,

Schliemann was still unable to excavate.[134] In the London *Times* he railed about the maddening interferences, but he lingered in the Troad until finally abandoning his excavation plans in late June.[135] Willing to try anything, Schliemann published an obsequious letter, dated 11 July 1876, in a Constantinople daily paper. There he claimed from beginning to end that Safvet Pasha was his benefactor and praised his wisdom, noble enthusiasm, and initiative.[136] By December, Schliemann's efforts to put diplomatic pressure on the Turks finally succeeded, and the grand vizier gave strictest orders to the governor, or pasha, of the Dardanelles not to throw obstacles in Schliemann's path, but to help in every possible way.[137]

But Schliemann would not waste more time on Troy's account, and he returned to Greece to excavate Mycenae in the summer of 1876. For this, Calvert was once again unnecessary, and Schliemann left him alone. For the next few months Schliemann made history at Mycenae, where he again invited Burnouf and his daughter Louise to join him.[138] The Greek Archaeological Society held the excavation permit, but because they were short of funds, Schliemann was retained to excavate on their behalf at his own expense.[139] Panayiotis Stamatakis was their representative. Schliemann again began by excavating in the "Treasury of Atreus" and around the threshold of the Lion Gate. His wife, Sophia, excavated the "Tomb of Clytemnestra," another *tholos*, or beehive tomb. Although his permit stipulated that he open one area at a time and employ a limited number of workmen, by August he had sixty-three workmen digging in three teams in three separate areas.[140]

Ruthless with regard to evidence of later habitation, again Schliemann dug for the Homeric remains. Stamatakis railed that he "eagerly demolishes everything Roman and Greek, in order to lay bare the Pelasgian [Homeric] walls. If we find Greek or Roman vases, he looks at them in disgust, and if such fragments come into his hands, he lets them fall."[141] Yet he fought to retain the prehistoric sherds.[142]

Max Müller later said that "he had the scent of a truffle dog for hidden treasures."[143] By 2 November, while working in an area behind and to the right of the Lion Gate, Schliemann uncovered the first of five shaft graves. The kilograms of gold and silver artifacts that he unearthed there instantly became legendary. Greek newspapers wrote about his "lucky fingers."[144] The *Times* stationed correspondents, including William "Crimean" Simpson, to cover the latest news as soon as he had finished excavating.[145] The excitement was palpable, and when the finds were immediately exhibited in Athens, they drew great crowds.[146] Some were skeptical, however. Charles Merlin, the British consul at Piraeus, distrusted the excavator's hyperbole, writing to Newton that "Schliemann's geese are all swans" and noting that Ernst Curtius did not think much of the finds.[147] Upon seeing the golden jewelry for himself, however, Merlin, for one, retracted his earlier skepticism. The director of the German Archaeological Institute in Athens suggested that the "un-Greek, barbarian stamp" of the finds was partly responsible for the classicists' initial mistrust of Schliemann's discovery. "The astonishing, shocking, I may say even anguishing quality of these finds lies not in their oriental characteristics but in their exclusively oriental character. In seeing them, one has the feeling as if one were suddenly thrown into a foreign, barbarian world in which one searched in vain for a familiar face, for an accustomed article."[148]

In these years, Schliemann had become the toast of Europe. This fact was not lost on Schliemann himself. Long before his fame was consolidated, Schliemann decided he could wield "Priam's Treasure and my large collection as a weapon" to get permission to excavate Olympia and Mycenae.[149] In 1873, he had presented the Greek government with a bargain whereby he would get permission to excavate these two sites in return for his construction of a museum to house all the finds, including those from Troy, "under the condition that the museum should bear my name."[150] But because they had decided instead to award the Olympia concession to Ernst Curtius, he thought of abandoning Greece for excavation opportunities in southern Italy or Sicily that would, he thought, present themselves if he volunteered to build a museum for whatever he found there.[151] In another letter, he wrote that he gladly would give the Trojan Collection to Italy.[152]

Although Schliemann once had written to Calvert that he never would sell his collection, within months he was marketing it on a larger scale than Calvert could have dreamed and using it to further his archaeological goals.[153] By 26 July 1873, he sought in strictest confidence, through Newton, to sell his collection to the British Museum, noting "by the discovery of Troy I have a claim to the gratitude of the whole civilized world."[154] Newton responded that the government might consider its acquisition if the collection were put on view.[155] Schliemann gave Newton an estimated value of £50,000, twenty-five times the indemnity he had given to the Ottoman government.[156] Changing his position weekly, he also considered the Louvre.[157] Letters ricocheted back and forth across Europe when it appeared that the treasure and collection were endangered by the lawsuit.

By June 1876, Schliemann had promised Gladstone he would exhibit the Trojan Collection in London for a year.[158] Although Schliemann had wished to exhibit it at the British Museum, the trustees had declined, "owing to the present crowded state of the museum,"[159] so he accepted Gladstone's suggestion of the South Kensington Museum (now the Victoria and Albert). On 22 March 1877, this time introduced by Gladstone himself, Schliemann addressed the Society of Antiquaries and was immediately voted an honorary member. Later he became honorary member of the Royal Archaeological Institute. Schliemann happily complained that the reception in London was too warm and he "had to leave London to save his life."[160] At the same time, because of Schliemann's promised exhibition, Murray was able to convince Gladstone to write the preface for *Mycenae*.[161] Schliemann then announced in the *Times* that he would exhibit his Trojan Collection for the first time in London.

While Schliemann was enjoying his fame and using his collection to extract favors from British luminaries, Frank Calvert grew increasingly isolated, especially after Frederick's death in July 1876[162] and Charles's a year later. He lived in his brother's unfinished house at the Dardanelles with his spinster sister, while his brother's widow and their three daughters lived at Batak Farm. Meanwhile, the Calvert Collection languished in both locations. Although the Calverts originally had talked of establishing a "museum" as early as 1853, Frederick's misfortunes and the attendant financial disaster had made that impossible. As early as 1870, after his failed negotiations to sell the collection to the Ottomans, Calvert had looked to Europe.[163] At that point, Schliemann had advised him to send his "museum" to London in order to sell it to the British Museum, for they paid very high prices and bought constantly and had urged him to come with his antiquities and bring a letter of introduction from Mr. Newton.[164] But Calvert, from bitter experience, had been skeptical.[165] On 10 June 1874, Calvert contacted Newton, presumably because he had no other options or because he thought Newton might support him now that Hisarlık's worth had been amply demonstrated and Schliemann no longer could excavate in Turkey. Calvert sought advice from Newton about the collection and about proposed collaborative excavations with the museum. Newton, not wishing to offend Schliemann by encouraging his enemy to excavate at the site that had made him famous, discreetly deflected Calvert's collaboration. He did not think the present time "favorable for starting new explorations in Turkey at the public expense," but added, "if you should at some future time send over your Troad Collection to England, I think we might come to terms."[166] Prompted by this offer, but hesitant to act while Frederick was alive, Calvert waited until 1877, a year after Frederick's death, when urgency may have been compounded by the Russo-Turkish War. He sent some finds as a gift to Washington, D.C.[167] The cream of the collection, however, went to London. But by then, no one focused on Calvert or his collection.

Calvert decided not to sell directly to Newton, but instead sent his collection to the auction house of Sotheby, Wilkinson, and Hodge, which set the sale of the Calvert Collection for 2 August 1877.[168] It was announced by a *Catalogue of the Interesting Collection of Trojan Antiquities and Prehistoric Remains, Discovered at Hissarlik and in the Troad by Mr. Frank Calvert, of the Dardanelles.*[169] The British Library's copy of the sale catalogue has on the left margin the names of all the buyers of the lots placed for sale, on the right, the prices fetched at auction.

Rollin Feuardent, the firm that frequently supplied the British Museum, bought twenty-one glass vessels from Cyzicus, Abydos, and the Troad. It also purchased

> an interesting collection of upwards of 300 Trojan antiquities, discovered by Mr. Frank Calvert at Hissarlik, supposed by Dr. Schliemann, to be the site of Ilium, consisting of objects of Ilium Novum: stone, bronze, and terra cotta in whorls, amulets, cylinders, hammers, perforated stones, vases and fragments, numbering 219. Also there are 91 specimens of Greek painted terra cotta vases and fragments from Mysia, the Troad, and other places, all of which have the localities marked on them.

On specific instructions from Newton, Rollin purchased the bronze lion weight from Abydos and the inscription from Sestos, which he most coveted for the Department of Greek and Roman Antiquities. Museum correspondence shows that he had convinced the trustees to pay as much as £300 for these two pieces alone,[170] but in the end, they were sold for as little as £95. Rollin paid a total of £124.7 for his acquisitions, of which less than half went to the British Museum. The register of the Greek and Roman Department recorded that on 30 September 1877, forty-six of Calvert's objects were presented by the antiquarian and collector Sir Augustus Wollaston Franks (1826–1897), the keeper of the Department of Medieval and Later Antiquities from 1866 to 1896 and an avid follower of Schliemann's excavations.[171] Once acquired by the museum, their original provenance as part of the famous Calvert Collection was largely forgotten, while Franks's name was preserved.[172]

In September, Schliemann came to London to prepare his promised Trojan exhibit. Max Müller helped him order the objects, which were "in wild confusion." The Indo-Europeanist's wife recalled a conversation in London: "Max Müller was busy over a case of the lowest stratum, he found a piece of pottery from the highest. 'Que voulez-vous?' said Schliemann, 'it has tumbled down!' Not long after, in a box of the highest stratum appeared a piece of rough pottery from the lowest. 'Que voulez-vous?' said the imperturbable Doctor, 'it has tumbled up!' "[173]

Schliemann's Trojan Collection went on view on 20 December 1877 and ran through December 1880. Positive reviews appeared in the London *Times* on 20 December 1877, the *Archaeological Journal,* and the *Illustrated London News.* The reviewer for the *Academy,* however, noted that it was "disappointing to the last degree."[174] More than four thousand objects were exhibited in the South Court of the museum, with Priam's Treasure at the center, protected by heavy glass, police, and detectives.[175] The exhibit filled twenty or thirty cases and still consisted of only a small fraction of the total collection.[176] The exhibition caused a sensation, as did the Mycenae finds, which were being exhibited simultaneously to crowds in Athens.[177] To add to the excitement, *Mycenae* was published in the same month. Honors followed Schliemann, and through Virchow he was made an honorary member of the German Anthropological Society in Berlin at the end of 1877.[178]

Although the prehistoric artifacts appeared odd and threatening to German classical archaeologists, Schliemann and his prehistoric finds were embraced by the anthropologists in that country. Long rebuffed by the same entrenched philological giants who had rejected Schliemann,[179] these students of the prehistory of northern and central Europe rallied to his side.[180] For them, he had liberated a new world of research, for which ancient texts were not the only guide.

By 1873, Calvert had been relegated to the shadows by Schliemann, who would remain in the limelight for the rest of his life. Politicians and personnel of the world's most noteworthy museums angled to acquire his collection. Priam's Treasure and the Trojan Collection, which Schliemann valued at £50,000, drew crowds in London. By contrast, the Calvert Collection, once estimated to be worth £1000,[181] had been decimated by auction and brought only a small fraction of the expected amount.[182] It was completely upstaged, and henceforth what remained at the Dardanelles and at the farm would be kept hidden. During the years that followed, Calvert would, from time to time, contribute articles or correspondence in protest to newspapers and learned journals, but he had been completely overshadowed. The eclipse of Frank Calvert and the Calvert Collection was complete.

CHAPTER NINE

"The hatchet . . . buried"
Rapprochement and Cooperation

Despite his public fame and the respect of many professionals, Schliemann could not silence his critics. From 1873 on, their volleys had zeroed in on Schliemann's behavior and the authenticity of Priam's Treasure. In 1878, Schliemann's accounts of its discovery were challenged by those of other witnesses. And the problem of the thousand-year gap remained, throwing into question Schliemann's fundamental claim—that he had found the walls of Homer's Troy. Behind the scenes, Calvert pointed out to visitors the flaws in Schliemann's problematic interpretations. For Schliemann, these controversies meant he needed to mount a new campaign. They also meant, he realized, that he once again needed to reconcile with Frank Calvert.

Even before Schliemann exhibited Priam's Treasure to the public, there were rumblings of dissension. In July 1877, the prominent British war artist William "Crimean" Simpson described his recent visit to "the Schliemannic Ilium."[1] Simpson had recorded the Dardanelles in 1854 on his way to the Crimea. Now he visited the site of one of history's most famous wars, as chronicled by Homer, whom he called "the first special correspondent." Simpson was predisposed to believe that Hisarlık was the site of Troy, if it had ever existed. He had reported on the Mycenae excavations and had read *Troy and Its Remains*. Full of expectancy, he stood on the brink of the chasm that "Dr. Schliemann's 'intelligent spade' . . . had produced . . . looking into the deep cutting for a railway . . . walls of houses, paved streets, and larger walls, of fortifications,—all in seeming confusion beneath"[Figure 31].[2] Simpson regarded the mud brick "hovels" as "a joke" and thought Schliemann's "very beautiful Palace of Priam" more likely to be "Priam's pigsty."[3] Following Schliemann's plan, Simpson noted that the so-called palace would have blocked the "Scaean Gate" of his "so-called Troy." In fact, the two were not contemporary, for the building obstructing the gate had been built after the entrance had gone out of use [Figure 26b, no.7].[4] He accused Schliemann of "unbalanced imagination in order to explain the creations . . . produced at Hissarlik."[5] Yet he concluded that even if Schliemann were "incapacitated by his overabundance of imagination and enthusiasm for the calmer sphere of reflection and judicial investigation, on the other hand, his energy and instinct which never seems to go wrong, when excavating has to be done, entitle him to the highest place in that field of labour."[6]

The eminent classical archaeologist Karl Bernhard Stark was less generous. He had visited the Troad with Ernst Curtius in 1871 and knew the degree to which Schliemann was indebted to Calvert. In November 1877, he reviewed the scholarship on Troy,[7] noting that Schliemann's *Trojanische Alterthümer* was full of criticisms of Calvert and empty of the grateful acknowledgment due him. He recorded Calvert's initial assessment of the Hisarlık excavations and his defense against Schliemann's unmerited attacks.[8] He corroborated that Calvert had indeed indicated Hisarlık to Schliemann and repeated Calvert's concerns over the devastation made of the upper levels and the inaccuracy of the seemingly precise indications of depths of finds.[9]

In 1878, the British antiquarian William Copeland Borlase (1829–1914) published Yannakis's eyewitness account of the discovery of Priam's Treasure, which differed from Schliemann's.[10] Schliemann's former paymaster had guided Borlase on a disappointing trip to the Troad in August 1875. His 1878 account, removed by five years from the actual discovery, contains certain inaccuracies of its own but remains an important corrective to Schliemann's story. In language reminiscent of the anonymous September 1873 *Levant Herald* article, Borlase accused Schliemann of "compromising the reputation of every archaeologist who has ever worked on Turkish soil."[11] He berated Schliemann's own defense of his "breaking agreements and carrying off the 'lion's share'" as "only copying the example set him by all the great English, French, German, and American archaeologists who have ever made archaeological researches in Turkey and whereas everyone swears to uphold the agreement with the Ottoman Government to give one half of their discoveries, none of them have ever thought of fulfilling this convention."[12] Looking into Schliemann's trenches, Borlase, like Simpson, felt that he had been "taken in."[13] By contrast, he cited Frank Calvert in glowing terms as the person "to whom, more than any other resident in the district, the thanks of the antiquarian are due for the light his researches have thrown on the whereabouts of the ancient mounds—and the structure and contents of the tumuli."[14] Concerning the identification of Hisarlık as Troy, Borlase wrote:

> It was the opinion of Maclaren, Eckenbrecher, as also of Frank Calvert. . . . It was at the insistence of the latter that Herr Schliemann was induced to adopt this view, and as he tells us, to set about 'digging away a hill at his own cost.' As Herr Schliemann has denied that it was Mr. Calvert who indicated to him that Hissarlik was the site of Troy, the reader is referred to a communication made by Calvert in the *Levant Herald*, Sept. 8, 1875, wherein Herr Schliemann's own letters are brought forward as convincing proofs that it was so.[15]

Furthermore, Borlase credited Calvert with excavating major monuments of the site. "Portions of well-fitting walls, columns of a fine Temple of Apollo or Minerva, bas-reliefs and inscriptions—identifying the site with that of Ilium Novum—such have been the objects which have rewarded the labours of Mr. Frank Calvert and Herr Schliemann passing through them."[16] He called Schliemann a "prevaricator," the excavator who "dug *through* the remarkable remains which had been previously excavated by Calvert!"

Schliemann knew that Calvert's criticisms lay behind all attacks and continued to denounce him. Privately, Schliemann maligned Calvert as "a foul fiend" to Max Müller. "Calvert has been libelling me for years . . . he is of bad faith and a liar. . . . Never daunted, he now enrages the English travellers against me by his ill representation and explications of the ruins at Hissarlik and persuades them to attack me."[17] Schliemann enlisted Max Müller to defend him in the scholarly world against seven specific charges, the second being "that Fr Calvert first showed me Troy-Hissarlik. This he indeed maintained in the *Levant Herald*, but I proved in the *Guardian* his falsehood . . . many eminent men have long ago maintained that theory; Maclaren already in 1822."[18] Clearly, in 1878, he still was unable to credit Calvert for his help.

On 19 July, Calvert, no better disposed toward Schliemann than Schliemann was to him, wrote to Simpson, "I am fully aware Schliemann[19] has not spared me for we had a great tussle—everyone here who saw through him he called—either '*thieves, liars, or brigands.*'" He reassured Simpson, "I do not leave an opportunity escape to open people's eyes to the humbug of Schliemann." Then he noted that high-ranking diplomats had described Schliemann to him as a "charlatan" and "an impostor."[20] Calvert claimed that he had "indoctrinated" a correspondent from the London *Times* so that he had called Schliemann "the greatest impostor of the day" and wrote an exposé for the *Times* that was, according to Calvert, considerably altered before publication.[21] Calvert enclosed excerpts of Schliemann's own writings to illustrate his "fawning or biting venomously to suit his purpose" and then concluded, betraying his obvious jealousy, "We must do our duty and try to dispatch the Doctor off his elevated peg."[22]

Insecure as ever, despite his fame, Schliemann could not see that he in fact had far surpassed Calvert's achievements by this time, and he remained oddly competitive with Calvert for many years. Perhaps this was one of the reasons he sought passionately to become U.S. consul for Athens. Another was his wish to be the government's representative at the ethnographic section of the Universal Exhibition in Paris. For this purpose he employed the prominent American journalist Kate Field (1838–1896) as a conduit to the United States government. In March 1878 he made another of his not-so-veiled promises, holding out the possibility of rewarding "the Smithsonian Hall in Washington by gifts of antiquities" in exchange for the position.[23] She recommended him to the government, noting that "he can be of great assistance to American art museums now in process of formation."[24]

At the same time, Schliemann neared completion on Iliou Melathron, a "palazzo [with extensive gardens] . . . close to the Royal Palace, in the very best part of town"[Figure 34].[25] Designed by Ernst Ziller in 1871,[26] the compelling and grandiose structure in Athens makes a similarly bold statement in reply to the twenty-two-room consular mansion that Frederick Calvert built at the Dardanelles. Both neoclassical residences dwarfed all other nearby buildings, and both had as a prized feature extensive walled gardens.[27] But now Frederick Calvert was dead, and his house remained unfinished.

In 1878, Schliemann, in answer to his detractors, again planned to mount excavations at Hisarlık, but his 1876 *firman* had expired. By 30 July, he was negotiating for a new permit. This time he enlisted Austen Henry Layard, the excavator of Nineveh and Nimrud, and British ambassador to Turkey from 1877 to 1880.[28] He confided his frustrations to Layard. By 3 August, someone still was interfering with his promised *firman,* "probably the same person who endeavoured to obtain it in order to sell it to me."[29] On 14 August, Calvert gossiped to Simpson that Schliemann had appeared with a *firman* for Hisarlık and had demanded a bodyguard of fifty men. After his request was refused, Schliemann left for Athens, planning to return shortly to commence operations. "Priam's Palace, that damning piece of evidence, will form, I suppose, the first object to be destroyed by his pick." Calvert also reported that Schliemann apparently had agreed to give up everything he found in the projected excavations to the Ottoman government, adding: "this information may be incorrect—if it be true he is up to some dodge."[30]

Whatever his private feelings were, as an American citizen, Schliemann needed to have a good relationship with the U.S. consular agent at the Dardanelles, even if, inconveniently, that agent was Frank Calvert. If Calvert would not render the wide range of services that he had provided in the past or even negotiate access to the eastern half of the mound, which Calvert still owned, Schliemann still required his help as consul. Even in the thick of their past quarrels, Calvert had pledged that he would not obstruct Schliemann in his excavations and would help him as the local representative of the U.S. government. Now Schliemann had to depend on the man he had so maligned and mistreated.

Calvert was no longer the same naive gentleman who had invited Schliemann to dig at Hisarlık. A decade of dealing with Schliemann had conditioned him. But if Schliemann once again needed Calvert at this point, Calvert, for many of the same reasons as before, also needed Schliemann. The recession that had had begun in 1873 made life difficult at the Dardanelles. Meanwhile, the Russo-Turkish War of 1877–78 had brought a flood of refugees from Bulgaria and Circassia.[31] With them came diseases that ravaged the local livestock.[32] Even after peace was declared, refugees kept streaming across the straits, further taxing the area.[33] Calvert was in financial difficulties again. His income as consular agent was nil, and his mines, which required tremendous capital to develop, had not paid off yet. He still believed in the cause of archaeology as a science and in a gentleman's duty to uphold it. Calvert still owned Hisarlık and still was convinced that Homer's Troy lay there, where he had commenced his original excavations. He also was all but alone after the deaths of his elder brothers Frederick and Charles and after

Figure 34. Schliemann's mansion in Athens, Iliou Melathron. Courtesy of George S. Korres.

James's move to Constantinople. Save for the business brought by the U.S. consular agency and the Moss Steamship agency, the big house was virtually empty. Only Calvert and his increasingly frail sister remained. Schliemann was both a link to the past and a connection to whatever the future might hold. The ties that bound Schliemann and Calvert were in the end not so easy to break.

They reconciled. How Schliemann and Calvert effected this difficult rapprochement is not preserved in their correspondence.[34] For one thing, though, both decided to recognize Maclaren's 1822 identification of the mound as the original one and not bicker publicly about their own.[35] And for a change, their relationship was reciprocal. Schliemann was going to provide assistance to Calvert in carrying out his own plans for excavations, not just demand assistance from him. The proposed cooperation involved not only Hisarlık, but also Hanay Tepe, where Schliemann had agreed to underwrite the costs of Calvert's renewed excavations. This suited both men, for each was interested in Trojan topography and especially those sites that might be contemporary with Hisarlık. Hanay Tepe was a perfect choice. In return for funding, Calvert promised to give Schliemann half of the finds from the site and to refrain from publishing or giving out any information until Schliemann's own book was published.[36] Thus, they began a genuine collaboration in place of their previous contentious relationship, a limited partnership that was to continue until Schliemann's death in 1890.

Schliemann excavated on government land from 30 September through 26 November 1878. Along with Yannakis, three overseers, and a large number of workmen, Schliemann employed ten "gensdarmes," not only to guard against brigands, but also to keep the workmen honest. No treasures would escape his grasp this time.[37] As Calvert and Simpson correctly had predicted, he concentrated his efforts to the north and northwest of the "Scaean" gateway and in the area of the north platform and demolished the mud-brick structure above "Priam's Palace" that had blocked the earlier gateway [Figure 26b, no. 7].[38] During the last weeks of the season, in the elaborate structure northwest of the gateway, he uncovered one large and three small treasures consisting mainly of gold jewelry and bronze weapons.[39] These treasures, like Priam's Treasure, came from the second stratum.[40]

Schliemann resumed work on 1 March 1879 with 150 men.[41] For the first time he brought experts into the field. Emile Burnouf came in early April to prepare the maps and plans of the site. Together they would determine what course should be taken. Rudolf Virchow also came for a month to study the flora, fauna, and geological characteristics of the plain of Troy to put the site into context.[42] This signaled the beginning of a lifelong collaboration between Schliemann and Virchow. They shared an interest in the remains of the preliterate world that ran counter to prevailing classical interests in nineteenth-century German academia.[43] Schliemann, to be sure, was looking to validate Homer, but in the meantime, he had to make sense of 14 meters of prehistoric deposits at Hisarlık. Virchow's experience with prehistoric sites in Germany and interest in face urns in particular made him naturally curious about Schliemann's owl-faced "Athenas" at Troy. Schliemann, in return, could use the intellectual backing of the founder of the Berlin Society for Anthropology, Ethnography, and Prehistory and the editor of its journal, the *Zeitschrift für Ethnologie*. Virchow also had attended the first Congress of Prehistory in 1867.

Workmen cleared the fortification walls to the east and southwest of the gate as Schliemann explored Calvert's land on the northeastern part of the mound. He excavated two more treasures.[44] Meanwhile, Schliemann secured a permit to explore the tumuli in the plain and excavated several.[45] In the 1879 season, Schliemann noted a new stratum sandwiched between the prehistoric ones and the Greco-Roman upper level. It generally lay 2 meters below the surface but seemed only to be preserved outside the walls of the second stratum, on the slopes of the prehistoric citadel, where it could extend down from 3 to 6 meters. Now he recognized that the Greeks had indeed leveled the mound, particularly under the Temple of Athena, where they had laid the foundations on much earlier prehistoric strata.[46] Although previously he may have excavated architecture belonging to this new stratum in the western and northwestern soundings of 1870, he had decided that it was from too late a period to be Homer's Troy. This time he hesitated to label the material either prehistoric or historic, and because its pottery resembled that of the Etruscans more than anything found before or after at Hisarlık itself, he called it "Lydian," after the traditional cultural connection between the Lydians and Etruria, dating it, according to tradition, to about 1044 B.C. Its gray and tan pottery was both handmade and thrown on a wheel [Figure 35a].[47]

Schliemann was satisfied with his season. He believed he had corroborated his identification of Priam's Troy with the additional discovery of four treasures of the second stratum in 1878 and four more in 1879. He had uncovered a substantial area of that stratum, including a major portion of its fortification wall. Moreover, he had involved scholars of international standing in his project, scholars whose specialist studies would place Troy in relation to its landscape and elevate its status—and his—in the fast-developing world of scientific archaeology. When he left, he felt that he had accomplished his mission and once again was finished with Troy forever.[48]

In June, two young Americans visited the excavations and met Schliemann: Francis Henry Bacon (1856–1940) and Joseph Thacher Clarke (1856–1921). Clarke was writing a history of the Doric order, and Bacon was documenting the trip with an illustrated journal while the two scouted possible excavation sites for the fledgling Archaeological Institute of America, founded in 1879.[49] Bacon noted that Hisarlık "looked like the rubbish shoot of a mine! The acropolis is all dug out." Of Schliemann, Bacon remarked, "He swears by Homer!" Within two years, the young men would be back excavating at Assos (1881–1883),[50] the first Mediterranean excavation sponsored by the Archaeological Institute of America, founded in 1879.[51] Bacon's life thereafter was bound up with Assos, the Troad, and, because he later joined the Calvert family, Schliemann. The visit of the young Americans may have reminded Schliemann of his suit for the U.S. consulship, and he wrote again to Kate Field, noting that the U.S. government probably did not "see how advantageous that could be to the U.S. museums . . . I possess the richest and most wonderful collection in the world, which is *not* for sale and which I do not think to take with me to the grave."[52] But still no answer came.

Schliemann sent to London his share of the finds on government land, one-third under the terms of this *firman*. The remaining two-thirds went to the Imperial Ottoman Museum. However, Schliemann had no better opinion of the Constantinople museum in 1879 than he had had in 1873. To Layard, now regarded as "the patriarch of all British explorers,"[53] he wrote: "The Turkish Museum is anything but public and . . . the Trojan jewels are of no value to science as long as they remain in the hands of the Turks."[54] After several months of excavation in 1879, he recruited Layard's aid to secure broken pot fragments from Hisarlık for his own collection, convinced that if they went to the museum, they would be *"forever* lost

Figures 35a–b. 35a. Local pottery from the "Lydian" sixth stratum at Hisarlık. After Schliemann (1881a), Figure 1384, 594. 35b. Fragmentary vase from the middle stratum at Hanay Tepe. Redrawn by author, after Calvert (1859), 4.

to science . . . nothing but ballast."[55] Two days later he continued: "Old Dr. Déthier, the director of the *not* existing museum, told me that they had *no* use whatsoever for the *broken* Trojan pottery . . . they would put here [in his house at Hisarlık] a clerk to sell the potsherds to travellers. . . . In my hands . . . the potsherds become gold to science."[56] Schliemann's interest in pot sherds, which began in Mycenae in 1876, was unusual for his time, and in this particular case his concerns were valid. After the 1879 division, some of the material that was given to the museum was stolen.[57]

After the close of the 1879 season, Schliemann took stock of his life. To a supporter he wrote, "An explorer must be a selftaught man, excavation being an art by itself which cannot be learned in colleges."[58] Although he now received offers to excavate sites across the globe, he declined to leave the niche he had created for himself. He had spent the last decade working in "Homeric Archaeology" and thought he should remain in it for the rest of his life.[59]

During the same period, Calvert summed up his own achievements for Schliemann, listing sites that he had excavated: Neandria, Cebren, Scepsis, Ophryneion, Dardanus, Colonae, Larisa, Abydos, Thymbra, Hanay Tepe and Mal Tepe, Rhoeteum (Paleokastro), Aianteion (Tavolia), Ilion, Sigeum, Gergis, Achilleion, Berytis (Akköy), Sestos (Ak Baş), Cardia (Crittna), Cyzicus (Artaki), and unascertained sites at Adakeliş, Gâvur Hisar, Karayur, Kaz Dağ (near Köşedere), Çamlıca, Dumbrek Rachi, Kayalı Dağ, Hisarlık (opposite Pınarbaşı/

Ballı Dağ), Kossak Dağ, Kemer, Hisarlık (near Kuş Çayır), Ovacık, and some other localities the names of which he could not remember [Figures 36a and 36b]. Of these, he had identified twelve and discovered sixteen.[60]

The reconciliation of 1878 yielded in 1879 to a cautious rapprochement and mutual, though guarded, support.[61] Evidence for this comes primarily from Calvert's enthusiastic and cordial letters to Schliemann from 1879 on. Nevertheless, the voluminous correspondence between Schliemann and Calvert shows their mutual dependence as well as a certain reserve not present in their correspondence with others such as Rudolf Virchow.

Bridges were not mended overnight, and the chasm they sometimes shakily spanned between the two men remained. Just as the ties that bound Schliemann and Calvert were in the end not so easy to break, the differences that kept them at odds were not easy to overcome. One can infer from Schliemann's letters to others that he continued to exploit the weaker man, for example. But now, from past experience, Calvert treated Schliemann extremely cautiously. To Virchow, Calvert later described his position toward Schliemann as "peculiar." "I must be very careful not to give cause for his observations."[62] In spite of the missing correspondence for July 1878 to July 1879, Schliemann's later correspondence with Virchow and Richard Schöne (1840–1922), general director of the Berlin Museums from 1880 to 1905, discloses the extent to which, as always, in this relationship, Schliemann principally looked out for Schliemann.[63] He drove a hard bargain, never giving the slightest bit without getting something greater in return. The reason he attempted to keep Calvert happy was that Calvert always could be "useful."[64] He sought to secure a decoration for Calvert in exchange for Calvert's donation of his half of the Hanay Tepe material to Berlin, and he funded Calvert's excavations at Hanay Tepe in exchange for the right to control their publication.[65]

Calvert always had been limited in his archaeological work by his lack of capital. Because of Frederick's interest in building up a collection, if Frank ever located a cemetery, he excavated tombs, where he would find whole vases, rather than the accompanying settlement, with its scrappy remains.[66] With Schliemann's support and with additional manpower, at Hanay Tepe Calvert undertook the more strenuous demands of the systematic excavation of a settlement.[67] Since Schliemann's excavations had revealed such a wealth of prehistoric material at Hisarlık, Calvert welcomed the opportunity to reinterpret analogous material from the Hanay Tepe site (shown in Figure 37a in relation to Batak or Thymbra Farm and the Thymbrios and Scamander Rivers).

Calvert proceeded methodically and uninterruptedly with eight to ten workmen. From west to east he cut a trench 3.5 meters wide diagonally across the middle of the roughly rectangular site [Figure 37b].[68] To the south lay his earlier probe of the mound, from which he had taken the north-south section. By April 1879, he had proceeded 24 meters into the mound and had unearthed numerous skeletons from various levels, which he later gave to Virchow for analysis.[69] Calvert asked Schliemann: "What are your wishes—to continue the excavations and thor-

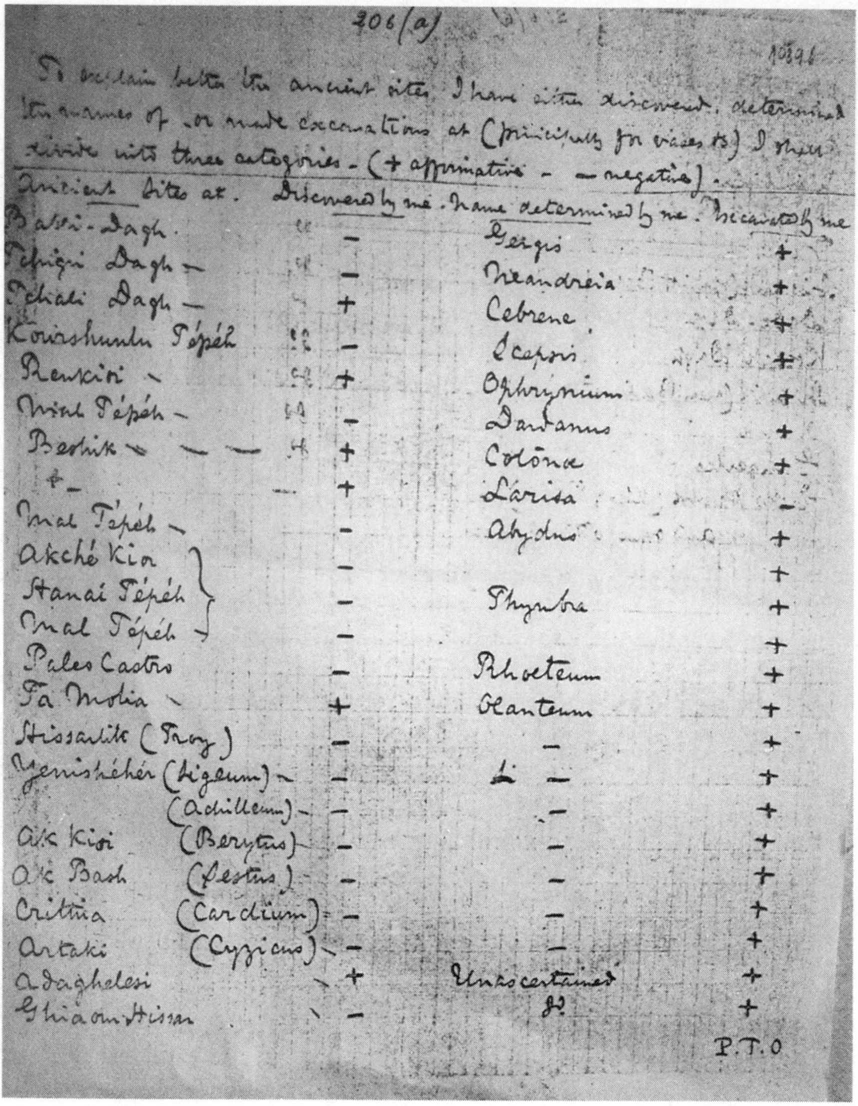

306(a)

10396

To explain better the ancient sites I have either discovered, determined the names of, or made excavations at (principally for vases &c) I shall divide into three categories — (+ affirmative — — negative).

Ancient Sites at.	Discovered by me.	Name determined by me.	Excavated by me
Balli-Dagh.	—	Gergis	+
Tchigri Dagh —	—	Neandreia	+
Tchali Dagh —	+	Cebrene	+
Kourshunlu Tépéh	—	Scepsis	+
Renkioi —	+	Ophrynium	+
Mal Tépéh —	—	Dardanus	+
Beshik — —	+	Colonae	+
+ —	+	Larisa	—
Mal Tépéh —	—	Abydos	+
Akché Kioi	—		+
Hanai Tépéh	—	Thymbra	+
Mal Tépéh	—		+
Paleo Castro	—	Rhoeteum	+
Ta Molia —	+	Aianteum	+
Hissarlik (Troy)	—	—	+
Yenishéher (Sigeum) —	—	—	+
(Achilleum) —	—	—	+
Ak Kioi (Berytus) —	—	—	+
Ak Bash (Sestus) —	—	—	+
Crithia (Cardium) —	—	—	+
Artaki (Cyzicus) —	—	—	+
Adaghelesi —	+	Unascertained	+
Ghiaour Hissar —	—	do.	+

P.T.O

Figures 36a–b. List of sites discovered, identified, and/or excavated by Frank Calvert. Courtesy of the Gennadius Library of the American School of Classical Studies, Athens.

oughly examine the mound so as to leave no doubt as to the origin—or to cease the works?"[70]

Schliemann kept control of the operation and at several points stopped paying Calvert altogether.[71] Meanwhile, clearly needing more funds to complete his excavations, Calvert wrote to Schliemann that "I have confined myself strictly to the tracing of the walls, as you desire—I shall continue as long as the funds last."[72] Exasperated by the time Calvert was taking to excavate the site and the paucity of dramatic finds, the impatient Schliemann again cut off funds.[73] Calvert wrote to Virchow, "I have received an intimation from the Pasha, who has new orders from Cple to stop the works at Hanai Tepeh. I do not know who the *kind friend* can be who has given the information to Consple—notwithstanding I shall try to bring the excavations to a successful termination."[74] Only a fraction of the site had been

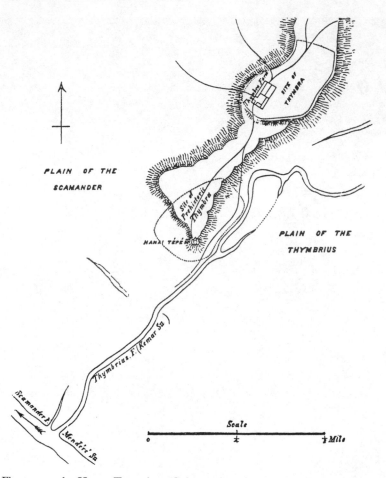

Figures 37a–b. Hanay Tepe plans. Calvert (1881), figures 1538 and 1539.

brought to light by October 1880, yet Calvert thought further excavations crucial to clarify the date of the middle stratum, with "the pottery of the age between the stone axes and the Syro-Phoenecian."[75]

A new tug-of-war now began between Schliemann and Calvert concerning the writing of the Hanay Tepe report. As early as 16 October 1879, Schliemann had requested a description of Calvert's excavations for *Ilios*. He noted that he would publish Calvert's report as it was sent but reserved the right to add a small section on the pottery.[76] On 16 December 1879, Calvert, disappointed by Schliemann's control over the proposed minimalist presentation of his excavation, responded:

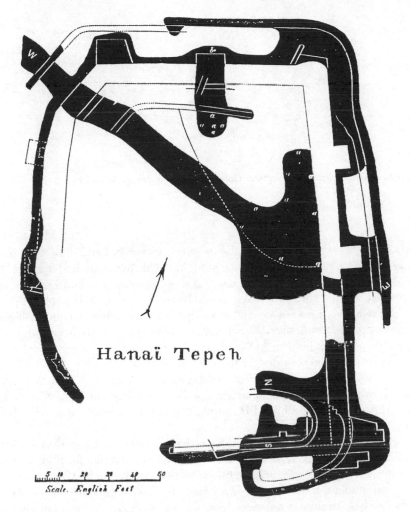

Hanaï Tepeh

Scale. *English Feet*

"If I understand you rightly you wish the description of the actual work at Hanai Tepé to be a brief summary of facts—for the introduction—and an enlargement on the results for the body of your work."[77]

By January 1880, Schliemann had written that he wanted not more than twenty pages because the book was already too thick.[78] On 16 March 1880, Calvert had provided scaled plans and sections, as well as copious illustrations of constructional details, all clearly designed to illustrate a much longer paper.[79] Schliemann refused to send some of Calvert's drawings to the publisher and complained about the time and money needed for the engraving of Calvert's plan.[80]

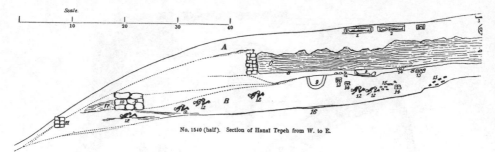

Figures 38a–b. Hanay Tepe section. Calvert (1881), figures 1540a and 1540b.

Calvert's cross-section drawing of the mound was excellent and showed his sensitivity to stratigraphy [Figures 38a and 38b]. Yet Schliemann advised the publisher to "do it roughly and cheaply, because it is most unimportant, and I merely do it to please Calvert." He added that it should be reproduced on one page, not two,[81] thereby reducing it excessively and rendering it almost completely unintelligible. Even the publisher protested.[82] Schliemann hounded Calvert from January to June 1880 to submit his text.[83] Distraught over an economic disaster at the farm,[84] Calvert relinquished control over the final product and sent his notes to Schliemann to work up himself. Schliemann's displeasure is clear from his letter to Virchow, in which he describes the submission as "in no way worthy of *Ilios.*"[85] The Oxford Assyriologist Archibald H. Sayce (1845–1933), as editor, worked to bring Calvert's material into order.[86]

After the end of the 1879 season, Sayce had visited the early prehistoric levels at Hisarlık and Hanay Tepe with Calvert.[87] Sayce praised him for his knowledge of historic and prehistoric sites and his excavation experience.[88] After viewing the finds and stratigraphy at Hisarlık, Sayce suggested to Calvert and Schliemann that its first or base stratum, 5.5 meters thick, should be divided in two. This, in turn, now made five prehistoric levels at Hisarlık. The level that Schliemann had labeled "Lydian" now would be a sixth [Figure 28].[89]

Calvert needed to absorb these changes before presenting his own thesis on Hanay Tepe. In his first report to Schliemann, Calvert laid out the three major strata of Hanay Tepe, two major prehistoric levels and a disturbed historic level on the surface. His assessment of Hanay Tepe was critical because of the similarity between black, hand-polished pottery from the lowest, or first, stratum of Hisarlık and that from the lowest stratum of Hanay Tepe. Likewise, the middle stratum at Hanay Tepe, with its ribbed *pithoi* and gray pottery with animal handles, seemed similar to Schliemann's newly recognized Lydian stratum at Hisarlık.[90] So whatever Calvert concluded regarding the dating of Hanay Tepe would affect the dating of analogous levels at Troy.

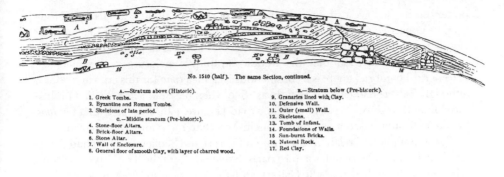

No. 1510 (half). The same Section, continued.

A.—Stratum above (Historic).

1. Greek Tombs.
2. Byzantine and Roman Tombs.
3. Skeletons of late period.

c.—Middle stratum (Pre-historic).

4. Stone-floor Altars.
5. Brick-floor Altars.
6. Stone Altar.
7. Wall of Enclosure.
8. General floor of smooth Clay, with layer of charred wood.

B.— Stratum below (Pre-historic).

9. Granaries lined with Clay.
10. Defensive Wall.
11. Outer (small) Wall.
12. Skeletons.
13. Tomb of Infant.
14. Foundations of Walls.
15 Sun-burnt Bricks.
16. Natural Rock.
17. Red Clay.

In the fourth appendix of Schliemann's *Ilios*, Calvert presented the Hanay Tepe mound as the nucleus of a larger settlement, fortified with massive inner and outer walls. As at Hisarlık, the sequence of building levels showed repeated destruction by fire. Calvert reported the presence in the lowest stratum of a multiphased settlement characterized by intramural burials, a considerable number and variety of plastered granaries, and copious faunal remains. In the first phase of the lowest stratum, the town lay unprotected. Then it was fortified with a stone wall and an outer wall of stone and mud brick. Later the settlement was taken by force. After being abandoned, the area inside the walls was reused. This was the middle stratum, which Calvert had connected with the Trojan heroes as early as 1859. He no longer believed it held the ashes of heroes, however. He now interpreted it as a sacred enclosure because of the tremendous accumulation of ash over built altars.[91] These brick and stone circular hearth altars had been laid one on top of the other to a depth of more than 2 meters. As layers of ash exceeded the space of the enclosure, they spilled out over the fortification wall, showing its disuse. Calvert suggested that the enclosure was dedicated to Thymbraean Apollo, in whose legendary temple Achilles died.[92] Calvert identified this site as ancient Thymbra (*Iliad* 10.430), where, according to later authors, Achilles ambushed the young Trojan prince, Troilus, about whom it was prophesied that Troy would not fall if he reached the age of twenty. Thus Thymbra Farm got its name.[93] After the altars were abandoned, simple dwellings were erected. Finally, the area served as an extension of the Archaic and Classical period necropolis, which was used from the seventh century to the fourth century B.C.[94] This had extended from nearby Akça Köy as far as Hanay Tepe and partly overlain the prehistoric settlement. In Byzantine and Ottoman times it still occasionally served as a place of burial.

Schliemann appended a note to the end of the report in which he differentiated the people of Hanay Tepe and Hisarlık by noting the different methods of interment used at each. He also tried to highlight differences between the black-polished pottery from the lowest stratum at Hanay Tepe and the pottery at Hisarlık. However, he conceded that the dull gray pottery of the middle stratum at Hanay Tepe closely resembled that from the Lydian settlement at Hisarlık [Figure 35a].[95] Aside from Calvert's assertion that the middle stratum's enclosure represented the "Homeric Thymbra," there is a conspicuous lack of a date for this critical stratum, although Calvert had dated it as early as 1859 when he established the first prehistoric (Late Bronze Age) vessel from the Troad [Figure 35b]. It is likely that for *Ilios*, Schliemann suppressed it and other conclusions than ran counter to his own.

In the complicated relationship between Calvert and Schliemann that had developed, there was little room for a third party. Skeletons from the Troad and common scientific interests had brought Calvert and the pathologist Virchow together in 1874, a year before Schliemann and Virchow met, and this gave Schliemann fits of anxiety. As always, he simultaneously knew he needed Calvert and felt he needed to keep Calvert under his own personal control. Schliemann seems to have suspected Calvert and Virchow of communicating directly, and indeed, Calvert at first would not exchange information directly with Virchow, probably because he feared Schliemann's retribution.[96] In March 1880, Calvert loyally reported to Schliemann that Virchow was preparing a separate publication on Hanay Tepe, focusing on skeletal remains.[97] Instantly, a crisis arose.[98] Schliemann, who thought he had total control over what would be said about the site, was shocked and duplicitously wrote Virchow that it was Calvert who was dismayed at the intended publication. Schliemann also threatened to denounce Virchow before "the tribunal of the civilized world" if he proceeded.[99] Calvert tried to placate Schliemann: "Virchow will make the final publication of Hanay Tepe for the subject is much too large and extended for giving all details in your forthcoming work." At the same time, he tried to heal the wounds. "I regret your misunderstanding with Virchow—perhaps he will not interfere with your book. What he publishes is not for the general reader."[100]

Schliemann tried to cover his overreaction by exaggerating Calvert's concerns to Virchow. To save face, he later put the blame for the incident on Calvert,[101] who seems not to have been upset by Virchow's designs. After all, Schliemann already had insisted that he wanted just a brief summary. Ironically, Schliemann's misrepresentation to both Calvert and Virchow encouraged them to communicate independently of Schliemann.[102]

Although Schliemann told Calvert that Virchow would stop his own plan to publish on Hanay Tepe,[103] in fact, it was only delayed, and Calvert contributed to it. The postponement, which lasted until after *Ilios* appeared, once again mainly served Schliemann, who maintained control over the initial publication. Perhaps the more detailed, scholarly treatment that Calvert originally had intended to submit can be appreciated in light of Virchow's subsequent publication, which gives a complete synopsis of Calvert's excavation and which was favorably reviewed in the *American Journal of Archaeology* by Joseph Thacher Clarke in 1886: "An important amplification of Calvert's reports concerning Hanai-Tepeh occupies the latter part of the book, this being the first adequate publication of a contribution to prehistoric ceramics scarcely less important than that derived from Troy itself. . . . Accurate, intelligent, and objective, it forms a happy contrast to the style of Schliemann's *Ilios* and *Troja*," Schliemann's accounts of his 1879 and 1882 excavations.[104]

Always wary of their relationship, the insecure Schliemann continually denigrated Calvert's archaeological expertise to Virchow. On 5 July 1880 he complained that Calvert, who was the first to identify Bronze Age ceramics in the Troad, had no understanding of ceramic material and couldn't tell prehistoric from historic pottery. He curiously continued in the same letter, "But I cannot write against him and must hold my tongue."[105] Each was extremely leery of the other, and they perhaps agreed to support each other in public once the truce was settled.

Even Schliemann's apparent acts of kindness toward Calvert had ulterior motives. Schliemann's publication of *Ilios* in 1881, for example, gave more recognition to Calvert. In his introduction, Virchow acknowledged that Calvert had conducted the first archaeological excavations at Hisarlık but qualified his acknowledgment by saying that "these excavations, however, were confined to the surface."[106] Schliemann himself credited Calvert with the identification of Neandria, Scamandria, Eskı Hisarlık, the ancient bed of the Scamander River in the Kalafatlı Asmak, the region of Aianteion, and the port of Karanlık.[107] This seeming generosity allowed him to keep in the background Calvert's earlier work at Hisarlık, which he still minimized as "two small ditches" that had brought to light some remains of the Macedonian and Roman periods. He still neglected any mention of Calvert's excavation and identification of the Temple of Athena or of his finds from the Archaic period.[108]

In 1879, Schliemann repeatedly tried directly and indirectly through Virchow to procure a decoration for Calvert from the German government.[109] In response to a letter from Schliemann concerning the delay, Calvert, ever the gentleman, graciously replied, "I have never sought this kind of honour—my idea is that the time is not far distant when men will be judged by their actions, not by the number of stars they carry on their breasts."[110] To Virchow, Calvert wrote, "I am not a vain man. . . . My sincerest thanks are due to you for your kind intention. It proves that I have gained a friend, who, to me is more valuable than a decoration."[111]

Later, clearly depressed, Calvert wrote to Schliemann, "Many thanks for the kind interest you have taken on my behalf to obtain a decoration from the German government—I do not however expect to receive it if the intention has been communicated to the British govt." The British government had mistreated the family in the past, and Calvert did not expect fairness in the future.[112] Elsewhere, Calvert's letters concerning the stalled recognition betray a pessimism not present in earlier documents: "I have often been disappointed in life and now, unless the *fait* is *accompli*, place no hopes on possibilities. I am prepared for negative results, like a philosopher."[113]

In another letter, Calvert resigned himself to a modicum of compensation. "I thank you most sincerely for the great interest you have taken to obtain for me the decoration or other acknowledgement from the German govt. and also for the acknowledgement of any suggestion I may give you regarding the Troad. At the same time I regret you have alluded to the past. I was under the impression that the hatchet had been buried and the calumet of peace smoked after all your kindness I shall not reply and give cause to cases for any further discussion in the matter."[114] Of course, acknowledgment is exactly what Schliemann had neglected with Calvert's most important identification based on archaeological field work—that of Hisarlık as Troy.

In fact, this effort to secure a decoration for Calvert was a calculated ploy to get Calvert to donate his own share of the excavated finds from Hanay Tepe to the Royal Museum in Berlin, an otherwise unlikely choice for a British citizen.[115] Calvert did not intend to give up his entire portion,[116] but when he and Schliemann were again interested in the same pieces, he did so rather than risk further unpleasantness with Schliemann at any cost. Calvert's letters to Schliemann clearly stipulated that the Hanay Tepe gift would be made in their joint names.[117] Whereas Calvert seems to have donated his finds, Schliemann, at least, saw this as an exchange for the decoration for Calvert.[118]

In spite of Calvert's gift to Berlin of his share of the finds—from his own excavations on his own land—he never received the promised decoration. With the exception of a little letter from Crown Prince Bernhard of Saxe-Meiningen (1851–1926) and one from the education minister, Paul Falk (1827–1909), Schliemann appears to have been unsuccessful in securing any recognition for Calvert from Germany.[119] Virchow was still trying in 1883, but Calvert's "gift" went unrequited.[120]

The first shipment of Hanay Tepe artifacts to Berlin was plagued with problems. Miscommunication and Schliemann's haste resulted in unnecessary damage.[121] Rather than accept the blame himself, Schliemann berated Calvert for carelessness. Because the Royal Museum was full, the collection went first to the Museum of Applied Art and Design and finally to the new Ethnographical Museum.[122] Virchow celebrated this acquisition with a presentation at the academy of science on 22 January 1880.[123]

Sometime after 21 August 1879, when John M. Francis, former United States minister to Greece, had written to the secretary of state on his behalf, Schliemann indirectly received a negative reply from the U.S. secretary of state to his application for the consulship.[124] He quickly abandoned his plan of buying the consulship with his collection and later explained to Field that he could not do otherwise than give his Trojan Collection to the German nation, "since the U.S. government refused to appoint me as their consul; had they done so the collection would long ago have been in the Smithsonian and it has been received in Germany with immense enthusiasm . . . for all ages to come it will attract to Berlin thousands of people from all parts of the world."[125]

By the time the Hanay Tepe material arrived in Berlin, Schliemann already secretly had willed his Trojan Collection to the German people.[126] It was only a question of when it would come. A year after the Hanay Tepe finds were received in Berlin, the director of the South Kensington Museum, in which Schliemann's Trojan Collection was being exhibited, asked him to remove it within a month because of space shortage.[127] Although Schliemann originally had been prejudiced against Germany and especially against Berlin,[128] the indignant excavator quickly offered the Trojan Collection to the people of Berlin in a letter to Crown Prince Bernhard of 11 December 1880 on the condition "that all the rooms in which it is exhibited bear my name."[129] It was Virchow who on 20 December discussed the matter with Richard Schöne, laid the matter before the minister and the German Parliament, and received the go-ahead that evening. This was indeed a coup for Schöne, who aggressively promoted acquisitions from Asia Minor in a concerted effort to outdo the collections of London and Paris.[130]

Because of the gift of the Trojan Collection, the joint gift of antiquities from Hanay Tepe was immediately and forever overshadowed. Calvert's generous gift was subsumed into the much larger collection of Schliemann's antiquities from Troy and known simply as the Schliemann Collection. From now on the gift was not only unrequited, but also unacknowledged.

But if Calvert had renewed his ties with Schliemann in the hope that they would open up future opportunities for him, his hope was rewarded. Rudolf Virchow breathed new life into Calvert's studies. Calvert and Virchow had similar interests.[131] In fact, they had corresponded since 1874, when Gustav Hirschfeld, later professor of archaeology at the University of Königsberg, had acquainted the pathologist with Calvert's article on Ophryneion and perhaps with his 1873 article on the remote prehistory of the Troad. Virchow had requested permission to work on the skeletal material, and Calvert sent it off himself.[132] Occasionally, Calvert, who did not read a word of German, would publish articles in the *Zeitschrift für Ethnologie*, the journal of the Berlin Society for Anthropology, Ethnography, and Prehistory, which Virchow edited. Unlike Newton in Calvert's early career, Virchow responded quickly to Calvert's queries, read Calvert's material carefully, and offered considered criticism and support. This was the sort of colleague Calvert had been looking for.

At the same time that Calvert was finding new support and recognition in the scholarly world, however, the role he could play in that world was being circumscribed by the growing professionalization of archaeological research and knowledge. Virchow, through the Berlin society, put Calvert into contact with a number of German scientists, scholars in a professionalized world, but Calvert was relegated to the periphery of their endeavors by virtue of his remote situation at the Dardanelles and his need to make a living outside the profession. Calvert would in effect serve in an accessory role for these professionals. Increasingly, he would provide the samples for interpretation by the professional scientists. In the world of late-nineteenth-century science, one needed institutional support for necessary equipment, libraries, and colleagues in order to remain active in one's field. The learned societies provided Calvert with colleagues, but he lacked the other requirements of scholarly scientific research. In this way he reverted to the role of the antiquarian. His primary occupation was the collection of data and the equally antiquarian participation in collective works.

A good example is Calvert's work on the remote prehistory of the Troad.[133] In 1873, Calvert had written an article on an exciting find from remote prehistory, not for a scholarly journal, but for the *Levant Herald*, where it appeared in both the daily and weekly editions and was reprinted in Europe.[134] Thanks to Edmund Calvert, who forwarded a copy to Sir John Lubbock, first president of the Royal Anthropological Institute of Great Britain and Ireland, it was read three weeks later at the Anthropological Institute in London, on 31 March 1873. Only then was it published in the newly founded *Journal of the Anthropological Institute*, where it was seen by many prehistorians.[135]

The remains Calvert had found came from well before the Bronze and Stone Ages, from geological time—the Miocene epoch, dated thirteen to twenty-five million years before the present. Calvert wrote that he had found a bone of the long-extinct deinotherium, or mastodon, on which had been carved the figure of a horned quadruped, along with seven or eight other figures. Nearby in the same cliff he had come upon a flint flake with animal bones split lengthwise for the extraction of marrow. Worn flint and jasper tools gave proof of human existence in drift deposits. But the scientific validation of the find and its assimilation into the growing body of professional knowledge concerning remote prehistory was done by others. His mentor, Tchihatcheff, had determined the geological age of the cliff, and Sir John Lubbock sent the bones and shells Calvert found for analysis by experts, who identified them as of the same age.

In his later excavations at Ophryneion, Abydos, and Tavolia and in general observation of landslides along the northern coast, Calvert found more prehistoric remains under the Classical period sites. At some sites, he encountered significant fossils, as well as stone and bone tools indicative of very early human activity.[136] Calvert refrained from excavating the promising site until the proper specialist arrived, realizing the importance of the fossils. In 1874, the paleontologist Melchior Neumayr, a member of the Berlin Society for Anthropology, Ethnography, and Prehistory, journeyed to the Troad, and their joint work on this early prehistoric material began.[137] Calvert supplied the fossils, analyzed geological deposits, and drafted plans of the geomorphology of early coastal sites. But it was Neumayr who studied the fossils and presented their co-authored material to the mathematical-natural scientific gathering of the Imperial Viennese Academy in January 1880.[138] In subsequent work on raised gravel beds, Calvert found early stone tools but demurred from publishing them, humbly wishing "to have a more competent authority than my own."[139] His need to earn his livelihood as a merchant had made it virtually impossible for him to participate independently in the professionalized scientific scholarship of the late nineteenth century.

Calvert had become a corresponding member of the Berlin Society for Anthropology, Ethnography, and Prehistory in 1875, along with Huxley, Evans, Lubbock, and Franks in England and Worsaae in Denmark.[140] Calvert regularly reported finds and forwarded local articles of interest to the society's group on the subject of excavations in Asia Minor. One such was his *Athenaeum* review of *Troy and Its Remains,* which Virchow summarized for the gathering months before he met Schliemann.[141]

Both Calvert and Virchow wanted to put Hisarlık into context geologically. Synthesizing years of observations of landslides, of ancient walls then under water, and of ancient towns and graves from Abydos to Ophryneion, Calvert devised a theory of geological change for the region that focused on coastal erosion of the Hellespontine shore and disputed the theory of the encroachment of the sea into the Trojan plain. Virchow and his son translated and presented Calvert's paper at the society on 20 December 1879. Then Virchow published it in the society's journal.[142]

Virchow's support encouraged Calvert to prepare other scientific contributions.[143] From this point on, Calvert published almost all of his articles in Germany. He began sending artifacts and submissions on remote prehistory to Virchow for feedback. As Calvert struggled with locust infestation at Thymbra Farm, he wrote an article on the insect for Virchow.[144]

Calvert and Virchow did not always agree, but each could tolerate opposition better than Schliemann.[145] Calvert's thesis on coastal erosion of the northern coast of the Troad opposed the general consensus but has been borne out by recent geological research.[146] He had observed both gradual erosion and the cataclysmic effect of landslides in which more than a million cubic yards of earth had collapsed from a height of a hundred feet.[147] Because he also had witnessed dramatic changes to the bay of the Dardanelles and the Menderes River as a result of flash flooding, Calvert rejected Strabo's view (13.1.36) that the embayment had shrunk over time and concurred with Maclaren, who had argued that it was basically static.[148] Schliemann and Virchow originally followed Strabo, thinking that Troy was much closer to the water before the large inlet of the sea filled in with silt from the Scamander. But as a result of test pits Virchow dug around the Trojan plain, Virchow sided with Calvert, claiming that the topography had not changed significantly in the past 4000 years,[149] although on this point they erred.[150]

Inspired by his successful scholarly collaboration with Neumayr, Calvert decided to compile his observations and produce a geological map of the Hellespontine coast and hinterland. He announced his intentions to Schliemann in 1880 and asked to borrow Schliemann's copy of Tchichatcheff, his English admiralty maps, a barometer, and other equipment.[151] When Schliemann voiced concerns about Calvert's inadequacy,[152] Calvert responded that he simply wished to compile many observations that he had had the opportunity of making over time.[153] Considering Calvert's proposal ill advised and too demanding, Schliemann misrepresented his requests to Virchow. But Virchow expressed his provisional support for Calvert's proposition as long as he would send his geological samples off to Vienna or Berlin for testing.[154] After all, Calvert was not a novice. He already had published on the geology of the coastal formation of the shores of the Hellespont and specific archaeological sites.[155] Because Schliemann planned to bring architects with surveying instruments on his 1882 campaign, he promised Calvert access to the necessary equipment for his own research.[156] However, since local authorities seized the equipment before any work could be done, Calvert never compiled his map.[157]

Calvert had explored ancient mines by the late 1860s. Putting his geological expertise to work, he and his brother James even had secured several mining concessions. But the development of such finds was notoriously difficult in Turkey. There was no governmental support, no infrastructure coordinating the industry, and it was difficult to find capital and transport ores to market.[158] One mine was in the Balıkesır area to the southeast, another lay to the south, around Edremit, and still another lay at Hassan Alan, at the foot of Çığrı Dağ between Geyikli and Ezine.[159] A boracite mine engaged him near Panderma and there was an argentiferous lead mine near Lapsekı (Lampsakos).[160] Undoubtedly, those for which he had no concession went unmentioned. A rich deposit excavated by Calvert lay at Bergaz, ancient Perkote.[161] In another mine, he found fossils embedded in limestone between immense mineral veins of iron, copper, and lead that had been worked in antiquity.[162] But the Calverts' pride was the ancient gold mine of Astyra, southeast of Çanakkale, for which they obtained a concession for ninety-nine years in 1877. There, Calvert had found ancient galleries, traces of working, the ruins of a fortress, and fortification walls to protect the ancient miners.[163]

With the exception of the Astyra mine, it is difficult to connect Calvert's vague references to his mining efforts with actual locations of mines now known in the Troad and areas of Edremit and Balıkesır.[164] In his 1879 report, Calvert noted the presence in Biğa province (Çanakkale district) of "gold, silver, copper, lead, zinc, iron, chromate of iron, manganese, sulfur, lignite, alum, sulfate of iron, salt and gypsum." However, only three of these minerals were exported (among them, lead and manganese to the United Kingdom).[165] The mines are many, but with the exception of Astyra, it is difficult to prove that any of these were worked by Calvert because those who have researched them know nothing or next to nothing about Calvert's work.[166] But they were critically important to the ancient world, as well as to Calvert's livelihood. Silver used in important treasures from Near Eastern capitals contemporary with Bronze Age levels at Troy has been traced to deposits in the Troad.[167] Both the Bergaz mine and that of Balya Maden (in the Balıkesır region) have been suggested as sources of the silver found at Troy itself.[168] Extensive traces of old workings have been found in the Balıkesır mine, which contains one of the most important deposits of silver in Asia Minor.[169] Several authorities have referred vaguely to silver deposits with old shafts northeast of Mount Ida (Kaz Dağ), one area suggested for Calvert's Cave of Andeira. Other mines, a number of which were worked and abandoned,[170] contain copper, lead, iron, and sundry other ores.[171] Orpiment, or yellow arsenic, a highly prized commodity in long-distance trade during the Bronze Age, also has been found in area mines worked in antiquity.[172] Until more documentation surfaces, the true extent of his efforts and any benefits Calvert derived from them, as well as the significance of his discoveries, will not be known.

As soon as Calvert met Virchow in 1879, Calvert also began to collect botanical specimens for Virchow's herbarium in Berlin. Virchow, in turn, through the Society for Anthropology, Ethnography, and Prehistory, put him in touch with Berlin botanist Paul Ascherson (1834–1913).[173] For his contribution of thirty-one species of plants in 1879 and 1880, Ascherson, Theodor von Heldreich (1822–1902), and F. Kurtz singled out Calvert in their appendix to *Ilios*, "Catalogue of the Plants of the Troad. . . ."[174] The material they studied came from the collections of Virchow, Calvert, and the astronomer Julius Schmidt, who had dug with von Hahn at Pınarbaşı. Between 1880 and 1882, Calvert's collaboration with Ascherson resulted in an expanded treatment of the flora of the Troad, which Ascherson published in 1883.[175] In the introduction, Ascherson praised Calvert's own extensive collection and expert botanical knowledge.[176] Between 1880 and 1884, Calvert contributed more than seven hundred prepared samples of more than one hundred species to the Royal Botanical Museum in Berlin and provided the common names in Turkish and modern Greek. These he had obtained by trekking and scrutinizing the landscape from Cyzicus (Artaki), along the Simois River, and south to Balıkesır. Thus, he added significantly to the previous research of Tchihatcheff. Ascherson noted that many of the species had not been observed before Calvert's work. Just as with Neumayr, Calvert had supplied the critical samples that subsequently were analyzed by professionals. His collaborator praised his meticulous fieldwork, observation, and local experience.[177]

But among all those with whom Frank Calvert collaborated in their investigations of his beloved Troad, the most important remained Heinrich Schliemann. Almost immediately after publishing *Ilios*, Schliemann had become skeptical respecting the extent of the settlement that he had connected with Homer. He was plagued by thought that in Homer's accurate description of the landscape, Hisarlık itself was out of scale: "a few hundred men might have taken it in a few days, and the whole Trojan war . . . would easily have been a total fiction."[178] He wanted to be absolutely sure there were no other candidates for Homeric Troy in the area. At the same time, both Schliemann and Calvert were perplexed at the similarity of the pottery from the lowest stratum at Hisarlık and Hanay Tepe and yet the difference in burial techniques. Schliemann was particularly concerned about locating the cemetery of the prehistoric inhabitants of Troy.[179] Calvert, on the other hand, was concerned about dating the middle level at Hanay Tepe. In 1856, he had suggested that it was Homeric in date. In 1879, he had dated it as contemporary with Schliemann's "Lydian" level at Hisarlık. Because of the implications for dating the remains at Hisarlık, he now wanted to establish the age of the pottery of this level.

As early as July 1879, however, Schliemann was looking ahead and asking Calvert what his excavation plans were after Hanay Tepe.[180] Roughly a year later, Calvert proposed a campaign of strategic exploratory digging to address target localities worthy of further excavation when Schliemann returned with the next *firman*. This way, both men could satisfy their personal scholarly objectives while contributing to a common solution. Excavations were necessary to secure good dates because "our knowledge is very imperfect on this subject," and Calvert recommended tombs as the cheapest way of obtaining the relevant data.[181] Together they planned a wide-ranging cooperative archaeological venture at numerous sites throughout the Troad that would use Calvert's time, knowledge, and expertise and Schliemann's money.[182]

This, of course, had been the basis of their relationship from the start. What was different about it this time was that because they had as yet no *firman*, the new excavations were to be clandestine. The government was to know nothing about them, and Schliemann was to share the proceeds equally with Calvert. Schliemann's 1878–79 permit had expired, and he foresaw renewed troubles inherent in getting a new one. This was a dangerous way to proceed with their legitimate inquiries.[183]

Calvert wrote to Schliemann on 10 November 1880 that

> *pioneer* work should be undertaken now with not more than six men in the necropoli of ancient towns—this I can do without attracting attention—this method will save you much time—by the results the most likely localities can be selected as no share will be given to the govt., I propose the proceeds should be shared by us equally. I give my time and knowledge, you the funds. I promise nothing shall be published of the discoveries which should be numbered and record kept of locality [e]tc. I anticipate in preliminary point of view you will be no loser, for the value of the objects, I think, to come from your share will be amply represented vs. amount expended.[184]

In the spring of 1881, Schliemann approached Otto von Bismarck (1815–1898), chancellor of imperial Germany, to aid in his suit to get a permit to excavate not only Hisarlık and the lower plateau of Ilium Novum, but also throughout the Troad, and on liberal terms,[185] after which he said he planned to explore the region for the rest of his life. While they were waiting for the permit, Calvert proceeded to excavate. After a brief interlude at Orchomenos in the spring, Schliemann returned to the Troad, where he reviewed the sites with Calvert. From 11 May to 21 May 1881, Schliemann traveled throughout the Troad. After the trip, he wrote, "I was pleased with my journey for I now know for certain that, whilst at Hissarlik the accumulation of prehistoric ruins, 14 metres deep, is succeeded by a layer of Hellenic ruins and debris two metres deep, there is in the whole Troad, between the Hellespont, the Gulf of Adramyttium, and the Chain of Ida, no site containing prehistoric ruins, except at Hanai Tepeh and Besik Tepeh."[186]

That summer, Schliemann was in Berlin, setting up the exhibition of the Trojan Collection.[187] In July 1881, he was made an honorary citizen of the city. Meanwhile, Calvert had targeted a number of localities where it would be advantageous to dig, looking for burial sites and sites contemporary with the middle stratum at Hanay Tepe and the Lydian stratum at Hisarlık.[188] On 9 July, Schliemann expressed his and Virchow's interest in Calvert's finds and enclosed a check to cover expenses, begging him to continue the excavations throughout the Troad until he arrived. But, Schliemann stipulated, "do *not* dig either on Hissarlik or on the site of the Lower City of Ilium."[189] Schliemann asked to be informed about Calvert's activities.[190] He planned to resume exploration in Calvert's field, where he hoped to find more marble sculpture from the Temple of Athena, in the theater, where he also anticipated rich finds, and in the plateau below the citadel, where he hoped to find the prehistoric cemetery.[191] The permit finally came through in October 1881.[192]

Meanwhile, Calvert was pursuing their clandestine project. "The results of the diggings are satisfactory on the whole so far. I mark all the objects discovered so that you can see where they have been found, at a glance. There are a number of localities where it would be desirable for you to dig, but you must not be impatient, for it is prudent not to put too many men to work at a time."[193] On 1 September 1881, Calvert vaguely mentioned excavations that he lately had made. Among the sites Calvert had targeted were Ophryneion, where he excavated a well to a depth of 6 meters, and the Bay of Artaki, where Calvert found underwater ruins of Cyzicus.[194] In October, Calvert urged Schliemann to excavate at Pınarbaşı on the Ballı Dağ "to crush once and for all the Bounarbashi theory." The necropolis would furnish objects of interest, and several spots looked promising.[195]

Schliemann seems to have been most interested in two cemeteries, Köprü Başı, near Ezine,[196] and Çamlıca, two hours from Thymbra Farm.[197] Three noteworthy bronze fibulae, that is, brooches or clasps, ancient, but not as old as the prehistoric remains at Hisarlık, had been found at Köprü Başı. Virchow, who had been advancing a pet theory based on similar brooches from the Caucasus, was keen to study them in Berlin.[198] Schliemann wished to acquire them for the Schliemann Collection.[199] At the same time, Schliemann asked Calvert to send the finds from the last excavations at Hanay Tepe to Berlin to be added to the Trojan Collection.[200]

Meanwhile, Calvert continued scouting sites for Schliemann in 1882, reporting that he had "found five ancient sites in the area [of Balıkesır], but having no book with me, I am unable to identify them."[201] In July of that year, he recommended that Schliemann excavate at Astyra and Abydos.[202] Astyra was particularly promising, with large dumps and a network of underground passages. According to Calvert, this was Priam's gold mine, worked already long before Strabo's time.[203] But these were too far from Schliemann's primary goal, Hisarlık, where he had resumed excavations in the spring.[204]

The clandestine campaign is one of the first underhanded dealings in which Frank Calvert engaged. His scholarly interest in finding sites contemporary with the middle stratum at Hanay Tepe, which he strongly believed was Homeric in date, and in examining prehistoric grave types in the Troad only partly explains his motivation for such an obviously illegal course of action. His reasons may have been economic as well as intellectual. Calvert again was short of money.[205]

Valonia prices were down, and a small crop was predicted.[206] Schliemann's correspondence with Virchow may best reveal Calvert's motivation. There, Schliemann mentioned that in June 1882 Calvert still wanted to continue the excavations at Hanay Tepe as soon as Schliemann would give him the money.[207] But Schliemann was displeased with the quality of the mostly fragmentary finds and thought it a waste of time. And Calvert never resumed excavating the partially opened site.

In his preface to *Ilios,* Virchow had written: "Whoever has himself made an excavation knows that minor errors can hardly be avoided, and that the progress of an investigation almost always corrects some of the results of earlier stages of the enquiry." He noted Schliemann's succession settlements at Hisarlık, which by now totaled seven, but cautioned that "order of succession is not yet chronology." The deeper that one descended at Hisarlık, the fewer correspondences there were that one could cross-date with datable material elsewhere. For this reason, he maintained that adaptation of a foreign chronology to Hisarlık seemed "in the highest degree dangerous."[208] Schliemann never had given dates to the prehistoric settlements because he would have had to explain why several settlements intervened between Homeric Troy and the Lydian settlement only 180 years later. When Schliemann returned in March 1882, he once more would be absorbed with questions arising from Calvert's thousand-year gap, in addition to his nagging doubts about the size of the stratum in which he had discovered all of the treasures, the one he claimed belonged to Priam.

Schliemann began in March with 150 laborers, as before. This time, however, Schliemann concentrated on the hitherto largely neglected eastern half, Calvert's property.[209] At Richard Schöne's suggestion, he brought two architects, Wilhelm Dörpfeld (1853–1940), from Berlin, who had been working at Olympia, and Josef Höfler, from Vienna, and three overseers, one of whom was Gustav Batthus, Calvert's man.[210] Dörpfeld was hired to produce accurate maps and plans of the site with surveying instruments [Figure 39], but for more than six months the Turks forbade their use and prevented them from taking measurements of any sort.

Schliemann concentrated his efforts in the theater on Calvert's land to the northeast of the citadel and in the northeast corner of the acropolis, where he noted a magnificent wall of Macedonian construction. The wall Schliemann encountered was the massive wall that had stopped Calvert almost twenty years earlier. Schliemann had his men destroy the large blocks with hammers so they could be moved.[211] He wished to find sculpted blocks comparable to the Helios Metope but did not succeed, although he did uncover a Roman medallion of Romulus, Remus, and the she-wolf in the Augustan theater.[212] In the central area, he and Dörpfeld uncovered a series of *megarons,* or axial architectural complexes with porches, vestibules, and interior chambers in the burnt stratum.[213] Then he excavated several trenches in the plateau below the citadel, looking in vain for the prehistoric cemetery and attempting to gauge the size of the settlement.

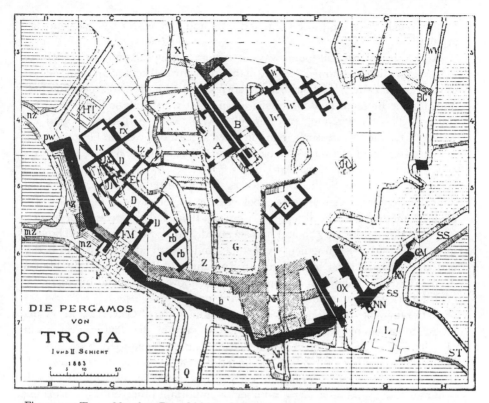

Figure 39. Troy, 1882 plan. Dörpfeld (1902), Figure 5, p. 13.

Expanding his focus in order to understand more about the as-yet-undiscovered cemeteries of Hisarlık, he excavated tumuli in the plain: those of Achilles, previously opened by Choiseul-Gouffier, and Patroclus at Sigeum,[214] Protesilaos on the Chersonese, and three barren mounds near the so-called Tomb of Ajax. Then he struck out to the south, excavating one of four tumuli and the site of Pınarbaşı on the Ballı Dağ. He continued by exploring Eskı Hisarlık on the opposite bank of the Scamander, Fulu Dağ, Kurşunlu Tepe (near Beiramiç), and Cebrene sites all previously excavated by Frank Calvert.

In many ways, the season was a success. Dörpfeld and Höfler had begun to help clear up the stratigraphy of the mound.[215] Instead of subdividing the lowest stratum, they split the level above the burned second stratum of Priam's Treasure in two, thus maintaining but renumbering the six prehistoric strata [Figure 28].[216] After the season was over, Schliemann, ill with fever,[217] chastised Calvert for lack of enthusiasm.[218] Calvert, who was nursing his dying brother Henry, responded, "You complain of my indifference to archaeology—this is unkind of you, for circumstances prevent me from doing more in my favourite pursuit. . . .

Unfortunately, I have not the unlimited time and means you have at your disposal."[219]

As before, Schliemann found ways of circumventing the authorities with regard to exporting his finds.[220] Already in the spring he had kept them from the Ottoman government.[221] He and Schöne corresponded on how to secure the best finds for the museum in Berlin while leaving the worst for the Turks (and for Calvert). The division took place in July, with twenty-two crates bound for Berlin.[222] Of the two treasures found in 1882, at least one went to Germany in a secret consignment of twenty-one baskets via Athens with the help of Emilio Vitalis, Italian vice-consul at the Dardanelles.[223]

At the same time, Schliemann once again capitalized on Calvert's financial difficulties to purchase his antiquities below value, as, for example, in the case of a gladiator metope from the Temple of Athena at Ilion. Calvert, pressed for money, had offered it to him for £70 and had accepted £30.[224] Schliemann also bought from Calvert two other fragmentary metopes and forwarded all of them to Berlin with the Augustan relief medallion with Romulus and Remus[225] and the fibulae from Köprü Başı. Although the brooches were above and beyond his share, he prided himself on getting them from Calvert for free.[226]

At this time they also discussed Schliemann's inclusion of Calvert's study of the mountain stronghold Neandria in *Troja,* the account of the 1882 excavations at Hisarlık. Calvert had identified the site decades earlier, thanks to its description by Demetrius of Scepsis.[227] He had conducted the earliest archaeological research there, excavating the necropolis with early graves of the late eighth and seventh centuries B.C.[228] and amassing a number of important observations concerning the connections of successive architectural styles and ceramics with Troy that he subsequently had communicated to Newton, Schliemann, and others. It was this pottery that was crucial to understanding the thousand-year gap that still plagued efforts to identify Homer's Troy at Hisarlık. Calvert believed that it linked both the prehistoric Lydian city of Troy and the middle stratum of Hanay Tepe with the Archaic period Greek remains from the seventh to sixth centuries B.C. at both sites.[229] Unfortunately, Calvert and Schliemann did not agree on the dating.[230] Perhaps for this reason, although Schliemann gave a different excuse, Calvert's report was not included in *Troja,* and his ideas had to wait a decade to be published by Robert Koldewey (1855–1925), a young member of the Assos excavation team, who later excavated Neandria.[231]

By January 1883, Schliemann's eyes were again on Knossos, Crete, "still virgin soil to archaeology."[232] On 15 April, he wrote his American publisher, "I have now terminated for ever the excavations on the site of sacred Ilios . . . as Troy is now entirely excavated, and as there is no other Troy to excavate, the life of this book will last as long as men will love divine Homer,—that is to say as long as our globe will be inhabited by men."[233] Schliemann also wrote to Gladstone in advance of his copy of *Troja,* due out in November, "I have brought to light all what remained of the Homeric Ilios . . . this is my last book on Troy, for my work is terminated there for ever."[234] In recognition of his tremendous achievements, he was made a fellow of Sayce's college—Queens College, Oxford.[235]

Although Schliemann initially had feared that Virchow would interfere with the hold he exerted over Calvert, in the long run, the presence of the third man helped dampen the severity of the others' conflicts. Virchow had helped to raise Schliemann's opinion of Calvert, and thanks to Virchow, a personal friendship eventually grew between Calvert and Schliemann. In 1883, Schliemann invited Calvert to Athens, and the visit was apparently a success. Calvert responded that it "left very pleasant reminiscences."[236]

In March 1885 Schliemann received the gold medal of the Royal Institute of Architects from Queen Victoria for his work at Hisarlık, Mycenae, Orchomenos, and Tiryns and for his publications. With this "incessant personal exertion" and "lavish expenditure of his own money, Dr. Schliemann has succeeded in recovering a lost chapter in the history of the arts of the world and in rehabilitating to the scientific mind what have been considered as the mystic arts of ancient Greece."[237] Calvert congratulated him: "May you long live to enjoy the satisfaction of wearing this crowning point of your labours."[238] He already had forwarded the news to the *Eastern Express*, successor to the *Levant Herald*.

The growing friendship soon involved the next Calvert generation and Francis Henry Bacon, as well. From 1881 to 1883, Bacon worked as architect at the Assos excavations, which Calvert facilitated in many ways. There Bacon first met Calvert and his nieces, Edith and Laura (1862–1942).[239] By then Bacon was less in awe of Schliemann and assessed him candidly: "He wouldn't talk about anything but prehistoric remains and cared nothing for our work here."[240] By late summer 1883, Bacon had enjoyed Calvert hospitality at the Dardanelles and Thymbra Farm and ascended Mount Ida with the Calvert sisters and Koldewey, his German colleague at Assos.[241] In June 1885, when Bacon wed Alice Calvert, Schliemann sent wedding presents and a year later congratulations on the birth of their son, Frederick.[242] Frederick R. J. Calvert (1853–1927), the only son and the namesake of the late consul, followed his father into the British consular service. When his consulate at Adrianople (Edirne) burned to the ground and he and his sisters lost everything, Schliemann thoughtfully sent aid.[243] But of all the children, it was Edith Calvert who was most interested in Schliemann's work.[244] She developed a lively correspondence with him, read his books, and visited his excavations. In turn, Schliemann always asked to be remembered to her.[245]

In 1883, Calvert graciously had commended Schliemann for *Troja*. "It will crown the great work of your labours at Troy—the extensive excavations will not be obliterated by time, but remain a standing monument to the energy and perseverance of a distinguished devotée to archaeological science."[246] This was Calvert's highest praise—the kind that he would have wished for his own life's work. But that was not to be. Schliemann had far surpassed Calvert and had obliterated the traces of Calvert's own excavations, leaving no standing monument to their excavator.

CHAPTER TEN

"More remains buried than has been brought to light" Homer's Troy

In 1885, Schliemann grandly declared to a friend that "wherever I hitherto put the spade into the ground, I always discovered new worlds for archaeology at Troy, Mycenae, Orchomenos, Tiryns, each of them brought to light wonders. . . . I ought to imitate Rossini, who stopped after having composed a few but splendid operas, which can never be excelled."[1] But Schliemann was as wrong to assume that his archaeological labors were at an end as he had been when he told Gladstone that his work at Hisarlık was finished.

Schliemann still was haunted by the problem posed by Calvert's thousand-year gap. In 1879, Schliemann partially had closed the gap with the recognition of a sixth stratum, the one he had called "Lydian" and had dated, according to historical tradition, to approximately 1044 B.C. Now he needed to link Hisarlık firmly to the Homeric citadels of Greece at Tiryns and Mycenae, which were well known thanks to his own excavations. But he had found very little at Hisarlık that compared to the Homeric levels of either town, and of the precious few objects he could compare, the similarities were more between material from the Lydian stratum than from the second stratum at Hisarlık. Even more troublesome was vicious and repeated criticism from a German amateur, Ernst Bötticher. So Schliemann again returned to Troy for one last try at disproving his critics and at establishing, beyond the possibility of objection, his claim to have discovered Homeric Troy.

The years that preceded Schliemann's finale were quiet ones for Hisarlık and the Calverts. Since 1881, Calvert had been helping the fledgling American expedition at Assos, a town that figured in both Homer and Strabo.[2] Calvert enjoyed his association with the Americans, who valued his expertise and saved for him the honor of opening certain graves at Assos. When Clarke found a rare Aeolic column capital at Neandria in 1882, Calvert helped him move it to Thymbra Farm for study before it became part of the collection of the Imperial Ottoman Museum.[3] Calvert also helped expedite the legitimate export of the American share of the Assos finds, which the Archaeological Institute of America gave to the Museum of Fine Arts, established in 1870 in Boston. In 1883, after the close of the excavations, the Archaeological Institute of America officially recognized Calvert's generous efforts on behalf of their expedition. For his "constant kindness" and for "attentions which have contributed . . . to the success of their work," they presented him with a large flag of the United States.[4] Calvert treasured the flag and flew it from the roof of the consular mansion on the Fourth of July and other special occasions.[5]

It had become increasingly hard for foreign excavators to work in Turkey. To protect cultural patrimony and channel it toward the Imperial Ottoman Museum, the Ottoman government enacted a tighter antiquities law in February 1884, basically a reproduction of the long-standing regulations employed by Greece, whereby the state forbade the exportation of all works of art and declared that all objects found belonged by right to the state.[6] This time they were adamant. The reason for the new regulations had not so much to do with Schliemann's smuggling as with much larger "exportations."[7] Calvert wrote to Schliemann of this setback on 13 March 1884: "exportation is prohibited of all relics and consuls are not allowed to excavate within their jurisdiction." But he added sanguinely, "I expect the same number of antiquities will find their way out of the country as before."[8] In its first issue, the *American Journal of Archaeology* summarized the new antiquities law.[9] Pessimistically, the editor predicted a complete cessation of the enterprising activity at Pergamon, Halicarnassus, and Assos.[10] Reverend Joseph Hirst of Smyrna repeated Calvert's concerns in a letter of October 1885 to the Archaeological Institute in London that the Turkish government had "withdrawn all permission given to Englishmen and other foreigners to excavate ancient sites within the Sultan's dominions, and also that large quantities of finely sculptured pillars, walls, and stones are being sold and utilized for modern building purposes."[11]

Calvert, meanwhile, lacked direction, latching like an antiquarian onto assorted projects rather than focusing on a larger goal. He wrote Virchow that because of his absence from the Dardanelles for many months, in Balıkesir and London, he had had little time for archaeological pursuits. Still, he had managed to write a brief article on the braziers or cooking stoves of the earliest stratum of Hanay Tepe, which he sent to Virchow for comments.[12] He also forwarded to his German colleague a paper on coal at an archaeological site in a bituminous region, which he planned to publish in America.[13]

Schliemann was restless, too. With his health beginning to fail, he eyed Crete for his next conquest and wished in vain to sink his spade into the hill at Knossos where a local antiquarian had made profitable excavations in 1878 and 1879. Instead, in March 1884 he resumed the important excavations begun at Tiryns in 1876. With Dörpfeld, he made sense of the palace plan and fortification system and brought out the site volume, *Tiryns*, a year later.[14]

Although Calvert was keenly interested in the location of Troy, his net was wider than Schliemann's, and he was equally interested in classical sites and their contexts. At forty-one, he had wanted to clear up as much as possible in his life-time the archaeology of the Troad.[15] Despite his other commitments, he had spent most of his life doing just that. In 1885, at fifty-six, he again wrote optimisti-cally to Schliemann: "Far from the mine of scientific riches being exhausted in this portion of Asia Minor . . . more remains buried than has been brought to light." But he believed that by means of the new regulations, "Hamdi Bey has effectively closed the road of the archaeologist."[16] Hamdi Bey had assumed the directorship of the Imperial Ottoman Museum in Constantinople after Déthier's death in 1881. Calvert complained that he was "putting the screw on. The excavation by any person competent to preserve from ruin precious relics is surrounded by great difficulties. Stringent orders have been sent to all governors to prevent any exca-vation—all antiquities are confiscated. On the other hand wholesale destruction of ancient remains by the peasantry is freely permitted. Such is the logic of Hamdy's ideas on archaeology."[17] Still, Calvert encouraged Schliemann and then confided to him that permission to excavate could be obtained: "My excavations are limited to a very small scale—examination of tombs *sub rosa*."[18]

In fact, Hamdi Edhem Bey (1842–1910), whose task it was to administer the ex-cavation and recovery of archaeological finds on Turkish soil, was highly edu-cated, a distinguished painter and archaeologist and an alumnus of the Ecole des Beaux Arts, Paris, where he had studied with Jean-Léon Gérôme, France's most renowned "Orientalist" painter.[19] As grand vizier, his father, Edhem Pasha, had tried to force English archaeologists in Mesopotamia to yield their finds to the Im-perial Ottoman Museum in 1878–1879, as their *firmans* dictated, but was thwarted by Ambassador Layard.

But Hamdi Bey was in a difficult position. He and his brother Halil, who later succeeded him as museum director from 1910 to 1931, were Western-educated and Western-oriented Muslim patriots.[20] As such, they, too, sought to preserve antiq-uities found on Turkish soil for their nation, even as the Ottoman world was crum-bling around them. Hamdi Bey wished to elevate the Imperial Ottoman Museum to the stature of the great European museums. Their antiquities legislation had followed the wholesale removal of the Pergamon altar. Other major European ex-propriations would follow because Sultan Abdul Hamid II (1842–1909), who had come to power in 1876, had no interest whatsoever in Greek or early Christian re-mains, and the Porte, although not the antiquities administration, was willing "to barter antiquities for Western support" to guarantee Ottoman sovereignty.[21] Hos-tility consequently was directed toward the antiquities administration by the sul-tan, as well as by the peasantry. The department was understaffed, and Hamdi Bey was forbidden to leave the walls of Constantinople for a decade because of his politics.[22] Although he had added clauses to the legislation for the protection of ancient monuments, he could not enforce them, and the extraction of excavation *firmans* by foreigners began to be seen as an "incipient form of colonial rule."[23] Perhaps because of his stressful position, he also was volatile. One friend described him as capable of "working himself into a rage over a triviality and ten minutes later dancing the cancan."[24] The job of protecting Ottoman antiquities from the predations of sultan, peasantry, and foreign archaeologists thus was difficult socially and politically. When whole walls of squared stone of the Greek and Roman eras at Hisarlık disappeared for a new mosque at Kum Kale, Calvert blamed, undeservedly, the "archaeological humbug, Hamdi Bey."[25] Schliemann attempted to protect the site by securing a new *firman.*[26]

In February 1886, the *Levant Herald and Eastern Express* ran an editorial corroborating Calvert's predictions concerning the effects of the 1884 antiquities law and concluded that it largely had failed in its objectives to enrich the Imperial Ottoman Museum and to prevent the destruction of monuments, clandestine excavation, and the illegal export of antiquities. Because of the law's strictness, it noted, legitimate archaeologists, Schliemann among them, were looking elsewhere.[27] Meanwhile, it pointed out, a new industry had sprung up in Smyrna devoted to the fabrication of spurious terra-cottas to supply an avid market.

In Schliemann's absence, Calvert continued to publish when he could. He completed an article on meteor showers, documenting the remarkable coincidence of the fall of six meteors within a radius of 24 kilometers in the Troad and the Chersonese from 467 B.C. to 1886. He sent it on to Virchow, who translated it and saw that it got published in Germany in 1886.[28]

Calvert's personal circumstances had their ups and downs. After a long convalescence, Calvert's sister died during the summer of 1886.[29] Perhaps temporarily freed of responsibilities, and in defiance of Hamdi Bey's legislation, Calvert scouted for new and promising archaeological sites. He was finding antiquities in the ancient workings of his gold mine and noting the ancients' mining technology.[30] He was concerned about Schliemann's health and cautioned him to slow down.[31] Disagreeing with Schliemann's pessimistic assessment of the number of prehistoric sites in the Troad, Calvert correctly advised him, "To find a great depth of accumulated material as at Hissarlik is exceptional. There are prehistoric settlements on which no other subsequent buildings were placed. These are not in the form of a mound and are difficult to detect by the unpracticed eye."[32] But Schliemann, still wary of the new law code, coveted rich Knossos and took Dörpfeld with him to examine the site that summer.

Forest fires, locust infestation, brigandage, and disease stalked the recently fortified Dardanelles. An earthquake wracked the town in mid-May of 1887, causing a minaret to collapse, but also providing the opportunity for building a new school and a military hospital, and for widening the street and expanding the town along the bay to the east.[33] In June, the town celebrated Queen Victoria's jubilee. All consulates flew their flags, and the British colony attended a reception with the highest Ottoman civil and military officials. "God Save the Queen" and a royal salute echoed through the streets. On the night of the jubilee, Calvert, who once again was the acting British consul, opened his garden to the public. The family had hung the trees with lights, giving "a fairy-like appearance," while the lofty terrace of the Calvert mansion glowed with a double row of lights. The still waters

of the straits reflected myriad lights illuminating the houses of the smug British inhabitants.[34]

By contrast with Victoria's jubilee, 1888 was a slow year, and permission to excavate indeed was becoming more difficult.[35] In January 1887, Schliemann again
had expressed reservations to Calvert about reopening excavations at Troy.[36] In
1888, in response to Calvert's renewed questions about a campaign at Hisarlık,
Schliemann wrote that he was helpless without Yannakis, his old paymaster and
servant, who had drowned in the Scamander in 1884.[37] Furthermore, he was busy
arranging the Trojan Collection at the Ethnographical Museum in Berlin.

Schliemann was still hoping to excavate at Knossos, where he and Dörpfeld
had seen "the walls of a prehistoric palace" with "heaps of potsherds of the Mycenaean type and age (1400 B.C.)."[38] His understanding of the importance of such
evidence is clear from his statement that "comparative pottery is just as important
as comparative philology."[39] He left for Crete in February 1889 to complete his
purchase of the mound but a month later reported that Crete was "a no go."[40]
Meanwhile, Calvert finally published a note on his gold mines at Astyra, which
Strabo had attributed to Priam,[41] and sold his mining concession to an English
company.[42] This triumph increased Schliemann's estimation of Calvert, and he
now consulted with him about the existence of minerals needed in Germany,
which was interested in exploiting its friendship with the Sublime Porte to obtain
raw materials.[43] And the German archaeologist Robert Koldewey had begun to
probe Calvert's site of Neandria.[44]

But this lull was coming to an end. New critics were questioning Schliemann's
claims about Troy. Again the war waged between the proponents of Hisarlık versus the loyal followers of Chevalier, who still championed Pınarbaşı. In April 1887,
Calvert reported to the *Levant Herald and Eastern Express* that the southernmost tumulus near Pınarbaşı on the Ballı Dağ had been opened at night on 6/7 March by
a group of Turks with their imam, or priest.[45] Unlike the other three, which had
been excavated by Calvert, Schliemann, and Lubbock, this one had remained untouched and was rich in grave goods: a golden diadem with oak leaves and acorns,
three thin golden fillets with embossed figured and geometric decoration, fine
strips of gold, fragments of a bronze mirror case, and fragments of alabaster oil
flasks, sprigs of myrtle on lead stems with gilt berries, and bronze patera, or shallow bowls.[46] Calvert regretted that the tomb had been excavated by incompetent
persons but credited the Ottoman authorities for rescuing the treasure "from the
melting pot." In spite of Calvert's claim that this later treasure would be conclusive proof against the argument that the Pınarbaşı tumuli were those of Priam,
Hector, and the Trojans, Calvert and Schliemann had still not yet silenced those
who preferred Pınarbaşı. Instead, the editor of the *American Journal of Archaeology*
predicted that it would "revive the archaeological war" about Troy.[47] It certainly
revived Schliemann's interest. On 24 April, Schliemann arrived with Carl Schuchhardt (1859–1943), a German archaeologist working on the Pergamon excavations.
Immediately suspicious of Schliemann's motives, the authorities demanded to see

Schliemann's *firman*. Because he had none, they prevented him from visiting Hisarlık, to which he had walked from the Dardanelles, and made him return unsatisfied.[48]

Much more crucial for Schliemann was the mounting disturbance caused by Ernst Bötticher. As a member of the Society for Anthropology, Ethnography, and Prehistory, the former German artillery officer published his first communication in the pages of Virchow's own journal in 1883.[49] On 17 December, he began a barrage, attacking Schliemann's entire interpretation of the site. Like Calvert, Bötticher focused on the second stratum. But unlike Calvert's reasoned, disinterested review in the *Levant Herald*, Bötticher's was ad hominem. He questioned the character and function of the site, accusing Schliemann and Dörpfeld of purposely misrepresenting Hisarlık. Schliemann's walls, temples, towers, and palaces were an illusion, Bötticher claimed, not Homer's Troy. Instead, Bötticher saw the ashes, cinerary urns, and half-burned bones of the second stratum as a huge crematorium. According to Bötticher, who was firmly in the Pınarbaşı camp, the mound at Hisarlık, with its network of crosswalls, was not a settlement at all, but rather a huge urn necropolis.[50] His argument rested on the depth of the ash deposit of the second stratum and the fact that there were no traces of the city outside the walls. Like Schliemann himself, Bötticher aimed to engage and persuade the public.

Schliemann was devastated by the assault. Although Bötticher's criticisms were, in fact, ridiculous, they struck a nerve with Schliemann, who for years had been concerned that he had not yet found Hisarlık's prehistoric cemeteries and was desperate to find evidence to increase the modest size of the second settlement. Virchow immediately spoke up at the 16 February meeting of the society, and his remarks were printed in the journal. But Bötticher was determined. In 1884 alone he published seven different articles, letters, and pamphlets. Dörpfeld stepped in to rebut him in October 1884. Undeterred, Bötticher always had the last word: there were nine more communications in 1885 alone.

After his 1886 attempt to challenge Schliemann was ignored, Bötticher retreated, but then, reinforced by the recent finds at Pınarbaşı, in 1888 he resumed his attack. By October 1889, eight more letters, articles, reviews, and pamphlets had been published. Schliemann had nagging questions of his own and felt seriously threatened. Dörpfeld fought back in the Berlin papers; Virchow did so as well, but Bötticher could not be silenced. Schliemann was older now, and increasingly unwell. Of all the attacks mounted by Bötticher, not one rebuttal was by Schliemann himself.

It is an index of the height of Schliemann's reputation, which was now jeopardized, and of the public's keen interest in Troy that these communications had been printed in numerous journals and newspapers, including one by Schliemann's own publisher, Brockhaus.[51] Learned societies also reported the controversy: in the proceedings of the German Anthropological Society in Breslau (1884) and Karlsruhe (1885); at the general meeting of the German Anthropological Society (5–10 August 1889);[52] and at the International Congress of Anthropology and Prehistoric Archaeology in Paris (19–26 August 1889). Schliemann belonged to the public, and they pitched their camps on one side or the other. Schliemann, the maverick whose money afforded him the privilege of independence from institutions and patrons, saw his life's work collapsing as major intellectual figures began to succumb to Bötticher's rhetoric. Bötticher, as much as or more than Schliemann, was a master at using the press. The fact that Bötticher's writings would be accepted for publication in such journals as the *Berlin Philological Weekly* shows the extent to which traditional classicists in academic hierarchies still hated and envied Schliemann.

Bötticher attacked Schliemann's associates, calling Virchow "Schliemann's employee" and Dörpfeld a "falsifier and forger" who broke away many walls "of furnaces in order to get plans for palaces."[53] To Schliemann's chagrin, Bötticher had a following and was converting serious scholars and archaeologists such as Salomon Reinach (1858–1932) of the Institut de France, whom Hamdi Bey had charged with the formal classification and cataloguing of the collection of the Imperial Ottoman Museum.[54]

Unable to silence Bötticher, to answer his accusations, Schliemann requested another permit from Constantinople.[55] On the same day, he wrote to Virchow that Pallas Athena had appeared to him in a dream. Virchow recommended that he send Calvert out to make a *sondage* with the hope of finding the cemetery at Hisarlık, which so far had eluded Schliemann, in order to disprove Bötticher's contention that the site itself was a necropolis.[56] Schliemann asked Calvert to help on 11 October.[57] A week later, the *firman* for Hisarlık was ready, and on 31 October 1889, Calvert was in the field, excavating a necropolis from the fourth century B.C.[58] Schliemann requested Calvert to keep absolute secrecy about this rich find so as not to jeopardize the ongoing negotiations for a *firman* to excavate ancient cemeteries in the Troad.[59]

After building a small village of wooden huts on the mound, known as "Schliemannopolis" or "Schliemannburg,"[60] Schliemann requested that the Academies of Berlin and Vienna send delegates to a gathering at the site to decide the question of the character of the remains of the second stratum. At stake was Schliemann's and Dörpfeld's integrity, for they had been accused of inventing the walls, towers, palaces, and temples in order to disguise the fact that the mound was a vast cinerary urn field.

In December 1889 and in the spring of 1890, Schliemann convened conferences of scholars at Hisarlık.[61] He paid their expenses so they could see for themselves where the truth lay between him and Bötticher. He desperately wanted Reinach to attend, but he was unavailable.[62] The December conference included Bötticher, Dörpfeld, Georg Niemann (1841–1912), an architect and professor at the Vienna Academy of Fine Arts,[63] Halil Bey of the Imperial Ottoman Museum, and Major Bernhard Steffen (1844–1991) of the Prussian artillery in Cassel, a cartographer who had worked with Habbo Gerhardus Lolling to produce maps of Mycenae. Calvert, still notarizing letters and procuring timber and builders for

Schliemann, participated in both conferences, noting, "I shall assist with greatest interest at the conference and thank you for giving me the opportunity of hearing the arguments on the important questions of Troy."[64] He entertained distinguished visitors at Thymbra Farm and escorted them to Hanay Tepe on 5 and 6 December [Figure 40]. Steffen and Niemann enthusiastically signed the protocol in defense of Schliemann, stating that they believed the remains to be those of a town including temple and halls. But they did not give dates for the stratum, nor did they substantiate Schliemann's claim that Hisarlık was Homer's Troy. Bötticher retracted his accusations that Schliemann had tampered with the remains but left without signing.[65]

It was not a clear-cut victory for Schliemann, and in spite of his retraction, Bötticher continued to attack Schliemann's interpretation, if not his integrity.[66] Because of this, Schliemann hosted a second, larger, international conference from 23 March to 7 April 1890 [Figure 41]. Participants included Friedrich von Duhn (1851–1930), a professor of archaeology from Heidelberg,[67] Carl Humann (1839–1896), excavator of Pergamon and director of the royal museums in Berlin,[68] Charles Waldstein (1856–1927), director of the American School of Classical Studies from 1888 to 1892, representing the Smithsonian Institution and Archaeological Institute of America [Figure 42],[69] Charles L. H. Babin (1860–1932), Near Eastern archaeologist and engineer and a member of the Académie des Inscriptions et Belles Lettres, Paris, Dr. Wilhelm Grempler (1826–1907), a member of Virchow's Society for Anthropology, Ethnography, and Prehistory and chair of the Society for Silesian Antiquities, from Breslau, Hamdi Bey, and Frank Calvert. Along with the other distinguished guests, Calvert discussed the results of the excavations and Schliemann's interpretations of them and signed the 30 March protocol.[70] The scholars supported Schliemann and Dörpfeld and wrote that their plans "correspond accurately to the existing remains. . . . We affirm that in no part of the ruins have we found any signs of the burning of corpses."[71]

But Salomon Reinach was not persuaded.[72] Bötticher was still not satisfied and responded that Calvert, the first excavator, was himself not convinced of Hisarlık's identity with Troy. After the protocol, he noted that Waldstein had lectured to the Royal Society that "it remained unproven whether Hisarlik was the Ilium of Homer or no. At least it was a walled town; and Dr. Schliemann may console himself with the certainty that [at] one time or another it saw wars of the Homeric type." Bötticher himself awaited the verdict of the 1890 season. As late as 1895, he remained unconvinced of Schliemann's and Dörpfeld's theories.[73]

Schliemann commenced excavations on 1 November 1889 but was forced to stop because of December weather. This time he wished to expose all of the house walls of the second settlement in order to make a plan. His other objectives were to continue to probe outward from the three gates in his second-stratum fortification walls, especially in the lower part of the mound to the south and west of the walls. He and Dörpfeld wished to determine the fortification walls of each stratum, to study the ground plan of the sixth, or Lydian, and upper Archaic, Hel-

Figure 40. Calvert, Steffen, Schliemann, Halil Bey, and Niemann at the 1889 Hisarlık Conference. Copyright Deutsche Archäologische Institut, Athens, Neg. No. Troja 120.

Figure 41. 1890 Hisarlık Conference. Seated, from left: Calvert, Hamdi Bey, and Waldstein. Standing: Virchow, Grempler, Halil Bey, Schliemann, Edith Calvert, Dörpfeld, Madame Babin, Babin, Von Duhn, and Humann. Courtesy of the Museum für Ur- und Frühgeschichte, Berlin.

Figure 42. Virchow and Waldstein at Thymbra Farm, 1890 Hisarlık Conference. By Edith Calvert, courtesy of Elizabeth Bacon.

lenic, and Roman strata, and to search for the early tombs. In late February, Schliemann recommenced with Dörpfeld, eighty workmen, and two railways to facilitate the removal of debris.[74] By March, he had secured a *firman* to excavate wherever he pleased within the circumference of a two-day journey, provided he respected the 1884 antiquities law.[75]

Schliemann had partial success in his search for a cemetery and a city below the citadel. Outside the Roman circuit wall of the lower city he found a great number of Roman graves, either built with slabs or hewn into the rock. Schliemann intended to excavate the second stratum's lower city south of its citadel walls in 1890 but was hindered by later deposits that were 15.2 meters deep.[76] He dug trenches 98.75 meters into a large mound on the south and west sides and found walls of massive buildings with Corinthian columns.[77]

Here the Romans had not leveled the older strata, as they had on the top of the mound. Instead, they built on top of them, thereby preserving earlier walls up to 1.21 meters high. Walls of four distinct settlements—Roman, Hellenic, Archaic, and "Lydian"—above the five prehistoric ones were visible for the first time in a stratified sequence [see Figures 28 and 29].[78] Schliemann wrote: "Sandwiched between these strata was one most noteworthy on account of its buildings' mode of huge dressed blocks, the fourth settlement from top," the sixth from the bottom, with gray pottery that once he had called "Lydian." In March, he asked Calvert to come and see the walls.[79] It is impossible to know whether Calvert and Schliemann recognized the similarities between these well-constructed cut-stone walls and those that Schliemann had uncovered long before, below the later walls with builders' marks. If they had, it would have been a bittersweet moment at best. Neither ever acknowledged that earlier he had found walls dating to the same stratum.

Schliemann discovered the pottery on the west side, beyond the second-stratum Pergamos, but within the Greco-Roman acropolis, in a deposit that was 2.1 meters deep and 7 meters down from the surface.[80] By 1890, like Calvert, he had found this same gray pottery in early levels at Pınarbaşı, Ballı Dağ, Fulu Dağ, Kurşunlu Tepe, Scepsis, and Cebrene and shared Calvert's opinion that it was local [Figure 35a]. But here, for the first time, it occurred with the painted ceramics of Mycenae, such as the stirrup jar [Figure 43].[81] Moreover, a *megaron*, as at Tiryns, and fortification walls 4.8 meters wide and 3.9 meters high seemed to belong to this settlement.[82]

On 27 July 1890, Schliemann wrote King George I of Greece with the exciting news that in the sixth settlement, where he had found the gray ware called "Lydian," there were many vessels of Mycenaean type, including that characteristic shape, the stirrup jar imported from Greece. These jars, found in tombs dating to the time of Ramses II in Egypt (1350 B.C.), could indicate the chronology of Troy.[83] Schliemann had confided in Virchow as early as May about these welcome, yet disturbing, finds: "Very noteworthy are the Mycenaean ceramics, which indicate the high age of the prehistoric remains. At least contemporary with the Mycenaean exists the pottery called Lydian by me, which one finds in great masses."[84] They proved that Schliemann must be closing in on Homer's Troy at last. Unfortunately, they also seemed to prove once again that his previous claims had been wrong.

Schuchhardt, now director of the museum in Hannover, visited Hisarlık that summer in the course of writing a book on Schliemann's excavations. There he noted the impressive sixth-settlement buildings. "Since the sixth stratum was contemporary with Mycenae, Dörpfeld regarded it as the Troy destroyed by Agamemnon. Schliemann did not want to accept this and looked with displeasure on every stirrup jar that emerged from the earth."[85] Dörpfeld delicately noted in his report on the architecture of the 1890 season that "the second stratum must be older than this stratum with Mycenaean vases."[86]

More than fifteen years earlier, Schliemann had admitted that one of his greatest difficulties was to make the enormous accumulation of debris at Troy agree with chronology.[87] Now he would have to rethink his entire intellectual construct for the stratigraphy of Hisarlık. The second stratum could not possibly be Homer's Troy. The Mycenaean pottery proved that Homer's Troy had to be in the level that previously he had called "Lydian." After searching for twenty years to find the level contemporary with the palaces of Mycenae and Tiryns, he finally had found it. But he had just dug through this stratum and removed its fine new

Figure 43. Mycenaean stirrup jar from the "Lydian" sixth stratum at Hisarlik. Redrawn by author, after Schliemann (1891b), plate 1.

buildings. In doing so, he had destroyed as surely as Homer's Greeks had done before him the city most likely to have been the site of the Trojan War.

The *American Journal of Archaeology* quoted Schliemann's statement that the sixth level "may be contemporary in date with the palaces of Mykenai and Tiryns."[88] Struggling with this assessment, he suggested that the users of Mycenaean-style pottery were Aeolians who had migrated to the Troad after the Dorian migration and the destructions of the twelfth century at Mycenae and Tiryns and "became naturalized at Ilion." He inferred a continuing local presence at the site because of the presence of masses of the local gray ware he once had called "Lydian."[89] In compiling his own report weeks later, Dörpfeld wrote cryptically that the number of fragments of Mycenaean vases gave "a clue to their date."[90] The second stratum was indeed vastly earlier. Thus, the thousand-year gap that had haunted Schliemann for almost twenty years became his private nightmare. Calvert's thousand-year gap had been a reality all along, and Calvert's observations were about to be vindicated.

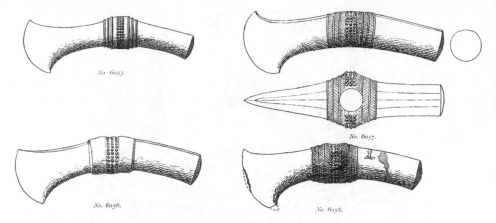

Figure 44. Ceremonial axes from Treasure L, Hisarlık, 1890. Schmidt (1902),
figures 6055–6059.

Perhaps as a perverted form of revenge, Schliemann may unconsciously have
wished to punish Calvert for his prescience. While excavating on Calvert's land in
July, Schliemann uncovered one last treasure in an area 0.5 meter square near the
eastern city wall of his second stratum. Schliemann wrote in his diary for 8 July that
it included "especially four splendid new axes of nephrite, three are green and one
grey, polished and so smooth that at first we thought they were of glass" [Figure
44], four scepter knobs of crystal, fifty pieces of crystal (lenses), two round plaques
of crystal, a scepter knob of iron, small gold objects, small gold rings and nails, and
two clumps of bronze fragments with numerous gold trinkets.[91] This was a lap-
idary's hoard, and the crystal hemispheres were magnification lenses for stone carv-
ing and the production of intricate jewelry. On the same day, he wrote a confidential letter to Virchow, describing how Athena had led him to the treasure, one of
inestimable worth, more valuable than anything he had found at Mycenae.[92]
Schliemann's hyperbole and his vision of Athena leading him to the treasure may
have been unconscious defensive measures to divert himself as well as others from
the much larger story that was now unfolding in his last months of life.

Rather than sharing it with Calvert, the proprietor of the land and once again
his ally, or with the Ottoman government, whose 1884 law he had promised to
obey, Schliemann quietly smuggled it out of the country with the help of Calvert's
colleague Agis de Caravel, the Italian vice-consul,[93] whom Schliemann called the
"Saviour (*soter*) of Trojan Antiquities" for his help with other "exportations."[94]
Schliemann had intimated to Virchow that he would pass the ceremonial axes off
"as coming from Egypt." Indeed, Calvert never knew about this treasure found on
his own land, and he continued to stand by Schliemann.

He would stay until 21 July in hopes of locating the royal tombs. Unsuccessful
in that quest, he reported his season's results on 20 July to Alexander Conze
(1831–1914), the secretary general of the German Archaeological Institute.[95] On

23 August he wrote to Virchow that he was updating his will to include the last treasure.[96] Schliemann wrote to Carl Humann and Gustav von Gößler, education minister in Berlin, about the new treasure, which he promised to will to the Royal Museum in Berlin, and asked to have Caravel decorated for his services.[97] Then he notified Richard Schöne. In a postscript to his letter, he noted that the sixth settlement, which he now held to be local, had flourished at the same time as the Mycenaean royal tombs.[98] To Alexander Conze, he again maintained that he had been guided by Athena and that, as he had said to Carl Humann, word of the treasure could not be leaked because the authorities in Constantinople would revoke his *firman* and stop his excavations forever.[99]

Schliemann did not complete his objective in 1890 and planned to excavate for two more years at Hisarlık, targeting the lower city in 1891.[100] But this was to be his finale, and there would be no encore. After other summers, he had claimed he had finished excavating Troy forever. Now, he finally had. After a poor recovery from an operation in Germany to correct an ear infection, he collapsed in the streets of Naples on Christmas, 1890, and succumbed the next day from an abscess on the brain. He died at sixty-eight, twenty years after he first began to excavate Hisarlık. He had earned twenty-nine degrees and diplomas from academic societies, museums, and universities. His funeral in Athens drew the king of Greece, government ministers, diplomats, and Athenian society. Dörpfeld's eulogy enjoined him to "rest in peace, you have done enough."[101]

Yet Schliemann's life work remained unfinished. Before his death he had found pottery and had recognized house walls of the correct era, but he died before he could articulate to the world just what he had discovered. Ironically, for once, he had not explicitly claimed to have found the walls of Homer's Troy. The citadel that had eluded him for twenty years he had found in the last months of his life, but by then he lacked the health and energy to continue.

Dörpfeld was the one who reaped the glory of the momentous discovery only hinted at by Schliemann in private letters to Berlin archaeologists, museum directors, and the king of Greece [Figure 45]. After Schliemann's death, Dörpfeld would continue precisely where Calvert first had begun to dig. With the financial backing of Sophia Schliemann, Dörpfeld returned to Hisarlık in 1893. He chose to excavate in the southeast on Calvert's land, in fact, in the area of Calvert's first trench. It was a wild success. Immediately he came down on the magnificent fortification walls of the sixth stratum. He revealed three gates, towers, and a door [Figure 46]. In 1894, Kaiser Wilhelm II himself funded the excavations.[102] Dörpfeld cleared the massive northeast tower (18 meters wide and 9 meters high) that protected the water supply [Figure 47]. Beyond the citadel, Dörpfeld located the first few graves of the sixth stratum south of the Greco-Roman city wall and found sparse evidence of a lower city in Mycenaean times.[103] The *American Journal of Archaeology* reported: "Dörpfeld discerned, in one of the layers of ruins (discovered but disregarded by Schliemann), a city which must be the Ilios of Priam contemporaneous with the Mykenai of Agamemnon; he removed the surrounding walls, the towers, and some of the houses

Figure 45. Wilhelm Dörpfeld at Thymbra Farm. 1890 Hisarlık
Conference. By Edith Calvert, courtesy of Elizabeth Bacon.

that filled it. It is to be understood that this little acropolis, analogous to that of
Tiryns, is not the whole of the city, but simply its citadel, which Homer called *Pergamos*. It was surrounded, lower down, by a city."[104]

Calvert was characteristically soft-spoken about Dörpfeld's discoveries. On 7
July 1894, in an important summary of work at Troy to date for the *Levant Herald
and Eastern Express*, he noted that his own northeastern trench had hit a Roman
wall, but had it "continued a few metres would have led to the Trojan tower [Fig-
ure 47] on which it abutted." Later, when Dörpfeld excavated Schliemann's

Figure 46. The walls of Troy. Dörpfeld (1902), Supplement 15, opposite 112.

Figure 47. The walls of Troy. Dörpfeld (1902), Supplement 20, opposite 136.

dumps encircling the tiny fortified settlement of the second stratum, he found walls 5 to 6 meters in breadth covered with material from the previous excavation. Calvert concluded: "Undoubtedly the identity of the Sixth City, the Troy or Ilium of Homer, has been established."[105]

In 1895, Calvert declared to British writer Samuel Butler (1835–1902) that "the excavations at Hissarlik in 1893 and 1894 by Dr. Dörpfeld have decided the question of Troy—It is now proved that the sixth city of Dr. Schliemann and not the second is Homer's Troy—As to Bounarbaschi's claim to the site the theory has collapsed."[106] He also forwarded to Butler a copy of his 7 July 1894 *Levant Herald and Eastern Express* article, "The Discovery of Troy."[107] The *American Journal of Archaeology* reported that "Schliemann, carried away by his zeal, had overlooked the very end which he wished to attain, and that the burnt city which he thought to be the real Troia, is a more ancient foundation going back beyond the year 2000 B.C."[108] Calvert's dating of the second stratum seventeen years earlier to between 2200 and 1800 B.C. was accurate. And although others had followed him, Calvert had been the first to have the courage to offer a date for the prehistoric material. Yet it was a bittersweet triumph.

But as always, there was more to Calvert's life than Homer, Troy, and Schliemann. Archaeology remained his avocation, but he had to make a living. At the consular agency, where the office always was open from eight in the morning until sunset, Calvert collected fees for notary services, bills of health, and visas and continued to file invoices, service vessels of war and travelers, protect American citizens, and furnish reports on shipping, commerce, and the agricultural produce of the Troad for the U.S. State Department.[109] He also served on a commission to examine and report on shipping *practique,* the communications between ships with clean bills of health and the shore. Meanwhile, the family picnicked at Troy with tea in Schliemann's cut. In April 1893, Calvert's niece Laura married Henry Bacon (1866–1924), brother of Francis Bacon and later architect of the Lincoln Memorial.[110] They honeymooned at Thymbra Farm and left for the United States.

As the century waned, Calvert made a bid for recognition. In 1900, he gave 9 acres of land at Hisarlik to the Imperial Ottoman Museum.[111] In recognition of his gift, Hamdi Edhem Bey, the director general of the museum, forwarded to Calvert the brooch and insignia of Commander of the Imperial Order of Merit conferred by Sultan Abdul Hamid II, the highest honorary distinction.[112] Yet according to Charles M. Dickinson (1842–1924), the U.S. consul general from 1897 to 1906, the highest possible imperial recognition seemed "inadequate in view of the material and historical value" of his gift.[113] But Calvert was pleased. He had sought unsuccessfully to sell the land. Now in his lifetime he gave it away freely and basked in the glory of his generosity.

Still, Calvert's isolation deepened. James died in 1896, and except for Edith and Edmund, the Dardanelles was a lonely place. Of the ten thousand inhabitants, there were no more than fifty foreigners.[114] At Thymbra Farm, cut off by the flooding Scamander, the Calverts mourned the death of Queen Victoria. Frank

Calvert's nephew, Frederick R. J. Calvert, wrote on 25 February 1901: "The passing of our great Queen and the end of the Victorian era find us, still, as you see, denizens of Thymbra Farm."[115]

Calvert continued to publish archaeological notes and articles, adding to his collection objects from excavations of hitherto unknown and extremely rich sites around the Troad and Balıkesır. Although he published only a fraction of these sites, he did contribute notes to the *John Murray Handbook* until his death.[116] In 1900, he was investigating Kilia, a rich site on the Chersonese.[117] Three large Greco-Roman cemeteries, with *pithos* and cist graves and one with sarcophagi, produced chiefly Hellenistic finds: one hundred lamps, vases, terra-cotta figurines, bronzes, and glass vessels, pierced stone axes, and an inscribed grave relief.[118] There also were prehistoric remains, and Calvert published an alabaster figurine from Kilia similar to one from the lowest stratum at Hanay Tepe.[119]

In 1902, Calvert summed up his archaeological work along the north coast of the Troad and once again refuted Schliemann's identifications for sites that did not agree with his own. He focused on three sites that he had been investigating for one to five decades: Rhoeteum, Ophryneion, and Tavolia.[120] Rhoeteum was a fortified settlement west of Erenköy, with an acropolis, necropolis, and harbor installations. At Ophryneion, he had found earlier pottery that extended its history back to the seventh century B.C.[121] He had located Tavolia east of Karanlık Limanı and suggested that because it was well protected from the brutal Hellespont winds, it must have been Ilion's ancient harbor and necropolis. There he found underwater harbor installations, remains of a small settlement, and a huge and rich necropolis with tombs ranging in date from the sixth century B.C. to the Roman era, a necropolis much larger and more significant than any graves found at Hisarlık.[122] In the site's lower levels, he found prehistoric remains comparable to the deeper strata of Hisarlık. This was Calvert's last published scholarship, and Hermann Thiersch (1874–1939)[123] celebrated Calvert's contributions to the field in his commentary on it. But he disagreed with Calvert's conclusions, since Tavolia's richest graves were of the fifth to fourth centuries B.C., a time of little consequence at Ilion. Instead, he associated the harbor with the sites of Aianteion and Rhoeteum to the east.[124]

In 1902, Dörpfeld published *Troja und Ilion*, using for the second stratum a chronology similar to what Calvert had put forth almost thirty years earlier. In his foreword, he graciously acknowledged his debt to Calvert for permission to excavate his land and for his help as an expert authority and as a friend.[125] By subdividing Schliemann's Lydian level into a sixth and a seventh stratum and by combining Schliemann's Archaic and "Hellenic" levels, Dörpfeld maintained there were a total of nine major strata [Figure 48]. He concluded that his sixth stratum was Homer's Troy and clarified the size of that settlement in his master plan [Figure 49, and see Figures 28 and 29]. At the same time, members of Dörpfeld's Troy team undertook the study and cataloguing of Calvert's collection. His assistant, Alfred Brückner (1861–1936), had begun the catalogue in 1894, and R. Rohrert photographed it.[126] With support from the German Archaeological Institute, of

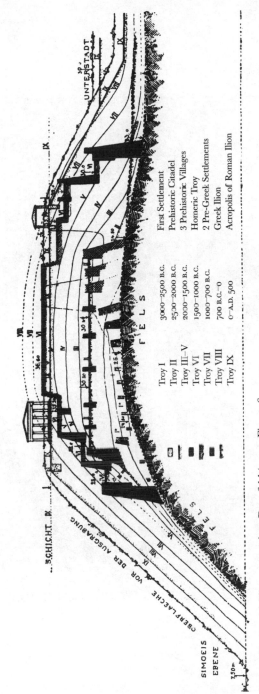

Troy I   3000–2500 B.C.   First Settlement
Troy II   2500–2000 B.C.   Prehistoric Citadel
Troy III–V   2000–1500 B.C.   3 Prehistoric Villages
Troy VI   1500–1000 B.C.   Homeric Troy
Troy VII   1000–700 B.C.   2 Pre-Greek Settlements
Troy VIII   700 B.C.–0   Greek Ilion
Troy IX   0–A.D. 500   Acropolis of Roman Ilion

Figure 48. Dörpfeld's 1902 section. Dörpfeld (1902). Figure 6, p. 32.

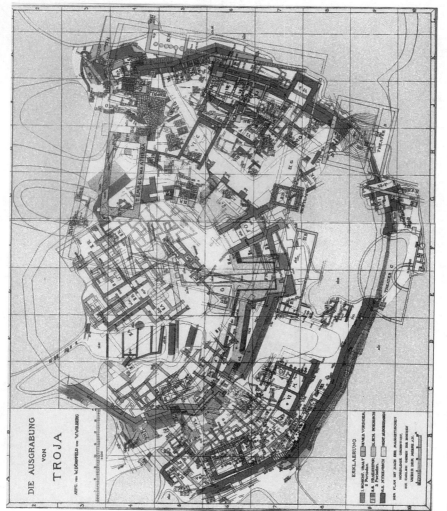

Figure 49. Dörpfeld's plan of Hisarlık. Théater C is the Odeion; Theater B is the Bouleuterion. Dörpfeld (1902), Plate 3.

Figure 50. The Schliemann mausoleum, First Cemetery, Athens. Courtesy of
George S. Korres.

which Calvert was a member, Thiersch compiled the collection of some sixteen hundred artifacts into a manuscript catalogue, but it never was published.[127]

On the night of 12 August 1908, Frank Calvert died at Thymbra Farm, a week after his elder brother Edmund.[128] He was buried near his brothers in the small family cemetery south of the Calvert garden at the Dardanelles. An obituary appeared in the 15 August *Levant Herald and Eastern Express:*

> we regret to announce [the death] . . . of Mr. Frank Calvert for many years U.S. Consular Agent at the Dardanelles, but better known as an authority in Trojan Archaeology. Mr. Calvert was an advocate for the claim of Hissarlik as the real site of Troy at a time when most archaeologists placed it at Balli Dagh, and it was at his instigation that the late Dr. Schliemann decided upon excavating the former place, with such success that the true position of Homer's Troy is now established beyond question. Mr. Calvert was a corresponding member of the Archaeological Societies of London and Berlin, and his loss will be felt in the antiquarian world.[129]

Apparently ignored in England, Calvert's passing was mourned in the learned societies of Berlin, of which he was a member and to which he had been a contributor. The Society of Anthropology, Ethnography, and Prehistory eulogized Calvert's almost sixty years of research on the question of Homeric sites in the Troad and commemorated his excavations of "a temple" at Hisarlık prior to Schliemann's excavations, as well as his demonstration of his finds to his successor. "So that in many respects he claimed honor with justification." At the Archaeological Society of Berlin, Alfred Brückner expressed the society's debt to Calvert for his work at Neandria, which had inspired Koldewey to excavate there, and for championing the Hisarlık claim, "which showed Schliemann the way." He mourned that Calvert had not published a synthesis of his vast knowledge of the landscape but took heart from the existence of his collection, since it could fill in the gaps.[130] Even in death Calvert's name was inextricably linked with Schliemann's.

Calvert's and Schliemann's final resting places contrasted as much as their personalities did in life. Ernst Ziller, who had introduced Schliemann to the Pınarbaşı theory in 1868, designed Schliemann's mausoleum [Figure 50].[131] This temple to Schliemann bore on its podium a sculpted frieze. On the east were scenes from the *Odyssey,* on the south, the *Iliad* and related sagas of Troy from Aulis to the death of Agamemnon, on the west, the walls of Tiryns. On the north, Schliemann himself was depicted, Homer in hand, supervising the excavations at Troy with his wife Sophia by his side. Calvert's modest tombstone quietly stated: "I am the resurrection and the life. He that believeth in me though he were dead yet shall he live and whosoever liveth and believeth in me shall never die" [Figure 51].[132]

TO THE MEMORY OF
FRANK CALVERT
BORN AT MALTA
SEPTEMBER 3 1828
DIED AT THE DARDANELLES
AUGUST 12 1908

I AM THE RESURRECTION
AND THE LIFE HE THAT
BELIEVETH IN ME THOUGH
HE WERE DEAD YET SHALL
HE LIVE AND WHOSOEVER
LIVETH AND BELIEVETH
IN ME SHALL NEVER DIE

Figure 51. Calvert's grave, Chanak Consular Cemetery, Çanakkale (the Dardanelles). Photo by the author.

CHAPTER ELEVEN

"Wolf scalps" and War Booty
The Fate of the Collections

Like the men who amassed them, the collections of antiquities assembled by Frank Calvert and Heinrich Schliemann suffered very different fates. Schliemann's, begun with deceit, theft, and secrecy and then ardently sought by all the museums of Europe and used by Schliemann during his lifetime to get what he wanted, went on to have a history as spectacular as Schliemann's self-promoting accounts of his own life, a history that fully lived up to its origins. The tangible heritage of Calvert's archaeological endeavors, by contrast, was dispersed and disseminated, some of it lost to catastrophes, some of it languishing in obscurity, like Calvert himself.

Frank Calvert continued to accumulate antiquities long after the sale of part of his collection, as such, in London in 1877. In the 1890s, Calvert had formed a friendship with a very American American, Alexander Watkins Terrell (1827–1912), a noted Texas politician and judge and U.S. minister to Turkey from 1893 to 1897.[1] Terrell thought he saw in Calvert's situation an opportunity to pick up some priceless European culture cheap and to ship it back to Texas, a state that was considered as exotic as Egypt by Victorian travelers.[2]

In mid-November 1894, Terrell proceeded to the Dardanelles in the sultan's launch and, surrounded by a cavalry escort, visited Hisarlık with Calvert [Figure 52]. Terrell immediately wrote to his brother: "Long before Shleiman began his work of excavating Mr. Calvert announced that Troy once occupied that spot, and he was the first to begin excavations there. The lack of means alone prevented him from doing all that Schleiman did."[3] To his colleagues in Texas he wrote that Calvert was "the quiet sort . . . who after being the *real* discoverer of ancient Troy, found his money exhausted when within a *few feet* of the walls, and had the mortification of seeing *Scleimann* (who he authorized to excavate) reap all the glory of a discoverer and get most of the treasure."[4]

Calvert's exhaustive description of Schliemann's stratigraphy prompted the judge to write that archaeologists could be just like "some people on the witness

Figure 52. Frank Calvert ascending the walls of Troy with Alexander Watkins Terrell. Courtesy of Candace Bacon Cordella.

stand, and know more than there is."[5] Still, even Terrell had become enthralled with Calvert's story, Troy, and archaeology, removing a boar's tusk and a quern from the mound[6] and buying an inscribed marble fragment for less than $3.00 from what he called, with a provincial's Shakespearean erudition, a "turbaned Turk." Concerning the inscription, he notes that "Shleman found nothing more interesting."[7] From Calvert he received a number of "souvenirs from the remote past," which Terrell wished to present to "some American University that has or will establish a Museum." For effect, to seal the letter he sent back home with this news, he used an engraved stone that Calvert had excavated at Thymbra Farm.[8] Apparently Terrell saw Frank Calvert's collection at the Dardanelles and also Frederick's at Thymbra.[9] Almost immediately, Terrell wished to purchase Calvert's collection for the University of Texas, which he had helped to establish only eleven years earlier.[10]

Calvert sent Terrell a copy of his article on the discovery of Troy from the recent *Levant Herald and Eastern Express*. Evidently the two men also discussed the sale of

Calvert's land at Hisarlık, for Calvert enclosed an estimate of the extent of his land "on the plateau inside and outside the walls of Troy." At that time, he owned about 80 acres, valued for taxation purposes at $6500.00. He honestly noted that this valuation was high for farmland, but it was taxed at a higher rate because of the antiquities contained therein. He would accept £1000, or $5000.00, "a moderate sum considering the very interesting remains therein discovered and to be discovered. Were I a younger man with the chance of a longer life, I would not part with my property, but now I would like it to pass to competent hands to do it justice."[11] Terrell asked for an estimate and requested that Calvert produce "a catalogue of the entire collection," including dates and provenances for each article.[12] For this reason, Calvert had Dörpfeld's assistant, Alfred Brückner, catalogue the collection in 1894.

Terrell tried to interest Texans in purchasing the collection for the university. He noted that the excavations at Troy really had just begun, and only the acropolis, or citadel, had been explored. "I presume as always Legislatures had rather waste ten dollars for wolf scalps than to invest one for a museum of antiquities," he grumbled.[13] He described Calvert's corpus as "the rarest collection of archaeological curios and treasures in private hands anywhere" and noted that Calvert needed money and would "fix a price on it."[14] Although he noted elsewhere that most items had not been cleaned and still possessed an encrustation of lime, he estimated its worth at between $3000 and $5000 and noted that this estimate was less than one-third of what it would bring in any European capital.[15] In a letter written on 12 December 1894, he repeated that times were hard there, and he could get "the nucleus of a museum of antiquities that Texas would not take a fortune for hereafter." He himself had bought a golden bowl from Troy, and he noted "this craze for research will soon be exhausted."[16]

To Colonel George Breckenridge of the university, he explained that "all antiquities belong to the Sultan, now found, and none can be exported without his consent—For this cause Calvert's Collection is a secret from archaeologists—It is kept in a secret chamber entered only by him."[17] Regarding Calvert's "prehistoric antiques . . . *certainly* no such collection of Trojan antiques [exists] *in private hands* in the world. If the University acts it must move *without* noise." In a postscript, Terrell explained how this wonderful collection had escaped notice. First, Calvert had concealed his archaeological treasures

> to avoid the Turkish chief of the Museum from claiming it—Next Calvert is an archaeological crank, who has the modesty of a woman, and except for a German is the only Christian living at the Dardanelles. He has been digging in the ground for relics and the like for 25 years, and has about spent his substance at it—He is an old batchelor living with his Sister, and not only never offered his collection for sale, but he tells me he had never contemplated selling it. Now hard up it is my opinion that if it were in hands able to keep it that collection would fetch $10,000 in America—It is a rich collection from the Stone age—the prehistoric Trojan—Trojan—Mycenae, Greco, Roman, and Roman periods with vases, lamps, lachrymal urns, bowls, painted vases, dishes, [e]tc. terra cottas, gods, idols . . . not much statuary.

He begged Breckenridge to get someone from the university to discuss it "with some fool professor (if they are unfortunate in having one)" and secure this nucleus for a museum.[18]

According to Terrell, Calvert's collection at this time consisted of "bowls, pitchers, vases, lachrymal urns, lamps + [e]tc. with bronze utensils, hatchets, hammers, moulds, daggers (steelyards? but made of *copper*) Terra cotta . . . statues and bone and ivory utensils and implements, with gold necklaces and rings. Dr. Long,[19] Professor of Archaeology here at Robert College, says there is no such *private* collection of Antiques 1200 B.C. in Europe. Everything was found by Calvert."

"Europe *shall not* have Calverts Collection," Terrell declared. "I believe it to be worth 4 times what he asks." He threatened to interest "some northern university" if his own refused to act. "Outside the Smithsonian Institute there would be nothing like it in America, and no such collection of *Trojan* antiques away from Berlin."[20] Indeed, he tried to intercede with the Smithsonian, strongly believing that the collection should come to the United States. But the Smithsonian declined, "having no funds of its own" with which to purchase the collection, and so it remained in Turkey.[21] In high irony, Terrell wrote: "I am here in a position to obtain exceptional favors from the Sultan in exporting antiques, and therefore able to buy them for a song," but he could not move the board of regents of the University of Texas.

Eventually Terrell admitted defeat. Whether or not he ever pursued his threat to interest a northern school is not known. He returned to Texas and donated the inscription found at Troy to the university in 1898.[22] On 13 April 1912, he promised to bequeath "three antique, genuine Trojan vases, presented to me by my consular agent Mr. Frank Calvert, who lived at the Dardanelles and owned the site of Troy."[23] Nothing more was said about the purchase of Calvert's collection, so one must assume that the university declined the offer. Thus, much of the collection remained closeted at the Dardanelles.

Nevertheless, in the last decade of his life, Calvert watched many prize objects from his collection travel to the United States. Terrell had strengthened Calvert's connection with America. Francis Henry Bacon narrowed his focus to the Boston area. For years, the upper portion of a tall slender grave stele dating to around 500 B.C. that Calvert had found at or near the "Tumulus of Ajax" near Karanlık Limanı on the Hellespont had stood outside the Thymbra farmhouse.[24] Known as the Calvert Stele, the remarkable Archaic period marble gravestone with a beautifully carved *anthemion,* or floral ornament, was purchased by Bacon's neighbor, the Boston collector Edward Perry Warren in 1903 for the Museum of Fine Arts in Boston, where it joined sculptured friezes from Assos.[25] The stele already was well known to several classical archaeologists in Boston who had excavated with Bacon at Assos. Among them was the museum's director, Edward Robinson (1858–1931).[26]

In 1905, Calvert sold over sixty pieces from his collection to the Worcester Art Museum, in Worcester, Massachusetts, through Francis Henry Bacon.[27] Thus, the largest number of objects collected by Calvert known outside Turkey came to Worcester, where they have for the most part languished in storage since their purchase in 1905. The glass, bronze, alabaster, terra-cotta, and ivory objects date from the third millennium B.C. to the Roman Imperial era and come from Troy, Neandria, Berytis, Madytos, Kilia, and Tavolia. These gradually are being placed on exhibit.

Meanwhile, Henry and Laura Calvert Bacon were living in New York City, surrounded by objects from her uncle's past. The architect William Partridge described the Bacons' apartment in New York: "Greek vases, toilet articles, gold wreaths, even the Metropolitan Museum could not rival the quality of the collection crowding the shelves of the Bacons' living room."[28] Although perhaps apocryphal, Partridge's memoirs of life at the Bacons in New York give the flavor of the time.

> The Turkish law against exporting any archaeological treasures was very severe but Schliemann in gratitude to the Calverts gave them many of the beautiful treasures unearthed. Some of these were smuggled out to the Henry Bacons in New York. These were first wrapped in oiled silk and suspended in a crock of melted Jujube paste. When this cooled it became a perfect packing material. On arrival in New York the jar was placed on a slow fire and when the paste melted the package was fished out, unharmed.

They displayed their heirloom antiquities on the living room mantle and nearby shelves, while lush oriental carpets covered the floors.[29] Henry Bacon, who had been profoundly influenced by the necropolis and classical architecture of Assos, spent his life designing elegant, classically inspired monuments. "Small wonder Bacon had a flair for the Greek Classic when his wife's family owned ancient Troy," Partridge mused.[30] In his crowning achievement, Bacon designed the Lincoln Memorial and in recognition received the gold medal of the American Institute of Architects from President Warren G. Harding in May 1923, but he died a year later.[31] When Laura Calvert Bacon fell on hard times, her portion of the antiquities collection was dispersed, and its whereabouts are now unknown. In the end, the greatest number of objects from Calvert's collection outside the Troad came to the country he had served for half his life.

Between 1900 and 1925, the Dardanelles passed through several periods of political and economic disaster, mitigated by very brief respites of normal life and prosperity. The process of revolution and counterrevolution that attended the demise of the 640 years of Ottoman rule began three weeks before Calvert's death. And almost exactly four years after his death, an earthquake "so violent that it upset the needle of the seismograph" wracked the Dardanelles. Contemporary newspapers record that the Calverts lost priceless treasures in that cataclysm.[32] Edith Calvert described the 9 August 1912 earthquake in her vividly detailed letter of 10 August. Hot springs erupted throughout the town. Stone houses such as the Calvert mansion suffered the worst damage. Houses facing the water lost their seaside facades, and parapets plummeted into the strait. Inside the Calverts' own house, floors collapsed one upon the other from the roof to the basement, while the exterior walls stood intact, appearing as if "gutted by fire." Crowds of people took refuge in the garden, tenting on the tennis court and under the pine trees. Edith Calvert despaired. "Our house is a perfect ruin," she wrote. Her uncle's office had been less affected by the disaster, although his collection had suffered a grave blow. "A great number of the glass vases and other antiquities have been smashed to atoms. In fact, the damage is incalculable."[33]

After the 1912 quake, the family made do in reduced circumstances with makeshift wooden shanties inside the garden, fondly nicknamed the "Jamlik," or glass house, the "Tekke," or inn, and the "Kiosk," or small house. No longer able to maintain the family cemetery, the sisters appealed to the British government to take it over. All around them, refugees flooded into the Dardanelles, along with the wounded from the first and second Balkan Wars (1912–1913), once more bringing tuberculosis, smallpox, and typhoid with them.[34] There were skirmishes between the Greek and Turkish fleets at Imbros. Frederick R. J. Calvert lived with his wife, Hélène, and son, Gerald, at Thymbra Farm. Their daughter, Winifred, had married Godfrey Whittall (1882–1957), grandson of her grandfather's friend James Whittall of Smyrna, and lived in a house just outside the family's walled garden at the Dardanelles.[35]

As war approached in 1914, Thymbra Farm and the Dardanelles were threatened and then became inaccessible. The Turks mined the strait between Dardanos and Kilid Bahr and fortified the hills of the Asiatic shore facing the British to the north. The Calverts, the Whittalls, and Alice Calvert Bacon were among the last Europeans to evacuate the war zone in 1914, dreading what would happen to their beloved farm, gardens, and antiquities collection.[36] Unwillingly, they evacuated in December 1914, with Alice remaining in Constantinople so as not to lose her patrimony, the Dardanelles property alone, consisting of the mansion, walled garden, and 6 acres of vegetable and fruit gardens in the center of the city, being valued at £10,000.[37] Then, the Dardanelles and Gallipoli became a battlefield. Months later, in the 1915 bombardment, a shell fell in the garden, and two Ottoman divisions were billeted at Thymbra Farm. As the Ottoman forces successfully defended the strait, a young officer named Mustafa Kemal (1881–1938) rose to prominence in the surge of nationalist sentiment that followed the unexpected victory over the British at Gallipoli. Following the battle in 1915, the strait was demilitarized. Meanwhile, what remained of the collection was hidden away inside the old mansion.

The end of World War 1 did not signal the end of troubles in Turkey. After the November 1918 armistice, the strait was occupied by troops from Great Britain, France, and Italy. With this apparent security, the families returned to the Dardanelles. But less than a year later, the Greco-Turkish War began. The Greeks invaded Smyrna, sanctioned by two of the occupying countries and the United

States.[38] In 1920 Smyrna, Imbros, and Tenedos, eastern Thrace, and the Gallipoli peninsula were ceded to Greece.[39] In September 1921, both sides of the Dardanelles were declared a neutral zone, and British forces suppressed brigandage. Though humiliating to the Turks, the occupation brought a false sense of security to foreigners, but the increased stability and prosperity they enjoyed was short-lived.[40]

On 26 August, the Turks under Kemal, the hero of Gallipoli, began to repulse the Greeks, who by this time had pushed far into Anatolia. In less than two weeks the Turks had recaptured Balıkesır and Smyrna. On 10 September, they recaptured Bursa, on the fourteenth, Bergama (Pergamon). Thus, the Calverts and Bacons again found themselves in a war zone as the Kemalist forces proceeded north, driving lines of refugees ahead of them like cattle. Desperately, Frederick R. J. Calvert and his wife, Hélène, tried in vain to bring in the harvest before the devastation of the advancing troops was upon them. Thymbra, stripped of its produce, again found itself in no-man's-land, and the Calvert family was forced to evacuate, leaving not only the farm to be despoiled by the troops, but also the hidden collection. Rumors circulated regarding confiscation of property if foreigners left the country.[41] Alice Calvert Bacon and her siblings remained to guard their rights to the strategic and valuable real estate. Kemal arrived at the neutralized Dardanelles on 24 September in a direct confrontation with the British, the only remaining occupying force.

Meanwhile in Smyrna, the Turks drove the Greeks into the sea.[42] To add to the tragedy of lost lives on both sides, a devastating fire erupted, consuming as many as twenty-five thousand houses and half of the center of the city, making the sack of Troy pale by comparison.[43] A portion of the Calverts' collection that had been given to Alfred van Lennep, Alice's cousin from Smyrna on the Abbott side, may have perished in the great fire of Smyrna and in the subsequent confusion and looting there and in the outlying communities.[44] But the loss of art and artifacts was insignificant compared with the devastating loss of life.[45] To prevent further bloodshed, the English commander of the Dardanelles conceded to the Nationalist demands, and peace was declared. On 8 October, the Nationalists withdrew to a distance of 10 kilometers from the Dardanelles.[46] Within weeks, they had seized power and the sultan had fled. An enforced exchange of populations followed. All Greeks in Turkey outside of Constantinople and all Turks in Greece, excepting Thrace, were forced to migrate to their country of ethnic origin. In an area like the Dardanelles, with a large Greek population in the city as well as in the surrounding villages such as Erenköy, Yenişehir, and Madytos, this caused massive disruption, tearing the fabric of the old communities and introducing "foreigners" into the ghost towns left by departing Greeks.[47] Imbros and Tenedos reverted to Turkey, as did eastern Thrace and the Gallipoli peninsula. On 24 July 1923, the last instrument of the treaty between Greece and Turkey was ratified, and the British troops began to evacuate. Although properties such as Thymbra Farm that had been confiscated during the war were returned, the situation grew increasingly tenuous for foreigners like the Calverts and Bacons.[48]

Francis Henry Bacon was an indefatigable diarist, photographer, and chronicler of life at the Dardanelles. After witnessing the devastation endured at Thymbra Farm and the Dardanelles in one short decade, he decided to act quickly on behalf of posterity. He had had close relations with the American School of Classical Studies in Athens since its founding in 1882.[49] Two days after the ratification of the peace treaty that had brought about the population exchanges, massive exchanges of territory, and significant curtailment of rights of foreigners in Turkey, Bacon sent an important package to the director of the school. Always championing Calvert's cause with the Americans, Bacon gave the surviving Schliemann letters from Calvert's study to the Gennadius Library. In his 26 July 1923 letter to the director, Bacon wrote: "I think Mr. Calvert did not quite like it because Dr. Schliemann never gave him credit for directing him to Hissarlik." Ironically, this formed the seed of the major collection now known as the Schliemann Archive.[50]

By necessity, the Bacons retired at the Dardanelles to protect their property.[51] With her war indemnity, Alice Calvert Bacon restored a waterfront residence known as "Sea View," just west of the old mansion.[52] Then, in 1932, a fire forced them to abandon this house for a smaller residence whose back gate opened onto the garden.[53]

During the 1930s, excavators again looked to the Troad with new questions. The American archaeologist Carl Blegen (1887–1971), known for his tripartite chronology for the Early, Middle, and Late Bronze Age of mainland Greece, reopened excavations at Hisarlık in 1932.[54] Like generations before him, Blegen enjoyed Calvert hospitality.[55] In town, periodic persecutions of ethnic minorities continued, and many non-Muslims left. During this grim time and perhaps at Blegen's suggestion, Edith Calvert and Alice Calvert Bacon gave what remained of Calvert's collection at Thymbra Farm and the Dardanelles to the Çanakkale Archaeological Museum, located in the former Armenian church.[56] In October 1934 the family began deaccessioning the collection by giving objects to the museum.[57] After another sharp earthquake rocked the Dardanelles and probably further damaged the big house on 4 January 1935, the sisters gave away the remainder of the Calvert Collection.[58] This would ensure its preservation in uncertain times ahead no matter what happened to the increasingly vulnerable Calverts and Bacons still resident in Turkey.[59]

Thus, the majority of Calvert's vast collection never left the Dardanelles. Meanwhile, the Istanbul Archaeological Museum, once the Imperial Ottoman Museum, had acquired the catalogue to the collection, which Dorothy Thompson, John L. Caskey, and John M. Cook studied in the 1960s.[60] In 1971, the catalogue and more pieces from the Calvert Collection were transferred from Istanbul to Çanakkale.[61]

As war again loomed in Europe, the American excavators left, and the Calverts finally lost their privileged status. Erenköy had been "shot to pieces" in the 1915 bombardment. "Only dogs and cats prowled around."[62] Thymbra Farm was seized by the government in 1939.[63] The sisters sold the ruined family mansion to a *vakif,* or pious foundation, which passed it to the municipality on 24 July 1939.[64] Within weeks, the family's garden was seized for a public park.[65]

After this, the family virtually disappeared as that generation died out. Francis Henry Bacon died at the Dardanelles in 1940, leaving the elderly sisters alone less than six months after the seizure of the garden.[66] Alice Calvert Bacon died at 91 in 1949 and Edith, apparently known locally as "Kokana," died at 93 in 1952. Both are buried in the Calvert cemetery. After Edith's death, the Garden Villa went out of family hands.[67] Although Remzi Arik, the government representative during the Blegen years, had chronicled Calvert's achievements at Troy and throughout the Troad in 1953, and objects still were labeled "Gift of Miss Calvert,"[68] memory of Edith barely survived when Cook began his fieldwork in 1959.[69] The next generation grew up far from Troy—in England, Canada, the United States, and Rhodesia, still cherishing their forebear's role. The mansion was demolished as part of a reconfiguration of the waterfront by the garrison commander in the 1940s. Eventually the *vilayet,* or province, of Çanakkale built its government offices on what was once Calvert property to the southeast of the consular mansion.[70] Benches now look out at the straits from the paved site of the razed structure.[71] The family's famous gardens became the city park of Çanakkale in 1941, and the unacknowledged Calvert Collection is the core of the Çanakkale Archaeological Museum. Calvert's name still is not mentioned anywhere in the museum, nor is his nieces' generous gift publicly credited.[72] In fact, none of these venues commemorate the family who built and tended them for almost a century.

Although the majority of Calvert's collection never left the Troad, the rest is now dispersed in museums on three continents and rarely identified with the man who created it. Like the archaeologist himself, the collection of artifacts discovered in Frank Calvert's archaeological excavations—once the most important collection of excavated antiquities of the Troad—has never received the recognition and respect it deserves. It is no wonder, then, that the descendants of Frank Calvert's brother Frederick referred to his story and that of the collection as "a family myth."[73]

The characteristically more vivid story of the Schliemann Collection's fate is a happier one.[74] For years, Schliemann's Trojan Collection was thought lost, destroyed in the Battle of Berlin. Hoping for the survival of Priam's Treasure was akin to believing in the survival of Czar Nicholas III's daughter Anastasia. Then, in 1991 and 1993, with the end of the Cold War came dramatic disclosures from the former Soviet Union. Documentation indicated that the Red Army had taken Schliemann's treasures to the USSR after the fall of Berlin. Priam's Treasure miraculously had survived for fifty years, veiled in secrecy behind the Iron Curtain. The loss and rediscovery of Schliemann's Troy treasures thus is no less dramatic than its original discovery and spiriting out of Turkey, and the ending has yet to be written.

Schliemann's Trojan Collection and the Hanay Tepe finds, which had resided in Berlin since 1881, had been moved between two museums, the Museum of Applied Arts and Design, located in the Martin Gropius Building, built in 1877, and the adjacent Ethnographical Museum, where a room had been dedicated to Schliemann since the building's construction in 1885.[75] From 1896 to 1900, Hubert Schmidt (1864–1933), catalogued 9704 inventoried pieces.[76] As the Museum of Ethnography expanded, the Museum of Applied Arts and Design moved out, and in 1921, the Prehistoric Section returned to the Gropius Building, eventually becoming the Museum for Prehistory and Early History.[77] In 1926, Wilhelm Unverzagt (1892–1971), later a Nazi Party member, became director.[78]

Across the street from Unverzagt's museum, the rallies and meetings begun by Hitler and Goebbels in 1932 quickly escalated. The Martin Gropius Building soon found itself in the government quarter of Hitler's SS state, across the street from Himmler's Gestapo and SS headquarters. Göring's Luftwaffe was less than a block away to the northwest. Consequently, when the bombing began during World War II, this was not a safe place to be. And when the Red Army arrived at the end of the war, chaos reigned.

That is why everyone thought the Troy treasures had been lost, destroyed in the Battle of Berlin, looted, or melted down by the Nazis.[79] Then, in 1971, Dr. Klaus Goldmann, a curator at the Prehistory and Early History Museum in Berlin, began to prepare a permanent installation on the Bronze Age. Through Unverzagt's widow, he acquired microfilm records of the collection that had been prepared during the war on Hitler's orders. According to Unverzagt's information, Schliemann's collection had been transferred to his museum in 1932. But with the division of the city into East and West Berlin in 1949, the museum moved from the gutted Martin Gropius Building to the Charlottenburg Palace in the western sector. After the central district had been cleansed of buildings from the recent Nazi past, the old museum stood alone in no-man's-land, with the Berlin Wall running right down the street at its front door. During the Cold War, the few records and objects from the Schliemann Collection that still could be found in Germany were split between East and West. Yet Goldmann slowly pieced together the twentieth-century history of the Schliemann Collection prior to May 1945.[80]

As Hitler prepared for war in 1934, all works of art in Berlin were categorized as Class 1 (Irreplaceable), Class 2 (Very Valuable), and Class 3 (Other). Schliemann's Trojan Collection fell into all three classes.[81] At the same time, Hitler was equally methodical in classifying which masterpieces he wished to acquire for the museum of world art that he intended to create in his birthplace of Linz, Austria. These would be systematically looted from major European museums and private collections during the course of the war and brought to special art repositories in Berlin.[82]

One week before the invasion of Poland in 1939, Unverzagt closed the museum and put his staff on alert. The crating began.[83] They placed the museum's most valuable Class 1 objects in crates labeled MVF 1 through 3 and secreted them in the basement of the Gropius Building for security purposes. MVF 1 contained all of the gold from Priam's Treasure and four silver vessels, three ceremonial axes (in

Treasure L from Calvert's land), and various other golden artifacts. The Helios Metope (Class 1) and the best Class 2 objects of silver, bronze, and pottery were also boxed and taken to the cellar. Soon they became separated, some for good.[84] The Allies dropped the first bombs in August 1940. Basement windows were walled up and the cellar was used as safe storage until January 1941, when Unverzagt got the Class 1 material transferred to the safe at the Prussian Maritime Commerce Bank.[85] Class 2 objects went to the cellar of the New Mint, part of the Reichsbank.[86]

In November 1941, Unverzagt had the three numbered crates taken to the "Flakturm Zoo," the largest of the massive anti-aircraft towers built between 1941 and 1942.[87] The concrete fortress took up one city block on the grounds of the Berlin Zoo and stood 40 meters high, with walls 2.4 meters thick. Well protected against Allied bombing assaults by a roof installation of anti-aircraft guns, the thirteen-story structure, equipped with its own water and electricity supply, was designed to accommodate the civilian population of the city and housed a hospital, air-raid shelter, and military garrison.[88] The first floor, rooms 10 and 11, took Nefertiti's portrait head, Humann's disassembled Altar of Zeus from Pergamon, and, on 2 September 1941, Schliemann's treasures in MVF 1 and thirty other cases. These lay in a 1500-square-meter depot, accompanied by hundreds of paintings, cabinets of gems,[89] and the coin collection that had belonged to Kaiser Wilhelm II.

The Allied bombardment of Berlin intensified in December 1943, with daily and nightly missions and tremendous civilian casualties.[90] Unverzagt secured more space in the tower. In 1943, Hitler had ordered museums to microfilm lists of their holdings. Unverzagt placed them in the flak tower and soon took up residence there himself.[91] He sought to secure the remainder of his museum's holdings outside the city in three different locations: Lebus on the Oder River, to which he sent crated objects by barge in the autumn of 1943,[92] the salt mine at Schönebeck, and a castle near Berlin.[93] More went to the third floor of the flak tower.[94] As the net closed around Berlin and danger of Allied assaults mounted, numerous plans called for the evacuation of the priceless works of art held in the concrete fortress. On 1 February 1945, two high-ranking officials ordered the immediate evacuation of the treasures of the Berlin repositories to the west. One official noted, "This is foreign currency."[95] Meanwhile, museum staff, bankers, librarians, and archivists panicked as they sought safe havens for their charges in any way possible. Two days later, Allied bombs gutted what remained of Unverzagt's museum, incinerating some four hundred boxes still awaiting evacuation.[96]

By February, works were already being sent to salt mines in Bavaria, caves, castles, and monasteries. But responsibility weighed heavily on Unverzagt, and he was loathe to let his prizes go. That spring, Unverzagt evacuated fifty crates to mines at Schönebeck, Grasleben, and Merkers, soon to be taken by the advancing American troops.[97] Many of the crates sat near Schönebeck, half-unloaded until the end of the war. The last transport left for the Grasleben salt mines on 7 April 1945.[98] Although they were on the list to be transported, crates MVF 1 through 3 were not among the works shipped.[99]

Now the Red Army was fast approaching from the east. They had seized East Prussia in two weeks and by 27 January were within one hundred miles of Berlin. At 5:00 A.M. on 16 April, Moscow time, General Georgii Zhukov (1896–1974) launched the Soviet offensive on Berlin with a massive bombardment. Blinding the Berliners with 143 spotlights stationed 200 meters apart along the front, Zhukov sent a million and a half men forward in an assault that would take the lives of three hundred thousand of his own troops and one hundred and twenty-five thousand civilians before it was over. On 20 April, Hitler's fifty-sixth birthday, Zhukov was on the outskirts of Berlin. As May approached, the Red Army was poised to invade Berlin. By agreement, the Allies held back west of the Elbe River, and the Soviets entered the conquered city first. When they reached the zoo, the flak tower was still standing. On 30 April, Hitler committed suicide. The flak tower surrendered, and the Soviets raised their flag on the Reichstag on 1 May. Thus, when the Allies ceded the fate of Berlin to the Soviets, they ceded them the fate of the Schliemann Collection as well.[100]

Despite Unverzagt's later declaration that he had handed over the Schliemann Collection to the Soviets,[101] some mistrusted him because of his ties to Hitler's *Ahnenerbe*, the archaeological wing of the SS.[102] Some Berlin depots were burned and officials responsible for the transporting of artworks died; cover-ups were suspected. Pillaging was rampant. The black market thrived.[103] Had the material gone to the West, as intended in the last shipment of 7 April 1945? If it had been stored in a mine, the Americans would have found it, as they found most of the hidden masterpieces.[104] Could it be in America?

During the German invasion of the Soviet Union, the Nazis ruthlessly had looted the artistic and cultural treasures of their former allies.[105] An expert on the Leningrad collections selected objects for Hitler's museum.[106] Others removed the famed amber panels from the Amber Room in Catherine the Great's palace, a gift to Peter the Great from Frederick William II of Prussia. From the Summer Palace of Peter the Great the Nazis removed some thirty-four thousand art objects.[107] "They took anything they could pry loose from the myriad palaces and pavilions around Leningrad, right down to the parquet floors. They opened packed crates and helped themselves to the contents. Mirrors were smashed or machine gunned, brocades and silks ripped from the walls."[108] Cathedrals were pillaged, churches destroyed, museums and libraries ransacked. German troops stripped Kiev's libraries and museums and pillaged and desecrated the houses, graves, and museums of famous figures.[109] According to one estimate, the Nazis removed, destroyed, or damaged 564,723 museum objects worth over five billion rubles, or one and a quarter billion dollars.[110]

The Nazi aggression and brutality practiced on Leningrad, Kiev, and other Soviet cities invited quick retribution. In November 1943, Josef Stalin (1879–1953) signed an edict establishing an emergency state committee. A "Trophy Commission" sanctioned the removal to the Soviet Union of European art collections and state and private libraries. In particular, trophy brigades composed of art historians, artists, and restorers would collect any useful portable goods, from art to food and industrial installations, as reparations for the depredations suffered by the Soviet people at the hands of Nazi Germany.[111] In January 1945, Stalin authorized the massive removal of cultural property for his own proposed museum in Moscow.

During May and June 1945, the Soviets had their run of Berlin. On 3 May, escorted by Dr. Otto Kümmel (1874–1952), director of the Berlin museums, the Soviets toured the flak tower and the museums. On 5 May, they made Unverzagt "director of the Flak Tower Museum," and two days later the evacuation of art began in the western repositories, which soon would be in the British and American zones. All objects were taken to a collection point deep within the future Soviet zone.[112] On 12 May, Unverzagt was permitted to visit his museum. Sealed boxes were opened and resealed. The zoo flak tower, which lay in Britain's zone, would take a month to empty. Unverzagt remained on hand.[113]

Soviet troops removed the frieze from the Pergamene Altar of Zeus. Seven thousand Greek vases, nine thousand antique gems, sixty-five hundred terracottas, and thousands of lesser objects came from the Department of Greek Antiquities alone.[114] On 17 June, a trophy brigade inventoried the contents and trucked three large crates from the zoo flak tower to a special depot east of Berlin.[115] Unverzagt met with the Soviets a last time on 26 June. Lists in Russian, discovered at Potsdam, give military transport numbers identical with those of the three crates.[116] Around 30 June, a military airplane bound for Moscow was loaded with hostages from the flak tower: paintings by Degas, Monet, Cézanne, Renoir, and El Greco, a Velázquez from Hitler's private collection, a hoard of fur coats, and the same three crates.[117] The same officer who supervised the deportation of the Pergamon Altar signed off on the other loot from Unverzagt's museum.[118] Delayed for eight days at the Moscow airport, they were finally admitted and signed for by the senior curator of the Pushkin State Museum of Fine Arts on 9 July.[119] There were three boxes of pictures and one of gems, as well as three containing gold, silver, and other archaeological objects from the Stone Age to the early Middle Ages: in one was the cream of the Schliemann Collection.

On the same day, junior curator Irina Antonova, then in her 20s, cosigned for Schliemann's treasure when it arrived at the Pushkin Museum.[120] On 12 July, the contents of box MVF 1 were inventoried in Protocol No. 83 as containing 259 items.[121] The numbers on the Pushkin Museum documents matched those of Potsdam.[122] In 1956, a curator at the Pushkin Museum inventoried the contents of the crates.[123]

The Schliemann Collection remained hidden from the world by the Soviets, just as its centerpiece, Priam's Treasure, repeatedly had been hidden from the Turks. Then, with the new openness of glasnost, the tightly guarded Soviet Central Archives became public. In April 1991, Konstantin Akinsha, an art historian and journalist, and Grigorii Kozlov, a former museum inspector for Russia's Department of Museums and curator of a museum affiliated with the Pushkin, broke the story of the Soviet "special repositories" for the spoils of war, secret art depots hidden in monasteries, museums, and castles within the former Soviet Union. Among the works said to have been brought back to the Soviet Union were the treasures of Troy. They alleged that hundreds of thousands of artworks lay hidden in secret repositories in Kiev, Moscow, and Saint Petersburg. More than two and a half years later, Evgeny Sidorov, the minister of culture of Russia, finally announced in August 1993 that the Troy treasures indeed had survived and were in the protective custody of the Pushkin Museum in Moscow, where they once again had been transported "for safekeeping."

But the parallels with the earlier history of Priam's Treasure do not end there. According to Goldmann, the Germans had sent an identical set of copies of the Schliemann gold to the Pushkin Museum before 1917.[124] Were those now in the Pushkin Museum the original treasures that were smuggled out of Turkey in 1873, or were these the German duplicates? Or were they the duplicates in gold that Schliemann himself had explored the possibility of making—cheap, untraceable copies to give the Turks should he be threatened with litigation? At the time of the original discovery, rumors had circulated in Constantinople that the original Priam's Treasure had been fabricated, although Calvert had maintained its authenticity.[125] Thus questioned at the start, Priam's Treasure faced questions about its authenticity again. In October and November 1994, a handful of Turkish, European, and American archaeologists were permitted to examine the objects in Moscow, including most of the gold and silver, the 1890 finds: ceremonial axes, rock-crystal lenses, the lead figurine, and the lump of meteoric iron.[126] The group reached consensus that the objects in fact are all authentic. At the same time, they reported that 414 additional objects, mainly bronzes, had survived at the Hermitage.[127] Despite almost unanimous support for the genuineness of the material, however, some scholars still question discrepancies in the various treasures, while others urge that they be tested.[128]

But whose are they? Here too, as when they were first discovered, the ownership of Schliemann's finds is being contested. In 1986, a symposium of scholars at Bryn Mawr College reviewed the evidence for a historic Trojan War as it stood prior to the resumption of excavations by a joint U.S.-German team at Hisarlık. The consensus was that there was not one Trojan War, but several throughout the Bronze Age.[129] Now, at the end of the second millennium A.D., East and West are waging perhaps the last Trojan War. The booty is Priam's Treasure.

In January 1995, a conference was held at the Bard Graduate Center in New York City entitled "The Spoils of War." Inspired by issues arising from Lynn Nicholas's *Rape of Europa* (1994), it featured sixty-five speakers from Europe, the former Soviet Republics, and the United States and drew an audience of three hundred, spellbound by the magnitude of the problems involved and the sheer drama of it all.[130] Simultaneous translation eased communication. Central to the conference were thorny issues such as the repatriation of archaeological finds, and Priam's Treasure became a case study. The question is, to which nation or individual should it be returned? One observer noted that after fifty years, "the wounds are still so raw." Repatriation still seems a long way off.

Because of the vicissitudes of war, parts of Schliemann's collection are now located in Berlin, Saint Petersburg, Moscow, Istanbul, and Athens.[131] Some of the more common pieces, of which he had many examples, went to the Smithsonian, the British Museum, and study collections throughout Germany. In all, he excavated twenty-one "treasures," which Schmidt labeled with the letters "A" to "S" when he catalogued the small finds of the collection in 1902.[132] All eight treasures excavated in 1872 and 1873, including Treasure A, Priam's Treasure, were smuggled from Turkey and given by Schliemann to the German people after he had won his lawsuit with the Ottoman government.[133] A portion of Treasure C, stolen by the workmen in 1873 and recovered by the government, remains in the Istanbul Archaeological Museum, along with remains of four of the nine others excavated in 1878 and 1879. Apparently all of the treasures found in the 1882 and 1890 seasons were smuggled to Berlin.[134] Since the 1884 law stipulated that all antiquities belonged solely to the Ottoman government, so did Treasure L, although found on Calvert's land in 1890. So Schliemann did not have a clear title to all of the Trojan Collection that came to Berlin. Today, several states and individuals claim that they do.

Germany's claim rests on the gift by Schliemann of his Trojan Collection to the German people. Yet he clearly did not have a legitimate claim to all of the material, and according to the Ottoman ministerial decree of 1872, he had no permission to export finds, whether or not they fell in his half.[135] It is not clear whether he finally willed the later material to the German people, but if he did, he certainly seems not to have had any legal basis for doing so.

In order to buy support for the invasion of Hungary, Stalin gave back to East Germany more than one and a half million art objects and five hundred boxes of archaeological material in 1957.[136] Among the objects returned to East Berlin that year were Schliemann's Helios Metope and the Pergamon Altar. Both remain in the Pergamon Museum.

The Turkish argument rests on the ministerial decree of 1872 as affecting the 1873 finds. According to Easton, treasures excavated in 1878 and 1879 seem for the most part to have been divided legitimately.[137] If one ignores the prohibition against export in effect since 1872, then Germany does have a right to Schliemann's half of that split. But Turkey has a valid claim to two-thirds of the treasures excavated in 1882 and all of Treasure L of 1890, and it may have a claim on half of those excavated earlier.[138]

The Russians argue that since after Hitler's defeat there was no legitimate government in Germany, and since the Soviet Union was the legitimate governing authority in its occupation zone, it had every right to remove cultural property.[139]

But the zoo was not in its legitimate zone, it was in Britain's. This is why the Soviet troops worked night and day to empty it as quickly as they did.

While they seek an honorable solution, the Russian government does not intend to give priceless material away for nothing.[140] They want returns to be made on a reciprocal basis. However, the Germans have little to return, since most of the cultural material looted from the former Soviet Union that still exists was stolen by private individuals, sold by East German trophy squads looking for cash in hard currency, or returned long ago by the Allies. Still, they could give money, services, or comparable art to replace the thousands of works that were looted or systematically destroyed.

Germany has proposed that the parties submit to binding arbitration by the World Court at The Hague. There, the Turks could argue for the return of their portions of the two treasures excavated in 1882 and the return in full of Treasure L, further dividing the collection. But in the end, Easton foresees a political, rather than a legal, solution, in which the treasures go for cash to the highest bidder, Germany.[141]

The Calvert family in London also seeks redress for decades of exploitation.[142] Had the 1884 antiquities law not stipulated that all antiquities belonged to the state, they would have been entitled to one-third of Treasure L, which Schliemann found more valuable than anything he had found at Mycenae.[143] But unless additional 1884 clauses specify the continuing rights of proprietors to antiquities excavated on their land, even though the Calverts have a moral claim, they have no legal right to the treasure. This point still awaits interpretation by legal experts. Traill has argued that Treasure C was found on the eastern half of the mound in March 1873.[144] If so, the Calvert family has a legal right to their half, although they could not export it from Turkey. Since this would be difficult to prove, it would be unlikely that the Istanbul Archaeological Museum would be willing to surrender any part of its meager portion of Schliemann's treasures. Perhaps the Calverts might be given the opportunity to place their half of this material on permanent loan to the Archaeological Museum or to donate it, as their forebears did, but this time in return for some sort of public acknowledgment of both the gift and Frank Calvert's role in the archaeological exploration of Troy. Finally, the family believes that Schliemann falsified his records so as to locate all of the other treasures on the western half of the mound, that is, on government property. Whereas Traill has proven that Schliemann did alter the reported locations of finds to suit his circumstances, there is no proof of this other than in the case of Treasures R and C. And certainly, Moscow would give little more than a nod of recognition without hard proof as to the provenance of the finds. Yet it is interesting to note that Schliemann found all of his treasures during years when he was excavating on Calvert's land, and none in 1870 and 1871, when he excavated only the western half of the mound. Whatever solution is reached in Moscow, an acknowledgment of Calvert and the Calvert family will be in order.

The author and journalist Karl Meyer noted that in 1945, American officers warned "that disputes over captured spoils can sow enduring acrimony," an ironic parallel with the *Iliad:* Agamemnon and Achilles fall into a deadly dispute over war prizes that Agamemnon takes for himself.[145] Irina Antonova, the junior curator who signed for Priam's Treasure in 1945 and now director of the Pushkin State Museum of Fine Arts, has declared, "The war has not truly ended as long as we have not settled the issues in the area of cultural property."[146] Nor, it seems, has the "Trojan War."

The British archaeologist Donald Easton stresses the merits of keeping the collection intact and near the site of Troy, where it could be consulted and studied by scholars investigating the site. This makes a great deal of sense. In 1996, the area around Troy and the Trojan plain, from Calvert's site of Ophryneion on the Hellespont to Beşika Bay, including both Calvert farms and Pınarbaşı, was declared a national historic park to protect it in perpetuity from pillage and damage by developers.[147] The beleaguered area that has seen so many wars once again has been demilitarized and the horrors of no-man's-land finally dispelled. In 1997, the Turkish government granted $3 million for the construction of a new museum for the Trojan finds, which could be designated "humankind museum property."[148] It is hoped that in 1998 Troy will join UNESCO's list for world heritage sites. At the Bard Conference, speakers stressed archaeological, historical, and scientific reasons for having the material in close proximity to the site. Calvert's collection is already almost entirely nearby in Çanakkale. Schliemann's would come from Russia, Germany, and Greece. If the Russians contributed the Trojan material in their possession, it certainly would be the jewel in the crown.[149] Morally, this would be the right solution, considering the unquestionable 1872 prohibition on export.

On 15 April 1996, the Pushkin Museum unveiled Schliemann's sequestered treasures to an appreciative international crowd for the first time in more than half a century.[150] Soon, the treasures of the Hermitage also will be shown. After the current and proposed exhibitions, an international committee may be formed to coordinate and arrange conservation.[151] Then perhaps the exhibition could travel to each of the countries that would be contributing part of its collection to the international whole, finally returning home to Troy, to the internationally sponsored museum where it perhaps would be on permanent loan from all concerned.[152] Since Russia would be contributing the lion's share in terms of monetary value, it could be spared international monetary contributions of another sort. At the same time, Germany and Russia would be free to negotiate over matters more integral to their own cultural patrimony.[153]

This solution would mean international recognition of Hisarlık beyond the scope of Calvert's wildest dreams. If the museum were to be built on his land, Calvert could receive the recognition he deserves along with Schliemann and his precious treasures, which to date have been hidden for longer than they have been displayed. The park and museum would be a wonderful celebration of their tremendous achievements.

Epilogue
Finding the Walls of Troy Today

As the world awaits the outcome of the international disputes over possession of the Troy treasures, a last inscription on the Trojan palimpsest is being written year by year in the reports of the joint German-American excavations that have been carried out at Hisarlık since 1988.[1] Whereas some of the earliest investigators merely hypothesized from the comfort of their studies in the British Isles and northern Europe about the location of Troy based on reading Homer or Strabo, Calvert, Schliemann, Dörpfeld, and Blegen penetrated the mound of Hisarlık itself, excavating to find the walls of Troy. The present excavators are using new technology to solve many of the same questions that puzzled earlier excavators. Although the team continues to excavate strategic areas of the citadel and its slopes with pickaxes and shovels as before, remote-sensing technology has now enabled them to probe the vast area of the lower city without destroying what lies buried beneath it.[2]

Still struggling, like his predecessors, with the chronology of the early strata at Hisarlık, Manfred Korfmann has chosen to group the prehistoric levels together using cultural affinities [Figure 28]. Thus, for the first three strata, he speaks of a "Maritime Troia Culture" that had over a dozen building phases and lasted over six hundred years, from 2920 to 2300 B.C.[3] The similarities in the pottery from these three levels and the continuity in their use of architecture, especially the fortification wall, ramp, and gates, make all the more palpable the break between these and the fourth and fifth strata, the ones that Schliemann characterized as "stone period debris." In addition, Korfmann now posits an abandonment of about one hundred years between the earlier culture and the fourth and fifth levels.[4] Because these last two levels have more parallels with the Anatolian hinterland, Korfmann calls them the "Anatolian Troia Culture, 2000–1750 B.C." These five strata, along with the lower phases of the sixth stratum, make up the Early and Middle Bronze Age periods at Hisarlık.

What has captivated the world with the Troy excavations, of course, is the connection with Homer. The sixth and seventh strata at Hisarlık are those connected with Homer by Dörpfeld and Blegen, respectively [Figure 29]. This powerful Late Bronze Age settlement Korfmann calls "High Troia Culture, 1700–1180 B.C." It is in these strata that the advances of the present team are easiest to measure. But Korfmann is less interested in proving the validity of Homer's account than his predecessors. He does not seek to find the shield of Achilles or the remains of the Trojan Horse; rather, he wants to understand the major Bronze Age Anatolian and Classical site that arose in such a strategic spot.[5]

Since 1993, the excavators have used remote sensing to trace the defenses of a lower city large enough to answer the prayers of Calvert and Schliemann. It is comparable in size to its counterparts on the Greek mainland and related to, but smaller than, the central Anatolian "palace-temple-cities" of the Hittites.[6] South of the citadel at Hisarlık, the present team has discerned an expansive elliptical lower town. Encircling the town are two concentric ditches 3 meters wide cut into the bedrock with three or four gateways, 10 meters wide, forming causeways giving access to the lower town. These were dug to prevent chariots and siege engines from attacking the vulnerable lower city [Figure 53]. A wooden palisade with a gateway 5 meters wide located 3.5 meters behind the inner ditch further impeded attack. The first ditch encircled an area large enough to increase the total size of the city from 20,000 to 200,000 square meters.[7] The second ditch, found in 1995, which lies 80 to 100 meters south of the first, will increase the expanse exponentially.[8] Moreover, in 1995, the first traces of a stone fortification wall for at least a part of the lower city were found enclosing the northeast bastion, whose ample water supply now seems to have served the lower city.[9]

The lower city itself has been found like "negative architecture" underneath the grid plan of a vast Roman city laid out on the plateau in the time of Augustus.[10] The remains were almost completely destroyed by later building or eroded away, and what remained were post holes from wooden houses. Six of the houses excavated in this area had unusually high concentrations of Mycenaean pottery. The team also found bronze missiles hurled by hostile forces into the beleaguered city of wooden houses, ample tinder for the blaze that destroyed it. But who were the inhabitants, and did they include Priam, Hecuba, Hector, and Paris?

With the existence of a lower city now securely fixed, the citadel has become an acropolis worthy of "Priam's Pergamos," contemporary in date with its Mycenaean counterparts on the Greek mainland. Surely, then, this is Troy. The high citadel with its elite buildings, the walls, the provisions for chariot warfare, the size of the rich sixth settlement, with a projected population of between six and seven thousand individuals,[11] and the character of the landscape as now understood reflect Homer's description and thus reinforce if not confirm outright the identification of this site with the bard's Troy. Moreover, the most recent excavators have shown that the walls of the sixth settlement were still visible in the eighth century B.C., when Homer putatively lived and might have visited the site. The devastated

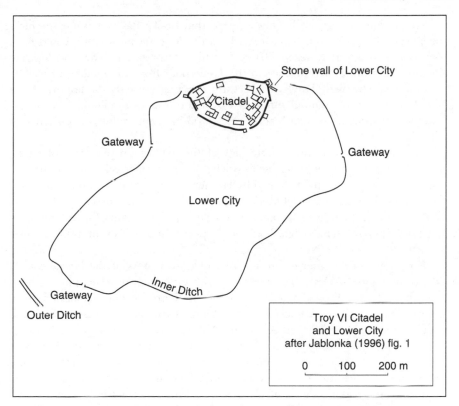

Figure 53. Troy. The citadel and lower city, 1995. After Jablonka (1996), Figure 1.

Anatolian citadel, then only sparsely inhabited in the shadow of the towering earlier walls, well could have inspired the tradition of war and heroes wasted at that ghostly spot in the fertile plain.

Was the Trojan War an actual event? Pottery from Late Bronze Age levels at Hisarlık does suggest significant contact with the Mycenaeans to the west in the fourteenth through thirteenth centuries B.C.[12] On the coast just southwest of Troy a headland projects into the Aegean, creating a protected anchorage at Beşik Tepe.[13] It has sheltered mariners as far back as history can record and has remained the favored harbor in the nineteenth and twentieth centuries. In the 1980s, Korfmann excavated scanty traces of a Late Bronze Age settlement on the eroded promontory. On the edge of the ancient bay below he uncovered a Late Bronze Age cemetery with eclectic grave types and rich remains of Mycenaean and local pottery and trade goods.[14] Above Beşika Bay, a tumulus now thought to date to the Late Bronze Age period has been connected by the excavator with the tumulus that the Greeks thought belonged to Achilles, the one most likely visited by Xerxes and Alexander. He has asserted that Beşika Bay represents the most likely site of Troy's ancient harbor, where the Mycenaean Greeks would have been camped during a siege of Troy.[15] In his interpretation, Troy was a pirate fortress controlling the entrance to the Hellespont from the citadel, as well as from Beşik Tepe, with Troy's architecture reflecting not only the import of the site, but also the continuous threat of extinction over two millennia that its inhabitants felt due to its wealth and strategic position controlling the entrance to the Hellespont.[16]

But this does not prove the historicity of the specific ten-year siege of which Homer sang. Nor does it prove the historicity of figures such as Priam and the various heroes so poignantly described by Homer. To lift the veil of prehistory once and for all, the excavators will need to find the palace archive or some other written proof of the identity of the ancient town and its inhabitants, for without texts, the association of archaeological finds with specific historical events is notoriously difficult.[17]

Far away, in the center of ancient Anatolia, excavators of the Hittite capital found thousands of clay tablets inscribed with the annals of an empire contemporary with Late Bronze Age Troy. Some of these do indeed mention royal names that have been associated with Priam (Pariamu) and Alexander/Paris (Alaksandus/Pariya). Even the Achaeans (Ahhiyawa) and names for Hisarlık may be preserved in these documents—Troy (Taruisa) and Ilios (Wilusa)—but these are subject to a wide array of interpretations.[18] The Alaksandus Treaty of the early thirteenth century B.C. in the Hittite Archives mentions a town in the west named Wilusa and gives a list of its gods, who witnessed the treaty. The first was "the Stormgod of the Army," and next, after a lost name, came Appaliunas.[19] Perhaps Homer knew more than we think: the chief god of his Trojans was Apollo, who decimated the Achaeans with plague and built the city's famous walls. After male and female gods, mountains, and rivers (springs), came the "subterranean stream of Wilusa."[20] This could be the source of the Scamander, high up the slopes of Mount Ida, where it flows out of the rock after passing through a long tunnel-like fissure at a place where tradition has placed the fatal judgment of Paris.[21] It seems far more likely, however, that the subterranean stream refers to the "latomie" first explored by Frank Calvert between 1863 and 1865, then by Schliemann. The latomie, or cave, lies below the lower city, gaping and mysterious, much more intimately connected with Wilusa itself than the source of the Scamander several days' journey from the site by foot or by horse. Although Korfmann and Rose explored it in 1997, there still is no hard proof. In the end, one again needs confirmation from inscriptions at Troy to corroborate these tantalizing clues.

The first linguistic clue to the identity of the inhabitants who lived behind the walls was found in 1995. A seal dating anywhere from 1280 to 1175 B.C. and inscribed in the hieroglyphic script of the Hittites has given proof that the inhabitants of the citadel were operating in an Anatolian cultural sphere, bilingual perhaps, but rooted in Anatolia.[22] The script generally was used for monumental stone inscriptions in the Luvian language of ancient Anatolia. Another text in that language records a ritual song sung in the sixteenth century B.C. that opens with: "When they came from steep Wilusa."[23] Thus, Hittite (Luvian) and Homeric Wilusa had similar epithets, and the language of the song seems to match the language of the seal.

Dates suggested for "The Trojan War" in the last decade alone have ranged from the fifteenth to the eleventh century B.C.[24] As many students of Troy's history have noted, the excavations themselves show that there have been many Trojan wars. Violent destruction occurred in both the sixth and seventh strata. For the destruction found in the sixth stratum, explanations range from earthquake (Blegen), to attack from outside (Dörpfeld), to social upheaval, or all of the above.[25] Recently, Korfmann has noted the evidence of fire and a subsequent "military event" in the thick deposit of ash that covered the seventh settlement in the lower town.[26] According to carbon 14 dating, the catastrophe occurred around 1180 B.C., a date remarkably close to the one given by Eratosthenes, 1183, which was accepted by Calvert in 1873.

Some scholars have claimed pessimistically that for Greeks of the eighth century, the thread to their Homeric past was "irretrievably broken" and have called modern attempts to match ancient Greek dates with archaeological remains "an exercise in illusion."[27] But Korfmann has noted that the Luvian language survived the collapse of the palace civilizations at the end of the thirteenth century B.C., particularly in the area around Izmir (Smyrna), Homer's milieu. Thus, he suggests that the story of Wilusa may have been handed down in local languages, both orally and in written form. But all we have is one small seal. It was found in a late deposit of the seventh stratum.[28] If not an heirloom, it might suggest that literacy survived at Troy into what have come to be called the Dark Ages.[29]

The period of the Dark Ages at Troy, between the high civilization of Troy in the Late Bronze Age and that of the Aeolic village in the seventh century B.C., long has been the black hole of Trojan archaeology [Figure 29]. It is part of Calvert's thousand-year gap. This transition period has attracted the scrutiny of Brian Rose, director of the present post–Bronze Age excavations at Troy. Along with his work on the Roman lower city, Rose repeatedly has focused on the deep deposits near Blegen's western sanctuary. There he has uncovered remains of a millennium of worship, beginning with such tenuous clues to contact with central Anatolia as a bronze "standing warrior" figurine from the seventh stratum, perhaps the "Stormgod of the Army,"[30] and a fragmentary Anatolian stag statuette, then continuing with a geometric temple and Archaic and Hellenistic successors.

In 1996 and 1997, Rose found paltry but significant remains of strata absent on the inner citadel. Following Blegen's division of Dörpfeld's nine major strata into forty-six levels, the present team has discerned the last three centuries (1040/1000 to 750/700 B.C.) missing in Calvert's thousand-year gap. In the excavator's words, the gap is finally "beginning to close."[31]

As excavations continue at Troy, Korfmann also has targeted Calvert's and Schliemann's excavation dumps, hoping to sift through the detritus left by his predecessors and get down to that left by the Greek and Roman builders who truncated Troy to build their own monuments. This is one area where fruitful excavations still might uncover the archival evidence to clinch the historical issues that still engage us. Lovers of Homer can only wait and hope for the retrieval of an archive or some written proof at Troy itself. It is possible and perhaps probable that the answers will emerge in the course of the present excavation campaign. Until then, "faith in the historicity of at least a core tradition on an historical Trojan War" remains just that.[32] Yet at this majestic spot on the plain of Troy the hopes of Calvert and Schliemann have already been realized in the full reemergence of Troy itself.[33]

NOTES

PROLOGUE

1. Calder (1972), 343.
2. Schliemann (1874), 4.
3. Schliemann (1881), 3.
4. Freud compared his success with psychoanalysis to Schliemann's discovery of Troy. Gay (1988), 172, noted by Calder (1990), 361.
5. Calder (1990), 360 n. 47.
6. Easton (1982), 95. For Ludwig, see Calder (1990), 362–69, for the reaction of Alexander Melas, Schliemann's descendant, quoted by Lynn and Gray Poole in *One Passion, Two Loves: The Story of Heinrich and Sophia Schliemann, Discoverers of Troy* (New York, 1966), viii; see Calder (1990), 360 n. 47.
7. For Georg Karo, see Calder (1990), 362–69, and Traill (1995), 8. For the letter from Theodor Wiegand (1864–1936) to Dörpfeld, 17 May 1932, see Calder (1990), 368 n. 50.
8. John A. Scott, quoted in Calder (1990), 368 n. 48.
9. Meyer (1953), 7, and (1958), 406; Calder (1986), 21 n. 16, and (1990), 370–78; Witte (1990), 39.
10. There are numerous errors of transmission. Calder (1990), 372; Calder (1986), 21–22.
11. Calder (1990), 370 n. 56.
12. Meyer (1936), 25. Translated in Calder (1990), 371.
13. Calder (1972). Calder spoke in private because the Communist government had forbidden him to deliver a public lecture. Calder, foreword to Traill (1993).
14. Calder (1972), 350.
15. Most of the diaries and letters are housed at the Gennadius Library of the American School of Classical Studies at Athens. The letters are catalogued B, BB, and BBB with file and letter number. They are quoted here with the kind permission of the director, Haris Kalligas.
16. Traill (1993 and 1995). Reviewed in Allen (1997b), 598–99, Calder, foreword to Traill (1993). David Turner has called Traill's work "a disturbing example of biographical

methodology" that concentrates on scrutinizing inconsistencies while using material conducive to his argument, yet suppressing documents that provide a more balanced view and overlooking others. According to Turner, much of the fictional in Schliemann's life, such as the childhood dream of excavating Troy, "is probably the most important *fact* of his life," a way into his mind. Turner's review of Traill (1995) is in *Journal of Hellenic Studies* (1996), 235–37. In fact, there are disturbing lacunae in his book.

17. Traill (1995). Korres (1975). On 6 January 1997, the occasion of the 175th anniversary of Schliemann's birth, both Calder and Traill received medals in Neubukow for their work on Schliemann.

18. Korres (1975) and (1974). An updated edition of the latter is forthcoming.

19. Easton (1990). Easton also has chronicled the history of the Schliemann Archive in (1982), 93–110.

20. The American Germanist Mark Lehrer and the British scholar David Turner scrutinized Schliemann's 1868 diary in order to assess Traill's interpretation and also arrived at an interpretation more sympathetic to Schliemann (1989).

21. Akinsha and Kozlov (1991a), 130–41.

22. Traill (1993), 22–25, recently has reviewed his decade-long debate with Easton. Easton is currently preparing a volume dedicated to Priam's Treasure.

23. Since this book focuses largely on Europeans in Turkey, European names for cities are used rather than the Turkish names that were in use since the time of the Ottoman conquest of Constantinople in 1453, e.g., the Dardanelles (Çanakkale), Smyrna (Izmir), and Constantinople (Istanbul). Transliterations from Turkish follow Cook (1973).

24. Leaf (1923), 230.

25. Ludwig (1931), 191; Calvert (1873a, 1874a and 1874b, 1875).

26. In 1953, Remzi Arik wrote a book in which he noted Calvert's contributions prominently. Arik (1953), 21. Arik may have been stimulated by the surfacing in 1943 of the unpublished manuscript catalogue of the Calvert Collection, Thiersch (1902a). Unfortunately, his book was not widely read, and Cook, for one, was not aware of it.

27. Thiersch (1902a). Cook had learned of its existence in 1960 through his student, Nicholas Bayne. Professor Cook kindly gave me his and Bayne's notes. The catalogue is now in the Çanakkale Archaeological Museum being studied and published by Gustav Gamer (1992) and Coşkün Özgünel.

28. Cook (1973), 36.

29. Ibid., 219.

30. Ibid., 36, 95.

31. Lascarides (1977), 63–65. This site was known variously as Bounarbashi, Bunarbashi, Bounarbaschi, and Ballı Dağ.

32. These were collected and edited by Calder in Traill (1993).

33. Ibid., 22–23.

34. Wood (1996), 31.

35. Wood (1985), rev. ed. (1996); Easton (1990). These are housed in the Manuscript Division of the British Library (BLMS), the British Museum Central Archive (BMCA), and the Keeper's Archive of the Department of Greek and Roman Antiquities in the British Museum (BMGR).

36. Several ongoing projects now focus on Schliemann's predecessor: see Gamer (1992), Allen (1993, 1994, 1995a, 1995b, 1996a, 1996b, 1997a, and 1998a). Robinson (1990, 1994: 167,

and 1995: 340) discovered critical diplomatic correspondence concerning the Calverts in the Foreign Office Archives of the Public Record Office, Kew, England (PRO/FO) and National Archives (NARA), Washington, D.C. and is working on a biography of Calvert. Allen has hitherto focused on Calvert's archaeological method and collection (1993–1998a).

37. Easton (1991), 121. Cobet (1990), 144 n. 166, discovered Ziller's handwritten autobiography in a private collection in Athens. In it he noted, "I lent this brochure to Dr. Schliemann when he came to Athens and wanted to go to Troy for the first time." Russack (1942), 153.

38. Lehrer and Turner (1989) translated and published excerpts of Schliemann's 1868 diary housed in the Gennadius Library of the American School of Classical Studies in Athens. Of concern here are the sections in modern Greek dealing with Greece, the Troad, and Constantinople. Subsequent references will include citations of their translations.

39. Schliemann's 1868 diary; Lehrer and Turner (1989), 237.

40. Again his description borrowed heavily from Murray (1854).

41. Von Hahn (1865) and Nicoläides (1867), as noted by Lehrer and Turner (1989), 240. Von Hahn's colleague, the astronomer Julius Schmidt, also gave an account of the 1864 excavations. Schmidt (1864), 591.

42. Even Murray (1854) recommended that the traveler visit the British consul at the Dardanelles before proceeding to the Troad. If Schliemann had done so, he certainly would have been passed to Frank Calvert, with whom the British vice-consul, William H. Wrench, had a good relationship.

43. Schliemann probably did this either because of his Crimean War affiliation or his Russian family.

44. Here, too, the Calverts maintained the most prominent residence, but Schliemann did not encounter them.

45. Schliemann's 1868 diary, 137; Lehrer and Turner (1989), 241.

46. It had been partly excavated by Calvert.

47. Schliemann's 1868 diary, 139; Lehrer and Turner (1989), 242. Cyclopean masonry is a primitive style of stonework using massive, irregularly cut stones. It was named for the Cyclops, the three one-eyed sons of Gaea and Uranus, who were said to have built the walls of Mycenae.

48. Nicoläides noted: "The principal objection is that Ilium Novum is too close to the Hellespont" (1867), 47.

49. Nicoläides (1867), 83 nn. 1, 85 noted that "Calvart" (his brother Frederick, not Frank) had opened one of the three tumuli at Sigeum in 1855, not the Erenköy tumulus. Lehrer and Turner (1989), 256.

50. Schliemann's 1868 diary, 142; Lehrer and Turner (1989), 243.

51. Nicoläides (1867), 83 n. 1.

52. Schliemann's 1868 diary, 144; Lehrer and Turner (1989), 244. Lehrer and Turner questioned when the entries for 11 and 12 August were written but came to no conclusion (1989), 257.

53. Schliemann's 1868 diary, 144; Lehrer and Turner (1989), 244.

54. Traill (1993), 79 n. 19.

55. Schliemann's 1868 diary, 144; Lehrer and Turner (1989), 244.

56. In 1984, Traill was the first to suggest that Schliemann had written his 14 August entry after his meeting with Calvert and then had back-dated it to cover his tracks. Traill (1993), 78, 88–89.

57. Lehrer and Turner (1989), 244–45; Traill (1993), 78.

58. Traill (1993), 89.

59. Schliemann's 1868 diary, 148; The 16 August entry is cited only by Traill (1993), 79.

60. Untitled memoir by William Partridge, an associate of Henry Bacon's, in the Partridge Papers, William Robert Ware Collection, Division of Drawings and Archives, Avery Architectural and Fine Arts Library, Columbia University in the City of New York. Quoted here with the kind permission of Angela Giral, Librarian. I thank Elizabeth Gwaim, Wesleyan University, for bringing this source to my attention and also Thomas (1990), 21 n. 3, 45 n. 24.

61. Calvert (1875).

62. Traill has illuminated the sequence of events as altered by Schliemann (1869), 161–62, and the manipulation of his diary entries; Traill (1993), 73–90.

63. Schliemann's 1868 diary, 148; Lehrer and Turner (1989), 245. The weight is discussed in Calvert (1860a), 199–200.

64. In his later publication of his journey, he described "the rich collection of ancient vases and other curious objects which the ingenious and indefatigable archaeologist Frank Calvert found in his numerous excavations." Schliemann (1869), 213.

CHAPTER 1

1. De Kay (1863), 64.

2. Hunt, in Walpole (1817), 95; De Kay (1833), 64; Walsh (1836), 2:37; Cuinet (1893), 3:702.

3. Major Sir Grenville Temple with fifty-five other vessels attempted to beat the current and tacked for fourteen hours, only to advance one and a half miles before admitting defeat and anchoring for eleven days. Temple (1836), 1:292.

4. Fellows (1839), 57.

5. Temple (1836), 1:289.

6. Turner (1820), 1:43.

7. Simpson (1854), 11 November 1854. I thank Peter Harrington, curator of the Ann S. K. Brown Military Collection of Brown University, for bringing Simpson's sketchbook to my attention. *Dictionary of National Biography*, s.v. "Simpson, William."

8. Views of the strait by L. F. Cassas and Corneille Le Brun (1714) document the castles and their tiny towns.

9. Fellows (1839), 56–57. The term "Dardanelles" originated in the area's association with ancient Dardanos, about five miles southwest of the city, at Barber's Point. Slade (1854), 18. Apparently, Europeans also referred to it fancifully as "Abydos." Turner (1820), 3:215. The Greeks called it *ta mesa Kastra*, from its position between the castles. Walpole (1817), 92.

10. Durbin (1849), 2:182–84.

11. Frederick Calvert to Stratford de Redcliffe, 14 July 1854, PRO/FO 195 391, also NARA RG84 Dard. 4. For the hospital, see De Kay (1833), 465. The *Levant Herald and Eastern Express* of 2 August 1892 recorded cholera at the Dardanelles in 1848, 1854, and 1865. NARA RG84 Dard. 8. Walsh noted that whenever plague was epidemic elsewhere, it was particularly mortal there. Walsh (1836), 2:39.

12. Murray (1875), 160.

13. Cotton and wool were produced on the plain of Troy beginning in the nineteenth century. Hunt in Walpole (1817), 99. In 1857, one million pounds of cotton were produced annually in the region, of which only four hundred thousand were consumed. Frederick Calvert to the earl of Clarendon (1800–1870), 31 December 1857, PRO/FO 78 1309.

14. Pottery production already was declining in 1867. Cuinet (1893), 3:725–26. Three factories still produced coarse pottery in 1910, but transport remained a problem.

15. Ten thousand pounds were produced a year according to Hunt in Walpole (1817), 99.

16. Murray (1878), 129. For insight into the conduct of trade between local communities in the Ottoman Empire and Europe, see Frangakis (1985), 27–41. In the early nineteenth century, "morrocco leather, hare skins, wax madder root and gall nuts" were exported. Dearborn (1819), 2:41–42. In 1910, the Dardanelles exported fifty-five hundred tons of valonia to Austria, Italy, Germany, Belgium, France, and Romania, as well as considerable quantities of oak, pine, and fir to Greece and Egypt. Report of C. Xanthopoulos to the U.S. consul general, 26 October 1910, NARA RG84 Dard. 6. According to Cuinet, 41,117 hectares were fields of wheat and other grains or of beans, 1,547 of olive groves, 838 of vineyards, and 266,510 of valonia; 196,901 hectares were state-owned forests, and 243,087 were uncultivated mountain pasturages. Cuinet (1893), 3:689–90, 731. One hectare equals 2.471 acres.

17. Fellows (1839), 83.

18. Durbin (1849), 2:182–84; Smith (1851), 55–56.

19. Murray (1854), 127, 140. Cuinet (1893), 3:720. Temple, who also enjoyed the local shellfish, noted that the Roman poet Catullus had lavished praise on the Hellespontian bivalve. Temple (1836), 1:292.

20. Temple (1836), 1:283; Murray (1878), 140.

21. Hunt's memoir in Walpole (1817), 94.

22. Clarke (1817), 3:89. *Dictionary of National Biography*, s.v. "Clarke, Edward Daniel."

23. It was the capital of the Archipelago before 1876 and of Biğa province after 1880. Its area in later times was approximately 750,000 hectares, or 300,000 acres. Cuinet (1893), 3:111, 3:692, 3:743.

24. De Kay (1833), 66; Borlase (1878), 228.

25. Borlase (1878), 228.

26. The British consulate twice had been destroyed by fire by 1851, with many of its records burned. PRO/FO 78 1105.

27. Fellows (1839), 56–57.

28. Durbin (1849), 2:183; Smith (1851), 55.

29. Murray (1854), 125–26.

30. Hunt's memoir in Walpole (1817), 93; Cuinet (1893), 3:745.

31. Cuinet (1893), 3:606, 3:740, 3:748, 3:762.

32. Other intended improvements consisted of prison reform, better organization of the police, encouragement of native agriculture, and road construction. Frederick Calvert to Charles Allison, chargé d'affaires at the British embassy, Constantinople, 10 January 1858, PRO/FO 195 602.

33. Senior (1859), 183. This may have been an attempt to segregate religious groups as well, for in Smyrna, the Muslims' houses were built of wood, and those of the Christians were built in stone. Murray (1840), 262, and (1845), 281.

34. Koça Çay. Cook (1973), 53.

35. Dearborn (1819), 2:41–42.

36. Turner (1820), 2:215, and Temple (1836), 1:286.

37. Broughton (1813), 804, and Broughton (1817), 2:216.

38. The pasha, who enjoyed hunting, had his kiosk, or lodge, outside town. Across the strait, his harem would resort for the day to the lovely valley near Kilid Bahr. Temple (1836), 1:289, 2:215.

39. The term *raya* was defined according to differing degrees of specificity. Karpat notes that only Christians could be *raya*. Karpat (1985), 114. However, in nineteenth-century accounts of the Dardanelles, Jews also were referred to as *raya*.

40. Turner (1820), 215. Cuinet (1893), 3:745.

41. Register of the British consulate at the Dardanelles, 31 December 1844, PRO/FO 78 570. Robinson notes that in 1872 there were 32 Englishmen, but does not cite a source for the information. Robinson (1994), 157. The U.S. consular agency did not count American women and children until 19 January 1908. NARA RG84 Dard. 1.

42. There were in Kalaisultaniye 2208 Muslims and 4614 *raya*. There were 58 consular personnel—all Jews, according to the 1831 census "Ottoman Population in Rumili and Anatolia in 1831." Karpat (1985), 114. The "Ottoman General Census in 1881/1882–1893" recorded a population for Çanakkale of 4093 Muslim females and 4225 males; 2532 Greek females and 2407 males; 432 Armenian females and 532 males; 766 Jewish females and 729 males; 19 Protestant females and 27 males; and 125 foreign females and 167 males. Karpat (1985), 130–31.

43. The population was 11,062 in 1890, with 3551 Muslims, 2577 Orthodox Greeks, 956 Armenians, 1805 Jews, and 2173 foreign subjects and protégés, of which 8 were Protestants. Cuinet (1893), 3:746. Armenians dealt in Greek vases in Artaki (Erdek) or Cyzicus. Dr. Hunt in Walpole (1817), 91. By 1910, the population had risen to 11,875. The number of Greeks (largely agriculturists) was declining as they moved to Egypt or the United States to avoid conscription. More than 500 Jews remained in 1909. C. Xanthopoulos to the U.S. consul general, 26 October 1910, NARA RG84 Dard. 6.

44. Cuinet (1893) , 3:607, 3:727, 3:729.

45. Murray (1840), 213; Broughton (1817), 2:216; Dearborn (1819), 2:41. Frangakis-Syrett has shown how from 1780 to 1820 the *raya* communities in the eastern Mediterranean took over a large part of the trade that hitherto had been almost monopolized by the Europeans through outfits like the Levant Company, which existed from 1581 to 1825. Frangakis-Syrett (1987), 74.

46. Clarke (1817), 3:85; Cuinet (1893), 3:731.

47. Hunt's memoir in Walpole (1817), 93, mentions a female statue from Çıplak that he procured in this way for Lord Elgin and that was in his collection. He later notes the Sigean inscription (hitherto used by a local priest for exorcisms) and a fragment of exquisite sculpture that were removed in 1799 for Lord Elgin (1817), 97.

48. Turner (1820), 2:214. For a history of the Levant Company, see Wood (1964).

49. Ibid., 2:219.

50. Ibid., 2:42, 214–15. According to Lord Broughton, they had represented the British for a century. Broughton (1817), 2:216. Rumors of the family's sudden enrichment by skimming off profits from illegal grain trades may have led to their being replaced by British subjects such as Lander.

51. Slade (1837), 2:214.

52. Carlisle notes it in October 1853. Carlisle (1855), 130. Frederick Calvert to Stratford de Redcliffe, 4 June 1853, PRO/FO 195 391.

53. Paid for by Frederick Calvert on behalf of Lander's heirs. Arthur Raby, memo to the Foreign Office, 10 September 1863. George Henry Clifton to Lord Lyons, 9 December

1865, PRO/FO 195 775, referred to by Robinson (1994), 167. The land was owned by a *raya*, Vacuzzo Russo, who disclaimed any interest in it.

54. Frederick Calvert alluded to the pasha's objections as frivolous and untenable. Frederick Calvert to Stratford de Redcliffe, 4 June 1853, PRO/FO 195 391. But apparently part of this was government land, "Vacoof property of Sultan Mahmoud the Conqueror, Evkaf Register." The *Evkaf* was the government's administrative department responsible for the land owned by pious foundations. Randall Callander to the Foreign Office, 9 April 1864, PRO/FO 195 775. Since the garden and warehouses were built on land belonging to Vacuzzo Russo, this was very creative financing indeed.

55. Varying reports suggested that in 1853, seven warehouses were transferred by way of security to "Messrs. Abbott of Salonica." Unspecified buildings used as washhouses and stables were transferred to Lander's heirs informally as payment of a debt in 1858. Callander to the Foreign Office, 9 April 1864, PRO/FO 195 775.

56. Senior (1859), 156, 182, recorded that Frederick had been British consul for ten years prior to 1857. Frederick's tombstone in Çanakkale noted that he served as consul for seventeen years.

57. Frederick Calvert entertained General Sir John Henry Lefroy at his house at Sestos during the Crimean War. *The Autobiography of General Sir John Henry Lefroy* (privately circulated), 273–76; courtesy of Ken Horton via Ibrahim Aksu.

58. Weston visited Calvert in 1845. Weston (1894), 120–24, in Easton (1991), 119. Because Muslims would not eat shot-slain animals and the *rayas* could not carry arms, the Europeans had an unbounded range. Slade (1837), 2:213. George Lawson, a physician during the Crimean War, recounted a splendid visit to the local pasha in Frederick's company. Bonham-Carter (1968), 48.

59. Carlisle (1855), 127. When Frederick fell from his horse in 1851, because the Dardanelles had no surgeon, he had to travel to London, where he stayed for eighteen months, through 1852, when their father died, until spring 1853, when he returned to work. Frederick Calvert to the Foreign Office, various letters, PRO/FO 195 391 and 492 and PRO/FO 78 867 and 903. Frangakis-Syrett discusses chronic monetary shortages that encouraged money lending in the Ottoman Empire. Frangakis-Syrett (1991a), 409. For Lander's loans, see Senior (1859), 156. Carlisle, (1854), 97, noted that after a bad experience lending money to Turks, Calvert lent money only to local Greeks, at 20 percent interest. See also Senior (1859), 157. Although there is no direct evidence for the Calvert family being active in collecting tithes and tax farming, one may perhaps infer that Frederick soon entered this sphere, in which his father-in-law had great experience. For Abbott and the lucrative practice of tithe collecting and tax farming by British consuls in western Anatolia, see Frangakis-Syrett (1992). This system was still intact in 1910. NARA RG84 Dard. 6.

60. George Henry Clifton to Lord Lyons, 9 December 1865, PRO/FO 195 775.

61. Frederick Calvert's correspondence with foreign secretary Lord John Russell (1792–1878), later Earl Russell, PRO/FO 78 1525, and Carlisle (1855), 127.

62. E. Whitaker, British vice-consul of Gallipoli, wrote of a "few educated foreigners who have bought estates in Turkey and are cultivating them under their own supervision . . . not only does their more sc. knowledge of their calling enable them to set examples . . . but they may also, if not thwarted by the officials, exercise a wholesome moral influence on the country and they prove most efficient pioneers to those measures of reform." E. Whitaker to William H. Wrench, 16 July 1870, PRO/FO 195 938.

63. *Dictionary of National Biography*, s.v. "Howard, George William Frederick," seventh earl of Carlisle.

64. *Dictionary of National Biography*, s.v. "Canning, Stratford, first Viscount Stratford de Redcliffe"; Lane-Poole (1890).

65. Carlisle (1855), 125.

66. Carlisle (1854), 97.

67. Ibid., 98.

68. Baumeister (1854), 511.

69. "A large house to the northeast, a small but unfinished palace by the sea, with a little park lying on the other side of the street." (Stark 1874a), 173. My translation from German.

70. Grimm (1964), 357 n. 2267. For Belgian and Dutch positions, see Frederick Calvert to Stratford de Redcliffe, 4 June 1853, PRO/FO 195 391. See also James Calvert to Nicholas Vitalis, 24 November 1862 and 28 May 1863, NARA RG84 Dard. 1. It was common for consuls to reside at their place of employment. Foster (1906), 1:216–17. The rank of the U.S. official at the Dardanelles seems at first to have been that of vice-consul, but in accordance with Charles Calvert's wishes, the title was changed to "consular agent" in 1843. George A. Porter to Abel P. Upshur, secretary of state, 16 December 1843, NARA RG84 Dard. 1.

71. Stark (1874a), 173. Schliemann referred to "the enjoyment of hearing the divine voice of your ladies" in a letter to James Calvert on 4 October 1871, BB 2.4/4.

72. It is currently maintained by the British Commonwealth War Graves Commission.

73. Corroborated by Stark (1874a), 173.

74. Francis H. Bacon to "K.B.," his sister Kate, from Assos, 28 July 1883, partly published by Congdon (1974), 83–95. Kind thanks to Cornelius and Emily Vermeule for alerting me to this wonderful manuscript, "An Archaeological Expedition to Asia Minor: Letters and Journals of Francis H. Bacon 1881–1882–1883," 56. Allen, Congdon, and Landry, eds. (forthcoming).

75. The village is also known as Frankrein, Erinkein, Eren Keuy, Renkioi, Aring Kuy, Arenkioi, Ghiaourkeui, "village of infidels" (Walpole 1817), 95, Eet Guelmess, and, most recently, In Tepe. See also Giannokopoulos (1995); Fellows (1839), 57; Carlisle (1854), 95; Senior (1859), 168; and Cook (1973), 390.

76. Turner (1820), 2:220.

77. Ibid.

78. Cook (1973), 630.

79. Temple (1836), 1:289; Napier (1840), 297.

80. Senior (1859), 168. The locations of the villa and vineyards were shown on a plan (by John Brunton) that accompanied Calvert's article on the nearby site of Ophryneion. Calvert (1860b). The original Brunton chart for the entire area is shown in Toppin (1981), 20. The house apparently had marble stairs and a kiosk in the center of the garden. Giannokopoulos (1995), 24–25.

81. Temple (1836), 1:289.

82. Slade (1837), 2:207, 2:232.

83. The Calverts held the property as trustee for Lander's heirs. Charles Calvert to Lord Palmerston, 22 April 1850, PRO/FO 78 837, and Arthur Raby to the Foreign Office, 10 September 1863, PRO/FO 195 775.

84. Murray noted that the British consul resided here: Murray (1840), 267; (1845), 286; and (1854), 170.

85. Carlisle (1854), 76–77.

86. Slade (1837), 2:207.

87. It was designed by Isambard Brunel for the War Office and shipped out from England. Toppin (1981), 2–18. The British railway engineer John Brunton supervised its assembly. Clapham (1939), 47, 64, and Parkes (1857). By November 1855, it was the central medical depot south of the Bosphorus and "greatly superior to the others." Vulliamy (1939), 218, and Toppin (1981), 16. The first railway in Asia Minor serviced the hospital. For Frederick's role, see Frederick Calvert to Stratford de Redcliffe, 18 August 1855, PRO/FO 195 492. Frederick later acquired it. Frederick Calvert to the earl of Clarendon, 24 November 1856, PRO/FO 195 492. By 1884, the hospital site was home to a British steam mill for the grinding of oak-apple bolls and pine bark for use in British tanneries. Frank Calvert's report 172 to the consul general, 29 November 1884, NARA RG84 Dard. 6.

88. One of Lander's daughters married a British officer, Major William Chads, who had control of British military positions at the strait. Frederick also gave asylum there to a Wallachian refugee (from present-day Romania) who was working as an artist. Carlisle (1854), 76, 95–97.

89. Randall Callander to the Foreign Office, 9 April 1864, PRO/FO 195 391.

90. Frank Calvert to Schliemann, 23 February 1870 and 13 September 1871, B 65/77 and B 66/216.

91. Maclaren (1863), 222, in reference to himself.

92. Cuinet (1893), 3:707. The highest peak rises 5797 feet. On this mountain, also known locally as "Olympus," Hera bedded Zeus during a critical stage of the Trojan War (*Iliad* 14.292–353).

93. Napier (1840), 298. Bears also used to frequent Mount Ida.

94. Newton (1865), 126.

95. Clarke (1817), 3:110.

96. One observer pronounced that the Scamander and Simois had "too little water for a goose to swim in." Belon (1553), quoted in Maclaren (1863), 6. According to Aeschines, the Athenian orator who visited the Troad in the fourth century B.C., virgins bathed in the Scamander prior to marriage, offering their virginity first to the river god. Napier (1840), 300. In the first or second century A.D., sculptors depicted the reclining god. Sevinç (1992), 60. The sculpture is now in Istanbul.

97. Napier (1840), 293; Temple (1836), 1:273.

98. Senior (1859), 164–65.

99. Carlisle (1854), 97. It is not known whether or not Frederick did purchase the estate.

100. Carlisle (1854), 77, 97. Frederick Calvert referred to his "Kilid Bahar farm near the European Coast" in Frederick Calvert to Stratford de Redcliffe, 7 May 1857, PRO/FO 195 492. The exact location of Frederick's property is unknown. It may have been "Lebera" *çiftlik*, the deserted estate northwest of the fortress and Madytos (Eceabat) that Picard and Reinach visited in 1910, or located in a valley known as Ziblik just west of the fortress, or the estate once owned by a Mr. Willis and visited by Lords Byron and Broughton in 1810. Broughton (1817), 2:214.

101. On 18 July 1853, Carlisle noted a size "in excess of 3000 acres." Carlisle (1854), 77–78. Senior estimated "2000 to 3000 acres." Senior (1859), 162. Frederick W. Calvert as trustee for his heirs purchased this land with Lander's money. It contained 2448 square kilometers of land in forty-three fields. Arthur Raby to the Foreign Office, 10 September 1863, and *mazbatta*, or minutes of official reports, of the Council of Biğa, 19 January 1864, PRO/FO 195 775. The 2000 to 3000 acres are said to have cost £400. Senior (1859), 168–69.

102. Maclaren (1863), 39; Strabo, 13.1.35.

103. İnalçik (1985), 123. Urban investors paid agricultural workers or sharecroppers seasonal wages for labor at harvest time, especially for export crops. Besides the landlord's mansion and a large courtyard, a typical *çiftlik* included shacks for workers, storage buildings, stables, mills, slaughterhouses, presses, and oxen for plowing. Large herds of sheep, cattle, and horses were bred. It was a plantationlike farm in its purpose and organization and varied in size from approximately 74 to 1,235 acres.

104. Calvert (1881), 719. Gell (1804), plate 33, illustrated the village in 1801.

105. Forschammer (1842), 36–39; Calvert (1859), 1; Newton (1865), 134, 355 n. 62.

106. Carlisle (1854), 77–78, 92, 97; Senior (1859), 165, 156, 160. This is supported by *mazbatta* of the Council of Biğa, 19 January 1864, PRO/FO 195 775.

107. Newton (1865), 125.

108. In 1852 and 1880, workers at Batak, later Thymbra, collected tons of locusts and apparently did not make a dent in the problem. Frank Calvert to Schliemann, 15 May 1880, B 83/398.

109. Francis H. Bacon to "K.B.," his sister Kate, 28 July 1883, Congdon (1974), 83–95. For the complete edition, see Allen, Congdon, and Landry, eds. (forthcoming).

110. Schuchhardt (1891), 87. By this time, Frank Calvert had identified the necropolis as that of ancient Thymbra, hence Batak became Thymbra Farm.

111. Easton (1991), 119.

112. Murray (1840), xviii, and Frangakis-Syrett (1991a), 395.

113. The senior Calvert's 1838 and 1839 correspondence is preserved in BLMS no. 36470, 63, 188–207, and no. 36468, 432–34. He corresponded with Lord Broughton (John Hobhouse), among others, in January 1839. James Calvert to Hobhouse, 4 April 1839, BLMS no. 36470, 188.

114. Edmund Calvert painted an undated watercolor of this view from the balcony of the house. Uluer collection, Çanakkale. Information comes in part from the Calvert cemetery at the Dardanelles and in part (for James Calvert's death date in 1852) from an unpublished genealogy prepared by Donald F. Easton.

115. Newton (1865), 125. For Maitland, see *Dictionary of National Biography*, s.v. "Maitland, Sir Thomas." While commander in chief, he lived in a palace on Corfu and was affectionately known as "King Tom." Walsh (1836), 1:74, and Carlisle (1855), 201. Apparently the Calverts once visited there in 1850. Landscape in the Uluer collection, Çanakkale.

116. A possible portrait of James Calvert, Sr., who died in 1852, may have been discovered at Çanakkale in 1997. The undated chiaroscuro portrait by Edmund Calvert bears a strong family resemblance but cannot be Charles, James, or Frank Calvert. The patriarchal figure wears a long cloak. Uluer collection, Çanakkale.

117. Frederick J. Calvert kindly gave me considerable information on all the paintings, derived from labels placed on their backs after the death of Frederick R. J. Calvert in 1927. All paintings originally were at Erenköy. Their fate after 1927 is unknown.

118. Lander to John Bidwell, superintendent of the Consular Office, London, 30 October 1844, PRO/FO 78 570.

119. Prince de Talleyrand, in a eulogy to Count Reinhard, who had been consul, director of foreign affairs, and ambassador. De Lesseps (1888), 283.

120. Spencer (1851), 2:296–300.

121. Spencer noted that their power was often abused, among others, "by some who represent Great Britain; such things would not be borne by any Government but that of poor enfeebled Turkey." Spencer (1851), 2:296–300.

122. By far, most professionals on Malta were likewise employed in government offices. Senior (1882), 235.

123. Davy (1842),1:45, 2:114–15. According to Senior (1882), 235, one-sixth of the children in the population were educated. Senior also gives an alternate, though biased, opinion on the quality of local education in 1856. Senior (1882), 271–74; Murray (1840), xxiv. The exchange contained commercial reading rooms, which were well supplied with English and other journals, and the Union Club offered reading rooms and news rooms. Murray (1840), xxii–xxiii.

124. Slade (1837), 1:123.

125. Edmund Calvert documented current Maltese fashions in watercolor sketches. Uluer collection, Çanakkale.

126. Slade (1837), 1:124, 1:129.

127. Davy reported that among infants one to two years of age, 238 boys and 201 girls died in 1830. In one and a half years, smallpox claimed more than 1,500 lives. Davy (1842), 1:266–67, 1:383, 1:323–67.

128. Sattin (1988), 9.

129. Numerous errors have crept into the scanty literature on the family. Henry Calvert is frequently omitted. Cook (1973), 35, and Traill (1993), 167 n. 3. Easton (1991), 119, mistakes the order of the brothers. Georg Grimm thought that the family was American and that Lavinia was Frank's wife. See Grimm (1964), 356–57 n. 2264; Lascarides (1977), 63. Gamer (1992), 38–39, contains similar errors.

130. *Illustrated London News,* 19 August 1882, 197 98. He had learned to sketch before leaving Malta, documenting several Maltese views in pen and ink. He commemorated Ezerum and other Armenian landscapes at Tortoom, Saghir, and Hasan Kaleh around 1838. Uluer Collection, Çanakkale.

131. PRO/FO 78 4122. He painted and sketched the British consulate at Trebizond, Trebizond itself, Zillah, and Samsoon. Uluer collection, Çanakkale.

132. Senior (1859), 33–44, 122–23, records his presence at the British embassy in Constantinople in 1857. It was during his second tour of duty in Constantinople that he helped push for the *firman* for Heinrich Schliemann. Meyer (1953), 328 n. 240.

133. Edmund served in Adalia, Kaisaria, Erzerum, Monastir, and Adrianople (Edirne). Obituary, *Levant Herald and Eastern Express,* 14 August 1908; *Constantinople Messenger,* 9 August 1878; Sayce (1923), 180. Some of these vice-consulates in the interior of Turkey were established after the 1838 Anglo-Turkish Convention in order to facilitate British trade with the interior. Frangakis-Syrett (1992), 106–7.

134. Robinson (1994), 153–54.

135. Napier (1840), 289, 297.

136. Frederick J. Calvert of London has informed me that the connection between the present descendants of Frederick Calvert and the Lords Baltimore may be closer than previously known. Aside from the reuse of names such as Charles, Frederick, and Henry in the family, when the line became extinct with the death of the last Lord Baltimore in Naples in 1771, certain family heirlooms may have been passed to this lateral branch of the family—in particular, a dinner service with the family motto "Fatti Maschi: Parole Femine," "Deeds

for a man, words for a woman." Foster and Manakee (1961), 12. It may be this dinner service that is shown in an unpublished photograph of the Calvert dining room at the Dardanelles. Searches for the family silver in Çanakkale have just begun.

137. Stewart (1955), 1–2; Frangakis-Syrett (1987), 82, and Wood (1964).

138. Frangakis-Syrett (1991a), 407; Welcker (1865), 224–227.

139. Napier (1840), 297; Temple (1836), 1:282, 1:289–90. Curzon reported staying at the newly completed residence in town when it was completely bare of furniture in 1833. Curzon (1849), 295. In 1838, Lander's wooden house in town was destroyed by fire twice within a year, and in the second fire, he lost a valuable library. Fellows (1839), 57.

140. Napier (1840), 297; Slade (1837), 2:214.

141. Temple (1836), 1:282.

142. They had three daughters: Louisa, named after Lander's sister; Mary Campbell, named for Lander's mother; and Sophy. Slade (1837), 2:205–40. Of these, Mary Lander was an accomplished watercolorist. Landscape of 8 April 1848 documenting a trip to England after her father's death in 1846. Uluer collection, Çanakkale. A label on the back of the elder Mary Campbell Lander's portrait noted her relation to the Duneaves and Campbell branch of the ducal family. *Burke's Peerage* for 1856 further noted that this was a branch of the great house of Argyll through that of Breadalbane (113). In 1997 I discovered a curious family tree written by Frank Calvert. Calvert notes that his mother's and sisters' names were Luisa. He notes the years 1808–1814, 1831, and 1883 without saying why. He omits Henry and Charles, who already had died without issue. For that reason it must have been written before 1886, when his sister died.

143. Slade (1837), 2:165–66, 2:205–6, 2:232.

144. Spencer (1851), 2:296–300.

145. De Lesseps (1888), 279–83.

146. Senior recorded that Frederick had been British consul for ten years prior to 1857. Senior (1859), 156, 182. Frederick's tombstone in Çanakkale noted that he served as consul for seventeen years.

147. Nicolas Vitalis to Charles Calvert as consul of the United States, 14 February 1844, NARA RG84 Dard. 4. Prior to 4 February 1832, when the United States opened its consulate at the Dardanelles, U.S. interests were served by the British Levant Company. Stewart (1954), 2. After a hiatus, the office was reopened in 1843 with a vice-consul. George A. Porter to Secretary of State Abel P. Upshur, 16 December 1843, NARA RG84; U.S. consul general John H. Goodenow to William Hunter, second assistant secretary of state, 10 April 1875. Porter's letter makes it clear that Charles Calvert had requested the title of "consular agent" so as to be on an equal par with his colleagues. NARA RG84 Dard 1.

148. Charles Calvert's appointment as acting consul of Damascus is discussed in his letter to Lord Palmerston, 22 April 1850, PRO/FO 78 837. Carlisle (1855), 188, mentioned him in Beirut. For his later posts, PRO/FO 78 1030 and 1302.

149. Louisa was Frank Calvert's long-standing companion, well loved in her community and universally respected for her charitable work with the poor. Obituary, *Levant Herald and Eastern Express*, 26 May 1886.

150. James served as acting British consul for eighteen months, from 1851 to 1853 and during 1854 and 1855, when the U.S. consular office was closed. PRO/FO 78 903, several letters. He wrote and spoke English, Greek, French, and Italian, and he knew Turkish. James was writing letters as consul by 1849. NARA RG84 Dard. files.

151. James began signing correspondence as the vice-consul to Mr. John P. Brown on 29 August 1849. The status of his position was unclear, as indicated by official letters addressed to him as acting U.S. consul, consul, and vice-consul. NARA RG84 Dard. 1. Part of the confusion arose because the U.S. consulate in Constantinople was closed by the president from 1853 to 1856 and was destroyed by fire in 1870, when all records were lost except the few stored in a safe. Stewart (1954), 1–2. James first departed the Dardanelles in 1872. A portrait of Lavinia Abbott, his wife, is preserved in the Uluer collection, Çanakkale. He died and was buried in Constantinople.

152. He served as acting consul from 31 July 1845 to 16 January 1847, when he was formally appointed. Frederick Calvert to Lord Palmerston, 16 January 1847, PRO/FO 700 28.

153. The organized pillaging of archaeological sites for available building material began as early as the sixteenth century at Alexandria Troas and Sigeum.

154. Napier (1840), 297. Hunt remarked about a pyramidal pile of granite shot for the huge cannon at Çanakkale and was told by Lander's predecessor, Tarragano, that they had come from Alexandria Troas. Walpole (1817), 92. Turner (1820), 1:43, reported that they weighed about 144 pounds each. In 1857, Senior noted that they weighed between 500 and 700 pounds. Senior (1859), 181–82. The stone had been removed from the ancient gymnasium. See also De Kay (1833), 464; Walsh (1836), 2:214; Temple (1836), 2:288; and Fellows (139), 58, to name a few.

155. Slade (1837), 2:214.

156. PRO/FO 78 1208, etc. (also in Italian), and NARA RG84 Dard. 1, 4.

157. PRO/FO 195 492, while James was acting British consul.

158. 13 April 1856, PRO/FO 195 602, and 19 April 1858, PRO/FO 78 1209.

159. According to the U.S. State Department List of Consular Officers for the Dardanelles, he assumed the post on 10 June 1874.

160. They advertised daily in the *Constantinople Messenger* and the *Levant Herald and Eastern Express*. James Whittall was their agent in Smyrna.

161. NARA RG84 Dard. and ABBAW, Virchow, 335.

162. Contrary to Lascarides (1977), 63, and Grimm (1964), 356.

CHAPTER 2

1. Ovid, *Ars Amatoria*, 3.176, in A. Pauly, Georg Wissowa, and Wilhelm Kroll, eds., *Paulys Real-Encyclopädie der Altertumswissenschaft* 8 (Stuttgart, 1912), 159–63; and *Ovid: The Art of Love and Other Poems*, with an English translation by J. M. Mozley (Cambridge, Mass., 1957), 130–31.

2. Ibid., 2.249, 82–83; *Amores* 2.16, 31, in A. Pauly, Georg Wissowa, and Wilhelm Kroll, eds., *Paulys Real-Encyclopädie der Altertumswissenschaft* 8 (Stuttgart, 1912), 904–16; and *Ovid: Heroides and Amores*, with an English translation by Grant Showerman (New York, 1914), 430–31.

3. Actually, Byron failed in his first attempt on 16 April 1810. Broughton (1813), 806–8. Travelers reported that a local youth had swum the Hellespont in order to win the hand of the girl he loved. Temple (1836), 291. Another unsubstantiated rumor claimed that a Jewish servant of the imperial consul had swum the distance in both directions. Turner (1820), 1:44. Following in Byron's footsteps, Rev. Walsh was so inspired that he plunged in and began to swim but noticed to his chagrin that his ship had since departed; there was no wind, so he was able to catch up. Walsh (1836), 2:38. To my delight, I joined Byron's followers in swimming the Hellespont in 1997. Allen (1998b), 37.

4. For recent scholarship on Homer and the periods related to the *Iliad* and *Odyssey*, see Latacz (1996), Carter and Morris (1995), Nagy (1996), Raaflaub (1998), and Thomas (1998), 26–33.

5. *Webster's Biographical Dictionary*, s.v. "Chikhatchev, Pëtr Aleksandrovich."

6. *Dictionary of National Biography*, s.v. "Maclaren, Charles"; Cox and Nichol (1894).

7. Maclaren (1863), 222–23.

8. Because the ancient dates spanned a period of over four hundred years, at least one scholar recently has concluded that the Greeks "knew nothing about the dates of the Trojan War." Beyond the eleventh to tenth centuries B.C. "there was a blank." Burkert also suggests that "the precision of the calculations should not disguise the fact that they were nothing but guesses . . . that one or the other figure should agree" with the destruction of the Homeric Troy "is . . . inescapable coincidence." Burkert (1995), 146. Raaflaub (1998) has posed the question whether for political purposes the heroic story was constructed in the ninth to eighth centuries B.C. to validate the emergent Panhellenic world reborn at the end of the Trojan Dark Age—a deliberate archaism, rather than a genuine survival.

9. Duris of Samos suggested 1334, a millennium before Alexander, as the date. Felix Jacoby, ed., *Fragmente der griechischen Historiker* (Berlin, 1923), 76 F41. The Marmor Parium gave 1218 to 1208. *Fragmente der griechischen Historiker* 239 ep. 23.24. And Ephoros gave 1149. *Fragmente der griechischen Historiker* 70 F223, 234.

10. Herodotus, 2.145, in *Herodotus*, vols. 1–2, with an English translation by A. D. Godley (Cambridge, Mass., 1982), 452–53. To arrive at his date, long before the development of historical consciousness and in a society of oral histories, Herodotus used the chronological framework given by Near Eastern king lists. His dating recently has been examined by Burkert (1995), 141–48.

11. Calvert (1873a). For Eratosthenes, it occurred 407 years before the first Olympiad; see *Fragmente der griechischen Historiker* 241 F1, 244 F61.

12. Strabo, 13.1.25, maintained that it had been established around the time of Croesus.

13. Strabo, 13.1.22. For recent translations of the ancient authors whose works touch on Ilion, see Rose (1992), 60.

14. Herodotus, 7.43.

15. Herodotus, 1.4–5.

16. Senior (1859), 155. This had been excavated by the Turks during the Crimean War as they fortified Abydos.

17. Walsh (1836), 1:216, 2:37. The ships were in fact recent casualties of the dangerous strait.

18. Plutarch, *Alexander*, 8.2, 26.1, in *Plutarch's Lives*, vol. 7., with an English translation by Bernadette Perrin (Cambridge, Mass, 1971), 242–43, 298–99. *Moralia* 327f–28a, 331d, in *Plutarch's Moralia*, vol. 4, with an English translation by Frank C. Babbitt (Cambridge, Mass., 1957), 390–91, 410–11.

19. "Furthermore, the gravestone of Achilles he anointed with oil, ran a race by it with his companions, naked, as is the custom, and then crowned it with garlands, pronouncing the hero happy in having, while he lived, a faithful friend, and after death, a great herald of his fame." Plutarch, *Alexander*, 15.2; Arrian, *Anabasis*, 1.11–12.2, in Arrian, *Anabasis Alexandri*, with an English translation by P. A. Brunt (Cambridge, Mass., 1976), 49–51. Rook's translation, quoted by Maclaren (1863), 185; Strabo, 13.1.8. Cook (1973), 167, suggested that these tumuli were raised in Persian times for their pro-Persian supporters. The temple itself was "small and cheap," according to Strabo, 13.1.26.

20. Curtius, 4.6.29, cited in Cohen (1995), 485 n. 20.

21. Rose (1992), 44; Vermeule (1995), 468.

22. Strabo, 13.1.26. Maclaren noted that the identifications of Lysimachus's wall had been challenged by Grote (1846), 441, who considered Alexandria Troas as its recipient. Maclaren supported this with his own observations (1863), 31. Rose (1992), 44 n. 10, notes the continuing scholarly dissension on the date of the wall. The iconography of the Temple of Athena Ilias apparently imitated that of the Parthenon in Athens. Holden (1964), 28.

23. Alexandria Troas was in turn deserted in Byzantine times after its harbor silted up.

24. Strabo, 13.1.27. He compared his success on the eleventh day to Agamemnon's in the tenth year.

25. Lucan, *De Bellum Civile*, 9.954–99, in *Lucan: Civil War,* with an English translation by J. D. Duff (Oxford, 1977), 576–79.

26. Suetonius, *De vita Caesarum*, 79, in *Suetonius: Works,* vol. 1, with an English translation by J. C. Rolfe (Cambridge, Mass., 1940), 104–5. The coin had Aphrodite/Venus on the obverse and the Flight of Aeneas on the reverse, with the Trojan prince carrying his father, Anchises, and the Palladium. Vermeule (1995), 471 n. 51.

27. Rose (1992), 44. Germanicus inspected the remains at Ilium Novum in A.D. 18. Tacitus, *Annalia,* 2.54, in *Tacitus: The Annals,* with an English translation by J. Jackson (Cambridge, Mass., 1962), 468–69.

28. Vermeule (1995), 471–73. A portrait of Augustus was discovered at the site in 1997. Hoffman (1998), 26–31. In 1993, a magnificent full portrait of Hadrian was found in the Odeion. Rose (1998), fig. 6. In A.D. 147, nine hundred years after the founding of Rome, the theater at Ilium was refurbished, with embellishments celebrating the blood ties between the two cities.

29. Vermeule (1995), 476.

30. Herodian, 4.8.3–5, in *Herodian,* vol. 1, with an English translation by C. R. Whitaker (Cambridge, Mass., 1969), 416–17. Dio Cassius, 78.16.7, in *Dio's Roman History,* vol. 9, with an English translation by E. Cary (Cambridge, Mass., 1969), 322–23. Maclaren (1863), 189.

31. Strabo, 13.1.26; Maclaren (1863), 189; Rose (1992), 44.

32. Zosimus, 2.30.1, in *Zosime: Histoire nouvelle I. Livres I et II,* edited and translated by F. Paschoud (Paris, 1971), 102–3.

33. Visitors to the Byzantine capital would say that they were going to "The City," or polis (εἰς τὴν πόλιν), hence the name "Istanbul."

34. Geraldus Cambrensis, *History of the British People,* written for Henry II. Gerald of Wales, *The Journey through Wales and the Description of Wales* (London, 1978), 1, 7. Geoffrey of Monmouth, *History of the Kings of Britain,* vol. 2.1. I owe this reference to Vronwy Hankey.

35. Geoffrey of Monmouth, *History of the Kings of Britain,* vol. 2.1.

36. I owe this insight to Vronwy Hankey.

37. Vaughan (1954), 66. Pero Tafur noted a folk etymology whereby Turci, Turcae came from Teucri. Letts (1926), 137.

38. Critoboulos of Imbros, *Historiae,* 4.11.5. *Critobuli imbriotae historiae,* ed. Dieter R. Reinsch (Berlin, 1983). Raby (1980), 242–46, and (1982), 3–8.

39. Strabo, 13.1.35.

40. *Iliad* 5.815–77, in *Homer: The Iliad,* with an English translation by A. T. Murray (Cambridge, Mass., 1954).

41. Grote (1849), 449 n. 451.

42. Strabo, 13.1.27, 35. Maclaren (1863), 193, disposed of Demetrius's theory.

43. There is a reference to a "road to Troy" in *Early Travels in Palestine* (Bohn's Antiquarian Library, 1848). It mentions that in 1432–33 Bertrandon de la Brocquière, a liege man of the Duke of Burgundy, traveled home overland from Palestine. He described his trip "in a [spice] caravan of 400 to 500 persons, with 600 or 700 camels and mules." After quitting "the caravansera [at Kutahya], I took the road to Bursa, leaving that leading to Troy on my left, between the south and west points." I owe this reference to Vronwy Hankey.

44. Alexandria Troas was still being shown as Troy in 1820. Easton (1991), 111.

45. This site had been diminished by those removing stone for construction in Constantinople as early as the beginning of the sixteenth century. Apparently the mosques of Suleiman the Magnificent and the Sultan Ahmet, or "Blue" Mosque, were built with stone and columns from Alexandria Troas. Robert Wood wrote of his visit in 1750, "they are daily employed in carrying away everything that is valuable to Constantinople to build the new mosque." In 1812, Turner recorded the disappearance of masses of ruins of the aqueduct. Turner (1820), 1:224. Because of the expense of iron, cannonballs continually were being cut from columns and sarcophagi on the spot. Cook (1973), 200–201. Columns of red jasper and red and white marble also were taken for the Yeni Cami in Constantinople. Cuinet (1993), 3:769.

46. As did the great naturalist Pierre Belon du Mans (ca. 1517–1564) in 1548, who opted for Alexandria Troas as Troy. *Les observations de plusieurs singularitez et choses memorables,* vol. 2. (Paris, 1553), 82–84.

47. I thank David Thomas for information concerning English-Ottoman relations at this time. Elizabeth I ruled from 1558 to 1603, and Mehmet III ruled from 1595 to 1603.

48. Bent (1893), 46–49, and Vaughan (1954), 72. Another traveler extended the circumference of Troy some three hundred miles, with gates as far away as Cyzicus and Cape Adramyttion (Edremit). Easton (1991), 113.

49. Lascarides (1977), 9, noted that it was plundered for the construction of the fort at Kum Kale in the late 1650s.

50. Hill (1709), 205–6.

51. *Letters of the Right Honourable Lady Mary Wortley Montagu Written during Her Travels in Europe, Asia, and Africa* (London, 1763). Letter 31.7.1718. *Webster's Biographical Dictionary,* s.v. "Montagu, Lady Mary Wortley."

52. Murat III ruled from 1574 to 1595. *Webster's Biographical Dictionary,* s.v "Murad III."

53. Wood (1964).

54. George Sandys, *Relation of a Journey Begun An Dom 1610* (London, 1627, 3rd ed.), and Cook (1973), 159.

55. Lascarides (1977), 25. The Society of the Dilettanti was founded in 1733 in London as a men's eating establishment for those who had undertaken the Grand Tour but soon metamorphosed into a club that promoted the arts and neoclassicism. Lionel Cust, *History of the Society of the Dilettanti* (London, 1914); De Grummond (1996), 1037–38.

56. Cook reconstructed this from Wood's published works and unpublished diaries (1973), 20–1, and Cobet (1990), 150. For Wood, see de Grummond (1996), 1202–4, with portrait.

57. *Dictionaire de biographie française,* s.v. "Choiseul [Beaupré] (Marie-Gabriel-Florent-Auguste de) Gouffier"; Easton (1991), 113; de Grummond (1996), 279–80, with portrait;

Abbé Martin, *Voyage à Constantinople, fait à l'occasion de l'ámbassade de M. le compte de Choiseul Gouffier* (Paris, 1821).

58. *Webster's Biographical Dictionary*, s.v. "Le Chevalier, Jean-Baptiste."

59. Easton has pointed out that although Chevalier's map did not show the mound at Hisarlık, it did place the best route to Pınarbaşı from Kum Kale through the village of Çıplak, the closest habitation to Hisarlık itself. Thus, travelers were encouraged to pass by the eminence and eventually noticed it. Easton (1991), 114.

60. Chevalier (1791). The reaction was such that in 1792, a German translation was published, and in 1794, the original French text was republished with notes by Andrew Dalzel, followed in 1798 by an expanded treatment in French by Dalzel. Cook (1973), 22. Calvert used *Voyage de [sic] le Troade* (1802, 3rd ed.).

61. During this time, Choiseul-Gouffier's own manuscript was published in German by Carl Lenz in 1798.

62. It was published in two installments in 1809 and posthumously with notes by J. D. Barbié du Bocage in 1822.

63. Easton (1991), 114. An *asmak* is a seasonal torrent, full of water in the winter and dry in the summer.

64. Easton (1991), 114–15. According to Easton, Clarke's imminent publication of his identification of Hisarlık with Ilium Novum apparently caused Choiseul-Gouffier to send Dubois back to the Troad to document the remains at the site more completely in 1814. Choiseul-Gouffier (1822), 422 n. 4.

65. Choiseul-Gouffier (1822), plate 36.

66. Choiseul-Gouffier noted the mound's original height as 29 French feet (between 31 and 32 English feet) above the original ground level, but only 20 feet above that of his own day. Cook (1973), 162. Choiseul-Gouffier (1822), 319, 322, 325.

67. Choiseul-Gouffier (1822), 322.

68. Shown intact in Choiseul-Gouffier (1822), plate 30. Choiseul-Gouffier suggested that it might be the tomb of Festus. Ibid., and Cook (1973), 162.

69. Hunt in Walpole (1817), 100.

70. Ibid.; Broughton (1817), 160–62. One of these was the traveler and antiquary Edward Daniel Clarke, who later defamed Gormezano by suggesting that his "Jewish brethren of the Dardanelles had substituted antiquities in the place of relics which they had been told they might find in the tomb." Clarke (1817), 3:209–10. The location of the objects is not known, although some were reportedly brought to England in 1799 by Henry Philip Hope. Cook (1973), 26. In the same year, Dr. Philip Hunt (1772–1838) visited the Troad twice with his patron, Lord Elgin (1766–1841). In 1801, he returned to remove the "granite block" for Lord Elgin's collection, along with an important early boustrophedon inscription and bas-relief from Sigeum. British Museum inscriptions 1002 and 789; Lascarides (1977), 30. Hunt in Walpole (1817), 100, recounted that the "granite block" was in fact a marble inscription of an epitaph: "Herakleia, wife or daughter of Lucius, farewell." Lord Elgin would achieve notoriety for removing the pedimental sculptures, metopes, and frieze blocks from the Parthenon in Athens between 1803 and 1812. They were acquired by an act of Parliament for £35,000 in 1816.

71. Gell was educated at Cambridge and wrote on the antiquities of Ithaca and his travels in Greece. *Webster's Biographical Dictionary* s.v. "Gell, William."

72. *Edinburgh Review* (1805), 271.

73. *Webster's Biographical Dictionary*, s.v. "Byron, George Gordon, 6th Baron Byron."

74. *Webster's Biographical Dictionary,* s.v. "Hobhouse, John Cam, Baron Broughton de Gyfford."

75. Cook (1973), 29.

76. Marchand (1996), 119.

77. Diary entry, 1 November 1821, in *George Gordon Noel Byron, Born for Opposition: Letters and Journals,* vol. 8, ed. Leslie A. Marchand (London, 1978), 21.

78. Clarke, Gell, and Lords Byron and Broughton all attended Cambridge and communicated their ideas about the Troad. Clarke preceded Gell in the Troad by nine months but did not publish his ideas until 1812 and 1817.

79. Clarke (1817), 3:151–52.

80. Ibid., 130.

81. Ibid., 131–32, and Easton (1991), 117.

82. Clarke (1817), 130–33. James Rennell noted that Chevalier had placed Ilium Novum one and a half miles southeast of Çıplak, where pottery, columns, and a cemetery appear on his 1814 map. Rennell (1814), 4, 111, 115.

83. John B. S. Morritt agreed with Clarke's identification of Hisarlık with Ilium Novum but refused to accept that the situation could also agree with Homer's Troy. Morritt to Clarke, August 1812, in Walpole (1817), 579.

84. *Webster's Biographical Dictionary,* s.v. "Bruce, Thomas, 7th earl of Elgin."

85. Walpole (1817), 108. Calvert used a second edition of Walpole.

86. Walpole (1817), 109. It is not clear whether he ever visited Palaio Kalafatlı. He did note a very ancient Turkish burial ground filled with the scattered ruins of a temple and numerous inscribed marbles one mile southeast of Çıplak (Walpole [1817], 105), but this was just the Çıplak cemetery.

87. Bröndsted (1844), 280, 288, 332, 337. Translated in Mejer (1990), 302.

88. De Grummond (1996), 198–99.

89. Bröndsted (1844). Translated in Mejer (1990), 302.

90. Rennell (1814), 53. Yet Rennell misidentified the Simois.

91. Rennell (1814), 141.

92. Ibid., 125.

93. Maclaren (1863), 222, in reference to himself.

94. Turner (1820), 3:221. *Dictionary of National Biography,* s.v. "Turner, William."

95. Turner (1820), 1:37.

96. Ibid., 1:226.

CHAPTER 3

1. He wrote letters for his brothers in French and Italian, in addition to English.

2. Calvert (1860a), 199.

3. De Grummond (1996), 1037–38. A plan of the Pompeii excavation site already had been published in 1828. Ibid., 415.

4. A museum was established at Kerch (Panticapaion) in the Crimea in 1828. Excavations had begun in 1816, with the opening of the Royal Kurgan and Kul Oba following quickly thereafter. Finds were sent to the Hermitage. Peter the Great (1696–1725) passed a decree in 1718 ordering the "collection from earth and water of old inscriptions, ancient weapons, dishes, and everything old and unusual." De Grummond (1996), 183, 589.

5. *Webster's Biographical Dictionary*, s.v. "Botta, Paul Emile."

6. Calder and Kramer (1992), 1665–67; *Dictionary of National Biography*, s.v. "Layard, Sir Austen Henry." Canning was keenly interested in archaeology and obtained a *firman* for Layard and gave him an annual salary of £200 with additional funds for excavation. For Canning's support, see Lane-Poole (1890), 225–29, and Layard's own tribute to his patron in Layard (1849).

7. Lloyd (1980), 108. Layard to Henry Ellis, 20 August 1849: "I must . . . observe that the funds placed at my disposal for excavations and researches are much smaller than I could possibly have anticipated." BLMS 38942/1. The British Museum's lack of interest in funding his efforts and shipping his finds was symptomatic of its general lack of sympathy with the manifold problems of excavation.

8. Later, remains at the site were identified as the northwest palace of Assurnasirpal II, the southeast palace, or Burned Palace, and Fort Shalmaneser. Lane-Poole (1890), 225–29.

9. Transportation of the huge works of art was tremendously difficult. One contemporary's solution to the problem of transporting one of the colossal stone sculptures of winged bulls was simply to saw it in half. Stiebing (1993), figure 4.

10. 2 Kings 18–19. Layard (1849), 35, describes tunneling through the mound.

11. Trigger (1989), 40–45.

12. Ibid.

13. Lane-Poole (1890), 225–31.

14. Nyerup (1806), quoted by Daniel (1950), 51. It was Nyerup who proposed the creation of a Danish national museum in 1806. See Kristiansen (1981), 21.

15. Trigger (1989), 53.

16. Thomsen (1848), 25–104; de Grummond (1996), 325, 1099–1100.

17. *Webster's Biographical Dictionary*, s.v. "Worsaae, Jens Jacob Assmussen." The mounds first had been documented in 1591, and the first to become interested in them was Ole Worm (1588–1654). See Trigger (1989), 49.

18. Worsaae, quoted by Daniel (1950), 48. Schliemann met Worsaae in Paris at the exposition of 1867. He wrote Worsaae on 18 December 1879. Meyer (1958), #58, 84.

19. Worsaae (1849), 156, reviewed in *Archaeological Journal* 7 (1850): 101–5.

20. Daniel (1950), 54; Levine (1986), 19.

21. Lyell's *Principles of Geology* appeared in 1830–1833. Lyell read classics at Oxford. *Dictionary of National Biography*, s.v. "Lyell, Sir Charles."

22. Lubbock later became a banker and vice-chancellor of the University of London. For his popular works on archaeology and entomology he was created Baron Avebury in 1900. *Dictionary of National Biography*, s.v. "Lubbock, Sir John William."

23. Frank Calvert would be the first to make similar finds in Turkey. Calvert (1873b), 93, and (1873c), 127–29. British Museum records show the acquisition from the Calverts of a fossil skull of *elephas Nanadas* on 12 October 1860, perhaps among the remains from Ophryneion mentioned by Calvert (1860b), 292.

24. This was not immediately accepted. Rudolf Virchow, Schliemann's later collaborator, declared the Neander remains those of a pathological idiot. Daniel (1950), 59.

25. These had been preceded by finds of flints and animal bones under stalagmite at Kent's Cavern in Cornwall, but then the flints were not accepted as being of human workmanship. In the 1830s, human skulls were found with rhinoceros and mammoth skulls under a stalagmite crust at a cave near Liège. Daniel (1950), 58–59.

26. Stocking (1987), 150–51.

27. Charles Roach Smith, quoting an after-dinner speech by Sir John Simeon, ca. 1859. Levine (1986), 12. In the first annual report of the British Archaeological Association, Alfred Dunkin wrote that "the true antiquary does not confine himself to one single branch of archaeology; but in a comprehensive view surveys every fact." Ibid., 13.

28. This discussion is dependent on Levine (1986), 1–40.

29. Of Calvert's associates, Layard could not attend public school or university and went to work in London at age sixteen. Sir John Lubbock was educated at Eton and went to work at his father's bank at age sixteen. Hutchinson (1914), 1–20. John Turtle Wood (1821–1890), the excavator of the Temple of Artemis at Ephesus, had no academic training. Nor did Sir John Evans (1823–1908), an eminent British prehistorian. *Webster's Biographical Dictionary*, s.v. "Evans, Sir John." Naiditch (1989), 143. The same is true of George Dennis (1814–1898), author of *Cities and Cemeteries of Etruria* (1848), who worked as a clerk in the Excise Office for nineteen years before joining the Colonial Service in 1849 and embarking on a consular career in 1864. Rhodes (1985), xviii. Charles Maclaren also was self-educated.

30. Naiditch (1989), 125. The year before, John Disney gave a major collection of Greek and Roman marbles gathered in Italy to the Fitzwilliam Museum at Cambridge. De Grummond (1996), 442. Clarke's collection of antiquities also went to the Fitzwilliam.

31. Marchand (1996), 41.

32. Unte (1990), 310–20; For Müller's portrait, see Lullies and Schiering (1988), 23.

33. De Grummond (1996), 773–74; Unte (1990), 310–20. Until they were translated, these works did not have a wide readership in England because most English at that period did not read German. There is no evidence that Calvert owned or read these books, but Charles Newton would have.

34. Hermann (1981), 129; Marchand (1996), 1–74; Sichtermann (1996), 9–20.

35. Although Lubbock had studied Greek, Latin, and geography at Eton, his relationship with Darwin was far more significant. Darwin encouraged him to read biology and geology while he was not working at his father's bank. Darwin also encouraged his father to buy him a microscope. Hutchinson (1914), 15.

36. Ibid., 28–43.

37. Evans, a numismatist, used his study of coins in the development of typologies for prehistoric artifacts.

38. Stocking (1987), 152.

39. Lubbock's father, a mathematician and astronomer as well as a banker, had served as treasurer of the Royal Society. Ibid., 150.

40. For British classical education in the nineteenth century, see Clarke (1959), 78, 87; Goldstrom (1972); and Birchenough (1914). I thank Paul Naiditch for these references. In England, the target market of parents influenced the curricula in most cases. Schools varied tremendously in their curricula, although methods often were similar. Christopher Stray, personal communication. At Eton and Harrow, for instance, "Latin and Greek were flogged into little boys, and the bigger boys spent about 23 hours a week in classical work. At Eton, Latin verse is introduced to a boy before he is 14 . . . before he is 17 he is quite familiar with Latin authors." Barry (1928), 255.

41. Davy (1842), 2:102–3, 2:114; Murray (1840), xxii.

42. Napier (1840), 289; Boisgelin (1805), 36–37. The library was begun by the Knights of Malta, who were bound to bequeath to it their personal libraries. Although the library

contained over seventy thousand volumes before the British conquest, it was poorly arranged and uncatalogued. It was supported by subscription and lent its modern works. Murray (1840), xxii.

43. None of the Calverts ever learned German. It was not offered as a subject of study at their school. Among the major English sources were George Grote's *History of Greece* (1846; rev. ed. 1849) and William Smith's *Dictionary of Greek and Roman Biography and Mythology* (1844). Calvert used both.

44. When Sir Charles Fellows (1799–1860), leader of an archaeological expedition to Lycia for the British Museum, visited Lander in 1838, he noted that Lander protected a rich resident who had discovered a tomb at Abydos while plowing but dared not make it known. The superstitious discoverer gave Fellows a female statuette and sent two others to the museum in Athens. Lander assumed the responsibility of announcing the find. Fellows (1839), 60. Fellows was knighted after bringing back to England the Nereid Monument of Xanthus, now reerected in the British Museum. *Dictionary of National Biography*, s.v. "Fellows, Charles."

45. Frank Calvert sent Henry a letter of introduction to Newton on 30 May 1866. BMGR. Schliemann to Frank Calvert, 12 August 1871, discussed the inscription. BB 2.3/3.

46. Henry Calvert to Hekekyan Bey, 2 May 1865, BLMS 36468, 302, also noted his sketching of oriental latticework in Jedda. Joseph Hekekyan Bey (1807–1875) was an English-educated Armenian civil engineer who served the Egyptian government and conducted the first recorded excavation in Egypt in 1852 and 1853. His understanding of stratigraphy was the result of a training in geology. Thompson (1992), 249.

47. Henry Calvert to Layard, 4 May 1851, BLMS 38980, 53.

48. "I have been botanizing. So well have I explored the neighbourhood [Erzerum] that rarely do I meet with a plant which does not exist in my herbarium." Henry Calvert to Layard, 4 May 1851, BLMS 38980, 53. Both Tchihatcheff (1860), 3:xxvii–xxviii, and Henry Calvert's obituary in the *Illustrated London News*, 19 August 1882, 197–98, record his botanical collection. He also had a notable conchological collection.

49. Obituary, *Levant Herald and Eastern Express*, 14 August 1908. His drawings are in the Uluer collection, Çanakkale.

50. Charles wrote from Monastir to the secretary of the British Museum concerning a statue of Hercules. Letter of 1 August 1868, BMCA.

51. Although Waddington was a distinguished scholar, he devoted most of his life to diplomacy. Waddington represented France at negotiations leading to the Treaty of Paris, at the end of the Franco-Prussian War. *Webster's Biographical Dictionary*, s.v. "Waddington, William Henry."

52. According to Frank Calvert (1873a), Frederick excavated the two tumuli at Sigeum and Erenköy from 1857 to 1859. Kossatz-Pompé (1992), 171–83, esp. 177, incorrectly assigns the excavation of the Erenköy tumulus to Frank Calvert.

53. Frank Calvert (1860b), 295.

54. Senior (1859), 179, records that by November 1857, "Mr. Calvert" already had excavated it.

55. Calvert (1873a).

56. Considerable confusion exists concerning which brother actually excavated these mounds. Frank Calvert gave the credit to Frederick. Frederick Calvert's reasons for not excavating two of the four tumuli mentioned by Baumeister were that the tumulus of Achilles

already had been probed and that of Ajax had collapsed. Baumeister (1854), 511. Cook attributes the excavation of the Patroclus tumulus to Frank. Cook (1973), 36. Confusion certainly existed. Nicoläides (1867), 85. Schliemann wrote that Calvert had excavated it in 1855 with officers of the British fleet. See Schliemann (1884), 251, and Schliemann to Virchow in Herrmann and Maaß (1990), #283, 301. If true, this must have been Frederick, or else he confused the Calverts with the British engineer John Brunton.

57. "My sister takes great interest in your excavations." Frederick Calvert to Schliemann, 31 March 1873, B 68/104.

58. The first two are mentioned in a letter from Frederick Calvert to Schliemann, 2 April 1873, B 68/107, and Lavinia Calvert made at least two trips, on 19 and 25 October 1871. Schliemann to James Calvert, 20 October 1871; James Calvert to Schliemann, 25 October 1871, BB 2.4/6, B 66/261.

59. He would have been entertained at Erenköy. Frederick did not purchase Batak Farm until 1847, and the Dardanelles house had not yet been built.

60. Cox and Nichol (1894), 1–25.

61. Ibid., 202–5.

62. Ibid., 447–49.

63. Later that summer, the Calverts escorted American friends of John P. Brown, U.S. consul general at Constantinople, to Pınarbaşı, Alexandria Troas, and Çığrı Dağ. James Calvert to John P. Brown, 27 August 1849, NARA RG84 Dard. 1.

64. Tchihatcheff (1853), ix.

65. MacAdam (1991), 286. Waddington noted that Greeks and Armenians dealt in gold and silver coins. Waddington (1853), 3. His collection later would be purchased by the Cabinet des Médailles of the Bibliothèque Nationale, Paris, and published in Babelon (1898).

66. Perrot (1909), 76–77.

67. Waddington (1853), 2.

68. "The discovery of a gold or silver coin does not prove much for the name of the town, because of the value of the precious metal itself which tends to render its value more longlived. But when one finds a great quantity of bronze coins among the ruins, they almost certainly identify the city." Waddington (1853), 2.

69. Count Alfred de Nieuwerkerke, director general of the imperial museums of France, to "Mr. Calvert," as British consul, 24 January 1855. This letter shows that Calvert facilitated the export of inscriptions from Cyzicus out of Asia Minor for Waddington, who subsequently gave them to the Louvre. The letter, preserved in the Archives des Musées Nationaux, Paris, is mentioned with kind permission of I. le Masne de Chermont. Adrien de Longperier and J. de Witte (1855), 60, 1–6, published the stelai, Louvre acquisition numbers 2851–56. I thank Dr. Marianne Hamiaux, Department of Greek and Roman Antiquities, Louvre, for this information.

70. Frank Calvert to Charles Newton, 12 February 1862, BMGR. Calvert to Newton, 24 September 1863, shows that Calvert already had written to Waddington about his Hisarlık discoveries, including the Athena Ilias temple. BMGR. James Calvert corresponded with Newton concerning the acquisition of two statues that he previously had offered to Waddington. Letter of 25 August 1868, BMGR.

71. *Ilium Vetus,* inscription #*1038,* from Pınarbaşı, 1845. "An employee of the British consulate made a copy that he sent to Constantinople in September 1846." *Ilium Novum* inscriptions include #*1040,* from Haliléh, "found by M. Calvert, consul of England at the Dar-

danelles, who sent me this impression." Le Bas and Waddington (1870), 2:267. Also, *#1743:*
"I published the new text of this inscription after a facsimile, from M. Frank Calvert, pro-
prietor at the Dardanelles. The stone was found in the cemetery of the village of Haliléh."
Ibid., 416. *#1743b:* "Copy from Mr. Calvert—in the cemetery of Tchiplak." *#1743c,* from
Yeni Köy: "Copy and impression from Mr. Calvert." *#1743d:* "Copy and impression from
Mr. Calvert." *#1743e:* "Copy from M. Calvert. Stone found in the ruins of Ilium." *#1743f:*
"Copy from M. Calvert. On column found at Haliléh." Ibid., 417. *#1743g:* "Copy from M.
Calvert. Mutilated fragment found in the ruins of Ilium." Ibid., 418. *#1743h:* "Copy from M.
Calvert. Stone found at *Haliléh."* *#1743i:* "Fragment found near Akça Köy." *#1743k:* "Impression sent by M. Calvert." *#1743l:* "Impression sent by M. Calvert. Fragment from the
necropolis of *Hanai Tepe in the Plain of Troy."* *#1743m:* "Impression sent by M. Calvert." Ibid,
418. *Abydos* inscriptions include the following. *#1743n:* "Copy made by a Greek and communicated to M. Calvert. The stone was found at the Dardanelles and was transported into the
interior in order to be used in the construction of an oil press." Ibid., 419. *#1743o:* "Copy
from M. Calvert. Stone found at *Saradjik* in the Dardanelles Plain." *#1743p:* "Copy from M.
Calvert. On a column at *Gangherli* on the route from the Dardanelles to Lampsacus. Ibid,
419. My translations from the French original. See also Reinach (1913), 168 nn. 2–3, and
Lolling (1884), 69, 71; (1881a), 118–20; and (1881b), 227–28.

72. Frank Calvert is the only one known to have made copies.

73. Calvert (1859), 3 n. 1. In 1856, Calvert described a huge *pithos* burial with some
smaller vases, which he recovered. *Illustrated London News,* 26 April 1856. These vases are described by Stark (1874a), 377; Thiersch (1902a), 13, site no. 5; Cook (1973), 58; and Allen
(1996b), 150 n. 44 *Xenophon: The Hellenica and Anabasis,* 3.1.9–10, vol. 1, books 1–4, with an
English translation by C. L. Brownson (Cambridge, Mass., 1968), 180–81.

74. Calvert's trip with the Americans included Pınarbaşı, Alexandria Troas, and Çığrı
Dağ. James Calvert to John P. Brown, 27 August 1849, NARA RG84 Dard. 1.

75. Carlisle (1854), 72–75, described a harrowing forced march with Frank Calvert up
Çığrı Dağ to the summit, where Carlisle "took the liberty, on this spur of Ida, of imitating
the oft repeated example of Jupiter on its summit" and fell asleep *(Iliad* 14.350–53).

76. Newton (1865), 134; Carlisle (1854), 92–93; Tozer (1869), 45.

77. He co-authored the *Catalogue of the Greek and Etruscan Vases in the British Museum* (London, 1851), with Samuel Birch.

78. Newton (1851), 1–26, esp. 25–26.

79. Gardner (1896), 133.

80. Newton (1865), 126, reprinted in Hildesheim in 1989.

81. Newton (1865), 132, discussed by Easton (1991), 15–16.

82. The account in Newton (1865), 126, appeared after Calvert's and is based heavily on
Calvert's article (1860b), 286, 291–96.

83. Newton (1865), 128–30.

84. Although Newton frequently devoted as much of his narrative to odd customs or
the deportment of Turkish servants as he did to an archaeological site, his remarks were
nonetheless insightful. Newton (1865), 126–27.

85. Pottery from Mycenae was known "thanks to Thomas Burgon." Newton (1865),
126. Burgon (1787–1858), once a Levant Company merchant, joined the British Museum in
1841. *Dictionary of National Biography,* s.v. "Burgon, John William," his son. This great collector excavated on Melos and published a description of three vase fragments with spiral dec-

oration from Mycenae and the pattern of spiral ornament from the treasury of Atreus at Mycenae and dated them somewhat before 1200 B.C. Burgon (1847), 258. The British Museum's department of antiquities acquired the Burgon Collection in 1842, so Newton would have worked with it and would have familiarized himself with the Mycenaean sherds.

86. Newton (1865), 132.

87. Other travelers in 1853 also recorded Frank Calvert's work here: Carlisle (1854), 92–93; and Tozer (1869), 45. Calvert noted his excavation methods. Calvert (1859), 1, 3. See Allen (1995b), 387. Calvert (1873a) dated a second campaign to 1856.

88. Newton (1865), 134. Newton probably by this time had heard Worsaae speak on excavating Danish mounds at the Society of Antiquaries in London on 24 April 1852. Levine (1986), 19. Certainly he would have known of the criticisms of Gormezano's work. And since 1816, excavators in the Crimea had plumbed tumuli for generations, as at Panticapaion (Kerch).

89. Newton (1865), 134 n. 61.

90. Calvert had not yet committed himself to an identification of the site, although he later followed Broughton (1813), 753, who identified the remains at Akça Köy as ancient Thymbra.

91. Newton (1865), 134–35, 355 n. 62; Calvert (1859), 1–6. In 1857, Senior recounted the excavation of a *pithos* burial before breakfast. Senior (1859), 170, and (1861), 151. Initially, Calvert followed Captain Thomas Spratt's and Peter Wilhelm Forschammer's error in misidentifying the rivers near Hanay Tepe. Forschammer (1839), 29–33; Calvert (1859), 1. The result can be seen in Map 4.

92. *Neue deutsche Biographie*, s.v. "Baumeister, Karl August."

93. Curiously, Senior mentioned the site but included nothing on a Calvert excavation. Senior (1859), 179.

94. Baumeister (1854), 511. Calvert (1864 and 1873a) dated his Pınarbaşı excavation to 1863. There is no corroborating source for the first two excavations.

95. Senior (1859), 163; Thiersch (1902a), site no. 5, plate 13; Allen (1996b), 150 n. 44. Calvert (1859), 3 n. 1, records vases that he found in a *pithos* grave. A sketch of this *pithos* burial already had appeared in the *Illustrated London News*, 26 April 1856. He could have been led here by earlier discoveries at the site by Brunton's men, who also worked at the site.

96. Calvert (1860b and 1873a). Material from this site is in the British Museum. See also Thiersch (1902a), site no. 17, 155–63, and Allen (1996b), 155–57.

97. Herodotus, 7.43; Xenophon, *Anabasis*, 7.8.5, in *Xenophon: The Hellenica and Anabasis*, with an English translation by C. L. Brownson (Cambridge, Mass., 1950), 3:618–19; Strabo 13.1.29.

98. Newton (1865), 132–33. Calvert (1860b), 293 and plan.

99. Calvert (1860b), 296.

100. PRO/FO 195 492.

101. For Calvert's work at Pınarbaşı, see Baumeister (1854), 511. Calvert obtained permission from the Sublime Porte to excavate on the Ballı Dağ in 1856. Calvert (1894). Georges Perrot, who visited on 28 July 1856, noted that on the first plateau, one of the tumuli recently had been opened. It was "formed of rough stones thrown with earth one on top of the other." Perrot (1856), 66, my translation. See also a vague reference to activity at the site in the 1850s in Schuchhardt (1891), 85. Tozer's account of his 1853 travels mentions Calvert's work at the site but does not date it, other than to say that it occurred "some years ago." Tozer (1869), 34.

102. Forschammer (1842), 28–44, quoted by Calvert (1859). For Forschammer, see Lullies and Schiering (1988), 27.

103. Stratum 1, Turkish tombs, to Stratum 2 with classical and Archaic jar burials, to Stratum 3, deep deposit of calcined bones, to Stratum 4, wood ashes and fragments of pottery, and Stratum 5, another earth level with skeleton. Calvert (1859), 1–6. The excavations occurred in 1853 and 1856. Easton has unduly criticized the section drawing [Figure 15] as largely extrapolated from Calvert's limited discoveries. Easton (1991), 122.

104. He ably recognized the effects of the environment on finds, such as a skeleton that was well preserved "owing to the exclusion of air and damp."

105. Senior (1859), 160–61, 170. Calvert referred to *pithos* burials found by Colonel Munro near Balaclava in the Crimea. Calvert (1859), 2.

106. These are the first published description and illustration (to scale) of Bronze Age pottery in the Troad. See Figure 35b.

107. Calvert (1859), 5. Frank Calvert already had purchased acreage around Ilium Novum on the plain of Troy, indicating that his attention may have been changing direction around that time. Senior (1859), 163.

108. Calvert (1859), 4–6.

109. Ibid., 2.

110. Thiersch (1902a), site no. 3, 11.

111. Strabo, 13.1.46–48; Xenophon, *Hellenica*, 3.1.13, 16; Thucydides, *History of the Peloponnesian War*, 8.101, in Calvert (1861), 253–55. *Thucydides*, with an English translation by Charles Foster Smith (Cambridge, Mass., 1958), 4:378–81.

112. Calvert (1860b) and Thiersch (1902a), site no. 12, 98–102. Some finds are in the British Museum (Allen [1996b], 150, nn. 46–48).

113. Calvert (1860b), 287–91.

114. Chandler (1776), 32–34; de Grummond (1996), 270; Broughton (1813), 684.

115. Leaf (1923), 223–24, plate 11b.

116. Calvert wrote it on 8 September 1856, and it was presented on 3 December 1859. Calvert may even have sent it off to Newton, who could have forwarded it for him, but this is only conjecture.

117. The *Classical Museum* published articles, for example, Newton's article "On the Sculptures from the Mausoleum at Halicarnassus" (5:170–201), and reviews, such as Grote's *History of Greece* (5:125–70), and translated articles by F. G. Welcker on the pediments of the Parthenon (2:367–404, 6:279–96) and reviews by Heinrich N. Ulrichs (3:194–202), among others. But it was a tight group of contributors, and 7 percent of them accounted for 40 percent of the text. It was discontinued in 1849. The *Museum of Classical Antiquities*, which appeared in 1851, continued to accept articles through April 1853. After that, it issued only reprinted versions of the earlier volumes. The *Journal of Classical and Sacred Philology* published art and archaeology articles only occasionally. Naiditch (1989), 133–43.

118. Calvert (1859), 6, postscript.

119. Though not preserved, this letter is mentioned in Calvert to Newton, 12 February 1862, BMGR.

120. Tozer (1869), 47.

121. Calvert (1860a), 199–200. The report included a well-executed drawing of the weight that Calvert must have drafted. His article referred to Layard's publication of *Nineveh and Babylon* (London, 1851), 601, and discussed similar weights found by Layard there.

122. Calvert (1860b), 287–91; Allen (1996b), 150 n. 48.

123. Barker Webb (1844), 35; Forschammer (1842), 61.

124. Calvert (1860b), 286, 291–96. Calvert returned to this site in 1881. Calvert to Schliemann, 16 June and 2 July 1881, B 86/306 and B 86/370.

125. Calvert's plan (1860b), 293 [Figure 6], was based on the "Chart of Renkioi British Hospital and part of the country adjacent on the shore of the Dardanelles," by John Brunton. Toppin (1981), plan. Calvert pointed out mistakes introduced by the compiler, where the ancient remains were placed on the site of the hospital itself.

126. Calvert (1860b), 291–96. Below the site was a lower platform and an ancient mole, which appears on Calvert's plan (1860b), 286. Newton's account (1865), 132–33, is largely based on Calvert's but records a platform where he saw marble fragments, sherds, and wall foundations. In deep ravines to the southwest, Calvert located terra-cotta water pipes. To the southeast was a long wall of travertine blocks with rubble fill.

127. Calvert (1860b), 291–96. The Greek and Roman coins and Greek terra-cottas and bronzes that he found in the settlement became part of his growing collection, as did material from the extensive necropolis. Thiersch (1902a), site no. 17, 155–63. Material from this site is now in the British Museum. Allen (1996b), 150 n. 49. The nearby artificial mound above Erenköy was shown by Frederick's excavation not to have been sepulchral. Calvert (1860b), 295, and *Levant Herald,* 4 February 1873.

128. Herodotus, 7.43. As a tribute to Calvert's acuity, scholars still accept both identifications. Calvert (1860b), 293.

129. Greaves (1861), 363.

130. (1860b), 287. A close reading of Calvert's letter to Newton on 12 February 1862 suggests that Newton may have interceded on Calvert's behalf in facilitating this honor.

131. Calvert (1861), 253–55; Barker Webb (1844), 70, 73; Gell (1804), 19; Broughton (1813), 684. Gell had identified Liman Tepe as Colonae.

132. Strabo, 13.1.46–48 and Xenophon, *Hellenica,* 3.1.13, 16, 17.

133. *Athenaeum* 1750, 11 May 1861, 683.

134. Marchand (1941), 1, 16, 96.

135. The earliest preserved letter to Newton dates from 12 February 1862, although it is clear that the men corresponded in 1860, when Newton was still in Rome. For Newton in Rome, see Evans (1956), 303.

136. Calvert is listed as a corresponding member of the institute in 1860–61. Then there is no more mention of Calvert at the institute.

137. Marchand (1996), 54 n. 60.

138. De Grummond (1996), 608–10.

139. Newton was appointed in January 1861. Evans (1956), 303. Calvert to Newton, 12 February 1862, BMGR.

140. In Vaux (1863), 398.

141. *Athenaeum* 1799, 19 April 1862, 533. Newton was preoccupied with the publication of his opus on the mausoleum, due to be published that year.

142. Leaf (1923), 172, plate 10a. Strabo, 13.1.33–34, 47. Xenophon, *Hellenica,* 3.1.17.

143. Calvert never published this find, but Joseph T. Clarke, a member of the later Assos expedition, mentioned examining ancient mines in the mountain east of Çal Dağ near Cebrene and identified these with the Cave of Andeira, probably with information from Calvert. Clarke (1888), 317.

144. He clearly needed sources for comparison, although his brother Edmund had the *Horae Aegypt.* Poole (1851). Robinson suggests that he found Cebrene in 1860 (1995), 327.

145. Calvert never published Rhoeteum (Strabo, 13.1.30, 42), but he did make finds there. Thiersch (1902a), 170–71. Since he took Newton there in 1853, he probably had found it earlier. Newton (1865), 133.

146. Calvert had found a coin of Zeleia, a city in the Aesepus region to the northeast. Calvert to Newton, 12 February 1862, BMGR. Strabo, 13.1.45; *Iliad* 2.824; Xenophon, *Hellenica*, 1.1.2; Arrian, *Anabasis*, 1.12.8. Mentioned by Leaf (1923), 66–67.

147. Calvert (1860a), 198–200. Calvert (1859), 2, credited the villagers with finding the tremendous *pithos* burial at Dardanos, from which he removed a number of vases uninteresting to the locals.

148. Tchihatcheff (1860), 3:xxvii–xxviii; Allen (1996b), 148.

149. Gelzer (1874), 6.

150. Baumeister (1854), 510–12. Cook (1973), 390, further records that the Calverts kept inscriptions at Erenköy, though he does not cite his source.

151. Schliemann noted that the gladiator metope was in the courtyard of the Batak farmhouse. Schliemann (1884), 200; Dörpfeld (1902), 433. This metope was first mentioned by Calvert in his communication to Greaves (1865b), 337.

152. Schliemann's 1868 diary, 148; Schliemann (1869), 213.

153. Stark (1874a), 160, 173–74, 374–79.

154. Newton (1865) 45.

155. According to Newton, who knew Ismail Pasha well during his time as acting consul on Rhodes, the Turk possessed a clear idea of the coins as articles of commerce but completely overlooked their historical interest. Carlisle (1855), 103–8; Newton (1865), 45.

156. Senior (1859), 205. Whittall's coin collection, kept at his country house in Bournabat, was the most notable in Smyrna in 1878. Many of his coins are now in the British Museum. McKernan (1997), 2. His oldest son, Sir (James) William Whittall (1838–1860), of Constantinople, was also a collector. His antiquities collection was later sold to Count A. J. von Nelidow in Saint Petersburg. Pollak (1955), preface. The Smyrna collection of Chevalier M. Ivanoff, once the Russian consul, was sold in 1864. Newton (1865), 46; Murray (1878), 252. At that time, Smyrna was a "numismatic capital" and supplied "the cabinets of Europe" with Persian, Greek, Roman, and early medieval coins. Because coin collectors always were exchanging and selling, the size of their collections always was in flux. Most were unpublished. By 1875, James Whittall had the largest. Others were heirlooms started by previous generations of numismatists, such as that of O. Borrell. Murray (1875), 267.

There were numerous collectors of other artifacts. In Gallipoli, Newton noted "some interesting antiquities" in the house of the consular agent, Sitrides, comprising a marble group sculpture, a golden brooch with the head of Medusa, and gold and silver "temple treasure" from Lampsacus, part of which was already in the British Museum. Newton (1865), 125. In the course of trying to protect the ancient architecture of Smyrna from total destruction, the Swedish consul in Smyrna, F. Spiegelthal, bought up much of the ancient city around the temple of Asklepios. He developed a large collection of ancient bronzes, terra-cottas, and marbles between 1850 and 1857. Newton (1865), 123–24. It was passed over by *The Murray Handbook.* Newton promptly published some of his pieces in *Archäologische Zeitung* 11–12 (1854): 512–13. Spiegelthal is also mentioned by Baumeister in connection with the Lydian Alyattes tumulus. Baumeister (1854), 511. Senior noted that in 1857, Spiegelthal was packing his collection for sale in London and previously had sent a colossal bust to Berlin. Senior (1859), 191–94. Calvert may have considered Berlin a good market for antiquities sales because of Spiegelthal.

De Kay mentions Reverend Arundel's small but exceedingly valuable collection of minerals and antiquities, some of which he had gathered from Ephesus. De Kay also mentions a gentleman named Henry Borell, an antiquarian, numismatist, and collector "profoundly versed in numismatics" and possessed of a library "perhaps more extensive and complete than any similar private collection in the world." Mac Farlane (1850), 1:24. According to De Kay, he recently had sold one of his collections for $30,000 and worked on his investigations with untiring zeal. De Kay (1833), 479–80.

157. "A small bronze mouse, now in the collection of Mr. Frank Calvert, was found here [at Lisgyar, near Alexandria Troas]. From the nearness of the spot to the Sminthium, the seat of worship of Apollo Sminthius, there can be hardly a doubt that this mouse was dedicated to that deity, who on a coin of Alexandria Troas is represented holding a mouse in his hand." Newton (1865), 130, 132. While discussing Ophryneion, Newton mentioned coins of Ophryneion, Neandria, Sigeum, Ilium Novum, and Megiste, either seen with Calvert or gleaned from him. These previously had been noted in Calvert (1860b), 293.

158. Of Calvert's excavation of a *pithos* burial at Akça Köy, Newton noted, "One jar contained eight small vases mixed with bones. The figures painted on some of the vases were in black on a red ground, others red, on a black ground; all seemed of a very late period." Newton (1865), 135. Presumably these vases, noted by Carlisle in 1853, became the seed of the Calvert Collection.

159. Described in Carlisle (1855), 127.

160. Journal entry, 23 July 1853, Carlisle (1854), 96–97.

161. Baumeister (1854), 511, referred to in Stark (1874a), 374. Baumeister noted "a handsome collection" in his letter submitted on 24 November. Baumeister (1854), 510–11. He mentioned one inscribed fragment, which he read as "ΑΦΡΟΔΙΤΗ ΣΤΕΦΑΝΗΦΟ-ΡΟΣ," now in the British Museum, BMGR acc. no. 1877.9–30. 41. Calvert's correct reading of the inscription is ΑΦΡΟΔΙΤΗ ΧΡΥΣΟΣΤΕΦΑ[ΝΟ]. Calvert (1860b), 294. Stark followed Calvert (1874a), 377–78.

162. Allen (1996b), 150 n. 47; Calvert (1860b), 290.

163. Calvert (1860b), 290. Thiersch (1902a), site no. 12, 98–102. Cook noted the site and finds: an east Greek orientalizing oinochoe, gray ware, red figure vases, an Attic black-glaze bowl, and terra-cottas from the early sixth to the early fourth centuries B.C. Cook (1973), 216–21. Stark (1874a), 378, described the vase with the ΧΟΤΡΙΝΑΣ inscription, now in the British Museum, BMGR acc. no. 1877.9–30. 40.

164. See Hartkopf (1983) for a history of the Prussian Academy. Allen (1996b), 145–65, plates 18–21. Curtius (1873), 113. On 26–28 April 1871, Professors Georg Niemann and Alois Hauser (1841–1896), later architects on Alexander Conze's excavations at Samothrace, visited.

165. Gelzer, Stark, and Carl Curtius made rubbings and impressions of the Sestos inscription and others. C. Curtius (1873), 113–39; and Stark (1874a), 174, 374–76.

166. Ernst Curtius was professor of classical philology at the University of Berlin and later directed the German excavations at Olympia from 1875 to 1881. Mortimer Chambers, "Ernst Curtius, 2 September 1814—11 July 1896," in Briggs and Calder (1992), 37–42; Calder and Kramer (1992), 1091–94. For a portrait, see Lullies and Schiering (1988), 39.

167. *Webster's Biographical Dictionary*, s.v. "Gelzer, Johann Heinrich"; Calder and Kramer (1992), 1281.

168. Curtius (1872), 52 n. 6. Adler was a professor of architectural history who worked with Curtius at Olympia from 1874 to 1881. A member of the German Archaeological Institute and the Prussian Academy of Art, he was one of the few German scholars who recognized early the importance of Schliemann's work. *Neue deutsches Biographie* and *Webster's Biographical Dictionary*, s.v. "Adler, Johann Heinrich Friedrich." His daughter married Wilhelm Dörpfeld. For a portrait, see Lullies and Schiering (1988), 53.

169. Stark was a professor of classical archaeology and wrote the influential *Systematik und Geschichte der Archaeologie der Kunst* (Leipzig, 1880). For a portrait, see Lullies and Schiering (1988), 49.

170. There they found a fragment of the frieze of the mausoleum of Halicarnassus, a notable sarcophagus, and other reliefs. Published by Frick in the *Archäologische Zeitung* (1857). Ernst Curtius to his wife, Clara, 5 September 1871, in Curtius (1903), 606. German original.

171. Curtius (1872), 53. At Smyrna, they visited the German consul von Gonzenbach, who had a large collection of antiquities. Curtius (1872), 65–66.

172. Ernst Curtius to Clara Curtius, 5 September 1871. German original in Curtius (1903), 606. Calvert wrote Schliemann that his collection interested them greatly. Letter of 13 September 1871, BB 66/216.

173. Gelzer (1874), 6. Stark recorded that they did not visit Batak Farm and its collection (1874a), 160, German original. Consequently they left no description of it for posterity.

174. Stark (1874a), 173–74, 374–79. It was in one of the same attic rooms of the ruined Dardanelles residence where Calvert later kept his "Schliemann correspondence." Francis H. Bacon to Bert H. Hill, 26 July 1923, MSS 70.40; Allen (1995b), 379–80.

175. The crowding of the material in that year may have resulted from the clearing out of the Erenköy house, which the family seems at this point to have abandoned. Stark (1874a), 374–79.

176. For the Sestos inscription, see Curtius (1873). According to Stark, architectural sculpture consisted of Ionic capitals from Alexandria Troas, and from Ilion, moldings with dentil and egg-and-dart friezes and a frieze with volutes and acanthus. Large frieze fragments showed a hero and another figure in high relief and centaurs from the temple. Stark (1874a), 374. These are discussed in Holden (1964). See also Chapter 5 below.

177. Stark (1874a), 379. Eighty glass vessels were sold at the Sotheby's sale of August 1877. The present whereabouts of fewer than two dozen of these is known.

178. The Persian weight had an Aramaic inscription on the handle. Calvert (1860a), 198–200; Budge (1922), 171.

179. Stark (1874a), 379; Thiersch (1902a), site no. 1, 1. Castellani, the collector and creator of archaeological jewelry, sold the diadem in 1884. Allen (1996b), 154 n. 80. Greifenhagen (1884), 34, figures 1, 2; 35, no. 22, no. 23; Conze (1884), 92–94; Leroi (1884), 106, 110. 802. It is presently in the collection of the Victoria and Albert Museum. Neg. no. 31574. Room 2, case 11, 8.

180. Stark (1874a), 379. Calvert to Charles Newton, 8 October 1863, BMGR, speaks of a hoard of silver coins. So do Calvert to Schliemann, 3 February 1869 and 4 May 1872, B 64/49 and B 67/156.

181. Calvert (1873b), 93, not of interest to Stark.

182. Calvert (1873b), 93; Calvert and Neumayr (1880), 357–78. Some of these are on display in the Çanakkale Archaeological Museum.

183. That is, from Lesbos, Abydos, tombs discovered at Dardanos, Ophryneion, Akça Köy, Colonae, the furthest point being Cyzicus. Stark (1874a), 379. The Calverts long had been aware of the riches of Cyzicus, to the northeast of the Troad, where, according to their unpublished correspondence, they had discovered sculpture, vases, and coins. Stark himself catalogued their grave reliefs. Calvert's activity on Lesbos is harder to document.

184. Speech at the Winckelmann Anniversary, 9 December 1871. Curtius (1872), 58, German original. The Archaeological Society of Berlin was founded in 1842 by Eduard Gerhard (1795–1867). Their journal was the *Archäologische Zeitung.* See Borbein (1993), 28–36, and Sichtermann (1996), 414. Newton had been a member since 1849.

CHAPTER 4

1. They were stationed with the British fleet in the harbor of Beşika Bay on the west coast of the Troad. Spratt measured and Forschammer noted antiquities. Retaining Chevalier's identifications, they placed "Ilium Recens" (Ilium Novum) at Hisarlık. Forschammer (1842), 28–44. Calvert used Forschammer's 1842 article. In 1840, Napier sketched a useful map employing the new system of identifications. Napier (1840), 289–310.

2. Senior illustrated this wall on his map [see Map 4]. Senior (1859), map.

3. In this scheme, the Dümrek became the Thymbrios. Forschammer (1842), 43. The scheme was perpetuated in Senior's map [Map 4].

4. Senior (1859), 163, documents this.

5. By restoring the identity of the Simois to the Dümrek, Barker Webb could correct Chevalier. Barker Webb's original 1821 book in Italian was largely unknown and was inaccessible until reissued in French in 1844.

6. Barker Webb (1844) incorporated some of Maclaren's ideas but placed the site to the east. Grote (1849) and Smith (1873), 34, corroborated Maclaren in their revised editions. Apparently unaware of Maclaren's work, the Smyrna physician Gustav von Eckenbrecher visited the plain of Troy in 1840–1841, rejected Chevalier's thesis, and suggested that Troy was located south of Çıplak by two to three kilometers. Von Eckenbrecher was confused— he thought that this was where Clarke had placed Ilium Novum. Von Eckenbrecher (1843), 1–49, and (1845). See also Cook (1973), 33, 106–7 n. 5, for other travelers to the spot.

7. *Admiralty Chart* 1608 of 1840.

8. Cox and Nichol (1894), 449 n.

9. Maclaren's little-circulated 1822 volume was in Calvert's personal library five years later.

10. Senior (1859), 171.

11. Ibid., 174. Although Senior occasionally gives Frank Calvert's full given name in his account, he also refers to "the consul," to "Mr. F. Calvert," or simply to "Mr. Calvert." The ambiguity common to other treatments of the brothers and their interests continues here. It may be that "Mr. Calvert" refers to the consul, or Frederick, who often used his middle name of William, and that "Mr. F. Calvert" was a way of distinguishing Frank. In that case, the Pınarbaşı excursion, as well as that to Akça Köy, would have been undertaken with Frederick, and the ideas shared would have been Frederick's, not Frank's. Senior (1859), 168–75.

12. Ibid., 171–75.

13. Ibid., 173.

14. Rennell (1814), 124–25.

15. Leake (1824), 275, *Webster's Biographical Dictionary*, s.v. "Leake, William Martin." He visited the area in 1800.

16. Ulrichs (1845), 591–93, and (1847), 103–78.

17. Senior (1859), 164, 168; Schliemann (1881a), figure 15.

18. He and Freeman owned the original parcel in the name of Elias Frangi, a necessary formality because foreign men could not own land in Turkey. Shaw and Shaw (1977), 394, 399, 401. Calvert held the land in the name of Frangi and his brother Christo, and he had purchased the fields piecemeal over a number of years. Calvert to Schliemann, 23 February 1871, B 66/41. Frangi worked for Frederick Calvert as superintendent of the Erenköy farm for fifteen years. Deposition of 17 July 1862, PRO/FO 78 2066. For nineteenth-century equivalents between English pounds sterling, French francs, and Turkish lire, see Pamuk (1994), 972, table A9.

19. Contrary to Cook (1973), 95. See Senior (1859), 164, 168. Recent deed research in Çanakkale has not produced any record of the date of purchase of this land.

20. Frederick's last known land acquisition was the Erenköy hospital in 1856. Frederick Calvert to the earl of Clarendon, 28 March and 24 November 1856, PRO/FO 195 492.

21. Easton (1991), 120, based on Senior (1859), 164, 168.

22. Frederick Calvert's influence with the pasha silenced their protests. Senior (1859), 165.

23. Easton (1991), 120. Robinson (1995), 325, correctly notes that there are no letters posted from the farm.

24. If Frederick helped Frank acquire the higher part of the site, this could only have been between October 1860, when Frederick Calvert was paid his back commission and reimbursements from the War Office, and September 1863, when he wrote to Newton of his excavations there.

25. Leake (1824), 274–75.

26. Clarke (1817), 3:131.

27. Forschammer (1842), 39.

28. Von Eckenbrecher (1843), 39.

29. Newton (1865), 132.

30. Easton noted that Maclaren transposed north and south in his commentary. Easton (1991), 117. The error has been corrected in these discussions.

31. Brunton in Clapham (1939), 59–66.

32. He and Frank witnessed Louisa Lander's wedding to Major William J. Chads, who was in charge of British military establishments in the neighborhood, on 25 August 1856. Ellis and Ellis to James Murray, 22 November 1867, PRO/FO 78 5084.

33. The hospital housed some sixteen hundred patients. Clapham (1939), 68–69.

34. He had experienced first-hand problems with mutinous troops in July 1855. PRO/FO 195 492.

35. Easton (1991), 121.

36. The Greeks later removed the mosaic for the church at Kalafatli. Clapham (1939), 68–69; Cook (1973), 58, 137. Dörpfeld (1902), 230–34, noted that the colored floor had been removed by villagers. Brunton's fragments are now in the British Museum, BMGR Register, 1856. 12–8.30–33.

37. Frederick Calvert was asked to sell off the property by the war secretary, Lord Panmure (1801–1874). Calvert to Stratford de Redcliffe, 5 July 1856, PRO/FO 195 492.

38. Clapham (1939), 73. The 1 August 1856 sale notice mentioned 300 acres of land and at least thirty-nine buildings. PRO/FO 195 492.

39. Sir Anthony Panizzi (1797–1879) was the principal librarian, or director, of the British Museum from 1856 to 1866. His greatest acquisitions were archaeological: the Temple Collection, the Farnese sculptures, the excavated remains of Halicarnassus, Camirus, and Carthage, and the Christy Collection of prehistoric antiquities. *Dictionary of National Biography*, s.v. "Panizzi, Sir Anthony."

40. Clapham (1939), 80–81. Lord Panmure, the war secretary, facilitated the presentation on 8 December 1856. BMGR Register, 1856. 12–8.1–58. Lord Panmure later would investigate Frederick Calvert's wartime dealings with the Land Transport Corps. Foreign Office to Frederick Calvert, 9 April 1857, PRO/FO 78 1309.

41. BMGR Register, 1856. 12–8.1–58. Newton (1865), 355 n. 64, mentions Brunton's excavations at Dardanos.

42. Cook (1973), 37. It is also possible that by the "Necropolis of Troy," Brunton meant the plateau with tumuli at Pınarbaşı. See the confused later story of Calvert excavating a tumulus in 1855 with officers of the British fleet in Nicoläides (1867), 85, later repeated in Schliemann (1884), 251.

43. It does not appear that Brunton excavated on the acropolis itself, but rather around its base, presumably in the southeast area. For this reason, one must wonder whether Frank Calvert owned any part of the mound itself before 1860.

44. Carlisle (1854), 97, recorded that Frederick was interested in purchasing land in this locale, but no documents are preserved to corroborate a purchase.

45. Frank Calvert generously mentioned Gormezano in his retrospective article (1873a).

46. Easton (1991), 121. Although Brunton never specifically mentioned that he dug at Hisarlık, one assumes that this is where he set his disgruntled men to work.

47. He did cite Brunton's Erenköy hospital chart in his later article on Ophryneion, though he also pointed out its errors. Calvert (1859), plan.

48. This was on 27 July 1856. Perrot (1874), 61–62. *Webster's Biographical Dictionary*, s.v. "Perrot, Georges."

49. Perrot (1874), 61.

50. This would have been in the area of the Athena Ilias temple quarried by Turks. Brunton's "temple," with its Corinthian capital, cannot have been Lysimachus's Temple of Athena because Corinthian finds were concentrated in the south, according to the excavators. It seems more likely that they found a garbled lot of architectural members.

51. Tozer (1869), 48–49.

52. Schliemann's finds in 1890 on the southeastern slope and in the lower city matched these in character.

53. On 13 April 1856 (PRO/FO 78 1208) and 19 April 1858 (PRO/FO 195 492), Frank Calvert took over the consulate as acting British consul in his brother's absence. During the war and in 1857, he was constantly writing letters for his brothers. In 1860–61, he was again writing for Frederick.

54. Greaves (1861), 364. The Reverend Hugh A. J. Munro had edited Lucretius. *Webster's Biographical Dictionary*, s.v. "Munro, Hugh Andrew Johnstone." Cited in Easton (1991), 122.

55. Schliemann (1875a), map.

56. Frederick Calvert in Greaves (1861), 363. Frederick held on to this idea a decade later. Schliemann to James Calvert, 10 November 1871, BB 2.4/11. Following Leake (1824),

Schliemann agreed that the site was Strabo's Ilion Kome, but assuming by then that Strabo was incorrect as a source, he did not accept that it was Homer's Troy. Schliemann (1875a), 51; (1881a), 99, 108; Virchow (1880), 21.

57. He even mentioned it to Schliemann as the hottest spring in the plain in his 1 November 1868 letter, B 63/450.

58. James Calvert was skeptical about Frederick Calvert's theory, apparently siding with Frank. James Calvert to Schliemann, 11 November 1871, B 66/265.

59. Because the Archaeological Institute had no scheduled meetings, his article was not presented and published until February 1864. Calvert (1864), 46–53.

60. Although Easton (1991), 122–23, and Traill (1993), 102, note that Calvert excavated Pınarbaşı after reading Maclaren in 1863, Baumeister (1054), 511, already had recorded his work. See Perrot (1874), 66. Senior (1859), 173, also mentioned Calvert's having opened up the "Tomb of Priam." Calvert may have returned in 1863 to reevaluate it. Calvert (1864), 46–53; Calvert (1894).

61. Calvert quoted Hunt's idea that the stonework on the summit of the central tumulus was the foundation of an altar or shrine. Walpole (1817), 108.

62. Chevalier (1791).

63. Newton (1865), 126–27.

64. Calvert (1864) and (1873a). Anne-Ulrike Kossatz-Pompé (1992), 171, now inclines toward a Late Bronze Age date for the tumuli, with a later period of reuse in the fifth to third centuries B.C.

65. Xenophon, *Hellenica*, 3.1.15, and Strabo, 13.1.19, 70. Calvert (1873a). Tozer supported Calvert's attribution. Tozer (1869), 43 n. 30. Cook (1973), 140, 347–51, disagreed with this attribution and placed Gergis at Karıncalı, but he was not followed by Kossatz-Pompé (1992). Cook (1973), 347–51.

66. Maclaren (1863). Maclaren also wrote an article on Troy for the *Encyclopaedia Britannica* (1860), 8th edition.

67. Choiseul-Gouffier (1822), plate 35; Admiralty Chart 1608 of 1840.

68. See the Scottish Homeric scholar J. S. Blackie's review of Maclaren's book in *The Scotsman*, 11 May 1863, reprinted in Cox and Nicol (1894), 450.

69. Maclaren (1863), 5.

70. Ibid., 4.

71. Ibid., 76.

72. Frank Calvert credited Maclaren in (1874a), 610–11.

73. The extent of Calvert's property on the mound in 1863 is not known. If he was digging on his own land prior to his critical letter to Charles Newton of 23 September 1863, then he already owned both the northeastern summit of the tell and its southeastern slope as well, probably the entire eastern half of the mound.

CHAPTER 5

1. Senior (1859), 156; Slade (1837), 2:214.

2. Friedrich Gottlieb Welcker (1784–1868), a professor of classical philology and archaeology in Bonn and editor of the *Rheinisches Museum für Philologie*, met Lander while traveling through the Troad. He alone mentioned a younger "Mr. Lander." Welcker (1865), 224–27. He is not heard of afterward or mentioned in the papers con-

cerning Lander's children, which note three daughters. George Henry Clifton to Stratford de Redcliffe, 9 December 1865, PRO/FO 195 775. He inherits no property, consulships, or business. Lander's "son" must have been Frederick Calvert. *Biographisches Wörterbuch zur deutschen Geschichte,* s.v. "Welcker, Karl Theodor," his brother; Sichtermann (1996), 210, 414.

3. George Henry Clifton to Lord Lyons (1817–1887), British ambassador at Constantinople from 1865 to 1867, 9 December 1865, PRO/FO 195 775. Robinson (1994), 153–54.

4. Frederick Calvert, acting consul, to John Bidwell, 31 December 1845, PRO/FO 78 612. Lord Palmerston (1784–1865), foreign secretary from 1846 to 1851 and prime minister from 1855 to 1858, formally appointed Calvert in his letter of 28 January 1847, PRO/FO 78 700. Shortly thereafter, Calvert was absent for one and a half months settling Lander's estate. Frederick Calvert to John Bidwell, 30 June 1847.

5. According to General Sir John Henry Lefroy, Miss Abbott spoke Greek, Italian, and French, as well as her native English. Private memoir, circulated by Ken Horton to Ibrahim Aksu. In 1997, I found a watercolor portrait of Eveline Abbott in the Uluer collection, Çanakkale.

6. Grimm (1964), 357 n. 2267. For the Belgian and Dutch vice-consulships, see Frederick Calvert to Stratford de Redcliffe, 4 June 1853, PRO/FO 195 391 and NARA RG84 Dard. 4.

7. Frederick Calvert to Stratford de Redcliffe, 22 May 1857, PRO/FO 195 492.

8. The Abbotts had sixteen children. Carlisle (1855), 102. Like the Calverts, the sons entered the diplomatic service. Richard J. W. Abbott worked for Frederick Calvert as British vice-consul at Gallipoli. Subsequently he became a banker in Constantinople. William G. Abbott, who previously had managed the Erzerum consulate, took over the Dardanelles consulate for Frederick Calvert from 1858 to 1860. One Abbott daughter married Charles Wood, the British consul at Smyrna who witnessed Frederick's wedding; another married Charles van Lennep, a Dutch subject and the Swedish consul at Smyrna, and a third married E. Whitaker, who replaced Richard J. W. Abbott as vice-consul at Gallipoli. Another branch of the Abbott family lived in Salonica. G. F. Abbott served as consular agent there in the 1840s, and later a B. F. Abbott worked as an interpreter at the British consulate. Frederick Calvert transferred by way of security some of the Dardanelles warehouses to the Abbotts from Salonica. George A. Porter to Abel P. Upshur, 16 December 1843, NARA RG 84 Dard. 1; Arthur Raby to the Foreign Office, 10 September 1863, PRO/FO 195 775. The Abbott commercial house had branches in Constantinople, Salonica, and Smyrna. PRO/FO 83 111; *List of British Mercantile Houses in Constantinople, Salonica, and Izmir,* 1842, 1848; Frangakis-Syrett (1992), 99.

9. Spencer (1851), 2:296.

10. Most of the luxuries of England and France were available in its bazaar, and Smyrna had a good circulating library. Murray (1840), 261. There were two or three printing presses, a local French newspaper, and a third-rate theater for Italian opera. Murray (1875), 266.

11. Spencer (1851), 296–97. Security was an issue. "The fronts of their houses are protected by ponderous gates, secured at night with locks and chains; and from the back part to the bay, terraces, forming the roofs of magazines for merchandise, serve as walks, whence they have a full view of the harbour, shipping, and surrounding countryside. Consuls hav-

ing ambassadors at Constantinople live here in great style and magnificence." Dearborn (1819), 2:57. Murray (1840), 262.

12. Murray (1840), 262.

13. In the hills cradling Smyrna, they hunted wild boar, leopard, partridge, snipe, woodcock, and hares.

14. Murray (1875), 269.

15. De Kay remarked that in the gaming rooms, the European gentlemen's stakes were much higher than they should be. De Kay (1833), 478–79. The casino was "supported by subscriptions of the most respectable inhabitants of the city." Dearborn (1819), 2:66. See also Slade (1837), 2:259, and Stephens (1838), 1:195. Generally, there were three public balls at the casino during carnival, as well as private ones. The most popular dance was the waltz. De Kay (1833), 478–79. Even during the troubled years of the Greek War of Independence, while the "lower classes" were rioting in the streets of Smyrna, the "better classes" were attending a great ball at the casino. Walsh (1836), 2:43.

16. The Turks were on higher ground to the west. The Armenians were central, and the Jews wedged between the two. The Greeks were along the shore, south of the so-called English Scala. Murray (1840), 262.

17. Felicia M. F. Skene, wife of the British vice-consul in Constantinople, wrote of Sundays as "a day which it is perhaps more important to keep abroad than at home, in order that there may not seem to be any inconsistency in our conduct to those who have witnessed the strictness of its observance in England." Skene (1849), 174. Senior (1859), 220, heard J. T. Wolter preach in accented English. He also preached in Greek and Turkish. Wolter was the same German missionary who officiated at the marriage of Lander's daughter at the Dardanelles on 25 August 1856. Inquiry 169, 22 November 1867, PRO/FO 78 1998. Walsh wrote that Reverend Arundel had been the chaplain during his visit in the 1820s. Walsh (1836), 2:44.

18. Fellows (1839), 9, and Dearborn (1829), 2:56, respectively. Related to the Franks were the Levantines, who were descended from *raya* Greeks, Armenians, and Jews. "There were very few pure English." Murray (1840), 262–63, and (1878), 254. Turkey's chief exports were figs, raisins, valonia, madder, opium and other drugs, cotton, sponges, emery, chrome ore, and licorice. Englishman C. W. Hall had madder presses and also dealt in figs, valonia, and cotton. The Abbotts and J. B. Patterson were agents for the emery trade. Murray (1878), 255, 256.

19. Walsh (1836), 2:44. M. Çınar Atay, *19 Yüzyıl İzmir Fotoğrafları* (Istanbul, 1997).

20. Senior also was a member of the Athenaeum Club in London, along with Charles Darwin, Charles Lyell, George Grote, George Rawlinson, and Austen Henry Layard. The club was a highly desirable residence in London for those visiting from the East because it provided marvelous social opportunities.

21. Senior (1859), 187.

22. Lord Palmerston wrote on 28 January 1847 advising him that his annual salary would be £300, with liberty to engage in commercial pursuits in lieu of being entitled to any pension upon retirement. PRO/FO 700 28.

23. See, for example, Frangakis-Syrett (1987), 73–86, esp. 73.

24. PRO/FO 195 721; also James Calvert to the U.S. consul general, Constantinople, 10 June 1867, NARA RG84 Dard. 19. Frederick was in league with the Manchester Cotton Association to produce cotton in the Troad during the critical blockade of Southern states in the American Civil War. Frederick Calvert to Lord John Russell, 24 December 1860, PRO/FO 78 1525.

25. Carlisle noted that Frederick Calvert lent money to locals at 20 percent interest. Carlisle (1854), 97. According to Kasaba (1988), 81, this was an acceptable rate for short-term loans. For Lander's loans, see Senior (1859), 156. Carlisle noted that after a bad experience lending to Turks, Calvert lent money only to Greeks and at 20 percent interest. Carlisle (1854), 97; Senior (1859), 157. Frangakis-Syrett (1991a), 409, discusses chronic monetary shortages that encouraged money lending in the Ottoman Empire. See discussion in chapter 1, note 59.

26. Senior (1859), 207–8; London *Times,* 29 August 1862. This was common practice among the consuls of western Anatolia.

27. According to Senior, "Mr. Whittall's great grandmother was 'the Queen of Bournabat, and ruled her subjects with a kindness by no means unmixed with severity.'" Senior (1859), 221. The Whittalls were from Worcester and Liverpool. James Whittall's father, Charlton (1791–1867), had left Liverpool in 1809 for Smyrna, where he founded C. Whittall and Co. in 1811. He was joined in Smyrna by two of his five siblings and began a dynasty there that continues to the present day. McKernan (1997), 1–2; courtesy of his descendant, Brian Giraud. By 1891, they were known as "the principal transit agents" of goods from western Europe to Smyrna and exported raw materials from Turkey to Europe. They ran a local coastal service with lighters, or small boats, and imported coal from Britain to power larger ships. Frangakis-Syrett (1991b), 208.

28. Senior (1859), 207.

29. Slade (1837), 2:298; Senior (1859), 157.

30. At Bulair, where the British troops were stationed, "men swam in the sea, fished and hunted buffalo and wild bear." Christian Hibbert, *The Destruction of Lord Raglan: A Tragedy of the Crimean War* (London, 1961), 29. Later, many would freeze and starve in the cruel Crimean winter.

31. Russell (1858b), 25–30; Sweetman (1984), 45. Of the forty-four agents, Filder had only two experienced subordinates. McNeill and Tulloch (1856), 379.

32. Sweetman (1984), 45.

33. The London *Times* correspondent, William Henry Russell, wrote approvingly of Calvert's efforts on behalf of the British cause. Russell (1858b), 25–30. There were to be 15,000 troops stationed north of Gallipoli at Bulair, of which Frederick volunteered to billet 5000 around the Dardanelles. Frederick Calvert to Stratford de Redcliffe, 18 March 1854, PRO/FO 195 391. He met with Deputy Commissary General Smith on 27 March, and on 6 April suggested using the Abydos lazaretto as the chief depot. Foreign Office documents explicate his activities at this time in exhaustive detail. As a bystander, Russell noted the ineptitude of the Commissariat Corps. Russell (1858b), 25–30. Frederick asked for increased personnel. Calvert to the earl of Clarendon, 25 January 1855, PRO/FO 78 1105. He subsequently installed his brother-in-law, Richard J. W. Abbott, as vice-consul at Gallipoli. Frederick Calvert to Charles Allison, 26 December 1857, PRO/FO 495 192. Sweetman (1984), 45, noted Calvert's excellent planning, which resulted in having all supplies on hand before the troops arrived.

34. Sweetman (1984), 45.

35. Frederick Calvert to Field Marshal Lord Raglan, commander in chief, 25 January 1855, PRO/FO 195 391.

36. Frederick Calvert to the superintendent of consular services, 30 June 1855, and to the earl of Clarendon, 24 November 1856, PRO/FO 78 1105. The Land Transport Corps was instituted to facilitate Commissariat Corps arrangements. When Frederick Calvert was

absent, he placed James Calvert in charge while he assisted Lieutenant Ogilvy of the Land Transport Corps. PRO/FO 195 492.

37. Russell (1858b), 25–30. Walsh had recommended as early as 1833 that merchants in Constantinople band together to sponsor a steam vessel to tow ships through the dangerous passage. Walsh (1833), 2–3, 64–65; (1836), 1:37.

38. Frederick Calvert to Stratford de Redcliffe, 19 and 30 March 1854, PRO/FO 195 391. He even pressed his father-in-law, Richard B. Abbott, into service, having him purchase horses and mules. Frederick Calvert to Stratford de Redcliffe, 18 May and 15 November 1855, PRO/FO 195 492.

39. Pemberton (1962), 167. *Dictionary of National Biography*, s.v. "McMurdo, Sir William Montagu Scott." Panmure Papers 1, 92–95, Scottish Record Office.

40. His remarks were quoted in a letter from Frederick Calvert to Stratford de Redcliffe, 26 January 1856, PRO/FO 195 391.

41. McNeill and Tulloch (1856), 17. Problems arose over payments for a tremendous shipment of hay for Col. McMurdo. Frederick Calvert to the Foreign Office, 4 October 1855, PRO/FO 78 1105. Frederick Calvert to Stratford de Redcliffe, 5 March 1856; PRO/FO 195 492. Frederick Calvert to the earl of Clarendon, 24 November 1856, PRO/FO 195 492. Apparently this risky habit of buying in advance and on credit was common in peacetime in the British communities of western Anatolia. Frangakis-Syrett (1991b), 195.

42. Whittall's 1857 memoir, in Senior (1859), 207.

43. Frederick Calvert to the earl of Clarendon, 9 May 1855, PRO/FO 78 1105.

44. Testimony of James Filder to John McNeill and Alexander Tulloch, 15 May 1856. McNeill and Tulloch (1856), 372. On 20 October, Frederick Calvert was commended by his superior.

45. McNeill and Tulloch (1856), 17. Commissary General Filder reported that large quantities of hay accumulated along the coast from the Dardanelles to the Bay of Salonica. One reason the Commissariat could not move it was that the hay was unpressed. The Commissariat could move only pressed hay but had no presses available. Thus, Calvert was left with debts to his suppliers, and the government would not pay for the hay, because, although gathered, it had not been delivered to the press through its own lack of organization and its inefficiency. McNeill and Tulloch (1856), 372, 378.

46. James Filder to the Treasury Department, 13 September 1854, requesting funds for 2,000 tons of hay, the delivery of which took nine months. Sweetman (1984), 50. Part of the problem was the lack of financial support. Trevelyan admitted that many of Filder's letters had been ignored. Sweetman (1984), 58.

47. For Lord Panmure (1801–1874), see *Dictionary of National Biography*, s.v. "Maule, Fox, second Baron Panmure." McNeill and Tulloch (1856), 17.

48. Conacher (1987), 82. After the critical report was published, the officers who had been criticized protested and were largely exonerated. Sweetman (1984), 44–59. For the chain of command, see Sweetman (1984), chart inside cover.

49. McNeill and Tulloch (1856), 17.

50. Frederick Calvert's response to Smith's inquiry "as to what share . . . or otherwise I may personally have in this transaction" was that "I derive no pecuniary benefit whatsoever from the affair in question." Frederick Calvert to Stratford de Redcliffe, 1 January 1856, PRO/FO 195 492.

51. Whittall's 1857 memoir, in Senior (1859), 207.

52. Calvert to Brigadier General Mansfield, 26 January 1856, PRO/FO 195 492.

53. See the plan of the compound and its relation to the topography in Calvert (1881), figure 1538. In July 1855, Batak Farm was ransacked by marauding mutinous Bashi Bazouks, who plundered everything, destroying crops and attacking the overseer. Frederick Calvert to the Foreign Office, 8 July 1855, PRO/FO 195 391. Frederick Calvert to Stratford de Redcliffe, 8 July 1855, PRO/FO 195 391. At the same time, brigands had attacked Calvert's farms near Kilid Bahr, where the house was quite vulnerable. Frederick Calvert to Stratford de Redcliffe, 7 May 1857, PRO/FO 195 492. John Brunton warned Calvert of an intended raid by mutinous troops set on plundering Calvert's villa at Erenköy in July 1855. Clapham (1939), 47, 64. Frederick Calvert's correspondence to the Foreign Office on 7, 8, and 10 July recorded the general destruction by these Bashi Bazouks. They were also known as "Beatson's Horse," after Colonel Beatson, their commander, and Beatson himself was known briefly as "the Darling of the Bashi Bazouks." Skene (1883), 48–50. When Beatson was removed following a clash with the French at Gallipoli in October 1855, the Bashi Bazouks plagued the area. Schroeder (1972), 268, 342, and PRO/FO 78 1086, 690.

54. "The trade with which I was previously engaged with most satisfactory results to myself, has now fallen into other hands; all my property has been mortgaged, and that, for the purposes of fully and honourably liquidating all my affairs, I have assigned also the amount of my commission which I am entitled to receive in compensation for my services to the Land Transport Corps." Frederick Calvert to the earl of Clarendon, 24 November 1856, PRO/FO 195 492. Smith withheld payment.

55. Frederick Calvert to the earl of Clarendon, 10 March 1856, and to Stratford de Redcliffe, 29 March 1856, PRO/FO 78 1208 and 195 492.

56. Frederick Calvert to Stratford de Redcliffe, 3 July 1856, PRO/FO 195 492. When Henry Calvert was appointed British vice-consul at Alexandria, he chose not to have trading privileges, probably as a result of Frederick's experience. Henry Calvert to the earl of Clarendon, 17 December 1856, PRO/FO 78 1208.

57. Senior (1859), 207–8; London *Times,* 29 August 1862.

58. Records exist in the Public Record Office of the three-day auction on 15 September 1856. They give a description of the object, name of purchase, and amount in Turkish piasters. According to Ken Horton, the 300 acres of land was valued at £15,763.7.2, nurses' dormitories at £30, and lady nurses' dormitories at £60.

59. Brunton's memoir, in Clapham (1939), 71–72. The delay of Lord Panmure's investigation of the Commissariat Corps also plagued Frederick Calvert.

60. Arthur Perkins noted a deficit of £800 having to do with the shipment of hay supplied at Salonica to Calvert's agent and brought him to court in March 1857, PRO/FO 78 1309. On 31 October 1857 he was instructed by the Foreign Office to pay Perkins £1010. PRO/FO 78 1309; Sweetman (1984), 58. Lord Panmure requested his accounting for the sale of the Erenköy hospital and the transfer of money apparently still in his possession. Lord Panmure to Frederick Calvert, 9 April 1857, PRO/FO 78 1309. At this time, Frank Calvert must have been painfully aware of his brother's plight, since he was writing most of his brother's letters.

61. PRO/FO 195 602. On 6 January 1860, Frederick wrote to James Calvert accusing a local individual in the employ of the U.S. consular agency of fraudulently ap-

propriating a large sum of money—several thousand pounds sterling while engaged in the services of the Land Transport Corps during the Crimean War. NARA RG84 Dard. 4.

62. In the Queen's Prison, Southwark. PRO/FO 78 1457 contains several letters from Frederick Calvert there, e.g. to the earl of Malmesbury, 14 February 1859. Frederick Calvert to Lord John Russell, 18 November 1859, PRO/FO 78 1457.

63. Frederick Calvert to Lord John Russell, 31 January and 24 December 1860, PRO/FO 78 1525. Russell offered Calvert the British consulship at Damascus at more than twice his present salary (£700) in 1860, but Calvert attached so many conditions to his acceptance (such as health and the fragility of his commercial credit; 24 December 1860, PRO/FO 78 1525) that Russell treated his conditions as a refusal in 1861. PRO/FO 78 1592.

64. James Murray wrote to Lord John Russell on 8 February 1860 in reference to the Calvert claim of 31 January 1860, PRO/FO 78 1525. Calvert had written to Russell from 118 Cambridge Street, London, the address of his wife's uncle, the timber merchant William Abbott.

65. Hoffray (or Hoffey—it is spelled both ways in the documents), assistant paymaster of the British Treasury, reported on 18 August 1860 that Calvert should receive £2000 in commission and £2851.11.2 in allowance and interest. PRO/FO 78 1525. Hoffray blamed the War Office for not sending out experienced personnel as Calvert had requested, and he found that there was no evidence to justify negligence on Calvert's part.

66. Petition of 1 June 1868, PRO/FO 78 2066.

67. It is at this point that Frederick might have been able to forward funds to Frank Calvert for the purchase of part of the acropolis of Ilium Novum.

68. Senior (1859), 164–65.

69. In 1840, an English merchant from Constantinople bought 5000 acres in Bursa and brought in "adequate stocks of ploughs and farming equipment from England." Kasaba (1988), 145 n. 196; 28 January 1841, PRO/FO 78 441, 240–45. Frederick Calvert mentioned a magnificent estate of 20,000 acres near Cyzicus belonging to a pasha's heirs that could be bought for £5000. Senior (1859), 165.

70. Few attempts at large-scale cultivation were profitable because labor was scarce and costly, and without good roads, it was difficult to get crops to market.

71. Approximately eight miles south of the Dardanelles on the Chersonese, Lords Broughton and Byron observed an estate laid out by a Mr. Willis, an English gentleman, in European taste along a bay near a narrow valley. There was a neat building with offices attached, a courtyard, and many implements and conveniences of an English farm. Willis had transported fruit and garden trees from England, employed an English gardener, and had "created on the shore of the Hellespont a country seat not to be rivalled by any villa on the banks of the Thames." But by 1810 he had lost it to a Muslim. Broughton (1817), 2:214. Land speculations and investments during the cotton boom of the 1860s rarely ended up as long-term ventures. Kasaba (1988), 145 n. 196; 28 July 1860, PRO/FO 78 1533, 273–76. In Smyrna, there were the bankruptcies of G. Maltass in 1853 (PRO/FO 626 1) and Frederick Whittall (1821–1863) in 1861 (PRO/FO 626 3).

72. Senior (1859), 206.

73. Amounts exceeded £24,000, and of this, £14,000 represented simple loans from private individuals. Kasaba (1988), 72–73.

74. Mac Farlane noted the recent decline of British influence—the loss of shipping to the Greeks and Russians, and with it the decline of the British commercial and military fleets. He was convinced that British supremacy on the seas was gone, and that as a result it would be "good night not only to greatness but also to the liberty and independence of Old England." Mac Farlane (1850), 1:27.

75. Frederick Calvert to the Foreign Office, 4 May 1857, PRO/FO 78 1309.

76. He was prone to fever, having suffered from an extreme febrile condition in 1852, and Syria had a dangerous climate. Furthermore, he was needed at home.

77. Of the seven Calvert siblings, only Frederick produced heirs. He had one son, Frederick Richard James Calvert, born in 1853, and three daughters: Alice, born in 1858, Edith, born in 1859, and Laura Florence, born in 1862.

78. Consular reports reflect a series of bad harvests resulting in the Sublime Porte having to send funds to agriculturists for relief in 1861. Frederick Calvert to Sir Henry Bulwer (1801–1872), British ambassador to Constantinople from 1858 to 1865, 21 January 1861, PRO/FO 195 680. And a major fire in 1860 had destroyed the European casino and 120 buildings, including the French, Austrian, Sardinian, Greek, and Danish consulates, and had damaged the customs house, telegraph office, and *khan*, or inn. Damage estimates ran between £60,000 and £70,000. PRO/FO 195 602.

79. Calvert declared: "I feel far more keenly such a humiliating position than the material losses and injury I have sustained whilst conscientiously performing my duty to my Queen and country." Frederick Calvert to Lord John Russell, 1 February 1861, PRO/FO 78 1592.

80. Frederick Calvert to Bulwer, 25 August 1861, PRO/FO 195 680.

81. London *Times*, 29 August 1862, 8, discovered by Robinson (1995), 340.

82. Ibid., 30 August 1862, cited by Robinson (1994), 156, and (1995), 327–28.

83. As Lloyd's agent, Calvert notified the Constantinople office of the report on 28 April. London *Times*, 29 August 1862, 8.

84. Frederick Calvert to William Abbott, 5, 9, and 12 February 1862, published in the London *Times*, 30 August 1862.

85. The Register of Correspondence of the Constantinople Consular Court to the Foreign Office records a petition of 31 March 1862 by Abbott Bros. and correspondence regarding *Abbott Bros.* v. *Consul Calvert* on 11 March and 5 April 1862, PRO/FO 780 380. The actual correspondence has not been located by the author. Robinson (1995), 340.

86. *Dictionary of National Biography*, s.v. "Bulwer, William Henry Lytton, Earle, Baron Dalling and Bulwer."

87. A. Carlton Cumberbatch, consul general, to Frederick Calvert, 25 March 1862, PRO/FO 78 2066. File 2066 discovered by Robinson (1995), 327–28, 340.

88. Cumberbatch to Murray, Foreign Office, 16 April 1862, PRO/FO 78 2066.

89. Murray to Cumberbatch, 28 April 1862, PRO/FO 78 2066.

90. Frederick Calvert to Cumberbatch, 30 April 1862, PRO/FO 78 2066.

91. Foreign Office to Henry Bulwer, 30 April 1862, PRO/FO 78 2066.

92. Cumberbatch to Earl Russell, 4 May 1862, PRO/FO 78 2066.

93. Bulwer would have been partial to the family, since Edmund Calvert for years had been his secretary.

94. Henry Bulwer to Earl Russell, 9 May 1862, PRO/FO 78 2066.

95. Henry Bulwer to Earl Russell, 14 May 1862, PRO/FO 78 2066.

96. Edward VII (1841–1910) had just toured Egypt, where he had presented Frederick's eldest brother, Henry, vice-consul at Alexandria, with a jeweled box containing gold and ruby cufflinks. Passed down for generations in the Calvert family, they recently have resurfaced. Personal communication from Philip Whittall.

97. White (1845), 1:147–48.

98. Henry Bulwer to Earl Russell and Foreign Office to Bulwer, 27 May 1862, PRO/FO 78 2066.

99. Henry Bulwer to Earl Russell, 7 June 1862, PRO/FO 78 2066. London *Times*, 29 and 30 August 1862. Presumably he took up residence somewhere in the Troad with one of the countless local individuals who were in his debt. His reasons for taking such a futile course of action remain unknown. He had wished to carry on his investigation without publicity so as to be able to catch the culprits whom he said had set him up. He apparently was unsuccessful. Why he stayed in hiding for five years is also not known, although it may have been related to the expiration of the statute of limitations for claims on the underwriters mentioned in the Foreign Office memo of 31 October 1867, PRO/FO 78 1998.

100. Henry Bulwer to Earl Russell, 4 July 1862, PRO/FO 78 2006.

101. Foreign Office to Henry Bulwer, 30 June 1862, PRO/FO 78 2066.

102. Grimm (1964), 357 n. 2267.

103. Bulwer to the Foreign Office, 27 May 1862, PRO/FO 78 2066. The warrant was issued on 29 July 1862. PRO/FO 78 2066, cited in a memo of 27 November 1867, PRO/FO 78 1998. The Foreign Office recommended Francis as qualified to examine witnesses by his long service in the Levant.

104. John Fraser to Henry Bulwer, 5 August 1862, PRO/FO 195 21. He lost the Belgian and Dutch positions before the year was out. N. Vitalis and A. Bohor Sidi to James Calvert, 24 November 1862 to January 1863 and 28 May 1863, NARA RG84 Dard. 4.

105. Shamed in society and thwarted in business, James left the Dardanelles for good, fixed his residence in Constantinople in 1872, and resigned his consular office in 1874.

106. PRO/FO 78 4122.

107. James Calvert to John Fraser, 24 July 1862; Hassan Pasha, governor of Biğa Province, to acting British consul John Fraser, 1 August 1862; James Calvert to E. M. Erskine, chargé d'affaires, 18 November 1862. PRO/FO 195 721. James Calvert protested that Turkish officials were impeding his logging operations at Çan, from which he intended to float the fir logs down the Scamander. Cuinet (1894), 3:705.

108. Consular appeal of Fraser's refusal to admit James Calvert as the attorney for Frederick Calvert, "Bankrupt," 10 October 1862, sent by Earl Russell to the Foreign Office, PRO/FO 780/380, correspondence register, no. 14. Because Fraser had omitted "every legal requisite for that purpose," the judgment was annulled on appeal.

109. London *Daily News*, 25 November 1862.

110. *Levant Herald*, 5 and 10 December 1862, PRO/FO 802 614; London *Daily News*, 25 November 1862, discovered by Robinson (1994), 156, and (1995), 327–28. This injustice did not escape the Foreign Office, which received a copy of the article on 10 December 1862. After studying the 8 December report of the trial, Earl Russell wrote to Sir Edmund Hornby on 29 January 1863 relative to the proceedings of the Consular Court in *The Queen* v. *Frank Calvert*. PRO/FO 78 1757. It was Russell, the

British foreign minister, who declared himself not certain if the insult even had been worthy of a misdemeanor, and he noted critically that oral defamation was not often made the subject of a proceeding.

111. Frank Calvert to Charles Newton, 12 February 1862, attests to Calvert's continued connection with Newton. BMGR.

112. Evans (1956), 288. Newton had been sent to the Aegean by Lord Granville of the Foreign Office. Carlisle (1855), 103. Carlisle recorded his visits with Newton to the sites of Lalysos and Trianda on Rhodes before the archaeologist left for his first excavation on Calymnus. This was funded in 1854–55 by Stratford de Redcliffe, who also secured Newton's *firman* while Newton served as acting consul of Rhodes in 1853. Gardner (1896), 133. In 1856, Newton published a site report on Calymnus in volume 13 of the *Archaeological Journal.* After discovering the site of the mausoleum of Halicarnassus at Bodrum, Newton excavated the site and its colossal statues with the generous support of £2000 from the British government. Ibid., 135. A decade later, he would publish his excavations at Halicarnassus, in which he assumed a developmental approach to Greek archaeology that was influenced by Lyell. Turner (1981), 65. He excavated at Cnidus in 1858–59 and Miletus. In 1855, Lord Palmerston had offered him the Regius Professorship of Greek at Oxford in order to create a school of students in Archaeology, but he refused it. *Dictionary of National Biography,* s.v. "Newton, Sir Charles."

113. The letter is not preserved but is mentioned in Calvert's letter to Newton, 24 September 1863, BMGR. Easton (1991), 123–24.

114. Grote (1849), 1:43, 312. Grote also was a trustee of the British Museum. Briggs and Calder (1992), 119–26.

115. *Iliad* 6.242–375.

116. These Zeus had originally given to the king of Troy in exchange for his son Ganymede. The first sack of Troy occurred when the king's descendant, Laomedon, refused to hand over the horses to Herakles as payment for Apollo's and Poseidon's construction of the citadel walls (*Iliad* 5.637–51).

117. Dörpfeld (1902), 230–34; Rose (1992), 49–50. Easton (1991), 125, explains the larger exposed area—Schliemann (1874b), plate 116—as due to Brunton's manpower. See Figure 26a.

118. Easton (1991), 121, 123, suggested that Calvert (1863) and Schliemann (1873) excavated Brunton's trench in square J8 of Dörpfeld's excavation grid, finding Corinthian pillars, sculptured blocks, and inscriptions. Figure 49: Dörpfeld (1902), plate 3. See also Goethert's and Schleif's plan (1962). In Figure 8, Eveline Calvert sits on a Corinthian capital from this area.

119. Callander took charge on 16 September, according to his letter of 12 October 1863 to Henry Bulwer, PRO/FO 195 775.

120. Easton (1991), 124.

121. This would have been in grid squares G–H 3–4. Schliemann later referred to this temple in a letter of 2 May 1872, BB 2.3/17. Cook (1973), 36, 95, and Traill (1993), 102, report wrongly that Calvert began at Troy in 1865. Easton has noted that in Calvert's 13 January 1869 letter to Schliemann, he claimed that he had encountered the pavement of the temple at a depth of "10 to 12 feet." Meyer (1953), #113, 144. In his stratigraphical study, Easton has had difficulty associating this level with any known floor. Easton (1991), 125.

122. The extent of Calvert's property on the mound in 1863 is not known. If he added to the land between 1860 and 1863, he still did not own the higher, western half. Recent re-

search in the Ottoman deeds office at Çanakkale has failed to discover the originals. If he indeed owned the eastern half at this time, then he may have been suing to purchase the higher, western half, the very portion that later eluded Schliemann's grasp, as well. (See chapter 4, note 73.)

123. Easton published part of the letter (1991), 123–24. Wood suggested that Calvert had found a part of the Late Bronze Age city wall on the south slope that he probably thought was classical. Wood (1985), 45. This is in the area of the *bouleuterion,* which straddled it. This is possible, because although Calvert at this point was familiar with prehistoric pottery from Hanay Tepe, he would not necessarily have recognized the walls as prehistoric because they were not cyclopean. Later, Calvert wrote that he thought he had hit bedrock in this area.

124. This is corroborated by Arthur Raby to the Foreign Office, 1 April 1863, PRO/FO 195 775. For the tribunal, see Cuinet, 3:693.

125. This correspondence and the proposal itself were discovered by Wood (1985), 43, 45, and published by Easton (1991), 123. This is also discussed by Traill (1993), 31. Calvert (1874a), 610.

126. Calvert's 1875 statement that he did not attach "any great merit" to the idea of discovering Troy must be interpreted not as his true feeling, but as a rationalization of his subsequent failure to achieve this dream. Calvert (1875).

127. Robinson (1995) emphasizes Newton's omission of Calvert's offer to give all antiquities to the museum as evidence of his trying to discourage the trustees, but Calvert's own letter had been forwarded with Newton's, so this would have been redundant.

128. Calvert had invited Newton at the end of his 24 September 1863 letter. See above.

129. This information comes from Calvert to Newton, 6 November 1863, BMGR. I disagree with Robinson (1995), 329, who sees duplicity in Newton's actions.

130. Minutes of the Standing Committee 10/430, BMCA.

131. Ibid., 10/431.

132. Index to Minutes, vol. 5, January 1858 to December 1865, 120, BMCA, quoted with permission of Christopher Date. Robinson (1995), 340.

133. Calvert wrote on 24 September 1863 (BMCA), 8 October 1863, and 24 January 1864 (BMGR).

134. Strabo, 13.1.11, 42.

135. He also communicated with Newton on 8 October 1863.

136. Charles Newton to Calvert, 3 February 1864, BMGR, Easton (1991), 125, n. 26. Records do not survive to indicate how Panizzi decided to decline Calvert's proposal.

137. Here again, Robinson (1995), 330, has overinterpreted the sources, reading into Newton's correspondence duplicity and prejudice that cannot be proven. There is absolutely no evidence to suggest that Newton caused the trustees to reject Calvert's proposal.

138. De Grummond (1996), 193. This was R. Murdoch Smith.

139. Dyck (1990), 323.

140. Miller (1974), 301–2.

141. Robinson, (1995), 326, overstates the situation when she argues that Newton formed "an instant and apparently lasting mistrust of Calvert's abilities," believing his archaeological abilities "limited" and his education "deficient." His attitude toward the family, reflected in his 1865 publication, was more likely colored by general attitudes after the scandal.

142. Vaux (1863), 398. He referred it before news of the Calvert scandal.

143. Newton may have related the Smyrna/Constantinople gossip to Panizzi privately, but no written record exists between the two from October 1863 to February 1864.

144. B. Routh to Henry Bulwer, 19 July 1864, PRO/FO 195 775. Although Frederick had been declared bankrupt and attempts had been made to seize his property, in fact, little actually belonged to him. The Dardanelles house and subsidiary buildings belonged to Lander's heirs. The villa at Erenköy and its vineyards likewise belonged to them. In each case, Frederick was simply a trustee. Batak Farm also had been purchased with Lander funds. Because a Mr. Carr in London had sued Frederick for £47,000, the deeds were in the hands of Charles van Lennep of Smyrna, the Swedish consul and Frederick's brother-in-law. B. Routh to D. M. Logie, British consul general at Constantinople, 11 March 1865, PRO/FO 195 775.

145. B. Routh to Lord Lyons, 23 January 1866, PRO/FO 195 775.

146. Frank Calvert to Charles Newton, 30 May 1866, BMGR.

147. Korres (1977), 82. For Ziller, see Papastamou (1973); Russack (1942).

148. He used this system because of "the poverty and uncertainty of the topographical data in the *Iliad* and also to avoid the critical objections that an arbitrary choice of ancient names might cause." Although he suggested that he had named features after those "learned writers who had fixed Balli Dagh as the site of the Homeric Pergamus," he knew that Calvert had already refuted it. Von Hahn (1865), Traill (1977), 169–89. Cook (1973), 36, 95. Penny Wilson, librarian of the British School at Athens, graciously showed me an unpublished letter from von Hahn to the ancient historian George Finlay (1799–1875), dated 10 January 1865, which concerned the implications of Calvert's work and the Gergis identification for Pınarbaşı's claim, supported by coins found by von Hahn. Calvert stressed the similarities in wall construction at the Cığrı Dağ site.

149. Calvert (1874a), 610. One cannot imagine, however, that such a purchase could have been possible.

150. Calvert's four trenches are marked "n. 5" on Adolphe Laurent's 1872 plan [Figure 26a]. Schliemann (1874b), plate 116, described by Easton (1990), 433, as "purely impressionistic." These correspond to G 3–4, H 3–4, J–K 3–5, and J 8 in Dörpfeld's (1902) grid, plate 3.

151. Calvert (1873a).

152. Figure 8 on the wall behind Eveline Calvert. Goethert and Schleif (1962), plate 33a.

153. Raking *sima* fragment illustrated in Allen (1996b), plate 20b, with Francis Henry Bacon at the Dardanelles. Goethert and Schleif (1962), plate 15b.

154. Calvert (1875).

155. Easton (1991), 125. Calvert (1874a), 610–11. He also referred to this wall in Calvert (1873a). Easton concluded that it was Roman due to the builder's marks, also found on Dörpfeld's Roman wall in IXM and N (1902), 215–16, which must have extended from Calvert's excavated portion. Easton conjectures that he possibly may have encountered sections of Late Bronze Age fortification walls in his northern trenches.

156. Calvert (1875). These later were obliterated by Schliemann's northern platform.

157. Schliemann (1874b). Easton concludes that Calvert must have come down on the angle of masonry of the superstructure of the northern end of the city wall up to point "c" in Dörpfeld (1902), 144, figure 52. Easton (1991), 125. But significant discrepancies in the size and shape of the northeastern trench, as well as in the inconsistent placement within it of the crucial angle of masonry in later plans, render this issue moot. Adolphe Laurent's plans show an enlarged northeastern trench, probably as a result of Schliemann's extending the

trench to the south. In it, the masonry of the bastion is plotted more to the south. They also show the trench (31) as much smaller, although the angle of the wall is still within the limit of the trench. Schliemann (1874b), 215, also shows a narrower trench and does not include the masonry in it, but it seems to abut it on the south, perhaps the reason why the sounding was not more broad. Laurent's 1872 plans appear in Figures 26a and 26b and Schliemann (1874b), plates 116 and 214, respectively.

158. Calvert (1874a), 611. According to Schliemann, Calvert entered it around 1861. Schliemann subsequently excavated it, finding a vaulted, rock-cut area 18.4 meters long and divided into three passages. During the Roman era, water collected in a central trench and flowed out into a clay pipe, apparently a type of cistern. Schliemann (1881a), 625–26. Korfmann cleared and reexcavated this area and found that it went back about 23 meters. Information courtesy of Maureen Basedow.

159. Calvert (1873a).

160. Calvert, in Greaves (1865b), 337.

161. The gladiator metope stood in the courtyard at Batak Farm for many years. Holden (1964), plate 1, figure 1. Schmidt (1902), nos. 9582–84.

162. "Proceedings," *Athenaeum* 1969, 22 July 1865, 119.

163. Calvert (1874a), 610–11.

164. Calvert, in Vaux (1863), 394–98. A photograph of the site appeared in Leaf (1923), plate 10a, 172.

165. Calvert (1865), 51–57; Thiersch (1902a), site no. 11, 95–97; *Athenaeum* 1960, 20 May 1865, 687. Hence the mistake in the July issue.

166. Namely, the work of Leake, Clarke, and Barker Webb.

167. The descriptions are in Xenophon, *Hellenica*, 3.1.15–28, *Pliny: Natural History*, with an English translation by H. Rackham (Cambridge, Mass., 1958), and Strabo.

168. The article is mentioned in a 12 February 1862 letter to Newton, BMGR.

169. Strabo, 13.1.52–55, Xenophon, *Hellenica*, 3.1.15–28. Calvert (1865a), 53. An illustration of the site appeared in Leaf (1923), plate 16.

170. Thiersch (1902a), 179–80, confirms that Calvert excavated there.

171. Calvert discovered Scepsis on a large, dome-shaped hill commanding the approach to the upper valley of the Scamander River. Clarke had seen remains of a large marble temple of the Doric order there and had bought statues from the site in the nearby town of Bayramiç. Clarke (1817), 3:163–68, 185; Fitzwilliam Museum: nos. 91 and 94; Cook (1973), 345 n. 5. The site was completely pillaged by the 1860s, when Pullan noted only foundations and a few Doric fragments.

172. In 1857, Pullan surveyed the mausoleum remains after Newton's campaign of 1854–56. Then he went to Cnidus in 1857. With the Society of the Dilettanti, he excavated at Teos (1862), the Smintheum in the Troad (1866), and Priene (1869). Pullan noted, "The Troad is full of unidentified sites." He used Smyrna as his base. There, he and his wife lived with John Turtle Wood, who was then working as an architect on the Smyrna-Aydin railway. It was Pullan who introduced Wood to Newton, who later obtained for him the support of the British Museum for his Ephesus excavations. Pullan (1886), 1–10, esp. 8. *Dictionary of National Biography*, s.v. "Pullan, Richard Popplewell." Pullan, who had been a guest at Batak Farm, did not visit the Kurşunlu Tepe site until 1866 and claimed to have identified Scepsis by its position and coins. He ignored Calvert's identification and later gave Calvert's notes to a *John Murray Handbook*. Murray (1878), 148; Pullan (1886), 8–9. Calvert thus never

got credit for the identification; Pullan did, although Calvert had published the identification (embedded though it was) before Pullan arrived. Later Pullan found thirty to forty coins on the site, of which half were of Scepsis. Cook (1973), 345; Pullan (1915), 32, citing a November 1866 letter. Leaf (1923), 270, wrongly credited Pullan with the identification, recording that Calvert agreed with him.

173. Walther Judeich confirmed it with the on-site discovery of a decree naming Scepsis in 1896. Judeich (1898), 231; Robert (1951), 13–15; Cook (1973), 345.

174. An illustration of the site appeared in Leaf (1923), plate 12b. Calvert mentioned the site in letters of 30 May 1866 and 12 August 1874 to Newton and referred to it in his publication of Cebrene. BMGR and Calvert (1865), 53.

175. Murray (1878), 148–49. In 1864, before he learned of his rejection by the museum, Calvert had asked Newton for his opinion and had promised to send Newton a "memoir" on Neandria, but he seems never to have done so. He never published his manuscript on Çığrı. Some finds are in Worcester. Thiersch (1902a), site no. 16, 130–55. Koldewey (1891), 6, credited Calvert with the site identification.

176. He mentioned an argentiferous lead mine on Çığrı Dağ in the notes he gave to Pullan in 1866. Murray (1878), 148.

177. Since the antiquities laws had not changed, presumably Frederick Calvert's previous status had given Frank Calvert a certain immunity with local officials.

178. The French already had established themselves at Salonica, Samothrace, and Assos through architect Edmond Duthoit (1837–1889), who had excavated for the Louvre on Cyprus. Randall Callander to William Stuart, Foreign Office, 2 January 1865, PRO/FO 195 775. See *Dictionnaire de Biographie Française*, s. v. "Duthoit, Edmond-Armand-Marie."

179. Likewise, when the acting British consul at the Dardanelles asked for a leave, Callander noted the only capable stand-ins were the brothers of "his predecessor," both of whom were "perfectly competent and fit for the duty," but he did not even bother to submit their names because they would not have been considered. Randall Callander to William Stuart, 17 February 1865, PRO/FO 195 775. Contrary to Robinson (1995), 334, there is no earlier permit.

180. Calvert to Schliemann, 8 March 1869, B 63/142. The Prince of Wales, as patron of the Archaeological Institute, may also have been personally familiar with Calvert's work. J. F. A. Maling to Lord Lyons, 24 April 1865, PRO/FO 195 775.

181. The *Murray Handbook* for 1878 directed English-speaking tourists, after being "properly introduced," to visit Calvert and see his collection of coins and other antiquities. Murray (1878), 140. Robinson (1994), 159.

182. Greaves (1865a), 171–73, and BLMS 44406. Robinson (1995), 340; Curtius (1873), 133–39; Allen (1996b), 153 n. 69. See *Webster's Biographical Dictionary*, s.v. "Gladstone, William Ewert." Calvert mentioned in his 30 May 1866 letter to Newton that Duthoit, who had traveled with Waddington in Syria, also had tried to secure the "Sestos Inscription" at Yalova, near Sestos, for the Louvre, but that Calvert had gotten there first. BMGR. Allen (1996b), 169. Perrot (1909), 83.

183. *Athenaeum* 1960, 20 May 1865. 687.

184. Frank Calvert to acting British consul J. F. A. Maling, 2 June 1866, confirmed by a vizierial letter of 28 June, and William H. Wrench to Lord Lyons, 6 July 1866, PRO/FO 195 775.

185. James Calvert mentioned the interests of predatory locals in taking advantage of the family. James Calvert to the U.S. consul general, 2 June 1869, NARA RG84 Dard. 1.

The town itself was plagued by cholera in July and a devastating fire in August that left fifteen hundred people homeless and 139 shops destroyed. PRO/FO 78 1937.

186. George Dennis to Lord Stanley, 20 July 1867, PRO/FO 78 1998.

187. The Treasury to the principal librarian of the British Museum, John W. Jones, 2 September 1867, PRO/FO 78 1998. It was not an easy relationship. Dennis called it "a thankless office to work for the Trustees of the British Museum . . . they treat me as though they did me too much honour by allowing me to labour for them, snubbing me at every turn as if I were a clerk in their pay . . . although the claim I make on them, and which they refuse to accept, is only about £100." George Dennis to James Murray, 18 January 1869. Elsewhere he wrote, "To labour for the British Museum, is to return good for evil." Rhodes (1973), 102–3, 106.

188. According to a letter from W. H. Wrench to Lord Lyons, 5 July 1867, Frederick returned to the Dardanelles and was staying at Erenköy as of 16 June. PRO/FO 195 775. Actually, a letter written in Frederick's hand on Calvert Bros. stationery to John H. Goodenow, the U.S. consul general at Constantinople, on 10 June and signed by James proves his earlier presence. Louisa Ann Lander, Mrs. James Calvert, Sr., died on 23 July 1867.

189. James Lane to Lord Stanley and Philip Francis, 9 December 1867, PRO/FO 78 2055. Files 2055 was discovered by Robinson (1995), 332, 340.

190. "The Supreme Consular Court," *Levant Herald*, 19 February 1868, 6.

191. Memo 7828, 31 October 1867, PRO/FO 78 1998.

192. Lord Stanley to Philip Francis, 27 November 1867, case 5084, PRO/FO 78 2055.

193. James Lane to Lord Stanley, 9 December 1867 and 30 January 1868, PRO/FO 78 2055.

194. Lord Stanley to James Lane, 9 January 1868, PRO/FO 780 370.

195. June 1868 petition by Constantinople residents, PRO/FO 78 2066.

196. Acting judge James Lane to Lord Stanley, 26 February 1868, PRO/FO 78 2055.

197. "The Supreme Consular Court," *Levant Herald*, 19 February 1868, 14.

198. Acting judge James Lane to Lord Stanley, 26 February 1868, PRO/FO 78 2055.

199. Ibid.

200. Ibid.

201. Philip Francis to Lord Stanley, 22 March 1868, PRO/FO 78 2055.

202. Ibid.

203. James Murray to Philip Francis, 2 May 1868, PRO/FO 78 2066.

204. Philip Francis to Lord Stanley, 15 August 1868, PRO/FO 78 2055.

205. Philip Francis to Lord Stanley, 23 September 1868, PRO/FO 78 2055. Other complaints about the exorbitant costs were made on 27 November 1867. James Murray for Lord Stanley, PRO/FO 780 370.

206. PRO/FO 78 2066. These were penned by James and Frank Calvert, who identified themselves as merchants on the Dardanelles petition. Robinson (1995), 332.

CHAPTER 6

1. Schliemann was named for a brother who had died in infancy. Calder (1986), 37.

2. Biographical details are from Traill (1993) and (1995). David Turner attributes Schliemann's motivation in the pursuit of fame for discovering Troy to a desire to expunge the shame cast on his family by his father's actions. Turner (1996), 42.

3. Traill (1995), 17.

4. Ibid.

5. See Marchand (1996).

6. Schliemann (1881a), 7.

7. Ibid., 8, and letter to his sisters, 20 February 1842, in Meyer (1953), #1, 27. German original.

8. Traill (1995), 22.

9. Ibid., 23.

10. Ibid., 24 n. 39.

11. Ibid., 25.

12. Ibid. In addition to Sergius, or "Sergei" (1855–1940), there was Natalia (1858–1869) and Nadeshda (1861–1889). At the same time, the Frederick Calverts were having their family.

13. Ironically, his opposition to the Calverts began early.

14. Turner (1990), 40, and Traill (1995), 25.

15. *The Routledge Guide to the Crystal Palace, the Ten Chief Courts of the Sydenham Palace and the Official Guide of 1854;* O. Jones, *Description of the Egyptian Court,* 1854. Curl (1994), 244 n. 24, figures 136, 137.

16. The letter is dated 17 March 1856. Meyer (1953), #47, 81.

17. Turner (1996), 236, quotes a passage from July 1856.

18. Turner (1990), 40.

19. Schliemann (1881a), 15; Schliemann to his aunt, 31 December 1856, in German. In Traill (1995), 27.

20. Draft from before 9 January 1858 of a letter sent on that date to Carl Andress. The passage was shortened in the actual letter. Turner (1996), 236.

21. He left his wife alone with a newborn and a toddler.

22. He focused his attention on Egypt, where he acquired Arabic. Traill (1995), 27.

23. Traill (1995), 27–31, suggests that his campaign to acquire culture originated in his desire to please his wife, but it is truly hard to see that he ever placed her high in his consciousness.

24. Meyer (1953), #62, 95.

25. Meyer (1953), #67, 99.

26. Traill (1995), 28. This experience presumably helped him in later legal difficulties.

27. Meyer (1953), #67, 111. Frederick Calvert had begun to grow cotton at Batak Farm for the same reason.

28. Schliemann to E. Wirths, 10 December 1871, in Meyer (1953), #166, 197.

29. From Carthage, he detoured to Bologna, Florence, Naples, Capri, and Paestum.

30. Not able to resist business temptations, he bought fifty chests of prime-grade indigo in Calcutta. Traill (1995), 29.

31. In Java he had his first ear operation. Traill (1995), 29.

32. Heinrich Schliemann, *La Chine et le Japon* (Paris, 1867); Keyser (1990), 225–36; Carvalho (1992), 29–35.

33. Turner (1990), 41. He later purchased Nicoläides' *La topographie et plan strategique de l'Iliade,* which favored Pınarbaşı as Troy and cited Calvert as an authority. Traill (1995), 32.

34. Schliemann to M. Schröder, 11 February 1868, BBB 27/261; Schliemann to Sergei Schliemann, 20 March 1868. Translated from the French in Traill (1995), 35.

35. On 20 March, a lecturer reviewed von Hahn's excavations on the Ballı Dağ. Turner (1990), 41. It is not known whether Schliemann attended.

36. Schliemann to Sergei Schliemann, 4 April and 27 April 1868, BBB 27/368 and 402.

37. Schliemann to Johanna Diestel, 18 April 1868. Lehrer and Turner (1989), 223.

38. I rely on the analysis of the 1868 diary by Lehrer and Turner (1989). The diary traces Schliemann's growing interest in archaeology as he progressed from Rome to Pompeii and finally to Greece and Turkey.

39. Traill (1995), 37, from Schliemann's Rome diary, 7 May 1868. *Webster's Biographical Dictionary*, s.v. "Fiorelli, Giuseppe." De Grummond (1996), 441–42.

40. *Murray's Guide to Rome and Its Environs.* The Roman section took up seventy out of ninety-two pages. Lehrer and Turner (1989), 224–27; Traill (1993), 5.

41. Lehrer and Turner (1989), 229.

42. Fiorelli had begun work at Pompeii in 1860 and developed his pioneering technique of pouring plaster into voids in the ash in 1864.

43. Lehrer and Turner (1989), 229.

44. "Despite fatigue and hunger I was filled with tremendous joy to find myself in the fatherland of the very hero whose adventures I had read and reread with such fervent enthusiasm." Schliemann (1869), 14.

45. Lehrer and Turner (1989), 231–36.

46. Murray (1854), 86; Lehrer and Turner (1989), 232.

47. Traill (1995), 44.

48. Ibid., 42.

49. But because no other archaeologist has found graves on the site, and because Schliemann later altered and rearranged aspects of the excavation in a published account, Traill suspects the authenticity of his finds and suggests that they were among those that he bought. Traill (1995), 44–46.

50. To protect the remarkable henge monument at Avebury, Lubbock bought the land. For his popular works on archaeology and entomology he was created Baron Avebury in 1899. Stocking (1987), 151.

51. Hutchinson (1914), 51; Stocking (1987), 152–53.

52. Lubbock (1865), 2.

53. Hutchinson (1914), 82.

54. Calvert (1875).

55. Schliemann (1875a), 8, preface dated 31 December 1868.

56. Meyer (1936), #6, 112, in German. Translated in Traill (1995), 56.

57. Calvert to Schliemann, 1 November 1868, B 63/450. Only a portion of the letter was published in Meyer (1953), #110, 140. The entire letter is published in Lehrer and Turner (1989), #1, 263–65.

58. Easton (1982), 93–110, esp. 99. Lehrer and Turner (1989), #2, 265–66, published the letter of 29 October 1868. That of 10 October is lost.

59. Lehrer and Turner (1989), #1, 262–65.

60. Frank Calvert to Schliemann, 11 November 1868, B 63/462; Lehrer and Turner (1989), #3, 266.

61. Published in Meyer (1953), #112, 141–42.

62. Calvert to Schliemann, 13 January 1869, B 63/11. Robinson (1995), 334.

63. This letter (now lost) was published in Meyer (1953), #113, 142–44. Responding also to Schliemann's practical questions, Calvert advised him on wheelbarrows, shovels, and firearms. He then continued: "Coffee and sugar you will find here but not *tea*. The Dardanelles is deficient in luxuries of all kinds if you require them. Good lamb is to be procured at Easter and partly all the year round. Other meat is indifferent."

64. Frank Calvert to Schliemann, 3 February 1869, B 63/49.

65. This was obscured by my misdating to 1868 of the 27 December 1869 letter, B65/317, misfiled at the Gennadius Library. Allen (1995b), 394.

66. The former permit dated not from 1863, as Robinson (1995), 328–29, 334, surmises, but from 1865.

67. Frank Calvert to William H. Wrench, 18 January 1869, PRO/FO 195 938.

68. William H. Wrench to the British ambassador, Henry Elliot, 20 January 1869, PRO/FO 195 938. Cited by Robinson (1995), 334, 340.

69. The Dardanelles position was demoted from full to vice-consul with the appointment of William H. Wrench. Foreign Office to Wrench, 20 March 1866, PRO/FO 78 1937. By 1870, the Ottomans, too, were downsizing their administration after removing Cyprus from the *vilayet*, or province, of the archipelago. William H. Wrench to the British Ambassador, Henry Elliott, 7 July 1870 and 28 November 1871, PRO/FO 195 938.

70. PRO/FO 195 938. It is not known how quickly Calvert heard how it would affect him. The law is dated to March 1869 in Aristarchi Bey (1874), 161, and Young (1905), 388.

71. The museum, which originally comprised the sultan's collection of Eastern arms and military equipment, was housed in St. Irene church until it was moved in 1875 to Tchinli Kiosk. Fehti Ahmed Pasha began collecting works of art in the mid-nineteenth century. De Grummond (1996), 216. The present structure, the Istanbul Archaeological Museum, was built in 1891. Young (1905), 388.

72. Calvert's idea of funding the excavation with the sale of antiquities had been forced on him by hard times.

73. Schliemann to Calvert, 26 December 1868, in Meyer (1953), #112, 141.

74. Calvert to Schliemann, 13 January 1869, Meyer (1953), #113, 142–44, and B 63/11. There are several errors in the published version. In his 3 February 1869 letter, Calvert noted that Lysimachus had rebuilt the temple of Minerva and that the structure "may have still contained some of the materials of the Homeric period." B 63/49. Here he may be referring to an earlier "temple floor" of the Archaic period at a depth of ten to twelve feet in his 13 January 1869 letter. Elsewhere, he wrote that he had hit bedrock under part of the temple foundation.

75. The information is preserved in Calvert (1875).

76. Layard, too, was pressured by finances and later resorted simply to digging for architecture and excavating walls down to the floor, leaving important, but less lucrative, deposits in the interior spaces unexcavated.

77. Schliemann followed this advice in his brief 1870 season.

78. Calvert (1875). By October 10, Schliemann still had not gotten hold of the work of Eckenbrecher or Maclaren.

79. This letter is now lost, but fortunately Calvert quoted it. Calvert (1875). It has been carefully analyzed by Traill. Traill has corrected "July 1869" to be "Jany" (January) of the same year. Traill (1993), 36 n. 26 and 85 n. 36. Thus, he dates it to the time of Schliemann's study in Paris. He notes that the apparatus of learned arguments that Schliemann later ad-

duced in support of his claimed identification of Hisarlık as Troy is not in the diary. Traill (1993), 81. Calvert supplied it in the autumn of 1868 and early 1869.

80. Lehrer and Turner (1989), 232.

81. Lehrer and Turner suggest that at least one or two of the Troad entries were written in Constantinople. They further note that in the 1868 diary Schliemann wrote all the Troad entries in pencil and then in midword on page 148 in the 17 August entry switched to pen. Lehrer and Turner (1989), 245 n. 85.

82. Traill has proved that Schliemann wrote it on 24 August and back-dated it to 12 August. Meyer (1958), #6, 31. Traill (1993), 87–89; Lehrer and Turner (1989), 254 nn. 114–15.

83. John H. Goodenow, the U.S. consul general at Constantinople, had in fact confused Charles Calvert with Frederick in a letter to Hamilton Fish, the secretary of state. NARA RG84, dispatches.

84. Schliemann to George Henry Boker, U.S. minister to Turkey, 4 November 1874, NARA RG84 USLT vol. 287, French original. The entirety of this libelous letter will be published in a catalogue of Schliemann and Boker correspondence. Allen (forthcoming).

85. 8 September 1868. NARA RG84 Dard. 1.

86. Schliemann to Bétolaud de la Drable, 17 September 1868, BBB 27. French original. My translation.

87. Schliemann to Janssen, 30 September 1868, BBB 27. French original. My translation.

88. Schliemann to Adolph Schliemann, 24 October 1868, BBB 27.

89. Schliemann to Calvert, 29 October 1868, BBB 27, and published in Lehrer and Turner (1989), #2, 265–66.

90. Schliemann to Sergei Schliemann, 1 November 1868, BBB 27, and in Meyer (1953), #109, 139. Translated from French original in Traill (1995), 57.

91. Schliemann to Sergei Schliemann, 30 November 1868, BBB 27. French original. My translation.

92. Schliemann to Ernst Schliemann, 9 December 1868, in Meyer (1953), #111, 140.

93. Schliemann (1869), 175.

94. Traill has discussed the lack of correspondence between this account and the diary. Traill (1993), 79–89. See also Lehrer and Turner (1989) and Traill (1993), 29–40 and 73–89. Lehrer and Turner have further shown how Schliemann gave a verbatim recitation of material from von Hahn's report in (1869). They also question whether the Pınarbaşı diary entries of 11 and 12 August may have been written after Schliemann's meeting with Calvert but do not arrive at any conclusion. Lehrer and Turner (1989), 256–57.

95. Schliemann to Calvert, 26 December 1868, in Meyer (1953), #112, 141–42.

96. A "vade mecum" is a guidebook, like a Murray or a Baedeker, literally a "go with me."

97. Calvert to Schliemann, 8 March 1869, B 63/143.

98. James Calvert had to defend the right to keep the family mansion at 21 Hastakhane (Hospital) Street, now in Lavinia Calvert's name, to Ahmed Pasha, the governor general of the archipelago. James Calvert to the U.S. consul general, 2 July 1869, NARA RG84 Dard. 1.

99. James Calvert had asked the U.S. consul general at Constantinople for promotion to the rank of consul with a salary of $750, noting that he had for twenty years served at that post in a subordinate consular capacity. James Calvert to John H. Goodenow, 1 June 1867, NARA RG84 Dard. 1. He was refused on 4 June. Henry Calvert was "exiled" in Jedda and repeatedly denied promotion. Henry Calvert to Hekekyan Bey, 2 May 1865, BLMS

36468/302; Henry Calvert to Austin H. Layard, 2 November 1861, BLMS 39101/217; Henry Calvert to the earl of Clarendon, 7 December 1868, PRO/FO 78 2043. Edmund, unable to find employment, became dependent on the family. Charles Calvert's name also was tainted by the scandal.

100. Frank Calvert to Schliemann, 3 February 1869, B 63/49.

101. James Calvert to Charles Newton, 25 August 1868, BMGR. No response by Newton to Calvert's letter is preserved.

102. Calvert to Schliemann, 1 November 1868, B 63/450. Lehrer and Turner (1989), #1, 263–65.

103. Schliemann to Baron J. J. de Witte, 16 December 1868, BBB 27. French original. My translation. De Witte was a cofounder of the *Gazette Archéologique* in 1875. Schliemann to J. Lichtenstein, 16 December 1868, BBB 27. Their responses were received on 30 January 1869, B 63/39, and 5 February 1869, B 63/63, respectively.

104. Schliemann's sources were correct. Between 1864 and 1874, Newton purchased five important collections, two from Castellani, plus the Farnese, Pourtales, and Blacas Collections for more than one hundred thousand pounds. Calvert's collection was diminutive by comparison. "They gave me at the same time the following names, Mr. Julius Friedländer director of the museum of Berlin; Mr. I. Gredianow Director of the museum of St. Petersburg; Mr. le Comte de Nieuwerkerke director of the museum at Paris." Schliemann to Calvert, 24 December 1868, BBB 27. It is not known whether Calvert ever corresponded with Friedländer or Gredianow. Either he or Frederick already had corresponded with the director of the Imperial Museum of France as much as thirteen years earlier. There are no later letters preserved at the Louvre from Calvert.

105. Ibid. It is not likely that Schliemann pursued individuals in the art world during the unhappy trip to Saint Petersburg that precipitated the dissolution of his marriage in December 1868. Traill (1995), 59–60.

106. Calvert to Schliemann, 13 January 1869, B 63/11.

107. "There are few consulates here of which I have not at one time or another had the 'gerance' [management]." Calvert to Schliemann, 8 March 1869, B 63/143.

108. Schliemann to Calvert, 12 March 1869, BBB 28, inserted loose sheet. Lehrer and Turner (1989), #5, 262 n. 141, 267. He wrote again on 14 April 1869: "I am exceedingly sorrow not being able to assist you in any way to obtain the Prussian v. consulate for I have neither relations nor acquaintances at Berlin." Partially published by Meyer (1953), #118, 147.

109. Traill (1993), 65–71.

110. His cousin, Adolph Schliemann, had friends at the University of Rostock and had given a copy of *Ithaque* to a professor there. Schliemann further submitted on request Greek and Latin versions of the autobiographical introduction to the work. Schliemann to Adolph Schliemann, 12 March, in Meyer (1936), #7, 112, and Traill (1995), 64.

111. Traill (1995), 64, notes that the examiners awarded it because of the topographical discussion of Ithaca, not knowing that the very topographical descriptions and commentary for which he received the degree were in some cases "mere translations of Murray" and in others "moulded from beginning to end by the poetic depiction of the island in Murray's guide." Lehrer and Turner (1989), 235. For his Latin *vita, see* Calder (1973/1974), 271–82, and (1975/1976), 117–18.

112. Traill (1995), 63, accuses Schliemann of producing false testimony.

113. On 29 July 1869. Chambers (1990), 403 n. 31.

114. They wed on 23 September and honeymooned in October. Traill (1990), 430.

115. Frank was writing letters in Italian for James Calvert. NARA RG84 Dard. 1. James wrote on 8 September 1869 to thank Schliemann for some information he had sent for Frank on terra-cottas from Tarsus and the tumuli of Panticapaion (Kerch), now being excavated by Treister and Tolstikov. B 64/334.

116. He stated that Schliemann's letters of 29 October and 6 December had been received. They have not, however, been preserved. In early December, Schliemann's elder daughter, Natalia, died at the age of eleven in Saint Petersburg. Schliemann tried to divert grief into action.

117. Calvert congratulated Schliemann on his marriage and noted that he never had visited Greece himself. He also reminded Schliemann of his promise to make inquiries on his behalf concerning the Tarsus terra-cottas in the Louvre. B 65/317.

CHAPTER 7

1. Calvert had volunteered to persuade them to allow excavation already in 1869. Frank Calvert to Schliemann, 13 January 1869, B 63/11.

2. Meyer (1953), #131, 164; Schliemann (1870), 2301. Translated in Traill (1995), 78.

3. Schliemann's 1870–1872 diary in the Gennadius Library of the American School of Classical Studies in Athens, French original, 28/9 April 1870, 66. Traill's analysis of Schliemann's excavations in 1870 is highly selective and omits important evidence for understanding his development as an archaeologist. In addition to its many lacunae, his account is exceedingly biased. Traill (1995), 74–83.

4. Meyer (1953), #129, 163–64. Schliemann explained himself later in a letter to Calvert on 2 May 1872: "The other half being higher, it struck me there ought to be the king's palace." BB 2.4/17.

5. Schliemann to Frank Calvert, 17 February 1870, BBB 29/20–21, partially published in Meyer (1953), #129, 161.

6. "Perhaps without the firman excavations might be made although always there would be the possibility of the works being stopped, and I do not like advising you to undertake the enterprise unless everything is clear." Frank Calvert to Schliemann, 23 February 1870, B 65/77.

7. Schliemann to Frank Calvert, 26 February 1870, BBB 29/23.

8. Schliemann's 1870–1872 diary, 65–67; Calvert to Schliemann, 16 April 1870, B 65/123.

9. Schliemann's 1870–1872 diary, 66, 70, 72; Schliemann to Frank Calvert, 21 November 1870, BBB 29/288.

10. Schliemann's 1870–1872 diary, 80. The Turks returned the money and once again ordered him to refill the trenches.

11. Schliemann (1875a), 316. This oblong sounding was obliterated by Schliemann's 1871 excavations in the same area.

12. Schliemann's 1870–1872 diary, 66–69.

13. Schliemann's 1870–1872 diary, 69–70. Translation in Traill (1995), 78.

14. Schliemann's 1870–1872 diary, 76–84.

15. According to Donald Easton, both of these are Late Bronze Age structures (the fortification wall segment in Dörpfeld's grid D–E 3–4 and the structure later named "VIB Megaron" in A–B 4–5). Both are recorded in Schliemann's plan 2 (1875a), where the struc-

ture (later called Megaron VIB), Figure 26b, no. 36, is Schliemann's "Hellenic Tower." Easton (1990), 436.

16. Schliemann, "Les fouilles de Troie," *Levant Herald,* 3 June 1870, 142. This article and one with the same title printed on June 2 were translations of Schliemann (1870), a selective rewriting of his diary entries.

17. Although he mentions anticipating a visit from Frank Calvert during his excavations, he does not note whether Calvert came, or if he did, what they discussed.

18. Calvert (1874a) and Calvert to William Simpson 19 July 1878, Simpson Collection, the Mitchell Library, Glasgow. The *Augsburger Allgemeine Zeitung* printed Schliemann's article in its 24 May 1870 edition.

19. Frank Calvert to Schliemann, 16 April 1870, B 65/123.

20. Calvert (1874a). It is not clear whether Calvert actually visited the mound at that time.

21. Frank Calvert to Schliemann, 3/15 April 1870, B 65/121.

22. Schliemann to Frank Calvert, 14/26 April, BBB 29/60–61, partially published in Meyer (1953), #133, 169–70.

23. Schliemann's 1870–1872 diary, 89–91. Their sojourn at the Sublime Porte was from 29 April to 3 May 1870.

24. James Calvert to Schliemann, 27 April 1870, B 66/213, partially published in Meyer (1953), #134, 170. Because this letter apparently was lost, he repeated his observations in a later letter.

25. Ibid.; Frank Calvert to Schliemann, 11 May 1870, B 66/105.

26. Schliemann to Frank Calvert, 2 June 1870, B 2.3/1 and BBB 29/97; partially published in Meyer (1953), #136, 171–72; Schliemann to Frank Calvert, 10 June 1870, BBB 29/101.

27. Schliemann to Frank Calvert, 12 July 1870, BBB 29/152.

28. Frank Calvert to Schliemann, 20 July 1870, B 65/213, partially published in Meyer (1953), #139, 173.

29. Frank Calvert to Schliemann, 11 May 1870, B 66/105, partially published in Meyer (1953), #1, 171. His efforts are mentioned in a number of subsequent letters, for example 20 July 1870, B 65/213, in Meyer (1953), #139, 173. On 2 June 1870, Calvert had lobbied William H. Wrench to bring pillaging to the attention of the British ambassador. Wrench did so on 4 June. In that letter, he credited Calvert with twice stopping the destruction of Alexandria Troas and with suspending the demolition of Assos indefinitely. "Orientals in general look upon ancient buildings solely as quarries where the stones have providentially been prepared for their use. . . . Alexandria Troas and Assos have suffered more from the Acts of the Government itself than by the depredations of the peasants . . . villagers threatened to demolish remains of ancient city walls at Ilium Novum to build a bridge in the neighbourhood, walls supposed by some persons to be those of ancient Troy, the site of which was subsequently occupied by Ilium Novum." PRO/FO 195 938. As a result of his efforts, Ambassador Elliott recommended action. Robinson (1995), 340.

30. Schliemann to Frank Calvert, 14/26 April 1870, BBB 29/60–61, partially published in Meyer (1953), #133, 169–70. Frank Calvert to Schliemann, 14 June 1870, B 65/77, partially published in Meyer (1953), 328 n. 237.

31. Frank Calvert to Schliemann, 23 February 1870, B 65/77; Schliemann to Frank Calvert, 2 June 1870, BB 2.3/1, partially published in Meyer (1953), #136, 171–72.

32. Schliemann (1870), 2301–2.

33. Schliemann, "Les fouilles de Troie," *Levant Herald*, 3 June 1870, 142.

34. Frank Calvert to Schliemann, 20 July 1870, B 65/214; partially published in Meyer (1953), #39, 173 and 328 n. 241. Frank Calvert's source in Constantinople was his brother Edmund.

35. Frank Calvert to Schliemann, 10 August 1870, B 65/242.

36. Meanwhile, Schliemann had sent an engraving to Edmund Calvert, an amateur artist. Edmund was facilitating the *firman* process in Constantinople. Frank Calvert to Schliemann, 10 August 1870, B 65/242.

37. Edmund's remarks are quoted in Frank Calvert to Schliemann, 17 August 1870, B 65/246.

38. Frank Calvert to Schliemann, 17 August 1870, B 66/246. As late as 21 September, however, Edmund Calvert reported that Safvet Pasha was "inabordable" and Mr. Goold, the museum director, was much "*froissé*" because of his actions and the articles he had written about them. Edmund Calvert to Schliemann, 21 September 1870, B 65/270; Meyer (1953), #39, 178 and 328 n. 240.

39. Schliemann to Frank Calvert, 29 July and 25 August 1870, BBB 29/188, BBB 29/189, partially published in Meyer (1953), #140, #142, 174–75.

40. Edmund Calvert found a teacher for him. Edmund Calvert to Schliemann, 28 December 1870, B 65/320. By 1 January 1871 he knew some six thousand words. Schliemann to Sophia Schliemann, in Meyer (1953), #144, 177. French original. Schliemann arrived on 6/18 December 1870. On 9/21 December, he met Frederick Calvert, who recently had been released from prison. Schliemann's 1870–1872 diary, 134, 138.

41. Schliemann had bargained the Kum Kale Turks down to 5000 piasters and expected to purchase their half when he discovered that Safvet Pasha got them to sell for 3000 piasters. Schliemann to George Henry Boker, 4 November 1873, NARA RG84 USLT 287. On the same trip he visited John Turtle Wood's excavations at Ephesus.

42. Schliemann wrote Frank Calvert concerning the purchase of the Turks' land on 14/26 April; 2, 10, June; 29 July; and 25 August 1870. Meyer (1953), #133, #136, #140, #142, 171–72, 174, 175, 328 n. 239. The letter of 10 June 1870 is unpublished, BBB 29/101, #142.

43. This fund had been established in 1865 to aid in the funding of excavations in the Holy Land. Evans (1956), 288.

44. One *dönüm* is the equivalent of 0.247 acre, or more roughly one-quarter of an acre. İnalçık (1978), 227; Shaw (1976), 120. Calvert's desire to keep the pasturage on the plain suggests a possible intention to farm the land in the future. Frank Calvert to Schliemann, 11 May 1870, B 66/105. Calvert reiterated his offer. Frank Calvert to Schliemann, 14 June 1870, B 65/77. Robinson (1994), 160, and (1995), 335.

45. Schliemann to Frank Calvert 23 June 1870, BBB 29/127. The property originally had cost only £300. Senior (1859), 164. But he had added to it piecemeal. The additional expenditures are unknown. Although he may subsequently have purchased his half of the acropolis in 1860–61, no deeds have surfaced to confirm this.

46. Schliemann to Frank Calvert, 21 November 1870, BBB 29/288 89.

47. Frank Calvert to Schliemann, 20 July 1870, B 65/214.

48. Frank Calvert to Schliemann, 23 February 1871, B 66/41. Perhaps Calvert had approached the Ottoman government about selling his collection in 1870 to finance the same project, but since that had fallen through thanks to Schliemann, he needed to seek other funding sources.

49. Because mining was a risky business needing considerable capital and organization before returns were realized, the activity was dominated by a relatively small number of well-capitalized entrepreneurs. Frangakis-Syrett (1991), 214–19, discusses British mining concerns in Smyrna. She focuses on the activities of Ernest Abbott, who was active in mining in western Anatolia beginning in 1849–50, when he received his first concessions for antimony, zinc, and lead. Although emery was his largest product, Abbott also mined chrome, antimony, manganese, zinc, silver, lead, lignite, mercury, copper, and gold. Although Calvert's exact relationship to Abbott is not known, the two men were at least close friends, if not associates, and Calvert stayed with Abbott when he was in Constantinople. Frank Calvert to Schliemann, 23 March 1873, B 68/91.

50. Frank Calvert to Schliemann, 23 February 1871, B 66/41.

51. He proceeded in the letter to outline just how a foreign male could go about purchasing the land. Frank Calvert to Schliemann, 12 December 1871, BB 66/296, partially published in Meyer (1953), #167, 197–98. In fact, British capitalist farmers had bought as much as one-third of all cultivable land in the Smyrna hinterland, thanks to a modification of the Ottoman land code in 1866. Pamuk (1994), 198.

52. He wrote, "For, if I succeed to find Troy—of which I feel confident—I will at once get up a society, and I will then do all in my power to get you a very big price for your half of the Pergamos of Priamos." Schliemann to Frank Calvert, 3 January 1872, BB 2.3/4, partially published in Meyer (1936), #17, 119. On 11 August 1874 a protocol was signed enabling U.S. citizens to own real estate in the Ottoman Empire. V. Stamatiades, U.S. vice-consul general in Constantinople, to Frank Calvert, 25 August 1874, NARA RG84.

53. In the same letter, he wrote that James had left the Dardanelles for Constantinople for good. Frank Calvert to Schliemann, 6 March 1872, B 67/96.

54. Frank Calvert to Schliemann, 4 May 1872, B 67/156.

55. "I . . . am sorry to see that we cannot combine anything together about my land." Frank Calvert to Schliemann, 7 May 1872, B67/160. Contrary to Robinson (1995), 335–36, Calvert did genuinely need the money, and he was obliged to sell his land. By 1894 he had only eighty acres left.

56. Schliemann to Frank Calvert, 12 March 1871, in Meyer (1953), #150, 183–84.

57. Mac Veagh, a jurist from Pennsylvania, served as U.S. minister to Turkey in 1870 and 1871. *Webster's Biographical Dictionary,* s.v. "Mac Veagh, Wayne Isaac." The United States was not yet among the top powers and so had only a minister, not an ambassador. It is not known whether Schliemann made gifts of antiquities to Mac Veagh, as he later did to his successor, George Henry Boker.

58. Schliemann to Mac Veagh, 12 March 1871, in Meyer (1953), #151, 184–85.

59. Schliemann to Safvet Pasha, 18 June 1871, in Meyer (1953), #153, 186.

60. "Since I last had the pleasure of seeing you, I visited your excavations at Hissarlik." Frank Calvert to Schliemann, 10 May 1871, B 66/103; Calvert (1874a).

61. As a consequence of their relative elevation in the section [Figure 27], Calvert must have been referring to buildings in the top meter of earth.

62. The thick walls on the northern perimeter were the same, but only the marble superstructure dated to the Hellenistic or Roman era. At least a part was founded on remains of the Bronze Age. Eventually, Schliemann called the section of the fortification wall a "bastion," a "splendid wall, a tower, of large hewn stones from the first period of the Greek colony." The marble blocks on the top he dated to the time of Lysimachus. Reports of 10 May and 17 June 1873, in Schliemann (1875a), 316, 322–23.

63. Schliemann to Frank Calvert, 31 May 1871, BBB 29/300. Andromache Schliemann was originally called "little Clytemnestra." Schliemann to Wayne Mac Veagh, 29 May 1871, BBB 29/287. For erosion, see Calvert to Schliemann, 12 December 1871.

64. Frank Calvert to Schliemann, 13 September 1871, B 66/216, partially published in Meyer (1953), #155, 187 and 329 n. 255. For Schliemann's long and difficult relationship with the Prussian Academy, see Hermann (1990), 144–56.

65. Schliemann to Frank Calvert, 25 April 1871, BB 2.3/2, partially published in Meyer (1936), #12, 116.

66. Schliemann to Frank Calvert, 19 June 1871, BBB 29/312.

67. Schliemann to John P. Brown, 3 June 1871, BBB 29/302. Schliemann to Frank Calvert, 7/19 June 1871, BBB 29/312.

68. Schliemann to Brown, 11 July 1871, BBB 29/340.

69. The considerable correspondence between Schliemann and Brown at the Gennadius Library of the American School of Classical Studies is largely unpublished. See Allen (forthcoming).

70. Schliemann to Frank Calvert, 12 August 1871, BB 2.3/3.

71. Schliemann to John Brown, 5 October 1871, in Meyer (1953), #156, 187–88.

72. Schliemann to John Brown, 8 October 1871, in Meyer (1953), #157, 188–89.

73. Schliemann to Frank Calvert, 12 August 1871, BB 2.3/3, partially published in Meyer (1953), #154, 186.

74. Schliemann to John Brown, 5 October 1871, in Meyer (1953), #156, 88.

75. Schliemann to John Brown, 8 October 1871, in Meyer (1953), #157, 188–89.

76. Although he later reported that Sophia was present from morning to night at the excavations, she never arrived. Schliemann (1875a), 61–63; Traill (1995), 86, 88. In fact, she had just had a baby.

77. Schliemann (1875a), 63–64. Nicholas Zaphyros Yannakis acted as his personal servant and paymaster.

78. Ibid., 61–64; Schliemann to John Brown, 5 and 8 October 1871, in Meyer (1953), #156, #157, 188–89.

79. Schliemann to James Calvert, 29 October 1871, BB 2.4/8.

80. Schliemann to James Calvert, 30 October 1871, BB 2.4/9, partially published in Meyer (1936), #14, 117–18.

81. Schliemann to James Calvert, 7 November 1871, BB 2.4/10; partially published in Meyer (1953), #160, 190–91.

82. Schliemann (1875a), 43, 92; Frederick Calvert to Schliemann, 19 November 1871, B 66/277. Presuming Frederick served his full prison sentence, he would have returned in the spring of 1870, although he did not meet Schliemann until December. Schliemann's 1868 diary, 138. As was Schliemann's custom, he wooed Frederick with antiquities. Frederick responded on 19 November 1871: "Half a dozen objects which you do not require will be quite sufficient for me. I wish to house them here in a room which I shall actually reserve for all objects of antiquity found in the neighborhood." B66/277.

83. Schliemann to James Calvert, 18 November 1871, BB 2.4/13.

84. James Calvert to Schliemann, 8 November 1871, BB 66/261, partially published in Meyer (1953), #161, 192–93.

85. Schliemann (1875a), 62–74. Easton has suggested that the quadrangular building might have been the temple visited by Alexander, the precursor to Lysimachus's temple. Easton (1990), 437.

86. Report of 3 November 1871, in Schliemann (1875a), 77–80.

87. Schliemann to James Calvert, 7 November 1871, BB 2.4/10.

88. Frank Calvert to Schliemann, 7 and 16 July 1872, B 67/186 and B 67/233.

89. Schliemann's 1870–1872 diary, 242. Translated in Traill (1995), 89–90.

90. James Calvert cited nineteenth-century ethnographic parallels for the use of stone tools. James Calvert to Schliemann, 8 November 1871, B 66/261.

91. Schliemann (1875a), 81–85, figures 45a–g and 46.

92. Schliemann to John Brown, 11 November 1871, in Meyer (1953), #162, 193.

93. Schliemann to James Calvert, 14 November 1871, BB 2.4/12, partially published in Meyer (1936), #15, 118; Schliemann (1875a), 70–71, 92–97.

94. James Calvert to Schliemann, 11 November and 15 November 1871, B 66/265, B 66/277.

95. Schliemann to James Calvert, 7 November 1871, BB 2.4/10. Report of 18 November 1871, in Schliemann (1875a), 92. Cook places Ilion Kome at Kara Tepe about 12 kilometers northeast of Pınarbaşı and 10 east of Hisarlık. Cook (1973), 109–11.

96. Report of 24 November 1871, in Schliemann (1875a), 92–97.

97. Frustrated by the immense problem of disposal of dumped soil, Schliemann continued, "I shall build there a tramway [as he had witnessed at Pompeii] and carry on those diggings on a vast scale, for my success at Troy makes me a 1000 times more joy than the most lucky business-operation I ever made in my life." Schliemann to E. Wirths, 11 November 1871, in Meyer (1953), #166, 197. He did not build the tramway until the 1880s.

98. Report of 18 November 1871, in Schliemann (1875a), 82–85.

99. Schliemann to James Calvert, 14 November 1871, BB 2.4/12, partially published in Meyer (1936), #15, 118. "The deeper I dig the more civilisation I find." Schliemann to James Calvert, 19 November 1871, BB 2.4/14.

100. "Already now they write me enthusiastic letters, offering me every assistance, but, of course, I decline all help because for these small excavations I do not require it. But to clear away all the rubbish from above the virgin soil of the hill, that I had better leave to the Σύλλογος, and am merely the director of the works." In the same letter he offered Frank the opportunity "to pick out whatever he may wish to have for his museum." Schliemann to James Calvert, 21 November 1871, Schliemann, BB 2.4/15; partially published in Meyer (1936), #16, 118–19. But all that he had left were undecorated coarse wares.

101. Frank Calvert to Schliemann, 12 December 1871, in Meyer (1953), #167, 197. Wood incorrectly credited Newton with leading Schliemann to use pottery dating (1985), 66. Neither Döhl (1986) nor Bloedow (1992), who both have praised Schliemann for his observation of pottery, have admitted Frank Calvert's contributions to Schliemann's later methodology. See Allen (1995b), 398. The letter from Emile Burnouf (1821–1907), director of the Ecole Française Archéologique d'Athènes from 1867 to 1875, which Bloedow cites as crucial for Schliemann's development, postdates those from Calvert. Burnouf had told Schliemann that "you must save these large vases, always with an indication of the stratum in the earth where you found them. This is very important in connection with all the objects which you discover . . . because . . . it will be necessary for you to put back together everything which you have found, namely into the same level. Otherwise you will not be able to draw any specific conclusions from your magnificent discoveries. . . . Only the position occupied by an object in the excavations can truly indicate its date." Burnouf to Schliemann, 8 May 1872, in Meyer (1953), #179, 209. French original. Translated in Traill (1995), 93–94. For

Burnouf, see Masson (1995), 36–37, and *Webster's Biographical Dictionary*, s.v. "Burnouf, Emile Louis."

102. Schliemann to Frank Calvert, 3 January 1872, BB 30/174.

103. Two years earlier, Schliemann had written to Frank Calvert that he would bring from Rome or Pompeii "a pioneer in the excavating-business—or perhaps better an engineer so as to accomplish the grand work with greatest possible success." Schliemann to Frank Calvert, 14/26 April 1870, in Meyer (1953), #133, 169–70. Laurent had worked on the Athens-Piraeus railway. Meyer (1936), 123 n. 3.

104. Report of 5 April 1872, in Schliemann (1875a), 98–99; Schliemann to John Turtle Wood, 26 April 1872, in Dyck (1990), #1, 331.

105. Report of 25 April 1872, in Schliemann (1875a), 107.

106. Schliemann to Brown, 26 April 1872, BBB 30/374.

107. Schliemann to Brown, 19 March 1872, BBB 30/328.

108. Report of 25 April 1872, in Schliemann (1875a), 108.

109. Philip Smith, "Preface," Schliemann (1875a), vii. Smith was the son of William Smith, whose *Dictionary of Greek and Roman Biography and Mythology* (1844) was one of Frank Calvert's standard references.

110. Report of 25 April 1872, figure 71, in Schliemann (1875a), 110.

111. Report of 13 July 1872, in Schliemann (1875a), 194.

112. Frank Calvert to Schliemann, 8 April 1872, B 67/131.

113. Schliemann to Frank Calvert, 21 April 1872, BB 2.3/8.

114. In a letter to John Turtle Wood, Schliemann claimed that he never said that he had found Troy. If the city existed—and he was willing to swear that it had—he now claimed that the mound in which he was digging was its acropolis. Schliemann to Wood, 26 April 1872, in Dyck (1990), 329–30. His denial is rather odd, considering that in 1870 his *Augsburger Allgemeine Zeitung* article claiming to have found Priam's Pergamos was entitled "Excavations in Troy." Schliemann (1870), 3309.

115. Schliemann to Frank Calvert, 17/29 April 1872, BB 2.3/9, partially published in Meyer (1936), #18, 119.

116. Frank Calvert to Schliemann, 30 April 1872, B 67/149.

117. Schliemann to Frank Calvert, 2 May 1872, BB 2.3/10, partially published in Meyer (1936), #19, 120.

118. Schliemann to Frank Calvert, 6 May 1972, B 67/153; partially published in Meyer (1936), #19, 120.

119. Report of 25 April 1872, in Schliemann (1875a), 109.

120. Frank Calvert to Schliemann, 13 April and 16 July 1872, B 67/135 and B 67/233.

121. Report of 25 April 1872, in Schliemann (1875a), 117.

122. Report of 23 May 1872, in Schliemann (1875a), 133. Blegen (1964), 91, dated it to between 2200 and 2050 B.C. and believed it to be the palace of Troy's third stratum.

123. There is some confusion here, for Traill records a pin, an earring, and three rings. Traill (1995), 99, 100. Easton admits Schliemann occasionally bundled his finds in 1872. In this case, the gold from the second stratum is combined with a female skeleton found on 16 July. Report of 4 August 1872, in Schliemann (1875a), 210; Schliemann's 1870–1872 diary, 17–18; Easton (1984b), 200–201.

124. He did not announce the find in his 23 May, 18 June, or 23 July 1872 reports and freely admitted to Wood that he had not mentioned these items to the Turks. Schliemann

to John Turtle Wood, 6 August 1872, in Dyck (1990), #2, 332–33. Later, this was known as "Treasure R." Götze (1902), 246–47. The story appeared in the 8/20 August 1872 issue of *Ephemeris ton syzeteseon*. This casual behavior is all the more strange since he had just received Emile Burnouf's admonition to note carefully the exact spot of finds.

125. Schliemann to Frank Calvert, 25/6 June 1972, BB 2.3/15, partially published in Meyer (1953), #183, 210–11.

126. Schliemann (1875a), 170–72.

127. Report of 11 May 1872, in Schliemann (1875a), 128.

128. Schliemann (1875a), 166–67.

129. Report of 18 June 1872, in Schliemann (1875a), 149–50, figures 111–12, 149, 164–65. Fortunately, at Burnouf's urging, he began to indicate the depth of significant finds in his diary, although he later revised some by five meters. Easton (1984b), 200–201.

130. Schliemann (1875a), 153–57, figures 83–110.

131. Schliemann's 1870–1872 diary, 379. Translated in Traill (1995), 94.

132. In 1872, he submitted nine, in Greek only, to the Athenian paper; he intended to publish a book in German. Schliemann to Sir John Lubbock, 14 November 1872, in Hutchinson (1914), 142.

133. Traill (1995), 92 n. 14. The accounts in the diary match the published reports rather well. Traill (1995), 101, meticulously notes when they disagree, despite his selective treatment of Schliemann's 1870 excavations. For the listing of Schliemann's articles, see Korres (1974).

134. Report of 11 May 1872, in Schliemann (1875a), 34–35, 113–15, figures 10–13, 70.

135. Bloedow (1992), 211.

136. "What period would you attribute to the fine pottery you find at such tremendous depth? this would certainly be a guide to your discovery in what age you are working." Frank Calvert to Schliemann, 7 June 1872, B 67/221.

137. Frank Calvert to Schliemann, 10 June 1872, B 67/188.

138. Reports of 25 April and 18 June 1872, in Schliemann (1875a), 116, 147. Photidas, a resident of Paxos, had considerable experience in mining and tunneling, which Schliemann believed would be quite useful at Hisarlık. Photidas also copied the Greek reports for the newspapers.

139. Published in Schliemann (1874b). This was fortunate for Frank Calvert, since Schliemann later denied their existence. Schliemann (1875a), 273.

140. Report of 18 June 1872, in Schliemann (1875a), 144.

141. Schliemann followed Calvert's Lysimachean date. Reports of 18 June 1872 and 15 March 1873, in Schliemann (1875a), 147, 240. Easton suggests, however, that Schliemann's large quadrangular building of hewn stone with three inscriptions may have been an earlier temple. Easton (1990), 436.

142. Report of 18 June 1872, in Schliemann (1875a), 145; Frank Calvert to Schliemann, 14 June 1872, B 67/196; Traill (1993), 97–124. In 1986, Traill published a detailed study of the correspondence surrounding the discovery of the metope. Reprinted in Traill (1993), 97–125.

143. Frank Calvert to Schliemann, 14 June 1872, B 67/197.

144. Published in Traill (1993), 103–4.

145. Frank Calvert to Schliemann, 16 July 1872, B 67/233. One wonders if Calvert actually transacted sales with Newton.

146. Schliemann to Frank Calvert, 18 July 1872, published in Traill (1993), 104.

147. On 19 July 1872. Traill (1993), 104.

148. On 21 July 1872. Ibid.

149. Ibid., 105.

150. Frank Calvert to Schliemann, 8 July 1872, B 67/223.

151. Frank Calvert to Schliemann, 16 July 1872, B 67/233.

152. Schliemann to Frank Calvert, 13 July 1872, in Meyer (1936), #21, 121–22.

153. Report of 4 August 1872, in Schliemann (1875a), 203. It was part of the second stratum's fortifications at Troy.

154. Frank Calvert to Schliemann, 24 July 1872, B 67/241.

155. In his 7 August 1872 letter to Schliemann, Frank Calvert wrote: "I am sure you will do it [divide the finds] as if I were there myself." Schliemann responded, "You will please come at all events yourself for you attach to certain objects a greater value than I do." Schliemann to Frank Calvert, 8/20 August 1872, BB 2.3/29, partially published in Meyer (1936), #23, 123.

156. Report of 4 August 1872, in Schliemann (1875a), 204. Even before his first legitimate season, Schliemann fantasized that the British Museum or German emperor might underwrite his excavations once well begun. Schliemann to John Brown, 5 October 1871, in Meyer (1953), #156, 187–88.

157. Curtius to Schliemann, 17 September 1872, in Meyer (1953), #189, 215–16.

158. "I make a drawing each evening of every one of the objects which have been found during the day, and more especially the pictorial symbols, with greatest exactness. Every article which can have any interest for the learned world shall be photographed . . . and published." Ibid., 219. Report of 14 August 1872, in Schliemann (1875a), 218.

159. Schliemann (1875a), 97.

160. Report of 4 August 1872, in Schliemann (1875a), 211.

161. Schliemann to Frank Calvert, 1 October 1872, in Meyer (1936), #24, 123–24; report of 22 February 1873, in Schliemann (1875a), 224. While Schliemann was absent, the pillaging continued, and Schliemann continued to complain about it. But stone disappeared not only for a belfry in the Greek village of Yenişehir, but also for the walls of Schliemann's own stone house on the site.

162. Frank Calvert to Schliemann, 16 October 1872, B 67/306; Schliemann to Frank Calvert, 23 October 1872, BB 2.3/34. Lubbock related his stay with Frank Calvert in the Troad from 12 to 17 October 1872 in an unusually lengthy account in his diary. Lubbock's diary, in Hutchinson (1914), 139–40. Immediately Lubbock apprised Gladstone, the prime minister and a Homeric scholar, of his trip. Lubbock to Gladstone, 30 November 1872, BLMS 44436 58.

163. Schliemann to John Lubbock, 14 November 1872, in Hutchinson (1914), 142–44. He confirmed that he had just perused the objects from the prehistoric houses of Thera and Therassia (2000 to 1500 B.C.) and had found no parallels with Trojan material, although the houses were of rubble masonry as in the pre-Hellenic levels at Troy, which he thought to be not later than 1500 B.C. Schliemann (1875a), 204.

164. George Henry Boker to Schliemann, 29 December 1872, in Allen (1995b), 397. The Philadelphia playwright was appointed on 3 November 1871 and arrived the following March. He served until 1875. *Dictionary of American Biography*, s.v. "Boker, George Henry"; Bradley (1927), 283–86. Schliemann to Frederick Calvert, 20 November 1872, BBB 30/345.

Almost none of the important correspondence between Boker and Schliemann has been published. It will appear in Allen (forthcoming).

165. Traill (1995), 76. He also purchased petrified cheese, two terra-cotta lamps, a small, coarse vase, and from a local goldsmith a marble bust, gemstone, and twenty coins. According to his letter to the president of the Institut de France of 21 April 1870, he intended to place these in his little museum in Paris. Meyer (1953), #131, 168.

166. Schliemann to Frank Calvert, 12 August 1871, BB 2.3/3. Such moral inhibitions would not trouble him later.

167. Schliemann to Wood, 6 August 1872, in Dyck (1990), 332.

168. Schliemann to Charles Newton, 12 October 1872, in Fitton (1991), 6. It was not shipped by 4 September 1873. Ibid., 14. Schliemann to Alexander Conze, 28 December 1873, in Meyer (1953), #223, 244. German original. Translated in Vaio (1990), 416. Another copy arrived at the Smithsonian Institution and was acknowledged by Joseph Henry in a letter to Schliemann of 19 May 1873.

169. Schliemann to Frank Calvert, 7 November 1872, in Meyer (1936), #27, 125; Newton to Schliemann, 22 October 1872, in Fitton (1991), 6. He did not visit until December 1873, after the discovery of Priam's Treasure.

170. Frederick Calvert to Schliemann, 26 October 1872, in Meyer (1953), #192, 218. Frederick Calvert reported showing the Hisarlık excavations and the Calvert Collection to the crown prince of Saxe Meiningen in October. He noted in the same letter that the prince would be proceeding to Athens to see Schliemann's collection. In his letter of 30 October to Schliemann, Frederick noted that he had convinced the prince's tutor to favor Schliemann over Curtius on the location of Troy. Meyer (1953), 339 n. 305. As if in competition, in November, Schliemann responded that the prince had visited. Habicht (1985), 170, noted that Bernhard, the crown prince of Saxe Meiningen, traveled through the Peloponnese in the spring of 1873 with the classicist Ulrich von Wilamowitz-Moellendorff.

171. This was exactly what he accused Frederick Calvert of doing in his 4 November 1873 letter to Boker, NARA RG84 USLT 287.

172. Traill (1993), 105, publishes a letter from Schliemann to Frank Calvert on the inscriptions dated 18 March 1873 and a letter to Emile Burnouf from Schliemann on 23 February 1873.

173. Frank Calvert to Schliemann, 24 February 1872, B 67/61.

174. Calvert (1873a).

175. Frank Calvert to Schliemann, 5 February 1873, B 68/46.

176. The editor printed it in both the daily and the weekly editions. Calvert (1873a).

177. Calvert (1873a). After mentioning Choiseul-Gouffier's 1787 probe, he discussed the significance of the excavations at sites around the Troad that he and Frederick had made. He omitted Brunton's digging at Hisarlık and elsewhere, which should have figured in a history of excavation in the Troad.

178. Because of the severity of the fire destruction, he assumed that the houses were formed of combustible materials.

179. Then he cited François Lenormant's *History of the East* (Paris, 1869), 358–59. Lenormant had based his argument on the excavations of Col. J. E. Taylor, British consul at Basra from 1854 to 1855, who had excavated Tell Mukayyar (Ur), finding the ziggurat and the inscribed cylinders that had facilitated Rawlinson's identification of the site. Taylor also had excavated the palace and halls, which were filled with pottery, some made by hand and

some thrown on a wheel. Geologist and traveler W. K. Loftus explored the nearby sites of Uruk and Larsa in 1849 and 1850.

180. His cross-dating with Near Eastern parallels was accepted only after Schliemann's death, when Dörpfeld (1902), 31, dated the second stratum to between 2500 and 2000 B.C.

181. The treasures subsequently discovered at both sites have only strengthened this parallel.

182. This statement has been proven by Korfmann (1995), 173–83.

183. Frank Calvert to Schliemann, 5 February 1873, B 68/46. This was followed a month later by the news that Philipp Déthier, director of the Imperial Ottoman Museum, intended to annul Schliemann's permit because he had written openly about the smuggled metope.

184. Schliemann to Frank Calvert, 9 February 1873, BBB 32/2.

185. Soon Lenormant would himself join Frank Calvert in declaring the second stratum at Troy to be too early to be Priam's in articles in the *Academy* of 5 March 1874. Lenormant (1874), 314–16, 343–58.

186. Frank Calvert to Schliemann, 12 February 1873, B 68/51.

187. Schliemann continued to try to convince Calvert, but Calvert had no time for owlish Athenas. He was completing another article on an exciting find from remote prehistory.

188. On 19 March 1873, Schliemann argued that one significant relief was not historical and therefore not valuable, but later he claimed that the historical value could not be denied. By 21 March, Calvert had accepted Schliemann's terms yet again. He had a different agenda now. Traill (1993), 105–6. Frank Calvert to Schliemann, 23 March 1973, B 68/91.

189. Schliemann to Frank Calvert, 27 March 1873, BB 2.3/48, partially published in Meyer (1936), #32, 129–30.

190. Schliemann to Frank Calvert, 29 March 1873, in Meyer (1953), #202, 225–26.

191. Report of 29 March 1873, in Schliemann (1875a), 270–74.

192. Ibid., 272.

193. Schliemann to Heinrich Brockhaus, 1 April 1873, in Meyer (1936), #33, 130–31.

194. Frank Calvert to Schliemann, 23 March 1873, B 68/91. Calvert was related to Abbott through his sisters-in-law, but he also may have consulted with Abbott about mining affairs. C. Xanthopoulos to the U.S. consul general, 26 October 1910, NARA RG84 Dard. 6. Because mining was a risky business needing considerable capital and organization before returns were realized, the sector was dominated by a relatively small number of well-capitalized entrepreneurs. The Abbott family was active in mining in western Anatolia beginning in 1849–50, when it received its first concessions for antimony, zinc, and lead. Although emery was their largest product, Ernest Abbott also mined chrome, antimony, manganese, zinc, silver, lead, lignite, mercury, copper, and gold. Frangakis-Syrett (1991b), 214–19.

195. Frank Calvert to Schliemann, 7 April 1873. Traill (1993), 107.

196. Traill (1995), 107 n. 11.

197. Because the prospective litigants were of two different nations, the plaintiff, Frank Calvert, first would have had to apply to his own chancery or embassy. His claim, having been verified, would have been notified to the defendant, then the cause would have been heard before the defendant's tribunal and judged by three persons, two belonging to the debtor's nation and the third to that of the plaintiff. White (1845), 1:147–48.

198. In Traill (1993), 107.

199. Traill (1993), 107 n. 18. The Turkish lire was equivalent to £1.10, or 4.3 French francs. Pamuk (1994), 972, table A.

200. Schliemann to Emile Burnouf, 17 April 1873, in Meyer (1953), #204, 227. French original. My translation.

201. Frank Calvert to Schliemann, 17 April 1873, in Traill (1993), 107.

202. Frank Calvert to Schliemann, 20 April 1873, BB 2.2.

203. Report of 10 May, 1873, in Schliemann (1875a), 318.

204. The letter is dated by position to 24 April, BBB 32/208. Translated and published in Traill (1993), 109–110.

205. James Calvert to Schliemann, 30 April 1873, in Traill (1993), 111.

206. BBB 32/209–12. The letter probably was fired off as soon as Schliemann received Frank Calvert's response.

207. Frank Calvert to Schliemann, 25 April 1873, B68/131, and Traill (1993), 110–111.

208. Schliemann to Frank Calvert, 4 May 1873, preserved in the copybook cited above and translated in Traill (1993), 111–12.

CHAPTER 8

1. The discovery of Priam's Treasure was not announced until 5 August 1873 in the *Augsburger Allgemeine Zeitung*. Traill (1993), 127–66; Easton (1984b), 200–202.

2. The Rt. Hon. Robert Lowe suggested that the funds might, however, be raised by public subscription. Evans (1956), 288–89. Charles Merlin, the British consul at Piraeus, wrote Newton that Schliemann "had a bee in his bonnet" regarding Troy. Merlin to Charles Newton, 6 November 1872, in Fitton (1990), 7.

3. Schliemann to Calvert, 5/17 February 1873, in Meyer (1936), #30, 127–28; report of 22 February 1873, in Schliemann (1875a), 224–25.

4. Report of 1 March 1873, in Schliemann (1875a), 233. He complained about "removing all the stones of a temple which is about 288 feet long and 72 1/2 broad." Report of 15 March 1873, in Schliemann (1875a), 249.

5. Report of 15 March, 1873, in Schliemann (1875a), 257.

6. Report of 17 June 1873, in Schliemann (1875a), 348.

7. Reports of 16 April and 10 May 1873, in Schliemann (1875a), 287, 291, 304–5.

8. Report of 10 May 1873, in Schliemann (1875a), 305–6. To Lubbock, he wrote a joyous letter on 20 May 1873 proclaiming the gate and "the house of Priamos" to the northwest of it. Hutchinson (1914), 149.

9. Report of 16 April 1873, in Schliemann (1875a), 289.

10. Reports of 22 February, 1 and 29 March 1873, in Schliemann (1875a), 231, 244, 247, 266–69.

11. Report of 17 June 1873, in Schliemann (1875a), 344–45.

12. Report of 13–14 June 1873. This was later designated "Treasure B" by Götze (1902), 331, and Schmidt (1902), 5973–75a.

13. Schliemann to Sergei Schliemann, 30 May 1873, in Meyer (1953), #209, 231.

14. Traill (1993), 141, established the date. Schliemann to Nikolaos Didymos, first dragoman and political agent of the Ottoman government at the Dardanelles, 7/19 August 1873, in Meyer (1953), #214, 236–37; Schliemann (1881a), 66.

15. Götze (1902), 326–31; Schmidt (1902), 225–37. Easton wonders if Treasure B originally might have been part of the nearby Treasure A. Easton (1984a), 162–66, and (1997), 196 n. 13.

16. Borlase (1878), 178–79; Traill (1993), 156–57 nn. 8, 11; Schliemann (1874a), 290; (1875a), 323. Traill has shown that Schliemann originally wished to claim that he had found it in Priam's Palace and only changed his mind once he had checked Laurent's plans, which showed the correct spot. Traill (1995), 111–14. Apparently it was covered by a deposit of red, yellow, and black "calcined debris" 2 meters thick. Schliemann (1873b), 3309; (1874a), 290; Easton (1984a), 146.

17. Report of 17 June 1873, in Schliemann (1875a), 323–24.

18. Schliemann admitted her absence in a letter to Newton, 27 December 1873, in Fitton (1990), 24, and in one to E. Wirths, 7 May 1873, BBB 32/236; Traill (1995), 109. Traill suggests that the death of Sophia's father was brought on by an insensitive letter in which Schliemann announced an attempted rape of Sophia by George Photidas. Schliemann to George Engastromenos, 24 April 1873, BBB 32/226, quoted in Traill (1995), 108–9. Schliemann, who maintained Sophia's presence at the find, said of Photidas that he was obliged to dismiss him "for urgent reasons." Report of 10 May 1873, in Schliemann (1875a), 318. Schliemann to Alexander Conze, 14 May 1873, in Meyer (1953), #207, 229, and Schliemann's 1873 diary, 7 May 1873, 223, confirm this. Traill (1993), 238 n. 10.

19. Schliemann to E. Wirths, 5 July 1873, in Traill (1993), 156 n. 11; Schliemann to Nikolaos Didymos, 7/19 August 1873, in Meyer (1953), #214, 236–37.

20. Frederick Calvert to Schliemann, 31 May 1873, in Traill (1993), 157–58.

21. Schliemann to Frederick Calvert, 31 May 1873, BB 2.3/49, partially published in Meyer (1936), #35, 132.

22. Eckenbrecher (1874), 251–55, also noted Sophia's absence. Cited and translated in Traill (1993), 158–59 n. 16.

23. Schliemann showed them the site the next morning, after which Frederick Calvert collected Bulthaupt. Traill (1993), 160 n. 19.

24. Meyer (1953), #210, 231–33; Traill (1993), 130.

25. Schliemann's 1873 diary, 270. Translated in Easton (1981), 183. On June 2, "Mr. Frederick Calvert," who recently had drained the marsh, "called and reported on the temperatures of the springs, which he had been testing with a thermometer." These were the Duden springs near Ilion Kome. Although they may have discussed the transport arrangements and the goods, Frederick Calvert clearly was ill informed about what it contained until July. Frederick Calvert to Schliemann, 23 July 1873, B 68/236.

26. The ship, the *Taxiarches*, used the harbor at Karanlık Limanı. Traill (1993), 168–70; (1995), 111.

27. Traill (1993), 168.

28. Schliemann to George Henry Boker, 10 June 1873, BBB 32/364.

29. Schliemann found two additional inscriptions under his wooden dig house, but no more treasure. Report of 17 June 1873, in Schliemann (1875a), 355–56.

30. Easton (1994a), 226. For a comparison of the different accounts of the discovery, see Traill (1993), 127–52, and Easton (1984a), 141–69. The jewelry Schliemann claimed to have found packed in hard earth contained in a silver jar (1875a), 300–15. See Tolstikov and Treister (1996) for a complete presentation.

31. Schliemann to Newton, 4 September 1873. Fitton (1991), 14–17.

32. Comnos (1874), 178. It "continues to attract crusades of people to my office where it is exposed." Schliemann to Frederick Calvert, 16 July 1873, BBB 32/419.

33. Schliemann to his sister Dorothea in Röbel, in Meyer (1936), #43, 139–40.

34. Schliemann to Frederick Calvert, 16 July 1873, BBB 32/419.

35. Slade (1854), 166–70.

36. One traveler noted that "the three plagues of Constantinople are Fire, Pestilence, and Dragomen." Pardoe (1837), vi.

37. Bradley (1927), 283–86. Brown had translated novels from Turkish into English in 1850 and had written a serious volume on dervish spirituality in 1868 and a guidebook, *Ancient and Modern Constantinople*, also published in 1868.

38. Schliemann to Brown, 12 March 1872, BBB 30/321. The document was *Règlement relatif à la création d'un musée à Constantinople*. In 1871, Brown had advised Schliemann about the problems of exporting antiquities: "The trouble with the new law is due to the actions of Cesnola who found a large quantity of antiquities from that island and sold them in London, Berlin, and St. Petersburg." Brown to Schliemann, 15 April 1871, B 66/95. For General Luigi Palma di Cesnola (1832–1904), U.S. consul in Cyprus, see Calder and Kramer (1992), 1050, and Masson (1994).

39. John Brown to Schliemann, 19 March 1872, B72, partially published in Traill (1993), 149. A new reading by Peter S. Allen differs from his and adds new information. Schliemann acknowledged receipt of Brown's "very interesting letter." Schliemann to Brown, 10 April 1872, BBB 30/346. Easton (1984b), 200–202, and (1997), 194 n. 6.

40. This was Treasure R. Götze (1902), 342; Schmidt (1902), 246–47, nos. 6141–45.

41. Easton has noted that if he had found an item that he wished to reserve to combine or bundle with later objects, he at least would have written about it in his diary, as he had with Treasure R. Easton (1984a), 200–203.

42. George Henry Boker to Schliemann, 28 June 1873, B 68/202.

43. Cesnola had given Boker a gold signet ring and other gold trinkets from his excavations. George Henry Boker to Schliemann, 18 July 1873, B 68/226. And in return, Boker secured the *firman* for Cesnola's continued "excavation" of Cypriot sites and arranged for the subsequent export of his antiquities collection. George Henry Boker to Secretary of State Hamilton Fish (1808–1893), 1 April 1873, NARA RG84 USLT Dispatch. The Sublime Porte had been inconsistent in its application of the law on antiquities and had allowed the British archaeologist Wood, excavating at Ephesus, to export his finds. Cesnola reciprocated with a vacation in Cyprus for Boker and his wife. Bradley (1927), 304.

44. George Henry Boker to Schliemann, 28 June 1873, B 68/20.

45. Schliemann to George Henry Boker, 29 July 1873, BBB 32/451–53.

46. His quotation from Horace, *Odes*, 3.3.49–50, appeared in his 16 June 1874 letter to the Greek classicist Athanasios Rhousopoulos, in Fitton (1991), 32. See *Horace: The Odes and Epodes*, with an English translation by C. E. Bennett (Cambridge, Mass., 1946), 182–83: "stronger to spurn undiscovered gold (better so bestowed, while Earth yet hides it) than to gather it for human uses with a hand that plunders everything."

47. Pemble (1987), 228.

48. Senior (1859), 224–25.

49. Sir Gardner Wilkinson, *Dalmatia and Montenegro* (London, 1848), 85–86, quoted in Thompson (1992), 176.

50. "Dr. Schliemann's Discoveries—Division of the Spoils," *Levant Herald*, 10 and 16 July 1873.

51. George Henry Boker to Schliemann, 18 July 1873, B 68/226. Boker repeated his advice to Schliemann on 29 September 1873, B 68/332.

52. Schliemann to George Henry Boker, 29 July 1873, BBB 32/451–53.

53. Frederick Calvert to Schliemann, 23 July 1873, B 68/236. Frederick Calvert had learned of "the precious objects" recently found by Schliemann at the close of his excavations from an Englishman named Warner, who had talked with Yannakis.

54. Schliemann (1873a), 3309–10.

55. Schliemann to George Henry Boker, 12 and 19 August 1873, BBB 32/473, and BBB 32/491, only partially published in Meyer (1936), #216, 237–38. Schliemann to George Henry Boker, 29 July 1873, BBB 32/451–53, was omitted by Meyer.

56. George Henry Boker to Schliemann, 30 August 1873, B 68/289.

57. Frederick Calvert to Schliemann, 27 August 1873, B 68/248. Schliemann had offered his share to Frederick Calvert on 31 May and 30 July, BB 2.3/49 and BBB 32/456. Also Schliemann to Frank Calvert, 30 July 1873, BBB 32/458.

58. In fact, when the British antiquary William Borlase traveled to the Troad in 1875 in order to inspect Schliemann's discoveries, he was made to accept an "escort," ostensibly because of the Turks' suspicion of foreign archaeologists, arising from Schliemann's behavior. Borlase (1878), 229.

59. Schliemann (1875c), supplement. Calvert (1875), 1024, responded that "there were, in fact, others at the Dardanelles who knew about archaeology and submitted articles to the *Levant Herald*" and that he was not their only correspondent.

60. "It is below my dignity to make any reply . . . a great man wrote to me some time since I would do better to throw them into the ocean than to give any particle of them to the Turks." He also declared that "the editor of the Levant Herald, Wietecker, is his [Calvert's] brother in law." Schliemann to George Henry Boker, 16 September 1873, NARA RG84 USLT 287 and Gennadius Library BBB 33/82. "Wietecker" probably is the same individual, Whitaker, who had served as Frederick Calvert's vice-consul at Gallipoli from 1859 to 1860. In an earlier letter, Schliemann had slanderously reported that "Wietecker" was "the brother in law of two of the Calverts," but that "Mrs. Wietecker [an Abbott] has been living for two years with Mr. Wrench, now appointed in the embassy in Constantinople." Schliemann assured Boker that "no tribunal in the world is competent to accept a suit between two foreigners for the infringement of a convention." Schliemann to George Henry Boker, 12 August 1873, BBB 32/473. To Frederick Calvert, he justified his actions by claiming he had "acted like all others who ever excavated in Turkey." He also asked him to let Whitaker know that he had stopped digging on Frank Calvert's land at the end of March. Schliemann to Frederick Calvert, 1/13 August 1873, BBB 32/475–76.

61. Schliemann (1875b), supplement.

62. Calvert later published his letter to Lubbock. Calvert (1875), 1024. This letter was discovered and analyzed by Traill (1993), 180–181.

63. *Academy* 5, 10 January 1874, 41.

64. Obviously frustrated about not being able to return to Turkey, Schliemann was aware that local people had been plundering the site and removing the pavement of the gateway. Schliemann to Charles Newton, 16 May 1874, in Fitton (1991), 30.

65. [Frank Calvert], "Important Discovery at Troy: Priam's Treasure No Fiction," *Levant Herald*, 4 January 1874. A more complete summary is "The Recent Archaeological Discovery in the Troad," *Levant Herald*, 28 January 1874. Schliemann (1881a), 43; Calvert (1874a), 610–11; Déthier (1876), 416–19; Götze (1902), 332. Schliemann later indicated that the workmen's treasure, later called "Treasure C," was found just north of Priam's Palace and a little

west of the well on the west side of the great north-south trench. Götze (1902), 332; Schmidt (1902), 239–40; Schliemann (1881a), 494–98. But Traill notes that Schliemann's reports do not indicate he worked there in March 1873, but rather at the point farther east, where his east-west trench intersected the great north-south trench. If Calvert was correct in the location, 150 yards from that of Priam's Treasure, then, Traill reasons, it could have been found only near the eastern end of the east-west trench. Schliemann (1875a), no. 186, 266–69. Traill (1995), 125–26, further suggests that many pieces attached to Priam's Treasure were actually found here and not recorded. Traill did not realize the implications of Treasure C as well as the previously unreported pendant being found on Calvert land. Treasure C and the pendant therefore belonged at least in part to Calvert as proprietor.

66. Schliemann to George Henry Boker, 13 January 1874, BBB 33/357.

67. Schliemann to Charles Newton, 4 September 1873, in Meyer (1953), #217, 238–39, and Fitton (1991), 14–17.

68. Calvert urged the establishment of a fund to finance "energetic able men" who could acquire the confidence of the Ottoman government and pursue a course of "intelligent investigations" at Hisarlık. Frank Calvert, "The Recent Archaeological Discovery in the Troad," *Levant Herald*, 28 January 1874.

69. Charles Newton, "Dr. Schliemann's Discoveries at Ilium novum," *Academy*, 93, 5, 14 February 1874, 173.

70. Lenormant placed the remains of Thera and Therassia, with their painted pottery and plastered walls, at a later stage, in the seventeenth century B.C. Lenormant (1874), 314–16. For Lenormant himself, see de Grummond (1996), 672–73.

71. Traill has shown this in (1993), 29–40.

72. The French volume and an atlas that accompanied the German edition were published in 1874. Schliemann (1874a and 1874b). The American and British volumes appeared a year later, entitled *Troy and Its Remains*. Schliemann (1875a). Schliemann made his displeasure with Calvert public in (1875a), 270–74, and Schliemann (1874a), 237.

73. See Korres (1974), 7–9, for citations of the reports.

74. Report of 29 March 1873, in Schliemann (1875a), 272. See Traill (1993), 33–36.

75. Philip Smith, whom Schliemann had employed to edit the British edition, seems to have been uncomfortable about the gravity of Calvert's criticism but unwilling to incur the wrath of his patron by incorporating Calvert's remarks. Smith, "Preface," Schliemann (1875a), xiii.

76. Schliemann to John M. Francis, undated (July 1874), BBB 34/58.

77. He was confirmed on 10 June 1874. U.S. State Department Consular Lists.

78. Calvert (1874a), 610–11.

79. Schliemann (1874b), plate 214.

80. Calvert (1874b), 644.

81. Schliemann to Boker, 2 December 1874, BBB 34/173, partially published in Meyer (1953), #253, 272.

82. Stark (1874b), 347–51; Schliemann (1875b), 109–10. In a letter of 18 October 1874 to Heinrich E. Brockhaus, Schliemann complained of Stark's "heinous libel." Meyer (1936), #51, 143–44. German original. See also Schliemann to Ernst Curtius, 30 January 1875, in Meyer (1953), #258, 276–77. German original.

83. Schliemann's argument in (1875c) is quoted and analyzed by Traill (1993), 35.

84. Calvert's letter to the *Guardian*, 11 August 1875. See Traill (1993), 36 n. 26 and 85 n. 36.

85. Schliemann to Charles Newton, 3 September 1875, in Fitton (1991), 36.

86. Max Müller to Schliemann, 11 February 1874, in Meyer (1953), #233, 252–53. German original.

87. Max Müller (1902), 449.

88. Schliemann relayed Déthier's request to Brockhaus, Schliemann's publisher, on 2 August 1873, along with his own refusal and his proposal of compensation for the Turks. Meyer (1936), #39, 137. He already had told Frederick Calvert of his strategy. Schliemann to Frederick Calvert, 30 July 1873, BBB 32/456.

89. He wrote privately to P. Beaurain, his agent in Paris, about the tremendous find and his anxiety over the Turks naturally wanting their share of the treasure. He inquired whether there was in Paris a goldsmith in whom he

> could place absolute confidence, confidence such that I could entrust to him all the objects . . . with an appearance of antiquity and naturally without affixing his stamp. But it is absolutely essential that he not betray me and that he do all the work at a moderate price. Perhaps he could also reproduce the silver vases in galvanized copper, which he could blacken.
>
> In the course of your enquiries please speak of objects found in Norway and in God's name don't mention the word "Troy."

He reiterated that he must be able to place absolute and unlimited confidence in the person. Schliemann to Beaurain, 28 June 1873. Traill discovered the letter and translated it. Traill (1993), 173–82. Although he was ready to have fakes produced in order to dupe the Turks, there is no evidence to suggest he ever acted on this impulse.

90. Schliemann to George Henry Boker, 16 September 1873, NARA RG84 USLT 287 and BBB 33/82–85.

91. Schliemann to Reschid Pasha via George Henry Boker, 4 November 1873, NARA RG84 USLT 287, French original. As far as is known, Frederick served his sentence in Corradino Prison. For the complete text of the letter and other Boker correspondence, see Allen (forthcoming).

92. Schliemann to Frederick Calvert, 31 May and 30 July 1873, BB 2.3/49 and BB 32/456.

93. George Henry Boker to Schliemann, 8 November 1873, B 68/368.

94. Schliemann to Newton, 19 March and 16 May 1874, in Fitton (1991), 27–29, 30.

95. Once again, he did not wait for the answer to his request, which he knew would be negative. Schliemann to Max Müller, 12 March 1874, BBB 33/442; published in Traill (1995), 128. In five days in late March 1874 he sank thirty-four trial trenches in different parts of the site. Emile Burnouf and his daughter Louise, a competent artist, assisted the Schliemanns. Schliemann to Dr. Wittener, 14 March 1874. Meyer (1953), #238, 261; Traill (1986), 127–28. Around the Lion Gate, six trenches reached bedrock at 14 to 20 feet. Schliemann found a great deal of pottery and terracotta figurines before he was stopped by the authorities. When it was discovered that he had no permit, all finds were confiscated. He had solicited and later received permission to excavate the site, but this was revoked because of the pending lawsuit. The permit was awarded to the Greek Archaeological Society, which then engaged Schliemann as its excavator.

96. Spyridon Comnos, the director of the National Library, exposed the court proceedings. Comnos (1874), 178.

97. "Mr. Wait the consul called on me when the danger appeared greatest and offered me to put the U.S. seal on my collection in order to save it." Schliemann to George Henry

Boker, 16 April 1874, BBB 33/486–87 and 33/488–89; Traill (1995), 129. He had referred to their "wealthy friends" Constantinos and Wait in earlier correspondence. Schliemann to George Henry Boker, BBB 34/174.

98. Schliemann recounted this to Newton in a shameless letter and asked him to undervalue to £1300 the collection that Schliemann previously had tried to sell him for £50,000. Schliemann to Newton, 7 June 1874, Fitton (1991), 31–32; Schliemann to Newton, 4 September 1873, ibid., 14. In the 7 June letter, he begged Newton not to mention that he ever had offered the collection to the British Museum. Newton came to inspect the collection in December 1873.

99. Although the offer of sale to the French was seriously entertained, the French Ministry of Finance stalled and Schliemann wrote that he no longer could sell it because of the lawsuit. However, Schliemann later offered to give it to the Louvre.

100. Comnos (1874), 178, Fitton (1991), 31; Meyer (1953), 355 n. 432.

101. *Débats*, 23 June 1874, quoted in Comnos (1874), 178. On 3 May 1874, Burnouf, on the expectation that Schliemann was giving the entire Trojan Collection to the Louvre, secretly hid it at the Ecole Française d'Athènes. But Schliemann annulled his offer less than ten days later and again offered the collection to the Greeks. Burnouf subsequently demanded that Schliemann remove it from the school's depot, although it may have rested there throughout the proceedings. Schliemann confided to Boker that it had "disappeared." Schliemann to George Henry Boker, 9 June 1874, BBB 34/34. In his letter to Newton of 18 April 1875, Schliemann wrote rather improbably that the treasure's location was known to hundreds of Greeks. Elsewhere, he noted that he had hidden it with Sophia's relatives. Amandry (1995), 74

102. Déthier to Schliemann, 13 February 1875, in Meyer (1953), #259, 279.

103. Schliemann to the amateur collector Eugène Piot (1812–1890), 3 December 1874, quoted in Amandry (1995), 80. In October 1876, he offered it to Russia for £80,000 but said that because of his having spent twenty years of his life in Saint Petersburg, he would accept £50,000. Amandry (1995), 81. In a letter of 17 January 1877 to the French philosopher and archaeologist Felix Ravaisson (1813–1900), he offered to exhibit it at the Louvre. Amandry (1995), 82.

104. Schliemann to George Henry Boker, 16 April 1874, BBB 33/489, 19 May 1874, BBB 34/17, and 14 October 1874, BBB 34/102–3.

105. George Henry Boker to Schliemann, 5 December 1874, B 69/446.

106. Schliemann to George Henry Boker, 16 December 1874, NARA RG84 USLT 287 and BBB 34/200–202. Meanwhile, Schliemann complained that the treasure was ruining his sleep. Schliemann to Ernst Schliemann, 7 February 1874, in Meyer (1953), #232, 252. To Boker, he wrote that the process "ruins me." Schliemann to George Henry Boker, 14 October 1874, BBB 34/102–3. No doubt due to the stress, Sophia suffered three miscarriages during the year of the suit. Schliemann to George Henry Boker, 16 March 1875, BBB 34/306. Ironically, the revisionist scholarship on Schliemann, which he certainly would have considered libel, has been centered in the United States.

107. Schliemann to Eugène Piot, 3 December 1874, in Amandry (1995), 80.

108. Schliemann to George Henry Boker, 18 April 1874, BBB 34/333; Schliemann to Wilhelm Rust, 24 April 1875, in Meyer (1936), #53, 143–44, and in Stoll (1958), #5, 250–52; Schliemann to an unknown addressee, 27 June 1875, in Meyer (1953), #264, 283.

109. Schliemann to Charles Newton, 18 April 1875, in Fitton (1991), 32; Schliemann to Wilhelm Rust, 24 April 1875, in Stoll (1958), #5, 250–52.

110. Easton (1994a), 229.

111. Schliemann to Newton, 18 April 1875, in Fitton (1991), 32.

112. Emile Burnouf to the minister of public instruction, 15 April 1875, in Amandry (1995), 79–80, and Traill (1995), 135.

113. Schliemann to Wilhelm Rust, 13 March 1875, in Stoll (1958), #4, 246–48.

114. Schliemann to Wilhelm Rust, 24 April 1875, in Meyer (1936), #53, 145–46, and Stoll (1958), #5, 250–52.

115. John Murray (1808–1892) had published a series of successful archaeological works, Dennis's *Cities and Cemeteries of Etruria*, Fellows's *Excursion in Asia Minor*, Hamilton's *Researches*, Layard's books on Nineveh, Lyell's *Antiquity of Man*, and Lubbock's *Prehistoric Times*. Schliemann was in very good company. Vaio (1990), 422–26, contextualizes Schliemann's London visit.

116. He spoke on 23 and 30 April 1874. Charles Newton, "On Dr. Schliemann's Discoveries on the Plain of Troy" and "On the Discoveries of the Remains of Troy," *Proceedings of the Society of Antiquaries of London*, 2d series 6 (1876): 202, 215–25. Evans (1956), 338 n. 3.

117. Newton to Schliemann, 20 August 1873, in Fitton (1991), 13. Gladstone wished "to recover as substantial personages, and to bring within the grasp of flesh and blood some of the pictures, and even of those persons whom Mr. Grote had dismissed to the Land of Shadow and Dream." Briggs and Calder (1990), 415–30; Vaio (1990), 415–29, and (1992), 73 76.

118. Vaio (1990), 416.

119. Gladstone reviewed Schliemann (1874a) in *Contemporary Review*, June 1874, 41.

120. Correspondence between the two began in August 1875. Meyer (1955), 435; Herrmann and Maaß (1990). *Biographisches Wörterbuch zur deutsches Geschichte*, s.v. "Virchow, Rudolf." Virchow's correspondence with Calvert began in 1874, when Gustav Hirschfeld acquainted him with Calvert's 1860 article on Ophryneion. Virchow (1875) and (1882), 5.

121. Lindenschmidt advocated drawing all finds and systematically studying all the funerary objects, coins, weapons, clothing, and pottery in order to interpret other finds and solve historical questions. Kyrieleis (1978), 74–91.

122. Schliemann to Charles Newton, 25 December 1875, in Fitton (1991), 39.

123. Schliemann to Stanhope, 19 July 1875, in Fitton (1991), 33–34.

124. J. Winter Jones to Schliemann, 16 September 1875; Schliemann to Charles Newton, 3 October 1875, in Fitton (1991), 37–38.

125. Schliemann to Gladstone, 27 June 1875, BLMS 44452/256.

126. Schliemann (1881a), 44–45; Easton (1994a), 229.

127. Schliemann to Gladstone, 8 May 1876, in Meyer (1958), #11, 40–42.

128. Schliemann to Knight Watson, secretary of the Society of Antiquaries, London, 8 May 1876, in Meyer (1958), #12, 42.

129. Schliemann to Frank Calvert, 20 May 1876. Italian original. Translated by R. R. Holloway, 21 and 29 May 1876, respectively. NARA RG84 USLT 287.

130. This presumably was the copy he had just received from Gladstone.

131. Calvert to Schliemann, 29 May 1876, B 71/168.

132. Schliemann to Reschid Pasha via George Henry Boker, 4 November 1873, NARA RG84 USLT 287. James (confused with Frederick) had been stricken from U.S. consular lists. U.S. consul general at Constantinople John H. Goodenow to W. Hunter, second assistant secretary of state, 30 April 1872. James never advanced beyond fourth clerk at the Constantinople consulate, a humble post for the best French scholar at the legation, a civil ser-

vant who also spoke Turkish, Greek, and Italian fluently. He had worked in the shipping department and was needed in legal affairs but could not be promoted. Henry Fawcett to Earl Granville, the British ambassador, 5 November 1880, PRO/FO 78 3160. It was to Boker that Frank Calvert would write on 2 May 1874 requesting to be considered for the position of U.S. consular agent recently vacated by his brother James. NARA RG84 Dard. 1.

133. Schliemann to Frank Calvert, 29 May 1876, BBB 35, published in Traill (1995), 142.

134. Schliemann to Philipp Déthier, 21 May 1876, in Meyer (1958), #15, 45 and 418 n. 47.

135. Schliemann's report on Ibrahim Pasha in the London *Times,* 30 June 1876, in Meyer (1958), #18, 47–48. Shortly thereafter, Schliemann asked Gladstone to request that Sir Henry Elliott (1817–1907), British ambassador to the Sublime Porte, intervene on his behalf. *Webster's Biographical Dictionary,* s.v. "Elliott, Sir Henry George." Gladstone did intervene through Frank Calvert, writing to let Schliemann know that the deed had been done. "The work has also been sent as you desired." Gladstone to Schliemann, 8 July 1876, in Meyer (1958), #20, 49–50. In the same letter, Gladstone recommended the South Kensington Museum as a site for an exhibition.

136. French original. It was reprinted by another daily, the *Stamboul,* whence it was copied by Frank Calvert and included in his 19 July 1878 letter to William Simpson. Simpson Collection, the Mitchell Library, Glasgow.

137. Schliemann to Gladstone, 28 December 1876, in Meyer (1958), #33, 66.

138. Schliemann to Burnouf, 19 July 1876, in Meyer (1958), #23, 52. All finds immediately would be handed over to the Greek government. Traill (1986).

139. Traill (1995), 144.

140. Stamatakis wrote that Schliemann was excavating simultaneously in seven areas. Traill (1986), 128 n. 21. By September, he had employed 120 workmen. Traill (1986), 160.

141. Quoted in Ludwig (1931), 168.

142. Kyrieleis (1978), 82.

143. Max Müller (1902), 447. Others were less generous. Theodor Mommsen apparently called him a "truffle pig." Ottaway (1973), 103.

144. *Stoa,* 14/26 November 1876, 2.

145. Meyer (1958), #27, 55–66.

146. Charles Merlin's snide letter of 22 December 1876 to Newton describes the scene at the site at the time of discovery: Schliemann "recognised Agamemnon's remains the minute he saw them, and the Greeks swear he rogered his wife in public on the spot, in an ecstasy of antiquarian delight. Luckily his wife was at hand, otherwise he might have 'atroced' one of the workmen, as the Yankees call it." In Fitton (1991), 43.

147. Ibid.

148. Ulrich Köhler, "Die Grabanlagen in Mykene und Sparta," *Mitteilungen des deutschen Archäologischen Instituts, athenische Abteilung* 3 (1874), 4. Translated in Marchand (1996), 122.

149. Schliemann to Frederick Calvert, 16 July 1873, BBB 32/419.

150. Schliemann to Charles Newton, 26 July 1873, in Meyer (1953), #213, 235–36, and in Fitton (1991), 9–11. Schliemann discussed the proposition with Heinrich E. Brockhaus, 30 August 1873. Meyer (1936), #40, 137–38. The complex politics behind the permit for Olympia were laid out by Schliemann in a letter to G. Bianconi of 19 July 1873. In Meyer (1953), #211, 233.

151. Schliemann to Heinrich E. Brockhaus, 25 October 1873 and 19 February 1874, in Meyer (1936), #41, 138–39, #47, 141.

152. Schliemann to Heinrich E. Brockhaus, 30 August 1873, in Amandry (1995), 46. He did excavate briefly in Sicily in the autumn of 1875. Isserlin (1968), 144–48.

153. Schliemann to Calvert, 17 April 1873, BBB 32/186–88.

154. Schliemann to Newton, 26 July 1873, in Meyer (1953), #213, 235–36, and Fitton (1991), 9–11.

155. Charles Newton to Schliemann, 20 August 1873, in Fitton (1991), 13.

156. Schliemann to Charles Newton, 4 September 1873. Ibid., 14.

157. Amandry (1995) has chronicled Schliemann's machinations with the French. On 1 August 1873, Burnouf wrote to the minister of the interior of Schliemann's wish to sell the collection to the Louvre. Schliemann to his sister, 24/26 December 1873, in Meyer (1936), #43, 139–40. Eugène Piot came from Paris to view the treasure. Schliemann to Max Müller, 18 January 1874, in Meyer (1953), #228, 248–49. In his 7 February 1874 letter to his brother Ernst, Schliemann wrote that he wished to sell the collection to the Louvre. In Meyer (1953), #232, 252. The offer was seriously considered.

158. Schliemann to R. S. Poole, 30 August 1876, in Fitton (1991), 39–40. Schliemann to John Murray, of 30 August 1877, mentioned Gladstone's acceptance. Traill (1995), 176.

159. J. Winter Jones, principal librarian, to Schliemann, 27 October 1876, in Fitton (1991), 41; Schliemann to Poole, 30 August 1876, in Fitton (1991), 40, 43.

160. Schliemann to Horace Maynard (1814–1882), U.S. minister to Turkey from 1875 to 1880, 29 June 1877, NARA RG84 USLT, 288; *Webster's Biographical Dictionary,* s.v. "Maynard, Horace."

161. Traill (1995), 176.

162. Frederick died on 26 July 1876. A short obituary appeared in the *Athenaeum,* again seeming to mistake Frederick for Frank: "Mr. F. Calvert, the Consul at the Dardanelles, well known to all visitors at the Troad and an occasional correspondent of this journal." *Athenaeum* 2546, 12 August 1876, 211.

163. Calvert had written to Waddington in 1870 about a possible sale to the Louvre but received no reply due to the Franco-Prussian War. On 10 August, Calvert asked Schliemann to help locate Waddington. B 66/242. Although both were members of the Geographical Society in Paris and had several acquaintances in common, Schliemann did not know him. Schliemann to Frank Calvert, 25 August 1870, BBB 293/188–89.

164. "I now tell you that it is my firm belief that the British Museum would give more than 400 pounds for this weight if you ask 800 pounds. Only ask always double of what you would accept. Come at all events here with your things and, if you can, bring a line of introduction from Mr. Newton or Mr. Burck." Schliemann to Frank Calvert, 12 August 1871, BB 2.3/3.

165. "From what I hear from other quarters the British Museum would not give any price for my collection of antiquities—for Mr. Newton (whom I know personally) *entre nous* is a great screw." Frank Calvert to Schliemann, 13 September 1871, B 66/216. By 1873, sales occurred, such as that of Calvert's fellow U.S. consul general Cesnola, whose collection of Cypriot antiquities went to London, Saint Petersburg, and Berlin. Hamilton Fish to George Henry Boker, 1 April 1873, NARA USLT Dispatches. Moreover, Newton had purchased major collections for the British Museum.

166. Newton to Frank Calvert, 12 August 1874, BMGR.

167. The uncertainties of the times probably also prompted Calvert to divest. The Russo-Turkish War had broken out in Bulgaria with large-scale massacres of Turkish peasants. Both

Edmund Calvert and his nephew, Frederick R. J. Calvert, were present at the fall of Adrianople (Edirne) on 20 January 1877. On 25 April 1877, Frank Calvert, as U.S. consular agent at the Dardanelles, presented the United States with a small collection of antiquities in order to honor the heroism of Henry H. Gorringe, commander of the U.S.S. *Gettysburg*, who had saved a Greek ship in peril at the straits. Calvert to "Venezzello," consul for the Greek king, NARA RG84 Dard. 1. This gift was acknowledged by a letter to Gorringe from Daniel Ammen (1819–1898), chief of the U.S. Bureau of Navigation, on 16 May 1877 and referred to Calvert with a note from Gorringe on 3 June 1877. I thank Donald F. Easton for sharing this information with me. By the time the gift arrived in Washington, D.C. two years later, it consisted only of a terra-cotta water pipe, a paving slab, one capital (order not specified), and one millstone, or quern, "from the Ruins of Ancient Cyzicus and Troy 3rd or 4th Century." These items are part of the Smithsonian Institution's permanent collections. Acc. no. 8034, 1 August 1879.

168. Lugt (1964), 130, no. 37636. See Allen (1996b), 155–57, for the Calvert sale.

169. Sale catalogue, Sotheby, Wilkinson, and Hodge, vol. 758, British Library. It is not known how the collection reached London.

170. Newton to the Trustees of the British Museum, 26 July 1877 and 9 October 1877, the latter confirming acquisition. BMCA.

171. Franks attended Cambridge and took an M.A. there in 1852. In 1851, he became assistant in the Department of Antiquities in the British Museum. Franks had attended Schliemann's 1877 Mycenae presentation at the Society of Antiquaries, illustrated in Fitton (1991), figure 6. *Dictionary of National Biography,* s.v. "Franks, Augustus Wollaston"; Wilson (1984).

172. By 1991, the link between Calvert and the objects he had excavated was all but obliterated. Special thanks to J. Lesley Fitton of the Department of Greek and Roman Antiquities for help in locating the pieces in 1993.

173. Max Müller (1902), 447.

174. Easton (1994a), 231. Olga Palagia had a similar reaction upon seeing the 1996 exhibition in Moscow. Communication to Aegeanet, 3 July 1997.

175. Easton (1994a), 230–31. The material, comprising a twentieth of that brought to light, filled between twenty and thirty cases. Hartshorne (1877), 291–96.

176. Ibid., 291.

177. Charles Merlin to Charles Newton, 1 February 1877, in Fitton (1991), 43.

178. Citation of 27 December 1877, in Meyer (1958), #40, 71–72.

179. See Curtius's attacks on Schliemann in Marchand (1996), 122.

180. Ibid., 122–24.

181. "People laughed at me at the Dardanelles, three years ago, when I expressed the opinion that your Museum was worth 1000 pounds and that your Phoenician weight alone had a value of more than 200 pounds. I now tell you that it is my firm belief that the British Museum would give more than 400 pounds for this weight if you ask 800 pounds." Schliemann to Calvert, 12 August 1871, BB 2.3/3.

182. It had brought £174.2.6. News of the sale reached Athens, where it was reported as "the precious archaeological collection of the British Consul at the Dardanelles, Frank Calvert. The British Museum bought the main objects of this collection, among which are prehistoric vases from Hisarlık similar to those found by Schliemann." *Deltion tis Estias* 33, 14 August 1877. My translation. I thank George S. Korres for this citation.

CHAPTER 9

1. Simpson (1877), 1–16. Nicholas Yannakis, Schliemann's majordomo, had been his dragoman. Simpson (1903), 274. Simpson referred to Chevalier as "Schliemann the first" and Schliemann as "Chevalier the second." Ibid., 275.

2. Simpson (1877), 4. See Harrington (1996), 100–109, for Simpson's career.

3. Simpson (1877), 5. Elsewhere, Simpson claimed that "the whole affair [had] the character of a farce." The sixty-two children of Priam and their spouses hardly could have been contained in Schliemann's "palace," with its three small rooms, "unless they had been packed like sardines in a box." He declared that he could more readily believe that it was the "Palace of Priam's pig." He later noted that as soon as Schliemann returned to Hisarlık in 1878, the offending structure was removed. Simpson (1903), 276.

4. Simpson (1877), 8. Traill suggested that plans in Schliemann (1875a) had mislabeled the structure. Traill (1995), 178. The offending building was the later palace of the third stratum and blocked the second-stratum gateway.

5. Simpson (1877), 6.

6. Ibid., 16.

7. Stark (1877), 665–78, esp. 676. German original.

8. Calvert (1873a) and (1874a), 610–11.

9. Stark (1877), 676.

10. The ways in which the testimony of Yannakis, Schliemann's assistant, differed from Schliemann's account included Sophia's absence, Yannakis's find of the treasure, the presence chiefly of bronze in the treasure, and the find spot itself. Borlase was scandalized and accused Schliemann of gross misrepresentation. Borlase (1878), 235.

11. Ibid., 229.

12. Schliemann in the *Athenaeum*, 7 November 1874.

13. Borlase (1878), 232.

14. Ibid., 228, 237.

15. Ibid., 236–37 n. 6. Reprint of Calvert (1875).

16. Borlase (1878), 236.

17. Schliemann to Max Müller, 25 February 1878, in Meyer (1962), #49, 97. Schliemann knew that Calvert had "given the text" to the correspondent of the *Times* as well as to Simpson. German original.

18. Ibid., 97–99, in reference to Borlase (1878), 231.

19. "Dr. Schliemann's tongue" in a June 1878 draft. Frank Calvert to Simpson [unnamed], 19 July 1878, BB 2.2. In the original draft, he had noted the circumstances of Schliemann's first excavations at Hisarlık and specified that his name not be used in print.

20. The diplomats he referred to were Dom Pedro II (1825–1891), emperor of Brazil, and Arthur de Gobineau (1816–1882), an Orientalist and the author of a racist sociological treatise on the superiority of the Aryan race. *Webster's Biographical Dictionary*, s.v. "Pedro II, dom" and "Gobineau, Comte Joseph Arthur de." It was de Gobineau who, upon visiting Troy on 16 October 1876, called Schliemann "an impudent charlatan"—and also "a liar" and "an idiot." Buenzod (1961), 186.

21. The article, "The Troad," appeared in the London *Times* on 5 June 1876. Meyer (1958), #19, 48–49.

22. Frank Calvert to Simpson, 19 July 1878, Simpson Archive, the Mitchell Library, Glasgow; Traill (1995), 179–80. Calvert thanked Simpson for his article, which he had circulated among friends "who take an interest in Trojan polemics."

23. Schliemann to Kate Field, 28 March 1878, Boston Public Library; Arndt (1981), 2–3.

24. Kate Field to General Noyes, 20 December 1878, NARA; Arndt (1981), 3–4.

25. Schliemann to Kate Field, 26 June 1878, Boston Public Library; Arndt (1981), 3. His son Agamemnon Schliemann was born on 16 March 1878. Traill (1995), 180.

26. It was planned from 1871 on, but built in 1880. Sold in 1926, from 1934 to 1981 it served as the Greek Supreme Court. Now it houses the Numismatic Collection of the National Museum. Korres (1977).

27. Calvert's gardens were, in fact, much larger. For Schliemann's neoclassical mansion, see Korres (1977) and (1988), 164–73.

28. Schliemann to Layard, 30 July 1878, BLMS 39021/132.

29. Schliemann to Layard, 3 August 1878, BLMS 39021/164.

30. Frank Calvert to Simpson, 14 August 1878, Simpson Archive, the Mitchell Library; Glasgow. Traill (1995), 182.

31. Edmund and Frederick R. J. Calvert, British vice-consul and later consul at Adrianople (Edirne) and Philippolis (Plovdiv), reported on Bulgarian atrocities against the Turks from their consulates in Turkish Thrace. *Constantinople Messenger*, 9 August 1878. Frederick R. J. Calvert suffered a "nervous disorder derangement" as a result. Edmund asked to be transferred. Edmund Calvert to Layard, 20 June 1879, PRO/FO 78 3909.

32. J. F. A. Maling to the marquis of Salisbury, 3 May 1878, PRO/FO 78 2869.

33. J. F. A. Maling to Layard, 30 July 1878, PRO/FO 195 1213.

34. Copybooks of Schliemann's correspondence for July 1878 to July 1879 are not preserved. Easton (1982), 99, 101, 106.

35. Lehrer and Turner (1989), 262. Each suppressed public criticism of the other.

36. Frank Calvert to Virchow, 27 March 1880, ABBAW, Virchow, 335. The Schliemann-Virchow correspondence has been published by Herrmann and Maaß (1990) and is housed mainly in the Gennadius Library in Athens and the Berlin-Brandenburgische Akademie der Wissenschaften in Berlin. All letters between Schliemann and Virchow are translated by me from the German. The correspondence between Virchow and Calvert is unpublished and is located in the Berlin-Brandenburgische Akademie der Wissenschaften (ABBAW).

37. Schliemann (1881a), 50–51.

38. Ibid., 51–52.

39. Schliemann to Virchow, 27 November 1878, in Meyer (1958), #43, 73. German original. Herrmann and Maaß (1990), #4, 85–86. Traill believes that Schliemann again bundled the spectacular finds so as to make a greater impact. Traill (1995), 184–85.

40. As a result of dividing the first stratum in two in 1879, Schliemann now referred to his "Homeric" level as the "third" stratum, or "Burnt Stratum," because it now was third from the bottom, but it remained in fact the same deposit that was considered earlier as the second stratum. Schliemann (1881a), 51–52. See Figure 28.

41. Schliemann wrote Virchow that he would begin excavations at Hisarlık on 1 March, continuing through May. Schliemann to Virchow, 26 January 1879, in Meyer (1936), #66, 158–59; Schliemann (1881a), 52; Herrmann and Maaß (1990), #6, 87–89.

42. Schliemann (1881a), 52, 55–58, and "Recent Discoveries at Ilium," *Archaeological Journal* 36 (1879): 170.

43. Marchand (1996), 121.

44. The treasures were Hb in the north-central area and J on the fortification wall to the east of "Priam's Palace" and another that was rescued from in a wheelbarrow of debris. Traill believes that Schliemann staged both the find and find spot, which were conveniently *not* on Calvert's land. Traill (1995), 189 n. 39. See also Easton (1997), 197.

45. He excavated Üjek Tepe, Beşik Tepe, Agios Demetrios Tepe, the Tomb of Ilus, and a tumulus at Pınarbaşı. Schliemann (1881a), 648–72.

46. Schliemann (1881a), 128–30, 587, 688. Among his finds that season was a bronze double ax that resembled two he had found at Mycenae. Schliemann (1881a), 606 n. 10, figures 1429 and 1430.

47. Allen (1990).

48. Schliemann to William Ewart Gladstone, 28 May 1879, in Meyer (1958), #48, 78. To Layard he claimed that Troy was fully excavated. Schliemann to Layard, 4 June 1879, BLMS 39026/205.

49. Bacon (1912), 87–88. See Thomas (1995–96), 28–33. Like a good traveler, Clarke first swam the Hellespont. When they arrived at the Dardanelles, Calvert was not to be found. Allen, Congdon, and Landry (forthcoming).

50. Congdon (1974). Two of Bacon's journals currently are being edited for publication by Allen, Congdon, and Landry (forthcoming).

51. Thomas (1995–96), 28–33. Sheftel (1979), 3–17.

52. Bacon's visit dated to 1–2 June. Bacon to Field, 19 June 1879; Arndt (1981), 1–8.

53. George Dennis to Layard, 19 July 1878, BLMS 39021.

54. Schliemann to Layard, 22 January 1879, BLMS 39024.

55. Schliemann to Layard, 15 May 1879, BLMS 39026/89.

56. Schliemann to Layard, 17 May 1879, BLMS 39026/101.

57. A small portion of five of the twenty-one treasures is still in the Istanbul Archaeological Museum. Saherwala, Goldmann, and Mahr (1993), 81, 225; Siebler (1994), 58–60. Treasures D, F, J, and O are represented, but some three hundred and thirty items once inventoried could not be found in 1902. Götze (1902), 237–47. Schliemann bought back some items. Saherwala, Goldmann, and Mahr (1993), 36–37.

58. Schliemann to "Sir A." [probably Augustus Wollaston Franks], 22 August 1879, in Meyer (1958), #53, 81.

59. Schliemann to Cesnola, 24 July 1879, in Meyer (1958), 425 n. 84.

60. Frank Calvert to Schliemann, 17 November 1879, B 81/974. The 1902 catalogue of the Calvert Collection added Alexandria Troas, Gergis, Imbros, Kilia, Lampsakos, Myrina, Perkote, Taşoba, Thasos, Çan, and the entire Troad. Thiersch (1902a) and notes sent me by Cook. Calvert elaborated on the previous list: Frank Calvert to Schliemann, undated, B 81/1039 a/b.

61. Allen (1993), (1994), (1995a), and (1995b). Lehrer and Turner had come to a similar conclusion: (1989), 262.

62. Frank Calvert to Virchow, 27 March 1880, ABBAW, Virchow, 335.

63. The Schliemann-Schöne correspondence has been published by Saherwala, Goldmann, and Mahr (1993) and Meyer (1936). For Schöne, see Pallat (1959). For Schöne's portrait, see Lullies and Schiering (1988), 75.

64. The term he used was *nützlich*. Schliemann to Virchow, 4 June 1879, in Meyer (1936), #65, 157, and Herrmann and Maaß (1990), #25, 104–6. "You must be good enough to work

out a little decoration for friend Calvert. Such finery has for him an immense worth and he can always be useful." Schliemann to Virchow, 19 June 1879, in Herrmann and Maaß (1990), #28, 109. In fact, the decoration was not important to Calvert. Rather, it was Schliemann who regarded such trappings so seriously.

65. Schliemann to Virchow, 21 July 1879, in Herrmann and Maaß (1990), #45, 126–27.

66. Frank Calvert to Schliemann, 13 October 1881, B 87/609; Calvert (1860b), 289–90.

67. Calvert (1881), 706–20. In his discussion of his surface survey, he alluded to hand mills, or querns, stone axes, sherds, spindle whorls, and flint flakes of the prehistoric settlement.

68. Calvert (1881), nos. 1538–40.

69. Calvert had sent specimens to Virchow since 1874–75. Virchow (1875) and (1882).

70. Frank Calvert to Schliemann, 1 May 1879, B 79/313. Calvert's frankness caused another contretemps, for which he later apologized: Frank Calvert to Schliemann, 4 May 1879, B 79/317.

71. In November, Calvert noted that he had recommenced excavations. A month later, he wrote: "The strike is nearly at an end I had 8 men at work at H. T. which is as many as I care to employ in the narrow trenches tracing out the walls. They go rather deep in places—towards the west—these walls are in places missing but the general plan at present can be traced." Frank Calvert to Schliemann, 13 November 1879 and 16 December 1879, B 81/962 and B 81/1039.

72. Frank Calvert to Schliemann, 7 December 1879, B 81/1018.

73. Schliemann to Frank Calvert, 17 December 1879, BBB 36/291–94.

74. Frank Calvert to Virchow, 15 January 1880, ABBAW, Virchow, 335.

75. Frank Calvert to Schliemann, 12 October 1880, B 84/857. He recommended excavating tombs as the quickest solution.

76. Schliemann to Frank Calvert, 16 October 1879, BBB 36/165.

77. Frank Calvert to Schliemann, 16 December 1879, B 81/1039. On December 28, Calvert complained that the engravings were too small. B 81/1079.

78. Schliemann to Frank Calvert, 1 January 1880. BBB 36/307. In the same letter (and in one of 10 February 1880, BBB 37/50) he refused to send up a number of Calvert's drawings to the publisher.

79. He also described the inhabitants' techniques of house building, noting such poignant details as a child's toe prints in once-fresh mud bricks. Pottery styles and manufacturing techniques are more than adequately noted, and he reconstructed the ancients' diet from animal bones and granaries at the site. Particularly illuminating are the discussions of the contents and contexts of two infant burials, which he saved for study by Virchow. Virchow (1882).

80. Schliemann to Frank Calvert, 10 February 1880, BBB 37/50. Schliemann requested that the plan be reduced by 80 percent. Schliemann to J. W. Whymper, 5 February 1880, BBB 37/41.

81. Schliemann to John Murray, 28 February 1880, in Traill (1995), 199.

82. Frank Calvert to Schliemann, 27 March 1880, B 82/201. J. W. Whymper to Schliemann, 16 February 1880, B 82/103.

83. Calvert responded to continual prodding by Schliemann in his letters of 6 January, 21 and 24 February, and 2 and 16 March 1880, B 82/21, B 82/114, B 82/116, B 82/133, and B 82/178.

84. Calvert had been busy with his mining enterprises in April and plagued by lost notes in April and locusts at the farm in May. "The locusts have come down from the hills like a sea." Frank Calvert to Schliemann, 8 April, 5 May, and 10 June 1880, B 82/232, B 82/304, B 82/398. By 15 May 1880, he had written ten pages of introduction. B 82/330.

85. Schliemann to Virchow, 30 July 1880, in Herrmann and Maaß (1990), #163, 216.

86. Schliemann to Sayce, 29 July 1880, BBB 37/292; quoted in Traill (1995), 199–201. Winifred Lamb praised the report more than fifty years later. Lamb (1932), 11–25.

87. Schliemann to Frank Calvert, 11 August 1879, BBB 36/201.

88. Sayce (1880), 75. He was sometimes employed by Schliemann. Traill (1993), 226–30.

89. Schliemann (1881a), viii.

90. Frank Calvert to Schliemann, 16 December 1879, B 81/1039. Winifred Lamb confirmed his dates in her article on prehistoric sites of the Troad. Lamb (1932), 120. Calvert noted that the second, fourth, and fifth prehistoric strata at Hisarlık were missing at Hanay Tepe. He had slightly revised his thinking in 1882 when he subdivided the lowest stratum B at Hanay Tepe into five phases. Frank Calvert to Virchow, 17 January 1880 and 24 October 1882, ABBAW, Virchow, 335.

91. Although he originally thought the calcined material was of human bone, he now concluded that it was ash from vegetal matter, with only accidental bone or shell.

92. Calvert (1881), 709–19. Sayce referred to it as "a temple . . . to manes of the dead." "The Troad," *Athenaeum* 2710, 4 October 1879, 440.

93. In this he sided with Lord Broughton and Barker Webb. Broughton (1813), 753; Barker Webb (1844), 50. One of Waddington's inscriptions (1743d) apparently came from the area associated with the temple. Le Bas and Waddington (1870), 2:417. Strabo (13.1.35) mentioned a Thymbraean plain and a Temple of Apollo Thymbraeus near the Thymbrios River. Calvert's previous Thymbra finds are in the British Museum (Allen 1996b), 147 n. 17. See Stark (1874a), 160, and Thiersch (1902a), site no. 26, 257–98. Cook disagreed with the attribution of the site to Thymbra due to the lack of numismatic evidence and simply records a sixth–fifth-century cemetery. Cook (1973), 119–22.

94. Calvert later attributed the upper part of the lower stratum (B4 and B5, the fortified levels), all of the middle stratum (C), and the lower part of the top stratum (A) to a civilization contemporary with the "Lydian" settlement at Hisarlık. Frank Calvert to Virchow, 17 January 1881 and 24 October 1882, ABBAW, Virchow, 335. Calvert (1881), 715, figure 1567.

95. Calvert (1881), 720. This resemblance even included the animal-head handles.

96. Frank Calvert to Virchow, 15 January 1880, ABBAW, Virchow, 335.

97. Frank Calvert to Schliemann, 2 March 1880, B 82/133.

98. "Publish nothing hanaitepe your publication would kill our friendship my love Germany." Schliemann telegraph to Virchow, 8 March 1880, in Herrmann and Maaß (1990), #98, 169. French original. Virchow responded by telegram on 9 March and in letters of 8 and 13 March 1880. In Herrmann and Maaß (1990), #99–101, 169–71. Schliemann reiterated his position ten days later. In Herrmann and Maaß (1990), #103, 173. French original. Other correspondence between the two cited here was in German. As with Calvert before, Schliemann probably used French to threaten his adversary.

99. Schliemann to Frank Calvert, 3 March 1880, BBB 37/83; Schliemann to Virchow, 18 March 1880, in Herrmann and Maaß (1990), #102, 172.

100. Frank Calvert to Schliemann, 16 March 1880, B 82/178.

101. Schliemann wrote to Virchow that his intended publication of Hanay Tepe had really upset Calvert. He declared that he had tried to keep Calvert quiet and had sent him a telegram in Virchow's name that Virchow had stopped publication. Schliemann to Virchow, 18 and 24 March 1880, in Herrmann and Maaß (1990), #102, 172, #106, 174–75. It was Schliemann who overreacted, not Calvert, as claimed by Traill (1995), 201–2. Traill has shown that Schliemann later put the blame on Sophia in order to extricate himself from another misunderstanding with Virchow. Traill (1995), 246–50.

102. "Our friend is too apt to take offences as I have learned by experience." Frank Calvert to Virchow, 10 June 1880, ABBAW, Virchow, 335.

103. Virchow (1882).

104. "In his *Beiträge zur Landeskunde der Troas,* which appeared in 1882 [sic], Virchow collected and compared all that was then known concerning the fauna of that region. He now makes various additions to these data, embodying much material hitherto unpublished." Clarke (1886), 195–202.

105. "Calvert's prehistoric sherds from Rhoeteum, Aeanteion, and Ophrynium are invented. . . . He can't tell the difference between historic and prehistoric." Schliemann to Virchow, 5 July 1880, in Herrmann and Maaß (1990), #154, 209. In all fairness, Cook himself (1973) was occasionally uncertain as to whether sherds at Ophryneion, Rhoeteum, and Aianteion were historic or prehistoric. Cook (1973), 77, 80, 86.

106. Virchow (1881), 681.

107. Ibid., 56, 57, 60, 99, 104.

108. Ibid., 20. Schliemann (1875a), 272, mentioned two small cuttings.

109. Schliemann to Virchow, 26 January and 6 July 1879, in Meyer (1936), #66, #67, 158–60, and Herrmann and Maaß (1990), #6, 87–89, #35, 115–16.

110. Frank Calvert to Schliemann, 15 July 1879, B 81/532. There Calvert mentioned an acknowledgment he had received from Paul Falk in advance of the gift.

111. Frank Calvert to Virchow, 14 July 1879, ABBAW, Virchow, 335.

112. Frank Calvert to Schliemann, 26 August 1879, B 81/674.

113. Frank Calvert to Schliemann, 28 December 1879, B 81/1079.

114. Frank Calvert to Schliemann, 17 November 1879, B 81/974.

115. In a letter to Virchow, Schliemann noted that he had promised Calvert a decoration for giving his half of the Hanay Tepe material to Berlin. Schliemann to Virchow, 4 June 1879, in Meyer (1936), #65, 157–58, and Herrmann and Maaß (1990), #25, 104–6. Schliemann wrote to Virchow that the government would not give a decoration to an Englishman. Schliemann to Virchow, 5 September 1879. In 1883, Schliemann was still trying to obtain it, through Virchow, but was unsuccessful because Calvert was English. Schliemann to Frank Calvert, 6 February 1883, NARA Dard. 11.

116. Frank Calvert to Schliemann, 4 May 1879, B 79/317. Earlier he had written concerning the division that he would like to keep the nephrite ax. In 1882, Calvert again wrote asking for the ax. Frank Calvert to Schliemann, 7 July 1882, B 89/425.

117. That his gift to the Berlin Museum should be made in their joint name is mentioned by Calvert to Schliemann in letters of 12 October 1880 and 10 November 1880, B 84/857 and B 84/908. Eight cases from the Hanay Tepe excavations were received by the museum. An inventory in Calvert's hand described the contents. From the lowest stratum (B): skulls and accompanying bones, pottery; millstones, weights, hammers, and the broken bones of animals, plus stone implements—flakes, shells, horns, jawbones, and sundries.

From the middle stratum (C): pottery, burned bones, bricks, calcined and vitrified stones, and charcoal. From the highest stratum (A): an infant skeleton, asbestos, pottery, a slate necklace of glass beads, an earring, and a ring of bronze. These objects were later placed with others given by Schliemann and put under the heading of the Schliemann Collection. Register of the Museum for Prehistory and Early History, Berlin. See also Schmidt (1902), preface, Zengel (1990), 151–58, and Bertram (1992), 397. Lamb (1932), 112–125, studied the Hanay Tepe material, and I did so in 1993.

118. Schliemann to Virchow, 4 June 1879, in Herrmann and Maaß (1990), #25, 104–5; Frank Calvert to Schliemann, 12 October 1880, B 84/857.

119. Schliemann approached the crown prince on 30 July 1879; mentioned in Frank Calvert to Schliemann, 13 November 1879, B 81/962. Paul Falk to Frank Calvert, 23 June 1879, in Saherwala, Goldmann, and Mahr (1993), 24 n. 110. The communication with Falk is noted in Frank Calvert to Schliemann, November 1879, B 81/962, and in Frank Calvert to Virchow, 14 July 1879, ABBAW, Virchow, 335.

120. Schliemann to Frank Calvert, 6 February 1883, NARA RG84 Dard. 11.

121. Schliemann's haste may in part have been prompted by a desire to avoid splitting the finds, humble as they were, with the Ottomans, for according to the 1874 antiquities law, the Ottoman government should have received one-third of the finds. Aristarchi (1874), 162. Calvert was treating the skulls and packing them carefully when he received Schliemann's orders to ship them immediately in July 1879. Because of disagreements between the German consul and Schliemann, however, they were not sent to Germany until the autumn. Because of Schliemann's impatience with the packing, some skulls were broken. Moreover, Schliemann told Virchow that he had not actually witnessed the sending of the packages and so could not say whether he had sent all of them, but thought so because he was "a correct man." Schliemann to Virchow, 29 October 1879, Herrmann and Maaß (1990), #77, 149.

122. The Ethnographical Museum is now the Museum for Prehistory and Early History. Bertram (1992), 397 n. 2. Schliemann to Virchow, 12 February 1880, in Meyer (1958), #64, 89, in Hermann and Maaß (1990), #92, 163, and in Saherwala, Goldmann, and Mahr (1993), 27; Schöne to Schliemann, 25 November, 17 December 1879, and 8 January 1880, in Saherwala, Goldmann, and Mahr (1993), 144–45.

123. Saherwala, Goldmann, and Mahr (1993), 26.

124. Secretary of State William Evarts to John M. Francis, 15 August 1879, referred to in Francis correspondence, 21 August 1979, NARA. Arndt (1981), 1–8.

125. Schliemann to Kate Field, 15 January 1881, Boston Public Library; Arndt (1981), 8.

126. Schliemann to Virchow, 9 September 1879, in Meyer (1936), #73, 164, and in Hermann and Maaß (1990), #59, 139–40; Schliemann to Schöne, 1 January 1880. Bertram (1992), 397. He virtually had announced the gift to Germany in Schliemann to Wilhelm Rust, 25 December 1879, in Saherwala, Goldmann, and Mahr (1993), 25, and Stoll (1962), #17, 268.

127. Schliemann to the London architect and architectural historian James Fergusson (1808–1886), 9 December 1880, in Meyer (1958), #90, 16.

128. His prejudice against his native land is clear from several letters he wrote to Wilhelm Rust. See Schliemann to Rust, 13 March and 24 April 1875, in Stoll (1958), #4, #5, 246–53. Interestingly enough, even as late as December 1878, Schliemann wrote of his Trojan Collection that it was not for sale, and even if he gave it to a German town, it certainly never would be to Berlin. Amandry (1995), 82.

129. Schliemann to Crown Prince Bernhard, 11 December 1880, in Meyer (1958), #91, 116–118. German original. To Max Müller, he again noted his conditions for this gift. Schliemann to Max Müller, 29 December 1880, in Meyer (1962), #28, 100. German original.

130. Virchow to Schliemann, 20 December 1880, in Meyer (1958), #92, 188–91, and Hermann and Maaß (1990), #195, 237–38; Ottaway (1973), 103–4. For Schöne, see Marchand (1996), 65, 74.

131. Frank Calvert to Virchow, 8 July 1879, ABBAW, Virchow, 335.

132. Calvert (1860b) and (1873b); Virchow (1882), 5, and (1875), 41, 90, 276.

133. He was well aware of Lyell's *Principles of Geology* (1830–33).

134. *Levant Herald*, 14 and 19 March, 1873. Calvert (1873b).

135. Frederick Calvert to Schliemann, 31 March 1873, B 68/104; Calvert (1873c), 127–29.

136. These sites are described in Calvert (1880), 31–39. He had encountered the prehistoric remains at Ophryneion (stone axes and prehistoric pottery) only after his 1860 article had been published. Frank Calvert to Virchow, 13 January 1881, ABBAW, Virchow, 335.

137. Calvert (1873b); Calvert and Neumayr (1880), 357.

138. Calvert and Neumayr (1880), 357–78 and plates 1 and 2.

139. Frank Calvert to Virchow, 13 December 1882, ABBAW, Virchow, 335.

140. The American explorer E. G. Squier of New York, consul Spiegelthal of Smyrna, the Swedish prehistorian Oskar Montelius (1843–1921), and Theodor von Heldreich, director of the Botanical Garden in Athens, also were corresponding members of the society. Regular members included several of Calvert's future collaborators: Professors Paul Ascherson, Melchior Neumayr, and F. Kurtz of Berlin.

141. It had appeared first in the 28 October 1874 *Levant Herald*. Virchow (1875), 276.

142. Virchow to Schliemann, 3 February and 13 March 1880, in Herrmann and Maaß (1990), #91, 162, and #101, 171. Apparently Virchow saw the paper through publication as a favor to Calvert and Schliemann, since he had been unsuccessful in obtaining a decoration for Calvert. Frank Calvert to Virchow, 10 June 1880, ABBAW, Virchow, 335. Calvert also had sent a copy to Sayce for comments, but only Virchow responded and helped him. Frank Calvert to Schliemann, 7 December 1879, B 81/1018. Calvert (1880), 31–39.

143. Frank Calvert to Virchow, 15 January 1880, ABBAW, Virchow, 335.

144. Frank Calvert to Virchow, 18 September 1880, ABBAW, Virchow, 335.

145. Frank Calvert to Virchow, 10 June 1880, ABBAW, Virchow, 335.

146. Rapp and Gifford (1982), 33, figures 13 and 14. Rapp and Gifford unfortunately ignored his pioneering research.

147. Calvert (1880), 31–39. Had Zangger been aware of Calvert's article, he might have found a measure of support for his unusual and improbable thesis on the destruction of Troy/Atlantis. Eberhard Zangger, *Flood from Heaven: Deciphering the Atlantis Legend* (London, 1992), 81–90.

148. Calvert (1880), 31–39; Maclaren (1863), 60.

149. Rapp and Gifford note that Virchow's pits (from 0.5 to 2 meters deep) were not deep enough to be conclusive. By contrast theirs were from 30 to 70 meters deep. Rapp and Gifford (1982), 17.

150. Ibid., 25, figure 9. For the latest research on the bay of Troy, see Kayan (1995), 221.

151. Frank Calvert to Schliemann, 25 October 1881, B 87/631. One senses Calvert's frustration at trying to conduct scholarly research without facilities nearby.

152. "I think what Calvert wants to do is rash. . . . Calvert is not really prepared for such work and how in the world can I get all those priceless things! I really do not know how I can make him get lost and I ask you to tell me how." Schliemann to Virchow, 29 October 1881, in Herrmann and Maaß (1990), #259, 283.

153. Frank Calvert to Schliemann, 15 November 1881, B 87/669.

154. "Calvert is a remarkable man, he can do a lot and I think it is good for him that he has the opportunity to inform himself in a geological way because he can then be quite useful." Virchow to Schliemann, 10 November 1881, in Herrmann and Maaß (1990), #260, 283–84.

155. Later Schliemann strongly supported his views: "Calvert proves beyond any doubt the cessation of growth of the land on the coast and the gradual invasion of the sea upon the land." Schliemann (1881a), 91 n. 4.

156. Schliemann to Frank Calvert, 25 November 1881, B 38/326.

157. Frank Calvert to Virchow, 13 December 1882, ABBAW, Virchow, 335.

158. A *Levant Herald* article on 5 May 1881 expressed the frustrations of one who had found a mine and had to go out looking for capital without any governmental support. Later *Levant Herald and Eastern Express* articles and editorials, on 9 June and 21 July 1886, expressed a desire for a financial and scientific center to coordinate the mining industry. A 1910 memo by Calvert's successor as consul noted the mineral wealth of the Troad but deplored the lack of transport. NARA RG84 Dard. 6.

159. Frank Calvert to Virchow, 24 August 1882, ABBAW, Virchow, 335. One was the "Adramite" (Adramyttion) mine. Frank Calvert to Schliemann, 15 July 1879, B 81/532. The first concession was given to a foreigner—a Frenchman—in 1856 for boracite mines in the Balıkesır area. Cuinet (1893), 3.iv, 3:18–19.

160. Frank Calvert to Schliemann, 13 November 1879, B 81/962. Strabo, 13.1.18, and Pliny, *Natural History*, 34.37, mentioned a mine at Lampsacus. Apparently Calvert had not spoken to Burnouf about the silver and lead mine there and sent an engineer named Serpieri. Calvert was setting up a company to develop the mine. Sixteen kilometers south of Lapseki, on the banks of the rivers Kory and Derındéré, Calvert had a concession for an argentiferous lead and copper mine. By 1983, an English syndicate was beginning preliminary work there. Cuinet (1893), 3:704, 3:761. Boracite was discovered and exploited by Calvert in the village of Yıldız, near Panderma. This, too, was exploited by an English company. It was closed by the government in 1962 after about a hundred years of mining. Bülent Coşkun, via Ibrahim Aksu; Cuinet (1893), 3:704.

161. Cook's notes to the catalogue of the Calvert Collection.

162. Frank Calvert to Virchow, 24 August 1882, ABBAW, Virchow, 335.

163. Reports to Frank Calvert from F. Bonnet, 15 January 1881; W. L. Storey, March 1881; and Gorkiewicz, a Polish excavation architect, 9 March 1881. Calvert to Virchow, 11 September and 12 December 1882, ABBAW, Virchow, 335. Strabo, 13.1.23, 65, 67, and Leaf (1923), 133–36. Their concession of 2177 acres was issued under an imperial *firman* for ninety-nine years from 13 March 1877. Calvert to Virchow, 12 December 1882, ABBAW, Virchow, 335. At one point, the Calverts had an offer from a London syndicate to form a company with a capital of £200,000 to exploit the auriferous quartz mine at Sevciler or Terziler and Osmanlar, out of which the Calverts would have received a large portion in cash, but an untimely glut of gold from India rendered this unfeasible, so Calvert approached Virchow to find an appropriate person to develop the mine. Frank Calvert to Virchow, 11 September 1882, ABBAW, Virchow, 335. Cuinet (1893), 3:748–49.

164. There were ten mines known in the *kaza,* or district, of Ezine: four of chrome at Pınarbaşı, Kemali, Dümrek, and Hissardji, five of manganese at Icıklar, Orman Tepe, Çamlı, Köprü Başı, and Kaz Burnu, and a sulfur mine at Kourmalar. Cuinet (1893) 3:704, 3:766.

165. Frank Calvert to U.S. consul general G. H. Heap, 16 January 1879, NARA RG84 Dard. 1.

166. The *Levant Herald and Eastern Express* of 20 October 1886 reported that two research permits had been granted, one for chrome, antimony, and argentiferous lead mines over an area of over 20,000 *dounoms* in the *kaza* of Panderma, and the other for iron, argentiferous lead, coal mines, and petroleum over an area of 40,000 *dounoms* in the *kaza* of Edremit. The first certainly must have been granted to Calvert, who was very active in this area. The second may well refer to him, as well.

167. The Tod treasure of Egypt, Annie Caubet, personal communication.

168. De Jesus (1980), 76. Ernst Pernicka currently is sampling silver ores from Trojan sources throughout the Troad. His reports appear in *Studia Troica.*

169. De Jesus (1980) 65, and 268, no. 116. Ryan (1957), 3, suggests that the remains date at least to the age of Pericles and that modern methods were introduced only in 1882, when according to de Jesus, the "Bonne Espérance" mine began to be worked by a French-owned company that exploited it until 1935. The mine was known as Hoca Gumuç. It exported four thousand tons annually by 1893 and employed four hundred persons. De Jesus (1980), 65. Cuinet 3:iv, 3:17.

170. Ibid., 236–37, 269–71; Ryan (1957).

171. A number of the mines could have produced Calvert's fossils. Copper deposits abound in the area of Çanakkale. Numerous such deposits were worked in the past, caved and tunneled and then abandoned. Another lead mine in the Çanakkale area preserves remnants of old mining activity. Antimony mines near Balıkesır that were worked as early as 1887 continue to have thousands of tons of reserves. For iron, Ryan lists a deposit near Lapseki with reserves of about one million tons. Manganese deposits were worked prior to World War I in the *kaza* of Edremit, where there remain reserves of between eight and ten thousand tons. Others exist around Balıkesır. For chromite, which was discovered in Turkey in 1848 and for which in the years 1860 to 1893 Turkey led the world's production, Ryan notes forty-eight deposits in Balıkesır, nineteen in Çanakkale. Bauxite and graphite were also mined. Ryan (1957), 27, 63, 80, 116, 131, 155–56, 177–78; de Jesus (1980), 269.

172. Ryan (1957), 5, 76, suggests that the mine at Balya Maden, which was exploited in antiquity, was also a source of orpiment in ancient times. He also suggested that certain mines in the Edremit area had the correct composition for orpiment. Ryan (1957), 66, 83. De Jesus (1980), 90–91, seconded Ryan's finds. Orpiment, or realgar, is an arsenic derivative, a yellow crystalline substance frequently found in association with lead as arsenopyrite. It was important in Bronze Age trade and recently has been found in an amphora on a Bronze Age shipwreck of approximately 1327 B.C. off the south coast of Turkey at Ulu Burun, near Kaş. Orpiment was used in antiquity by the Egyptians of the Eighteenth Dynasty as a common pigment in wall painting and an ingredient in ink used on papyri. Orpiment also was used to decorate the walls of Malkata, the mortuary temple of Amenophis III, the Egyptian pharaoh who had the most frequent contact with the Aegean. At Malkata, on the base of the fifth of ten statues depicting the pharaoh, there are fourteen Aegean place names, perhaps a geographical itinerary of a specific state visit. Cline (1994), 38–39. Ilios, or Troy, is included in this list, and if it was in control of re-

sources from mines such as Balya Maden, it may be seen as among Egypt's sources of this important raw material. In the Amarna Age, orpiment was used on portraits of Akhnaten and Nefertiti. A bag full of orpiment was found in the tomb of Tutankhamen. Later evidence shows that it was an important ingredient in glass manufacture, as well. Bass (1986), 278–79 nn. 37–42.

173. *Neue deutsche Biographie,* s.v. "Ascherson, Paul."

174. Frank Calvert to Schliemann, 12 October 1880, 16 June and 2 July 1881, B 86/306 and B 86/370; Cook (1973), 35; Ascherson, Heldreich, and Kurtz (1881), 727–36. All were members of the Society for Anthropology, Ethnography, and Prehistory.

175. Ascherson (1883), 339–65.

176. Ibid., 341. Calvert had contributed six hundred samples of plants and seeds between 1880 and 1882.

177. Ibid., 342–43.

178. Schliemann (1884), 2.

179. Calvert had suggested that the cemetery must lie outside, but close to the walls. He had found the Greco-Roman necropolis outside the much larger historic city. Frank Calvert to Schliemann, 30 November 1879, B 81/1001. He suggested that Schliemann work on the southeastern side of the acropolis. Schliemann later told Virchow that he would commence there. Schliemann to Virchow, 23 October 1881, in Herrmann and Maaß (1990), #258, 282.

180. Schliemann to Frank Calvert, 30 July 1879, BBB 36/116.

181. Frank Calvert to Schliemann, 12 October 1880, B 84/857.

182. Schliemann already was looking ahead in 1879. Schliemann to Frank Calvert, 30 July and 16 October 1879, BBB 36/116 and B 36/165.

183. Schliemann noted that he would have to make arrangements with all the landowners. Schliemann to Frank Calvert, 9 December 1879, referred to in Frank Calvert to Schliemann, 16 December 1879, B 81/1039. The compliant Calvert immediately gave him permission to search for prehistoric graves on his own land.

184. Frank Calvert to Schliemann, 10 November 1880, B 84/908. One wishes that the recorded master list, with objects and their provenances, were still preserved.

185. Schliemann (1884), 5.

186. Schliemann (1881b), 72. He was wrong. See Cook (1973) and Allen (1990).

187. Witte (1990), figure 7.

188. Frank Calvert to Schliemann, 2 July 1881, B 86/370.

189. Schliemann to Frank Calvert, 9 July 1881, BBB 38/144.

190. Schliemann to Frank Calvert, 29 July 1881, BBB 38/231.

191. Schliemann to Frank Calvert, 27 March, 11 and 21 October 1881, BBB 38/12, 38/265, and 38/282.

192. Schliemann to Frank Calvert, 11 October 1881, BBB 38/265.

193. Frank Calvert to Schliemann, 16 June 1881, B 86/306.

194. Calvert included a map in his letter to Schliemann of 14 December 1881, B 87/732.

195. Frank Calvert to Schliemann, 13 October 1881, 87/609.

196. "Calvert, to whom I gave some money to do some excavations found some graves made with crude stone plaques." Schliemann to Virchow, 4 December 1881, in Herrmann and Maaß (1990), #265, 286–87. Calvert had announced the finds to Schliemann on 10 November 1881. Calvert admitted to Virchow that he had not been present when the tombs

with the fibulae were opened. Frank Calvert to Virchow, 11 September 1882, ABBAW, Virchow, 335.

197. Schliemann to Virchow, 28 June 1882, mentioned that Calvert had found a stone ceremonial ax and pot with owl's head in tombs at Çamlıca. In Herrmann and Maaß, (1990), #302, 321. Schliemann mentioned these finds in *Troja* (1884), 325–27. Virchow (1882), 127.

198. Schliemann to Virchow, 4 and 22 December 1881, and 24 April and 23 May 1882, in Herrmann and Maaß (1990), #265, 286–87, #270, 290, #284, 301–3, #292, 308–10, Schmidt (1902), xviii–xix, and Virchow to Schliemann, 12 December 1881 and 13 April 1882 show intense interest in the pieces. In Herrmann and Maaß (1990), #267, 287–88, #282, 299–300. There is material from Çamlıca in the catalogue of the Calvert Collection, Thiersch (1902a), 298–301.

199. Schmidt did not include finds from sites other than Troy in his 1902 catalogue, but Goldmann (1992), 378, mentions a handwritten catalogue that contained the very numerous items not from Troy (Schmidt's numbers 4,705–11,879). The Köprü Başı fibulae were entered into the Schliemann Collection. Apparently, to protect Schliemann, Calvert had mislabeled the two fibulae (5581 and 5582) so that it appeared they came from Troy. Schliemann to Albert Voß (1837–1906), director of the Prehistoric section of the Ethnographic Museum and member of the Berlin Anthropological Society, 23 October 1887, in Saherwala, Goldmann, and Mahr (1993), 130.

200. Schliemann to Virchow, 3 June 1882, in Herrmann and Maaß (1990), #296, 312–13. German original.

201. Frank Calvert to Schliemann, 9 May 1882, B 89/295.

202. Frank Calvert to Schliemann, 5 July 1882, B 89/422. Calvert was himself active at both sites. Finds from Abydos (Strabo, 13.1.22) are in the catalogue of the Calvert Collection, Thiersch (1902a), 1, 3.

203. Calvert (1889), 174; Judeich (1898), 532–34; Leaf (1923), 133–35; Strabo, 14.5.8; de Jesus (1980), 83. Schliemann repeated this in (1884), 49–50.

204. Schliemann to Frank Calvert, 5 July 1882, B 89/422.

205. Responding to Schliemann's request for horses in 1879, Calvert apologized that all the rideable ones had been sold. By 1882, he was selling metopes from the temple of Athena at a bargain price for cash. Schliemann to Schöne, 26 July, in Meyer (1936), #126, 216, German original, and Saherwala, Goldmann, and Mahr (1993), 100–101.

206. *Levant Herald*, 10 March and 20 November 1880.

207. Schliemann told Virchow that Calvert "really wants to continue the excavations at Hanay Tepe when I give him the money. He thinks that in the lowest stratum he could find a lot of skulls, but I do not think so because he only found one even if the excavations were very important." Schliemann to Virchow, 3 June 1882, in Herrmann and Maaß (1990), #296, 313.

208. Virchow, "Preface" to Schliemann (1881), x.

209. Frank Calvert to Schliemann, 17 March and 12 and 19 October 1881, B 85/156, B 87/606, and B 87/619. On 12 October 1881, Calvert once again gave Schliemann permission to excavate his "land at Hissarlik, measuring 8 dounoms [about 2 acres], subject to conditions which Ottoman law exacts," with one-third of the finds going to Schliemann, one-third to the Ottoman government, and one-third to Calvert as landowner. B 87/606.

210. Schliemann (1884), 5. For Dörpfeld, see *Webster's Biographical Dictionary*, s.v. "Dörpfeld, Wilhelm."

211. Schliemann (1884), 18. He later estimated that the theater would have held around six thousand spectators.

212. Schliemann to Frank Calvert, 21 October 1881, BB 2.4/31. Rose (1998), 105.

213. One of these *megarons* was 110 meters long by 3 meters wide.

214. Schliemann's permit supplement came through in 1882. Schliemann (1884), 5, 10. He noted incorrectly that Frank Calvert had opened this tumulus and excavated with soldiers of the British fleet in 1855 but found nothing of any worth in the excavation, since pottery was not thought to be important then. Ibid., 251. That the Calverts did give attention to pottery at this time is clear from Carlisle (1854), Senior (1859), and Calvert (1859). Schliemann was simply mistaken.

215. Schliemann told Gladstone that he wished he had had such architects with him from the beginning. Schliemann to Gladstone, 3 May 1882, in Meyer (1958), #116, 142–44.

216. Sayce (1884), xiii. Schliemann now noted three phases in the long-lived second settlement.

217. Schliemann (1884), 27–28.

218. Letter (not preserved) to Calvert's niece Edith, with whom Schliemann corresponded, referred to in Frank Calvert to Schliemann, 7 July 1882, B 89/425.

219. Ibid. Henry died of typhoid on 29 July, a month after returning to the Dardanelles, after surviving terrible civilian riots and massacres in Alexandria, where he had served as British vice-consul for twenty-five years. Baron de Kusel, English chief of the European department of the Customs Service in Alexandria, recorded the anti-European sentiments that were rampant, the arrival of the British and French fleets to secure stability and "protect European nationals," which aggravated the situation, the flight within two weeks of fourteen thousand Europeans and their dependents, and the outbreak of rioting on 11 June. He had sought refuge in the gutted British consulate and found the consul, Charles Cookson, had been seriously wounded, and Henry Calvert, the vice-consul, was in a state of collapse from nervous fatigue. Approximately fifty Europeans and many more Egyptians had been killed or wounded. After subsequent bombardment by the British fleet, Alexandria was left to burn. Looters targeted foreign property. While some foreigners made their way to Malta, Spain, Greece, or Italy, Henry returned to the Dardanelles. His valuable botanical and conchological collections had been destroyed in the riot. The funeral was reported in the *Illustrated London News*, 19 August 1882. For de Kusel's memoir, see Sattin (1988), 107–10.

220. Now he used Nikolaos Didymos, dragoman of the Turkish governor at the Dardanelles, and Emilio Vitalis to smuggle out finds to Athens. Schliemann to Virchow, 19 October 1882 and 2 January 1883, in Herrmann and Maaß (1990), #319, 334–36, #329, 345. Schliemann to Schöne, 5, 12, and 17 May and 5 July 1882, in Saherwala, Goldmann, and Mahr (1993), 95–98. Apparently when their decorations were stalled in Berlin, Schliemann threatened Virchow that he would send the rest of the collection, which still was in Athens and Hisarlik, to Munich. He received the decorations the same month.

221. Schliemann to Virchow, 17 May 1882, in Herrmann and Maaß (1990), #271, 291.

222. Schliemann to Schöne, 17 June, 5 and 23 July, and 7 August 1882, in Saherwala, Goldmann, and Mahr (1993), 36, 96–99, 102–3.

223. Schliemann to Schöne, 23 July, 28 August, and list 5 of 31 August 1882, in Saher-wala, Goldmann, and Mahr (1993), 99, 105, 227. Easton (1997), 198 n. 51.

224. Schliemann to Schöne, 26 July 1882, in Meyer (1936), #126, 216, German original, and Saherwala, Goldmann, and Mahr (1993), 100–101. Schliemann's letter to Virchow of the same day conveys a different tone. In Meyer (1936), #127, 216–17, and Herrmann and Maaß (1990), #310, 328, both German originals. For Schöne's response to Schliemann's letters of 3 and 8 August and 8 September 1882, see Saherwala, Goldmann, and Mahr (1993), 174–75. The gladiator metope is now in the Pergamon Museum.

225. These metopes, mentioned in Calvert's 12 July 1882 letter to Schliemann, B 89/493, and in Schliemann (1884), 200, now are in the Pergamon Museum, Berlin. Holden (1964), 19 n. 1, plate 20, figure 37; 24, plate 26, figure 48. Others, such as ibid., 22, plate 24, figures 43 and 44, and 27, plate 30, figure 58, remained in the Calvert Collection and are now in the Çanakkale Archaeological Museum. Schliemann to Schöne, 26 July 1882, in Saherwala, Goldmann, and Mahr (1993), 101.

226. "I have already given a copy of the Caucasian fibula to Calvert, asking him to sell me both fibulae found near Ine. I already own one since he excavated with my money. These fibulae should enrich the Trojan collection." Schliemann to Virchow, 24 April 1882, in Herrmann and Maaß (1990), #284, 302. Thus, Schliemann again wrote: "Because Calvert made the excavation with my money I own one half of the results. I took both fibulae as my share because you are so interested in them." Schliemann to Virchow, 23 May 1882, in Herrmann and Maaß (1990), #292, 310.

227. Quoted in Strabo, 13.1.47. Murray (1875), 167.

228. Calvert (1860b), Thiersch (1902a), 16, 130–54, Koldewey (1891), 6 n. 11, and Schwerteim and Wiegartz (1994), 24 n. 18. Work continues at the site.

229. Calvert had written to Newton about resemblances between ceramics at Hisarlık and those at Neandria on 30 May 1866. Newton had asked him to write it up for *Transactions of the Royal Society of Literature*. Newton to Frank Calvert, 12 August 1874, BMGR. Calvert described his analysis of three architectural styles in the city walls of Neandria, based on his examination of the ruins and tombs. Frank Calvert to Schliemann, 1 February 1881, B 85/58.

230. To Virchow, he confided that Schliemann had misdated the Neandria remains to the Macedonian and Roman eras in *Ilios*. "My visits to Chigri have been frequent—and I have been as long as a fortnight at a time examining the ruins and tombs. I found three different styles of architecture in the city walls, but to none of these do I think so late a date as of Macedonian times can be given. I am of the opinion the pick, the marks of which are to be seen on the worked stone at Gergis (Balli Dagh) and Neandria (Chigri), was not of *iron*. this metal would not have made an impression on the hard stone—and steel was unknown. Why not hardened bronze. The pottery I discovered in the tombs, outside of the walls of Neandria, in different localities, are certainly not Macedonian, still less Roman. The vases and terra cottas are early and very remarkable." Frank Calvert to Virchow, 1 February 1881, ABBAW, Virchow, 335.

231. Koldewey (1891). He also excavated at Babylon from 1898 to 1917. *Neue deutsche Biographie* and *Webster's Biographical Dictionary*, s.v. "Koldewey, Robert." For a portrait sketched by Bacon, see Lullies and Schiering (1988), 116.

232. Schliemann to Ioannis Photiades, governor general of Crete from 1879 to 1885, 7 January and 6 March 1883, in Meyer (1958), #123, 150–51, #127, 154, #130, 156–57; Schliemann to Gladstone, 30 October 1883, in Meyer (1958), #141, 166.

233. Schliemann to Charles Scribner's Sons, in Meyer (1958), #133, 159.

234. Schliemann to Gladstone, 30 October 1883, in Meyer (1958), #141, 166.

235. Schliemann to Professor McGrath, chancellor of Queens College, Oxford, 13 May 1883, in Meyer (1958), #135, 160–61. The crown prince of Saxe Meiningen bemoaned the fact that no German university had so honored him. Crown Prince Bernhard to Schliemann, November 1883, in Meyer (1958), #142, 166–67.

236. Frank Calvert to Schliemann, 24 December 1883, B 93/1058.

237. Royal Institute of Architects to Schliemann, 16 March 1885, in Meyer (1958), #187, 206–7.

238. Frank Calvert to Schliemann, 29 April 1885, B 103/269.

239. Bacon's 30 September 1882 entry in "Assos Days," in Allen, Congdon, and Landry, (forthcoming).

240. "He told us about his lawsuit with the Turkish government. He is a knowing old chap, but I think a bit cracked." Bacon to "K.B.," his sister Kate, 16 May 1881, in Congdon (1974), 88, and Allen, Congdon, and Landry (forthcoming).

241. The account is in "Assos Days." Allen, Congdon, and Landry (forthcoming).

242. Schliemann to Frank Calvert, 14 September 1886, BB 2.4/34.

243. Calvert announced to Schliemann the wedding of his niece, 27 February 1885, B 96/135. Alice Calvert Bacon thanked Schliemann for his generosity to the couple on 25 April 1885, B 96/259, and her sister Edith thanked Schliemann for helping the family after an 1884 fire devastated the Adrianople consulate where her brother was consul. Edith Calvert to Schliemann, 26 September 1885, B 97/679.

244. She would translate German articles for her uncle. She also gave rare coins to the British Museum.

245. The letters are at the Gennadius Library. The diary is in a private London collection. Both are unpublished. Edith also gave finds to the British Museum. Departmental Records, Coins and Medals. Edith had a continuing correspondence with Schliemann, and her diary documents her privileged position vis-à-vis her uncle and Schliemann.

246. Frank Calvert to Schliemann, 24 December 1883, B 93/1058, misread by Meyer (1958), #144, 168.

CHAPTER 10

1. Schliemann to E. Wirths, 8 March 1885, in Meyer (1958), #185, 205–6.

2. Strabo, 13.1.57.

3. Clarke (1887), 2; Clarke, Bacon, and Koldewey (1902).

4. Edward H. Greenleaf, secretary of the Archaeological Institute of America, to Frank Calvert, 15 December 1883. Frank Calvert to Greenleaf, 17 May 1884, acknowledged the gift. NARA RG84 Dard. 1.

5. Frank Calvert to Edward Ozmun, U.S. consul general in Constantinople, 23 August 1907, NARA RG84 Dard. 1.

6. Frank Calvert to Schliemann, 24 December 1883, B 93/1058. For the text of the law, see Reinach (1884), 335–44.

7. In 1878, the German excavator Carl Humann and Alexander Conze, the new director of the Royal Museum's sculpture collection, had joined forces with Richard Schöne at the Ministry of Education and the German embassy in Constantinople to secure a royal

grant of 50,000 marks, to be matched by the museums. This deal as well as Humann's momentous discovery of the Pergamon altar was kept secret until 1880, when the Ottoman government sold the land to Humann for 20,000 francs. Thus, he outwitted the Turks, who otherwise could have claimed two-thirds of the finds from the site, and was able to claim the finds as his own property. Humann's first shipment of sculptures back to Germany weighed approximately three hundred and fifty tons. Marchand (1996), 95 n. 61, 96 n. 62.

8. Frank Calvert to Schliemann, 13 March 1884, B 94/165.

9. The new journal of the Archaeological Institute of America was to disseminate important work through regular correspondence from important archaeological centers, news reports of archaeological discoveries, book notices and reviews, summaries of principal archaeological periodicals (for those scholars who had no access to a research library), reports of proceedings of archaeological societies, and a bibliography of recent literature. *American Journal of Archaeology* 1 (1885): ii. The editor faithfully recorded news of the finds and controversies occurring in the Ottoman realm.

10. "Archaeological News," *American Journal of Archaeology* 1 (1885): 285. With respect to the cessation of activities at Assos, the editor was correct. The Archaeological Institute of America funded no more excavations at the site.

11. "Archaeological News," *American Journal of Archaeology* 2 (1886): 477.

12. Frank Calvert to Virchow, 26 May 1884, ABBAW, Virchow, 335. The article is dated 24 May 1884.

13. Frank Calvert to Virchow, 28 October 1885, ibid.

14. On 10 November 1885 Calvert received his copy.

15. Frank Calvert to Schliemann, 27 December 1869, B 64/317.

16. Frank Calvert to Schliemann, 27 February 1885, B 96/135.

17. Frank Calvert to Schliemann, 20 August 1885, B 96/549.

18. Frank Calvert to Schliemann, 27 February 1885, B 96/135.

19. Hamdi Bey excavated at Sidon (1887–88), founded the Turkish Ecole de Beaux Arts, and supervised the construction of the new Imperial Ottoman Museum. *Webster's Biographical Dictionary*, s.v. "Hamdi Bey, Osman."

20. Marchand (1996), 200.

21. In 1904 the sultan is reported to have exclaimed, "Look at these stupid foreigners. I pacify them with broken stones." Watzinger (1944), 170. In this way, the Ishtar Gate was successfully removed from Babylon and the Mschatta Gate from Syria. Thus, German *Kulturpolitik* and Ottoman foreign policy were brought together in a number of joint endeavors. After Germany's support of Turkey in the peace with Greece and Crete of 1898, the sultan had issued a *note verbale* announcing his authorization of the Berlin museums to keep half of the material excavated by the Germans in 1899. The elite German Orient Society had been formed in 1898 to steer the excavation/acquisition program. The Austrians at Ephesus already had negotiated to keep their choicest finds. And apparently the French and Russians also had arranged a favorable agreement with the sultan. Marchand (1996), 199–202.

22. Ibid.

23. Ibid., 205.

24. Ibid., 202.

25. Edmund and Frank Calvert had been out to Hisarlık and had witnessed its dismantled state. Frank Calvert to Schliemann, B 96/269.

26. Frank Calvert to Schliemann, 12 November 1885, B 96/788.

27. "The Law on Antiquities," *Levant Herald and Eastern Express*, 10 November 1886.

28. Frank Calvert to Virchow, 10 February 1885, ABBAW, Virchow, 335. Virchow read it at the mathematical and natural scientific section of the Prussian Academy on 22 July 1886, and it was published the same year. Calvert (1886), 673–74.

29. Louisa Calvert died on 21 May 1886. Frank Calvert to Schliemann, 14 August 1886, B 99/442.

30. Gustav Batthus, his foreman, to Frank Calvert, 4 May 1886, concerning the Astyra mine. BB 2.3. Frank Calvert to Virchow, 28 October 1885, ABBAW, Virchow, 335.

31. Frank Calvert to Schliemann, 23 February 1886, B 98/167.

32. Frank Calvert to Schliemann, 14 September 1886, B 99/504.

33. The years between 1878 and 1887 were difficult, with two years of "cattle plague" (1878 and 1879) and three years of locust infestation (1880 through 1882). By the summer of 1887, brigandage was on the rise, and in August, fires ravaged the forests of Mount Ida. *Levant Herald and Eastern Express*, 18 July, 10 and 17 August 1887.

34. *Levant Herald and Eastern Express*, 29 June 1887.

35. Frank Calvert to Schliemann, 24 December 1888, B 103. Frank Calvert served as acting British vice-consul for more than four months in 1887 and again in 1888. Calvert to Schliemann, 6 October 1887, B 101/359, and various documents, PRO/FO 78 4122. Schliemann and Virchow spent a February holiday on the Nile. Later that year, Edmund Calvert, his health broken, returned to the family home at the Dardanelles.

36. Frank Calvert to Schliemann, 12 February 1887, B 100/22.

37. Schliemann to Calvert, 17 May 1888, BBB 41/23. He sent money to his widow that year.

38. Schliemann to Frank Calvert, 3 January 1889, BBB 41/199.

39. Schliemann to Adolf Furtwangler (1853–1907), 10 April 1887, in response to Furtwangler's *Mykenische Vasen*. In Meyer (1958), #249, 265–68.

40. Schliemann to Frank Calvert, 13 February and 16 March 1889, BBB 41/232 and BBB 41/259.

41. Calvert (1889), 174. Judeich, who had traveled through the Troad in May, June, and July 1896, commented on Calvert's findings in (1898), 531–44.

42. Schliemann congratulated him on getting a very high price. Schliemann to Frank Calvert, 13 February 1889, BBB 41/232. The company had £180,000 in capital but encountered problems extracting the gold from the ore. The mine was still not in full operation in 1893, and operations halted in 1914. Cuinet (1893), 3:704, 3:749. *Arsenic, Mercury, Antinomy, and Gold Deposits of Turkey*, Report 123, Maden Tetkıkve Arama Enstitüsu (1970), 21. See also Report 508 (1900). Courtesy David Bickford.

43. Principally chromate of iron and pyrites. Schliemann to Frank Calvert, 16 March 1889, BBB 41/259. A subsequent letter promised that he would be liberally rewarded for his efforts. Schliemann to Frank Calvert, 31 March 1889, BBB 41/268.

44. Frank Calvert to Schliemann, 10 July 1889, B 105/259.

45. This was a fourth mound, known as Çobantepe, or the tomb of Paris, not those excavated by Calvert, Schliemann, or Lubbock.

46. Calvert sent in his report on 4 April. The newspaper printed it on 13 April. Calvert published another note on the rich tumulus at Pınarbaşı with an elevation of the tomb a decade later. Calvert (1897), 319–20.

47. "Archaeological News," *American Journal of Archaeology* 3 (1887): 435.

48. *Levant Herald and Eastern Express,* 4 May 1887. For Schuchhardt, see Grünert, in Herrmann (1992), 161–76.

49. Bötticher had published "Analogien der Funde von Hisarlik" in *Zeitschrift für Ethnologie* 15 (1883): 157–62.

50. Bötticher (1889), 46–47.

51. *Zeitschrift für Ethnologie; Das Ausland; Kölnische Zeitung; Zeitschrift für Museologie und Antiquitätenkunde,* Dresden; *Korrespondenz-Blatt des Gesamtvereins der deutschen Geschichte- und Altertumsvereine; Neue freie Presse; Neue freie Presse,* Vienna; *Allgemeine Zeitung,* Munich; *Berliner Philologische Wochenschrift; Le muséon,* an international review published by the Société des Lettres et des Sciences de Louvain; *Revue critique d'histoire et de littérature; Wochenschrift für klassischen Philologie; Berliner National-Zeitung; Annales de la société d'archéologie de Bruxelles; Mittheilungen der anthropologischen Gesellschaft in Wien; Kreuzzeitung; Zeitschrift für bildende Kunst, Kunstchronik; Zeitschrift für Volkskunde,* Leipzig; *Berliner Börsen Courier;* and *Jahrbücher des Vereins von Alterthumsfreunden im Rheinlande.* The ability to trace these publications and their ripple effect is thanks to Korres (1974), 83–102.

52. See Saherwala, Goldmann, and Mahr (1982) for a photo of participants in the Paris conference. Some of the delegates were Schliemann, Montelius, Salomon Reinach, and John Evans.

53. Schliemann to Frank Calvert, 11 October 1889, BBB 41/427.

54. Schliemann to Schöne, 10 October 1889, in Meyer (1936), #206, 290–92. Young (1905), 388. From 1880 to 1882, Reinach had codirected French excavations at Myrina on Lemnos. In 1902 he became director of the Musée Nationale de St. Germain. *Webster's Biographical Dictionary,* s.v. "Reinach, Salomon." Calder and Kramer (1992), 2052.

55. In spite of his agreeing to the 1884 regulations, Schliemann promised the Ethnographical Museum that Berlin would be the beneficiary of his new campaign. Schliemann to Hamdi Bey, 13 September 1889, BBB 41/387; Schliemann to Herbert von Bismarck (1849–1904), eldest son of the German chancellor and secretary of state, in Meyer (1936), #207, 293–94.

56. Virchow to Schliemann, 18 October 1889, in Herrmann and Maaß (1990), #547, 519–21.

57. Schliemann to Frank Calvert, 11 October 1889, BBB 41/427.

58. Schliemann to Virchow, 31 October and 14 November 1889, in Herrmann and Maaß (1990), #549, 522, and #553, 524–25.

59. Schliemann to Frank Calvert, 22 January 1890, BBB 42/116.

60. Herrmann and Maaß (1990), plate 14. Achieved largely with Calvert's help and advice, the construction was not yet complete on 11 November 1889. Schliemann to Frank Calvert, BBB 41/468.

61. Reported in "Archaeological News," *American Journal of Archaeology* 5 (1889): 489–91.

62. Reinach had served as a delegate to the 1889 Anthropological Conference in Paris, along with Schliemann, Oskar Montelius, and John Evans.

63. An excellent draftsman, Niemann taught perspective theory and the theory of design in Vienna. He had served as Conze's architect in the 1873 and 1875 Samothrace excavations and with Otto Benndorf in Lycia in 1881 and 1882. For his portrait, see Lullies and Schiering (1988), 80; also de Grummond (1996), 805–6.

64. Frank Calvert to Schliemann, 12 November and 8 December 1889, B 105/530 and B 105/608, published in Allen (1995b). Although Traill (1993), 18, neglected to mention

Calvert, Calvert did attend both events. Figure 40 shows the postprandial visit to Hanay Tepe.

65. "Archaeological News," *American Journal of Archaeology* 5 (1889): 489–90. Schliemann to Virchow, 13 December 1889, in Herrmann and Maaß (1990), #561, 531–32.

66. Calvert reported this to the *Levant Herald and Eastern Express.* Schliemann to Frank Calvert, 22 January 1890, BBB 42/116.

67. De Grummond (1996), 375–76; *Neue deutsche Biographie,* s.v. "Von Duhn, Friedrich." For his portrait, see Lullies and Schiering (1988), 100.

68. This self-taught engineer learned archaeology and topography in the field. After discovering two fragments of the Altar of Zeus in 1871, he began to dig at Pergamon in 1871 and excavated there until 1886. For his acquisition of the Pergamon sculptures, Humann was "received like a general who has returned from the battlefield, crowned with victory." Otto Kern, "Ernst Curtius und Karl Humann," *Deutsche Literaturzeitung* 34 (10 May 1913): 1159 61. *Neue deutsches Biographie,* s.v. "Humann, Carl." De Grummond (1996), 600. For a portrait, see Lullies and Schiering (1988), 69. Joseph Maria von Radowitz (1839–1912), the German ambassador to Turkey, had acclaimed Humann "the viceroy of Asia Minor" for his adept handling of the Turks, from the Ottoman court to the lowliest workman. Marchand (1996), 93 n. 56.

69. Waldstein, an American archaeologist and art historian later knighted in England as Sir Charles Walston, was professor of ancient art at the American School of Classical Studies in Athens from 1892 to 1897. He directed excavations at Eretria, Plataea, and the Argive Heraion. From 1916 to 1928, he was professor and director of the Fitzwilliam Museum at Cambridge University. *Webster's Biographical Dictionary,* s.v. "Walston, Sir Charles"; de Grummond (1996), 1184.

70. Calvert and his niece Edith, a fan of Schliemann's, are pictured in Figure 41. Another photograph, published by Herrmann and Maaß (1990), plate 17, shows the participants posing in the ruins themselves.

71. Quoted in Schliemann (1891b), 324.

72. Schliemann to Virchow, 30 July 1890, in Meyer (1958), #350, 376 77, and Herrmann and Maaß (1990), #587, 555.

73. Bötticher (1894).

74. "Archaeological News," *American Journal of Archaeology* 6 (1890): 348–51, 546–47; Schliemann to Frank Calvert, 21 October 1889, BBB 41/427. Perhaps with a prescient sense of urgency, he added another railway by May. Schliemann (1891b), 324. Schliemann to Otto Benndorf, in Meyer (1958), #335, 357–58.

75. Schliemann to Frank Calvert, 6 March 1890, in Meyer (1958), #331, 353. The law was quoted by Reinach (1884), 335–44.

76. Schliemann (1891b), 334.

77. He intended to continue in this area in 1891.

78. Schliemann (1891b), 330.

79. Schliemann to Frank Calvert, 6 March 1890, in Meyer (1958), #331, 353.

80. Schliemann (1891b), 331, plates 1 and 2.

81. "Archaeological News," *American Journal of Archaeology* 6 (1890): 348–51, 546–47. See Allen (1990), for gray ware.

82. "Archaeological News," *American Journal of Archaeology* 6 (1890): 348–51, 546–47; Schliemann (1891b), 332, figure 4.

83. Schliemann to Virchow, 10 May 1890, in Herrmann and Maaß (1990), #573, 542–43, reiterated in Schliemann to Virchow, 30 May 1890, in Herrmann and Maaß (1990), #576, 545–46.

84. Schliemann to King George I, in Meyer (1958), #337, 359–61. German original.

85. Schuchhardt (1944), 181. Translated in Traill (1995), 287.

86. Dörpfeld (1891), 349.

87. Schliemann (1875a), 12.

88. "Archaeological News," *American Journal of Archaeology* 6 (1890): 348–49, taken from Schliemann's announcement in the *Neue freie Presse* of 11 June 1890.

89. Allen (1990).

90. Quoted in "Archaeological News," *American Journal of Archaeology* 6 (1890): 547.

91. Translation of modern Greek from Schliemann's 1890 diary in the Gennadius Library, 59–61, in Easton (1984b), 199. Götze and Schmidt catalogued the sixty-five objects for the Schliemann Collection. Götze (1902), 338–40; Schmidt (1902), 242–44, nos. 6055–120. Korfmann (1994) emphasizes the importance of these precious axes for understanding long-distance trade and local ceremony.

92. Schliemann to Virchow, 15 July 1890, in Meyer (1958), #344, 367–68, and Herrmann and Maaß (1990), #584, 552.

93. Saherwala, Goldmann, and Mahr (1993), 142–43. Presumably Caravel didn't realize that he was helping Schliemann cheat Calvert, his colleague and friend. Photographs show the Caravels enjoying Calvert's hospitality in the family gardens in 1890.

94. Caravel had helped Schliemann smuggle out imperial portraits in marble heads earlier in 1890. Siebler (1994), figures 147–49. Schliemann to Crown Prince Bernhard of Saxe Meiningen, 16 June 1890, in Meyer (1958), #340, 363–65, 365 n. 392; Schliemann to Virchow, 8 July 1890, in Herrmann and Maaß (1990), #583, 551.

95. *Neue deutsche Biographie*, s.v. "Conze, Alexander." De Grummond (1996), 324. For portraits, see Lullies and Schiering (1988), 59, and Marchand (1996), figure 14.

96. Meyer (1958), 463 n. 413.

97. Schliemann to Gustav von Gößler (1838–1902), minister of culture from 1881 to 1891, 13 September 1890, in Meyer (1958), #353, 379–81. Schliemann to Humann, 20 August 1890, in Meyer (1958), #351, 377–78.

98. Schliemann to Schöne, 9 October 1890, in Meyer (1958), #356, 382–83. Saherwala, Goldmann, and Mahr (1993), 142.

99. Schliemann to Alexander Conze, 9 December 1890, in Meyer (1958), #363, 388–91. Schliemann promised Humann discretion and relied on Humann's friendship with Hamdi Bey in getting the *firmans* renewed.

100. Schliemann to the former U.S. minister to Greece, the journalist John M. Francis, 10 June 1890. He projected a season from March to November 1891. In Meyer (1958), #339, 362–63. Schliemann to Virchow, 20 August 1890, in Meyer (1958), #351, 377. He and Dörpfeld still suspected a lower city "annexed to the Pergamos." They hoped to find the royal tombs outside the city gate. Dörpfeld (1890), 226–29.

101. Hundreds of obituaries appeared, and Virchow eulogized his friend at a memorial service in Berlin in February 1891. Traill (1995), 296–97. In another eulogy across the Atlantic, an American professor noted: "It may as well be remembered that Troy was discovered under the protection of 'our flag.'" Chambers (1990), 405 nn. 41, 42.

102. The kaiser was an avid patron of archaeology and of *Kulturpolitik* in German-Ottoman relations.

103. Brückner, in Dörpfeld (1894), 121–23.

104. "Archaeological News," *American Journal of Archaeology* 9 (1896): 135–36.

105. Calvert (1894).

106. Frank Calvert to Samuel Butler, 3 June 1895, BLMS 44035/163.

107. Frank Calvert to Samuel Butler, 19 April 1895, BLMS 44035/114, and Calvert (1894).

108. "Archaeological News," *American Journal of Archaeology* 9 (1896): 135.

109. He reported on the cultivation of figs and raisins, olives, oranges, and lemons. Frank Calvert to James Waters, 23 January 1892 and 18 February 1894, NARA RG84 Dard. 7. Improbable as it seems, dog excrement was an export commodity. Dickinson to Frank Calvert, 25 May 1905, NARA RG84 Dard. 7, and 23 May 1892, NARA RG84 Dard. 8. Frank Calvert, report to Charles M. Dickinson, U.S. consul general at Constantinople, 4 November 1898, NARA RG84 Dard. 7. Official expenses for 1898 were $1.18.

110. According to the Partridge memoirs, the gold for Laura Calvert Bacon's wedding ring was mined at Astyra. Partridge Papers.

111. Frank Calvert to Charles M. Dickinson, 22 January 1900, NARA RG84 Dard. 1.

112. According to K. Gökkaya of Çanakkale Onsekiz Mart University, the decoration was the merit award of distinction "LIYAKAT NIŞANI." Ibrahim Aksu.

113. Charles M. Dickinson to Frank Calvert, 20 February 1900, NARA RG84 Dard. 1.

114. Frank Calvert, report to the U.S. consul general, 5 August 1890, NARA RG84 Dard. 8.

115. Frederick R. J. Calvert to Samuel Butler, BLMS 44041/52.

116. Robinson (1994), 157, and (1995), 332.

117. The necropolis was located about 0.8 kilometer from the shore, on the slopes of Mal Tepe, from the Lebera *çiftlik* to northeast of ancient Madytos (modern Maidos or Eceabat) and northwest of Kilia Bay. Picard and Reinach (1912), 296–97, published the site and the important pieces in Calvert's collection, some of which were bought from locals. The Lebera estate occupied part of the site in 1921, and two large purple granite sarcophagi, reused as part of the Christophorides fountain, still could be traced to it. Calvert's excavation to find the acropolis at Mal Tepe hit only rock. The area was shown in Choiseul-Gouffier (1822), plates 54–56. Thiersch (1902a), site no. 10, 59–95. Picard and Reinach (1912), 288–305. Some of Calvert's objects from the Kilios collection are in the Worcester Art Museum. Allen (1996b), 147, 160. Others remained at Thymbra until given to the Çanakkale Archaeological Museum. For inscriptions from the site, see Reinach (1913), 167.

118. According to Picard and Reinach, who published the most important finds, there was also a Mycenaean gold seal ring, which they thought suspect. Picard and Reinach (1912), 297 n. 4. Cook's personal notes mention that it was in the Berlin Antiquarium.

119. Bacon later gave the figurine to the American School of Classical Studies in Athens. Calvert (1901), 329–30; Caskey (1972), 192–93; Picard and Reinach (1912), 297 n. 2. It resembles others from the Neolithic period in Thessaly and from the Early Bronze Age in the Cyclades.

120. Cook (1973) and Virchow (1882), 112, consistently supported Calvert's identification of the north-coast sites.

121. Calvert (1880), 34–35, and (1902), 240–45. The necropolis of Tavolia, Ta Molia, or Çoban Tepe, was largely looted by Greeks. Cook (1973), 83; Blegen et al. (1950), figures 28 and 35. The finds are listed as "bought" in Thiersch (1902a), 181–255. The Calverts knew Karanlık Limanı well. The Helios Metope, the inscriptions, and Priam's Treasure all had been shipped from this spot. Thiersch (1902b), 15–16, noted that on 15 August 1887, Calvert had found a remarkable tomb of the late fifth to fourth century B.C. rich in terra-cottas.

122. As before, Calvert analyzed ancient testimonia, including Strabo, 13.1.30. Following Barker Webb and Maclaren, Schliemann mistakenly had put Ophryneion at this spot. The necropolis contained stone cists, or burial chambers, and tile graves. There were a few Greek coins. Cook followed Calvert (1973), 81. Calvert in turn had followed Leake (1821), who followed Choiseul-Gouffier (1822), plate 19. He had added a number of his recent discoveries at Ophryneion for Virchow (1882), 5–22.

123. Thiersch (1902b), 246. He later was professor of Archaeology at Freiburg and then at Göttingen. For his portrait, see Lullies and Schiering (1988), 144.

124. Thiersch (1902a), 23. Cook later suggested that it might be Traron. Cook (1973), 86.

125. Dörpfeld (1902), ix.

126. For Brückner's portrait, see Lullies and Schiering (1988), 144.

127. Calvert's fossils and early stone tools seem not to have been included in the catalogue. Thiersch (1902a). The catalogue will be published by Gamer and Özgünel. Gamer (1992), 41.

128. Alfred Grech, telegram to Edward Ozmun, U.S. consul general at Constantinople, 13 August 1908, NARA RG84 Dard. 1. For some reason, Frederick R. J. Calvert was passed over, and the consulship went outside the family to Grech, who also succeeded Calvert as agent for the Moss steamship line in the 1880s. The last photograph of Calvert was taken one month before he died.

129. The *Zeitschrift für Ethnologie* recalled Calvert's friendship with Virchow and how Calvert had preceded Schliemann at Hisarlık. It also noted that he was a collector and contributor to their journal of an important article on the ancient coastline in Homeric times. *Zeitschrift für Ethnologie* 50 (1908): 922.

130. Alfred Brückner, *Jahrbuch des deutschen archäologischen Instituts* 24 (1909): 34–35.

131. The mausoleum was built in 1893–94, crowning an eminence in Athens's First Cemetery, for 50,000 drachmas, while Dörpfeld was excavating at Hisarlık. Korres (1981), 133–73.

132. The former Calvert family cemetery is now the Chanak Consular Cemetery, administered by the Commonwealth War Graves Commission.

CHAPTER 11

1. Wallis (1937), 143–44; Chamberlain (1957), 557.

2. In the Victorian Home and Travellers' Library series, *Texas and the Gulf of Mexico; or, Yachting in the New World*, by a Mrs. Houstoun, published in 1845, was the first volume. It was followed by a volume on Egypt. See Fernea (forthcoming).

3. Terrell to his brother, 16 November 1894, Terrell Archives, Center for American History, University of Texas, Austin.

4. Terrell to "sir" (Dr. T. D. Wooten), 12 December 1894, Terrell Archives.

5. Terrell to his brother, 16 November 1894, Terrell Archives.

6. Wallis (1937), 138.

7. Terrell to Major Walter, 20 December 1894; Terrell to his brother, 16 November 1894, Terrell Archives; Terrell to Calvert, 25 November 1894, NARA RG84 Dard. 8; and Calvert to Terrell, 19 November 1894, Terrell Archives, all deal with the inscription. Terrell to Major Walter, 19 November 1894, describes the fragment as a "marble inscription with an oak wreath" encircling the words "the State and People of Ilium."

8. Terrell to General Charles Culberson, 25 November 1894, Terrell Archives. Of the souvenirs Terrell mentioned "lamps of clay, broken pottery, tiling, a funeral urn + two stone axes" taken for friends. Calvert also gave him small copper coins from Troy, "from his own cabinet." Terrell to his brother, 16 November 1894, Terrell Archives. He also took "some entire vessels." Terrell to Major Walter, 20 December 1894, Terrell Archives. He had received other gifts from the governor of the Dardanelles and the Division Commander.

9. Terrell to his wife, 7 December 1894, Terrell Archives, cited by Wallis (1932), 139.

10. Terrell to Calvert, 25 November 1894, NARA RG84 Dard. 8; Terrell to Major Walter, 20 December 1894, Terrell Archives; Wallis (1932), 141.

11. Calvert to Terrell, 19 November 1894, Terrell Archives. This is reminiscent of Calvert's correspondence with Schliemann on the same subject between 1870 and 1872. In 1857 Senior noted that Calvert owned 2000 acres with Mr. Freeman. Senior (1859), 164, 168. He must have sold considerable acreage over the years. The original purchase price for the land had been £300, but that did not include the acropolis. So Schliemann was correct in foreseeing that Calvert's land would rise in value, at least as far as the Ottoman government was concerned. But all this meant for Calvert was that his taxes went up.

12. Terrell to Calvert, 12 December 1894, NARA RG84 Dard. 8.

13. Terrell to Judge A. S. Walker, 8 November 1894, Terrell Archives.

14. Terrell to Charles Culberson, 25 November 1894, Terrell Archives. In a letter of 12 December 1894 addressed only to "sir," Terrell wrote that Calvert's nephew and sister seemed to be in good circumstances, but Calvert's were straitened. Terrell Archives.

15. Terrell to "sir," 12 December 1894, Terrell Archives. Wallis (1937), 139, noted that Terrell had purchased a collection for $400 that he valued at four times the amount. Terrell to his wife, 7 December 1894; Terrell to Colonel C. M. Terrell, Terrell Archives.

16. Of the "few antique vases + books of mementoes of what [he] had seen," most were given him by Calvert. Terrell to "Walter," 12 December 1894, Terrell Archives.

17. In another letter, Terrell wrote: "Few have ever seen it and no archaeologist perhaps knows of its existence." Furthermore, "an Imperial Iradé prohibits the exportation of all antiquities and all things excavated belong to the Sultan's Museum—For this reason, his collection is kept under lock." Terrell to "sir" (Dr. T. D. Wooten), 12 December 1894, Terrell Archives. In another letter, he noted that "Calvert's [collection] was secured before the order, but to avoid trouble he keeps it from sight." Terrell to Major Walter, 20 December 1894, Terrell Archives.

18. Terrell to Colonel George Breckenridge, 12 December 1894. Terrell obviously took no note of women in his unofficial census. The "Sister" he referred to must have been Calvert's sister-in-law, Eveline, or her daughter, Edith.

19. Albert L. Long taught at the American missionary school at Roumeli Hissar on the Bosphorus, north of Constantinople.

20. Terrell to Major Walter, 20 December 1894, Terrell Archives. In another letter he explained that the collection contained "a fair sample of everything found in each of the

several cities of Troy" and also material from Pınarbaşı and the islands. If the university didn't want it, perhaps a "Texas gentleman" might. Otherwise, he would see about the Smithsonian Institution or some better-endowed school. Terrell to "sir," 12 December 1894, Terrell Archives.

21. Samuel P. Langley, secretary of the Smithsonian, to Terrell, 3 January 1895, responding to Terrell's letter of 28 November 1894. Terrell Archives. In fact, some of Calvert's objects reached the Smithsonian almost twenty years later, but record of his name in connection with the gift did not survive.

22. Recently the inscription was found in a filing cabinet in the Department of Classics, University of Texas, Austin, and connected with Calvert by Ken Mayer. Harriman et al. (forthcoming).

23. Hargrave (1933), 77. One is an early black Trojan jug. Ken Mayer, personal communication.

24. Although documentation no longer exists, the stele may well have come from Tavolia, the rich cemetery just east of Karanlık Limanı, which Calvert had been excavating since at least 1887. Calvert (1902), 16–17. Cornelius Vermeule has suggested that the Roman emperor Hadrian, who visited Ilium in A.D. 124, during the restoration of the eroded tomb of Ajax, may have ornamented it with this stele. Vermeule (1995), 473. Vermeule's n. 80 contains garbled family information.

25. In 1900, Francis Bartlett gave $100,000 to the Boston Museum of Fine Arts for the purchase of classical antiquities. The stele was acquired with part of these funds. Bartlett Donation, no. 03.753; Körte (1895), 3–4. The 1.3 meter stele is on exhibit there. When Körte wrote his 1895 article, the stele was still at Thymbra Farm [Figure 8]. Allen (1996b), plate 21b. It already had been catalogued by Brückner, and the photograph had been registered at the German Archaeological Institute in Athens. Apparently Warren also owned two gold discs from the Calvert Collection. Oxford Archive, courtesy of Joan Haldenstein. Photograph no. 2411 of the German Archaeological Institute in Athens, Calvert Collection, no. 119. Caskey (1925), 25–26, no. 13.

26. William Robert Ware (1832–1915), a professor of architecture at Columbia University and Bacon's former professor at the Massachusetts Institute of Technology, visited Thymbra Farm in 1883 and posed next to the stele.

27. Worcester records note that the purchase cost $300. Otherwise, the only record of the 26 January 1905 acquisition is in a 10 June 1955 letter in the Worcester Art Museum, Worcester, Mass., from Bert Hodge Hill to Louisa Dresser of the museum explaining the significance of the collection and how it got to the museum. The circumstances surrounding the sale remain unclear. Oddly enough, Frank Calvert's name and details of the Calvert-Schliemann story had been introduced to Worcester three decades earlier when Stephen Salisbury, president of the American Antiquarian Society, gave an address on Troy, Homer, and Schliemann in 1875. Stephen Salisbury, *Troy and Homer: Remarks on the Discoveries of Heinrich Schliemann in the Troad* (Worcester, Mass., 1875), 15–16.

28. Partridge Papers. For a view of the apartment, see Allen (1996b), plate 21a.

29. Elizabeth Bacon remembers rolled carpets stacked in the apartment, part of Laura's patrimony from the Dardanelles.

30. Partridge's second installment, 8 March 1948. Partridge Papers.

31. When debts overtook Laura Calvert Bacon following the stock market crash, the New York chapter of the American Institute of Architects supported Mrs. Bacon until her

death in 1942. Partridge Memoir and Partridge's second installment, 8 March 1948. Partridge Papers. There is a long, illustrated obituary in the *New York Tribune*, 17 February 1924. Both were buried in Wilmington, N.C.

32. *Levant Herald and Eastern Express*, 10 August 1912.

33. An official report in 1913 noted that the structure was indeed beyond repair; £3000 would not cover the expenses. Vice-consul Palmer's report, 11 November 1913, cited a report of the Commonwealth War Graves Commission's Architect at Constantinople.

34. Alfred Grech to G. B. Ravndal, U.S. consul general, 31 August 1912, NARA RG84 Dard. 6. Ottomans had lost 82 percent of their land in Europe. Shaw and Shaw (1977), 298.

35. Hélène Adossides Calvert was the sister of Anastasios Adossides, Greek governor of Macedonia during and after the Balkan War, governor of the Cyclades and Samos during World War I, and later business liaison for the American School of Classical Studies, Athens. Merritt (1984), 6. In 1911, Winifred Calvert married Godfrey Whittall, grandson of James Whittall, himself a Lloyd's agent at the Dardanelles. Later they lived on the waterfront with their five children. McKernan (1997), 50. Gerald Calvert, who attended Sandhurst and fought with Serbia in the Macedonian campaigns of 1916–1918, married much later and inherited the farm. He had a son, Frederick J. Calvert, and a daughter, Beatrice Helen, of London, from whom this information comes.

36. In 1914, the family still owned approximately 2000 acres, valued at £11,370. That autumn, 250 Turkish soldiers were quartered in their barns and outbuildings, the Calverts' equipment was "borrowed" by the authorities, and 90,000 *okes* of grain, or over 25,000 pounds, were taken. Report by A. van Hemert Engert to G. B. Ravndal, 7 November 1914, and to Frederick R. J. Calvert, 14 December 1914, NARA RG84 Dard. 5.

37. Alice Calvert Bacon and her siblings had been forced to evacuate in December 1914. G. B. Ravndal to A. van Hemert Engert. 17 December 1914, NARA RG84 Dard. 5. Alice volunteered in the hospitals during the war while Constantinople, completely blockaded by sea, ran desperately short of food and fuel. A. van Hemert Engert to G. B. Ravndal, 7 November and 14 December 1914, NARA RG84 Dard. 5.

38. The Greek army, which otherwise would have remained on ships in Smyrna harbor, was requested by Woodrow Wilson to "occupy Smyrna to protect its Greek population" of six hundred thousand persons on 10 May 1919. Pentzopoulos (1962), 37. Thus twenty thousand troops invaded Smyrna as part of the *Megali Idea*, or plan for a greater Greece, encompassing the western coast of Asia Minor. Later, the powers sanctioned Venizelos "to restore order in all of northwestern Asia Minor." Ibid., 37. On 22 June, the Greek offensive began in Asia Minor.

39. The Treaty of Sèvres was signed on 10 August 1920.

40. Venizelos lost the election and did not stay in power. By 9 March 1921, all of the occupying forces with the exception of Great Britain had abandoned the Greeks.

41. Francis H. Bacon to Alice Calvert Bacon, 17 December 1922, Bacon family archive.

42. Greeks and Christians from western Asia Minor fled to the ports, "converging in a terrified mob on the city of Smyrna where they hoped either to get protection or to be evacuated." Macartney (1931), 79.

43. Ward Price, who was stationed on a ship in Smyrna harbor, telegraphed the London *Daily Mail* his distant view of the catastrophe on 19 September 1922: "What I see as I stand on

the deck of the Iron Duke is an unbroken wall of fire, two miles long, in which twenty distinct volcanoes of raging flames are throwing up jagged, writhing tongues to a height of a hundred feet. . . . From this intensely glowing mass of yellow, orange and crimson fire pour up thick clotted coils of oily black smoke that hide the moon at its zenith. . . . The sea glows a deep copper-red, and worst of all, from the densely packed mob of many thousands of refugees huddled on the narrow quay, between the advancing fiery death behind and the deep water in front, comes continuously such frantic screaming of sheer terror as can be heard miles away."

44. Reinach (1913), 167 n. 1, and Picard and Reinach (1912), 292 n. 4, note that Alfred van Lennep, the son of Eveline and Lavinia Calvert's sister had received terra-cotta figurines and lamps from Kilia.

45. Lascarides wrote incorrectly that most of the Calvert Collection was destroyed there. Lascarides (1977), 64, later repeated by Traill (1993), 79. However, none of the poignant letters describing the chaos and destruction endured by family and friends in Smyrna in 1922 mentions the destruction of antiquities, and certain British houses, such as those of the Whittalls in Bournabat, were relatively unscathed. Collection of documents kindly shared with me by Mrs. Elizabeth Bacon, preserved by Francis H. Bacon.

46. One estimate gave twelve thousand dead from the Smyrna fire alone. Macartney (1931), 79. Within a couple of weeks, three-quarters of a million refugees were "dumped like cattle" at the ports of Piraeus, Salonica, and Thrace. Morgenthau (1929), 48. Members of the Abbott family were evacuated to Malta as refugees.

47. The Turkish census of 1910 recorded 29,000 Greeks in Biğa (Dardanelles) province. That of the Greek patriarchate in Constantinople recorded 32,830 in 1912. Pentzopoulos (1962), 29–30. This represented between one-fifth and one-sixth of the total population of the province, according to either census. Ironically, in 1997, all the servants of the Whittall descendants speak Greek, being themselves descendants of Greek-speaking Turks from Crete.

48. The earlier rumors about confiscation had been confirmed in a Kemalist proclamation of 17 December 1922. The farm was still in no-man's-land on 4 June 1923.

49. According to Homer Thompson, a bench once stood in the garden at the school, inscribed in Bacon's honor.

50. Francis H. Bacon to Bert Hodge Hill, director of the American School of Classical Studies, 26 July 1923, almost fifteen years after Frank Calvert's death, Gennadius Library, Schliemann Archive, manuscript 70.40, files BB 2.1, 2.2, 2.3, and 2.4. Other Schliemann letters never were found, perhaps on purpose. Only in 1997 have additional Calvert papers come to light. Although these are not Frank Calvert's own manuscripts, they are of great value in reconstructing the family's existence at the Dardanelles, and further discoveries may be in store.

51. Bacon's interior design firm, FHB Co., managed by Frederick Calvert Bacon, experienced hard times. At the same time, in New York City, Laura Calvert Bacon was "selling her securities to live," less than a decade after the death of her illustrious husband.

52. There they entertained foreign scholars who came to study their collection, such as Winifred Lamb and Alfred Brückner in 1930.

53. They had purchased the "Garden Villa" on Alman Sokak from Winifred and Godfrey Whittall in 1926.

54. Blegen (1921). Blegen had excavated numerous Mycenaean sites on the Greek mainland before he came to Hisarlık and had established the chronology with his friend and col-

league Alan Wace (1879–1957). He previously had excavated at Kolophon, near Smyrna, in the ill-fated 1922 American expedition. Like Calvert, Schliemann, and Dörpfeld before him, Blegen wanted to prove the historicity of Homer's Troy. He located the rich cremation cemetery of the sixth-stratum settlement. The thirteenth-century graves yielded a high proportion of Mycenaean pottery, as well as gray ware. Allen (1990). But he decided that the first phase of the seventh-stratum settlement was the Troy of Homer. He also found a major Hellenistic sanctuary on the western and southwestern sides of the mound.

55. Blegen also reciprocated the Calverts' hospitality. He graciously acknowledged their help in each of his excavation reports from 1932 to 1938 in the *American Journal of Archaeology*. Blegen also gave Bacon his house and driver in Athens so that he could keep up his contacts with the American School of Classical Studies. It was on Bacon's final trip in 1935 that the young John Cook met the Assos excavator, so full of Troad lore, but as Cook later wrote me, that was long before his own interest in the Troad, and he never knew of Bacon's Calvert connection until our correspondence in 1992.

56. Francis H. Bacon to Frederick Calvert Bacon, his son, 16 February 1932. Bacon recorded the fire. Diary entry, 1 August 1934. Both in the Francis Henry Bacon archives. A view of the church can be found in Aksit (1971), n.p.

57. The Çanakkale Museum register records "60 years ago these things were dug up near Troy by the Englishman Calvert. Now Miss Calvert and Mrs. Bacon have given them as a gift." Translated by David Thomas. Museum Inventory 1:69, nos. 433–460. Given on 13 October 1934.

58. Çanakkale Museum register, nos. 537–1570. Given on 10 August 1936.

59. King Edward visited the Gallipoli cemeteries and tried to allay the fears of the British at the Dardanelles. Alice and Edith Calvert were photographed with him on 3 September 1936. Later that year, all foreigners were forced to sign a document acknowledging that the strait was now a military zone and were told to stay within city limits. Bacon mused, "The way to Troy was open under military escort. No more picnics and bicycle rides." On 10 December, Edward abdicated, and around the same time the cliffs on both sides of the Dardanelles were inscribed with 6-meter-high letters commemorating the British defeat and Turkish victory of 1915. The Bacons were now "prisoners . . . in Chanak." After reading the newly published *Gone with the Wind* in 1937, a friend noted: "One wonders that we have not learned the lesson of post war tragedy and seem to be preparing so blithely and fearlessly for the next one we are to be drawn into." Passages from Francis Henry Bacon's 1936 diary, with updates. Private collection, Çanakkale.

60. This was acquired by the Istanbul Archaeological Museum on 29 November 1943 and later transferred to Çanakkale. A copy also exists in Tübingen. Unfortunately, Rohrert's photographs are kept separately at the German Archaeological Institute in Athens. Thompson (1963), 5 n. 8; Caskey (1972), 192; Bert Hodge Hill to Louisa Dresser of the Worcester Art Museum, 10 June 1955; Cook (1973), 9.

61. The Istanbul Archaeological Museum transferred a portion of the Calvert Collection to the Çanakkale Archaeological Museum. "11 October, 1971 Istanbuldan göndariş den Calvert kalaksignu." Museum Inventory. The precise number of objects transferred has not been ascertained. The accession numbers used by the two museums are different. Over one thousand items may have been transferred from Istanbul. Çanakkale Museum acc. no. 1775–3248. It is not known when these objects were acquired by the Istanbul museum and whether they were bought or given, but it may be that Calvert finally did transact at least part of his intended sale

of 1870. Between the 1934 and 1936 gifts of 1170 objects and the 1971 transfer, well over two thousand objects from the Calvert Collection are present in the Çanakkale Museum.

62. Thomas Cook's 1923 guidebook noted the village as "a heap of ruins" and mentioned a short-lived return by Greek inhabitants and settlers. When the Renkiots abandoned the village, they settled in Greece and in the United States. Giannokopoulos (1995), 99–107. The later Turkish settlers found only empty houses and fields in the village they renamed In Tepe. Carl Blegen remarked that only ten years later, the destroyed mud-brick houses of the Greeks were in a state of preservation comparable to those he was excavating from the Bronze Age at Hisarlık. Peter S. Allen, personal communication.

63. Less than a month after the 20 July 1936 Treaty of Montreux, which permitted the Turks to fortify the previously demilitarized Dardanelles, Thymbra Farm, thanks to its size and proximity to the strait, was one of numerous properties that were seized as part of *istimlak*, the legal expropriation of land against payment. The properties thus taken could not be reacquired, and generally, owners did not receive full compensation. Information courtesy of Ibrahim Aksu. İnalçık records that by a 1945 law, all properties over 500 *dounoms* (125 acres) in size were nationalized for distribution to the peasantry. İnalçık (1978), 227. This certainly would have included the Calvert property if it hadn't been seized earlier. The government farm now located on the property and visited by the author in 1993 and 1997 is Kum Kale T.I.G.E.M. When the author visited it, the Calvert farmhouse and many buildings still stood.

64. Zeki Çakir, Municipality Public Improvements Planning Department (Tapu Dairesi). Translated by Ibrahim Aksu.

65. On 17 August 1939, the Calverts were offered one-eighth the assessed value of 40,000 Turkish lire and given fifteen days to accept. Bacon wrote: "To lose this wonderful garden planted near a hundred years ago by their father and full of their childhood memories seems unbelievable." On 22 August 1939, the mayor of Çanakkale gave them forty-eight hours to clear out and lock the garden gate. Although the family appealed and never accepted money from the government, the land was seized on 29 October 1939, along with Edith's cows and chickens. Francis Henry Bacon's 1936 diary. Private collection, Çanakkale.

66. Obituary, *New York Times*, 8 February 1940, 23.

67. Edith's possessions were auctioned off, with the proceeds going to the state, since she had no heirs. One of Bacon's diaries was acquired by a local resident. Paintings and drawings by the Calvert brothers and Lander sisters were bought by the ancestors of Ziya Uluer of Çanakkale, their present owner.

68. The label was noted by Dr. Gladys Weinberg and mentioned in the letter of 10 June 1955 from Bert Hodge Hill to Louisa Dresser of the Worcester Art Museum.

69. Cook (1973), 119 n. 6. Arik's information came from Leaf (1923), from first-hand knowledge of Calvert's own archaeological reports, and from conversation with Gerald Calvert, whom he photographed with Blegen and William and Louise Taft Semple of the University of Cincinnati, sponsor of the 1930 campaign. Arik (1953).

70. When I swam the Hellespont in 1997, I aimed for this building, imagining the Calvert family on their parapet. Allen (1998b), 37. *Vilayet* is the post-Ottoman term for *sançak*, or province.

71. After the seventy-fifth commemoration of the ANZAC landings at Gallipoli, the area was named Moorabbin Friendship Park, Moorabbin being a suburb of Melbourne, Australia. Information courtesy of Ibrahim Aksu.

72. The surprising lack of acknowledgment certainly will be corrected when Coşkün Özgünel and Gustav Gamer publish the catalogue and the Çanakkale collection. Gamer (1992), 41.

73. Kendall Bacon, personal communication.

74. Easton (1994), 141–69; Allen (1997a), 89–96.

75. The Museum of Applied Arts and Design, which opened in 1882, is shown in Witte (1990), figure 6. Witte's figure 7 shows the Schliemanns arranging the collection in Berlin. In 1885, Schliemann added the finds that he had purchased from the Imperial Ottoman Museum. The rest of his collection came after his death. Saherwala, Goldmann, and Mahr (1993), 31–39, 48.

76. Schmidt (1902); Bertram (1992), 398–99. Schmidt served as the curator of the Prehistoric Section of the Museum for Prehistory and Early History in Berlin and was a member of the Berlin Anthropological Society.

77. Saherwala, Goldmann, and Mahr (1993), 48. The Trojan Collection was there from 1881 to 1885 and 1922 to 1945. Goldmann (1992), 378.

78. Unverzagt succeeded Schuchhardt, director from 1908 to 1926. Kater (1974), 22.

79. Stone (1975), 449.

80. Goldmann (1990).

81. Goldmann (1992), 379.

82. These were more than documented by reams of paperwork and volumes of photographs at the Nuremberg trials. This effort (the ERR, or *Einsatzstab Reichsleiter*) was headed by Alfred Rosenberg, who used the Jeu de Paume Museum as his headquarters for western Europe. Nicholas (1994). In the autumn of 1940, he had gathered some twenty-one thousand works of art to be shipped to Berlin. Hitler was not the only collector. There was also Göring, and below him many others. In light of Hitler's plan to acquire works of art and his high estimation of Priam's Treasure, it is curious that when the Germans controlled Athens, he did not evacuate Schliemann's treasures from Troy and Mycenae stored there.

83. They were carefully packed, with meticulous documentation in duplicate, one copy for staff and one in the crate itself. Unverzagt (1988), 317; Goldmann (1992), 380. Also Easton (1994a), 221–43, on which some of the following discussion is dependent.

84. According to Easton, some of this material, three or four silver vessels, a bronze kettle, spearheads, and flat axes, remained in Berlin. Easton (1994a), 235.

85. Unverzagt (1988), 317; Goldmann (1992), 379–80.

86. It had held the treasure when it first arrived from Britain in 1881.

87. Meyer (1993), 28. "Flak" is from a German acronym, "FLAK," for *Flugabwehr-Kanone*. Siebler (1994), figure 71. The lading lists are shown in figures a–c.

88. Moorehead (1994), 260.

89. The other material was from the Altes Museum. Akinsha and Kozlov (1991a), 132.

90. Seventy-five thousand tons of high explosives and incendiary bombs were dropped on the city, resulting in between thirty-five thousand and fifty thousand dead and a million and a half homeless.

91. Unverzagt (1988); Goldmann (1992), 380. Siebler (1994), figures 70 a–d.

92. The Class 2 pottery and bronzes from Lebus went to the German Democratic Republic (East Germany), to the Academy of Sciences. Goldmann (1992).

93. Goldmann (1992), 381.

94. Ibid., 381–82, from Unverzagt (1988).

95. Ibid., 382, from Unverzagt (1988).

96. Moorehead (1994), 263, based on Unverzagt (1988). The bombed-out museum is shown in Siebler (1994), 72, in photos from 1945 and 1946.

97. Nicholas (1994). Of these, only the objects stored at the Merkers mine made it back to Berlin unscathed after the war, when the six crates sent to Merkers were returned. Both Grasleben (held by the Americans and then by the British) and Schönebeck (held by the Americans, the British, and finally the Soviets) were looted. Of the fifty crates that Unverzagt sent to Grasleben on 7 April 1945, thirty were returned to Berlin. Goldmann (1992), 383.

98. Nicholas (1994), 312.

99. Goldmann (1992), 383; Easton (1994a), 234.

100. Unverzagt (1988), 343; Cheney (1997).

101. Unverzagt (1988), 352–55.

102. Goldmann (1992), 385. For the *Ahnenerbe*, see Kater (1974); Sichtermann (1996), 426.

103. According to Goldmann, the two Trojan golden tassels that appeared on the black market in Berlin in autumn 1945 were not part of the Berlin holdings. Goldmann (1995).

104. Goldmann reported that Americans took charge of 80 percent of the 1700 known repositories. Meyer (1993), 31. Most were repatriated, although thefts occurred, such as the infamous vandalism by an American G.I., Joe Tom Meador, who mailed home priceless Carolingian gospels to Whitewright, Texas. Honan (1997).

105. See also the secret order of the chief of naval staff, Staff 1.a. No. 1601/41, of 29 December 1941, cited by Nicholas (1994), 189.

106. Akinsha and Kozlov (1991a), 132. Among the 50,000 Russians who starved in 1941 during the siege of Leningrad was Schliemann's son, Sergei (1855–1941). Antonova (1996), 7.

107. Akinsha and Kozlov (1991a), 132.

108. Nicholas (1994), 192.

109. Pushkin's house was ransacked, Tolstoy's manuscripts were burned, and Tchaikovsky's home was used as a motorcycle garage. Nicholas (1994), 193.

110. Akinsha and Kozlov (1991a), 132; Akinsha (1991), 112.

111. Akinsha and Kozlov (1991a), 134.

112. Nicholas (1994), 362.

113. Ibid.

114. Akinsha and Kozlov (1991a), 135.

115. Unverzagt (1988), 348. The inventory lists are shown in Siebler (1994), figures 75a–b. An archival photo shows a trophy brigade relaxing. Akinsha and Kozlov (1994), 159.

116. These were brought to Goldmann. Meyer (1993), 32.

117. Akinsha and Kozlov (1991a), 131.

118. Ibid.

119. Moorehead (1994), 279, based on interviews with Akinsha and Kozlov. Siebler (1994), figure 78.

120. Akinsha and Kozlov (1994), 69. Antonova's signature can be read on this document. Siebler (1994), figure 77. Antonova is shown in a 1945 photograph during the unloading of war loot. Akinsha and Kozlov (1994), 155, 158. See also Akinsha and Kozlov (1997), 162–65.

121. Akinsha and Kozlov (1994), 70.

122. Goldmann (1993), 51.

123. Meyer (1993), 31, from Akinsha and Kozlov (1991b), 119.

124. Goldmann (1991), 205. Irina Antonova, director of the Pushkin State Museum of Fine Arts, has corroborated the fact that when the Pushkin Museum's predecessor, the Tsvetaev Museum of Fine Arts, opened in Moscow in 1912, among the first exhibits were replicas of objects from Schliemann's excavations, although these seem to have been electrotypes of the Mycenae gold. Antonova (1996), 7; Easton (1995), 12.

125. Sir Edwin Pears (1835–1919), a British lawyer resident in Constantinople, wrote that "it is true that in many parts of Asia Minor to this day similar ornaments are found or are made, but the conservatism that exists in reference to manufacture, especially in the East, is a sufficient answer to the suggestion that because these ancient objects resemble modern ones, they are therefore not authentic." Toynbee (1916), 66. William M. Calder III brought this passage to my attention.

126. Easton (1995), 11.

127. Ibid., 12.

128. Traill (1995). Because of the apparent ease with which one could acquire gold ornaments in Constantinople in Schliemann's day, Calder strongly urges that the gold ornaments be tested. Personal communication from William M. Calder III.

129. Mellink (1986), "Postscript," 93–101.

130. Simpson, (1997); Akinsha and Kozlov (1997), 162–65.

131. The parts of three treasures that went to the National Museum in Athens must have been Sophia Schliemann's personal property: Treasures D, G (1878) and earrings from Treasure A. Konsola (1990), 79–87. Korfmann (1994) also mentions possible finds in Philadelphia. This gold jewelry in Philadelphia may have been gifts to the Philadelphian George Henry Boker by Schliemann and Cesnola, or if it indeed was "purchased at Çanakkale" in 1966, it may have been part of a hoard found in the last Calvert house, the Garden Villa on Alman Sokak. See George F. Bass, "Troy and Ur: Gold Links between Two Ancient Capitals." *Expedition* 8 (1966): 29, and "A Hoard of Trojan and Sumerian Jewelry," *American Journal of Archaeology* 74 (1970): 335, plate 86, figure 1.

132. Schmidt (1902), 225–47.

133. Treasures N, P, R1, and R2 (1872) and A, B, S1, and S2 (1873). Götze (1902), 325–43; Easton (1997), 194–99. These were exported from Greece with a valid permit dating from 1874. Saherwala, Goldmann, and Mahr (1996), 107.

134. Déthier (1876), 416–19. Parts of Treasures C (1873), D, F, and O (1878), and J (1879) remain at the Istanbul museum. The museum's holdings were diminished by theft before 1881 and Schliemann's buying back of Trojan material in 1885. Easton (1997), 194–99.

135. As Marchand has shown, even this decree never was universally enforced. Marchand (1996), 199–203.

136. Akinsha and Kozlov (1993), 141.

137. Easton (1997).

138. The 1882 Treasures K and Q were smuggled out in baskets. Saherwala, Goldmann, and Mahr (1993), 99; Easton (1997), 198 n. 51.

139. Meyer (1995), 47.

140. Mikhail Piotrovsky, Director of the Hermitage Museum, is committed to "identifying an honorable solution to the fate of these works."

141. Easton (1994a), 240.

142. Allen (1996a), 26–27, and (1998a), 21–35.

143. Schliemann to Virchow, 15 July 1890, in Herrmann and Maaß (1990), #584, 552.

144. Traill (1995).

145. Meyer (1995), 52.

146. Irinia Antonova, "Instances of Repatriation by the USSR," in Simpson (1997), 145–47.

147. Korfmann (1996), 16, figure 9.

148. Interview with Valery Kulishov, member of the State Commission on Restitution, conducted by Moscow *Times* reporter Anne Barnard. In Hoffman (1993), 39, and Brandau (1998), 24.

149. This is less and less likely since a national law was passed in Russia in 1997 declaring that all "trophy" art is "owned by the Russian Federation and . . . recognized as federal property." How this will fare internationally is another issue. Akinsha (1997), 65–66.

150. Hochfeld and Akinsha (1996), 75.

151. Easton (1995), 14.

152. Ibid.

153. A Moscow librarian suggested that rare German books and archives be returned. Meyer (1995), 52.

EPILOGUE

1. See Manfred Korfmann's annual reports of excavation progress in *Studia Troica*, a journal devoted to subjects pertaining to Troy.

2. The survey has been made with a cesium magnetometer and then confirmed through stratigraphic excavation of selected areas where anomalies in the patterns generated by computers indicated significant buried features. Eberl (1995), 16–22; Brandau (1998), 18.

3. Korfmann and Kromer (1993), 135–71. Korfmann's belief that Troy II was partly contemporary with Troy I has resulted in vastly different dates assigned to the Early Bronze Age:

Troy I 2920–2480/20 B.C.	Troy I 3000–2500 B.C.	Troy I 3000–2700 B.C.
Troy II 2600–2480/20 B.C.	Troy II 2500–2300 B.C.	Troy II 2700–2150 B.C.
Troy III 2480/20–2300 B.C.	Troy III–V 2300–1700 B.C.	Troy III 2150–2000 B.C.
Brandau (1997), 376	Korfmann and Mannsperger (1992), 33, 34, 36, 37	Easton (1990), figure 13

4. Brandau (1997), 377.

5. As Carter and Morris have recently asserted, "The history of the 'Trojan War' belongs not to Homer but to Anatolian archaeology." Carter and Morris (1995), 2.

6. Korfmann (1995), 181–82.

7. Ibid., 179.

8. Jablonka (1996), 66.

9. Korfmann (1996), 6–7.

10. Rose (1993), 112.

11. Korfmann (1995), 173–83, and (1996), 6–8, figures 33–36, plates 1, 4; Jablonka (1996), 66.

12. Local gray ware from levels VI and VII often imitates particular Mycenaean shapes, suggesting adoption of certain customs. Allen (1990).

13. Studies of coastal change estimate that the headland once may have projected as much as a mile into the sea. Kayan (1995), 221.

14. Korfmann found over fifty cremations similar to those of the sixth stratum that Blegen excavated at Hisarlık and also inhumations. One aristocrat was cremated and placed with his sword and five seal stones in a built stone tomb. One of the seals Korfmann believes to be Mycenaean, though it also has parallels on the Kaş/Ulu Burun ship. One elliptical cist burial has Thracian parallels, according to Maureen Basedow, who is publishing the cemetery.

15. However, Basedow, *Die Spätbronzezeitliche Graberfeld von Beşik Tepe* (forthcoming), disagrees and believes that Beşik Tepe represents a coastal trading emporium, no more and no less. She asserts its Anatolian parallels and downplays its demonstrable Aegean connections.

16. Allen (1990); Korfmann (1995), 173–83.

17. As Edgar J. Forsdyke put it, "Archaeological discovery may throw light upon the legends, but the use of legendary statements for historical interpretation of material is a reversal of proper procedure." Forsdyke (1956), 166.

18. Güterbock (1986), 33–44.

19. Ibid., 42. The equation was first made by Emil Forrer in "Apollon," *Revue Hittite et Asianique* 1, no. 5 (1931): 141–44. Recently, Korfmann presented an intriguing paper connecting Appaliunas, a Hittite god of gates, to the god of the Trojans represented in aniconic form in stelai set up at the south gate of the citadel. Korfmann (1998), 51–73; Brandau (1998), 23–24.

20. Güterbock (1986), 42. Korfmann suggests that the god was an underworld deity in general and affiliated with wells and springs. According to Korfmann, the Hittites built artificial grottoes near a sacred lake at their capital, Hattusa, for his cult. Brandau (1998), 24.

21. Wood (1996), 247. When Maclaren visited it in 1847, Ayazma, the source, was an object of pilgrimage. We visited 150 years later.

22. The ancient language was Luvian, the lingua franca of ancient Anatolia, including the area around Smyrna, the vicinity of Homer. Hittite was the language of the "upper crust." Korfmann (1998), 51–73.

23. Calvert Watkins, "The Language of the Trojans," in Mellink (1986), 45–62.

24. Emily Vermeule, "Priam's Castle Blazing: A Thousand Years of Trojan Memories," in Mellink (1986), 77–92; Hood (1995), 25–32.

25. Brandau (1998), 22.

26. Korfmann (1996), 7.

27. Burkert (1995), 139–48.

28. It was found in House 731, in an unexcavated "pinnacle" left by earlier excavators. Its context is the late twelfth century B.C. Hawkins and Easton (1996), 111, figures 1–3. If the find spot is original, there might be a shred of evidence for literacy (not yet proven for the site as a whole) as late as the late twelfth century B.C. Korfmann (1996), 7.

29. Ibid.

30. Ibid., 34, figure 27.

31. Rose (1995), 91. These scraps of evidence for sparse habitation he now assigns to Troy VIIb3 and 4.

32. Raaflaub (1998), 79–99.

33. It may appear in the end that poetic memories such as one finds in Homer owe more to imagination than to history. Carter and Morris (1995), 4.

SOURCES CITED

ARCHIVES

England

British Library, Manuscripts Department, London (BLMS).
British Museum, Central Archives, London (BMCA).
British Museum, Department of Greek and Roman Antiquities (BMGR).
Frederick J. Calvert Archives. Family records.
Public Record Office, Kew. Foreign Office Records (PRO/FO).

Germany

Akademiearkiv, Berlin-Brandenburgische Akademie der Wissenschaften (ABBAW).
Museum für Ur- und Frühgeschichte, Berlin.

Greece

Gennadius Library of the American School of Classical Studies at Athens.
    Letters received by Schliemann (B).
    Original letters sent by Schliemann and drafts of Frank Calvert's replies to him (BB).
    Copies of Schliemann's outgoing correspondence (BBB).
    Schliemann's diaries.

Scotland

William Simpson Collection, the Mitchell Library, Glasgow.

Turkey

Private collections in Çanakkale.
    Francis Henry Bacon diary.

Calvert family watercolors and pencil and pen-and-ink sketches.
Private collections in Izmir.
Whittall family archives.

United States

Center for American History, University of Texas, Austin, Terrell Archives.
Francis Henry Bacon archives. Bacon family members.
National Archives Research Administration, Washington, D.C. (NARA).
    U.S. Consular Agency (RG 84), Dardanelles, vols. 1–14.
    U.S. Consulate General, Constantinople (RG 84).
    U.S. Legation to Turkey, vols. 287 and 288.
William Partridge Papers in the William Robert Ware Collection, Division of Drawings and Archives, Avery Architectural and Fine Arts Library, Columbia University in the City of New York.

BIBLIOGRAPHY

Akin, Nur. 1993. "Osman Hamdi Bey Âsâr—ı Atîka Nizamnamesi ve Dönemin Koruma Anlayışı üzerine." In Rona (1993), 233–39.

Akinsha, Konstantin. 1991. "The Turmoil over Soviet War Treasures." *ARTnews*, December, 110–15.

———. 1997. "Duma Does It." *ARTNews*, April, 65–66.

Akinsha, Konstantin, and Grigorii Kozlov. 1991a. "Spoils of War: The Soviet Union's Hidden Art Treasures." *ARTnews*, April, 130–41.

———. 1991b. "The Soviets' War Treasures: A Growing Controversy." *ARTnews*, September, 112–19.

———. 1993. "Trojan Treasures Were Stolen from the British by Soviets." *The Observer*, 23 April.

———. 1994. "To Return or Not to Return." *ARTnews*, October, 154–59.

Aksit, Ilhan. 1971. *Çanakkale Rehberi*. Istanbul.

Allen, Susan H. 1990. "Northwestern Anatolian Grey Ware in the Late Bronze Age: Analysis and Distribution in the Eastern Mediterranean." Ph.D. diss., Brown University.

———. 1994. "Frank Calvert: The Man Who Would be Schliemann." *American Journal of Archaeology* 98: 325.

———. 1995a. "In Schliemann's Shadow: 'Rediscovering' Frank Calvert, the Unheralded and All-but-Forgotten Discoverer of Troy." *Archaeology* 48: 50–57.

———. 1995b. "'Finding the Walls of Troy': Frank Calvert, Excavator." *American Journal of Archaeology* 99: 379–407.

———. 1996a. "Calvert's Heirs Claim Schliemann Treasure." *Archaeology* 49: 26–27.

———. 1996b. "'Principally for Vases, etc.': The Formation and Dispersal of the Calvert Collection." *Anatolian Studies* 46: 145–65, plates 18–21.

———. 1997a. "The Later History of 'Priam's Treasure.'" *New England Classical Journal* 24: 89–96.

———. 1997b. Review of *Excavating Schliemann* and *Schliemann of Troy: Treasure and Deceit*, by David A. Traill. *American Journal of Archaeology* 101: 598–99.

————. 1998a. "A Personal Sacrifice in the Interest of Science: Calvert, Schliemann, and the Troy Treasures." In Boedeker (1998), 21–35.

————. 1998b. "Swimming with Heroes: Hellespont 1997." *Horizons* 27: 37.

————. Forthcoming. "Heinrich Schliemann and the American Diplomatic Community."

Allen, Susan H., Lenore O. K. Congdon, and Helen B. Landry, eds. Forthcoming. *Francis Henry Bacon's "The Log of the Dorian" and "Assos Days."*

Amandry, Pierre. 1995. "Schliemann, le 'Trésor de Priam,' et le Musée du Louvre." In *Le Trésor de Priam retrouvé. Dossiers d'archéologie* 206: 42–83.

Andree, Christian. 1990. "Heinrich Schliemann und Rudolf Virchow." In Calder and Cobet (1990), 256–95.

Antonova, Irina. 1996. "Introduction." In Tolstikov and Treister (1996), 7–8.

Arik, Remzi O. 1953. *Turuva Kılavuzu.* Istanbul.

Aristarchi Bey, Grégoire. 1874. *Legislation ottomane cu recueil des lois règlements, ordinances, traités, capitulations, et autres documents officiels de l'Empire.* Constantinople.

Arndt, Karl J. R. 1981. "Schliemann's Excavation of Troy and American Politics. . . ." *Yearbook of German-American Studies* 16: 1–8.

Arnott, W. G. 1978. "Schliemann's Epitaph." *Liverpool Classical Monthly* 3: 93.

Ascherson, Paul, Theodor von Heldreich, and F. Kurtz. 1881. "Catalogue of the Plants Hitherto Known of the Troad, Compiled According to the Collections of Professor Rudolf Virchow and Dr. Julius Schmidt, and from the Literary Sources." Appendix 6 in Schliemann (1881a), 727–36.

————. 1883. "Beitrag zur Flora des nordwestlichen Kleinasiens." *Jahrbuch des königlichen botanischen Gartens und des botanischen Museums zu Berlin* 2: 39–65.

Babelon, M. Ernest. 1898. *Inventaire sommaire de la collection Waddington acquise par l'Etat en 1897.* Paris.

Bacon, Francis H. 1912. "Extracts from 'The Log of the Dorian,' Part II." *Architectural Review* 1: 76–89.

Barker Webb, Philip. 1821. *Osservazione intorno allo stato antico e presente dell'agro Troiano.* Milan.

————. 1844. *Topographie de la Troade ancienne et moderne.* Paris.

Barry, A. 1928. "The Tradition of Classics in England." In *The Classics, Their History and Present Status in Education,* 252–58. Ed. F. Kirsch. Milwaukee.

Bass, George. 1986. "A Bronze Age Shipwreck at Ulu Burun (Kaş): 1984 Campaign." *American Journal of Archaeology* 90: 269–96.

Baumeister, August. 1854. "Reisen in Kleinasien." *Archäologische Zeitung* 11–12: 509–12.

Bent, John T., ed. 1893. *Early Voyages and Travels in the Levant.* London.

Bertram, Marion. 1992. "Zur Geschichte der Berliner Schliemann-Sammlung." In Herrmann (1992), 397–401.

Biographisches Wörterbuch zur deutschen Geschichte. 1973. Munich.

Birchenough, Charles. 1914. *History of Elementary Education in England and Wales from 1800 to the Present Day.* Baltimore.

Blegen, Carl W., John L. Caskey, and Marion Rawson. 1950. *Troy: Excavations Conducted by the University of Cincinnati, 1932–1938.* Vol. 1. *General Introduction: The First and Second Settlements.* Princeton.

————. 1953. *Troy: Excavations Conducted by the University of Cincinnati, 1932–1938.* Vol. 3. *The Sixth Settlement.* Princeton.

————. 1958. *Troy: Excavations Conducted by the University of Cincinnati, 1932–1938.* Vol. 4. *Settlements VIIa, VIIb, and VIII.* Princeton.

Blegen, Robert D., ed. 1995. *Carl W. Blegen: His Letters Home II—From Distant Fields.* Privately published.

Bloedow, Edmund. 1992. "Schliemann's Attitude to Pottery." In Herrmann (1992), 211–21.

Boedeker, Deborah, ed. 1998. *The World of Troy: Homer, Schliemann and the Treasures of Priam.* Washington, D.C.

Boisgelin, Louis. 1805. *Ancient and Modern Malta.* London

Bonham-Carter, Victor, ed. 1968. *Surgeon in the Crimea: The Experiences of George Lawson Recorded in Letters to His Family, 1854–1855.* London.

Borbein, Adolph. 1993. "150 Jahre Archäologische Gesellschaft zu Berlin." *Winckelmannsprogramm* 134: 28–34.

Borlase, William C. 1878. "A Visit to Dr. Schliemann's Troy." *Fraser's Magazine* 17, February, 228–39.

Bötticher, Ernst. 1888. "La Troie de Schliemann: Une nécropole à incinération." *Le Muséon* 7: 101–31, 226–46, 343–52, 489–502.

———.1890. *Hissarlik: Wie es ist. Funftes Sendschreiben über Schliemann's Troja.* Berlin.

———. 1894. *Troja im Jahre 1894.* Schwerin.

Bradley, Edward S. 1927. *Geo. Henry Boker: Poet and Artist.* Philadelphia.

Brandau, Brigit. 1997. *Troia: Eine Stadt und ihr Mythos. Die neuesten Entdeckungen.* Bergisch Gladback.

———. 1998. "Can Archaeology Discover Homer's Troy?" *Archaeology Odyssey* 1: 14–25.

Briggs, Ward W., and William M. Calder III, eds. 1990. *Classical Scholarship: A Biographical Encyclopedia.* New York.

Bröndsted, Peter O. 1844. *Reise in Groekenland i Aarene, 1810–1813.* Ed. N. B. Dorph. Copenhagen.

Broughton, Lord (John C. Hobhouse). 1813. *A Journey through Albania and Other Provinces of Turkey in Europe and Asia to Constantinople during the Years 1809 and 1810.* 2 vols. London.

———. 1817. *A Journey through Albania and Other Provinces of Turkey in Europe and Asia to Constantinople during the Years 1809 and 1810.* 2 vols. Boston.

Budge, E. A. Wallis. 1922. *Guide to Babylonian and Assyrian Antiquities in the British Museum.* London.

Buenzod, J., ed. 1961. *Arthur de Gobineau: Lettres d'un voyage en Russie, en Asie Mineure, et en Grèce.* Etudes de lettres, 2d series, vol. 4. Paris.

Burgon, Thomas. 1847. "An Attempt to Point Out the Vases of Greece Proper Which Belong to the Homeric Period." *Transactions of the Royal Society of Literature* 2, 2d series: 258–96.

Burkert, Walter. 1995. "Lydia between East and West; or, How to Date the Trojan War: A Study in Herodotus." In Carter and Morris (1995), 139–48.

Byron, Lord (George N. Gordon). 1978. *Born for Opposition: Letters and Journals.* Vol. 8. Ed. Leslie A. Marchand. London.

Calder, William M., III. 1972. "Schliemann on Schliemann: A Study in the Use of Sources." *Greek, Roman, and Byzantine Studies* 13: 335–53.

———. 1973/1974. "Heinrich Schliemann: An Unpublished Latin Vita." *Classical World* 67: 272–82.

———. 1975/1976. "Nonnulla Schliemanniana." *Clasical World* 69: 117–18.

———. 1986. "A New Picture of Heinrich Schliemann." In Calder and Traill (1986), 17–47.

———. 1990. "Apocolocyntosis: The Biographers and the Archaeologists." In Calder and Cobet (1990), 360–78.

Calder, William M., III, and Justus Cobet, eds. 1990. *Heinrich Schliemann nach hundert Jahren.* Frankfurt am Main.

Calder, William M., III, and Daniel J. Kramer, eds. 1992. *An Introductory Bibliography to the History of Classical Scholarship Chiefly in the XIXth and XXth Centuries.* Hildesheim.

Calder, William M., III, and David A. Traill, eds. 1986. *Myth, Scandal, and History: The Heinrich Schliemann Controversy.* Detroit.

Calvert, Frank. 1859. "The Tumulus of Hanai Tepe in the Troad." *Archaeological Journal* 16: 1–6.

————. 1860a. "On a Bronze Weight Found on the Site of Hellespontic Abydos." *Archaeological Journal* 17: 198–200.

————. 1860b. "Contributions to the Ancient Geography of the Troad. On the Site and Remains of Colonae. On the Site and Remains at Ophrynium." *Archaeological Journal* 17: 286–296.

————. 1861. "Contributions to the Ancient Geography of the Troad. On the Site and Remains of Larisa." *Archaeological Journal* 18: 253–55.

————. 1864. "Contributions towards the Ancient Geography of the Troad. On the Site of Gergithe." *Archaeological Journal* 21: 46–53.

————. 1865. "Contributions to the Ancient Geography of the Troad. On the Site and Remains of Cebrene." *Archaeological Journal* 22: 51–57.

————. 1873a. "Excavations in the Troad." *Levant Herald,* 4 February.

————. 1873b. "Important Scientific Discovery. Proof of Man's Existence during the Miocene Period." *Levant Herald,* 19 March.

————. 1873c. "On the Probable Existence of Man during the Miocene Period." *Journal of the Anthropological Institute* 3: 127–29.

————. 1874a. "Trojan Antiquities I." *Athenaeum* 2454, 7 November: 610–11.

————. 1874b. "Trojan Antiquities II." *Athenaeum* 2455, 14 November: 643–44.

————. 1875. "Mr. Calvert and Dr. Schliemann on Troy." *The Guardian,* 11 August, 1024.

————. 1880. "Über die asiatische Küste des Hellespont." Trans. Rudolf Virchow. *Zeitschrift für Ethnologie* 12: 31–39.

————. 1881. "Thymbra, Hanai Tepeh." Appendix 4 in Schliemann (1881a), 706–20.

————. 1886. "Meteorsteinfälle am Hellespont." *Mathematische und naturwissenschaftliche Mittheilungen aus den Sitzungsberichten der königlich-preussischen Akademie der Wissenschaften zu Berlin,* 441–42.

————. 1889. *L'Orient franco-hellenique,* 174.

————. 1894. "The Discovery of Homer's Troy." *Levant Herald and Eastern Express,* 7 July.

————. 1897. "On the Tumulus of Choban Tepeh in the Troad." *Journal of Hellenic Studies* 17: 319–320.

————. 1901. "Ein Idol vom thracischen Chersones." *Zeitschrift für Ethnologie* 33: 329–30.

————. 1902. "Beiträge zur Topographie der Troas." *Mitteilungen des deutschen Archäologischen Instituts, athenische Abteilung* 27: 239–45.

Calvert, Frank, and Melchior Neumayr. 1880. "Die jungen Ablangerungen am Hellespont." *Denkschriften der kaiserlichen Akademie der Wissenschaften. Mathematische naturwissenschaftliche Klasse* 40, 357–78.

Çamoglu, Samşettin. 1962. *Çanakkale Bogazı ve Savaşları.* Istanbul.

Carlisle, the earl of (George W. F. Howard). 1854. *Diary in Turkish and Greek Waters.* London.

————. 1855. *Diary in Turkish and Greek Waters.* Boston.

Carter, Jane B., and Sarah Morris. 1995. *The Ages of Homer: A Tribute to Emily Townsend Vermule.* Austin.

Carvalho, Elizabeth. 1992. "Schliemann in Asia." In Herrmann (1992), 29–35.

Caskey, John L. 1972. "The Figurine in the Roll-Top Desk." *American Journal of Archaeology* 76: 192–93.

Caskey, Lacey D. 1925. *Catalogue of Greek and Roman Sculpture.* Museum of Fine Arts. Cambridge, Mass.

Cezar, Mustafa. 1995. *Sannata Batya Açılış ve Osman Hamdi Bey.* Istanbul.

Chamberlin, Charles. 1957. "Alexander Watkins Terrell, Citizen." Ph.D. diss., University of Texas, Austin.

Chambers, Marylin. 1990. "Schliemann and America." In Calder and Cobet (1990), 397–414.

Chandler, Richard. 1764. *Travels in Asia Minor.* London.

Chaney, Otto P. 1997. *Zhukov.* Rev. ed. Princeton.

Chevalier, Jean-Baptiste. 1791. *Description of the Plain of Troy.* Trans. and ed. Andrew Dalzel. Edinburgh.

———. 1794. "Tableau de la Plaine de Troye: Accompagné d'une carte levée géometriquement en 1785 et 1786." *Transactions of the Royal Society of Edinburgh.* Vol. 3, part 2, *Papers of the Literary Class,* 3–92.

———. 1799. *Voyage dans la Troade, ou Tableau de la Plaine de Troie dans son état actuel.* Paris.

———. 1802. *Receuil des cartes, plans, vues, et médailles pour servir au voyage de la Troade.* Paris.

Choiseul-Gouffier, Marie G. F. A., Comte de. 1798. See Lenz (1798).

———. 1809. *Voyage pittoresque de la Grèce.* Vol. 2, part 1. Paris.

———. 1820. *Voyage pittoresque de la Grèce.* Vol. 2, part 1. Chapter 14. Ed. J. D. Barbié du Bocage. Paris.

———. 1822. *Voyage pittoresque de la Grèce.* Vol. 2, part 2. Ed. J. D. Barbié du Bocage and J. A. Letronne. Paris.

Clapham, John H., ed. 1939. *John Brunton's Book.* Cambridge.

Clarke, Edward D. 1817. *Travels in Various Countries of Europe, Asia and Africa, Greece, Egypt, and the Holy Land.* Parts 2.1 (vol. 3) and 2.3 (vol. 8). 2d ed. London.

Clarke, Joseph T. 1886. Review of "Beiträge zur Landeskunde der Troas," by Rudolf Virchow (1882b). *Abhandlungen der königlichen Akademie der Wissenschaften zu Berlin,* physikalische Klasse, no. 3. In *American Journal of Archaeology* 2: 195–202.

———. 1887. "A Proto-Ionic Capital from the Site of Neandreia." *American Journal of Archaeology* 2: 136–45.

———. 1888. "Gargara, Lamponia, and Pionia: Towns of the Troad." *American Journal of Archaeology* 4: 291–319.

Clarke, Joseph T., Francis H. Bacon, and Robert Koldewey. 1902. *Investigations at Assos: Drawings and Photographs of the Buildings and Objects Discovered during the Excavations of 1881–1882–1883.* Cambridge, Mass.

Clarke, M. L. 1959. *Classical Education in Britain.* Cambridge.

Cline, Eric H. 1994. *Sailing the Wine Dark Sea: International Trade and the Late Bronze Age Aegean.* British Archaeological Reports, international series 591. Oxford.

Cobet, Justus. 1990. "Troia vor Schliemann." In Calder and Cobet (1990), 118–51.

Cobet, Justus, Emre Madran, and Nimet Özgünel. 1991. "From Saewulf to Schliemann." *Studia Troica* 1: 101–9.

Cobet, Justus, and Barbara Patzek, eds. 1992. *Archäologie und historischen Erinnerung nach 100 Jahren Heinrich Schliemann.* Essen.

Cochran, William. 1887. *Pen and Pencil in Asia Minor; or, Notes from the Levant.* London.

Cohen, Ada. 1995. "Alexander and Achilles—Macedonians and Mycenaeans." In Carter and Morris (1995), 483–505.

Comnos, Spyridon. 1874. "Hissarlik and Mycenae." *Athenaeum* 2441, 8 August: 178–79.

Conacher, J. B. 1987. *Britain and the Crimea, 1855–1856: Problems of War and Peace.* New York.

Congdon, Lenore O. K., ed. 1974. "The Assos Journals of Francis H. Bacon." *Archaeology* 27: 83–95.

Conze, Alexander. 1884. "Goldschmuck kleinasiatischer Fundorte." *Archäologische Zeitung* 42: 90–94.

Cook, John M. 1973. *The Troad: An Archaeological and Topographical Study.* Oxford.

Cox, Robert, and James Nicol, eds. 1894. *Select Writings, Political, Scientific, Topographical, and Miscellaneous, of the Late Charles Maclaren.* 2 vols. Edinburgh.

Cuinet, Vital. 1894. *La Turquie d'Asie.* Vols. 3 and 4. Paris

Curl, James S. 1994. *Aegyptomania: The Egyptian Revival, a Recurring Theme in the History of Taste.* Manchester, England.

Curtius, Carl. 1873. "Inschrift aus Sestos." *Hermes* 7: 113–39.

Curtius, Ernst. 1872. "Ein Ausflug nach Kleinasien und Griechenland." *Preussische Jahrbücher* 29: 52–71.

Curtius, Friedrich E., ed. 1903. *Ernst Curtius: Ein Lebensbild in Briefen.* Berlin.

Curzon, Robert. 1849. *A Visit to the Monasteries in the Levant.* London.

Daniel, Glyn. 1950. *A Hundred Years of Archaeology.* Edinburgh.

———, ed. 1981. *Towards a History of Archaeology.* London.

Davy, John. 1842. *Notes and Observations on the Ionian Islands and Malta: With Some Remarks on Constantinople and Turkey and on the System of Quarantine as at Present Conducted.* Vol. 2. London.

Dearborn, Henry A. S. 1819. *A Memoir on the Commerce and Navigation of the Black Sea, and the Trade and Maritime Geography of Turkey and Egypt.* Vol. 2. Boston.

de Grummond, Nancy T. 1996. *An Encyclopedia of the History of Classical Archaeology.* Westport, Conn.

De Jesus, Prentiss S. 1980. *The Development of Prehistoric Mining and Metallurgy in Anatolia.* British Archaeological Reports, international series 74. Oxford.

De Kay, James E. 1833. *Sketches of Turkey in 1831 and 1832.* New York.

De Lesseps, Ferdinand. 1888. *Recollections of Forty Years.* New York.

Demakopoulou, Kaiti, ed. 1990. *Troja, Mykene, Tiryns, Orchomenos: Heinrich Schliemann zum 100. Todestag.* Athens.

Déthier, Philipp A. 1876. "Une partie du trésor Troyen au Musée de Constantinople." *Revue archéologique* 31: 416–19.

Dickinson, Oliver. 1994. *The Aegean Bronze Age.* Cambridge.

Dictionaire de biographie française. 1933–1989. Paris.

Dictionary of National Biography. 1937. London.

Döhl, Harmut. 1981. *Heinrich Schliemann: Mythos und Argernis.* Munich and Lucerne.

———. 1986. "Schliemann the Archaeologist." In Calder and Traill (1986), 95–109.

Dörpfeld, Wilhelm.1890. *Mitteilungen des deutschen Archäologischen Instituts, athenische Abteilung* 15: 226–29.

————. 1891. "The Buildings of Troy." In Schuchhardt (1891), 335–49.

————. 1894. *Troja 1893: Bericht über die im Jahre 1893 in Troja Veranstalteten Ausgrabungen.* Leipzig.

————. 1902. *Troja und Ilion: Ergebnisse der Ausgrabungen in den vorhistorischen und historischen Schichten von Ilion.* Athens.

Durbin, John P. 1849. *Observations in the East: Chiefly in Egypt, Palestine, Syria, and Asia Minor.* Vol. 2. New York.

Dyck, Andrew R. 1990. "Schliemann on the Excavations at Troy: Three Unpublished Letters." *Greek, Roman, and Byzantine Studies* 31: 323–37.

Easton, Donald F. 1981. "Schliemann's Discovery of Priam's Treasure: Two Enigmas." *Antiquity* 55, 179–83.

————. 1982. "The Schliemann Papers." *Annual of the British School of Athens* 77: 93–110.

————. 1984a. "Priam's Treasure." *Anatolian Studies* 34: 141–69.

————. 1984b. "Schliemann's Mendacity—A False Trail?" *Antiquity* 58: 197–204.

————. 1990. "Reconstructing Schliemann's Troy." In Calder and Cobet (1990), 431–47.

————. 1991. "Troy before Schliemann." *Studia Troica* 1: 111–29.

————. 1994a. "Priam's Gold: The Full Story." *Anatolian Studies* 44: 221–43.

————. 1994b. "Schliemann Did Admit the Mycenaean Date of Troia VI." *Studia Troica* 4: 173–75.

————. 1995. "The Troy Treasures in Russia." *Antiquity* 69: 11–14.

————. 1997. "The Excavation of the Trojan Treasures and Their History up to the Death of Schliemann in 1890." In Simpson (1997), 194–99.

Eberl, Ulrich. 1995. "Behind the Myth of Troy." *DaimlerBenz HighTech Report* 1: 16–22.

Eckenbrecher, Gustav von. 1843. "Über die Lage des homerischen Ilion." *Rheinisches Museum für Philologie* 2: 1–49.

————. 1874. "Ein Besuch bei Schliemann auf der Stätte des alten Troja." *Daheim* 10: 251–55.

Esin, Ufuk. 1993. "Yüzyıl Sonlarında Heinrich Schliemann'ın Troya Kazıları ve Osmanlılar 'la İlişkileri." In Rona (1993), 179–91.

Evans, Arthur. 1921. *The Palace of Minos.* Vol. 1. London.

Evans, Joan. 1956. *A History of the Society of Antiquaries.* Oxford.

Fellows, Charles. 1839. *A Journal Written during an Excursion in Asia Minor.* London.

Fernea, Elizabeth. Forthcoming. "Victorian Women's Views of the Exotic: Egypt and Texas."

Fitton, J. Lesley, ed. 1990. *Heinrich Schliemann and the British Museum.* British Museum Occasional Paper 83. London.

Forschammer, Peter W. 1842. "Observations on the Topography of Troy." *Journal of the Royal Geographical Society* 12: 28–44.

————. 1850. *Beschreibung der Ebene von Troja.* Frankfurt.

Forsdyke, Edgar J. 1956. *Greece before Homer.* London.

Foster, J. W. 1906. *The Practice of Diplomacy.* Boston.

Foster, James W., and Beta K. Manakee. 1961. *The Lords Baltimore: An Account of the Portraits of the Founder and the Five Proprietaries of the Colony of Maryland.* Baltimore.

Fox, Robin L. 1980. *The Search for Alexander.* Boston.

Franckland, Charles C. 1829. *Travels to and from Constantinople in the Years 1827 and 1828; or, Personal Narrative of a Journey from Vienna, through Hungary.* 2 vols. London.

Frangakis, Elena. 1985. "The Raya Communities of Smyrna in the 18th Century (1690–1820): Demography and Economic Activities." In *La ville néohellénique: Heritages ottomans et état grec. Actes du colloque intérnational d'histoire* 27-42. Athens.

Frangakis-Syrett, Elena. 1987. "Greek Mercantile Activities in the Eastern Mediterranean, 1780–1820." *Balkan Studies* 28: 73–86.

———. 1991a. "The Greek Mercantile Community of Izmir in the First Half of the Nineteenth Century." In *Les villes dans l'empire ottoman: Activités et sociétés,* 391–416. Ed. I. D. Panzac. Paris.

———. 1991b. "British Economic Activities in Izmir in the Second Half of the Nineteenth and Early Twentieth Centuries." *New Perspectives on Turkey* 5–6: 191–227.

———. 1992. "Implementation of the Anglo-Turkish Convention on Izmir's Trade: European and Minority Merchants." *New Perspectives on Turkey* 7: 91–112.

Frisch, Peter. 1975. *Die Inschriften von Ilion.* Bonn.

Gamer, Gustav. 1992. "Frank Calvert, ein Vorläufer Schliemanns: Wer hat Troia entdeckt?" In *Troia Brücke zwischen Orient und Okzident,* 34–50. Ed. Ingrid Gamer-Wallert. Tübingen.

Gardner, Percy. 1896. "Sir Charles Newton: Born 13. Sept. 1816 +28. Nov. 1894." *Biographisches Jahrbuch für Altertumskunde* 19: 132–42.

Gavrilow, Alexander. 1990. "Schliemann und Russland." In Calder and Cobet 1990, 379–96.

Gay, Peter. 1988. Freud. *A Life for Our Time.* New York.

Gell, William. 1804. *Topography of Troy and Its Vicinity.* London.

Gelzer, Heinrich. 1874. "Eine Wanderung nach Troja." *Offentlich Vorträge gehälten in der Schweiz* 2: 3-32.

Giannokopoulos, Giorgios A. 1995. *O teleutaios Ellenismos tou Renkioi (Ophryniou).* Asprobalta.

Goethert, Friedrich W., and Hans Schleif. 1962. *Der Athena Tempel von Ilion.* Berlin.

Goldmann, Klaus. 1992. "Der Schatz des Priamos: Zum Schicksal von Heinrich Schliemanns 'Sammlung Trojanischer Altertümer.'" In Herrmann (1992), 377–90.

———. 1993. "Heinrich Schliemanns 'Sammlung Trojanischer Altertümer.'" In *Staatliche Muzeen zu Berlin, Schliemanns Gold und die Schätze alteuropas aus dem Museum für Vor- und Frühgeschichte: Eine Dokumentation,* 13–15. Mainz.

———. 1994. "Das Schliemann-Gold vor Augen: Protokoll einer Dienstreise nach Moskau." *Antike Welt* 25. Unpaginated.

———. 1995. *Das Gold des Priamos: Geschichte einer Odyssee.* Leipzig.

Goldstrom, J. M. 1972. *Education: Elementary Education, 1780–1900.* New York.

Götze, Alfred. 1902. "Die Kleingeräte aus Metall, Steine, Knochen, und ähnliche Stoffen." In Dörpfeld (1902), 325–420.

Greaves, Charles S. 1861. "Proceedings." Meetings of the Archaeological Institute. *Archaeological Journal* 18: 363–64.

———. 1865a. "Proceedings." Meetings of the Archaeological Institute. *Archaeological Journal* 22: 171–73.

———. 1865b. "Proceedings." Meetings of the Archaeological Institute. *Archaeological Journal* 22: 337.

Grimm, Georg. 1964. *Johann Georg von Hahn.* Wiesbaden.

Grote, George. 1849. *A History of Greece.* 2d ed. London.

Grünert, Heinz. 1992. "Schliemann und Schuchhardt." In Herrmann (1992), 161–76.

Güterbock, Hans. 1986. "Troy in Hittite Texts? Wilusa, Ahhıyawa, and Hittite History." In Mellink (1986), 33–44.

Habicht, Christian, ed. 1985. *Pausanias' Guide to Ancient Greece*. Berkeley.

Hahn, Johann G. von. 1865. *Die Ausgrabungen auf der homerischen Pergamos in zwei Sendschreiben an Georg Finlay*. Leipzig.

Haines, George, IV. 1969. *Essays on German Influence upon English Education and Science, 1850–1919*. Hamden, Conn.

Hargrave, Helen. 1933. "List of Gifts, 1883–1932." *UT Bulletin* 3315, 15 April: 77.

Harriman, Martin, et al., eds. Forthcoming. "An Honorary Decree from Ilium."

Harrington, Peter. 1996. "The First True War Artist." *Quarterly Journal of Military History* 9: 100–109.

Hartkopf, Werner. 1983. *Die Akademie der Wissenschaften der DDR: Ein Beitrag zu ihrer Geschichte*. Berlin.

Hartshorne, Bertram. 1877. "Dr. Schliemann's Trojan Collection." *Archaeological Journal* 34: 291–96.

Hawkins, J. David, and Donald F. Easton. 1996. A Hieroglyphic Seal from Troia." *Studia Troica* 6: 111–18.

Herodotus. 1982. *Histories*. With an English translation by A. D. Godley. Vol. 3, books 5–7. Cambridge, Mass.

Herrmann, Joachim. 1981. "Heinrich Schliemann and Rudolf Virchow: Their Contributions towards Developing Historical Archaeology." In Daniel (1981),126–32.

———. 1990. "Heinrich Schliemann, Troja, und die Berliner Akademie der Wissenschaften." *Das Altertum* 36: 144–56.

———, ed. 1992. *Heinrich Schliemann: Grundlagen und Ergebnisse moderner Archäologie 100 Jahre nach Schliemanns Tod*. Berlin.

Herrmann, Joachim, and Evelin Maaß, eds. 1990. *Die Korrespondenz zwischen Heinrich Schliemann und Rudolf Virchow, 1876–1890*. Berlin.

Heyck, T. W. 1982. *The Transformation of Intellectual Life in Victorian England*. New York.

Higgins, Reynolds A. 1954. *Catalogue of Terra Cottas in the British Museum*. London.

Hill, Aaron. 1709. *A Full and Just Account of the Present State of the Ottoman Empire in All Its Branches. . . .* London.

Hochfeld, Sylvia, and Konstantin Akinsha. 1996. "A Question of Restitution." *ARTNews*, June, 75.

Hoffmann, Barbara. 1993. "The Spoils of War." *Archaeology* 46: 37–40.

Hoffman, Carey. 1998. "Piecing Together the Mysteries of Ancient Troy." *Horizons* (Winter): 26–31.

Holden, Beatrice M. 1964. *The Metopes of the Temple of Athena at Ilium*. Northampton, Mass.

Honan, William H. 1997. *Treasure Hunt: A "New York Times" Reporter Tracks the Quedlinburg Hoard*. New York.

Hood, Sinclair. 1995. "The Bronze Age Context of Homer." In Carter and Morris (1995), 25–32.

Hunt, Philip. 1817. "Journey from Parium to the Troad. Ascent to the Summit of Ida.— The Salt Springs of Tousla.—Ruins of Assos. From the Journals of Dr. Hunt." In Walpole (1817), 84–140.

Hutchinson, Horace G. 1914. *The Life of Sir John Lubbock, Lord Avebury*. 2 vols. London.

İnalçık, Halil. 1978. *The Ottoman Empire: Conquest, Organization, and Economy*. London.

————. 1994. "Weights and Measures." In İnalçık and Quataert (1994), 987–94.

————, ed. 1985. "The Emergence of Big Farms: Çiftlıks: State, Landlords, and Tenants." In *Studies in Ottoman Social and Economic History.* Ed. Halil İnalçık, 105–26. London.

İnalçık, Halil, with Donald Quataert. 1994. *An Economic and Social History of the Ottoman Empire, 1300–1914.* Cambridge.

Isserlin, B. S. J. 1968. "Schliemann at Motya." *Antiquity* 42: 144–48.

Jablonka, Peter. 1996. "Ausgrabungen im Süden der Unterstadt von Troia: Grabungsbericht 1995." *Studia Troica* 6: 65–96.

Jacoby, Felix, ed. 1926–57. *Fragmente der griechischen Historiker.* Berlin.

Jenkyns, Richard. 1980. *The Victorians and Ancient Greece.* Cambridge, Mass.

Judeich, Walther. 1898. "Bericht über die Reise im nordwestlichen Kleinasien." *Sitzungsberichte Deutsche Akademie der Wissenschaften zu Berlin*: 531–44.

Kahle, Paul, ed. and trans. 1926. *Piri Re'is: Das türkische Segelhandbuch für das Mittelländische Meer vom Jahre 1521.* Berlin.

Kannengiesser Pasha, Hans. 1926. *The Campaign in Gallipoli.* Trans. C. J. P. Ball. London.

Karpat, Kemal H. 1985. *Ottoman Population and Demographic and Social Characteristics.* Madison, Wisc.

Kasaba, Reşat. 1988. *The Ottoman Empire and World Economy: The Nineteenth Century.* Albany, N.Y.

Kater, Michael H. 1974. *"Das Ahnenerbe" der SS, 1935–1945.* Stuttgart.

Kayan, İlhan. 1995. "Troia Bay and Supposed Harbour Sites in the Bronze Age." *Studia Troica* 5: 211–35.

Keyser, Paul. 1990. "The Composition of *La Chine et le Japon*." In Calder and Cobet (1990), 225–36.

Kluwe, Ernst. 1992. "Schliemann und Dörpfeld." In Herrmann (1992), 153–60.

Koldewey, Robert. 1891. *Neandria. Winckelmannsprogram* 51. Berlin.

Konsola, Dora. 1990. "Die Trojanische Sammlung des Nationalmuseums Athen." In Demakopoulou (1990), 78–87.

Korfmann, Manfred. 1986. "Troy: Topography and Navigation." In Mellink (1986), 1–16.

————. 1994. "Die Schatzfunde in Moskau—Ein erster Eindruck." *Antike Welt* 25: unpaginated.

————. 1995. "Troia: A Residential and Trading City at the Dardanelles." In *Politeia: Society and State in the Aegean Bronze Age.* Eds. Robert Laffineur and Wolf-Dietrich Niemeier. Proceedings of the 5th International Aegean Conference. University of Heidelberg, 10–13 April 1994. Austin. In *Aegaeum* 12: 173–83, plates 23–32.

————. 1996. "Ausgrabungen 1995," *Studia Troica* 6: 1–63, plates 1–2.

————. 1998. "Troia, an Ancient Anatolian Palatial and Trading Center: Archaeological Evidence for the Period of Troia VI/VII." In Boedeker (1998), 51–73.

Korfmann, Manfred, and Bernd Kromer. 1993. "Demircihüyük Beşik-Tepe, Troia—eine Zwischenbilanz zur Chronologie dreier orte in Westantolien." *Studia Troica* 3: 135–71.

Korfmann, Manfred, and Dietrich Mannsperger. 1992. *Troia: Homer, the Iliad, and After.* Istanbul.

Korres, George S. 1974. *Bibliographia Errikou Sleman.* Athens.

————. 1975. "Epigraphai ex Attikes eis Katochen Errikou Sleman." *Athena* 75: 54–67, 492.

————. 1977. "To 'Iliou Melathron' os Ekphrasis tis Prosopikotitos kai tou Ergou tou Errikou Sliman." *Etaireia ton Philon tou Laou. Morphotikai Ekdoseis* 8.

————. 1981. "Das Mausoleum Heinrich Schliemanns auf dem Zentralfriedhof von Athen." *Boreas* 4: 133–73.

————. 1984. "Neues zum Mausoleum Heinrich Schliemanns in Athen." *Boreas* 7: 317–25.

————. 1988. "Heinrich Schliemanns Iliou Melathron in Athen." *Das Altertum* 34: 164–73.

Korres, George S., and Sophia N. D. Tarantou. 1988. "Iliou Melathron: To klassiko demiourgema tou Tsiller." *Armos Timitikos Tomos:* 943–81.

Körte, Anton. 1895. "Kleinasiatische Studien 1: Eine archaische Stele aus Dorylaion." *Mitteilungen des deutschen Archäologischen Instituts, athenische Abteilung* 20: 1–4.

Kossatz-Pompé, Anne-Ulrike. 1992. "Ballı Dağ, der Berg von Pınarbaşı: Eine Siedlung in der Troas." *Studia Troica* 2: 171–83.

Kristiansen, Kristian. 1981. "A Social History of Danish Archaeology (1805–1975)." In Daniel (1981), 20–44.

Kuniholm, Peter I., et al. 1996. "Anatolian Tree Rings and the Absolute Chronology of the Eastern Mediterranean, 2220–718 B.C." *Nature* 381: 780–83.

Kyrieleis, Helmut. 1978. "Schliemann in Griechenland." *Jahrbuch des Romisch-Germanischen Zentralmuseums zu Mainz* 25: 74–91.

Lamb, Winifred. 1932. "Schliemann's Prehistoric Sites in the Troad." *Prähistorische Zeitschrift* 23: 111–25.

Lane-Poole, Stanley. 1890. *The Life of Lord Stratford de Redcliffe.* London.

Lanjouw, J., and F. A. Stafleu. 1954. *Index herbariorum.* Utrecht.

Lascarides, A. C. 1977. *The Search for Troy: 1553–1874.* Lilly Library Publication 29. Bloomington, Ind.

Latacz, Joachim. 1996. *Homer, His Art, and His World.* Ann Arbor, Mich.

Layard, Austen H. 1849. *Nineveh and Its Remains.* London.

Leaf, Walter. 1912. *Troy: A Study in Homeric Geography.* London.

————. 1923. *Strabo on the Troad.* Cambridge.

Leake, William M. 1824. *Journal of a Tour in Asia Minor.* London.

Le Bas, Philippe, and William-Henry Waddington. 1872. *Explication des inscriptions grecques et latines recuillies en Grèce et en Asie Mineure.* Vol. 2. Paris.

Lehrer, Mark, and David Turner. 1989. "The Making of a Homeric Archaeologist: Schliemann's Diary of 1868." *Annual of the British School at Athens* 84: 221–68.

Lenormant, François. 1874. "Dr. Schliemann's Discoveries in the Troad." *Academy* (21 March) 98: 314–16; *Academy* (28 March) 99: 343–45.

Lenz, Carl G. 1798. *Die Ebene von Troja nach dem Grafen Choiseul Gouffier und anderen Reisenden.* Neustrelitz.

Le Roi, P. 1884. *Catalogue des objets d'art antiques du moyen-age et de la Renaissance dépendant de la succession Alessandro Castellani.* Paris.

Letts, Malcom, ed. 1926. *Pero Tafur Travels and Adventures.* London.

Levine, Philippa. 1986. *The Amateur and the Professional: Antiquarians, Historians, and Archaeologists in Nineteenth-Century England, 1838–1886.* Cambridge.

Lloyd, Seton. 1980. *Foundations in the Dust.* Rev. ed. Bristol.

Lolling, Habbo Gerhardus. 1881a. "Miscelle: Die Inschrift aus Kebrene." *Mitteilungen des deutschen Archäologischen Instituts, athenische Abteilung* 6: 118–20.

————. 1881b. "Mittheilungen aus Kleinasien." *Mitteilungen des deutschen Archäologischen Instituts, athenische Abteilung* 6: 217–32.

————. 1884. "Inschriften aus den Küstenstädten des Hellespont und der Propontis." *Mitteilungen des deutschen Archäologischen Instituts, athenische Abteilung* 9: 58–77.

Longperier, Adrien de, and J. de Witte. 1855. Untitled. *Bulletin archéologique de l'Athenaeum Français,* 60.

Lubbock, John. 1865. *Prehistoric Times.* London.

————. 1870. *Origins of Civilization.* London.

Ludwig, Emil. 1931. *Schliemann of Troy: The Story of a Goldseeker.* Trans. D. F. Tait. London.

Lugt, Felix. 1964. *Repertoire des catalogues de ventes publiques, 1861–1900.* La Haye.

Lullies, Reinhard, and Wolfgang Schiering. 1988. *Archäologenbildnisse: Portraits und Kartbibliographien von Klassischen Archäologen deutscher Sprache.* Mainz.

Mac Adam, Henry I. 1991. "William Henry Waddington: Orientalist and Diplomat, 1826–1894." In *Quest for Understanding: Arabic and Islamic Studies in Memory of Malcom H. Kerr,* 283–320. Eds. Samir Seikaly, R. Baalbaki, and Peter Dodd. Beirut.

Macartney, C. A. 1931. *Refugees—The Work of the League.* London.

Mac Farlane, Charles. 1850. *Turkey and Its Destiny: The Result of Journeys Made in 1847 and 1848 to Examine into the State of That Country.* 2 vols. Philadelphia.

Maclaren, Charles. 1822. *A Dissertation on the Topography of the Plain of Troy.* Edinburgh.

————. 1863. *The Plain of Troy Described.* Edinburgh.

Marchand, Leslie A. 1941. *The Athenaeum: A Mirror of Victorian Culture.* Chapel Hill.

Marchand, Suzanne L. 1996. *Down from Olympus: Archaeology and Philhellenism in Germany, 1750–1970.* Princeton.

Masson, Olivier. 1992. "Diplomates et amateurs d'antiquités à Chypre vers 1866–1878." *Journal des savants:* 123–54.

————. 1994. "L. Palma di Cesnola, H. Schliemann, et l'editeur John Murray." *Cahier du Centre d'Etudes Chypriotes* 21: 7–14.

————. 1995a. "Henry Schliemann à Paris et ses amis français." *Le Trésor de Priam retrouvé. Dossiers d'archéologie* 206: 28–41.

————. 1995b. "Recherches récentes sur Heinrich Schliemann." *Revue des études greques* 108: 593–600.

Max Müller, Lady Wanda, ed. 1902. *The Life and Letters of the Right Honourable Friedrich Max Müller.* Vol. 1. London.

McKernan, Betty. 1997. *The Whittall Family in Turkey.* London.

Mc Neill, John, and A. M. Tulloch. 1856. *Report on the Commission of Enquiry into Supplies of the British Army in the Crimea.* London.

Mejer, Jorgen. 1990. "Henrik Ibsen's Peer Gynt and Heinrich Schliemann: Fact and Fiction." In Calder and Cobet (1990), 296–325.

Mellink, Machteld, ed. 1986. *Troy and the Trojan War.* Bryn Mawr, Pa.

Merritt, Lucy Shoe. 1984. *A History of the American School of Classical Studies at Athens.* Princeton.

Meyer, Ernst. 1953. *Briefwechsel von Heinrich Schliemann,* Vol. 1. Berlin.

————. 1955. "Schliemann und Virchow." *Gymnasium* 62: 435.

————. 1969. *Heinrich Schliemann, Kaufmann und Forscher.* Berlin.

————, ed. 1936. *Briefe von Heinrich Schliemann.* Berlin.

————, ed. 1958. *Briefwechsel von Heinrich Schliemann.* Vol. 2. Berlin.

————, ed. 1962. "Schliemann's Letters to Max Müller in Oxford." *Journal of Hellenic Studies* 82: 75–105.

Meyer, Karl E. 1993. "The Hunt for Priam's Treasure: A Berlin Prehistorian Conducts a Search for Schliemann's Celebrated Trojan Gold." *Archaeology* 46: 26–32.

———. 1995. "Who Owns the Spoils of War?" *Archaeology* 48: 46–53.

Meyer, P. 1894. "Funerailles de M. Waddington." *Publications divers de l'Institut de France.* Paris.

Miller, Edward. 1974. *That Noble Cabinet: A History of the British Museum.* Athens, Ohio.

Money, Edward. 1857. *Twelve Months with the Bashi Bazouks.* London.

Moorehead, Caroline. 1994. *The Lost Treasures of Troy.* London.

Morgenthau, Henry. 1929. *I Was Sent to Athens.* Garden City, N.Y.

Müller, Karl O. 1835. *Handbuch der Archaeologie der Kunst.* 2d ed. Breslau.

Munn, Geoffrey G. 1990. "The Archaeologist, the Collector, and the Jeweller, 1820– 1900." In Calder and Cobet (1990), 326–34.

Murray, John. 1840, 1845, 1854, 1865, 1878. *A Handbook for Travellers in the Ionian Islands, Greece, Turkey, Asia Minor, and Constantinople.* London.

———. 1854. *Handbook for Travellers in Greece.* London.

———. 1875. *Handbook for Travellers in Turkey in Asia, Including Constantinople, the Bosphorus, Dardanelles, Brousa, and Plain of Troy.* London.

———. 1878. *Handbook for Travellers in Turkey.* 4th ed. London.

———. 1900. *Handbook for Travellers in Constantinople, Brusa, and the Troad.* London.

Nagy, Gregory. 1996. *Homeric Questions.* Austin.

Naiditch, Paul G. 1989. "Classical Studies in Nineteenth-Century Great Britain as Background to the Cambridge Ritualists." In *The Cambridge Ritualists Reconsidered,* 123–52. Ed. William M. Calder III. Atlanta.

Napier, Edward. 1840. "Remarks on Ancient Troy and the Modern Troad." *United Service Journal* 140: 289–310.

Neue Deutsche Biographie. 1953. Berlin.

Newton, Charles T. 1851. "On the Study of Archaeology." *Archaeological Journal* 8: 1–26.

———. 1865. *Travels and Discoveries in the Levant.* Vol. 1. London.

Nicholas, Lynn. 1994. *The Rape of Europa: The Fate of Europe's Treasures in the Third Reich and the Second World War.* New York.

Nicoläides, George. 1867. *La topographie et plan strategique de l'Iliade.* Paris.

Nyerup, R. 1806. *Oversyn over foedrelanders mindesmaerker faroldtiden.* Copenhagen.

Ottaway, James H. 1973. "Rudolf Virchow: An Appreciation." *Antiquity* 47: 101–8.

Pallat, Ludwig. 1959. *Richard Schöne: Generaldirector der Königlichen Muzeen in Berlin.* Berlin.

Pamuk, Sevket. 1987. "Commodity Production for World-Markets and Relations of Production in Ottoman Agriculture, 1840–1913." In *The Ottoman Empire and the World Economy,* 947–80. Ed. Huri İslamoğlu-İnan. Cambridge.

———. 1994. "Money in the Ottoman Empire, 1326–1914." Appendix in İnalçık (1994), 947–80.

Papastamou, D. 1973. *Ernestos Tziller.* Prospatheia Monographias. Athens.

Parkes, Edward A. 1857. *Report on the Formation and General Management of Renkioi Hospital.* London.

Patzek, Barbara. 1990. "Schliemann und die Geschichte der Archäologie in neunzehnten Jahrhundert: Von Entstehung einer Wissenschaft zür archäologischen Sensation." In Calder and Cobet (1990), 31–55.

Pemberton, W. Baring. 1962. *Battles of the Crimean War.* London.

Pemble, John. 1987. *The Mediterranean Passion: Victorians and Edwardians in the South.* Oxford.

Pentzopoulos, Dimitri. 1962. *The Balkan Exchange of Minorities and Its Impact on Greece.* Paris.

Perrot, Georges. 1874. "Excursion à Troie at aux sources du Menderé." *Annuaire de l'Association pour l'Encouragement des Etudes Grecques en France* 7: 58–74.

———. 1909. "Notice sur la vie et les travaux de W. H. Waddington." *Publications divers de l'Institut de France.* Paris.

Picard, Charles, and Adolphe J. Reinach. 1912. "Voyage dans la Chersonèse et aux îles de Thrace." *Bulletin de Correspondence Hellènique* 36: 275–352.

Pollak, Ludwig. 1955. *Klassisch-Antike Goldschmiede arbeiten im Besitze. Sr. Excellenz A. J. von Nelidow.* Leipzig.

Poole, R. Stanley 1851. *Horae Agyptiacae.* London.

Porter, David. 1835. *Constantinople and Its Environs in a Series of Letters.* New York.

Prime, Samuel I. 1855. *Travels in Europe and the East.* Vol. 2. New York.

Pullan, Richard P. 1865. *The Principal Ruins of Asia Minor.* London.

———. 1886 "Exploration and Excavation in Asia Minor." *Archaeological Journal* 43: 1–10.

Raaflaub, Kurt. 1998. "Homer, the Trojan War, and History." In Boedeker (1998), 79–99.

Raby, J. 1980. "Cyriacus of Ancona and the Ottoman Sultan Mehmed II." *Journal of the Warburg Institute* 43: 242–46.

———. 1982. "A Sultan of Paradox: Mehmed II the Conqueror as a Patron of the Arts." *Oxford Art Journal* 5: 3–8.

Rapp, George, Jr., and John A. Gifford. 1982. *Troy: The Archaeological Geology.* Troy Supplementary Monograph 4. Princeton.

Reinach, Adolphe. 1913. "Voyage épigraphique en Troade et en Eolide." *Revue Epigraphique,* n.s., 1: 166–89.

Reinach, Salomon. 1884. "Chronique d'Orient." *Revue Archéologique,* 3d series, 3: 335–344.

Reinach, Theodor. 1891. "Trois groupes en terres cuites de la Troade." *Revue Archéologique,* 3d series, 17: 289–97.

Renfrew, Colin. 1996. "Kings, Tree Rings, and the Old World." *Nature* 381: 733–34.

Rennell, James. 1814. *Observations on the Topography of the Plain of Troy: And on the Principal Objects Within and Around It Described, or Alluded to, in the "Iliad."* London.

Rhodes, Dennis, ed. 1973. *Dennis of Etruria.* London.

Robert, Louis. 1952. *Etudes de numismatiques grecque.* Paris.

Robinson, Marcelle. 1990. "Frank Calvert: The Pre-Schliemann Years." M.A. thesis, Harvard University Extension School.

———. 1994. "Pioneer, Scholar, and Victim: An Appreciation of Frank Calvert." *Anatolian Studies* 44: 153–68.

———. 1995. "Frank Calvert and the Discovery of Troia." *Studia Troica* 5: 323–41.

Rona, Zeynep, ed. 1993. *Osman Hamdi Bey ve Donemir.* Symposium, 17–18 December 1992. Istanbul.

Rose, C. Brian. 1992. "The 1991 Post–Bronze Age Excavations at Troia." *Studia Troica* 2: 43–60.

———. 1993. "The Post–Bronze Age Excavations at Troia." *Studia Troica* 3: 97–116.

———. 1995. "The 1994 Post–Bronze Age Excavations at Troia." *Studia Troica* 5: 81–105.

———. 1996. "The 1995 Post–Bronze Age Excavations at Troia." *Studia Troica* 6: 97–101.

———. 1998. "Troy and the Historical Imagination." In Boedeker (1998), 101–132.

Russack, Hans H. 1942. *Deutsche Bauen in Athen.* Berlin.

Russell, William H. 1858a. *Russell's Despatches from the Crimea.* Rev. ed. London.

———. 1858b. *The British Expedition to the Crimea.* London.

Ryan, C. W. 1960. *A Guide to the Known Minerals of Turkey.* Ankara.

Saherwala, Geraldine. 1982. *Troja: Heinrich Schliemanns Ausgrabungen und Funde*. Austellung des Museums für Vor- und Frühgeschichte Preußischer Kulturbesitz und Berliner Gesellschaft für Anthropologie, Ethnologie, und Urgeschichte. Berlin.

Saherwala, Geraldine, Klaus Goldmann, and Gustav Mahr, eds. 1993. *Heinrich Schliemanns "Sammlung trojanischer Altertümer": Beiträge zur Chronik einer grossen Erwerbung der Berliner Museen*. Berliner Beiträge zur Vor- und Frühgeschichte, n.s., 7. Berlin.

Satow, Ernest. 1922. *A Guide to Diplomatic Practice*. London.

Sattin, Anthony. 1988. *Lifting the Veil: British Society in Egypt, 1768–1956*. London.

Sayce, Archibald H. 1880. "Notes from Journeys in the Troad and Lydia." *Journal of Hellenic Studies* 1: 75–93.

———. 1884. "Preface." In Schliemann (1884), i–xxx.

Schliemann, Heinrich. 1869. *Ithaque, le Péloponnèse, et Troie*. Paris.

———. 1870. "Ausgrabungen in Troja im Frühjahr 1870." *Augsburger Allgemeine Zeitung*, 24 May, 2301–2.

———. 1873a. "Ausgrabungen in Troja." *Augsburger Allgemeine Zeitung* 165, 14 June, 2527–28.

———. 1873b. "Der Schatz von Priamos." *Augsburger Allgemeine Zeitung* 217, 5 August, 3309–10.

———. 1874a. *Antiquités troyennes*. Paris.

———. 1874b. *Atlas trojanische Alterthümer*. Leipzig.

———. 1875a. *Troy and Its Remains*. London.

———. 1875b. "Professor Stark und Troja." *Augsburger Allgemeine Zeitung*, 8 January, 109–10.

———. 1875c. "Dr. Schliemann and Mr. Calvert on Troy." Supplement to *The Guardian*, 31 March, no. 1530.

———. 1878. *Mycenae*. London.

———. 1881a. *Ilios: The City and Country of the Trojans*. London.

———. 1881b. *Reise in der Troas im Mai 1881*. Leipzig.

———. 1881c. "Orchomenos." *Journal of Hellenic Studies* 2: 122–63.

———. 1884. *Troja*. London.

———. 1885. *Tiryns*. London.

———. 1891a. *Bericht über die Ausgrabungen in Troja im Jahre 1890*. Leipzig.

———. 1891b. "Report on the Excavations at Troy in 1890." In Schuchhardt (1891), 323–34.

Schmidt, Hubert. 1902. *H. Schliemanns Sammlung trojanischer Altertümer*. Berlin.

Schmidt, Julius. 1864. "Dr. von Hahn's Ausgrabungen im Gebiete von Troja." *Rheinisches Museum für Philologie*, n.s. 19 (1864): 591.

Schroeder, Paul W. 1972. *Austria, Great Britain, and the Crimean War: The Destruction of the European Concert*. Ithaca, N.Y.

Schuchhardt, Carl. 1890. *Schliemanns Ausgrabungen in Troja, Tiryns, Mykenai, Orchomenos, Ithaka im Lichte der heutigen Wissenschaft*. Leipzig.

———. 1891. *Schliemann's Excavations: An Archaeological and Historical Study*. Trans. Eugenie Sellars. London.

———. 1944. *Aus Leben und Arbeit*. Berlin.

Schwertheim, Elmar, and Hans Wiegartz. 1994. *Neue Forschungen zu Neandria und Alexandria Troas I*. Asia Minor Studien 11. Bonn.

———. 1996. *Die Troas: Neue Forschungen zu Neandria und Alexandria Troas II*. Asia Minor Studien 22. Bonn.

Scott, John A. 1931. "Ludwig and Schliemann." *Classical Journal* 27: 15–22.

Senior, Nassau W. 1859. *A Journal Kept in Turkey and Greece*. London.

————. 1861. *La Turquie contemporaine.* Paris.

————. 1882. *Conversations and Journals in Egypt and Malta.* London.

Sevinç, Nurten. 1992. *Troia.* Istanbul.

————. 1996. "A New Sarcophagus of Polyxena from the Salvage Excavation at Gümüşçay." *Studia Troica* 6: 251–64.

Shaw, Stanford, and Ezel K. Shaw. 1977. *History of the Ottoman Empire and Modern Turkey.* Vol. 2. *Reform, Revolution, and Republic: The Rise of Modern Turkey.* Cambridge, Mass.

Sheftel, Phoebe S. 1979. "The Archaeological Institute of America, 1879–1979: A Centennial Review." *American Journal of Archaeology* 83: 3–17.

Shepherd, John. 1965/66. "The Civil Hospitals in the Crimea, 1855–1856." *Proceedings of the Royal Society of Medicine* 59: 19–24.

Sichtermann, Helmut. 1996. *Kulturgeschichte der klassischen Archäologie.* Munich.

Siebler, Michael. 1990. *Troia-Homer-Schliemann: Mythos und Wahrheit.* Mainz am Rhein.

————. 1994. *Troia: Geschichte-Grabungen-Kontroversen.* Mainz am Rhein.

Simpson, Elizabeth, ed. 1997. *The Spoils of War. World War II and Its Aftermath. The Loss, Reappearance, and Recovery of Cultural Property.* New York.

Simpson, William. 1854. Pencil Sketches of the Crimea—Marseilles—Voyage to the Crimea. Unpublished sketchbook. Ann S. K. Brown Military Collection, Hay Library, Brown University, Providence, R.I.

————. 1877. "The Schliemannic Ilium." *Fraser's Magazine* 16, 1–16.

————. 1903. *The Autobiography of William Simpson, R.I. (Crimean Simpson).* Ed. George Eyre-Todd. London.

Skene, Felicia M. F. 1849. *Wayfaring Sketches among the Greeks and Turks, and on the Shores of the Danube.* London.

Skene, James H. 1883. *With Lord Stratford in the Crimean War.* London.

Slade, Adolphus. 1833. *Turkey, Greece, and Malta.* 2 vols. London.

————. 1837. *Records of Travels in Turkey, Greece, etc., and a Cruise in the Black Sea, with Captain Pasha in the Years 1829, 1830, and 1831.* 2 vols. London.

————. 1854. *Slade's Travels in Turkey, Turkey and the Turks, and a Cruise in the Black Sea, with the Captain Pasha.* New York.

Smith, Albert R. 1851. *A Month at Constantinople.* London.

Smith, Charles H. 1896. *Catalogue of Greek and Etruscan Vases in the British Museum.* Vol. 3. *Vases of the Finest Period.* Oxford.

Spencer, Edmund. 1851. *Travels in European Turkey in 1850, through Bosnia, Servia, Bulgaria, Macedonia, Thrace, Albania, Epirus, with a Visit to Greece and the Ionian Isles.* 2 vols. London.

Sperling, Jerome. 1986. "Reminiscences of Troy." In Mellink (1986), 29–31.

Stark, Karl B. 1874a. *Nach dem griechischen Orient.* Heidelberg.

————. 1874b. Review of *Trojanische Alterthümer,* by Heinrich Schliemann, *Jenaer Literaturzeitung* 41, 347–51.

————. 1877. "Neueste Litteratur zur trojanischen Frage." *Jenaer Literaturzeitung* 44, 3 November, 665–79.

————. 1880. *Systematik und Geschichte der Archäologie der Kunst.* Leipzig.

Stephens, John L. 1838. *Incidents of Travel in Greece, Turkey, Russia, and Poland.* Vol. 1. New York.

Stewart, Laddie. 1954. Preliminary Inventory of the Records of the U.S. Consulate General in Constantinople (Istanbul) Turkey, 1855–1935. Record Group 84 (RG 84).

Stiebing, William H., Jr. 1993. *Uncovering the Past: A History of Archaeology.* Oxford.

Stocking, George W. 1987. *Victorian Anthropology.* New York.

Stoll, Heinrich A. 1958. *Abenteuer meines Lebens: Heinrich Schliemanns Berichte über seine Entdeckung in der griechischen Welt.* Leipzig.

Stone, Irving. 1975. *The Greek Treasure.* Garden City, N.Y.

Strabo. 1970. *The Geography of Strabo.* With an English translation by H. L. Jones. Books 8 and 9. Cambridge, Mass.

Sweetman, John. 1984. *War and Administration: The Significance of the Crimean War for the British Army.* Edinburgh.

Tchihatcheff, Peter de. 1853. *Asie Mineure, déscription physique, statistique, et archéologique de cette contrée.* Vols. 1 and 3. Paris.

Temple, Major Sir Grenville. 1836. *Travels in Greece and Turkey.* 2 vols. London.

Thiersch, Hermann. 1902a. Katalog der Sammlung Calvert in den Dardanellen und in Thymbra. Unpublished. Çanakkale Archaeological Museum.

———. 1902b. "Zusatz." *Mitteilungen des deutschen Archäologischen Instituts, athenische Abteilung* 27: 246–52.

Thomas, Carol G. 1998. "Searching for the Historical Homer." *Archaeology Odyssey* 1: 26–33.

Thomas, Christopher A. 1990. *The Lincoln Memorial and Its Architect (1866–1924).* New Haven, Conn.

———. 1995–96. "Francis H. Bacon: Master Draftsman as Archaeologist." *The Classicist* 2: 28–33.

Thompson, Dorothy B. 1963. *The Terracotta Figurines of the Hellenistic Period.* Troy Supplementary Monograph 3. Princeton.

Thompson, Jason. 1992. *Sir Gardner Wilkinson and His Circle.* Austin.

Thomsen, Christian J. 1836. *Ledetraad til nordisk Oldkyndighed.* Copenhagen.

———. 1848. *A Guide to Northern Archaeology.* Trans. Lord Ellesmere. London.

Tolstikov, Vladimir. 1996. "Heinrich Schliemann and Trojan Archaeology." In Tolstikov and Treister (1996), 15–23.

Tolstikov, Vladimir, and Mikhail Treister. 1996. *The Gold of Troy: Searching for Homer's Fabled City.* New York.

Toppin, David. 1981. "The British Hospital at Renkioi, 1855." *Arup Journal* 1–20.

Toynbee, Arnold J. 1916. *Forty Years in Constantinople: The Recollections of Sir Edwin Pears, 1873–1915.* London.

Tozer, Henry F. 1869. *Researches in the Highlands of Turkey.* Vol. 1. London.

Traill, David A. 1986. "Introduction" and "The Mycenaean Diary." In Calder and Traill (1986), 124–260.

———. 1993. *Excavating Schliemann.* Illinois Classical Studies, supplement 4. Ed. William M. Calder III. Atlanta.

———. 1995. *Schliemann of Troy: Treasure and Deceit.* New York.

———. 1997. "J. G. von Hahn's Report of His Excavations at Ballı Dağ in 1864: The Finlay Translation." *Annual of the British School at Athens* 92: 169–89.

Treister, Viktor. 1996. "The Trojan Treasures: Description, Chronology, Historical Context." In Tolstikov and Treister (1996), 197–234.

Trigger, Bruce. 1989. *A History of Archaeological Thought.* Cambridge.

Turner, David. 1990. "Heinrich Schliemann: The Man behind the Masks." *Archaeology* 43: 36–42.

———. 1996. Review of *Schliemann of Troy: Treasure and Deceit,* by David A. Traill. *Journal of Hellenic Studies* 116: 235–37.

Turner, Frank M. 1981. *The Greek Heritage in Victorian Britain.* New Haven.

Turner, William. 1820. *Journal of a Tour in the Levant*. 2 vols. London.

Ulrichs, Heinrich N. 1845. "Über die Lage Trojas." *Rheinisches Museum für Philologie*, n.s., 3: 573–608.

———. 1847. "An excursus on the Topography of the Homeric Ilium." *Transactions of the Royal Society of Literature*, 2d series, 3: 103–78.

Unte, Wolfhart. 1990. "Karl Otfried Müller. 28 August 1798—1 August 1840." In Briggs and Calder (1990), 310–20.

Unverzagt, Mechtild. 1988. "Materialen zur Geschichte des Staatlichen Museums für Vor- und Frühgeschichte zu Berlin während des Zeiten Welt Krieges—Zu seinen Bergungaktionen und seinen Verlusten." *Jahrbuch preußischer Kulturbesitz* 25: 315–84.

———, ed. 1985. *Wilhelm Unverzagt und die Pläne zur Gründung eines Instituts für die vorgeschichte Ostdeutschlands*. Mainz.

Urquhart, David. 1839. *The Spirit of the East, Illuminated in a Journal of Travels through Roumeli during an Eventful Period*. 2 vols. Philadelphia.

U.S. Agency for International Development. 1971. *Troy Historical National Park: Master Plan for Protection and Use*. Washington, D.C. and Ankara.

Vaio, John. 1990. "Gladstone and the Early Reception of Schliemann in England." In Calder and Cobet (1990), 415–30.

———. 1992. "Schliemann and Gladstone: New Light from Unpublished Documents." In Herrmann (1992), 73–76.

Vaughan, Dorothy. 1954. *Europe and the Turk: A Pattern of Alliances*. Liverpool.

Vaux, W. S. W. 1863. "Extracts from Letters, Etc." *Transactions of the Royal Society of Literature*, 2d series, 7: 398.

Vermeule, Cornelius C., III. 1995. "Neon Ilion and Ilium Novum: Kings, Soldiers, Citizens, and Tourists at Classical Troy." In Carter and Morris (1995), 467–82.

Virchow, Rudolf. 1875. *Zeitschrift für Ethnologie* 7.

———. 1879. "Beiträge zur Landeskunde der Troas." *Abhandlungen der königliche Akademie der Wissenschaften 1879*.

———. 1881. "Troy and Hissarlik." Appendix 1 in Schliemann (1881a), 673–85.

———. 1882. "Alttrojanische Gräber und Schädel." *Abhandlungen der königlichen Akademie der Wissenschaften zu Berlin*, physikalische Klasse, 2.

———. 1892. "Über den troischen Ida, die Skamander-Quelle, und die Porta von Zeitunli." *Sitzungberichte Akademie der Wissenschaften zu Berlin*, mathematische-physikalische Klasse, 969–82.

Vulliamy, C. E. 1939. *Crimea: The Campaign of 1854–1856*. London.

Waddington, William-Henry. 1853. *Voyage en Asie Mineure au point de vue numismatique*. Paris.

Wallis, Mary E. 1937. "The Life of Alexander Watkins Terrell." M.A. thesis, University of Texas, Austin.

Walpole, Robert. 1817. *Memoirs Relating to European and Asiatic Turkey*. London.

Walsh, Rev. Robert. 1836. *A Residence at Constantinople during a Period Including the Commencement, Progress, and Termination of the Greek and Turkish Revolutions*. Vol. 2. London.

Walters, H. B. 1893. *Catalogue of Greek and Etruscan Vases in the British Museum*. Vol. 2. *Black-Figured Vases*. London.

Ward, Humphrey. 1926. *History of the Athenaeum Club*. London.

Watzinger, Carl. 1944. *Theodor Wiegand: Ein deutsche Archäologe*. Munich.

Webster's Biographical Dictionary. 1964. Springfield, Mass.

Welcker, Friedrich G. 1865. *Tagebuch der Griechischen Reise*. Vol. 2. Berlin.

White, Charles. 1845. *Three Years in Constantinople; or, Domestic Manners of the Turks in 1844*. Vol. 1. London.

Williams, Dyfri, and Jack Ogden. 1994. *Greek Gold Jewellery of the Classical World*. London.

Wilson, David M. 1984. *The Forgotten Collector: Augustus Wollaston Franks of the British Museum*. New York.

Witte, Reinhard. 1990. "Schliemann und Berlin." *Das Altertum* 36: 133–43.

Wood, Alfred C. 1964. *A History of the Levant Company*. London.

Wood, Michael. 1985. *In Search of the Trojan War*. London. Rev. ed. 1996.

Wood, Robert. 1775. *An Essay on the Original Genius and Writings of Homer: With a Comparative View of the Ancient and Present State of the Troade*. London.

Worsaae, Jens J. A. 1843. *Danmarks Oldtid*. Copenhagen.

———. 1849. *The Primeval Antiquities of Denmark*. Trans. W. J. Thoms. London.

Wroth, William W. 1894. *Catalogue of the Greek Coins of Troas, Aeolis, and Lesbos. A Catalogue of Coins in the British Museum*. London.

Xenophon. 1950. *Hellenica and Anabasis*. Trans. Carleton L. Brownson. Cambridge, Mass.

Young, George. 1905. *Corps de droit Ottoman: Récueil des codes, lois, règlements, ordinances, et actes les plus importants du droit contumier de l'empire Ottoman*. Oxford.

Zengel, Eva. 1990a. "Die Geschichte der Schliemann-Sammlungen." *Das Altertum* 36: 157–66.

———. 1990b. "Troy, Mycenae, Tiryns, and Orchomenos." In Demakopoulou (1990), 51–78. Athens.

INDEX

NOTE: Locators in italics denote illustrations.

Designer: Ina Clausen
Compositor: Impressions Book and Journal Services, Inc.
Printer: Edwards Brothers
Binder: Edwards Brothers
Text: 10/12 Baskerville
Display: Baskerville